T0244572

FORBIDDEN DESIRE IN EARLY MODERN EUROPE

FORBIDDEN DESIRE IN EARLY MODERN EUROPE

MALE–MALE SEXUAL RELATIONS, 1400–1750

NOEL MALCOLM

OXFORD
UNIVERSITY PRESS

OXFORD
UNIVERSITY PRESS

Great Clarendon Street, Oxford, OX2 6DP,
United Kingdom

Oxford University Press is a department of the University of Oxford.
It furthers the University's objective of excellence in research, scholarship,
and education by publishing worldwide. Oxford is a registered trade mark of
Oxford University Press in the UK and in certain other countries

Published in the United States of America by Oxford University Press
198 Madison Avenue, New York, NY 10016, United States of America

British Library Cataloguing in Publication Data
Data available

Library of Congress Control Number: 2023944177

ISBN 978–0–19–888633–4

DOI: 10.1093/oso/9780198886334.001.0001

Printed and bound in the UK by
Clays Ltd, Elcograf S.p.A.

MIX
Paper | Supporting
responsible forestry
FSC
www.fsc.org   FSC® C018072

Contents

1. Gregorio and Gianesino   I

2. Diplomats, renegades and catamites   8

3. Prejudices   19

4. Ottoman realities   28

5. Western Mediterranean realities: men and boys   41

6. Contexts of sexual life   49

7. Typical and untypical   69

8. The Western Mediterranean lands   85

9. Theology and religion   107

10. Law and punishment   125

11. Literary works   142

12. Western Mediterranean attitudes   170

13. Ottoman religion, law and culture   195

14. Northern Europe: broad patterns   214

15. Northern Europe: forms of sexual behaviour   235

16. Northern Europe: contexts of sexual life   253

17. Northern Europe: literary works   277

18. European colonial societies   310

19. England after 1700   336

20. France and the Netherlands after 1700   355

21. Conclusion: from sodomy to homosexuality   380

    Afterword   414

Notes	421
List of Manuscripts	533
Bibliography	535
Index	581

I

Gregorio and Gianesino

In the summer of 1588, the Venetian *bailo* in Istanbul felt obliged to investigate a sexual scandal. The *bailo*, a Venetian nobleman sent out typically
to serve for three years, was roughly the equivalent of a resident ambassador,
though with some additional powers over the Venetian community there;
his residence, known as the 'bailate' and located in the outskirts of Galata
(also known as Pera), across the Golden Horn from Istanbul proper, functioned as the embassy. In addition to his official and domestic staff, it also
contained a small number of young men undergoing training as 'dragomans'
or interpreters.[1] And the scandal involved the strong suspicion that sexual
activity—acts of sodomy—had taken place between a trainee dragoman and
one of the junior members of the staff. (When present-day historians discuss
the period before the nineteenth century they generally avoid the terms
'homosexuality' and 'homosexual', which may carry anachronistic assumptions about a special type of personality or disposition. It is now standard for
historians to use the early modern terms 'sodomy' and 'sodomite'; that practice will be followed in this book.)

Since the 1550s, adolescents known as *giovani di lingua*, 'language youths',
had been sent from Venice to live in the bailate and learn Turkish from a
native speaker. The purpose of this scheme was to reduce dependence on
local interpreters in Istanbul, whose position as subjects of the Sultan raised
questions about their trustworthiness; but since the supply of suitable
Venetian youths was seldom sufficient, members of Italian-speaking Christian
families of Istanbul and Galata were also accepted. The trainee in this case,
Gianesino Salvego or Salvago, had such a background. His father, Matteca,
belonged to a local family of Genoese origin, and had served for many years
as a dragoman for the Venetian *baili*.[2] One difference between Gianesino
and the Venetian trainees was that, having been born and raised in Galata, he
had already become a fluent speaker of Turkish as a child; presumably his

Forbidden Desire in Early Modern Europe: Male–Male Sexual Relations, 1400–1750. Noel Malcolm, Oxford University Press.
© Noel Malcolm 2024. DOI: 10.1093/oso/9780198886334.003.0001

training in the bailate was devoted to learning how to read and write it. (A later Venetian envoy would note that he had no interest in learning other languages.)[3] In fact, he was first installed in the bailate not as a trainee but as an informal interpreter in the period 1582–5, when the *bailo* used him to deal with those Turks who turned up at the bailate every day.[4] But at some point thereafter he was designated by the Venetian Senate as a *giovane di lingua*; this meant that he would receive a small salary, and that he would live inside the bailate, even though he had a parental home not far away.[5] Lorenzo Bernardo, who served as *bailo* from 1585 to 1587, wrote in his final report that Gianesino had 'recently' become a *giovane di lingua*, and that he was 'of a very lively spirit'.[6] While there is no record of his age, the fact that he was performing a responsible job for the *bailo* some time before 1585 suggests that by 1588 he may have been in his early twenties.

The other person under suspicion in the summer of 1588 was the barber of the bailate, whose name is given only as Gregorio. He was a newcomer, having travelled to Istanbul in the entourage of the new *bailo*, Giovanni Moro, in September 1587. His origins were Venetian: during the investigation it was mentioned that the 'Dottore' (not a medical doctor; perhaps the *bailo*'s secretary) had urged Gregorio not to be a cause of shame to 'la Patria', the fatherland. The Dottore had also cited a letter sent by Gregorio's mother, telling him to behave well and not to do anything that would make people talk about him—a detail which suggests that Gregorio was quite young.[7] His job involved some technical skills, but would not have required long experience. Apart from hair-cutting and shaving, barbers performed a variety of simple medical tasks, such as blood-letting (a standard treatment for many illnesses), tending wounds and setting broken bones. There was a guild of barbers in Venice; a barber sent to the bailate in Istanbul would most probably have undergone an apprenticeship with the guild, but it is hard to assign precise ages to that process. One recent study of Venetian guilds in this period notes that most apprenticeships ended between the ages of 18 and 20.[8] So it may be that Gregorio was just a few years younger than Gianesino.

Some time before 8 July two disciplinary orders had been issued: first the two young men had been forbidden to speak to each other, and then Gianesino had been expelled from the bailate. (As the *bailo* put it in his report: 'having had people rebuke him, and having rebuked him myself several times, in the end I decided to dismiss him, as I had previously warned him that I would, if he did not change his way of life and his behaviour.')[9]

The initial reason for the formal questioning of members of staff was to find out whether it was true that contacts were persisting between the two; but this quickly turned into an investigation of their previous relationship.

On 8 July the stableman, Vido of Zadar, was questioned. Had he spoken to Gianesino since the latter was expelled? Yes: Gianesino had asked after Gregorio, and had told Vido to invite Gregorio to visit him at his home. And what did Gianesino want from his friend? 'I don't know; but many times I saw them kissing here in the house.' Had others seen this too? 'All those who eat in the servants' hall saw it, because they were kissing at the window of Mr Gianesino's little room; people standing in the servant's hall could see it.' Had he seen them kissing many times? Yes, many times. Asked further about the nature of their relationship, Vido said: 'I don't know, but I do know that everyone in the house said that they were performing shameful acts with each other.' What did he mean by 'shameful acts'? 'Your Excellency can well imagine.' Told to speak plainly, he said: 'as if they were having sex'. And where did they do this? 'I don't know, but many times they were locked in that little room, and the whole household could see.'[10]

The investigation resumed on 2 August with the questioning of the household tailor. He said that various people had told him that since Gianesino was expelled, Gregorio had been going to visit him at night in order—as they said—to have sex with him. Had he ever seen them give any sign of such behaviour when Gianesino was in the household? 'I saw them playing together, and running around after each other.' But when asked whether others had said they were having sex in the house, he said that he had heard such things from two servants, the baker, and 'everyone in the household'. Had he heard people talking about this outside the house? Yes, a lot, though he could not give a particular example. At the end of his interrogation he was sworn to silence.[11]

With one partial exception, the statements of the twelve other members of the household who were interrogated over the following three days conformed to this pattern: they had seen signs of intimacy and affection between the two men, but the claim that they were having sex was a matter of (widely held) assumption rather than evidential knowledge. One indication of their relationship was the fact that Gianesino had given Gregorio various keepsakes: a length of silk, a pair of white gloves made of satin or half-satin, a cap made of purple or dark blue satin, and also a knife.[12] Another was the way in which the barber had spoken about his friend: he had said to one servant that 'there was nothing that he would not do for him', and had told another that he would go to see him 'even if the gallows were prepared for him'.[13] (Such feelings appeared to be mutual. According to the kitchen boy, Gianesino had said that 'he would have laid down his life for him [sc. Gregorio]'; his overall description of the relationship was that 'the barber was in love with Gianesino, and Gianesino with him'.)[14] When they were at the dining table together, they had 'gazed longingly at each other'; and 'after Your Excellency forbade them to speak to each other, they made signs to each other, and if they could meet somewhere, they chatted too, but separated when they heard anyone coming.'[15] Some witnesses confirmed that several times after Gianesino's expulsion, Gregorio had left the building at night by climbing through a window, returning only in the morning. That window had finally been blocked; when Gregorio saw this, he stood there cursing, and uttered—according to the kitchen boy—the ominous words that he might as well lose his soul.[16]

Two more specific allegations were made. One servant reminded the *bailo* that he had warned him, during their journey from Dalmatia to Istanbul, that Gregorio would be 'the shame of the household'. Apparently a rumour had arisen about Gregorio and the Ottoman official who travelled with them: it was said that 'Gregorio had offered himself to him for sex, if he were willing to let him ride on the horse, and the Turk had refused, saying that he had a wife.'[17] And when the kitchen boy was asked whether Gregorio had 'fooled around' with anyone else, he said: 'he may have done with Mr Marc'Antonio, the carver [approximately: butler], since they went to the lavatory together, and stayed there for hours.'[18]

The most specific evidence of sexual activity between Gregorio and Gianesino came from the baker, Dominico of Vicenza. He was well placed to supply it, since he shared a bedroom—indeed, a bed—with Gregorio; yet the information was extracted only with difficulty. Dominico began by quoting Gregorio as saying that 'they loved each other, but not in a sinful way'. Had he seen them committing any shameful act? 'No, except that I saw them kissing each other.' Where had he seen that? 'Where didn't they kiss? In the hall, in the kitchen, and in the bakery.' Asked if they had slept together, he replied: 'I slept with the barber, and on some nights Mr Gianesino came, but I noticed only in the morning, when he wanted to get dressed.' Were they all in the same bed? 'I was on one side, and didn't take up much room; they slept on the other side. On a few occasions I noticed that he came in the evening, and for that reason I didn't want to sleep there any more.' Had he heard them moving during the night, or talking? 'I heard them talking, but I couldn't make out the words; they also seemed to be kissing, but if they did anything else I couldn't say for sure, but if it had been a woman I would have thought that they were doing that business [sc. sexual intercourse] together.'[19]

Finally, on 11 August, the *bailo* summoned Gregorio and asked what sort of friendship he had had with Gianesino. 'I shall tell you the truth,' Gregorio replied. 'I loved him greatly, I took pleasure in his company, and I slept with him several times.' Had he had carnal relations with him? 'I did kiss him, and anyone might think it was true [sc. that they had had carnal relations], but it was not like that.' The next question was notably direct: had he been the active partner, or the passive one? 'No, my lords.' (At least one other senior official was present at this interrogation.) Had he had carnal relations with anyone else? 'Yes, my lords, with Mr Antonio the carver.' How often? 'Twice, when he sought me out for it.'[20]

The questioning ended there; the record merely added that, on that same evening, Gregorio was put on a Venetian galleon, to be taken to Crete. One month later, when sending a copy of the interrogation records to Venice, the *bailo* explained that he would have dismissed Gregorio as soon as he found out about the scandal, were it not for the fact that the barber 'decided to let it be known that he would convert to Islam'. (That was apparently the significance of his remark, reported by the kitchen boy, that he might as well lose his soul.) For that reason, he wrote, 'I delayed taking action in order to obtain first of all an order allowing me to send him away in chains, so that he could not be taken off the ship on that pretext [sc. an intention to convert] or any other.' He also sent away the carver, and refused to accept Gianesino back into the bailate, despite the great need for his services.[21]

The full record of these interrogations, which runs to sixteen pages and gives the responses of fifteen members of the household and two Venetian merchants, provides evidence of an exceptionally detailed kind. Most of our knowledge of particular cases of same-sex relations in early modern Europe comes from judicial investigations by civil or ecclesiastical authorities. Those focused on determining whether specific acts took place: typically, the only people questioned were the accused and the small number of witnesses whose testimony was directly relevant to proving those facts. In this case, however, attention is paid not just to sexual acts, but to the whole nature of an affective relationship; and the questioning of a large number of people gives a much more general sense of the attitudes of Gregorio's colleagues towards his and Gianesino's behaviour. Several said that they thought the two men were having sex, and even more said that others among them made that claim. Two, on the other hand, gave it as their firm belief that the relationship had been affectionate but non-sexual. Zuanne Battista Jacioli, servant of the *bailo*'s assistant, when asked what sort of intimacy there had been between the two young men, replied: 'I'm not aware of any intimacy other than the sort that there is between the rest of us', saying that he had heard only that the two of them had kissed and slept together. And Giulio Ferrarese, a general servant, while agreeing that they had kissed and some-times shared a bed, denied that they performed any shameful acts, adding that 'sometimes they went to the serving-room and ran around after each other, having fun.' Even this last witness, however, had warned them to moderate their behaviour.[22]

The terms used by those who did accuse them of sexual relations were negative but mostly euphemistic: 'performing shameful acts', and so on. As we have seen, the baker was slow to condemn Gregorio, yielding the most serious evidence only after careful questioning. When asked whether any-one had warned Gregorio to stop behaving as he did, he replied: 'we all told him to stop, and I don't think there is anyone in the household who didn't warn him.'[23] Yet it may be that many of those warnings were made only after the household became aware that the *bailo* was trying to stamp out the affair: one person said he had reproved Gianesino especially because he had heard that the *bailo* had admonished him more than once.[24] Apparently the relationship had been going on for quite a long time without any of the staff making an effort to bring it to the *bailo*'s notice. Anyone who stood in the servants' hall had been able to observe—perhaps some with disapproval, some with indifference, and some with amusement—the spectacle of the two men kissing in Gianesino's room. At one point the baker had become upset, he said, at the fact that his colleagues 'were joking at my expense', poking fun at him for being aware of, or complicit in, sexual acts in his own bed.[25] Moralistic outrage was not the dominant attitude, even if some were genuinely disapproving.

The *bailo* was a product of the same Venetian world, and would have shared the same underlying assumptions. Yet, as the thoroughness of his investigation and the severity of his decisions show, his reaction was very different. One feature of his questioning may shed special light on this. In no fewer than eight of the interrogations, he asked whether they had heard the matter discussed outside the bailate. He received a range of answers. The tailor, as we have seen, said he had heard it discussed very widely; some others said no; the baker said he had heard that Gianesino 'was going around Galata boasting that he had had sex with the barber'. One person mentioned a Venetian merchant, Bernardo Agudi, who had come to the bailate: 'he asked me who was the barber who was said to be the object of Gianesino's love; understanding what he meant by that, I showed him another servant, and since that one had an ugly face, he began to laugh, and understood that I was not willing to show him to him.' Within a day, that merchant was himself hauled in for questioning, and asked whether he had heard the matter discussed more generally outside the bailate's walls.[26]

Why this strong, almost paranoid fear about the wagging of tongues in Galata and Istanbul? Same-sex relations between men were, as we shall see, far from unknown in Italian society during this period, and neither was their presence in Venetian society a secret so far as other West Europeans were concerned. It is hard to believe that a Venetian ambassador in Rome or Madrid would have felt so troubled by the existence of such an affair between two lowly employees, or by the thought of it becoming public knowledge.[27] But Istanbul was different. Built into the cultural and moral self-image of Western Christians was the idea that sodomy was prevalent in, and characteristic of, Muslim society generally and Ottoman society in particular. This was something that significantly distinguished 'them' from 'us'. To have the population outside the bailate—Christian or Muslim—gossiping about a sodomitical affair within it would be to undermine one of the assumptions of superiority on which the Venetians' attitude to the Ottomans was founded.

2

Diplomats, renegades and catamites

Diplomacy involves contact between cultures, and diplomats may be particularly exposed, or sensitive, to some cultural differences. Ottoman envoys and their entourages in Western Europe sometimes came under scrutiny for their 'unnatural' sexual interests. In Venice in 1483 three Turks, who were probably in the retinue of the Ottoman ambassador (they included a 'spahi' or cavalry officer), were put on trial, accused of sodomizing in the piazza San Marco a 'Christian boy, of fairly adult age'—meaning, probably, above the age of legal responsibility, which was fourteen. The officer was sent to prison, and the authorities decided to have him poisoned there; but the Ottoman ambassador intervened, presenting a request from the Sultan for the man's release, and was given permission to take him with him when he left Venice.[1] In 1520 the Venetian authorities exiled one of their citizens on the grounds that he had had sexual relations with Ahmed, an Ottoman envoy, and in 1533 they forbade another such envoy, Yunus, to take 'a beautiful boy' back with him to Istanbul.[2] Similarly, the senior official Ibrahim pasha, who went to Vienna in 1700 to organize the return of Ottoman prisoners of war after the Treaty of Karlowitz, was found to have included in his list of returnees a number of handsome young Germans to whom he had allegedly offered enticements.[3] In 1749 the Dutch authorities had to investigate the reasons for a demonstration in The Hague outside the residence of the ambassador of Tripoli, Ali Efendi, by hundreds of local Jews, protesting at the treatment of two young Jewish men who had entered the residence on business. According to the official report, one of them had been importuned by the ambassador himself, 'trying by all possible means to persuade him that he should go with him to the Ottoman Empire, with professions of the great love he had for him'; the other had been first

Forbidden Desire in Early Modern Europe: Male–Male Sexual Relations, 1400–1750. Noel Malcolm, Oxford University Press.
© Noel Malcolm 2024. DOI: 10.1093/oso/9780198886334.003.0002

assaulted by one member of the ambassador's entourage, and then locked in a room by another, who raped him while holding his mouth with 'great force'. The affair was handled delicately by the Dutch, so as not to upset the diplomatic relationship.[4] (A similar approach was taken by the French authorities in 1788, when a Parisian woman complained that her 15-year-old son had been sodomized by a member of the embassy sent by Tipu Sultan, the ruler of Mysore; the matter was settled quietly, with a payment to the indignant mother.)[5]

Such issues could also impinge on early modern Western diplomats in the Ottoman Empire. The Dutch traveller Joris van der Does, who was in Istanbul in 1597–8, noted an incident in which a good-looking youth was abducted in the street: 'For the beauty of such boys makes them liable throughout Istanbul to the ambushes of boy-kidnappers. This was experienced even by a certain Polish nobleman, who came to Istanbul with the ambassador of his king; a beautiful boy, of a fine character, entrusted to his guardianship and protection, was not able to escape the rapacious hands of the kidnappers. He was secretly seized in some unfrequented alleyway of the city, and carried off I don't know where.'[6] Here the sexual element of the story was assumed rather than proven, but in other cases there could be no mistake. In 1702 the young Aaron Hill was staying with the English Ambassador, Sir Robert Sutton, at a summer house on the riverside at Edirne, when they saw a middle-aged Turkish man lead 'a Boy of about Fourteen' to a point on the river-bank where they were out of sight of the village on other side. The man 'began...to prepare himself and his *consenting Catamite*' for sex; the Englishmen shouted at him, but he persisted until Hill threatened him with a gun.[7]

Roughly fifteen years later, at the English consulate in Algiers, an awkward misunderstanding arose when the young men of the consulate were working in the courtyard, wearing only their underwear because of the heat, with their shirts folded and placed on their heads to protect them against the sun. A button on one man's underwear failed, causing it to drop to the ground, and his colleagues then amused themselves by spanking his bare buttocks. In the words of a French consular official, a passing Turk heard their loud laughter, and entered the courtyard out of curiosity: 'He saw a young boy who was naked, with his shirt on his head, defending himself as best he could. He thought they were taking a different kind of pleasure, and wanted to have his share. He held out his half-sabre to push aside the other servants, and took possession of the man they were trying to spank.' The others quickly fetched the consul (who was in his office with the Frenchman), but even then 'we had great difficulty in getting the Turk to leave, and persuading him that the situation was not as he had thought.'[8]

★ ★ ★

If it was true that Gregorio the barber was thinking of converting to Islam, the prime reason would have been that he wanted not only to leave the bailate but also to free himself entirely from the *bailo*'s jurisdiction—though that might well have been combined with a wish to retaliate against the *bailo* by causing some reputational harm. From the *bailo*'s point of view, however, such action would have constituted a diplomatic incident in which disloyalty, unnatural sexual interests and Islam were all combined. Just five years later, the steward of the Imperial embassy—that is, the embassy of the Holy Roman Empire—in Istanbul, Ladislaus Mörth, did abandon his post and convert to Islam. Mörth, who had studied in Rome before embarking on a military career lasting roughly 20 years, was a senior figure in the embassy; after his departure and conversion, he did what he could to harm Imperial interests by leading an Ottoman raid on the embassy which found and confiscated secret documents. (He also offered to advise the Grand Vizier on how to conquer a Habsburg stronghold on the Croatian–Ottoman border.) His hostility against the Imperial ambassador may have had various causes, but prominent among them, according to early accounts, was the fact that the ambassador had punished him for having a sexual affair with one of the embassy's kitchen boys: Mörth himself was confined to his room, while the boy was kept in an unlit room 'in irons and chains'. Mörth escaped from the building, fleeing to Galata; when the ambassador used his diplomatic rights to have him arrested by janissaries, he quickly expressed a wish to convert to Islam, after which he was declared a free man by the Ottoman authorities. There survives a copy of a letter, apparently sent later by Mörth to the boy (whose name was Hansel), declaring that 'it is because of you that I have stayed in this country so that I could—and will—avenge you.'[9]

'Renegades' (converts to Islam) were commonly viewed by Westerners with great disapproval; guilty of both apostasy and the abandonment of all loyalty to their homeland, they were easily suspected of depravity more generally. But the association with sodomy was especially common. The French traveller Nicolas de Nicolay, visiting Algiers in 1551, noted that the renegades were 'all addicted to lewdness, sodomy, theft, and all other detestable vices'; the Portuguese cleric Antonio de Sosa, a captive there in the late

1570s, observed that their main reason for converting was 'to live as they please, wallowing in every kind of lust, sodomy and gluttony'.[10] Spanish texts of this period, while commenting on the prevalence of sodomy in North African society generally, portrayed the renegade Europeans as the worst offenders; one Spanish priest from a 'redemptionist' order—devoted to ransoming captives and bringing them back to Christendom—who had worked in North Africa in the 1590s wrote that many renegades were reluctant to return to Europe, because they were afraid of being recognized there, and denounced, by people who knew that they had been practitioners of sodomy.[11]

Such fears might well have been justified. When Inquisition tribunals in some parts of Southern Europe processed renegades (mostly ones who had been captured by Christian forces, not ones who had gone back to Christendom voluntarily), accusations of sodomy were quite often recorded. In 1570, for example, Pedro Justiniano, who had become an enthusiastic corsair for the ruler of Tunis after his conversion to Islam, was described during a hearing at the Sardinian Inquisition as having committed sodomy with 'Turks'; in 1589 the corsair captain Bartolomé Catalan was accused by the Sicilian Inquisition first of persuading a young captive to convert to Islam and then of making him his *paciente* (passive sexual partner) in Algiers.[12] Another such case involved a renegade called Mustafa, aged nineteen or 20, who was tried in 1578 by the Inquisition in Barcelona; he said he was originally from Corsica, but had been captured and taken to Algiers at the age of five. A witness stated that he had seen Mustafa in Algiers two years earlier: he was then a servant to another renegade called Mustafa, and 'his master kissed him, fondled him and slept with him...he served him as his catamite and passive partner, committing the sin of sodomy with him.'[13] Further cases involving renegades appear in other narratives by former captives. The Flemish merchant Emanuel d'Aranda, for example, who was captured—off the coast of Brittany—by North African corsairs and sold into slavery in Algiers, described how a rich Portuguese captive was permitted to live freely in the house of a merchant there, through whom he would organize a ransom payment, leaving his thirteen-year-old page as a hostage in the residence of the ruler of Algiers: in the master's absence, the boy was 'debauched by a Portuguese renegade', and then converted to Islam.[14] It would of course be hard to generalize from individual cases of this kind. But we do have some general statements from people at the time—and not only from censorious Christian observers. The renegade Jorge Mendes Morato

(Murad) was accused in 1576 by the Lisbon Inquisition of keeping two young converts as his catamites in Tangier. In his response, Morato openly declared: 'it is customary for all the renegades to keep boys for sexual pleasure instead of women; they commit the sin of sodomy with them, and boast about it.'[15]

As some of those cases illustrate, young male captives could be targeted for either or both of two very different purposes: sexual exploitation, and conversion to Islam. The latter was quite a common occurrence with captive boys. For the younger ones, it was Muslim practice not to require the converts' consent if they were below the age of reason, which was typically identified with the early teens; there was no strict age criterion—nor could there have been, when so many people did not know their precise ages—but in Algiers, for example, Laugier de Tassy observed that the threshold was around twelve.[16] Above the age of reason, conversion had to be voluntary, and although many of the renegades who ended up in Christendom claimed that they had converted under psychological and physical duress, corroborating evidence for this is quite hard to find—while the motive for making such a claim remains transparently obvious. From the point of view of the Muslim masters of Christian slaves, there was actually an economic disincentive to convert them: although conversion did not release them from their slave status, it meant, in legal theory at least, that the master was now forbidden to sell them on. (It also meant that they could no longer be ransomed—and, as Laugier de Tassy pointed out, ransoming played a major role in sustaining the financial value of such slaves.)[17] But a master who was a good Muslim would have regarded encouraging a Christian to convert to Islam as a meritorious act; on similar grounds such masters did often free such converted slaves in their wills. One basic difference between these Muslim societies and those of European Christendom in this period was that the former were less hierarchical and more assimilatory: a young household slave who showed talent could be taken into the master's family and, if converted, married to one of the master's daughters and treated like a favoured son, quite regardless of his social origin. Some were freed and converted on that sort of basis, and it is understandable that, with the prospect of enjoying a quality of life well beyond that of their previous existence in Europe, they were happy to follow such a path. Even those who did not receive any special favour from their masters may often have felt that, if they could gain their freedom, this society would offer them better opportunities for a good life than the society from which they had come.

The redemptionist priest Jerónimo Gracián de la Madre de Dios, writing about Algiers in the 1590s, observed that between half and three-quarters of all Christian captives converted sooner or later to Islam, and offered one simple explanation for the cases involving boys and youths: 'It's a marvel that any of the boys or beardless youths evade this: for the Muslims buy the apprentice sailors, or the poorest and most junior ones, at excessive prices, to commit their acts of wickedness with them, and from such an evil beginning it is easy to proceed to heresy.' Expanding further on this theme, he wrote: 'Especially as they normally take poor little boys, the sort who serve on ships, or look after sheep on Corsica, boys who have no food or clothing where they come from. And when they find themselves dressed in silk, with food in abundance, and loved by their master (who buys his slaves for evil purposes), they think it's a wonderful thing to deny the Christian faith— whose teachings they had never learned.'[18] Even more simply, listing reasons for conversion in Algiers, de Sosa said that in some cases it happened because 'since the time when they were boys, their masters got them acquainted with the vice of sodomy, which they then came to like.'[19]

No doubt there were many paths towards receiving better treatment, and a range of possible motives for wanting to assimilate more fully to the local society. Conversion to Islam did indeed facilitate such assimilation. Yet, where the renegades were concerned, these facts can yield only the most adventitious connection between sodomy and conversion to Islam, not an intrinsic link of any kind between them, and could not begin to justify the routine association between the two that was made by West European writers when they generalized so confidently and disapprovingly about these issues.

* * *

Whether or not they converted, there are many records of individual young captives being used as *bardaches*, catamites, by their masters—regardless, again, of whether those masters were themselves converts to Islam.[20] (The word, which was common to several European languages—*bardache* in French, *bardascia* or *bardassa* in Italian, *bardaxo* or *bardaje* in Spanish—has traditionally been thought to have come, via Arabic, from a Persian word for a captive, though recent research has suggested a broader European origin.)[21] Former captives could be questioned about this on their return to Christendom, with the interrogation focusing on whether such sexual relations had taken place under duress or willingly. In 1570 the Barcelona

Inquisition considered the case of Simon Ponz, a native of Seville, who had been a captive in Algiers: he was accused of converting to Islam, of rowing in a corsair galley 'against the Christians', and of having been the *bardaxe* of a Turk, 'albeit under duress'. The young Luis de Pedro, similarly questioned in Sardinia in 1584, insisted that his role as a *bardaxo* had been entirely unconsenting, even though it had continued for two years.[22] That captive youths could be used for sexual purposes was a common observation. As a high-ranking cleric from Antwerp (and Professor at the University of Louvain), Jean-Baptiste Gramaye, who was seized in the Mediterranean and taken to Algiers in 1619, wrote in his discussion of young male captives: 'the more good-looking ones are locked up and detained in their masters' homes for nefarious practices and horrible, unspeakable crimes, and in the end, to their most certain perdition, they are sent as presents to the Sultan and his ministers.'[23]

Certain galley captains had particular reputations for this. One renegade who returned to Spain by 1560, after a successful career in Algiers and Istanbul, had embarked on that career at the age of fourteen as a catamite to the most famous corsair of all, Hayreddin Barbarossa, *kapudan paşa* (admiral) of the Ottoman navy.[24] Two of the most important corsairs in the Ottoman navy in the later sixteenth century, Uluç Ali and Hasan Veneziano—both of them Italian renegades who had begun their careers as corsairs in Algiers— were said to have become bitter rivals over a boy.[25] An intelligence report, prepared by a Knight of Malta who spent time in Istanbul in 1575, described Uluç Ali (who was then based there, serving as *kapudan paşa* himself) as 'very much given to the unspeakable vice, taking pleasure in more than 300 page-boys'. It explained that when choosing slaves to serve on his own galley, he rejected ones who might want to return to Christendom, either because they were well-born or because they had wives and families there; instead he preferred 'men who are low-born and unmarried, and the more wicked they are, the more he likes them; thus he keeps more than 50 beardless boys to serve the appetites of these slaves, believing that if they are treated in that way they will have no wish to escape'.[26] In Algiers, according to de Sosa, 'sodomy is regarded as honourable, since the man who maintains the greatest number of boys is honoured most.' No Turk would go to war, he wrote, nor corsair embark on the *corso*, without his boy, 'who serves as his cook and his bed-mate'.[27]

Against this general background, accounts of pious Christian youths resisting the advances of their Muslim masters cannot be entirely dismissed, despite the obvious ulterior motives of the clerical authors who celebrated them. (Spanish authors, in particular, would have known of the tenth-century saint and martyr Pelagius of Cordoba, a beautiful boy who died resisting the sexual and conversionary advances of the Emir, 'Abd al-Rahman III; it was a story that could not fail to reinforce the association between conversion to Islam and 'unspeakable vice'.)[28] Thus an account of the future Jesuit Gerónimo López, who was sold to a Spanish renegade in Algiers in the early years of the seventeenth century, described how this 'extremely chaste youth' fought off the sexual advances of his master 'with his hands and teeth'.[29] Writing in the 1670s, the French Capuchin missionary Michel Febvre told the story of a young Polish slave in Aleppo who had not only beaten back his master but killed him, when the latter attempted to commit 'a shameful and abominable sin'. (The governor of the city decreed that the boy be executed and his body left to the dogs, but, in a miraculous sign triumphantly reported by Febvre, most dogs would not touch it, and the only one that did dropped dead.)[30] An account of the Franciscan mission in Tripoli in the late seventeenth century mentions that the friars, who were long-term residents there, tried to engage each young male Christian captive soon after his arrival in a 'very candid conversation' about the unspeakable vice of the Moors, urging resistance. They also boarded the vessels of Christian merchants, telling them not to allow their adolescents to leave the ship.[31]

★ ★ ★

It might be thought that the slave-owning societies of the North African ports, with their military and corsairing elites and their constant flow of new captives, were a special case; but the picture was broadly the same elsewhere in Ottoman territory. The teenaged Václav Vratislav, released from the 'Black Tower' prison outside Istanbul in 1596, was warned by an Ottoman official not to accompany the other freed prisoners to a meeting in the city, because 'on account of my youth, I might easily be seized by some pasha and converted to Islam. For the Turks, and above all the renegades, are disgraceful sodomites, and young people are in great danger.'[32] Joris van der Does, who was in the Ottoman capital during the following year, reported that the Turks had a particular passion for boys, and that consequently some fathers 'keep their sons locked up at home, until their chins are adorned with beard-down'.[33] In 1615 three Jews in Amsterdam drew up a document confirming the claim of a merchant company that 'there is an immeasurably great danger in travelling from this country to Istanbul, and other places in Turkey, for all people and above all for young adolescents aged from ten or twelve up to 18–20'; the danger was that they would be 'misused' [sc. sexually], 'especially if the youths are rather beautiful or attractive'. The three writers all had direct knowledge of conditions in the Ottoman Empire, and one of them, Samuel Cohen, 'was born in Turkey, and lived for many years in Istanbul'.[34] The 22-year-old Englishman Robert Bargrave, who was imprisoned in Istanbul in 1650, experienced the advances of his gaoler, which were 'unfitt to Discourse, & horrid to remember'.[35] According to a redemptionist friar who tended to them subsequently, captives (of both sexes, including children) in the Ottoman–Habsburg war of 1683–99 were subjected to sexual assaults by the slave-dealers who took them from Hungary to Istanbul.[36] As for the practice of keeping catamites: it was on the basis of a visit in 1579 to Istanbul that the traveller Jean Carlier reported that 'they [sc. the Turks] are very much given to the vice of sodomy, and the great men more than the common folk, given that there is hardly a single captain who does not have one or more catamites.'[37] In a similar vein, the English adventurer Thomas Sherley, who spent two years (1603–5) as a prisoner in Istanbul, commented that the Turks were 'Sodomittes, liars, & drunkardes, & for theyre Soddommerye they vse it soe publiquelye & impudentelye as an honest Christian would shame to companye with his wyffe as they doe with theyre buggeringe boyes'.[38]

In these cases, compulsion or slave-status was not necessarily a factor. The Lutheran pastor at the Imperial Embassy in Istanbul, Stephan Gerlach, recorded a conversation in 1577 with a Hungarian who was a slave in the household of a high official: 'he tells me what the Turks get up to, very shamefully, with boys. But the boys themselves dress up for it, and walk in front of the houses of the great lords, in order to be seen… they also receive large payments.'[39] Jacques de Villamont, visiting Ottoman Damascus in the early 1590s, had a conversation with a local janissary about the sexual mores of the inhabitants. After they had discussed polygamy, his interlocutor said: 'that is nothing in comparison with the catamites that they have in their homes; they are more jealous of them than of their actual wives, and when they go out into the fields, or off to war, they take them with them to serve them as wives.'[40] This practice of taking such boys on campaign was noted by several western observers. In 1634 the English traveller Sir Henry Blount, on the main east–west road through Bulgaria, encountered pashas leading their troops, each of them accompanied by his '*Catamites*, which are their serious loves...Boyes likely of twelue, or fourteene yeares old.'[41] And in 1709 the young writer Aaron Hill, who had spent roughly four years in the Ottoman Empire, made the same observation: 'They have their favourite *Pooshts*, or *Catamites*, as common as their Concubines, and ride attended to the Wars or distant Governments, by rich and splendid Numbers of these young *Male Prostitutes*.'[42]

Many Western writers on the Ottoman world generalized very freely on the subject of sodomy. Some of them, at least, were describing a society in which they had lived for years. The Greek author Theodore Spandounes, who in the late fifteenth century had spent part of his boyhood in Ottoman Macedonia, wrote that 'sodomy is commonly and openly practised without fear of God or man'; Luigi Bassano, writing in the 1540s on the basis of several years' residence (probably as a captive) in Ottoman territory, explained the high price of boys in the slave-market by saying that 'that nation is stained with the vice of sodomy.'[43] The English diplomat Paul Rycaut had lived in Istanbul for seven years when he published his influential book, *The Present State of the Ottoman Empire* (1668), in which he commented on Sultan Murad's paederastic affairs and described how the trainee youths in the Sultan's palace 'burn in lust one towards another'.[44] Such claims were taken up by Western travellers whose own experience was less immersive: Nicolas de Nicolay in the mid-sixteenth century, for example, who wrote of the Persians that 'like the Turks and all other Oriental nations, they are so addicted to the detestable sin against nature that they do not find it shameful', or Hans Jacob Breuning von Buchenbach (who had travelled in the Ottoman Empire in 1579), who noted that 'the Turks are great sodomites; that devilish vice is quite common in the high and low classes', or Jean Thévenot in the mid-seventeenth century, who declared that the Turks were 'great sodomites...it is an extremely common vice among them'.[45] Writers who did not indulge in such broad generalizations often included details here and there indicating the sort of role that such sexual behaviour was thought to play in Ottoman society; thus the traveller George Sandys, commenting on establishments that sold coffee ('coffa'), noted 'many of the coffa-men keeping beautifull boyes as stales [sc. bait] to procure them customers'.[46] And from such observational (or at least ostensibly observational) works as these, the theme was taken up by Western writers who lacked any direct experience of life in the Ottoman lands. Thus the historian Michel Baudier, in his widely read book about the nature of Islam in the Ottoman Empire, declared: 'they have fallen into the abominable vice of the sodomites, and into paederasty, to the point where male–male desire dominates their feelings so strongly that at the Sultan's court, and elsewhere, the great men discuss the beauty of their catamites in their most serious conversations.' In his equally popular book about the court of the Ottoman sultans, he added: 'they direct their feelings with abandon towards young boys; they caress them, and make use of them in place of women. This abominable vice is so common at the Sultan's court that you will hardly find a single pasha who is not, unfortunately, devoted to it.'[47]

3

Prejudices

What is the historian to make of such general claims? Some scepticism is required, for more than one reason. Obviously, the further removed these descriptions are from first-hand experience, the more suspect they become. Michel Baudier had never heard the 'great men' at the Sultan's court discussing 'the beauty of their catamites', and it is very unlikely that he had received information from anyone who had. Travellers who passed fairly briefly through the Ottoman lands may have acquired some of their generalizations from the Westerners they met there, who were resident for longer periods; but it would be hard to separate the elements of experience and prejudice that went into the original formation of those general statements, and it is also possible that the travellers selectively heightened them as they relayed them. What we now call 'confirmation bias' was unavoidably present in the minds of visitors—of all kinds, voluntary and involuntary— who spent time in a society which was unfamiliar to them, but about which they had already read or heard many things. And some of the statements made in narratives written by such people could themselves be copied from earlier, similar texts—even when appearing to relate their own experiences.

In any case, some observations, even if founded on genuine experience, might be open to alternative explanations. In Ottoman society it was normal, for example, for powerful men to display their status by employing large numbers of young male servants and pages; the fact that a pasha kept many such 'boys' did not necessarily mean that he was using them for sex. When Emanuel d'Aranda was brought to Algiers as a slave in 1640, and was placed in the household of the Italian renegade and corsair chief Ali Piccinin, he found there 40 boys aged between nine and fifteen who 'could not leave the residence, for fear of being debauched by the Turks; for Ali Piccinin, our master, was reputed to be strongly opposed to the abominable sin. And he kept these boys for show, just as great lords in Christendom keep pages,

Forbidden Desire in Early Modern Europe: Male–Male Sexual Relations, 1400–1750. Noel Malcolm, Oxford University Press.

lackeys, and household servants.'[1] (Note, however, that while this comment
may provide a useful corrective where some generalizations about young
male servants are concerned, it actually reinforces the standard assumptions
about the degree of sexual risk that was present outside the walls of the residence itself.) And sometimes even first-hand experience, quite accurately
recorded, might be open to more than one interpretation. When Diego
Galán was captured, as a fourteen-year-old boy, off the Algerian coast in
1589, one of the corsair captains 'began to show affection for me, running
his hand through my hair, and saying: "Don't be afraid, sir, that they will
harm you."' One modern scholar assumes from this that the man was pawing the boy with sexual intent, an assumption which may possibly have
been shared by Galán himself; yet there is nothing in his account here (or
subsequently) that would rule out an innocent explanation.[2]

★ ★ ★

What is undeniable is that Western Europeans in this period did harbour
strong prejudices and suspicions towards the people of the Ottoman lands
where same-sex relations were concerned. The most important element in
this prejudice was the idea that Islam condoned or even promoted such
behaviour. Since the Byzantine period, Christian anti-Muslim polemicists
had harped on the theme of lust and sensuality.[3] The fact that Islam allowed
polygamy, and the idea that the pleasures of sexual intercourse formed a key
part of the attraction of the Muslim paradise, encouraged these writers to
portray Islam as a pseudo-religion which gained its adherents, and ensured
their continuing loyalty, by pandering to the basest of human motives. Most
of the focus here was on male desire for women, and in that connection
there was much emphasis on the alleged venery of Muhammad himself.
This also included a highly prejudicial interpretation of a verse in the Koran
(2: 223), which said, in the words of the medieval Latin translation by Robert
of Ketton, 'take [or 'plough'] the women who are subjected to you entirely
as you please, wherever you might wish'. Christian writers seized on this
'wherever you might wish', arguing that it authorized Muslim men to
penetrate their women anally as well as vaginally. (When Theodor Bibliander
came to edit Robert of Ketton's translation in 1543, he added a marginal
note at this point: 'This passage has been twisted in a rather forced way by
Christians, as if it permitted nefarious acts, even though it goes on to say
"while fearing God".' Bibliander's scholarly scruples set him apart from
most other West European writers of the time.)[4] Among the handful of

mediaeval Christian scholars studying the Koran, it seems to have been the group that included Robert of Ketton, working in Toledo in the 1140s and supplying to Peter the Venerable, Abbot of Cluny, materials for an anti-Muslim treatise, that first seized on the possibility of using this verse to denigrate Islam and its prophet. One of them, Peter of Poitiers, wrote to Peter the Venerable assuring him that this shocking verse really did exist in the Koran, and offering a scheme for a refutation of Islam in which an entire chapter would be devoted to its apparent support for sodomizing women.[5]

From there it was only a short step to asserting that Islam permitted anal intercourse between men. Precisely how and when this step was taken is not clear; but it happened within a few generations, and we may suspect that several different causes played a role. One very general factor was the development of the concept of 'sodomy' in mediaeval European law and theology, which, as we shall see, tended to treat it as an overall category that included both male–male sexual relations and male–female anal sex; once this idea was established, it was almost sufficient just to say that Islam authorized sodomy. A much more specific factor was a text, the *Contrarietas elfolica*, written probably by a Christian Arab in Spain but surviving only in a Latin translation, which went so far as to interpolate a completely spurious verse into the Koran, telling Muslims that they should not have sex with men until those men were converted to Islam—thereby implying, apparently, that male–male sex was not wrong in itself.[6] The general background to this development in Christian anti-Muslim polemics also included a range of accounts, whether factually based or not, of actual behaviour by Muslims. The widely celebrated story of Saint Pelagius has already been mentioned; another influential text was a letter, purportedly by the Byzantine Emperor Alexius I, describing how the Muslim 'infidels' raped men and boys in the cities they conquered—most probably a document forged for propaganda purposes around the time of the First Crusade.[7] Readers familiar with such stories would have had no difficulty in accepting the claim that the Koran itself authorized sodomy, with men as well as women. Yet it was that claim itself that had the decisive effect: it persuaded Western Europeans that male–male sex was not just a practice of people who happened to be Muslims, but rather something explicitly permitted or recommended by Islam itself.

Thus we find the Dominican friar Riccoldo da Monte Croce (who in the late thirteenth century had spent time living in Baghdad) confidently asserting that the Koran permitted male Muslims to sodomize men as well as women; his work, written in c.1300, became one of the most influential texts about Islam in early modern Europe.[8] His younger contemporary Guillaume Adam, who passed through the lands of the 'Saracens' on a mission to Persia in c.1314, began his description of male prostitution there with the statement that 'In the Muslim sect any sexual act at all is not only not forbidden, but allowed and praised. So, as well as the innumerable prostitutes that there are among them, there are many effeminate men.'[9] In the late 1450s, when the Spanish Franciscan Alonso de Espina wrote his very influential treatise against the enemies of Christianity, *Fortalitium fidei*, he included in its anti-Muslim section the no less confident claim that Muhammad 'permits sodomy with both a man and a woman'.[10]

This prejudice became well entrenched in Spain, where the Moriscos (Muslims who had been forcibly converted to Christianity and were suspected of covert adherence to their former faith) became objects of particular suspicion on this score. In Granada, for example, a special investigation was held in 1528 into a suspected network of Morisco sodomites.[11] In Valencia the Inquisition targeted Moriscos when it could, issuing harsher penalties to them and handing over a disproportionate number of them to the secular authorities for execution.[12] 'Moors', North African Muslim slaves and ex-slaves, were also regarded with special suspicion, as were 'Turks' (a term that might cover a range of Ottoman Muslim subjects). Such people, when accused of sodomy, were sometimes questioned pointedly about its connection with Islam and the Muslim world. A freed Moor, charged in 1566 with dragging a youth into a hay-store to have sex with him, was asked by the Portuguese Inquisition whether sodomy was permitted by the law of 'Mafoma' (Muhammad); he replied that it was forbidden in his own country, but not in the land of the 'Turks'.[13] Sometimes, indeed, this habitual association may itself have led to the commission of the offence. Another Portuguese case, of 1557, involved a young Moor who said that a man had approached him in the town of Setúbal and had asked him whether it was true that Moors slept with boys; when he said that it was, the man gave him a coin and took him to an inn to have sex with him.[14] The general view that sodomy and Islam were connected became an active element in the anti-Morisco campaign which led to the mass expulsion of the Moriscos from Spain in 1609 and from Portugal in 1614. Indeed, one of the most prominent advocates of that policy, the friar Jaime Bleda, claimed that it was only thanks to Islam that sodomy had been introduced to Spain.[15]

That last point illustrates a much more general cultural–psychological syndrome: the desire to locate the origins of undesirable practices in societies other than one's own. Within Western Europe, as we shall see, the culprit most often identified as responsible for infecting other societies with this particular vice was Italy; but general claims were also made about cultures further to the east. Some argued that Crusaders had brought the practice of sodomy back to Europe from the Levant; in 1376 the English Parliament complained that Jewish and 'Saracen' merchants were introducing sodomy to London; in 1526 an anonymous German pamphleteer, adopting the persona of a Christian living in the Ottoman city of Edirne, wrote that 'this vice originated in Turkey, and from here it has also travelled to many other places in Christendom, as you may know.'[16] One modern scholar has coined the term 'xenohomophobia', applying it to the culture of Renaissance France; his main exemplar is the humanist Henri Estienne, whose hostility on this score was directed primarily at Italy, but also, in a secondary way, at the Ottoman Empire.[17] And this linking of Italians and Ottomans would become a long-lasting theme in West European discussions of these issues: as late as the 1730s a Dutch writer, Henricus van Byler, was still asserting that sodomy had come to Northern Europe from those two societies.[18]

To conclude on all these points: there are many different reasons why early modern European descriptions of, and claims about, sodomy in the Ottoman lands should be scrutinized with care and caution. Even apparently direct testimonies could be fallible, or borrowed in some way or other from previous writers; and a degree of prejudice was no doubt present in the mind of almost every Western observer. On such grounds it might be tempting to say that we should dismiss all the apparent evidence furnished by these early modern sources, taking as our default assumption the principle that Christian writers were always engaged in 'demonizing' the Muslims, often by projecting their own particular fears or fantasies onto them. That is indeed the tendency of much modern writing on these issues. One historian discusses Renaissance references to Ottoman sodomy under the heading 'sexual fantasies', arguing that Christian Europe was suffering an 'anxiety about homosexual passivity, as a metaphor for religious and military penetrability'; another declares that 'authors built on each other's descriptions to imagine ever more shameful acts... Long and vivid discussions of Turkish sexual depravities were often part of stories about Christians captured by Turkish forces, which both titillated and alarmed European readers', as if the possible cultural purposes served by these stories were fully sufficient to explain their actual contents.[19]

Yet evidence is evidence, and the fact that it all needs to be sifted does not mean that it is all to be dismissed on grounds of unreliability. While unacknowledged textual repetition may be a problem, valid opinions can be repeated no less than ill-founded ones; and where one finds that similar experiential claims are made across a wide range of different writers in different contexts, one must doubt whether they are all engaged in mere textual repetition. Deep prejudices, such as the idea that sodomy had some intrinsic connection with the Muslim faith, may well have influenced the attitudes of many Western visitors, making them both more inclined to notice signs of same-sex activity and more likely to generalize on the basis of such evidence. But that does not entitle us to say that the signs and the evidence did not exist; too much personal testimony suggests otherwise. Even if we confine ourselves to specific accounts by eye-witnesses and more general statements by those who had spent a long time in the Ottoman lands, making due allowance for possible prejudice and/or exaggeration, the quantity and the overall consistency of such evidence—of which only a very small sample has been presented above—are hard to gainsay.

★ ★ ★

Despite the existence of all this evidence, one line of argument for discounting it, and for dismissing almost any such testimony as mere 'demonization' of a stigmatized 'other', has become especially influential: the claim by Edward Said that Western European writers who gave negative portrayals of this kind were all engaged in a project of 'Orientalism'. This notion gathers together prejudices of various kinds (including specifically anti-Muslim ones), but reduces them all, ultimately, to a political basis. As Said puts it, the Orientalism that was present in all Western portrayals of the Muslim world was 'a kind of Western projection onto and will to govern over the Orient'. The underlying impulse here was a matter of power-relations; but the key way in which power was exerted was at the level of 'representation'. As Said explains, 'Like Walter Scott's Saracens, the European representation of the Muslim, Ottoman, or Arab was always a way of controlling the redoubtable Orient.' The nature of such representations was entirely determined by this power dynamic, not by any realities on the Oriental side: that was why 'Orientalism assumed an unchanging Orient, absolutely different...from the West.' So the need to depict a world that was both as different as possible and systematically inferior led Western writers to cultivate a 'cultural repertoire' of Oriental 'terrors, pleasures, desires'.[20] If this way of considering early modern Western writings about the Muslim world were correct, then it would be possible to dismiss all Western observations on a topic such as sodomy in the early modern Ottoman Empire as ideologically motivated fictions. But, as we shall see, there is more than enough non-Western evidence to render this approach unviable.

One modern scholar has presented an argument on this topic which, while remaining aligned with Said's view, makes some more specific claims. Nabil Matar's starting-point is the observation that the British in North America made accusations about sodomy against the native people there in order to justify subjugating them and taking their lands, in the same way that such charges had been made and exploited by the Iberian conquerors and colonists in territories further to the south. 'Sodomy became the devastating justification for conquest and possession; it served to distance, dehumanize, and ultimately render the Other illegitimate.' Matar also notes that some writers, commenting on the tribulations suffered by the native Americans—military defeat and devastation by disease—argued that these were God's punishments for their sodomitical sins. So, he concludes, when British writers referred to sodomy in Islamic societies, especially in North Africa, two main motives were at work. First, they hoped that if they could show that the Muslims were guilty of the same sins, those same divine punishments would sooner or later be inflicted on them. And secondly, writers wished to express or project an extra degree of hostility towards these Muslims precisely because they had not yet been defeated or devastated in such ways. 'Given that the North African Muslims had not been defeated as the Indians had, nor enslaved *en masse* as sub-Saharan Africans had, the need to demonize and alterize them became paramount.' Sodomy thus became an essential conceptual marker, distinguishing 'the Christian, civilized Briton' from the Muslim barbarian. But the reason for this was ultimately political: the purpose was either to invoke divine aid for the project of defeating these people, or to strengthen the resolve of those Western Christians who had failed to defeat them so far.[21]

Matar goes on to suggest that references to sodomy in British accounts of the Ottoman lands were all expressions of such *a priori* ideological prejudice, not of empirical observation (even when made by people who had spent time there as captives). This whole argument is unsatisfactory, not least because it has an *a priori* character of its own. It was hardly necessary, for political purposes, to 'demonize' Muslims by making sexual accusations; the idea that the Ottoman Empire, and/or the North African corsairs, posed a threat to Western Christians was sufficiently well established without resort to such ideological artifice. And when Christian Europeans did call for warfare against the Ottoman Empire, their main arguments and justifications did not in fact rest on claims about sexual depravity.[22] Nor, in any case, was there a parallelism between the aims of colonialists in America and those of opponents of the North African corsairs, who mostly sought to repress the corsairs' raiding activities by punitive action, not to take over their lands. Conversely, the fact that Western writers had some motives to give negative portrayals of these societies does not necessarily mean that the substance of those portrayals was systematically invented.[23] As for the actual claims about sodomy: Matar suggests that Thomas Sherley's testimony, quoted above, was a product of prejudice ('Shirley did not like the Turks'); he implies that another writer, George Manwaring, made the accusation because he had been beaten by a Turk ('an episode that understandably caused him to hate them'); he also dismisses the comments about sodomy by both Manwaring and one of his travelling companions on the grounds that a third person who travelled with them did not mention sodomy in his own account; and finally he refers to a passage in the book published by Adam Elliot in 1682 as 'the only actual description of an attempted homosexual seduction of a Christian Briton by a Muslim owner'.[24] There are in fact other first-hand accounts by British authors that relate individual experience, including the narrative of Robert Bargrave, already quoted, and that of the Catholic student William Atkins, who described how, when he and his fellow students were held below decks on a corsair ship, one of the 'Turks' came down into the hold, 'inflam'd with rageing lust upon the bodies of some of our more tender companie', and attempted to rape them.[25] But in any case, to narrow the field to writings by British authors is to set arbitrary and unjustifiable limits. Much more evidence is available, preserved in a multiplicity of texts in other European languages; as we shall see, there is also clear evidence deriving from Ottoman subjects themselves.

At one point, however, Matar sketches a different line of approach. Noting several fiercely disapproving references by British travellers to sodomy in Muslim lands, including one by William Lithgow, who said he had seen it performed openly in the marketplaces in Fez, he comments: 'The practice of sodomy was neither secretive nor clandestine but crudely public—much as it was in London, where Donne had satirized the "prostitute boy" (Satyre 1) and Shakespeare the "masculine whore" (*Troilus and Cressida*) . . . Neither did the Jacobean traveller seem to know of King James's public dalliances with male companions.'[26] By employing the *tu quoque* ('you too') argument to convict the travellers of hypocrisy, this may seem to acknowledge some reality, after all, on the Ottoman and North African side. But whereas the travellers' accounts cited here by Matar do report actual experiences, the historical evidence put forward on the British side is weak: two literary expressions, from a satire imitating Juvenal and a vituperative speech put in the mouth of an ancient Greek, plus the behaviour of King James towards his favourites—which, while it may challenge precise sexual–psychological classification to this day, certainly never involved sexual intercourse in public. That some acts of sodomy took place in early modern Britain is undeniable; that the practice was culturally prominent and widely observed is much harder to believe, as we shall see. But once again the argument here is greatly weakened by confining it to British evidence. In fact the *tu quoque* approach can be valid, to a significant degree, so long as it is applied to other, more relevant parts of Christian Europe. Before turning to those societies, however, it is necessary to do the one thing that most framers of Saidian arguments on this topic have failed to do. Because they have convinced themselves, seemingly *a priori*, that the Western accounts must be wrong, they have not felt the need to ask whether there is any non-Western evidence that corroborates those accounts. This leads to the strangely (and no doubt unintentionally) prejudicial attitude of treating the non-Western society as incapable of speaking for itself, as if the only real debate has to be about Western voices and Western intentions. The first thing we need to do, instead, is to consider the evidence about Ottoman sexual practices that has come down to us from the Ottomans themselves.

4

Ottoman realities

Male–male sexual relations were commonplace in early modern Ottoman society—widely existing, and widely known to exist. To state this fact is not to make a questionable extrapolation from Western reports; it is to recognize a reality which was attested to abundantly by the Ottomans themselves. The evidence can be found in written sources of many different kinds, including romances and love-poems in Turkish and Arabic. But since there are special questions of interpretation that arise over fictive literary texts, it should be emphasized from the outset that even when such literary works are excluded, there is no lack of evidence. In the words of the classic study by Khaled El-Rouayheb: 'the idea that pederastic liaisons were a common and visible part of the culture of the pre-modern Arab-Islamic East does not rest on the evidence of belles-lettres. It can be established solely on the basis of the biographical, homiletic, and juridical literature.'[1] El-Rouayheb's study concentrates on the urban culture of the Arab-speaking parts of the Empire; other works confirm that the situation in the Turkish-speaking parts was the same.[2]

It is worth pausing for a moment over the phrase 'pederastic liaisons'. Not all of these relationships involved sexual acts, even if in many cases there is strong evidence that they did. It was possible for an older man to be merely amorous with, or devoted to, a younger male, having been captivated by his beauty or behaviour. But in the overwhelming majority of cases, both sexual and non-sexual, age-differentiation was an essential condition of the relationship. The object of love or desire was almost always a teenaged boy—the key physical attribute being the lack of facial hair. There were various words for 'boy' in Arabic and Turkish, but one of the terms most frequently used in sexual or erotic contexts was *amrad* (in Arabic), meaning 'beardless boy'. (In the early years of the seventeenth century the pious Ottoman moralist Aḥmad al-Aqḥiṣārī wrote disapprovingly that sodomy

Forbidden Desire in Early Modern Europe: Male–Male Sexual Relations, 1400–1750. Noel Malcolm, Oxford University Press.
© Noel Malcolm 2024. DOI: 10.1093/oso/9780198886334.003.0004

'has spread in this Muhammadan community and expanded among its Arabs and its non-Arabs, its learned ones and its ignorant ones...It has reached such a point that they are proud of it and blame someone who has no beardless friend (*amrad*).')[3] Adopted into Turkish as *emred*, the word could have either that general sense, or the more specific meaning of a boy who was on the point of acquiring 'beard-down' on his cheeks. In the same-sex love poetry which was, as we shall see, such a major element of the literary culture, there was even a special genre of poem devoted to marking—often with a bittersweet combination of celebration and sadness—the first onset of beard-down on the face of the beloved. It seems that in the early modern period the underlying hormonal changes occurred later than they do today, probably for nutritional reasons; typically, a young man would develop facial hair around the age of 20, or perhaps one or two years before that. And since boys were thought to be potentially desirable from close to the age of ten, there was a target age-range of nearly a decade, with a common assumption that their beauty was at its greatest at or near the half-way point. El-Rouayheb notes as typical the comment by the late-seventeenth-century Egyptian writer Yūsuf al-Shirbīnī, who 'opined that a boy's attractiveness peaks at fifteen, declines after the age of eighteen, and disappears fully at twenty, by which time he will be fully hirsute: "So infatuation and passionate love is properly directed only at those of lithesome figure and sweet smile [among] those who are in their te[e]ns." '[4]

Once again, when al-Shirbīnī said that passionate love was 'properly' directed at such teenaged boys, he was not necessarily implying that sexual intercourse with them would be proper too. Religious and legal norms were, as we shall see, set clearly against sodomy (though we shall also see that the application of those norms could be limited in practice). For some writers, the love inspired by the beauty of a male youth was chaste and Platonic; they insisted that it differed from sexual desire.[5] But outside the more elevated literary genres that explored that idea, the passion which men felt for attractive boys was generally understood to be erotic—it was the very same feeling that did lead many men to perform sexual acts with their beloveds. Early modern Ottomans did not think there was anything unnatural about this desire itself. In the early 1530s the Chief Mufti, Kemalpaşazade, was asked to issue a *fatwa* or legal pronouncement on whether an imam could forbid a boy of fifteen or sixteen to stand in front of a group of men at prayer, on the grounds that they would be distracted by looking at him; his answer was yes, so long as the boy was *müşteha*, meaning sexually desirable.[6]

The existence of such desire was accepted as a fact of nature, and religious injunctions were concerned only with the extent to which men indulged in it or acted upon it.

The strictest Islamic jurists—a minority—argued that it was sinful even for a man to place himself in a situation where temptation might occur, arguing that it was prohibited to be alone with a beardless boy. Rigorists also stressed the need to protect such boys from unsuitable attentions: a prominent Palestinian jurist of the seventeenth century, Khayr al-Dīn al-Ramlī, declared that a father could not only require his son to live with him but also restrict his freedom of movement, if the son was a handsome youth.[7] (This chimes with Joris van der Does's earlier observation, in Istanbul, that some fathers 'keep their boys locked up at home, until their chins are adorned with beard-down'.)[8] During the sixteenth and seventeenth centuries, there were many criticisms of Sufis, accusing them of hypocrisy on the issue of admiration for young male beauty: it was said that their high-minded statements about contemplating divine perfection in a beautiful face were just a cover for seeking to have sex with the youths whom they inveigled into their religious orders. Yet even the most puritanical critics never questioned the idea that the boys' beauty did naturally render them objects of desire. Discussing one anti-Sufi treatise on this topic, by the seventeenth-century Palestinian scholar Muḥammad Abu al-Fatḥ al-Dajjāni, a modern historian comments on the author's clear assumption that for men to feel physically attracted to male youths as well as women was 'not only normal, but the norm. Nowhere in this treatise or in those of his contemporaries do we find a condemnation of the sentiment. Homoerotic attraction is never described as a deviation or an abnormal attraction, or even as something that defines a minority among men.'[9]

What was condemned as abnormal was sex between adult men. Intense disapproval was focused on the adult who willingly permitted himself to be sodomized. Such a person was known in Arabic as ma'būn, meaning that he suffered from ubnah, a disease or pathological condition which caused the man to gain pleasure from such a sexual act.[10] There was thus a radical distinction between an adult man who sodomized boys and a ma'būn: the former was doing what any normal man might do, while the latter was seeking something that the vast majority of men would not and could not desire. It is important to see how far these attitudes diverged from the ones associated with the modern notion of homosexuality. There was no concept of a single homosexual desire, differentiated only at a secondary level by whether its object was young or adult, or by whether it sought gratification from the active or the passive role. The desire of an adult man for a beardless boy was on a par with, and similar to, his desire for a woman. Male youths were attractive only so long as they were 'beardless'—that is, at the stage when they did not yet have all those properly male characteristics that would make them obviously undesirable. This point was emphasized by a rabbi in early-eighteenth-century Izmir (Smyrna), Eliyah haCohen, in his influential treatise *Shevet Mussar*. Discussing the sin of sodomy—which, as much evidence suggests, took the same form among Ottoman Jews as it did in Ottoman society more generally—he proposed a kind of psychological aversion therapy. Just as he had argued that a man tempted to fornicate with a woman should 'consider that when she will grow old... her face will wrinkle like a monkey', so he advised: 'if his inclination tempts him to lie with a man as with a woman, let him consider how when the partner's beard is full, and especially if they meet when they are both grown old, how much shame and embarrassment and disgrace and dishonour [they will feel] as they remember that they had lain with each other.'[11] To make a female object of desire seem repugnant, it was necessary to think of her as a withered crone; to do the same to a male object of desire, it was sufficient to picture him just as an adult with facial hair fully formed.

The idea that full, visible masculinity would render a man categorically undesirable in the eyes of other men was embedded in the culture. A special type of *ma'būn*, called a *mukhannath*, deliberately adopted feminine characteristics in his appearance and behaviour, plucking or shaving his beard; these men were generally accepted as occupying a special cultural niche, as musicians, entertainers and court jesters, but there was also some hostility towards them, on the assumption that they were sexually passive with other men.[12] Boys in their upper teens were also sometimes accused of shaving or plucking their first facial hairs—something seen as disreputable, as it implied that they enjoyed being the objects of the sexual desire of older men, and were in no hurry to make the transition to the active adult male role.[13] Some Islamic legal sources specifically instructed barbers not to shave the beards of either *mukhannath* men or teenaged boys.[14]

We have relatively little evidence of the attitudes and feelings of the boys themselves. The taboo against adults taking the passive role in male–male sex seems to have cast some sort of shadow over the adoption of that role at any age; certainly, men did not like to be reminded in their adult years that they had been passive partners when young. When the seventeenth-century traveller Evliya Çelebi wrote about his visit to the 'Fountain of Luck' near Sofia, an intermittent spring which allegedly refused to flow for any man who had been sodomized from his youth onwards, he described how people made fun of those for whom it stopped, or who were reluctant to try, commenting that out of 70 who tried while he was there, only five succeeded. (He himself was fearful, though he did in fact succeed.)[15] But the most negative aspect of the behaviour of a *ma'būn* was the fact that he wanted to be sodomized because it gave him pleasure. This, it seems, provided the essential objection to boys who went in search of sex with men: male youths were viewed as possessing at least a sort of 'potential manliness', which would be compromised if they showed any pleasure in being sexually penetrated.[16]

   As for the adults who sought out boys for sex: they were doing so entirely for their own satisfaction, without any thought of giving pleasure to the boys. In some cases their behaviour was purely predatory, taking no account of the wishes of their victims; there was a special term for the practice of committing a sexual assault on a sleeping youth, with some writers producing specific texts to advise men on the skills and techniques they would need to employ.[17] Even in cases where an adult man had romanticized his desire for a particular youth to the point of infatuation, getting the boy to yield sexually was seen essentially in terms of a conquest that brought the campaign to a satisfying conclusion—satisfying to the adult, that is—and not as a way of establishing a bond by sharing pleasure mutually. Discussing sexual relations between the older and younger trainee youths in the Sultan's palace, the late-sixteenth-century social commentator Mustafa Ali of Gallipoli wrote: 'Novice pages suffer that burden with an attitude that their turn to be used in this fashion has simply come, like mules or donkeys or cattle tethered to a revolving wheel.' In the same text, however, he also wrote disapprovingly of those trainees who developed a taste for being sodomized: 'Whenever one of the Inner Palace boys feels himself burning with a kind of fever, he makes a pact with another servant who is feeling the same . . . the anxious patient who is in need of a purgative sets out to procure one'— where the word for 'purgative', also meaning an enema-syringe, functions as a not very subtle *double entendre*.[18] (Mustafa Ali's whole account of these trainees' sexual relations validates the essential claim made about them by Paul Rycaut nearly 70 years later—a claim which has been characterized as mere stereotyping by one modern scholar, and as founded on 'hearsay and unfounded rumors more than anything else' by another.)[19]

That some boys were willing participants in such sexual relations is clear. Their motives could have extended beyond whatever physical pleasure they obtained thereby. For some, there were psychological satisfactions to be gained from being the object of attention and desire; a boy could enjoy imposing demands on his adult lover, or playing off one admirer against another, and the literary tradition gave a prominent role to the *beau garçon sans merci* who, in a dramatic reversal of the usual power-relations, reduced his lover to a state of abject servitude. Sometimes the boy's parents would be complicit in the development of a relationship with a higher-status man, who could offer patronage or financial subsidies. And it was common for lovers to present gifts to their beloveds; in some cases it became known that men had ruined themselves financially by showering gifts on the objects of their passion.[20]

The difference between seeking material rewards of this kind and actually prostituting oneself might have been hard, in some cases, to determine. Young male prostitutes were a well-known phenomenon. They had been a visible presence in the urban culture of mediaeval Islam: a study of sexual phrases and euphemisms by an eleventh-century Iraqi judge, al-Jurjāni, noted the word *ijāra*, which referred to the prostitution of youths under the age of 20; another judge from that region, al-Ṣaymarī, had written a full-length treatise on male prostitution two centuries earlier; as early as the eighth century, boys sold their sexual services 'more or less openly' in Baghdad.[21] The practice was also commonplace in the Muslim urban culture of mediaeval Andalusia; one modern scholar has written that 'Homosexuality—widespread and practised openly in all classes of society—was professionalized in several Andalusian cities', while another notes that in twelfth-century Seville the male prostitutes charged more than the female ones, 'and had a higher-class clientele'.[22] Writing at a princely court in western Anatolia at the beginning of the sixteenth century, Deli Birader referred to pimps and procurers who dealt equally in girls and boys.[23] Evliya Çelebi, whose travels in the mid-to-late-seventeenth century took him to many parts of the Ottoman world, encountered male prostitution repeatedly: Jewish boys in Galata ('there is no more despised group of catamites than they'), Tatar-speaking Karaite Jews in the Crimean town of Menkup ('men from all over Crimea who are fond of boys come here to engage in pederasty'), male youths in Cairo ('in the coffee-houses, *boza* shops and taverns, and in Rumeli Square, are to be found all the catamites'), and young prostitutes in the Egyptian town of Tanta ('there is a bazaar for boys in every coffee-house, where pretty boys are on display'). An anonymous late-seventeenth-century text on the subject of pimps and procurers also refers to the organized prostitution of boys in Istanbul.[24]

The association with taverns and coffee-houses was particularly strong. These were among a range of all-male commercial and social venues where men could go looking for boys. Taverns selling wine were to be found in all Ottoman cities; the proprietors would normally be non-Muslims, but Muslim men flocked to these places and enjoyed the somewhat rakish and transgressive culture that was to be found there. Mustafa Ali noted disapprovingly that after Friday prayers at the mosque, men would go to the tavern, 'clink their drinking bowls together and say, "It's the lucky day for giving a purgative!"' (again, using the administration of an enema as a crude *double entendre*). Others would go to these drinking-places for sexual trysts, making use of the rooms set aside for that purpose: 'Some come to the tavern with their boy lover, they eat and drink, and when evening falls they make their way over to the tavern's private room. According to the demands of their lust, they extract milk from the sugar cane [sc. ejaculate].'[25] Naturally these places were frequented by professional prostitutes looking for clients; but in other cases the boys' availability for sex was a secondary consequence of their employment there. Many taverns had musicians and dancing boys, known as *köçeks*; there was some overlap here with the *mukhannath* element of society, and the dancing boys, whose performance showed off their physical charms, often engaged in prostitution. (A work by the late-eighteenth-century poet Enderunlu Fazıl Bey celebrated several of them by name: 'Altıntop's bottom is always ready for his soul mates who are always grateful to him. You get erected as soon as you see Kanarya, he is distinctive. Girlish Memed, he is a wanderer, his property is his ass, he has thousands of husbands.')[26] Handsome young waiters were also objects of desire; in homoerotic literary works, a traditional comparison was made with the cupbearers in paradise.[27]

Much of the culture of the taverns was carried over to the coffee-houses, which became very popular places of male sociability. The moralist Aḥmad al-Aqhiṣārī condemned coffee-drinking because 'Using it necessarily forces one to observe these forbidden behaviours during gatherings, to mingle with the fools and the vile, to receive it from the hands of beardless youths, to touch their hands, and to commit acts of disobedience.'[28] One Syrian scholar, Muḥammad Najm al-Dīn al-Ghazzī, writing a little later in the first half of the seventeenth century, grudgingly conceded that drinking coffee was itself permissible under Islamic law; but, he added, 'As for passing it around like an alcoholic beverage, and playing musical instruments in association with it, and taking it from handsome beardless boys while looking at them and pinching their behinds, there is no doubt as to its prohibition.' The idea that coffee-houses hired beautiful boys to lure in the customers, as George Sandys related, seems entirely plausible, given the evidence that these waiters were indeed objects of erotic interest; in a court case in Jerusalem in 1608, the use of 'beardless youngsters' as waiters was singled out, with unmistakeably sexual significance, as a 'reprehensible act'.[29] And on the same basis it seems likely that Antonio de Sosa was reporting accurately when he said that in Algiers the barber-shops (another focus of all-male social life and gossip, with the additional element of some physical contact between staff and clientele) hired handsome boys to attract customers—though the truth of his comment that they were thus in effect 'public brothels' is harder to judge.[30]

The venue with the greatest opportunity for physical contact of a homoerotic kind, however, was the *hamam* or public bath, an institution which played a very significant role in Ottoman social and cultural life. *Hamams* opened at different hours or on different days for men and women, so were strictly single-sex at any given time; and the service for men involved the use of 'beardless boys' as bath attendants, who took the men's clothes when they undressed, and also administered massages and scrubs in semi-secluded cubicles. An early account of the *hamam* which was set up by Deli Birader in Istanbul in the late 1520s described how he staffed it with the most beautiful boys he could find, so that 'The beloveds of Istanbul streamed to that bath from all directions, and the lovers came, burning hotly…and in that bath they enflamed the wild horses of their hasty desire in the waters of lust.'[31] Deli Birader himself wrote that 'the ideal setting for masturbators is the bathhouse. There they can watch beautiful boys with ornate asses, [and] white and soft bodies and feel as if they are dying out of pleasure.' Such comments may well have been self-consciously exaggerated, but they were based on some elements of real experience: in 1585/6 the Sultan sent an order to the judges of the old Ottoman capital, Bursa, which said that 'I issued a decree that smooth-cheeked young men should not be in the bathhouses in order that nothing contrary to the *sharia* [sc. Islamic law] might issue from them. It has recently come to my attention that there are again boys in some bathhouses and [that] they are engaged in all manner of [morally] disruptive activities.'[32] (A generation earlier, Shah Tahmasb of

Persia had issued a decree, one of a series engraved on mosque walls, forbidding beardless boys to prostitute themselves in *hamams*.)[33]

In the early seventeenth century the Egyptian scholar 'Abd al-Ra'ūf al-Munāwī warned that since the use of beardless boys in the bathhouses led to improprieties that were 'as clear as the sun', the owners might find themselves, on the Day of Judgement, consigned by God to the category of pimps and procurers.[34] Later in that century, on his travels through the Ottoman Empire, Evliya Çelebi commented on the erotic nature of bathhouse behaviour both in Bursa ('In all these baths lovers dally freely with their darling boys, embracing them and going off to a corner. It is considered youthful exuberance and not improper behaviour') and in the Bulgarian city of Sofia ('I call this pool Lovers' Lair because everyone here embraces his darling boy uninhibitedly and they can go off in a corner to dally undisturbed... Others, meanwhile, are getting rubdowns with bathgloves and soap. This gets them very clean, though some who don't know the rules of ritual purity soil themselves (by ejaculating). It is altogether a marvellous scene, verging on mayhem').[35] These references are to men taking their own sexual partners to the baths; but sexual relations with the attendants there—above all, with those who specialized as masseurs—are also well attested. In the words of one modern scholar, 'the documentation for masseurs (*dellâk*), as well as barbers, acting as prostitutes is abundant; at any rate, adolescent masseurs were a favourite object of Ottoman homoerotic imagination.'[36]

Military life was another area in which such sexual relations seem to have been widely accepted. The comments of Western observers about Ottoman soldiers taking their catamites with them on campaigns are well supported by evidence from Ottoman sources. In his erotic compilation, Deli Birader included a dialogue between boy-fanciers and womanizers in which the spokesman for the former said: 'Beautiful boys are always with you on campaigns'; and the same point was also made by Mustafa Ali of Gallipoli, contrasting such boys with women, who could not perform that function.[37] This was something of a cultural trope; in the late tenth or early eleventh century the poet and medical writer Abū l-Faraj 'Alī b. Hindū had written: 'What a huge difference there is between a boy—who offers you company in travels and at home, is an adornment of your entourage when you ride out...[and acts like] a ferocious lion in the saddle of his horse and [like] a delicate gazelle under the blanket—and a woman.'[38] And the trope reflected social reality: in the mid-1660s the charismatic preacher Vani

Mehmed, who had acquired a strong influence at court, persuaded the Sultan to issue an order forbidding soldiers from taking non-combatant boys with them on campaign. As one modern historian puts it: 'In instituting the restriction, Vani had dared to outlaw a widely tolerated army perquisite. In the end, the practice proved to be as difficult to uproot as wine drinking and smoking.'[39]

The use of such boys was not confined to military campaigns. It was a feature of normal life for soldiers. In his detailed description of Cairo, composed in 1599, Mustafa Ali commented on the *jundīs*, uncouth salaried cavalrymen who exploited their local position as a privileged military caste. Each of them had a young Arab page-boy or servant, and sometimes, 'May God prevent it!—when they camp near a water they send word to each other to be ready. That night they all in concord engage in the act of the tribe of Lot [sc. sodomy].' In their leisure time they would 'stroll about eager to catch a game [sc. a boy]', and they were as likely to fight over a boy as over a horse; 'Their sensual appetite for the native beardless youths in their service is obvious.'[40] Such comments remind us that engaging in the sexual predation of boys, far from undermining the perpetrator's manliness, could be seen as a way of displaying it. Reports of soldiers taking special care, when they looted cities, to seize boys as captives, may attest—if the boys were used, as commonly alleged, for sexual purposes—to a special military ethos of swaggering masculinity. One study of early modern Damascus concludes that, for soldiers, 'a predilection for handsome boys seems to have been regarded as normal.' A report from 1606 described the mercenaries who looted the suburbs of Damascus as 'notorious pederasts'.[41] And the same may have been true of pirates, of whom Mustafa Ali wrote: 'They single out beardless boys and use them as did the people of Lot.'[42]

However willingly some of the youths in these categories—dancers, waiters, bathhouse attendants, military page-boys—may have accepted their sexual role, it is evident that they were acting, overall, under the influence of economic and social pressures: the need to earn a living, and the power dynamic that was inherent in such an age-stratified society, where teenaged boys, especially if separated from their own families, might enjoy little social or even legal protection. The same points would apply to apprentices and household servants. A rabbi in eighteenth-century Salonica warned that an unmarried craftsman should not take a young male apprentice, 'because Satan dances between them'; and as late as the nineteenth century a prominent rabbi in Izmir was insisting that poor Jewish boys should not be entered as apprentices with non-Jewish masters, because of the danger of sexual exploitation.[43] Where household servants were concerned, Mustafa Ali observed that 'Nowadays there are more dishonorable men who prefer beardless, smooth-cheeked, handsome, and sweet-tempered servant boys than there are men who prefer pretty and charming women'; he also expressed his disapproval of those servants who were guilty of 'bending over and sticking out their behind when serving, so as to make those present at the gathering hope for different joys and pleasures'.[44]

But the people who belonged to the most vulnerable and powerless category of all were the slaves. Against the whole background of social and sexual practices outlined above, it would be very surprising if male youths who had been captured and enslaved were not sometimes subjected to the sexual attentions of their masters. Under Islamic law, it was permitted for Muslim men to take female slaves as concubines; so the sexual exploitation of women in this situation could be more or less taken for granted. (Indeed, the treatment of female slaves could be even more exploitative than that: some slave-dealers would take such women from their owners on a promise to sell them, and, having hired them out intensively as prostitutes, return them several days later, claiming that they had found no buyers.)[45] This general attitude towards sex with female slaves may have influenced the behaviour of many men who owned young male slaves, making them feel that they had sexual rights, to some extent, over them too; some evidence suggests that the two cases were seen as morally equivalent.[46] There were legal scholars who argued that for a master to sodomize a male slave, or indeed to penetrate anally a female slave, was, although sinful, a less serious offence than it would be to act in such a way with a free person. The sixteenth-century Egyptian Sufi and medical writer 'Abd al-Wahhāb al-Sha'rānī complained bitterly of 'those scholars who have been led astray from the Holy Law and permitted the carnal penetration of a woman in her anus or carnal penetration of a male slave on the basis of ownership'.[47] As an honoured guest of the provincial governor of Tabriz, Evliya Çelebi was offered first wine—which, according to his later account, he refused as a good Muslim— and then his pick of the governor's young slaves: 'All his slaveboys—radiant as congealed light—embraced me and started kissing me. And I kissed them back.'[48] This may be one of the points where Evliya embroidered his narrative with some elements of fiction; but when he fictionalized, he was usually still aiming to be plausible. Here was a situation where a host was understood to be acting somewhat transgressively by offering alcohol, but where, as a slave-owner, he could offer one of his slave-boys to his guest—if not for sodomy, then at least for some degree of erotic pleasure.

Evliya's own attitude was also quite ambiguous. He was a man of the world (his pious refusal of wine on that occasion may have been a pose required by his status as an envoy), and his many passing comments on the beauties of male youths in the places he visited suggest that he shared those homoerotic feelings that were, by Ottoman standards, normal in adult men. His descriptions of the cavortings in the baths of Bursa and Sofia show that he was generally uncensorious; but at the same time he was quite reticent where his own sex life was concerned. In these ways, at least, he may have been fairly representative of his society. As Khaled El-Rouayheb has demonstrated, the love of boys was widely accepted, and in the educated, literary elite—which included religious scholars and jurists—no contradiction was felt between accepting that form of love as a social and cultural fact, and maintaining the official condemnation of male–male penetrative sex. A learned or high-status man who fell helplessly in love with a boy would be criticized, not on religious grounds, but for his loss of gravitas. (So long as dominance and control were properly maintained, on the other hand, such affairs were, in the words of a historian of eighteenth-century Damascus, 'matters for pride and not for remorse on the part of the notables'.)[49] As for actual sexual relations: one modern scholar concludes that these were generally tolerated, so long as they were conducted with discretion in reasonable 'semi-obscurity'; another notes that whilst 'congress between adult males and young boys was not construed as "homosexual" or aberrant', nevertheless that did not mean that it was 'uniformly or comfortably accepted'.[50]

For a final example of this ambiguous attitude, we need only return to Mustafa Ali of Gallipoli. Many of his disapproving remarks have been quoted above: on palace boys itching for sex, worshippers looking forward to sodomy after Friday prayers, men taking their lovers to private rooms at taverns, servants acting in sexually provocative ways, cavalrymen flaunting their sexual tastes in Cairo, and pirates sexually abusing beardless boys. In his treatise on social life, his fiercest denunciations were reserved for 'debauchees' who 'dally in the ass and deal in shit', and for 'Young men whose asses are aflame and who use them for profit'.[51] Yet, as we have also seen, he was happy to cite the standard justification for soldiers taking boys with them on campaign. Such a tangential acceptance of these paederastic sexual relations pales into insignificance, however, when one reads his long, lyrical and almost encyclopaedic description of the beauties and attractions of different types of boy:

> Now, the delectable morsels among beardless youth whom these dishonorable men favor are mostly bastards from Arabia and fathered by Turks from Anatolia on leave from the military. The true dancing boys from the European provinces are gentle, and the big and fierce-looking lads from Bosnia-Herzegovina always provide obedient service. Truly the beardless lads of no other country stay beautiful and comely as long as do they. Some of them do not sprout a hair on their face even at the age of thirty, still causing distraction of the mind to whoever sees them in the mirror of beauty. Yet the sweet-faced comeliness of Turkish youths and the agile lads of Arabia is shorter-lived than that of all the others. By the time they are twenty, they are no longer an object of desire by lovers.
>
> Nonetheless, the lads of the Inner Provinces, that is, the narrow-waisted boys of Edirne, Bursa, and Istanbul, surpass them in beauty, in perfection—in all ways. Those who lack in beauty and comeliness display a certain freshness and sweetness through the ingenious use of flirting and playfulness. And Kurdish boys, according to born roués, are said to be dedicated to submission and gentleness... When submitting themselves, they are said to exhibit gentleness with every member of their body. However, any one of the handsome lads of the Inner Provinces is said to vanquish all of them in outward gentleness and inward contrariness. It is said that they keep the lovers who flutter around them unfulfilled, dispossessing them of wealth and power... As for boys of Albanian blood, some are worthy of taking as a lover, but far too many are terribly contentious and obstinate.[52]

So wrote one of the most respected intellectuals of the late-sixteenth century in the Ottoman Empire: an eminent historian, moralist and senior administrator, who ended his career as the regional governor of Jeddah.

5

Western Mediterranean realities: men and boys

It is clear, then, that when Western travellers, diplomats and former captives wrote about sodomy in the Ottoman Empire, they were not simply engaging in malign fantasy, no matter how hostile their underlying attitudes may have been. They were describing a reality. Prejudice was certainly present in many of these accounts, especially where the presumed link with Islam was concerned; nevertheless, although any particular statement may have been unreliable for a variety of possible reasons, the overall picture drawn by these authors was reasonably accurate. But should we take their fierce condemnations as evidence that male–male sexual relations were, to them, a shockingly alien and unknown phenomenon? Or should we give some weight to the *tu quoque* argument here? Is it possible that in denouncing this phenomenon in the Ottoman world, they were at least partly engaging in a kind of psychological and moral projection, casting onto that society some of the disapproval which could have been applied, more uncomfortably, closer to home?

The answer to that last question is a simple 'yes', at least where people from the Christian lands of the Western Mediterranean were concerned. To summarize in advance a conclusion which will rapidly become inescapable: male–male sexual relations in the Western Mediterranean (a phrase which, for simplicity's sake, will be used here for Christian territories only, excluding the western part of North Africa) were essentially the same as those in the Eastern half. The striking fact, which has hardly been recognized at all in the modern historical literature, is that what we are looking at here was a single, pan-Mediterranean pattern of sexual behaviour.

It is only in the last few decades that historians have begun to realize the extent to which same-sex relations between males were part of the fabric of

Forbidden Desire in Early Modern Europe: Male–Male Sexual Relations, 1400–1750. Noel Malcolm, Oxford University Press.
© Noel Malcolm 2024. DOI: 10.1093/oso/9780198886334.003.0005

ordinary life in early modern Western Mediterranean societies. Michael Rocke's superbly researched *Forbidden Friendships* (1996) presented the most notable example: the case of Florence in the fifteenth and early sixteenth centuries, where a special magistrature, the 'Office of the Night', processed the accusations. Its rich archive enabled Rocke to calculate that in the period 1459–1502 more than 13,000 men and boys were implicated in, or accused of, such sexual relations, of whom at least 2,000 were convicted.[1] Subsequent monographs have shed light on sodomy in sixteenth-century Lucca, and on juvenile gangs and young male prostitution in early modern Rome; several studies (beginning in the 1980s) have illuminated the situation in Venice; and two articles have analysed the evidence from Bologna.[2] The patterns of behaviour revealed by all these Italian sources are remarkably consistent. And essentially the same picture has emerged from studies of Sicily (which was then under Spanish rule), Mallorca, several parts of mainland Spain, and Portugal.[3]

The great majority of these archival sources consist of judicial records—accusations by prosecutors, statements by witnesses, responses to these by the accused, and final judgments. The courts were of various kinds: special magistratures, ordinary criminal courts, and ecclesiastical tribunals, including, in some parts of Southern Europe, the courts of the Inquisition. Taken together, all these sources provide a wealth of documentation of individual cases, of a sort that is almost entirely lacking in the Ottoman lands. Where several tribunals are concerned, the quantity of evidence over extended periods makes it possible to conduct some kinds of statistical analysis. But although historians benefit hugely from this rich documentation, they need to bear in mind that it can have a distorting effect, by concentrating attention too heavily on the types of behaviour—and indeed the types of people—that were prosecuted and punished. Different factors, in different societies and at different times, may have affected the likelihood of cases being prosecuted in the first place; and different legal regimes, with different scales of punishment, may have had a significant influence too, not only on the willingness to prosecute, but also on the sexual behaviour itself.

★ ★ ★

In the Western Mediterranean, as in the Ottoman Empire, the most basic feature of male–male sexual relations was age differentiation. In Florence, 90 per cent of the passive partners were under the age of nineteen; if one excludes the very small number of boys aged twelve or below, and the even smaller number of young men aged between 21 and 26, the overwhelming majority of passive sexual partners were in the age-range 13–20, with an average age of sixteen. Of the active ones, 83 per cent were nineteen or over. The largest cohort (55 per cent) was in the age-range 19–30, with the next largest (18 per cent) aged between 31 and 40; fewer than 10 per cent of the active partners were older than that. These figures demonstrate that there was a transitional age-range, mostly located between eighteen and 21. They also suggest that the transition was asymmetrical overall: while the number of young men in their early 20s who were willing to remain passive was extremely small, the number of boys in their later teens who took on, if only experimentally, the active role was larger. It is understandable that some boys, as they approached the threshold of adulthood, may have regarded adopting the adult sexual role as an accomplishment that could bolster self-esteem; and in the great majority of such cases, the passive partner of an active teenager was another, younger, boy.[4]

In Lucca the pattern was broadly similar, with a watershed age of eighteen, above which 85 per cent of those prosecuted were accused of taking the active role. The age-range for active partners went up to 30, with no cases at all beyond that. (Only one person of a higher age was prosecuted, and he was a man in his 40s, accused of allowing himself to be sodomized by younger men.) The main difference between the Luccan statistics and the Florentine ones is that the former show a larger proportion of teenagers taking on the active role: in the age group between fifteen and seventeen (inclusive), 29 boys were accused of passive sex, 24 of active, and 21 of taking both roles. But precise comparisons are not possible; the total sample is much smaller in the Luccan case (a total of 259 individuals of all ages for whom the documents record both their age and the role they performed), and it may be that the magistrates there had a more particular concern with monitoring and reforming sexual behaviour among boys. Certainly the punishment regime, where boys were concerned, was much stricter in Lucca than it was in the Tuscan capital.[5]

In Bologna the statistical base is smaller again; here there was no special magistrature, only the regular criminal courts, so it is not surprising that the records yield a higher proportion of egregious sexual assaults on young children—the sort of case most likely to be brought to the attention of the courts, thanks to the efforts of aggrieved family members. In some cases the age of the victim was not recorded; in those where it was, during the fifteenth century, seven out of sixteen victims or passive partners were under the age of twelve, while the other nine were all in their teens. One adult man, tried in 1412, confessed to having sodomized, on thirteen different occasions, a variety of partners, the majority of them aged between fourteen and nineteen. In the sixteenth and seventeenth centuries, all the Bolognese cases that have been studied involved an age difference that correlates with the adoption of the active and passive roles.[6]

In Rome, in the records of the Governor's court (the main tribunal, though not the only one, dealing with such cases), 20 full indictments are preserved out of the 47 sodomy trials that are known to have taken place in the period 1560–85; of these indictments, seventeen involved the use of force against young or teenaged boys, and one concerned a consensual relationship between two people who lived together pretending to be 'father and son'. For the same court in the period 1600–66, a study of cases for which the ages of perpetrators and victims are recorded yields nine victims between the ages of thirteen and seventeen, none above that age, and sixteen who were aged twelve or less, including two four-year-olds. The perpetrators' ages ranged mostly from eighteen to 30, with the majority in the early-to-mid 20s, and just one 40-year-old and one 50-year-old.[7]

For Venice, although large numbers of cases are known—in the first half of the sixteenth century sodomy trials were running at more than five per year, often with several people accused—no statistical analyses of ages are available; but the great majority of reported cases fit the usual age-differentiated pattern. Confirmatory evidence comes from various provisions made by the Venetian authorities as they tried to clamp down on male–male sexual relations: the creation in 1458, for example, of a special group of anti-sodomy officers tasked with visiting taverns to investigate 'people keeping company of inappropriate ages, that is, grown-ups with youths'; the law of 1467 which required surgeons and barbers to report signs of anal damage in women and boys; or the crackdown in 1496, which involved special patrols searching for boys who were *patientes* (sc. passive partners), monitoring schools for fencing, dance and song, where youths might be found in the evenings, and once again looking for companions of unequal age.[8] It was in Venice that the libertine writer Antonio Rocco penned his dialogue in praise of paederasty, *Alcibiade* (c.1630), in which he declared that the time to enjoy boys sexually was when they were between the ages of nine and eighteen.[9]

The pattern was essentially the same in the Iberian peninsula. Rafael Carrasco, who pioneered the study of this subject in Spain, has referred to 'the eternal couple of adult man and attractive adolescent which runs like an Ariadne's thread through the trial records of the Inquisition'.[10] The most detailed documentation comes from the mainland territories of the Crown of Aragon—the only parts of Spain where the Inquisition exercised general jurisdiction over sodomy. A statistical analysis of these cases by Cristian Berco shows that the watershed age here was 20. If we leave aside the men and boys who were prosecuted for *mollities* (non-penetrative sexual acts, such as mutual masturbation), we find that 82 per cent of the under-20s were described as taking the passive role, while 80 per cent of the over-20s were said to have taken the active one. Carrasco's study of Valencia, which was one of the Aragonese Crown lands, has similarly given the age of 20 as the dividing-line; he notes that of those named in the trial documents who were between the ages of twelve and nineteen, the average age was fifteen and a half—within months of the average for Florence, cited above.[11]

While such statistical analyses are not available for Portugal, the impression given by the large number of cases that have been presented in the modern historical literature is that age-differentiation was the dominant pattern there too.[12] In some of these cases, where men enjoyed positions of social power, their age-differentiated preferences were displayed across a wide range of partners or victims. The Count of Vila Franca, whose residences in Lisbon and on the island of São Miguel in the Azores were staffed with numerous pages and servants, committed his first act of sodomy (as the active partner) with a 'young man' when he was eighteen (in 1612), and took his next passive partner when he was 21; by the age of 56 he had had sex with 46 partners (fifteen of them pages in his own household), and all those whose ages are given in the Inquisition trial records were between eleven and 20.[13] The last person to be burnt at the stake for sodomy in Portugal (in 1671) was a former priest, João da Costa, who had spent many years in Goa and other Portuguese trading stations in southern Asia; he had been sacristan of an important religious institution in Goa, the Santa Casa de Misericórdia, and had used his position there to indulge his sexual appetites. At two trials, in 1666 and 1671, he confessed to having had sex with a total of 49 boys, all aged between seven and seventeen.[14]

On the other hand, when reading many accounts of convicted sodomites in Portugal, one is struck by the number of cases—only a minority, but seemingly a significant proportion—where an active man sometimes also took the passive role. This was alleged of the Count of Vila Franca in the testimonies of two of his partners, though he hotly denied it.[15] It does emerge quite clearly from confessions made in other cases. In 1587 a 67-year-old priest, Dr Jorge Moreira, presented himself to the Inquisition in Coimbra and confessed that 'he had committed the unspeakable sin of con- summated sodomy over a period of seven years, committing that sin with other men actively and passively, as agent and patient, being the one on top and the one beneath'; the responsibility was primarily his, he admitted, because 'his accomplices were his servants, who lived in his house and served him.'[16] Dom Felipe de Moura, a senior military officer (and Knight of the Order of Christ) aged 42, made a confession to the Lisbon Inquisition in 1644, giving details of hundreds of acts of sodomy with nineteen different partners. The sequence he related had begun in Palermo when, aged approximately 20, he had sodomized a page of the Viceroy; since then he had been the active partner with various pages, soldiers and servants. But his most intensive sexual relationship had been with his personal retainer João de Lobão, with whom he had had sex 500 times over four years, taking both the active and the passive role; thereafter, on a long sea voyage, he had commit- ted sodomy 60 times with a page, again taking both roles.[17] The Carmelite friar António Soares, tried by the Lisbon Inquisition in 1630 when he was only 21, confessed that between the ages of eighteen and 20 he had had sex 200 times with another, slightly older, friar, both actively and passively, while during the same period also inviting older men to sodomize him, and also taking the initiative as the active partner with various youths aged under 20.[18] In this case one might be tempted to explain his sexual conduct simply in terms of an extended transitional phase. But such an explanation cannot apply to Felipe de Moura, who made no reference to having been passive in his youth (something that his high social status may, to some extent, have protected him against), and whose enjoyment of reciprocal sex clearly persisted far into his adult years. These are only individual cases, of course; but it does seem possible that, in Portugal, the Mediterranean pattern of male–male sexual relations, although predominant, applied rather less systematically.

Of the general nature of that pattern, within these societies, there can be no doubt. Here too, just as in the Ottoman territories, the key marker of sexual desirability in a male youth was the lack of facial hair. Michael Rocke refers to 'the age, around eighteen to twenty, at which the growth of a beard and the appearance of other secondary sexual traits became pronounced and [boys] began to lose what this society considered the beauty and erotic appeal of adolescence'.[19] Some Renaissance youths began to develop the first wisps of facial hair at seventeen, but later development was more common, even up to the age of 23 in some cases; it was on these physiological facts, evidently, that the statistical 'watershed' ages mentioned above were based.[20] Rocke cites an early-sixteenth-century Florentine novella describing a beautiful adolescent, Ridolfo: so long as he was smooth-faced, he was surrounded by suitors, 'But when a fuzzy down began to appear on his cheeks, Ridolfo was left no choice but to "attempt to deflower the boyhood of those younger than he, just as had been done to him".'[21] The significance of this liminal age is also illustrated by the fact that in Rome the juvenile criminal gangs were led by youths who were beginning to develop facial hair; while still young enough to be gang members, they were the ones who had sex with the younger boys, pimped them, and also arranged ambushes of the prostituted boys' clients, for purposes of extortion.[22]

In the Western Mediterranean lands, as in the Ottoman territories, there was a basic acceptance of the idea that male youths were, or could be, sexually attractive to adult men. The idea may have come easily to people at the 'libertine' end of the spectrum, but even those moralists and theologians who expressed the strongest disapproval of sodomy tended to make this assumption too. Thus Bernardino of Siena, the charismatic preacher whose sermons in Siena and Florence in the 1420s and 1430s inveighed passionately and repeatedly against sodomy, took it for granted that all the men who committed this sin were acting on the basis of such an attraction.[23] Cristian Berco concludes, from his study of the Aragonese trials, that although the Inquisitors abominated sodomy, they regarded the basic impulse to commit it as rooted in (male) human nature.[24] The Jesuit Giovanni Domenico Ottonelli, discussing boy actors in his widely read treatise on theatre (issued over several years in the mid-seventeenth century, and soon reprinted), cited as authoritative a statement by St Basil that looking at the beauty of boys was a means by which the Devil had succeeded in tempting many men.[25] And a generation later, the senior papal lawyer (and Cardinal) Giovanni Battista De Luca observed matter-of-factly that it was the general assumption of legal systems and jurists that men who sodomized adolescent boys did so because of 'a certain urge which is, as it were, natural'.[26]

The corollary of this assumption was, once again, the belief that there was something quite monstrous about an adult man wanting to be penetrated. Cardinal De Luca made the point just quoted in order to explain why it was that boys who had succumbed to the advances of adult sodomites were treated more leniently by the law. He immediately continued:

But if it were found to be true that the opposite happened (something which is rumoured to happen in some countries, and which honourable and correctly behaved people find impossible to believe), namely, that the passive role was taken by people of fully mature age, not because of that urge or indeed natural instinct which commonly arises towards good-looking boys, but rather because of a kind of sensuality which seems to partake of bestiality and excessive filthiness: in such a case judicial practice should take the opposite course, that is, using greater severity.[27]

The libertine Antonio Rocco, in his treatise in praise of paederasty, made a similar point, about the gross undesirability of an adult male body from the point of view of another adult man. When the boy, whom the tutor is trying to seduce, asks why it is that, if men get such natural pleasure from sex with boys, they do not also seek it with other men, the tutor replies: 'where the pleasures of love are concerned, both appearance and nature change with age. A baby goat is a fine-tasting food; but when it has grown into a billy-goat, it is utterly foul. Those who pay sexual attention to these big goatish men are rebelling against the principles of love—they are animals, whose desire is beastly and corrupt.'[28]

The widespread hostility to passive adult men was often reflected in legal systems and court judgments. At the beginning of the sixteenth century the Venetian authorities strengthened the penalty against adult men who allowed themselves to be sodomized: instead of being whipped and imprisoned for up to ten years, these miscreants were now to be executed. Another Venetian regulation on this subject, in 1516, referred to the adoption of the passive role by adult men as 'an absurd and unheard-of thing'; commenting on this new law, the diarist Girolamo Priuli denounced such behaviour as 'truly a wicked and abhorrent thing, never before heard of in our times, especially among old men'—resorting, just as De Luca did in the following century, to the self-comforting fiction that this was something which was, or had been, unknown in the writer's own society.[29] In mid-eighteenth-century Valencia, the Inquisitors went beyond their normal formulaic turns of phrase when condemning a nobleman who had taken the passive role, as well as the active, with a large number of adolescent boys: they said that he had engaged in 'perverting himself', extending further the 'irrational disorder' of his lust, and that 'not content with corrupting others, he procured the same opprobrium for himself.'[30]

6

Contexts of sexual life

For the most part, the existing bodies of evidence from these Western Mediterranean societies show that the nature of the sexual relationship that took place between adult men and male youths was merely physical—and often, indeed, quite casual. Rafael Carrasco even describes the Valencian trial documents as indicating 'a radical separation between affection and sex'.[1] Many of the Florentine records are about chance encounters between men who went out into the streets—typically in the period between dusk (when the working day ended) and the time, three or four hours later, when the taverns closed—and the boys they found there. A common game or ritual consisted of grabbing a boy's cap or hat and refusing to give it back until the boy had 'serviced' the man. The sexual act could then take place in a dark street or alleyway or covered doorway, or in the gardens and fields just outside the city walls, or in some other public place, such as a church. Rocke has calculated that such public venues were used in 28 per cent of all cases.[2] In Rome, the sites of such sexual activity included vineyards, gardens, city ramparts, and river banks; in Bologna and Barcelona, the area of the city walls; in Lisbon, streets, doorways and stables.[3] The episode witnessed by Hill and Sutton on the outskirts of Edirne fits this locational pattern; and William Lithgow's claim that in Fez he had seen buggery committed 'at mid-day, in the very Market places' (meaning, probably, the alleyways of the souk), would seem unusual only in respect of the time of day and therefore the literal visibility.[4]

The mentality or motive of the boys in these cases is generally harder to assess. Many of the youngest ones, probably, had no choice in the matter, having been tricked or simply seized. It may be that, for teenaged boys in a city such as Florence, the risk of being required to 'service' a man was just accepted as a hazard of spending time outside the home in the evening; and, of course, the older the boy, and the more closely he associated with a group

Forbidden Desire in Early Modern Europe: Male–Male Sexual Relations, 1400–1750. Noel Malcolm, Oxford University Press.
© Noel Malcolm 2024. DOI: 10.1093/oso/9780198886334.003.0006

of friends, the easier it was to resist such advances. But not all youths had homes to return to. Every early modern European city had an underclass of street-boys and beggars, who may have been especially targeted. In 1630, when the Bolognese authorities raided the house of Francesco Finetti, a tutor accused of abducting his sixteen-year-old pupil for sexual purposes, they found a ten-year-old German boy lying naked in his bed. It emerged that after that boy's parents had both died during their journey to Italy, he had come to Bologna to beg; Finetti had found him, brought him home, given him food and drink, and then raped him.[5] Several of the cases that came before the Roman court in the late sixteenth century involved men going in the evening to a church portico in order to select one of the beggar boys who slept there; if their *modus operandi* included giving the boy something to eat or drink, this may have been sufficient to gain willing consent. (More generally, Rocke notes that 'Men who took young friends to taverns usually paid the bill...Some accepted as little as a few sweets, fruit, bread, wine, or a meal.') In one case, a man took a seventeen-year-old beggar home every Sunday night between December 1570 and July 1571, paying him three *giuli* each time, and thus turning the relationship into one that looks more like a case of mutually accepted prostitution.[6]

The issue of gifts or payments is, however, a complicated one. In a society where gift-giving accompanied many kinds of social interaction (whether expressing the indulgence and patronage of a superior, or the respect and desire to ingratiate of an inferior), gifts were generally seen as signs of honour or gratitude, not as bribes or merely transactional payments. The tutor in Antonio Rocco's dialogue distinguishes indignantly between 'contract and fulfilment' or what he calls 'sordid trade' on the one hand, and, on the other hand, the interaction between a man's benign gift-giving to a boy and the boy's 'generous and courteous' (i.e. sexually compliant) response.[7] However suspect Rocco's idealistic language here may be, it was certainly true that where a man had a series of sexual encounters with the same youth it was normal for him to give presents: often they were items of clothing, including shoes, belts and hats, but other objects listed in the records include a chessboard, a birdcage, a bow for shooting birds, a fife, a drum and a lute. (The gifts presented by Gianesino to Gregorio the barber in the bailate in Istanbul were classic examples of this.) Money was also very commonly given, not so much as a payment but more in the spirit of a tip for a service rendered; over time this could add up to a significant extra income. Rocke gives the example of a seventeen-year-old tailor, questioned in 1502, who said that a priest had sodomized him 'many, many' times and had given him 'a large amount of money'.[8] In some other contexts, the use of money could have a different purpose. On a Spanish ship sailing to the Indies, when a sailor attempted to penetrate a thirteen-year-old page and the boy started calling for help, the sailor said he would pay him whatever he wanted if he remained silent. Similarly, in the case of one of the young boys sexually assaulted—in his sleep—by the Portuguese priest João da Costa in Goa, the victim was offered money as a bribe to stop him from crying out. But to another boy da Costa promised money in advance; and it seems that consent was then given for that reason.[9]

Whatever the basis on which payments had begun, if they then continued over an extended period it is reasonable to suppose that they may have become motivational. Rocke's analysis strongly suggests that many of the Florentine boys interrogated by the Office of the Night were engaging quite willingly in such sexual relations: while 25 per cent said they had had only one sexual partner in the previous year, 31 per cent were implicated with between three and six, and another 30 per cent with between seven and 20.[10] It would be surprising if economic self-interest were not one of the factors involved, even if a range of other interests were also present, including in some cases sexual pleasure, or a kind of game-playing, or the satisfaction of being praised and sought after, or the wider benefits that might have flowed from having intimate associations with higher-status men. (Such benefits could be appreciated by the boys' relations: there is clear evidence in the Florentine records of parents accepting or even encouraging a sexual liaison between their son and a rich or influential man, because of the advantages of patronage which this might bring to the whole family.)[11]

For some boys, prostitution is surely the correct description of what they were engaged in. Some were just acting independently, raking in the monetary and other benefits as they acquired them; perhaps the eight boys in the Florentine records who admitted to having had more than 30 sexual partners in the previous year were in this category. Others worked for procurers, such as the man who took a fifteen-year-old Florentine to Siena and prostituted him there.[12] Much of the procuring and pimping was quite informal and ad hoc. The example of junior gang members in Rome being pimped by their seniors has already been mentioned; in Lucca in 1605 the father of a fourteen-year-old boy, troubled by the fact that his son was showing the symptoms of syphilis, learned that the boy had spent time in an inn in Pisa, being hired out by an older youth (and, in the process, passing the infection to all his clients).[13]

In Seville in 1585, a black man called Machuco (probably a freed slave) was executed for being an *alcahuete* or procurer; the description of his activities which has come down to us portrays him as a kind of match-maker between youths, as he knew which of all the boys in town had a proclivity to sodomy, but it also describes him as 'very well known for the dealings he had with good-looking gentlemen', which suggests that he was supplying boys to adults.[14] At the Valencian Inquisition in 1625, the trial of a 20-year-old man called Nicolas Gonzales showed not only that he had been heavily engaged in prostitution himself, but also that he had been hiring out youths for sex, often to off-duty slaves; some impoverished teenagers were also dealing directly with these slaves, offering to be sodomized by them in return for a few coins or some food.[15] A few cases in early-seventeenth-century Seville reveal a more specialized form of prostitution: adult men receiving payment for sodomizing other adults (a rarer phenomenon, but one which is rendered understandable by the general distaste for adults who took the passive role).[16]

Nowhere in any of these legal records do we find a reference to what might be called a regular male brothel, on a par with the established heterosexual brothels which were a recognized element in many cities—though in 1424 Bernardino of Siena did refer, in one of his anti-sodomy sermons delivered in Florence, to 'the hidden places where people keep a public brothel of boys, like the ones with public prostitutes'.[17] The closest thing to this in the evidence studied by Rocke is to be found in four denunciations (between 1467 and 1510), in which individuals were accused of allowing or encouraging boys to come to their houses in Florence for sodomy and other immoral purposes, such as illegal gambling, on a regular basis. Also noteworthy is the fact that some of the most promiscuous boys were said to frequent the regular brothels, finding men there who were willing to sodomize them.[18]

There were, on the other hand, many taverns and inns where sexual encounters—some of them commercial—took place. The challenges to public morality posed by these places had been recognized by legislators for a long time. The Florentine statutes of 1322 forbade innkeepers to provide special delicacies that would stimulate unnatural lust between men and boys, and specified fines for those who served men suspected of sodomy; in mid-fifteenth-century Venice, as we have seen, officers patrolled the taverns looking for men with companions of unsuitable ages; and in sixteenth-century Palermo a standard decree was reissued almost every year, forbidding innkeepers to allow 'bearded men' and 'beardless boys' to share the same bed.[19] But the policing of such measures was generally quite inadequate. Many taverns in Rome had rooms specially set aside for sex. In 1605 a man complained to the governor's court that his wife's fifteen-year-old brother had been sodomized by a group of older youths, two of whom were to be found every day at a particular inn in Trastevere. 'As I understand it,' he said, 'all the innkeepers are well aware of that vice, and as they get business and profit from the sale of the goods [sc. boys] at their inns, they are complicit in it, and give them [sc. the sodomites] the facilities they desire.' In another Roman case, a boy who had been caught in flagrante being sodomized in a room at an inn explained that he had been summoned there by a procurer to service a client; this was apparently a regular arrangement ('several times he has asked me to go to the inn to let myself be buggered'), which may suggest also an ongoing understanding between the procurer and the innkeeper.[20] The general pattern of behaviour here seems identical to the Ottoman one, where, as Mustafa Ali put it, a man would take a boy to a tavern's private room to 'extract milk from the sugar cane'. So when a Catholic priest in Tunis wrote to the authorities in Rome in 1630 asking, among other questions, whether Christians working in inns sinned mortally if they offered customers 'some more private rooms for their meals, even though they know that those rooms are most commonly requested for the purpose of practising sodomy more conveniently', the issue would have been seen as a familiar one, not as a feature of an alien Muslim culture.[21]

The parallel with the Ottoman world seems less strong where public baths were concerned. They did exist in many West European cities, becoming increasingly popular from the twelfth century onwards. But they were much more utilitarian affairs, and did not have anything like the major social and cultural role that the *hamam* played in Ottoman society. The baths were also mixed-sex, with at most different areas set aside for men and women; male customers could receive scrub-downs from female assistants. It is not surprising, therefore, that in many cases they were well-known centres of heterosexual prostitution.[22] But there is some evidence that male–male sex also took place there. In 1493 the Florentine authorities issued a decree ordering the managers of public baths to refuse entry to 'suspect boys'. And in 1572 an elaborate trial in Lucca focused on the case of a fourteen-year-old boy who had been employed to wash male customers in a bathhouse, and had allegedly been sodomized by 42 men. One of the accused explained that the proprietor was simply using the boy to lure customers to his establishment.[23] The parallel here with the claim made by George Sandys about Ottoman coffee-house waiters, and that of Antonio de Sosa about barbers' assistants in Algiers, is very clear.

As for barber-shops in the Western Mediterranean: these do not feature significantly in the records as venues for sexual acts, but because they were foci for socializing and news-gathering (which may have included sexual gossip), attracting men who could linger to talk without paying for actual services, they could be places where contacts were made. In his study of Venice, Guido Ruggiero notes an anti-sodomy regulation of 1477 targeting apothecary shops, which were often run by barber-surgeons, and comments: 'Prosecution reveals a strong relationship between barbers and homosexuality, suggesting that they may have provided important links to the subculture. In an occupation breakdown they lead by far the list of the prosecuted.'[24] Studies of other cities and territories, however, do not show such a clear correlation. In Florence, barbers came fairly high on the list of occupations of men accused of sodomy—equal fifth, with butchers, at 3.7 per cent; in Lucca they came ninth, well below weavers and bakers; in Valencia barbers represented only 1.4 per cent of the total, as opposed to regular clergy (13.5), soldiers (7.0), sailors (4.6) or bakers (3.7).[25] Without background statistics on the relative sizes of these occupations or professions, of course, proper comparative analysis is not possible. Slight glimpses of attitudes or behaviour may be provided by anecdotal evidence. One of the most prominent cases in late-sixteenth-century Bologna involved a 'beardless' patrician boy and a 35-year-old Jewish merchant, who had regular sexual encounters over a period of three years; the trial records show that they had first met at a barber-shop.[26] And a story told by Pedro de León, the Jesuit from whom most of our information about sodomy in late-sixteenth- and early-seventeenth-century Seville is derived, may perhaps tell us something, despite its element of absurdity: he described how, before going to have his hair cut by an Italian barber, a young student had installed a basket around his buttocks.[27]

★ ★ ★

The prominence of soldiers and sailors in those Valencian statistics points towards two very male areas of life where sodomy was a familiar presence. In the Florentine documents there are several references to boys being sodomized by the soldiers whom they served as pages or servants; in one mid-fifteenth-century case, the magistrates cancelled the fine imposed on an active sodomite on the grounds that when he committed the offence 'he was at military service and frequented soldiers, who are commonly profligate in that vice.'[28] As with most professions that did not depend only on highly skilled workers, the military usually included boys performing menial tasks; these could be especially vulnerable in such a system of hierarchical authority. One striking case involves a group of eighteen soldiers described as 'Lombards' (meaning Italians, though a few were French or Burgundian), who were captured in 1474 when serving as mercenaries for the Duke of Burgundy, taken to Basel, and put on trial for sodomy. A majority admitted the offence; many said that they had been sodomized by their superiors, and that they had sodomized their own inferiors. Several said that these things had begun when they were young in Italy, claiming in some cases to have been raped by soldiers. Interpreting this evidence is not a straightforward task; the whole affair had something of the nature of a 'show trial', and the confessions were taken under torture (though retracted thereafter by only a minority). Modern historians have treated the whole trial as a merely propagandistic exercise.[29] Yet there is nothing intrinsically implausible about this picture of life within a close-knit group of Italian soldiers that included adolescent boys. Sodomy was widely seen as a vice that flourished among soldiers; one sixteenth-century military textbook, written by an experienced Venetian commander, began its list of soldiers' vices with blasphemy and irreligion, but next in order of importance was sodomy, which had to be 'driven out, and its practitioners harshly punished'.[30] Nor, of course, was it just within the army that such offences might occur. During the notorious sack of Prato in 1521, there were reports of Spanish soldiers raping the local boys; and eight years later fear of such rape was widespread when Florence itself was in danger of being attacked.[31] The Syrian mercenaries who sacked the suburbs of Damascus in the following century were behaving in just the same way.

If soldiering was—in these societies—conducive in some ways to sodomy, that was even more true of the kind of corsairing and galley warfare that took place in the Mediterranean, where an all-male social world was enclosed in the galley and its on-shore *bagno* (barrack-prison) of slave or convict rowers. As early as 1420, the Venetian authorities became concerned about the prevalence of sodomy in their fleet, noting that 'upon these [ships] it is committed to the greatest degree with no small infamy for us and manifest danger for every ship so that it is surprising that divine justice has not sunk them'.[32] A report, commissioned by the Pope, on the moral failings of the Christian fleet during the Lepanto campaign (1571) highlighted 'the gross vices of blasphemy and sodomy, which are normally just as prevalent among the galley crews as they are among soldiers'. As a general remedy for sodomy it recommended removing from the galleys all the boys who were not needed to perform essential tasks there; this, the author noted, would make it possible to exclude 'all the soldiers' boys'.[33] (War-galleys carried a large complement of soldiers, in addition to the crew and rowers.) A little later, the author returned to this topic, devoting a special section of his report to sodomy. Each galley had several boys on board, who were often brought there by senior officers for sexual purposes; 'many other wicked Christians, who are not sailors or junior officers, commit abominable acts with those youths, paying them money'; and the practice was 'so universal, that not only does it pass without punishment or reproof, but it is regarded as something honourable people do'. The author now suggested that only adults should be allowed on the galleys, to avoid 'the great dishonour to Christianity that comes from behaving like the Muslims, who bring youths on board'. (He even responded to the counter-argument which, he said, was put by some people, namely that if boys were excluded, men might commit this sin with other men—something which was evidently viewed as more disgraceful. His response was that that would be an improvement, since the practice would then be less public and less universal.)[34]

The problem was a familiar one; at the outset of the Lepanto campaign, the Pope had issued an order forbidding 'beardless boys' from boarding the papal vessels.[35] Such details suggest that the Christians did indeed behave like the Muslims. Many of the rowers on Christian vessels were Muslim slaves, and men in that category featured quite often in sodomy cases in Italian ports; in a Portuguese case of 1585, a sixteen-year-old Spanish boy was found to have been sodomized at least 40 times, over a period of four months, by a 'Turk' on a galley that was anchored at the entrance to the harbour at Lisbon.[36] But in any case the sexual culture of galley life was something entirely shared by Muslims and Christians. One of the claims mentioned previously, that in Algiers the galley captain Uluç Ali kept a supply of boys for his crew and rowers, may seem more extreme than anything known on the Italian or Iberian side; yet in late-seventeenth-century Marseille the convicts who rowed in the French naval galleys had their own catamites, street-boys aged between fourteen and eighteen, a hundred of whom slept in the barracks.[37] A few generations earlier, in 1631, a visitor to Toulon had noted that a recent order had forbidden the convict rowers from receiving visits from girls in their barracks, 'so that the only sinning that goes on there now consists of sodomy, masturbation, fellatio and other charming intimacies of that kind'.[38] Whether or not boys were specifically introduced to the *bagni* or the galleys for sexual purposes, it is clear that the younger rowers could also be targeted for sodomy. In 1575 a 20-year-old Frenchman, who was already in the royal prison (i.e. the city gaol) in Barcelona, was found to have incited another prisoner to sodomize him, explaining that many of the convict rowers had done this to him when he had served on the galleys.[39]

The punishment meted out to the Frenchman consisted, after a whipping of 200 lashes, of ten more years as a convict rower in the fleet. Being condemned to galley service was a common punishment for men convicted of sodomy. Cristian Berco has calculated that whereas 11.7 per cent of those tried by the Aragonese Inquisition were executed, 26.8 per cent were sent to the galleys (which, given the low life expectancy of convict and slave rowers, could often be a form of delayed death penalty). And the same statistics, re-calculated to exclude those who were released or whose fate is not recorded, show that galley service was inflicted on 38.5 per cent of all those who are known to have been convicted and punished.[40] Every Mediterranean naval power suffered a chronic shortage of rowers for its galley fleet; so the authorities generally ignored the obvious inconsistency between introducing sodomites to the galleys and at the same time fretting over the sinful sexual behaviour that was to be found there. Only Philip II of Spain, for whom no policy question was too small to investigate, seems to have been concerned by this. In a decree which he issued to Catalonia in 1585, he said that men found guilty of sodomy by the Inquisition should be handed over to the secular authorities to receive the legal punishment, which was death: 'one should not do what the Inquisitors nowadays do, when they condemn people guilty of such a gross crime only to the galleys—a practice which leads to many undesirable consequences, which it is not proper to explain because of the vileness and enormity of the crime.'[41]

The situation on the Spanish ships that made the long voyages to the New World was somewhat different; here there was no underclass of slaves or convicts, only a general hierarchy of naval ranks and functions. At the bottom of the regular hierarchy were the *grumetes*, 'grummets' or junior sailors, typically in their late teens; below them in age were the pages who accompanied some of the officers, and these could be as young as eight. The sexual exploitation of both groups was apparently quite common. One modern study, by Federico Garza Carvajal, notes that 'many seamen complained about the way in which ships' officers abused their positions of power and coerced them into performing sexual favors.' A typical example involved the 40-year-old boatswain on the master ship of the Indies fleet in 1566, who was accused of making sexual advances to at least ten pages and grummets, aged between fourteen and 20. Perhaps because of the prestige status of this fleet, the most senior officers did engage in strict disciplinary procedures when such cases came to their attention; and it may also be relevant that these ships had Catholic priests as chaplains, which was not normally the case on galleys in the Mediterranean. Investigations on board ship routinely used torture, and ostentatious capital punishment was used *pour encourager les autres*, sometimes with the subsequent burning of the corpse. There is some evidence that discipline was applied with particular severity to 'younger mariners, who practiced their own forms of sexual play with each other'.[42]

Some writers on the history of sodomy have invoked the concept of a 'total institution', developed by the sociologist Erving Goffman—an institution, that is, which is so all-encompassing and controlling that it eliminates the usual distinction between public and private behaviour.[43] The classic examples given in the modern literature are naval ships and prisons. There is some evidence of same-sex activity in early modern European prisons, but we need first to understand that the nature of these institutions was essentially quite different from that of modern gaols. Long-term incarceration as a form of punishment did take place, but it was more the exception than the rule; short-term confinement was a possible sentence (though we need to bear in mind that a 'prison' sentence issued by the Inquisition could simply mean being forbidden to leave one's house, district or town without the Inquisitors' permission), but many prisons operated primarily as holding-pens for people who had been arrested and were awaiting trial, or for those who had been convicted and were awaiting the application of their punishment.[44] There was little here to support the modern scenario of an established quasi-hierarchy among a large population of long-term inmates, with newer and younger ones made to submit to the sexual demands of their seniors. Cases of early modern prisoners trying to force themselves on other inmates are extremely rare, and must tell us more about those individuals' sexual psychology than they do about prison conditions generally.

One example would be that of the Portuguese friar António Soares, mentioned above, who took the passive and active roles with many partners when he was between the ages of eighteen and 21: among his trial documents is a note by the Inquisitors stating 'that he was extremely dissolute and that he had tried in the Inquisition cell with unheard-of daring to rape one or more of the three men with him'.[45]

Most sexual relations within the gaol had to be both low-key and consensual, not least because the general norm of disapproval seems to have been heightened by the desire of some inmates to ingratiate themselves with the authorities by reporting any such incidents. (The 20-year-old Frenchman, mentioned above, who invited another inmate to sodomize him, was reported by no fewer than five other prisoners.) Rafael Carrasco has written that in the Inquisition gaol in Valencia 'the prisoners spent their nights spying on one another.'[46] It is, of course, only the individuals who were caught whose cases survive in the records; but overall these tend to confirm the picture sketched here. In 1603 Gerónimo Juan Ponce, a mulatto sailor in his 20s who had been accused of repeated acts of sodomy in Spain and the New World, was held in the royal prison in Seville; while he was there, he struck up a relationship with an eighteen-year-old boy, sleeping with him and giving him gifts. Other inmates warned him to desist, with varying degrees of disapproval. When he was transferred to the prison of the Casa de Contratación, the Crown agency in Seville which managed the trade with the Indies, he began sharing sleeping quarters with a 20-year-old mulatto slave called Domingo López, who had also been accused of sodomy. Prompted, it seems, by some injudicious boasting by Domingo about Gerónimo's sexual interest in him, other prisoners then spied on them during the night. The evidence they gave to the authorities was not legally conclusive, but Gerónimo was nevertheless sentenced to be garrotted, with his body to be reduced subsequently to ashes.[47]

Such hostility seems to have prevailed in the prison culture of Iberia. Whether conditions were the same in Italy is not clear; but it may be doubted whether the experience of the intellectual and *libertin érudit* ('learned libertine') Jean-Jacques Bouchard, who in 1632 was briefly incarcerated in the city gaol of Salerno under suspicion of being a French spy, was typical. First he was left for a while in the gaoler's room, where he found a young boy lying naked on the gaoler's bed, 'who, to whatever small extent, sweetened the bitter and miserable situation in which I found myself, for so man is inclined by nature to physical pleasure'; then, introduced to the

room where the higher-class, fee-paying prisoners stayed, he learned that
they had sex quite often there, 'as the gaoler would bring them, for a fee,
girls and boys, either from outside the prison or from among those boys and
girls who were prisoners there'.[48]

★ ★ ★

Another type of 'total institution' in which men could be enclosed—much
less oppressive in its nature, but also tending to eliminate the distinction
between public and private behaviour—was the monastery or friary. The
accusation that sodomy was common among the clergy, and especially
among friars, was a cultural trope with a long history (which, again, does not
mean that there was no truth in it); this formed part of a broader range of
popular anticlerical sexual accusations, relating both to the alleged effects of
compulsory celibacy, and to the forms of privileged access which clergymen
could have to ordinary people of both sexes.[49] Certainly the records offer
some striking examples of early modern monks or friars with large numbers
of sexual partners. Those of the Portuguese Inquisition, for instance, give us
the cases of Agostinho do Monte Sion, from the Hieronymite Monastery in
Lisbon, who in 1681 supplied the names of the 62 partners, aged between
fourteen and 25, with whom he had had sex more than 300 times in the
previous eighteen years; João de Sousa, a 27-year-old Dominican, investigated in 1630, who had had 59; or indeed António Soares, the Carmelite
previously mentioned, who by 1630, aged only 21, had had 33. Some of the
partners in these cases were boys or men from the world outside the convent, but there is enough evidence to suggest that a significant amount of
sexual activity could take place within its walls. When Manoel da Costa, the
21-year-old sacristan of the Hieronymite Monastery, was questioned by the
Inquisition in 1682, he confessed to having had repeated sexual relations with
ten older monks, one of whom was Agostinho do Monte Sion. Eight years
later, a 40-year-old member of the same institution, Matthias de Mattos,
confessed to a sexual affair with a younger monk, in which they had alternated
between the active and passive roles.[50] Earlier in the century, a case was
brought by the Inquisition in Lima, Peru, against the head of the Dominican
province, who was accused of committing sodomy with a novice in the
Lima friary; the novice had wanted to leave the friary to avoid this man's
attentions, but the order refused permission for fear that he would publicize
what was going on there. Another Dominican, arrested for sodomy, also
accused the provincial, who finally resolved the situation by absconding.[51]

Sometimes the institutional connections furnished by the Church seem to have made possible the coming together of a group of clerics with a shared interest in sodomy. The most striking example is from Naples in 1591, where a number of priests and friars, with associated youths and boys, had formed what they called the 'Accademia Nobilissima e Onoratissima' ('Most noble and honoured academy'—an 'academy' in the Renaissance Italian sense, meaning a convivial literary society, not a formal place of instruction). It was led by a clergyman called Giuseppe Buono, known to his followers as the 'abbate Volpino' ('the crafty priest'), who was described as presiding over a 'brothel of catamites'. Reportedly, they spent their days going to see popular comedies; and among their other amusements they performed two so-called marriages between Augustinian friars and teenaged boys, and also drew up a mock-proclamation concerning the buggery of women. Two young men associated with this group had also been tried, one or two years earlier, for conducting a blasphemous parody of confession and penance, where one of them (acting as the penitent) knelt between the legs of the other, taking his erect penis in his hand; he confessed that he had allowed the other to kiss him, whereupon the 'confessor' assured him that that was not a sin, and he also confessed that he had promised to let the other sodomize him, receiving the same assurance.[52] While this self-styled academy was a very unusual phenomenon, it may perhaps serve as evidence of a more general tendency for sodomitical clergymen to act, among themselves, with some insouciance, feeling that they were protected by their special status.

One source from the early seventeenth century also depicts the Servite friary in Venice as a hotbed of male–male sexual relations, with—allegedly, and quite extraordinarily—the physical relationship between the active partner and his *cinedi* or catamites continuing long after the latter had reached adulthood. But the alleged sodomite in question here was Paolo Sarpi, the intellectual leader of the Venetian state's resistance to the papacy, and the allegation is found in an extremely hostile account of him addressed to the Pope and written by a papal agent who had tried to arrange Sarpi's assassination. He had every possible interest in denigrating the Venetian friar, declaring that he was 'the model of all wickednesses and the worst man in the world'; his inclusion of so many of the friars closest to Sarpi in the list of his catamites (such as his right-hand man Fulgenzio Micanzio, whom the writer described for good measure as having *cinedi* of his own) is open to severe doubt. So too is his claim to have been told by Sarpi's secretary that 'sometimes, in his presence and in that of those who had been his catamites, he walked around his room naked, with an erection, and took pleasure and delight in having himself seen, and in touching himself carnally in that way'. The sheer oddity of these claims seems much more likely to reflect the writer's desire to portray Sarpi as a monster, acting in ways that went far beyond the normal behaviour of sodomites, than to record any actual testimony. Only the background assumption, that readers would find it easy to suppose that some male–male sexual relations might take place in a friary, seems genuine; and the writer was a friar himself.[53]

Where the usual cases of monastic sodomy were concerned, involving the exploitation of novices and younger monks or friars by their seniors, the key factor was clearly the abuse of hierarchical power within the institution. Other cases concern friars exploiting the spiritual and social authority which inhered in their role as confessors for members of the general public. The offence of 'solicitation' in the confessional was far from unknown in the early modern Church; mostly it was associated with the seduction of female confessants, but a few male cases were also reported. In his monograph on solicitation in Spain, Stephen Haliczer explains this imbalance by pointing out that priests had almost unlimited opportunities to pursue relations with boys, whereas confession was the only occasion on which they could speak with complete privacy to girls and women. One of the Spanish cases involved a fifteen-year-old seminary student in Toledo, who went to see his confessor in the latter's cell (a location which suggests that the confessor was a friar); at some point during the confession, the confessor pushed him onto the bed and began to kiss and fondle him.[54] Similarly, when a boy in Lima confessed the sin of masturbation to an Augustinian friar, the friar invited him back to his cell and asked him to demonstrate; as the trial document recorded, 'at the request of the accused, the boy took out his shameful parts, and the accused rubbed them with his hand.'[55] It seems reasonable to assume that a friar who behaved in such a way would also have pursued sexual relations with other residents of the friary.

As for the involvement of the clergy more generally in same-sex relations: the evidence varies in accordance with the nature of the jurisdiction that generated it. Offences of this kind by clergymen were not normally handled by the secular courts; at most, some individuals might be implicated in passing by the testimonies of the laymen who were being questioned there. That is probably the main reason why priests do not feature at all prominently in the Florentine records.[56] Inquisition tribunals, on the other hand, could try the clergy; as we have seen, at the Valencian tribunal members of the regular clergy (that is, men belonging to religious orders) made up 13.5 per cent of the accused, a figure much larger than that for any other category. But ecclesiastics were seldom handed over by the Church to the secular authorities for punishment. In all but the most exceptional cases, this ruled out the death penalty and the galleys; the typical sentence was a period of close confinement in a monastic house, with degradation from the office of administering the sacraments. The relative mildness of the penalties handed down to clerical sodomites could be a source of resentment in the wider population.[57] Some people may well have believed that the clergy should be held to higher standards. Yet in most parts of the Catholic world, before and even long after the Counter-Reformation, it was a simple fact that many became priests or friars not out of a sense of spiritual vocation, but because it was a reliable career path that would bring job security and some social status. Generally, we might expect the sexual standards of the clergy to have been comparable to those of ordinary laymen. The key difference would lie in the extra opportunities given to some of these clergymen to pursue their sexual interests by exploiting their clerical status.

Similar opportunities existed for schoolmasters—some of whom could also be members of the clergy. The Barcelona Inquisition dealt with several such cases, including those of a distinguished teacher of Latin and Greek, accused of making sodomitical advances on his pupils in 1550, a nineteen-year-old schoolmaster who had molested a number of boys between the ages of seven and fifteen (1590), a grammar teacher who had got four of his pupils to masturbate him (1603), and a 26-year-old priest, employed to teach boys to read and sing, who attempted to have sex with at least five of them (1607).[58] A much more unusual case was heard by the Inquisition in Valencia in 1617, involving a 52-year-old who had previously been expelled from the order of Augustinian friars. According to the testimonies of several of his pupils, aged twelve and below, he not only tried to sodomize them but also made them undergo a strange kind of sexual training: 'the accused... taught those boys to be sodomites, making them know one another carnally, making them put their penises into one another's anuses alternately, with the accused taking their penises in his hands and placing them in the anuses of the passive ones, and making the active ones exert force until they got them inside', and even, according to one of the boys, 'making them say their prayers when they were engaged in those filthy acts'.[59] A case from Lisbon in 1639 concerned a schoolmaster accused by nine boys, aged between six and nine, of having molested them sexually while he was whipping them for offences against school discipline.[60]

These last two cases give an idea of the sense of power that may have enhanced the activities of some sodomitically inclined schoolmasters. But how typical were those individuals? Because of the nature of their job, pedagogues were of course easy targets for accusations; and there is some evidence from Italy of this charge being a cultural trope, if only as a reflex jibe. In his commentary on Dante, Boccaccio observed that people suspected teachers of sodomy because their pupils, being young and timorous, would obey 'the vicious as well as the virtuous commands of their masters'.[61] His slightly younger contemporary Benvenuto da Imola, commenting on the same text, said that 'literati' were likely to be stained with the vice of sodomy because 'they are lazy, and have the material for that vice ready-made, namely, plenty of boys.'[62] Writing to a friend from the University of Bologna in 1538, the young scholar Carlo Sigonio offered an over-the-top denunciation of all schoolmasters for their intense and notorious vices: 'it is public knowledge that they all practise most wickedly the sin of lust, and not only the natural variety, but also the sodomitical.'[63] A Florentine comic *novella* written probably in the 1540s by Antonfrancesco Grazzini involves the humiliation of a schoolmaster who has dared to woo a high-born young woman: her indignant brother gives him a severe beating, strips him, puts his clothes on a life-sized effigy and leaves it in a public square with a placard saying 'For betraying sodomy'—as if the man were punished for going against the normal sexual behaviour of his profession.[64]

And yet, overall, in these societies where boys could be thought sexually desirable from the age of about nine, what is striking is that the records do not furnish more examples of teachers exploiting their positions. It is also hard to find special regulations concerned with teachers and schools, comparable to the ones about, for example, taverns and inns. The 'schools' mentioned in the Venetian decree of 1496 were, apparently, places that offered lessons in fencing, dancing and singing: these were voluntary classes, more closely related to leisure activities than to education, held after working hours—which typically meant during the hours after dusk, the time most associated with male–male sexual liaisons. A similar law in Florence in 1494 specified that these schools must close at sundown; a new version of that law in 1502 required them to close at the singing of the Ave Maria in the evening. One scholar, commenting on the Venetian decree, has written that 'there is no reason to think that grammar schools, which were responsible for the teaching of Latin grammar and rhetoric, failed to cause a similar anxiety'; but while some anxiety may have existed in the general culture, it seems not to have been strong enough to generate any special practical measures.[65] The Florentine archive, which gives the names and professions of huge numbers of men accused of sodomy, yields only eight who were identified as schoolteachers; Michael Rocke comments that while there are a few cases of adolescents saying that they had been sodomized by their teachers, the striking thing is the 'scarcity' of such men in the records.[66] It may be that many schoolmasters refrained from seeking any kinds of sexual contact with the boys in their charge precisely because they lived in societies where the desire for such sexual relations was thought to be common, or even normal. This would have made them feel more exposed to the scrutiny of colleagues and parents—unlike teachers in societies where such desires were regarded as exceptional, unmentionable, or even unthinkable.

★ ★ ★

Almost all of the professions or institutions just mentioned—the army, galleys, the Indies fleet, monasteries, friaries, the clergy, schools—had their own systems of power and authority, of which use could be made by those who targeted sexually the young men or boys who were below them in the hierarchy. But the institution which embodied the most extreme kind of power relationship was, of course, that of slavery. Like galley warfare, this was a pan-Mediterranean phenomenon, and it was a significant presence in all the Christian countries that bordered the Mediterranean, with the partial exception of France. It has been estimated that in the sixteenth and seventeenth centuries there may have been between 40,000 and 50,000 slaves in Italy at any given time; estimates for Spain range between 50,000 and 100,000; sixteenth-century Portugal had at least 35,000; Malta had roughly 2,000, and in seventeenth-century France, despite a legal ban on slavery which went back to the early fourteenth century, at least 2,000 served in the Mediterranean fleet.[67] While more than half of the slaves in the Iberian peninsula were black Africans, nominally converted to Christianity, most of the rest, and the great majority of those in Italy and Malta, were Muslims from Ottoman and North African territories. (Many of these too had converted; but although changing faith in that way might bring some eventual advantages, it did not alter their slave status.) As we have already seen, there is much evidence of young male captives and slaves being used sexually by their masters in the Ottoman territories; given that so many of the practices, traditions and assumptions relating to this pan-Mediterranean institution were common to both sides, it is natural to suppose that slaves were also sexually exploited in the Western Mediterranean lands. In any case, given what is known of the sometimes predatory treatment of free youths by men in Italy and Iberia, it would be very surprising if some of the unfree ones were not similarly treated. The fact that very little direct evidence has come down to us is most probably just a consequence of the huge asymmetry in documentation: while we have a mass of first-person narratives and testimonies from Europeans who spent time as captives in North Africa and the Ottoman Empire, the equivalent records of the experiences of Muslim slaves in Europe are extremely meagre.

Lacking such accounts, we can extrapolate to some extent from other kinds of evidence, such as the treatise by a sixteenth-century Sicilian moralist which warned about the danger of keeping good-looking 'pages or slave-boys' (and cautioned masters not to let such boys sleep with the other servants).[68] It is known that some black male slaves in Seville had been bought for the purpose of hiring them out as prostitutes; this matched the practice of fifteenth-century Valencians who bought female slaves for the same reason.[69] Slave-women were commonly subjected to the sexual advances of their masters: in Ancona, for example, there were many cases of slaves made pregnant in this way, and the city's statutes of 1566 specifically forbade men from trying to have sexual relations, not with female slaves in general, but with ones who did not belong to them.[70] The relative acceptance of sex between masters and their slave-women is likely to have encouraged— rather as it did in Muslim societies, where that acceptance was legally correct—a more indulgent approach towards sex with a young male slave; and such sexual relations, protected both by the privilege of power and by the privacy of transactions within the master's home, were surely less likely to be reported to the authorities.

Clearer evidence comes from the more stratified slave-owning societies of the Spanish and Portuguese colonies in the New World. At the court of seventeenth-century La Plata (modern Sucre, in Bolivia), one slave testified that at the age of twelve or thirteen he had been regularly sodomized by a senior legal official there; but it was the slave, now charged with active sodomy as an adult, who was on trial, not the official.[71] The visitations of Bahia (in the north-east of modern Brazil) in the early seventeenth century uncovered several cases, including an owner of 30 black slaves who was 'notorious' for sodomizing them, and a rich plantation owner of whom a modern historian writes: 'From among the hundreds of slaves he possessed, he gave preference to Joseph and Bento, respectively fourteen- and fifteen-year-old mulattos whom he sodomized innumerable times.'[72] Overall, the Brazilian evidence reveals many cases of masters forcing their sexual attentions on their young male slaves; occasionally the slaves were able to bring accusations to the Inquisition, but for every case that generated a record of that kind, a large number must surely have gone unnoticed.[73] Some special factors may have applied to colonial societies of this kind; these will be considered in a separate chapter. But the basic social and cultural assumptions in the minds of the colonists were the ones that had been brought to the New World from their home societies in Iberia—where slaves were also present in large numbers.

As for domestic servants: in practical terms, their position in Western Mediterranean societies may not have differed greatly in some cases from that of domestic slaves, even though the legal situation was fundamentally different. A study of lawsuits brought for loss of virginity in early modern Spain shows that one third of the women in these cases were domestic servants; once again, this may encourage us to think that young male servants could also have been commonly targeted for sex.[74] Examples have already been given of upper-class Portuguese men exploiting the youths in their employment; in the words of Ronaldo Vainfas, 'It was common in Portugal to hear that "there is no chicken that does not lay eggs, nor servant that does not commit sodomy," a sign that the rendering of sexual services was a commonplace obligation of servants.'[75] Cases involving masters and servants were also quite common in Valencia.[76] But the most extreme cases seem to have involved men of high rank, who could employ a large number of young servants (some of whom might sleep, following aristocratic tradition, in the master's bedchamber), and whose elevated social status gave them a sense of relative impunity. A detailed record survives of the trial of the Catalan aristocrat Ponç Hug, Count of Empúries, in 1311–12: it shows that, as he enjoyed taking both the active and the passive role, he made much use of his servants and page-boys, often ordering them to rub his feet or legs in bed as a prelude to sexual intercourse. The Count was a demanding master; when one of the servants whom he had used for sex declared an intention to get married, he had him whipped. As one witness testified: 'it is public knowledge that with servants who let him do it, he commits this crime and favours these compliant ones, whereas with the ones who reject him, he wishes them ill, and dismisses them.'[77]

Beyond domestic service, there were other forms of employment that could give rise to opportunities for sexual exploitation. Apprentices would typically sleep in their master's house or shop; furthermore, they were under a particular bond of obligation, as their parents would have paid a fee for the privilege of having them trained up in a craft or trade. In one egregious case which came to trial in Rome in 1614, a thirteen-year-old boy came back to his parents, in need of medical attention, after only four months of apprenticeship; his master, a cap-maker, had sodomized him at least 30 times, either at night when the boy slept in his master's bed or in the daytime, in a room over the workshop—and, what is more, had begun renting the boy out to other interested men.[78] The Luccan records do contain some cases of apprentice boys being raped by their masters; cases in which they were sexually abused by older apprentices are much more common, though this archival imbalance may simply reflect the greater risk to a boy's career path that would come from denouncing his master.[79] Rocke's analysis of the Florentine data shows that only 5 per cent of the boys claimed to have been sodomized by either their employers (54 cases) or their co-workers (thirteen cases). He adds nevertheless that 'there are enough examples from a wide range of situations to suggest that working boys often had to give their employers their bodies as well as their labor', and cites the example of a doctor in San Miniato, just outside Florence, who was said to have taken four boys in turn into his service, each of whom left him for the same reason: he 'buggered him every night, and wouldn't let him sleep'.[80]

7

Typical and untypical

Hitherto, and especially in the previous chapter, an account has been given of the basic social conditions in which this pattern of sexual behaviour operated in Western Mediterranean countries. It may be helpful to add a little more detail here about the actual nature of the sexual relations. Once again, the distinction must be made between what was typical and what was untypical—with the latter category being, by its very nature, much more diverse than the former. The typical act involved penetrative sex committed by a man who was on top of, or behind, the youth he was penetrating. (Spanish witness statements often described the boy as being placed *boca abajo*, 'face down'.) Most of the testimony in the trials refers to anal penetration, whether actual or attempted; sometimes, especially with the younger boys, there were complaints about physical damage and bleeding. In Rome the court made regular use of surgeons to look for signs of such damage in alleged victims of sodomitical assaults; in Venice, as we have seen, surgeons were at all times required to report such injuries to the authorities.[1] However, as a kind of substitute for anal penetration, some men engaged in sex which was 'intercrural' or 'interfemoral' (between the thighs)—typically from behind, in order to simulate anal sex as closely as possible. Guido Ruggiero notes that interfemoral sex was quite common in Venice in the fourteenth and fifteenth centuries; a majority of those who practised it did not 'move on' to anal sex, while the behaviour of some sodomites was exclusively anal.[2] In the sodomy trials of the Valencian Inquisition, this position was also quite frequently reported.[3] In Portugal many of the accused insisted that they had engaged only in this type of sex; but there was a special reason for saying that, as the Inquisition's jurisdiction extended only to what was called 'perfect sodomy', that is, sodomy involving full penetration and ejaculation. (Much effort was spent at the Inquisition's tribunals on trying to prove or disprove the claim that this had taken place; Ronaldo Vainfas has

Forbidden Desire in Early Modern Europe: Male–Male Sexual Relations, 1400–1750. Noel Malcolm, Oxford University Press.
© Noel Malcolm 2024. DOI: 10.1093/oso/9780198886334.003.0007

commented that the Inquisition was 'held captive by its own morphology of acts'.)[4] Interfemoral sex was also known in the Ottoman world, where Sunni jurists apparently did not regard it as a major sin.[5] But overall, anal penetration remained the basic model; as we shall see, in Western Mediterranean societies this was the form of sodomy that predominated in the minds of theologians and lawyers, and also in popular culture.

The importance of age-differentiation in setting the framework for this whole pattern of sexual behaviour has already been discussed. Here we should consider the cases that diverged from that standard model. As we have seen, the typical active partner was a young adult man; in Florence the number of active sodomites in the records begins to tail off above the age of 30 (which was also the average age of marriage for a Florentine man), with only a small minority continuing beyond 40.[6] However, those records do reveal the existence of a relatively small number of men who were described as 'inveterate' or 'infamous' sodomites—persistent offenders over many years. Michael Rocke has calculated that their average age was close to 39, as opposed to the general average of 27, and judges that the great majority of them were 'probably unmarried'.[7] By not adapting or reverting to sex with women, continuing instead to pursue boys while (in some cases) in their 40s, 50s or even 60s, these men formed an aberrant minority within the larger cohort of active sodomites at any given time. A sense of the strong disapproval they attracted can be gained from the tariff of penalties set out in the Luccan statutes of 1539. For men between the ages of eighteen and 30 the punishment for a first offence was one year of imprisonment and a fine of 50 florins; each element there was doubled for the second offence, and capital punishment was decreed for the third. For men between 30 and 50, the first offence would already attract the double fine and two years of imprisonment, plus time in the pillory, with capital punishment for the second offence. But for anyone over the age of 50, immediate capital punishment was decreed.[8]

As for the minority of boys and adolescents who adopted the active role: the two most general reasons for this, namely, the existence of a transitional age-range, and the desire of some boys to 'jump the gun' by imitating the sexual behaviour of their seniors, have already been mentioned. Other psychological factors related to that second point are easy to imagine, such as the desire of one boy to exercise a kind of domination over another, younger boy. But much of this kind of sex might simply be classified as experimental. In Antonio Rocco's libertine dialogue, the boy, Alcibiade, while resisting almost to the end all his tutor's arguments in favour of paederastic sex, casually mentions at one point that he has tried out these pleasures (without gaining a high opinion of them) with 'boys the same age as me'.[9] Opportunities for this would not have been hard to find. Bed-sharing was common at all levels of society, especially where children were concerned. Some experiment-ation was caused by it; in late-sixteenth-century Pernambuco, for example, a man confessed that many years earlier, when he was a thirteen-year-old boy in northern Portugal sharing a bed with his fifteen-year-old brother, they had proceeded from 'feeling each other' to sexual intercourse, with the older boy sodomizing the younger.[10] But in other contexts boys might just engage in imitative behaviour. One example of this comes from a case brought to court in Guatemala City in 1609: an apprentice boy aged barely nine was said to have pushed himself on top of a young mulatto boy, 'moving his body as if they were engaged in the carnal act' and saying 'give me a kiss'.[11]

Sometimes a youth who took the active role with another boy might then alternate roles with that partner; this could perhaps be viewed as a form of shared experimentation, and one might expect it to have been more likely within the transitional age-range. Michael Rocke notes that such cases of reciprocal sex were rare, and arose only among adolescents of roughly the same age ('not two adults or companions of widely disparate ages'), concluding that 'the usually rigid norms of sexual role-playing loosened somewhat only when young coevals were involved.'[12] Beyond Florence, however, some cases of adult couples behaving reciprocally in this way can be found—for example, two Sicilian clergymen, both aged 25, who were accused in 1573 of sodomizing each other in the sacristy of a church, or the two inhabitants of Tortosa in Catalonia who, during the years preced-ing their trial in 1625, 'two or three times . . . had known each other carnally from behind, alternating one with the other', with an age-difference of c.25 years between them.[13] But such cases remain extremely rare.

This brings us back, again, to the category of passive adult males—the most scorned and reviled of all the minorities that diverged from the stand-ard pattern. These caused concern to the authorities whenever their exist-ence was noticed: in 1516, for example, the governing council of Venice was alarmed to learn that there were men in their 30s or above, even up to their 60s, who were willing to pay other men to sodomize them.[14] The number of passive adults in the records is so small that dividing them into sub-categories is something that can be done only with hesitancy. Some seem to have conducted their sexual relations only or predominantly with boys and youths, taking the active role most of the time while sometimes getting their young partners to sodomize them. Examples encountered already include Dom Felipe de Moura, the Portuguese military commander and prolific sexual offender, and the eighteenth-century Valencian nobleman who was specially censured by the Inquisition for seeking passive as well as active sex with adolescents; to these can be added the case of André de Freitas Lessa, a cobbler tried in Lisbon in 1593 for sexual relations—many of them active, but some passive too—with at least 31 male youths (whose known ages range from fifteen to eighteen) in the Brazilian city of Olinda.[15] Even if these men did seem to have conformed primarily to the 'normal' pattern of sodomitical activity, the addition of the passive role caused them to be viewed much more severely—as the comments of the Valencian Inquisitors showed. This is also demonstrated by the case of a notorious Florentine sodomite, Salvi di Niccolò Panuzzi, who was incriminated several times between the 1460s and the 1490s. When in 1492, as a repeat offender, he was found guilty of fondling the genitals of a young cleric in the cathedral during a sermon, he was given a heavy fine and exiled for three years. But when, four years later, at the age of 63, Panuzzi confessed not only to having sex with youths but also to asking several young men to sodomize him, he was sentenced to be executed and burnt. (This was then commuted to a large fine and confinement for life in a madhouse—though his family managed to extricate him from the latter element of the sentence.)[16]

If that was the attitude to men who simply extended their 'normal' relations with youths in this way, we can assume that an even more hostile view would have been taken of the rather different sub-category of adult couples who engaged in reciprocal sex. But the strongest disapproval of all was reserved for those adult men who took the passive role predominantly or exclusively. Given the disinclination of most men to penetrate another adult, it is understandable that some particular arrangement of circumstances may often have been needed for these passive males to find the sexual partners they desired. Payment was, no doubt, the simplest arrangement to make. A more elaborate strategy was allegedly adopted by a Venetian priest who was charged in 1608 with keeping female prostitutes in his house, in order to attract men to whom he could then submit passively himself.[17]

In some cases the passive adult encouraged the other to think of him as female: in the mid-seventeenth century, for example, a Portuguese friar and military chaplain, Lucas de Sousa, who persuaded a young man to sodomize him 200 times over a period of eighteen months, 'used to tell the boy that his anus was "a woman's passage," and should any blood flow, he explained it as "menstruation," which the boy admitted he believed, naïvely or cunningly, for some time'.[18] One case brought before the Valencian Inquisition involved a young married man, Francisco Roca, who, according to the testimony of one of his servants, invited soldiers to spend the night in his house and would dress as a woman in order to entice them to have sex with him. These two examples might be interpreted just at the level of tactics consciously adopted to achieve the desired effect. But in some other cases, the process of taking on some aspects of the female gender-role seems to have gone deeper than that.

In 1572 a Carmelite friar in Valencia, Pedro Pizarro, was denounced for trying to inveigle some of his brethren in the friary into performing sexual acts with him; one of the friars said that 'it's his normal habit to speak in a very effeminate way, and to imitate female behaviour, and so they have given him the nickname "la Pizarra"'.[19] In his treatise on physiognomy, published in 1598, the Neapolitan natural philosopher Giovanni Battista Della Porta included a section on effeminate men, in which he wrote: 'I saw one of them in Naples, who had a sparse beard or almost none, a small mouth, delicate and straight eyelashes [etc.] ... In short, with the body and gestures of a woman ... He was more womanly than the women themselves: he spoke like a woman, and always called himself "she" ... And the worst thing was that he submitted to the unspeakable kind of sex [sc. sodomy], worse than a woman.'[20] However, the issue of effeminacy, and of how it was conceptualized in early modern Europe, is complex; it will be discussed more fully in another chapter. Behaviour that was 'effeminate' in its sexual implications did not always coincide with a feminine physical appearance. In early modern Portugal there was a special term, *fanchono*, for young men whose behaviour signalled their preference for passive sex; one self-confessed *fanchono*, appearing before the Lisbon Inquisition in 1570, explained that 'the *fanchonos* are the passive partners, and one *fanchono* never commits this sin with another *fanchono*.' Yet this 25-year-old man, who admitted to having had sex with many partners, some older and some younger, was also described in the trial record as 'well bearded'.[21]

Beyond the standard practice of anal penetration, and the simulacrum of it performed between the thighs, there were some other forms of sexual activity that surface much less frequently in the records. In Western Mediterranean societies generally, fellatio seems to have been very rare; Rafael Carrasco found it mentioned only three times in all the trials held by the Valencian Inquisition.[22] It appears only occasionally in the Portuguese records; had it been a common practice, one might expect it to feature there much more prominently, since, surprisingly, it did not qualify as the offence of 'perfect sodomy', and so fell into the same category as kissing or fondling, which could be confessed quite easily. In the small number of cases that do mention it, fellatio seems to have been used as a complete form of sexual intercourse, not as something preliminary to anal penetration, and the 'active' partner, who initiated it and was in control, was the person doing the fellating—more often, a man fellating a youth, though in at least one case a man with another man.[23] The same pattern emerges in one case of a Spaniard in the New World, a priest in the Yucatán Peninsula who was charged with committing such an oral assault on a sixteen-year-old Mayan boy in 1609.[24] The Florentine evidence also conforms to this pattern (presenting only two exceptions to the rule, where the man required the boy to fellate him—in one of those cases, the notary described an act of that kind as particularly gross); but such sexual relations seem to have been less rare in Florence. Michael Rocke notes that, when men did fellate their young partners, this was 'apparently not their exclusive or even preferred sexual activity with boys'. He also observes that fellatio features disproportionately in the cases of 'older single men with long histories of sodomy'; this reinforces its untypicality overall, while suggesting that it appealed to a particular kind of sexual psychology. Whether Rocke has correctly identified that psychology, when he writes that such behaviour indicates 'a new ethos of mutual enjoyment in homoerotic interactions', seems more questionable; he has found one case of reciprocal fellatio over quite a long period, between an 83-year-old barber and an eighteen-year-old cook, but several of the Spanish and Portuguese cases seem to involve a man simply taking his own pleasure from the body of a youth. (That he derived his pleasure from a specifically masculine part of the boy's body may still suggest, however, that his psychology was different from that of most sodomites.)[25]

Masturbation seems also to have played only a minor role in these male–male sexual relations. As the classic form of *mollities*, it fell outside the jurisdiction of the Portuguese Inquisition, so could be mentioned fairly freely, as a sin but not a punishable offence; yet when it does surface in the records it appears to have functioned either as a prelude to sodomy or as a substitute for it when the boy had refused to comply.[26] There was in fact provision in

Portuguese secular law for the punishment of masturbation—whether mutual or solitary—as a criminal offence; but that element of the law was never applied in practice.[27] The situation was different in the kingdom of Castile, however. In Seville in 1579 two boys, aged approximately seventeen, were found guilty of 'immoral touchings' (a standard phrase for mutual masturbation) while 'frolicking' together in bed and 'talking immorally'; both were burnt at the stake.[28] Mutual stimulation or play of that kind may of course have been quite common among boys, and in the vast majority of such juvenile cases it would not leave any trace in the records. Guido Ruggiero notes that the authorities in Venice took no interest in masturbation in itself, and that even when two men were found to have masturbated in each other's presence, no punishment was applied because physical contact had not taken place.[29] Cases which did involve such contact seem sometimes to have occurred in situations where, practically speaking, masturbation may have been the most that could be accomplished: for example, a Dominican friar in Mallorca, tried by the Inquisition in 1605, who had engaged in 'solicitation' during confession, touching the genitals of six young men and encouraging them to fondle his (sometimes to the point of ejaculation).[30] Carrasco notes cases where mutual masturbation was adopted as a substitute for penetrative sex, when the circumstances would not allow behaviour that was 'more noisy or agitated'. He also observes that most commonly, in the cases where masturbation is mentioned, it arose because the older partner, frustrated by the refusal of the younger to accept penetration, then required the youth to masturbate him—again, an instance of substitution.[31]

Cases where men had manipulated the genitals of boys or men (non-mutually) were noticed in several of these jurisdictions, and the evidence thus generated suggests that such masturbation was seldom sought as a form of sexual activity in itself. In Florence, one of the 'inveterate' sodomites, the 63-year-old Salvi Panuzzi, did confess that 'he had fondled the genitals of numerous boys and youths'; it is not clear whether this was intended as a self-contained sexual activity or as a prelude to penetrative intercourse, but in any case the behaviour of such men cannot be assumed to have been typical.[32] Sometimes, where a sexually inexperienced youth was involved, masturbation was a way of loosening his inhibitions in order to prepare him for being penetrated—as in the case of a seventeen-year-old in Lisbon in 1703, invited to spend the night in the home of a shoemaker who began with 'the sin of *mollities*' and then persuaded him to lie face down.[33] Mutual or group masturbation as a primary end in itself, which—as we shall see—would be quite a common form of male–male sexual activity in some other parts of Europe, was very uncommon in these Mediterranean societies.

Group sex more generally was also a rare phenomenon. There were quite frequent cases where more than two people were implicated, but these typically involved an available boy being taken advantage of by a plurality of active partners. Thus in Rome in 1609, for example, two men picked up a thirteen-year-old boy, took him to an inn for dinner, and then retired to a bedroom to sodomize him in turn (where they happened to be discovered by a constable who was searching the inn for thieves); in a case brought before the Lisbon Inquisition in 1556, three men and a boy had met in a stable to sodomize another boy.[34] In such cases there are no indications of any sort of group interaction of a more complex kind. Guido Ruggiero has noticed in the fifteenth-century Venetian records a significant number of prosecutions of 'groups' of sodomites, with 32 cases involving three or more accused: for example, a group of thirteen individuals in 1464, or one consisting of two active men and four passive youths in 1474.[35] But again there is no specific evidence of 'group sex' in the fuller sense of that term; these may have been just networks of partners (some of them shared), such that one confession from the centre of the network might have a significant unravelling effect, implicating others. In Florence, where voluntary confession guaranteed the lightest punishments, it was quite common for groups of up to six men who shared the favours of a single boy—or, in some cases, of several boys—to present themselves to the magistrates together. 'Sometimes these self-disclosures occurred in chains, as word got around the circle of a boy's partners... Then the network of friends, singly or in groups, hurried to the officials to confess.'[36] Such discoveries of networks, albeit by much more involuntary methods, happened from time to time elsewhere: for example, in a sodomy trial of 1595 which revealed a group of at least ten men in Potosí and Sucre (in modern Bolivia) who had engaged in what a modern historian has described as a 'rotation of sexual couples', or in the prosecution of a number of men and boys, headed by the Count of Villamediana (whose prosecution actually followed his death by assassination), in Madrid in 1622, which ended with the execution of five youths.[37]

However, we cannot rule out the possibility that members of some of these groups did meet in particular venues where several of them might perform sexual acts at the same time. (Whether this might have involved the development of a 'subculture', with a degree of social self-identification, is a larger question which will be discussed later.) The fact that a diplomatic report from Venice in 1545 referred to the discovery there of 'a sect of sodomites' is possibly suggestive, but not at all decisive: this was the sort of negative language about sinister groups of people—real or imagined—that came most easily to mind.[38] But a minor example of what may have been a self-conscious group, meeting for sex, does emerge from a newsletter sent from Madrid in November 1655; it reported that four sodomites had been discovered together, after sunset, in a garden which belonged to one of them, 'lying down two by two', and said that they were now going to be tortured, 'in order to discover more of their accomplices'. The fact that all four were apparently adults may reinforce the impression that this was a sexual occasion deliberately arranged by a self-identified group, but it tells us nothing about the acts they may have performed.[39]

There is one striking example of a group that came together for sexual purposes, in a way that may well have involved some interchange of partners, or different couples having sexual relations in each other's presence. This was the set of eleven mostly Iberian men who were arrested at a church on the outskirts of Rome in July 1578, and charged not only with sodomy but also with trying to perform a male–male 'marriage'. The trial documents, discovered by Giuseppe Marcocci and analysed further by Gary Ferguson, are detailed enough to permit at least a partial reconstruction of the internal dynamics of this group, which, although it contained at least three youths, consisted mainly of adult men. Two of these had been companions for at least fifteen years: the passive partner, Battista, was a brawny boatman and former soldier, while the active one, Alfonso, was a former innkeeper. That active man also sodomized another passive adult, Gasparo, and had both active and passive sex—and masturbated—with another man, Bernardo, who himself sometimes sodomized one of the youths in the group. Gasparo had a friend from Spain, Antonio, who was the passive partner of another adult, Christopharo. Another man, Marco, who may have worked as a caretaker at the church, and confessed to being a habitual active sodomite, expressed a desire to 'marry' Christopharo (a term which in that instance was probably just a metaphor for sex); but the 'marriage' which brought the men together on the day of their arrest was apparently something more like a role-playing game, involving Gasparo and an adult friar—possibly a mock-ceremony, certainly to be followed by food and drink (for which provision had been made), and possibly to be followed also by sexual activities involving more than just that couple.[40] Beyond this one very unusual example—the untypical nature of which is heightened by the prominent roles played here by passive adults and reciprocal sex—it is hard to find significant cases of sexually interactive groups in the Western Mediterranean lands. Some examples do arise in the Iberian colonies in the New World, most notably the large social gatherings of sodomites in Mexico City in the 1650s; but these will be discussed later.

★ ★ ★

The standard pattern, then, involved sex between just two people, an adult and a youth. We have already noted Rafael Carrasco's comment that the interaction was a purely physical one, not involving affection. That does seem to have been the dominant model, even after one has made allowance for the fact that in some of these jurisdictions it was the cases of non-consensual sex—in effect, sexual assault—that were much more likely to be brought to court. (Most of the cases heard at the Roman criminal court were of that kind; Marina Baldassari concludes, not surprisingly, that the records of that court provide no signs of male-male sexual relations based on bonds of mutual affection.)[41] Nevertheless, there is enough evidence to demonstrate that in a minority of cases some sort of emotional relationship did develop.

'Demonstration' of such an emotional situation is, admittedly, a high hurdle to surpass, given that the judicial processes which generated most of the evidence were interested not in the feelings of the individuals involved, but only in whether certain acts had taken place. The fact that some of these sexual relationships were long-lasting and intensive—de Moura having sex with his personal servant 500 times over four years; the patrician Bolognese youth and the Jewish merchant having regular sex over three years; the shoemaker in Lisbon sodomizing his adolescent lodger twice a week for four years—does not necessarily mean that deep affection was involved, even if such prolonged relationships must surely have generated some sense of trust and intimacy. The fact that the older partner, in some cases, gave regular gifts to the younger one (as the Jewish merchant did) must also be considered in the context of a gift-giving society, where such behaviour was more a matter of convention than of the spontaneous expression of affection. Another problem affecting the interpretation of such evidence is that the nature of the judicial processes may sometimes have had the effect of causing people to misrepresent the nature of the relationship in which they had been involved. In his study of sodomy cases in the Spanish colonies in the New World, Zeb Tortorici comments: 'Archives also contain several cases that appear to depict consensual, sometimes long-term, sodomitical relationships in which, in an effort to negate one's own agency and free will, one partner would tell the authorities that he had been coerced into the sexual act by the other (which may or may not have been true).'[42]

Whatever degree of emotional depth one imputes to them, steady relationships between men and youths did exist in Florence, as the evidence analysed by Rocke clearly shows. Whereas Carrasco found sexual relationships that lasted for several months, but not—other than in a few cases that were 'extremely rare exceptions'—beyond a year, the Florentine evidence yields 52 cases that had lasted a full year, and fifteen that lasted significantly longer, including some with a duration of three, four, five, or even six years. And in roughly 16 per cent of all cases, the youth admitted to having had sex at least ten or 'many' times with his partner. Rocke concludes that ephemeral physical encounters were certainly not the only form of male-male sex in Florence: 'Men and boys commonly formed more stable, durable bonds that presumably furnished both partners with regular sexual pleasure as well as affection and companionship.' Denunciations by disapproving neighbours would sometimes refer to a man 'keeping' a boy 'for his use as a woman', and spending large amounts of money on him.[43] Such cases were thus common enough to be socially recognizable; but still, they were only a minority of cases, and the actual feelings of the users involved are generally unknown.

In a small subset of these cases, however, there is enough evidence to characterize the feelings of one party in the relationship—the older man. Several of these were described, in denunciations or witness statements, as being passionately in love. Of an unmarried weaver, whose young assistant worked in his shop by day and slept in his bed at night, an informant wrote that 'it's said he sees no other god but him.' A butcher was described as being hopelessly in love with his eighteen-year-old assistant, with whom he had sex every day in his shop; a doctor was said to be infatuated with a boy, for whom 'he commits the greatest follies in the world'. In one case the boy himself, when questioned, described his adult partner as being in love with him. But, as Rocke notes, examples of boys in love with older men are 'completely lacking'.[44] The case of Gregorio the barber, expressing his passionate feelings for Gianesino in the bailate in Istanbul, thus seems even more unusual. But although the evidence suggests that Gianesino was the older of the two, and the active partner, the age-difference between them was probably quite small; it seems that this was something more like an affair between equals—an impression strengthened by the kitchen boy's comment that 'the barber was in love with Gianesino, and Gianesino with him.'[45]

Of the kind of one-sided, older–younger love affair identified by Rocke, more examples can be found in the Iberian colonies. Doctor Gaspar González de Sosa, a canon of the cathedral at Sucre, rescued a poor boy from prison and installed him in his house as a servant; scandalized witnesses reported that they ate together, sometimes holding hands under the table, and that Gaspar would take a sip from his glass, or a bite from a piece of food, and then pass it to the boy. (He would also fly into a rage whenever the teenager stayed out late with a woman.) In another case from the same period, when the sexual relationship between Don Diego Díaz de Talavera and his young servant Luis de Herrera was discovered in 1603, and the latter was sent away to a different city, Don Diego reportedly pined for him and wrote him love letters.[46] In the territory of modern Colombia, at the cathedral of the city of Santa Fe de Antioquia, a friar was accused of sodomizing a novice and a singer in the choir; discussing with evident suspicion the man's relationship with another chorister, who had recently died, one witness said that the friar 'had made many excessive expressions of emotion' at his death.[47] The best-documented case is from late-seventeenth-century Brazil, where Luiz Delgado, a Portuguese man who had previously been tried for sodomy by the Inquisition at Évora, had a succession of passionate affairs. While working as a tobacco-seller in Rio de Janeiro, he became devoted to a teenaged boy; a neighbour testified that he had seen him 'treating him with singular affection... combing the younger one's hair and tying ribbons on the sleeves of his undershirt'. When the boy (who eventually confessed to the Inquisition that they had engaged in mutual masturbation and sodomy) announced that he was leaving for Angola, Luiz 'wept uncontrollably'. But he quickly found a new object of his affections, a sixteen-year-old, and eloped with him. One witness said that he called him 'my son, my love, and my sweetheart', and could be seen kissing and embracing him; another said that after he had settled in his new home, in the province of Bahia, he became intensely jealous, and would have the boy followed to make sure that he was not entering into relations with anyone else.[48]

Beyond the judicial records, traces of such feelings—which are so copiously documented in Arabic and Turkish poetry and prose literature—surface in a small number of texts from the Western Mediterranean lands. In sixteenth-century Italy, a handful of poets did write love poems addressed to boys; but they took care to avoid any directly sexual references, beyond the mention of apparently chaste kisses.[49] The Tuscan poet Francesco Berni sailed a little closer to the wind where references to male–male sex were concerned. In 1523 he wrote a passionate Latin poem and circulated it to his friends; entitled 'On a boy lying sick with the plague', and describing the poet as the boy's 'lover', it included lines such as these: 'I should have lain with you under the same sheets | And pressed my mouth to yours, | To suck the dreadful poison from that terrible wound, | And then to die along with you.'[50] Although extravagantly expressed, the sentiment here might conceivably be regarded as Platonic; but this was the same poet who, earlier in 1523, or possibly in the previous year, had written a burlesque 'comic encomium about a boy'—part of a series of comic encomia full of sexual innuendos—in which he said that he wished that some benefactor would give him a boy, as Maecenas had done to Vergil: 'Oh, rest assured, it's just a plaything, | To have a handsome boy, | To teach him what he should know, and to guide him!'—where the type of 'guidance' involved was unmistakeably implied.[51]

One of the strongest expressions of love for a boy in the literature of this period is to be found in the autobiography of Benvenuto Cellini. In his account of the period soon after his arrival in Rome in 1523 (coincidentally, the year of Berni's poem about his plague-stricken boy), when Cellini was himself 23 or 24, he wrote as follows:

> To help me I had only a young lad, whom I had taken on as my shop-boy, half against my will, in response to the very strong requests of my friends. This boy was aged roughly fourteen; his name was Paulino, and he was the son of a Roman citizen who lived on his own rental income. This Paulino was the best behaved, the most virtuous and the most beautiful boy that I had ever seen in my life. And it came about that, because of his virtuous actions and manners, and his infinite beauty, and the great love which he bore towards me, I felt for him as much love as any man can possibly contain in his breast. This helpless love was the reason why [I would play music], so that I could have more frequent opportunities to see that marvellous face—which was naturally virtuous and sad-looking—brighten up. As soon as I picked up my cornet, it suddenly developed a smile, so virtuous and so beautiful, that I am not at all surprised by those fables which the Greeks wrote about their heavenly gods. If this boy had lived in those days, he would perhaps have driven them even more to distraction.[52]

That description of Cellini's feelings is emphatically Platonic. Yet while reading it we need to bear in mind that in 1557 (many years after the period described here, but before the writing of the autobiography) a criminal court in Florence found Benvenuto Cellini 'guilty of keeping Fernando, son of Giovanni from Montepulciano, an adolescent, in his bed as his wife and using him carnally very many times in the nefarious act of sodomy for about the last five years'. He was sentenced to a heavy fine and four years in prison; the latter element was commuted on appeal to house arrest, but his artistic career suffered irreparable damage nevertheless.[53] The fact that Cellini was in his 50s when he had this sexual relationship with Fernando means that he belonged to the small minority known as inveterate sodomites—men who, as we have seen, continued to sodomize boys long after the age at which such sexual relations normally ceased. So, when a more than usually committed sodomite tells us that he was once passionately in love with a beautiful boy, it is reasonable to suspect that sex—or, at the very least, sexual desire—was involved. The suspicion can only be strengthened by the fact that his protestations of innocence here so obviously protest too much: the claim that he took on the boy reluctantly, only at the behest of others (why the reluctance, when the boy was charming and well behaved as well as beautiful?); the superfluous but carefully added details about the status and prosperity of the father (to remove the possibility that this was the sort of street-boy whom one could pick up and use as one pleased); the insistent repetition of the word *onesto* (a term which, in sixteenth-century Italian, under the influence of the Latin *honestus*, always referred primarily to behaviour that was morally correct: it is translated here as 'virtuous'); and finally, the reference—which Cellini makes as if he cannot help doing so, like a moth returning to the candle-flame—to the stories of the Greek gods (Zeus and Ganymede, etc.), where the erotic nature of the relationship was universally assumed.

Beyond such occasional examples of men lavishing affection on boys, there are just a few cases where the evidence suggests that strong emotional bonds existed between adults. One of the cases described as 'extremely rare exceptions' by Carrasco involved two men of the same age—34 at the time of their trial in 1574—who had been close friends since childhood, when they had often slept 'naked in the same bed'. While one had become a friar, the other had spent some time in Italy; but on his return to Spain he had sought out his old friend and resumed intensive sexual relations with him over a period of many years. Direct evidence of strong affection is not presented in the trial documents, but the whole nature of the story implies that it existed.[54] A more one-sided example comes from Portugal in 1664, where the sacristan of the cathedral in the city of Silves wrote a series of letters expressing his passionate feelings for a man who was a guitarist and a maker of musical instruments. The age of the sacristan (who said he was eager to take the passive role, interfemorally) is not known; the guitarist was presumably a young adult, as his recent engagement to be married is mentioned in one of the letters. Plaintively, the sacristan commented on that fact: 'I would have said that by Easter you would be betrothed to me. You implied that often, and you gave your word on it . . . And remembering your arms and the kiss you gave me, that is what torments me most! . . . There was no Lent for that heart [sc. penis] in your loins, when I touched it with my fingers, and instantly it sprang up! . . . Goodbye, my darling, my happiness, my true love!' Here, although the strength of these feelings was clearly not reciprocated (the letters survive because the guitarist passed them to the Inquisition tribunal at Évora), it seems that some sort of emotionally intimate relationship had existed, at least for a while. In another part of the same letter, the sacristan wrote: 'my feelings cannot rest an hour, either by day or by night, without bringing to mind your companionship and your sweet words that are continually reflected in my memory.'[55]

One other example, also from Portugal, was briefly mentioned before: the love affair between two monks in the Hieronymite monastery in Lisbon, investigated by the Inquisition in 1690. Again, very unusually, love letters apparently survive in the archive. The relationship was between a 40-year-old monk, Mathias de Mattos, and a younger man, Francisco, who sang in the choir. Luiz Mott, who discovered and published the letters, goes so far as to call him a 'young choirboy'. But Mathias's confession specified that, after 'many repeated acts of *mollities*' between them, it was the chorister who had taken the initiative and sodomized him (after which he reciprocated in turn); this suggests that the boy was at least in his later teens.[56] The letters are described by Mott as written by the younger man to the older one; this is hard to believe, given the nature of the terms of endearment which are scattered through them so liberally. 'My little bewitcher, my puppy', 'I saw you and your beautiful face . . . and your little mouth that I wanted to kiss with my tongue', 'Oh, my boy', 'my pretty, pretty boy', 'my little one', 'my child', 'my son', 'my darling, give me those arms, give me that little heart', and so on. At one point the writer says: 'How often when I was going to read the lesson in the choir stalls have I looked and missed what I so longed to see. How often have I looked at your place there and not seen my boy!' Since we know that the older monk still resided in the monastery at the time of the Inquisition hearing (which he had activated by making a voluntary confession), and since it is clear that the singer was, by that time, absent (he was referred to in the Inquisition document, but never questioned), it seems necessary to conclude that these letters were written by the older man after the departure of the younger. Nevertheless, their contents do strongly suggest that this had been a mutual affair of the heart, not just a one-sided infatuation. 'Oh, Jesus, what solace I feel now! To know what to say now, that you love me, love me excessively, excessively, excessively, love me so much and pay me in the same coin, because I love you so much, much, much. Ah, my puppy, you have already begun to kill me. I die, my dear! Help me; I die with longing for you!'[57]

8

The Western Mediterranean lands

Having looked at the typical forms of sexual behaviour, the typical contexts in which it took place, and the untypical variants, both sexual and psychological, that surface here and there in the records, it is worth considering what degree of variation there may have been, overall, between the different Western Mediterranean societies. Was this a general phenomenon, fairly evenly distributed across these territories, or was it more specific to some places than to others?

Many inhabitants of Southern Europe, if asked that question at the time, would have given a very definite answer: it was above all an Italian phenomenon. In Spain this was a standard cultural trope; a range of writers, including Quevedo, Alarcón and Góngora, explicitly associated sodomy with Italy.[1] In his collection of Spanish proverbs, published in 1659, James Howell included one which said: 'Three Italians: two buggers and an atheist'. (Another Spanish proverb, quoted in a remark attributed to the late Renaissance scholar Joseph Scaliger, said that 'In Spain the friars are buggers, in France the nobles, and in Italy everyone'; this became a popular saying, still repeated in late-seventeenth-century France and eighteenth-century Holland.)[2] Cristian Berco writes that in the Aragonese lands, 'So strong was the identification of Italians with sodomy that Italy itself was transformed into an imaginary pit of sodomitical desire', citing the case of a young servant who, when his master tried to seduce him, exclaimed: 'Am I perhaps in Italy that Your Grace wants to do this to me?'[3] At the royal court in Valencia, when a 27-year-old Frenchman was accused of sodomy in 1581, one of the first questions put to him was whether he had spent time in Italy.[4] In the Portuguese imagination, similarly, Italians were especially prone to this sin; when processing men accused of sodomy, the Inquisitors in Lisbon would

Forbidden Desire in Early Modern Europe: Male–Male Sexual Relations, 1400–1750. Noel Malcolm, Oxford University Press.
© Noel Malcolm 2024. DOI: 10.1093/oso/9780198886334.003.0008

question them much more closely if they learned that they had lived in Italy or even passed through it. People as far away as the territory of Minas Gerais, in south-eastern Brazil, used the phrase 'to fornicate the Italian way' to refer to anal intercourse.[5]

It was not only Southern Europeans who took this view. The association between Italy and sodomy was commonplace in French public opinion; in 1566 the Parisian scholar and printer Henri Estienne remarked that the French acquired the habit of sodomy either by going to Italy and the Ottoman Empire, or by associating with those who had done so, or with those who had learned it from them. According to him many Italians regarded it as a mere peccadillo.[6] English writers routinely alluded to this Italian connection; in early modern English, 'the Italian fashion' was a standard phrase for sodomy.[7] In the German lands, the idea that Italy was a hotbed of sodomy was well established. One of the commonest terms for 'to sodomize' was *florenzen*, 'to Florence'; when two men were executed for this offence in Nuremberg in 1594, a merchant's wife wrote to her husband that they had been 'burnt for the Florentine vice'.[8] The same view was held in the Netherlands, where the writer Joan Six van Chandelier published in 1657 a poem entitled 'Op de sodomiterye van Florencen', 'On the sodomy of Florence'; as late as the 1730s, if a man suspected of sodomy was found to have travelled in Italy, this was thought to be an incriminating detail.[9]

It is of course true that in Protestant territories there was a widespread presumption, dictated by religious prejudice, that this sort of serious moral vice was to be found in Italy, the heartland of the Catholic Church, and above all in Rome, where the papacy was located. As we shall see, this theme played a significant role in the inter-confessional 'culture wars'. Martin Luther—who liked to refer to acts of sodomy as 'Italian weddings'—harped constantly on this element of the depravity of the papal court, pointedly referring to Pope Paul III as 'Paulus tertia' (using the feminine form of the adjective) and describing him as surrounded by 'hermaphrodites, andro-gynes, catamites, buggers and suchlike monsters'.[10] But although the associ-ation of sodomy with Rome and Italy became a powerful reinforcing element in anti-Catholic prejudice, and was itself strengthened by that prejudice in turn, it was not simply a product of Reformation polemic, having preceded it for a long time. It was in the early fifteenth century that the Dutch poet Dirk Potter, who had spent much of 1411–12 in Rome, referred to God's punishment of the inhabitants of Sodom and Gomorrah and then added: 'Yet every day people behave like that | openly, in Italy'; it was in 1491 that the German scholar Conrad Peutinger wrote to a friend from Rome describing the papal court as 'this race which under the pretence of piety practises every sort of depravity and unspeakable vice'; it was in the 1490s that a group of German humanist poets in Regensburg borrowed the vocabulary of Roman sexual abuse to denounce Italians as buggers and 'pathics'; and it was in 1514, three years before the Reformation, that a plain-speaking Swiss mercenary declared that he would not serve the 'Lombards' (sc. Italians) because they were sodomites.[11]

It is obvious that, for some people, the fiction that sodomy was something done only by 'them', not by 'us' (and therefore that when it did occur in 'our' community, it must have been imported), was a very reassuring one. The Catalan historian and diarist Jeroni Pujades, commenting on the conviction of an Italian cook for sodomizing two boys in Barcelona in 1603, wrote: 'Evil race of Italians, who come to infect us with something of which, God be praised, Catalonia is completely free!'[12] That such a psychological mechanism of 'displacement' could play a powerful role in cultural politics has not escaped the attention of modern historians. Discussing this syndrome among Renaissance German writers, Helmut Puff observes: 'Displacement was never absolutely effective, however. Rather, displacement had to be continually rehearsed. On a geographical plane, the rejected practices were therefore often placed at a safe distance, south of the Alps or outside Christianity, though close enough to evoke anxiety about potential intrusions.'[13] The use of 'therefore' in that last sentence may suggest that this explanation is in itself sufficient to account for the prominence of both Italy and the Ottoman Empire in early modern Northern European references to sodomy. A similar line of argument is taken by a literary historian discussing Spanish writings on this theme: 'the nexus between... certain foreigners (especially Italians), long associated with homosexuality in Spain, and sodomy... was created by Spanish satirists and moralists as another discursive maneuver to evoke laughter and derision in their readers and spectators while guiding them to take seriously the perceived threat to heteronormative masculinity and sexuality.'[14] Prejudice clearly existed, and we need not doubt that it was strengthened by various mechanisms and manoeuvres of these kinds; but that does not necessarily mean that the basic assumptions on which it built had been invented out of nothing, simply to satisfy those mechanizing and manoeuvring purposes. If Spaniards had 'long associated' Italians with sodomy, might there not have been a reason for that?

The question is an open one; and, as it turns in effect on an assessment of the relative prevalence of sodomy in the two societies, it is difficult to answer. One possibly significant form of evidence is the high proportion of Italians who feature in the Inquisition trials in the Aragonese Crown lands. In Valencia they made up 13.5 per cent of all the defendants; in Catalonia, in the period 1580–1630, they were just over 35 per cent.[15] These were mostly poor men from the southern Italian lands, not well integrated in the local society, and often looking for work. Such people, viewed as outsiders and marginalized, are of course easily targeted. Yet the number of French immigrants in this part of Spain was larger, and they too had come in search of employment. (William Monter writes that 'even in the great port cities along the Mediterranean, Frenchmen were vastly more numerous than Italians throughout the Crown of Aragon.') Cristian Berco has calculated that, of all the foreigners prosecuted in these Aragonese sodomy trials, Italians made up 62.5 per cent, and Frenchmen only 32.8 per cent; Monter, who has also studied this evidence, describes the Italians as 'vastly overrepresented' in comparison with the French. One possible explanation— adopted by Berco—would be that this imbalance was simply the result of local people (both those making the denunciations and those conducting the prosecutions) 'stereotyping' Italians to a much greater degree.[16] But this theory is liable to two objections. The first is that while many more Italians were prosecuted for male–male sex, the opposite imbalance is found where prosecutions for bestiality are concerned: here Frenchmen heavily predominated. Both types of offence could be combined in the more general category of 'sodomy', and there is no clear evidence to suggest that the stereotyping of Italians discriminated so finely—nor, indeed, to show that Frenchmen suffered from a specific stereotype in relation to sex with animals.[17] And the second point is that when one reads a great many of these trial records, one gets no impression that Italians were being especially targeted by those who brought the cases to the attention of the authorities. The same kinds of denunciation, made by either victims or witnesses in the same kinds of circumstances, apply both to these cases and to ones involving local men.

One day in August 1637 a 20-year-old man from the city of Matera in the Kingdom of Naples entered a tavern in Barcelona. Asked by one of the customers where he was from, he said 'Naples', whereupon he received the reply: 'Are you from Naples? If you are, it's impossible that they haven't sodomized you, because the Neapolitans have a great reputation for being buggers.' Cristian Berco cites this exchange, but only to illustrate the intense anti-Italian prejudice that existed in this part of Spain; he does not mention what followed. Yes, said the young Italian, not only had he been sodomized in Naples, but only a short time ago he was sodomized by a monk, who was also Neapolitan, on a bed in his cell in the Benedictine monastery of Bages (an inland district of Catalonia); and, having said that, he proceeded to show them the position in which the monk had placed him on the bed in order to perform the act. Not surprisingly, he was then reported to the Inquisition by four witnesses (three scandalized women and a man). At the tribunal he admitted having uttered those words, and merely pleaded that he had done so 'as a joke'.[18] It is surely possible that, in addition to illustrating anti-Italian prejudice, this story may also be taken to indicate something else: that a man from southern Italy might have had a much laxer attitude concerning the sort of reference to one's own involvement in male–male sex that could be made—whether truthfully or in jest—in the company of strangers. And this difference might in turn signify a difference in social reality.

It is right to look at trial records and other reports in terms of the stereotypical assumptions and prejudices they may embody. But however limited by those prejudices they might be, they do also contain evidence about actual experience. Rafael Carrasco's study of the Valencian cases led him to suspect that in Sicily, and in other parts of Italy, opportunities for sodomy were more easily available than in the Aragonese lands: 'The testimonies of quite a number of Italy-loving Spanish sodomites confirm this suspicion. More than one traveller, ecclesiastic, soldier or pilgrim, who for one reason or another had spent time living in Genoa, Rome, Naples or Venice, admitted quite bluntly, in declarations that were not lacking in nostalgia, how easy it had been to find homosexual contacts in old Italy, contacts which were mostly based on payment, and with very young boys.'[19] The fact that among the men accused of sodomy in the criminal court in Seville, many stated 'that they were first seduced into committing sodomy by a foreigner, especially an Italian', might be a reflection of truth in some cases.[20] Similarly, the fact that a significant number of Swiss-German men accused of sodomy in the sixteenth and early seventeenth centuries 'claimed to have learned the practice of male–male sexuality from welsche, a derogatory term used primarily for Italians but also for other speakers of Romance languages' might also be a reflection of social reality. There is no particular reason to question the testimony of Hans Pröpstli, tried in Solothurn in 1525, who said that he had acquired the habit of sodomy while travelling in Italy (mentioning

Rome and Milan in particular); nor that of Johannes Nusser, tried five years earlier in Lucerne, who admitted having had sex with many boys and men, both laymen and monks, Italians and Germans, as well as with many women whom he had penetrated anally, while he was serving in the papal guard in Rome.[21]

Nothing like a proper survey of the distribution of sodomy in southern Europe can be attempted, as the sort of evidence that would be required for it simply does not exist. Nevertheless, the evidence which does exist can at least be summarized here. Pride of place goes to Florence, for reasons already mentioned. As Michael Rocke has calculated, between 1459 and 1502 an average of 350 people per year came to the notice of the 'Officers of the Night', having been mentioned in denunciations, testimonies and confessions—yielding a cumulative total of more than 13,000 such namings of individuals. Even allowing for the fact that only a small proportion— roughly 15 per cent—of these men and youths were actually convicted, the general figures are, as Rocke says, 'extraordinary'.[22] At one level of explan-ation, the exceptional numbers can easily be accounted for: from 1459 onwards, the authorities operated an unusually mild punishment regime, in which minors and passive partners were let off free, most men paid quite moderate fines, and the poorest among them were subjected either to short spells in prison or to brief episodes of ritualized public shaming.[23] On that basis it is not surprising that many Florentine citizens were willing to denounce themselves, and had few scruples about mentioning others in their confessions.

But this serves only to push the question back by one step: was the level of male–male sexual activity revealed by this liberal regime simply typical of an Italian city, or was there something unusual about Florence? There is some evidence that Florence and its region had a particular reputation. As early as 1305, a friar preaching in the city had exclaimed: 'Oh, how many sodomites are among the citizens! Or rather: all of them indulge in this vice.' Giving one of his fiery sermons in the early fifteenth century, Bernardino of Siena said that Tuscany had acquired such ill repute on this issue that Genoa had introduced a law forbidding the employment of Tuscan school-masters.[24] In 1496 Savonarola exclaimed in one of his sermons that he wished that he could keep in Florence only those who had obeyed God's laws, and expel the rest: 'May all those with the vice of sodomy depart!— Oh, how many would go away!'[25] A few years later the Venetian diarist Girolamo Priuli wrote despairingly that blasphemy and sodomy were becoming worse than ever in Venice, with the city exceeding even Florence in these sins.[26] Florentines also appear to have been disproportionately represented among men tried for sodomy elsewhere: in Venice in the period 1392–1402, for example, four out of the five sodomy cases involved men from Florence; Trevor Dean, in his study of fourteenth- and fifteenth-century Bologna, where outsiders outnumbered Bolognese citizens among those accused and convicted, has remarked that the 'frequent association' of this crime with Florence and Florentines is 'striking'. In the later part of the fifteenth century, he notes, the magistrates in Bologna repeatedly sent convicted sodomites to Florence to serve their prison sentence there.[27] Here too it may be possible to construct an argument which says that Florentines were victims of stereotyping; but there is enough evidence to suggest that any such stereotype was probably influenced by experience, and not simply generated by imagination.

In second place—if we attend only to the available statistics—comes Lucca, which had its equivalent of the Florentine 'Office of the Night', named the 'Office for Virtue'. Umberto Grassi has calculated that between 1539 and 1551, a period for which only summary records survive, roughly 571 men and boys were tried for sodomy, of whom 96 were convicted, while the fuller records for 1551–99 supply the figures of 596 accused and 368 found guilty. And these numbers represent only a selection from the larger quantity of people implicated: Mary Hewlett notes that during the period 1539–80 the Office undertook no fewer than 1,839 preliminary investigations. (Not all of these concerned sodomy, but a strong majority did; and each investigation could involve a number of accused individuals.) These figures are also extraordinary, for a city with a total population of roughly 20,000. And here too one significant element in the explanation must be the relatively liberal punishment regime, which became milder and milder from the mid-fifteenth century onwards: capital punishment was abandoned, and the typical sentences consisted of beatings (for the young), fines, imprisonment of up to two months, and banishment from the city— most typically for one year.[28] These were much less savage punishments than those inflicted in many other parts of Southern Europe; but they did apply to minors and to passive partners (unlike in Florence), and exile was not an inconsiderable penalty for citizens who did their business or trade in the city. The threshold of denunciation must therefore have been a rather more significant one to cross than its Florentine equivalent—which suggests that, if the even gentler punishment regime of Florence had applied here too, the totals could have been even greater. If some special factor existed that caused the level of sodomitical activity to be unusually high in Lucca, that factor has never been identified. Lucca was another Tuscan city (less than 40 miles in a straight line from Florence); the most obvious conclusion would be that such behaviour was simply very common in this part of Italy.

Elsewhere in the northern Italian territories, the best documented city is Venice. As we have seen, the authorities there showed a high degree of preoccupation with this issue in the fifteenth and early sixteenth centuries, issuing various laws and instituting special policing measures. After a major trial involving 35 individuals in 1406, jurisdiction over sodomy was transferred to a high-level governmental body, the Council of Ten, and in 1418 it set up a special tribunal called the 'Collegium contra sodomitas' or 'Collegium sodomitarum' (roughly: 'Sodomy commission') to investigate offenders.[29] The punishment regime here was much more severe than in the Tuscan capital. In 1464 the Council of Ten decreed decapitation, followed by the burning of the corpse, as the standard penalty; banishment—for at least two years, and sometimes for the rest of the person's life—was added as an alternative in 1470, and was more commonly applied to nobles; branding and mutilation were also inflicted, including the amputation of the nose; in 1500 the death penalty was re-affirmed for any passive man over the age of 20; and the alternative of years of forced labour in the galleys was introduced only as late as the 1530s or 1540s.[30] To denounce someone for sodomy was thus to set in train a process which might very possibly lead to his death. Yet during the fifteenth century 264 sodomy cases came to trial, involving 498 individuals; and in the early sixteenth century the frequency of these trials rose even higher, to more than five per year.[31]

In the case of Rome, we have a detailed study of the Governor's court for the years 1560–85; at least 47 sodomy trials are known to have taken place in that period, though fewer than half of those are fully documented. Marina Baldassari has found 114 between 1600 and 1666, with 103 of them in the period 1600–40. (Note, however, that an unspecified minority of these cases were concerned with the sodomizing of women.) Another court, that of the Cardinal Vicar, also handled sodomy cases, but its records for this period do not survive.[32] Nevertheless, the materials analysed by Baldassari are sufficient to conjure up a whole world of sexual activity, with its inns, taverns, gangs, male prostitutes, and sometimes predatory men. There is enough evidence here to add weight to the many anecdotal references to sodomy in

Rome by people who had visited the city or resided there—from the Dutch poet Dirk Potter, who disapproved so strongly, to the Swiss Guard Johannes Nusser, who had taken so many opportunities to have sex with men, boys and monks.

Beyond Florence, Lucca, Venice and Rome, evidence from the judicial records in Italy is patchy and thin. As Trevor Dean has noted, sample periods (ranging from years to decades) from the early- to mid-fifteenth century bring up no cases from the court records of Brescia, Viterbo, Terni and Mantua; Milan yields only one sodomy trial between 1385 and 1429; Spoleto offers just three in the period 1380–1449.[33] A study of the 293 executions that took place in Ferrara in the period 1441–1501 (or the 185 if one subtracts the punishments applied in several waves of convictions for treason) finds that eight of them were for sodomy; it is possible to assume that a larger number of people were convicted for this offence, as some death sentences would have been commuted, and it is highly likely that a greater quantity had been accused and investigated in the first place, but still the total seems modest—even though the number of men executed for rape was only slightly higher, at ten.[34] Bologna had a larger tally, with 30 recorded prosecutions in the fifteenth century. Most such Italian cities had statutes or laws specifying severe penalties for sodomy. In Bologna the statutes decreed death, and men were burnt or decapitated until the 1430s; thereafter, typical punishments included combinations of whippings, *strappados*, fines, imprisonment and banishment.[35] Strong disincentives to confession, or to the implication of one's acquaintances (unless one were motivated by malice) were thus clearly present—but perhaps no stronger than they were in Venice, where, allowing for the fact that its population was three or four times larger than that of Bologna, the rate of prosecution was at least twice as high.

Without much fuller studies of a range of cities, covering much longer periods—if complete runs of trial records exist, as they do not in many cases—it is not possible to draw any certain conclusions from this contrast. In some cases the lack of existing documentation for the periods cited by Dean may be misleading: he refers to a study which yields 'no trial, apparently, in Rome in the second half of the fifteenth century', but it is very hard to believe that the active sodomitical world that emerges so clearly from the sixteenth- and seventeenth-century Roman records had just sprung up out of nothing after 1500.[36] We should not exclude the possibility that sodomy really was more widely practised, and more socially accepted, in the Tuscan cities, and also in Venice, a cosmopolitan port-city of the Mediterranean, even though so much of their relative prominence clearly derives from their greater wealth of documentation. If we had no other evidence, it might be tempting to assume that sodomy was a relatively rare phenomenon outside the four best-documented cities. But other evidence does exist, in sources of various kinds.

One example is a comedy in Latin, written at the University of Pavia in 1437 and apparently intended to be performed by students there. Its author, Mercurino Ranzo, was a Piedmontese humanist notary, with a doctorate in law. Entitled 'De falso hypocrita', 'The False Hypocrite', it had a simple plot, concerned entirely with sodomitical desire. The hypocrite of the title is a priest, the sacristan of a local church, who makes sexual advances to a fourteen-year-old servant boy in the confessional. The boy tells his master, who is a student at the university, and the student's friends decide to entrap the man. One of them, Linius, goes to see the sacristan, persuades him that he shares his sexual tastes (explaining that he was corrupted when a boy by a Hieronymite monk, who taught him and slept with him), and invites him to his room, where they both undress and the priest prepares to be sodomized. Other students, who have been hiding, then rush into the room, seize the man and condemn him to punishment by public humiliation. That a respectable doctor of law should have thought this a suitable subject for performance by students—even though the work does of course have a moralizing message, condemning the priest's lust and hypocrisy—is in itself a remarkable fact, which must tell us something about the ambient culture of fifteenth-century Pavia. But some of the references to sodomitical practices in the play are even more striking. Before he goes to meet the sacristan, Linius has a close shave at the barber's, so that his smooth-cheeked appearance will make him 'pretty', stimulating the man's lust. Having established that the priest is the worst sort of sodomite, an adult who, in addition to sodomizing youths, is happy to be penetrated, Linius offers to bring a boy as well, so that 'you can be active and passive, whichever you wish.' When the priest is preparing to be sodomized by Linius, he makes the request: 'please do it gently, otherwise you will split my arse with your huge penis'; he also asks him to wait 'until I have made myself wet first with spit'.[37] Ranzo may have been a humanist, but this was not some remote literary exercise based only on classical Latin sources. It brought vividly to life some all-too-familiar aspects of contemporary experience, and one can only guess at the nature of the awkward laughter in the auditorium, as students recognized the behaviour portrayed, but may not have wanted their recognition to become too embarrassingly obvious. No study has yet been made of prosecutions for sodomy in the judicial records of fifteenth-century Pavia. But even if one were available, it is possible that this play might tell us rather more about the social and cultural conditions that existed there.

Again, while the relevant judicial documentation for Naples does not survive, there are other kinds of textual evidence. One generalizing comment was made by the Sienese ambassador there in 1466, after the city had suffered an earthquake. 'The cause of this miserable event is, according to some people, the sin of Sodom, about which the women have complained, and still complain to God. For that sin and terrible crime is, at the present time, strongly prevalent.'[38] But more detailed than that is a very informative text from the 1630s, the diary of the French libertine intellectual Jean-Jacques Bouchard, whose keen interest in sexual matters is amply attested in his writings. After spending eight months in Naples in 1632–3, he penned the following observation on the practice of sodomy there:

> Altogether, the petty nobility of Naples is the most notorious set of young people in Italy today. They have no other way of spending their time than this notorious business, which they even practise in public, standing around all day long at cross-roads and in the squares in order to attract passers-by; this is their only serious profession, and their most virtuous pastime. And in this matter they are so strongly imitated, and their example is followed so universally, by all the other young people—whether from the city or from outside it, from the provinces of the kingdom—who come to study in this town, that even if the number of buggers [sc. active sodomites] in Naples is exceeded by the number in Rome (as it certainly is, given that everybody is involved in it in Rome, but in Naples only the knights, philosophers and doctors of law, with the merchants, the craftsmen and the other inhabitants not being strongly inclined to do it), Naples does greatly exceed Rome both in the quantity of its catamites and in their beauty and cheapness. I have dwelt on these details, which I learned from what people told me in Naples, in order to let the reader judge which population is right, the Romans or the Neapolitans, when each accuses the other of sodomy—where I think that each of them is both right and wrong.[39]

Bouchard clearly took it for granted both that there were regional variations and specificities, where the social conditions of sodomy were concerned, in different parts of Italy, and that the basic sexual behaviour was the same. And this sense of a common underlying culture of male–male sexual practices is confirmed by other evidence, such as the discussion of sodomy, quoted above, in the report on the Christian fleet at Lepanto—a fleet which had contained rowers, sailors and soldiers from the territories of Venice, Urbino, the Papal States, the kingdoms of Naples and Sicily, Genoa, Tuscany, Savoy and Malta. William Lithgow, who travelled widely in Italy in 1609 and 1616, was a fierce anti-Catholic and thus not an unbiased observer; but the comment on sodomy which he added to his description of Padua (where he lived for three months, learning Italian) may have contained some truth: 'for beastly Sodomy, it is as rife here as in Rome, Naples, Florence, Bullogna, Venice, Ferrara, Genoa, Parma not being exempted, nor yet the smallest Village of Italy.'[40]

For the kingdom of Sicily, which like its sister-kingdom was a Spanish-ruled territory, some documentation of sodomy does survive in the archives of both the archiepiscopal court of Monreale (which, for historic feudal reasons, had criminal jurisdiction) and the Inquisition, even though the records of ordinary criminal courts are mostly lacking. Many people, including some of the administrators of the island, believed that sodomy was especially common there. Philip II issued a special decree-law for Sicily in 1569, demanding the death penalty and offering rewards to informers. It is clear from other territories that even when the law specified capital punishment, it was not always applied; nevertheless, a record of executions in Palermo specifies that 76 men were given this punishment for sodomy in the city between 1572 and 1640.[41] In a letter from Palermo in 1577 the Viceroy, the Prince of Castelvetrano (who was born there and spent most of his life in Sicily), wrote to Madrid that sodomy was a general phenomenon throughout the kingdom: even in the small town of San Filippo, he said, as many as 250 men were 'stained by this evil'.[42] The evidence of the Monreale trials, though statistically much slighter, tends to confirm that sodomy was quite a familiar feature of ordinary life in the Sicilian countryside.[43]

At the end of Philip's reign there was an attempt to put the offence under the jurisdiction of the Inquisition; this was blocked by the lobbying of influential Sicilians after his death, and the compromise was agreed that the Inquisition would try only its own 'familiars'—that is, the trusted local men who functioned as its officers and agents. In theory, only a pious married man of good standing could become a familiar.[44] But in practice, many of the familiars in Sicily were local noblemen keen to have a position which gave them immunity from arrest by royal officials and from punishment in the royal courts. The total number of familiars in the island in the late sixteenth century was just over 1,500; and in the period 1595–1634 no fewer than 173 of these were prosecuted by the Inquisition for sodomy. Given the social power exercised by many of these men (including, in some cases, the power to control or influence the process of denunciation to the Inquisition), and given the likelihood too that the Inquisition authorities were sometimes disinclined to expose the moral failings of their own officials, that statistic is truly remarkable. As William Monter has put it: 'the Sicilian Inquisition, which lacked formal jurisdiction over sodomy, nonetheless handled more sodomy trials per year during the first third of the seventeenth century than did the Barcelona Inquisition, which had full jurisdiction over this offense.' Since Sicily and the Kingdom of Naples were the parts of Italy with which the Aragonese had most contact, Monter concludes that there may after all have been good reasons why they particularly associated Italians with sodomy.[45]

★ ★ ★

As we have seen, the mainland territories of the Crown lands of Aragon were the only parts of Spain where the Inquisition had jurisdiction over sodomy; these made up roughly 20 per cent of the country. On the legal procedures employed by the Inquisition, more will be said in a later chapter. The surviving records are far from complete; for the Barcelona Inquisition we have only the summary reports sent to the Supreme Council of the Inquisition, not the original trial documents, and even the summaries are missing for most of the period 1640–57; a few entire years are missing from the Valencian records.[46] (Jurisdiction over sodomy had been granted to the Aragonese Inquisition by a papal breve in 1524.) The fullest modern analyses of these three tribunals—Barcelona, Valencia and Zaragoza—conclude that between 1540 and 1700 they held 691 sodomy trials (where each trial might have several accused individuals), and that between 1540 and 1776 they found 626 people guilty, sentencing 81 to be 'relaxed to the secular arm', that is, handed over to the civil authorities for execution, which was the standard penalty in Spanish law.[47] The main concentration of these cases occurred in the final decades of the sixteenth century and the early decades of the seventeenth; in the period 1571–1600, for example, there were 44 trials in Zaragoza, 59 in Barcelona and 107 in Valencia.[48] Other processes against suspected sodomites were taking place at the same time in other courts in these cities: in Zaragoza, Fernanda Molina has noted thirteen trials of ecclesiastics at the Archbishop's court between 1541 and 1600, while Jaume Riera i Sans has found sporadic records of sodomy trials in the royal court in Barcelona.[49] As we have seen, the punishments handed down by the Inquisition could be severe, with nearly 12 per cent of convicted sodomites sent to be executed, and almost 27 per cent condemned to years of galley service, during which many of them would die; other penalties included heavy floggings and banishment. So, once again, to denounce someone for sodomy was not an action to be undertaken lightly. The penalties for ecclesiastics were, almost always, much milder. But the sentences given out by the secular courts were much more severe.

  Our knowledge of cases that came before the ordinary criminal courts is much more limited, arising in some cases from contingent reports. Thus in Seville it is mostly thanks to Pedro de León, the Jesuit who acted as a confessor to condemned criminals, that we know that 71 people were burnt at the stake for sodomy between 1567 and 1616.[50] Enough documentation survives for the city of Malaga in the sixteenth and seventeenth centuries to show that sodomy cases made up 14 per cent of all criminal cases there—the third-ranking category, after murder and theft.[51] Elsewhere in the kingdom of Castile, however, the known evidence is very patchy; one historian comments that 'the documentary evidence from the secular courts of Castile has mostly disappeared.'[52] The Royal *Audiencia* and Chancery of Valladolid, which functioned as the highest appeal court for all or most of the kingdom, considered 27 sodomy cases between 1475 and 1516; but it seems that such cases were seldom taken to appeal, being dealt with by the local courts instead.[53] Six are specified in the surviving records of Ciudad Real in the period 1495–1521; in each of these the accused was found guilty and sentenced to death.[54] In Madrid, the records of the main criminal court mention 31 men tried for sodomy in the period 1581–1621, but not all sodomy cases were dealt with there. (Those 31 do not include, for example, the case noted by a chronicler in 1606: 'This year they burnt four men, because they had caught them dressed in friars' habits, sinning against nature with the sin of sodomy.') Combining information from newsletters, pamphlets and other sources, Rafael Carrasco has calculated that in the period 1580–1660 between 100 and 150 people were executed for sodomy in Madrid.[55]

No cases have been found in the court records of the Basque Country, unless one includes one case from there which was taken to Valladolid, that of a Genoese ship's captain, arrested in the port of San Sebastián in 1515 and accused of having committed sodomy with his page throughout the previous year: despite his claim (made under torture, and corroborated by witnesses) that he had only kissed and embraced the boy, he was sentenced to be 'burnt by live flames of fire until he died a natural death'.[56] Given the contrast between this paucity of cases from the northern coastal region of Spain and the relatively high frequency in Seville and Malaga, it might be possible to argue that the practice of sodomy, as described in previous chapters, was such a specifically Mediterranean one that its influence may have been much weaker in areas much further to the north. Emanuel d'Aranda, when writing his memoir of captivity in Algiers, mentioned two young men from the Basque Country who had been with him in the slave *bagno*, and said that he had been fearful about their innocence in these matters because they came from 'a country where sodomy is unknown'.[57] He had himself spent at least some time in the Basque Country, where, apparently, he had trading interests; it was on a voyage from San Sebastián that he was captured by the corsairs. But his characterization of it could not be literally true. In 1547 a local Inquisitor had asked the Supreme Council of the Inquisition for permission—which was refused—to try sodomy cases. During the following decade one man was brought before the local tribunal of the Inquisition for saying that sodomy was not a mortal sin (a heretical statement, which did fall fully within the Inquisition's jurisdiction). In the 1570s sodomy arose as a tangential issue in two cases being tried on other grounds; but one of these involved a priest from Seville, accused of having sex with a boy from Florence, and the other concerned attempted sodomy by a Benedictine monk whose origins are not recorded.[58]

In Portugal the Inquisition was granted jurisdiction over sodomy in 1562; as we have seen, this was taken to extend only to so-called 'perfect' sodomy, which had to involve both penetration and ejaculation.[59] This requirement greatly limited the possibility of conviction in many cases, as it was often impossible to disprove the claim that one or other of those things had not taken place. And the rules of the Inquisition were in any case quite favourable to the accused, in comparison with the practice of many criminal jurisdictions in early modern Europe. A set of instructions issued by the General Council of the Inquisition insisted: 'when in doubt, you should not presume that the crime or sin took place; and those factors or acts which could be interpreted for better or for worse should always be interpreted for the better. In accordance with these rules there is another, similar rule, namely, that when for some reason it is necessary to make a presumption of evil-doing, of any two evils you should always presume the lesser one.' So, it continued, when a man is found naked in bed with a boy, there can be a presumption of sodomy 'in cases where there is no family relationship between them, or other reason that would oblige them to sleep together'. Nevertheless, Inquisitors must apply the rule of the lesser evil: 'therefore so long as we do not hear anything that obliges us to take the contrary view, we must presume the sin of *mollities* or some other unusual pollution of the flesh, rather than the crime of sodomy, because the latter is the more serious and greater evil.'[60] (Note that the general category of sodomy here was taken to include *mollities*, non-penetrative sexual activity, while the 'crime' of sodomy was so-called perfect sodomy.)

As in the Kingdom of Aragon, here too the punishments meted out to sodomites could be heavy, even though they were much less severe, overall, than those laid down in the criminal law, which stipulated the death penalty for all convicted sodomites. It was also quite common for sentences handed down by the Portuguese Inquisition to be reduced later, on petition from the convicts after they had served out several years. But half the initial sentences involved serious physical punishment: roughly 8 per cent decreed the death penalty, while 42 per cent specified galley service, ranging typically between five and ten years.[61] So, once again, it was no light matter to report someone to the authorities for this offence.

In view of all these conditions and limitations, one might expect the number of prosecutions for sodomy to have been very small. But Luiz Mott has calculated that the total number of legal processes embarked on at the three Portuguese tribunals (Lisbon, Évora, Coimbra) up to the ending of these prosecutions in 1768 was 447. Relatively few cases were prosecuted in the eighteenth century; the total up to 1700 is given by Mott as 424. That figure should be increased slightly, as several more early cases, not noticed by him, have been found in the Coimbra archive. On the other hand we should bear in mind that a small but significant minority of the cases heard in Lisbon came from the Portuguese colonies. But what is really striking is the number of individuals who came initially to the attention of the Inquisition, having been denounced for this offence. In the Lisbon archive, the 'Repertórios do nefando' or 'Sodomy lists' specify 4,419 such people.[62] The existence of sodomy—primarily of the kind found in Italy and Spain, though perhaps, as we have seen, with a little more role-changing than in those societies—was a well-known cultural fact. Many of the testimonies given in the trial documents suggest that such sexual relations could quite easily be found or initiated on the streets of Lisbon; in one case from 1620 a witness referred to 'many people of that type' meeting in the room of a nobleman's servant, including a priest who was accused of organizing a ring of young male prostitutes.[63]

★ ★ ★

The evidence from Portugal almost concludes this brief survey of the distribution of sodomy in Western Mediterranean societies. (Geographically, Portugal is of course an Atlantic country, not a Mediterranean one; but the term is used in an extended sense here, given all the cultural and social commonalities between Portugal and the rest of the Iberian peninsula.) Detailed studies are lacking for Malta, though Godfrey Wettinger's magisterial account of slavery there does note several cases of Muslim slaves being punished for sodomy. He also quotes a decree issued by the Grand Master in 1691 which aimed to prevent 'the execrable crimes that are wont to be committed through the intercourse and friendships which such infidels had with young beardless youths', where the reference to friendships suggests that the authorities were concerned as much with consensual sex as with sexual assaults.[64] Given Malta's cosmopolitan Mediterranean connections, and its governing elite of corsairing knights (forbidden by their Order to marry, or ever to have been married), most of whom were from Italy and Spain, it would be surprising if sodomy had not been a component of sexual and social behaviour on the island. William Lithgow, who was there in 1616, was in no doubt about the matter. 'The fift day of my staying here, I saw a Spanish Souldier and a Maltezen boy burnt in ashes, for the publick profession of Sodomy, and long or [sc. ere, before] night, there were above a hundred Bardassoes, whoorish boyes that fled away to Sicilie in a Galleyot [sc. small galley], for feare of fire[;] but never one Bugeron [sc. active sodomite] stirred, being few or none there free of it.'[65]

Another small but significant Christian Mediterranean state was the Republic of Ragusa (Dubrovnik). Here there is very little direct evidence; yet the fact that sodomy was an issue of concern is clearly indicated by a law of 1474, which decreed that anyone found to have committed this offence, whether actively or passively, must be decapitated and his body burnt. To encourage prosecutions, it also stipulated that anyone who brought a successful accusation against another person should be rewarded: if he were also guilty himself, he would gain his freedom plus a monetary payment, and if he were not guilty of the crime he would receive a much greater payment. This legislation was confirmed in 1534; another law, issued in 1589 and reproclaimed in 1639, appointed five officials to 'inquire secretly about all those who may be marked...by the worst vice' in order to organize 'secret trials' of them.[66] Possibly the practice of conducting trials in secret, which may have entailed not entering the proceedings in the records, had already obtained for a long time—which might explain the lack of documented court cases. But cases involving defamation, at any rate, show that the accusation of sodomy was 'often mentioned as an insult among men'; sometimes a man would be accused of going to Tabor, a place outside the city, for such sexual encounters with 'Turks'.[67]

The most important territory to be largely missing from the available body of evidence is France—at least, those southern regions of France, such as Provence and Languedoc, which had a broadly Mediterranean culture. In the papal territory of Avignon a study of the limited and indirect evidence from the fourteenth and early-fifteenth centuries (a period for which the records of the criminal courts are not extant) has noted just a few cases; these are mostly age-differentiated, with boys or youths as the victims. To those can be added the mention in an English chronicle of a case of 1320, when a cook working for the Marshal of the Pope in Avignon was convicted of raping his fifteen-year-old servant boy.[68] Elsewhere in the whole southern region, the sort of sifting for records of sodomy cases that has been carried out in some other parts of southern Europe has only recently begun. In Languedoc, where actual records of trials are entirely missing before the seventeenth century, painstaking research by Damien Bouliau has uncovered a limited quantity of cases: fifteen men or boys accused of sodomy in the sixteenth century, three in the seventeenth, and five in the eighteenth. Age-differentiation was a factor in many cases, with a schoolboy, several choristers and some pages or servants among the partners or victims. The small number of perpetrators whose ages were specified were all in the classic Mediterranean age-range of 20–29.[69] However, several of the accused were not from this area: they included an Italian, a native of Limoges (the humanist scholar Marc-Antoine Muret) and an Englishman (Anthony Bacon, brother of the lawyer and philosopher). And one conviction may have been on a trumped-up charge: after the Inquisitor, a senior Dominican called Louis Rochette, was tried for heresy by the Parlement de Toulouse in 1538 and executed, his deputy was convicted of sodomy by the Vicar General of the archdiocese of Toulouse and several judges of the Parlement, and sentenced to death in what seems to have been the ruthless pursuit of a larger jurisdictional and doctrinal conflict.[70]

Otherwise, in the absence of any detailed study of early modern Provence, only a few indicative pieces of evidence can be mentioned. The fact that the galley-convicts in late-seventeenth-century Marseille had as many as a hundred catamites, aged between fourteen and eighteen, who slept with them in their barracks, is strongly suggestive of conditions in that port-city more generally: these were typically abandoned or orphaned children who had lived on the streets, and it would be surprising if the sort of sexual relationship they had with the convict rowers were quite unrelated to their previous street-life experiences.[71] As we have also seen, when Swiss Germans alleged that sodomy was particularly rife among the *Welsche*, they included in that term not only the Italians but also the French; and many of these were from the neighbouring south-eastern French region. A man tried for theft and sodomy in Zurich in the early sixteenth century declared that an honest person should not 'send his children to the *welsch*, neither the French, the Savoyards nor others since they ... introduce such viciousness to us'; he himself was found to have had, in Helmut Puff's words, 'a string of lucrative erotic liaisons with ... notaries, academics, and merchants, mostly in France'.[72]

The best-known sodomy case from southern France is that of Arnaud de Verniolles, a subdeacon, aged c.32, living in the town of Pamiers (south of Toulouse), who was tried by Bishop Jacques Fournier in 1323–4. The accusations against him were primarily religious: he had posed as a priest, and he had also uttered heretical statements, including the claim that sodomy with another man was a less serious sin than fornication with a woman. But from the testimonies of witnesses, including several teenaged boys, and from his own interrogation, quite a detailed picture emerged of his sexual activities. He said that he had first been introduced to male–male sex at the age of ten or twelve, by an older boy—old enough to have begun shaving—at his grammar school, who, when sharing a bed with him, had regularly ejaculated between his thighs. Thereafter, Arnaud had evidently had sex with women as well as men: defending his claim that it was natural to seek sexual release, he said that he felt ill if he went for longer than a week or two without having sex with a woman or a man. He seems to have had little difficulty in acquiring young male sexual partners, whom he would penetrate interfemorally, and invite to do the same to him. (It was apparently this form of sex, as opposed to 'perfect' sodomy, that he had described as a lesser sin.) With one fourteen-year-old boy, his seduction technique involved telling him that he could get a place for him as a lodger with a cleric who was a canon of Toulouse, while explaining that the canon had the habit of sodomizing his manservant interfemorally; he then offered to demonstrate what was involved—and, according to his account, the boy agreed and joined him, naked, on his bed.[73] Although this is just one case-history, it does suggest the presence of a larger context of sexual behaviour which, at least qualitatively, fits the Mediterranean pattern that has been broadly described above. However, until much further research has been carried out in the archives, much uncertainty must remain about sodomy in southern France in the early modern period; the evidence, mentioned above, that Frenchmen were prosecuted more frequently for bestiality than for sodomy in the Aragonese territories does suggest that—unless many of these men were from northern France—there was some difference between the sexual cultures of southern France and Italy at this time.[74]

★ ★ ★

In sum: no definite conclusions can be drawn about the relative prevalence of sodomy in different parts of southern Europe, although there are some plausible reasons to believe that it was rather more common in Italy than in Spain, and especially widespread in Tuscany and Sicily. There are too many gaps in the evidence, and too many (mostly fragmentary) bodies of evidence deriving from judicial regimes so different that the case-loads they generated cannot be properly compared. Even if it were possible to bring together detailed statistics from two different cities or territories that operated exactly the same investigative and judicial regime, there would still be the problem of adjusting for the size and nature of the population: not only do we have only very rough estimates of population totals in many cases, but where the jurisdiction included areas of countryside beyond the city walls, we do not know what adjustment to make for a difference in intensity between the urban and rural policing of such offences. The territory covered by the Valencia tribunal of the Aragonese Inquisition, for example, was large and mostly rural, with an estimated population of 360,000 in the late sixteenth century. Rafael Carrasco notes that of the 1,638 familiars of the Inquisition listed in 1567, only 183 resided in the city of Valencia itself; more than 55 per cent of the familiars lived in small settlements with populations below 200. He concludes that this represented 'very strict vigilance over the rural population'. Yet, as André Fernandez has calculated, 40 per cent of all the arrests were made in the city. An analysis of the places of residence of people accused by the Toledo Inquisition (across its whole range of offences, which however did not include sodomy) shows that towns predominated, out of all proportion to the relative sizes of the urban and rural populations: 'the pressure exerted by the Inquisition on the towns was four to five times greater than that to which the countryside was subjected.'[75]

One obvious consequence of this imbalance—if we assume that it obtained more generally—is that when some historians characterize sodomy in this period as an essentially urban phenomenon, they may be reflecting, to a significant extent, a bias in their evidence. In some cases (but not many) there are more specific reasons for linking the behaviour of particular sodomites with towns: in his study of sodomy at the Lisbon Inquisition tribunal, for example, João José Alves Dias notes that some people who lived in the countryside outside Lisbon would visit the city in order to find a sexual partner and then return home.[76] Youths who made money as prostitutes would naturally have preferred to live in places that furnished a large potential clientele, including transient trade. And the concept of a sodomitical 'subculture' does seem to require a mostly urban context—though the extent to which the existence of such a phenomenon can be assumed for this period is an issue to be discussed later. But on the other hand, if there is some truth in the idea that young men had sex with boys as a substitute for sex with women (another issue for later consideration), it must be relevant to point out that female prostitutes were also more available in towns, and that the urban population included more poor working women whose economic activity outside the home could have made them seem more viable targets of male desire and exploitation.[77]

The idea that sodomy was an 'overwhelmingly' urban form of sexual behaviour should be treated with some caution, not only because of intrinsic bias of the processes by which the surviving evidence was collected, but also because it may sometimes involve the projection of more recent assumptions and conditions onto the past. This seems to have been the case in the classic study of mediaeval sodomy by John Boswell, where he argued, in a somewhat *a priori* way, that an urban society would by its very nature generate a more tolerant atmosphere, and that this had played a key role in the development of a 'gay culture'. Against this, Bernd-Ulrich Hergemöller has pointed out that it was precisely in the cities of late mediaeval Western Europe that the most drastic regimes of punishment for sodomy were introduced.[78] The notion that cities can offer anonymity to those who go to live there seems to rest primarily on nineteenth- and twentieth-century experience; neighbourhoods in late mediaeval and early modern cities had quite cohesive communities, into which new entrants would soon be absorbed.

Indeed, the greater density of population meant that there was more scope for the mutual monitoring of behaviour. Town houses—sometimes in multiple occupancy, and often containing young bachelors still living with their parents—did not guarantee privacy, which must be one reason why so many of the sexual encounters recorded in the Florentine records took place outside the home.[79] Some rural inhabitants may actually have had an easier time finding venues for sex, as they could make use of barns and stables or retire to secluded woods and fields. And while Michael Rocke has found that sodomy in Florence was built into certain kinds of male sociability there, Nicola Pizzolato's study of sodomy in rural Sicily observes that 'in the countryside, sodomy was inscribed in the social relations that arose from the agricultural and pastoral economy', with overseers taking advantage of young workers, or youths experimenting sexually with younger boys while tending flocks or herds on remote hillsides.[80] The only conclusion that can safely be made is that the patterns of behaviour we have been considering here ran through entire societies.

9

Theology and religion

One large question that remains to be addressed is: what were the general attitudes of people in these societies towards this kind of sexual behaviour? As we have seen, in the mostly Muslim societies of the Ottoman Empire there was a degree of public tolerance in practice, despite the existence of significant moral and religious disapproval. Assessing the actual attitudes of ordinary people, as opposed to the official attitudes which are easily to be found in texts, is not a straightforward matter. But before attempting that task, we need to consider the official norms, both religious and legal, as these exerted strong influences on most people's judgements about what was good or bad, right or wrong.

In Christian theology, the foundation of all thinking about same-sex relations was to be found in a number of biblical passages. Most prominent among these was the story of the city of Sodom in Genesis 19. Abraham's nephew, Lot, who was living there as a resident non-citizen, encountered two angels (disguised as men) who had just arrived in the city, and invited them to stay the night with his family. But before the evening ended, the men of the city gathered in front of his house 'and said unto him, Where are the men which came in to thee this night? Bring them out unto us, that we may know them.' Lot begged them to let the two men be, as they were his guests; instead, he offered to send out his daughters. 'Behold now, I have two daughters which have not known man; let me, I pray you, bring them out unto you, and do ye to them as is good in your eyes.' The angels pulled Lot back into the house, struck the men in the crowd with blindness, and then explained to Lot that he and his family must leave the city in the morning, as God had sent them to destroy it for its iniquity. The next day, after they had left, 'the Lord rained upon Sodom and upon Gomorrah brimstone and fire from the Lord out of heaven.'

Forbidden Desire in Early Modern Europe: Male–Male Sexual Relations, 1400–1750. Noel Malcolm, Oxford University Press.
© Noel Malcolm 2024. DOI: 10.1093/oso/9780198886334.003.0009

It is understandable that many Christian readers should have thought that this story focused on the desire of the men of Sodom to have sex with the two male visitors. The use of the verb 'know' to mean 'have sexual intercourse with' was familiar from at least ten other passages in the Hebrew Bible; attempts by some modern scholars to deny it that meaning here are unconvincing, given the reference to the virginity of the daughters.[1] (There is also the shocking story in Judges 19: 16–30 of the Levite and the men of Gibeah, which consciously echoes the Sodom episode: the host, who has given the Levite hospitality for the night, offers his daughter to the crowd of men demanding to 'know' the visitor, but in the end it is the Levite's concubine who is handed over, 'and they knew her, and abused her all the night until the morning'.) However, other references to Sodom in the Hebrew Bible show that there was no tradition within that set of scriptures of identifying the sin of the men of Sodom with male–male sexual intercourse or desire. Even before the story of Lot and the angels is told in Genesis, readers have already learned that 'the men of Sodom were wicked and sinners before the Lord exceedingly' (Gen. 13: 13)—a description phrased in the most general terms. In some cases the sin of Sodom was associated just with acting sinfully in a particularly brazen way (Isa. 3: 9: 'they declare their sin as Sodom, they hide it not'). Often the destruction of Sodom and Gomorrah by fire and brimstone was invoked just to remind readers of the terrible power of God's judgement. The most detailed passage about the actual sins of Sodom comes in Ezekiel 16, where, after God has fiercely denounced the people of Jerusalem for their many transgressions, including fornication and idolatry, he says that they are even more sinful than the inhabitants of Sodom. 'Behold, this was the iniquity of thy sister Sodom, pride, fulness of bread, and abundance of idleness was in her and her daughters, neither did she strengthen the hand of the poor and needy' (Ezek. 16: 49). This list of four sins, interpreted as pride, gluttony, sloth and selfishness (or avarice), would quite often be what early modern Christian writers had in mind when they referred to the sins of Sodom—a fact which, as we shall see, has often escaped the attention of their modern commentators.

The clearest reference to male–male sexual relations in the Hebrew Bible comes in Leviticus, in the list of laws given by God, through Moses, to the priests and people of Israel. It appears twice: 'Thou shalt not lie with mankind, as with womankind: it is abomination' (Lev. 18: 22); and 'If a man also lie with mankind, as he lieth with a woman, both of them have committed an abomination: they shall surely be put to death; their blood shall be upon them' (Lev. 20: 13). Modern scholars point out that the word translated here as 'abomination' referred above all to things associated with the idolatrous cultic practices of the surrounding peoples; this injunction was thus more a rule to ensure religious purity—the avoidance of cultic pollution—than a simple statement about sexual morality.[2] (Some indirect confirmation of this can be found in references later in the Hebrew Bible to male prostitutes associated with other religions and their temples.)[3] But it is hardly surprising that mediaeval and early modern theologians took a more straightforward, literal view of the rule set out in Leviticus. And in doing so, they were able to draw also on a passage from the New Testament: the first chapter of St Paul's Epistle to the Romans. Here Paul described how the pagans, having descended into crude idolatry, were abandoned by God to 'uncleanness'. 'For this cause God gave them up unto vile affections: for even their women did change the natural use into that which is against nature: And likewise also the men, leaving the natural use of the woman, burned in their lust one toward another; men with men working that which is unseemly' (Rom. 1: 26–7).

The process by which, during the first five centuries of Christianity, the theologians known as the Fathers of the Church helped to form a Christian doctrine condemning male–male sexual relations was complex, and the doctrinal position thus arrived at was far from definitive. The connection between St Paul's condemnation and the story of the men of Sodom was made by Orosius and Augustine; what became known as the 'Alexandrian rule', namely, that sexual intercourse must be aimed at procreation, was set out by St Clement of Alexandria; and the idea that male–male sex was 'against nature' ('contra naturam' in the Vulgate translation of Rom. 1: 26) was gradually developed under the influence of Augustine, who viewed action against nature as wrong insofar as it was against God, the creator of nature. But 'nature' was not a very stable concept, given the corruption of human nature by the Fall, the difficulty of taking nature as normative in relation to practices such as priestly celibacy, and indeed the fact that sexual pleasure within Christian marriage seemed to some theologians quite natural in itself, which cast doubt on the narrow requirements of the 'Alexandrian rule'.[4] Moreover, some of the Eastern Fathers (including St Basil, as we have seen) continued to think that it was natural for men be erotically attracted to male youths; and when St John Chrysostom wrote a homily denouncing male–male sex, all his opprobrium was attached to the passive partner, apparently implying that the active one was following a natural inclination.[5]

Partly because of these various uncertainties, tensions and contradictions, the pioneering scholar John Boswell downplayed the formation of a Christian doctrine systematically hostile to sodomy in this early period. 'There is in fact little reason', he wrote, 'to assume that the specific objections of influential theologians played any major role in the development of anti-homosexual feelings in Christian society.'[6] In his view, attitudes remained broadly tolerant until much later in the Middle Ages. But this claim has been disproved by Pierre Payer and Hubertus Lutterbach, whose work on 'penitentials' (guides for confessors, laying down the penances to be applied for particular sins) demonstrates strong and consistent hostility to male–male sexual relations throughout the early Middle Ages. These manuals, which spread 'a relatively homogeneous code of sexual behaviour' throughout Europe, used the term 'sodomitae' to refer to men who practised anal intercourse with other males, and imposed heavy penances for their sin, typically of ten years' duration, but ranging from seven to 20 years.[7]

Nevertheless, although strong disapproval of sodomy was already institutionalized in this way in the Western Church, it is true that the range of negative theological arguments was significantly broadened and deepened from the eleventh century onwards. Some of the impulse for this may have come from a greater sensitivity about the issue within monastic communities, possibly because a raising of the entrance age for boys had brought into the monasteries youths who already had some experience of worldly vices. (The rules laid down by Lanfranc in the eleventh century said that 'When they go to bed the masters shall stand by them at night with lighted candles until they are covered up'; he also decreed that if a boy needed to wake the supervising adult in the night, he must use a clapper placed close to the adult's bed, thus avoiding the need to touch him.)[8] Reformers such as the Italian Benedictine Peter Damian were particularly concerned with challenging and eradicating the sins of the clergy, and it was for that purpose that he wrote a short polemical treatise, the 'Liber Gomorrhianus' or 'Book of Gomorrah' (c.1050), which analysed the sin of sodomy, adduced the relevant biblical passages, related this sin to the larger category of the sin of lust, and, for good measure, coined the Latin term 'sodomia' as an abstract noun.[9] Peter Damian addressed this work as an urgent appeal to the Pope; he may have been disappointed by the latter's moderate response, and indeed it has been argued that his influence on the Church's policy and practice has been generally exaggerated.[10] But he did help to stimulate a new kind of theorizing about the sin of sodomy in moral theology, and his classificatory scheme—dividing sodomy into four categories: solitary masturbation, mutual masturbation, interfemoral sex, and anal sex—would have a lasting influence.[11]

The developments that followed, at the hands of subsequent mediaeval theologians, can be summarized only briefly here. One important step was the creation of a link between sodomy and heresy. This connection appears to have been made by the latter part of the twelfth century, being particularly stimulated by the campaign against the dualist heretics known as Cathars in northern Italy and southern France. Most probably, the accusation of sodomy here (first recorded in 1170) was an opportunistic one, latching onto the fact that the elite among the Cathars practised a kind of asceticism which made them shun procreation.[12] But however fictitious the claim may have been, it became widely accepted in popular culture: among the poems of the mid-thirteenth-century *jongleur* Gautier le Leu we find one in which a widow links her second husband to the Cathars because he seems to have no sexual interest in women, and one in which a knight refers to a supposed sodomite as 'cel erite', 'this heretic'. As early as 1276, the statutes of the city of Augsburg used the word *Ketzer* (heretic) to mean 'sodomite'; the verb *ketzern*, 'to sodomize', would remain a standard German term well into the early modern period.[13] Likewise the French word *bougre*, originally meaning 'Bulgar' and referring to the Cathars' presumed teachers, the Bogomil dualists of the Balkans, acquired a long-lasting sexual meaning of its own, preserved also in its English derivative, 'bugger'.

The link with heresy, which may have been strengthened also by biblical verses associating sodomy with idolatry, was more psychological than formal. Sodomy itself was not defined as a heresy, and there was a clear general distinction between committing a sinful act of this kind and being a heretic. That is why Inquisition tribunals, which existed primarily to investigate and punish heretics, did not have jurisdiction over sodomy unless it was specifically granted to them by the Pope. Heresy involved the conscious adoption of, and wilful perseverance in, a significantly false theological belief. But from this it followed that if anyone said that sodomy was not a mortal sin, or not a sin at all, and persisted in that belief, that person was indeed guilty of heresy. In theory, inquisitors could have argued for an intrinsic link between belief and action; a model for this might have been found in the concept of a *factum hereticale* or 'heretical deed', which was created in the fourteenth century in order to assimilate the practice of ritual or ceremonial magic to heresy. There is some evidence that the concept was applied to sodomy, on a theoretical basis, in Spain and Portugal. (In fourteenth-century Navarre, one convicted sodomite was described as having committed heresy 'with his body'.) Yet although there are more signs of clerics—as opposed to laymen—being asked about their views on the sinfulness of sodomy when they were accused of committing it, one gets little sense that this method of treating action as an expression of belief was ever adopted in practice as a general way of drawing into the jurisdiction of the Inquisition suspects who would otherwise be outside it.[14] Rather, the connection with heresy—false belief, or even unbelief—was made in a way which seems indirect, but was not lacking in psychological force. As a Portuguese Inquisitor put it in 1623: 'sodomy brings on a suspicion of heresy', because no man will 'fall into such an abominable crime unless, in the faithlessness and foolishness of his heart, he has already begun to turn away from God to such an extent that he thinks and lives as if there is no God'.[15] A generation earlier, the French Professor of Theology Jean Benedicti had made a similar point, though putting it the other way round: he wrote that people who committed the sin of sodomy could soon fall into heresy, apostasy and atheism.[16]

If turning away from God was seen as something that could easily lead to—or follow from—sodomy, one might expect there to have been a close connection too with diabolism and witchcraft. That the Devil was in some way the author of sin, and that human beings could be actively drawn into the commission of sins by demons, were general assumptions; yet specific links between this particular sin and human contacts with demons were seldom made. Indeed, the standard view was that although people might be led by demons to commit the very worst sins, this particular one was offensive to the demons themselves, whose embarrassment in the face of it was proof that some element remained of their former angelic nature. The thirteenth-century Dominican writer Guillaume Perault (Peraldus) explained that angels and demons agreed about sodomy: it was a sin that made the demons blush.[17] Even the Devil himself was thought to share this residual sense of moral revulsion. As the Dutch legal writer Jan Matthijssen put it in c.1410, 'It is such a foul and nasty sin that whenever the Devil has induced someone to commit it, he turns around in order not to see the filthiness of the sin.'[18] One important consequence of this doctrine was that when, starting in the fifteenth century, many Western Christian societies became fixated on the idea of witchcraft as a form of contact between humans and demons, sodomy played hardly any role in the standard scenarios, even though sexual relations between demons and women would become a major theme of many accusations and confessions.

Heinrich Kramer, the German Dominican who had worked as an Inquisitor in Austria and the Czech lands, was emphatic on this point in his influential treatise on witchcraft, *Malleus maleficarum* (1486): 'it must be carefully noted that, though the Scripture speaks of Incubi and Succubi lusting after women, yet nowhere do we read that Incubi and Succubi fell into vices against nature. We do not speak only of sodomy, but of any other sin whereby the [sexual] act is wrongfully performed outside the rightful channel. And the very great enormity of such as sin in this way is shown by the fact that all devils equally, of whatsoever order, abominate and think [it] shame to commit such actions.'[19] (Later in this work Kramer told the story of a young Czech priest, possessed by a demon, who had been brought to Rome in the hope of obtaining an exorcism. Even in the presence of a powerful relic, which had the effect of forcing most demons to abandon their victims, this particular one declared that he would not leave the priest. 'And when he was asked why, he answered, Because of the Lombards. And being asked why he would not go forth because of the Lombards, he answered in the Italian tongue (although the poor priest did not understand that language), They all practise such and such things, naming the worst vice of lustfulness.' Modern scholars have struggled to explicate this story: Brigitte Spreitzer has suggested that 'Lombards' referred to Waldensian heretics, even though such people would have been few and far between in Rome, while Walter Stephens has identified them as usurers.[20] As we have seen, however, 'Lombards' was, for German speakers, a general term for Italians; this story is just another expression of the common view that sodomy was especially prevalent among Italians in general, and perhaps also among Romans in particular.)

In the case of witchcraft, therefore, unlike that of heresy, a strong connection with sodomy was never established. Only one writer attempted that task: Gianfrancesco Pico della Mirandola (nephew of the famous philosopher Giovanni Pico), whose treatise on witchcraft, *Strix*, was published in 1523. Pursuing an argument he had previously developed in other works, he explained that the classical pagan gods had all been demons. On that basis it was easy to show that sodomy—as practised by Zeus with Ganymede, etc.—was a demonic invention; from which it followed that when demons made contact with men at the present time, they might very well seek to sodomize them.[21] Yet although the work was widely read, this particular element of its argument was not taken up. The traditional idea that demons were offended by sins against nature may have been somewhat eroded by another early sixteenth-century writer on witchcraft, the Piedmontese theologian Silvestro Mazzolini da Prierio (known as 'Prierias'), who claimed that demons sometimes made use of bifurcated penises to penetrate women vaginally and anally at the same time; but the penetration of men hardly featured in the standard accounts.[22]

References to sodomy in witchcraft trials usually concerned demons having anal sex with women. The topic arises only once in the famous treatise on witchcraft by the Jesuit Martin Delrio (1600), where he quotes a judgment issued at Avignon in 1582 against a group of eighteen witches, both male and female; the overall judgment called them 'sodomites' (and fornicators, heretics, murderers, etc., etc.), but the more detailed charge-sheet said that 'you men fornicated with succubae, you women fornicated with incubi, you practised actual sodomy and the most unspeakable crime with them', which suggests that it was the incubi who had done the sodomizing.[23] Only very occasionally does the demonic penetration of men crop up in trial records. A general statement at an *auto-da-fé* in north-eastern Spain in 1610 declared that the devil sodomized both women and men; in a witchcraft trial in the archbishopric of Salzburg in 1678 a man was accused of committing sodomy 'with an unclean spirit and with animals', and in another case at the same tribunal it was said that the accused had had relations with the Devil in which he was 'constantly sodomized in his anus, which made him feel cold'.[24] One far from typical case involved a weaver executed for sodomy in Hamburg in 1657, who was accused not only of sexual assaults on several boys and girls, but also of sleeping with the Devil. However, given that the other offences he was charged with included sodomizing dogs and cats, and committing incest with his own mother, this seems to have been a case merely of throwing every conceivable accusation at the man (who happened also to be a Catholic—and a redhead) in order to ensure his conviction.[25]

Of course, people accused of sodomy might well say that the Devil had tempted, or inveigled, or somehow coerced them into committing it. At a trial of three young clerics accused of sodomizing a nine-year-old boy in Sicily in 1620, a witness reported that when he asked one of them what he had done, he answered: 'The Devil tricked me, I fucked Stassi's son.' A priest who appeared before the Inquisition in Seville in 1603, accused of uttering the heretical statement that sodomy was not sinful, said first that it was not a sin in his case because he had paid for it, then that someone had told him that the best remedy for haemorrhoids was to be sodomized by a man, and finally that the Devil had made him say those things. And in Lima in c.1584, a Dominican friar being tried for sodomy claimed that 'a demon tormented him and forced him to perform shameful acts, which he did not consider to be a mortal sin, saying that he had no liberty in the matter.' (Rather surprisingly, the judges then embarked on a serious debate about this point.)[26] These were all claims that could have been made, in principle, about any serious sin.

Sodomy was a special case among sins, however, and it was during the Middle Ages that its distinctive status emerged. One sign of this was the growth of what might be called theological legends, which spread from learned writers into the general culture. It was claimed that the Incarnation had been delayed because of the presence of sodomy in the world; this idea can be traced back at least as far as to Guillaume Perault in the thirteenth century. Another widespread belief was that all sodomites died at the moment when Jesus was born; this notion, derived apparently from a life of Mary written in c.1200, and later popularized in the mid-thirteenth-century collection of saints' lives known as the *Golden Legend*, was still being cited near the end of the sixteenth century by the Franciscan theologian Jean Benedicti. (It was a story which theologians could put to work: Bernardino of Siena, in his anti-sodomy sermons of the early fifteenth century, used it to explain why it was that Jesus made no reference to this particular sin in the Gospels.)[27] Also commonly repeated was the claim that Noah's Flood had been a divine punishment for sodomy.[28]

Indeed, floods and other disasters such as earthquakes and plagues were often seen as God's judgments on this sin. When the river Arno burst its banks in Florence in 1333, that was taken as a reason to introduce much harsher anti-sodomy laws; in the following century Antoninus of Florence, the Dominican friar who became Archbishop of that city in 1446, warned that God inflicted plagues as punishments for sodomy, adding that 'perhaps that is the reason why plagues frequently happen in many Italian cities, since that great vice is more prevalent there than in some other cities.'[29] Such a fear of divine punishment was widely felt. In 1466, as we have seen, an earthquake was blamed by the people of Naples on sodomy; in 1498 a prosecutor at a sodomy trial in Castile declared that this sin, if it went unpunished, caused 'famines and pestilences and other evils and harms'; in 1534 the renewed legislation against sodomy in Dubrovnik referred in its preamble to a recent plague as a reason for redoubling efforts to eradicate the offence. In 1542, when Duke Cosimo I introduced a new, much harsher anti-sodomy law in Florence, he was moved to do so by an earthquake and a recent lightning strike which had hit the cathedral and the government palace; in 1566, Pope Pius V issued a bull, *Cum primum Apostolatus*, against sodomy and other vices among the clergy, which explicitly said that sodomy was a cause of plague and other calamities. And as late as the first half of the eighteenth century, Dutch writers were blaming sodomites for floods, cattle diseases, a shipworm outbreak and even a financial crisis.[30] If some of these associations seem strangely far-fetched to modern eyes, we need to consider how strong the fear of divine judgement could be in the mind of an early modern religious believer. And we should recall that the total destruction of Sodom and Gomorrah was not only the most extreme example of divine punishment in the Old Testament, but also the one that was referred to elsewhere in the Bible as the archetype or symbol of such punishments in general.

A sign of the especially egregious nature of sodomy as a sin was the fact that from the Middle Ages onwards it was commonly described as the sin which should not be referred to or mentioned. The standard Latin term for this was 'nefandus', to which the English adjective closest in meaning is 'unspeakable'; but the equivalence is not exact, as 'nefandus' means that which should not or must not be spoken of, rather than that which cannot. (Some modern scholars—especially, for some reason, ones writing about sodomy in the Iberian territories—routinely translate the term as 'nefarious'; that is an error, associating it with a different Latin word which meant 'that which should not be done'.) One possible origin of this tradition was a law recorded in the *Institutes* of the Emperor Justinian, which condemned 'those who dare to exercise their unspeakable ['nefandam'] lust with men'— a use of the Latin adjective which may have reached back to Old Testament concepts of pollution and abomination.[31] But it was mediaeval theologians, especially in the thirteenth century, who developed this idea and made it both orthodox and commonplace. Paul of Hungary, in his *Summa de poenitentia* (c. 1220), wrote that sodomy was a sin which could not be spoken of without polluting both the mouth of the speaker and the ears of the listeners. Guillaume Perault, a generation later, insisted that 'no man should speak about this sin.'[32] Thomas Aquinas, writing in the 1250s, declared that lust 'against nature' was 'unnameable', referring to a passage in St Paul's Epistle to the Ephesians (5: 3): 'But fornication, and all uncleanness, or covetousness, let it not be once named among you, as becometh saints.'[33] (No such scruple developed, however, among mediaeval theologians about discussing fornication or covetousness.) Other writers drew on St Jerome's speculative etymology of 'Sodom' in his treatise on Hebrew names, where he gave its meaning as 'silent beast'. It became common practice to refer to sodomy as the 'mute sin'. The wrongness of speaking about it did seem to turn here into unspeakability, though Antoninus of Florence offered a more rational and psychological explanation: 'Sodomy is said to be mute because it makes a man mute, since he cannot excuse his behaviour, as he might in the case of some other evil actions.'[34]

To build up the taboo status of sodomy in this way was to create some practical problems for those clerics whose duty it was to guard the morals of their flocks. William of Auvergne, the influential theologian who became Bishop of Paris in 1228, insisted that preachers should never discuss this sin. Accordingly, Berthold of Regensburg (d. 1272), a Franciscan preacher famous throughout central Europe whose sermons survive in large quantities, mentioned sodomy only once, merely to say that it should not be named. [35] And at the end of the fourteenth century the Augustinian canon John Mirk was summarizing the standard view when he wrote, in his *Instructions for Parish Priests*, 'Also wryten wel I fynde | That of synne ageynes kynde | Thow schalt thy paresch no thynge teche, | Ny of that synne no thynge preche' ('Also, I find it well written that, where the sin against nature is concerned, you should not teach your parish anything about it, nor preach anything about that sin').[36] There were occasional dissidents. The extensive writings of Bernardino of Siena on sodomy in the early fifteenth century, which include nine sermons, show that he did not regard it as something to keep quiet about, even though he called it the worst of all sins. At the beginning of the sixteenth century the Strasbourg preacher Johannes Geiler acknowledged that some people criticized him for alluding explicitly to sodomy in his sermons, but defended himself by pointing out that St Paul had referred to it quite openly in his epistles. (Geiler was particularly troubled by the coming of syphilis to Strasbourg in 1496, which he saw as a divine punishment for sexual sins of all kinds.)[37] Nearly a century later, the French theologian Jean Benedicti defended the fact that he was discussing in print, in the vernacular, topics such as masturbation and nocturnal emissions, declaring that 'it is not from books that we learn our sins, but from our own—alas!—excessively corrupted nature'; yet a few pages later he would draw his discussion of sodomy to a close by saying that it was better, after all, to keep quiet about it.[38]

It was generally agreed among Catholics (including Martin Luther before 1517) that the best time or place for talking about sodomy was not in the pulpit but at confession.[39] Yet here too caution was required: mediaeval guides for confessors typically emphasized the need for discretion when broaching the topic.[40] In his manual, Antoninus recommended that boys and girls should be interrogated 'about carnal vices with males and females, committed either by them or mutually, which happen very frequently nowadays', but he added that 'they should be questioned very cautiously: far be it from you that they should learn things which they do not know.'[41] Earlier in the fifteenth century, the famous French theologian Jean Gerson had produced a little treatise for confessors on how to ask about the sin of *mollities* or masturbation. His probing questions were not aimed at children, but they began by asking about childhood experiences, obtaining the confidence of the penitent man by beginning with the most ordinary and innocent-seeming acts. First one should ask him if he remembered whether, at the age of ten or twelve, his penis was ever erect. Having obtained the answer 'yes', the confessor should then ask what he did about it: did he ever touch or rub it, 'in the way that boys normally do'? If the person says 'no', one should say that his statement is not believable. If 'yes', one should ask for how long he rubbed it: an hour, for example, or half an hour? And did he rub it until it ceased to be erect? If so, he should be informed that he had committed the sin of *mollities*, even if, because of his age, no 'pollution' (ejaculation) had occurred. Then the confessor must ask him 'whether he had rubbed the penis of another boy, a friend of his, in the same way, or whether someone had rubbed his—[with the questioning] proceeding thereafter to the more particular forms of sodomitical sin'.[42]

This gives some idea of the sort of careful probing that, ideally, a confessor could be expected to engage in. And the forms of sinful behaviour on which confessors were meant to focus extended far beyond the commission of physical acts such as masturbation or anal sex. In his manual for confessors, published soon after his death in 1498, the firebrand reformer Girolamo Savonarola wrote that a man should also be questioned about non-consummated sins of lust, such as touching or looking, or speaking shameful words or acting lasciviously in any way 'in order to please some woman, or some adolescent boy, whom he wants to induce to commit such a sin'—for this too was to sin mortally.[43] However, it was a common view among confessors that probing into sins of this kind was a risky business. As the Spanish theologian Martín de Azpilcueta wrote in his hugely influential *Manual de confesores, y penitentes* (1549), referring to the whole category of sins of lust: 'to dwell at length on questions about this subject is dangerous for the confessor, and for the penitent; for that reason he should deal with it quickly, asking only what is necessary, without particularizing or breaking it down into too much detail.'[44] The suggestion here of a risk to the confessor strikes a slightly unusual note; most probably Azpilcueta was aware that the grave sin of 'solicitation' was far from unknown in Spain. But the prime worry must have been about the risk to those who came to confess. As the Huguenot writer Henri Estienne would put it in his discussion of sodomy in 1566, 'all the more wicked are the priests, who in aural confession (as they call it) awaken people's thoughts by their questions, and give them the idea for evil deeds of various kinds.'[45]

★ ★ ★

However widely acknowledged these reasons for silence or reticence may have been, some theologians, especially in the latter part of the Middle Ages, did write at length on the sin of sodomy; and it was thanks to their work that a set of standard classifications arose which shaped the attitudes of clerics, legislators and lay people in late mediaeval and early modern Western Europe. The most important underlying principle was the idea of sinning sexually 'against nature', which tended to mean in a way that did not lead to procreation. Peter Damian, as we have seen, had been concerned with male-only sexual acts (masturbation, mutual masturbation, interfemoral penetration and anal sex), which were self-evidently non-procreative; but by the time Paul of Hungary was writing in the early thirteenth century, the argument had been extended to any sexual activity resulting in seminal emission anywhere outside a woman's vagina, a category which included not only anal sex with women but sex with animals too.[46] While scholastic theologians built up a detailed and carefully reasoned account of such 'sins against nature', however, they failed to establish—at least, in the wider culture—a single fixed meaning for the term 'sodomy', which some people used as a broad synonym for all these sexual sins against nature, and others as the label for a more limited subset of them. The ambiguities thus created would never be entirely resolved.

Thomas Aquinas, in his *Summa theologiae* (written in the 1260s and early 1270s), observed that the 'vice against nature' was a form of lust which was doubly repugnant, first because it was against 'right reason', and secondly because it was against 'the natural order of the sexual act'. It could take place in four different ways: masturbation, sex with an animal, intercourse with the improper sex ('for example, man with man, or woman with woman, as the Apostle [Paul] says in Romans 1, and this is called the vice of sodomy'), or finally 'if the natural way of having sex is not used, whether because the organ is improper, or through the use of other monstrous and beastly ways of having sex'.[47] This was a list of four different forms of unnatural vice, or perhaps five if one took the last two options separately: non-vaginal sex, and sex which was vaginal but in a 'monstrous' position, e.g. with the woman on top. (This last prohibition, we may note, diverged from the others by using a criterion of 'nature' which was not concerned with procreation. It exemplifies what Joan Cadden has called the mediaeval Church's 'shift toward the control of sexual behavior in general, including coital positions and clerical celibacy'.)[48] But only one of those forms of unnatural sin was classified by Aquinas as 'sodomy'.

Other writers broadened the meaning of that particular term, while adhering to the same general pattern of argument. The view expressed in many mediaeval guides for confessors was that sodomy consisted of same-sex relations and bestiality, with masturbation included by some and excluded by others. A very popular fourteenth-century German guide, based on the work of Johannes of Freiburg (d. 1314), defined sodomy as male–male or female–female sex, sex performed unnaturally between a man and a woman, and masturbation. And when Giovanni Boccaccio composed his commentary on Dante in the 1370s, he explained (in relation to the sodomites punished in Canto 15 of the *Inferno*) that there were three types of sodomy: same-sex intercourse, whether male–male or female–female; sex between man and woman if not 'in accordance with the normal rule of nature and also the laws of the Church'; and bestiality.[49] Some writers, on the other hand, limited the term to something much closer to Aquinas's restricted sense: the Sienese Dominican friar Agostino da Montalcino, in his very thorough guide for confessors (1590), insisted that 'sodomy' should be used only for sex 'between people of the same sex, consummated in any way at all'.[50]

Among modern historians who write about these matters it has become standard practice to refer to the concept of sodomy throughout the early modern period as—in a phrase first applied by Michel Foucault—'an utterly confused category'. This is quite misleading. Much careful ratiocination had gone into the construction of the category of sexual 'sins against nature'; the only uncertainty was about whether the term 'sodomy' should be used to cover all, or some, or only one, of those sins. The most constant element in general usage was the idea that male–male sexual intercourse was sodomy; definitional or classificatory statements would dutifully add female–female, in deference to Romans 1: 26–7 ('even their women did change the natural use into that which is against nature: And likewise also the men...'), but in ordinary life there was little reference to such cases, which were seldom encountered. The act of a man penetrating a woman anally was also commonly described as sodomy, perhaps not so much because of theological teachings about 'proper organs'—the parallel prohibition of improper positions was very rarely referred to—as because the physical act so closely resembled the main form of sexual intercourse between man and man. And this last point may have applied also to the description, which was very commonly made, of bestiality as another form of sodomy. (Again, cases of women inducing animals to penetrate them were not entirely unknown, but were much less common.) Certainly there was some conceptual slippage as the term 'sodomy' was differently applied across a range of subcategories. But to describe this in terms of sodomy itself being 'an utterly confused category' is to create unnecessary extra confusion.

The writings of Thomas Aquinas on these matters are important not just because he was one of the most influential mediaeval theologians, studied carefully by all scholastic writers well into the early modern period. In addition, he helped to develop a new approach to sexual sins, in which the emphasis was increasingly on the moral psychology of the sinner. When he wrote about non-procreative sex, he was concerned not simply with defining certain acts as incapable of causing conception, but rather with the nature of the desire which motivated a person to engage in those acts. 'The lustful person aims not at human procreation, but at sexual pleasure, which can be experienced without engaging in those acts that lead to human procreation. And that is the thing they seek when engaging in the vice against nature.'[51] This shifted the focus of theologians and moralists onto the nature of the erotic feelings and intentions of the sinner. In his commentary on Aquinas, Tommaso de Vio went in textbook fashion through the requirements for non-sinful sex (it must be penetrative, between humans, of the two sexes, using the proper organs, in the proper way), and then addressed the reasons why sinners fell away from one or other of those necessary conditions. 'The masturbator is motivated only by physical delight, the fulfilment of sexual pleasure', he observed, while 'the sodomite is motivated by a person of the improper sex.'[52] While Aquinas had taken an initial step towards psychologizing these sins, this moved the argument significantly further, implying that the sodomite was driven by a special kind of sexual desire—the desire for a person of the same sex. Pierre Hurteau has written perceptively about the importance of this change more generally: 'What was now the determining factor in establishing the gravity of an act was not primarily its objective nature, the parts of the body or the act involved, but, in true post-Tridentine fashion, it was the subjective factor, the feelings and desires that determined the meaning of acts.'[53] But the development was not in fact post-Tridentine; de Vio died in 1534, and his commentary was published in 1540, five years before the opening of the Council of Trent.

One aspect of this new approach was a particular interest in the nature of sexual fantasy. A special term was used, *delectatio morosa*, 'lingering delectation', which meant enjoying sexual excitement in the mind in a lingering way. (It was the lingering that made this a sin; a sexual thought or feeling might spring up involuntarily in the mind of any innocent person, who would then virtuously dismiss it, but to dwell on it and develop it, for the sake of extending the pleasure, was to involve the will and thus incur moral guilt. Many modern writers translate the adjective as 'morose', but this is an error: the Latin word here derives from a verb meaning 'to delay', and is best translated as 'lingering'.) De Vio discussed this in relation to masturbation, explaining that while masturbating simply for the sake of physical pleasure is already a grave sin, it is worse when 'subordinated to lingering delectation'; if the sexual fantasy involved is about another man's wife, for example, the sin takes on the character of adultery too.[54] This approach became a general one. Agostino da Montalcino declared that if a man had sex with a woman 'while thinking about males, he is a sodomite of the worst kind'. Jean Benedicti, writing in the 1590s, declared that if a man thought of a married woman while he masturbated, he was guilty of adultery, and if he thought of another man, he was guilty of the sin of sodomy.[55] The Spanish Jesuit Tomás Sánchez, writing less than a decade later, said that a man who thinks of another woman while having sex with his wife is guilty of a mortal sin.[56]

One of the questions posed by the German Jesuit Hermann Busenbaum in his popular treatise on moral theology, *Medulla theologiae moralis* (1645), was about whether same-sex 'mutual pollution' (i.e. mutual masturbation leading to ejaculation) was to be seen simply as *mollities*, or as a form of the sin of sodomy. He answered: 'If it is done only out of a desire for sexual enjoyment without intercourse, it is only *mollities*; but if it is done out of a desire for that person of the improper sex (especially if there is some joining and mixing together of the bodies), it is, with respect to its degree of evil intent, sodomy.'[57] Here we see both the original point about sexual intentionality made by Aquinas, and the further line of argument developed by de Vio, plus perhaps a nod in the direction of a more ordinary, popular understanding of what sodomy involved. Indeed, the distinction made by Aquinas remained indispensable. Tomás Sánchez pointed out that kissing and embracing could be innocent expressions of 'good will, and virtuous friendship, following the custom of the country', and said that sin would arise only if the actions aimed at sexual pleasure. 'We should add, *a fortiori*, that kisses and embraces between people of the same sex, if done because of the aforementioned sexual pleasure that they give rise to, are mortal sins.' To touch the genitals of someone of the same sex, for the sake of such pleasure, was the 'beginning' of sodomy. But, he noted, to look without desire was much less sinful, and some touching might be almost blameless—for example, boys 'grabbing one another's genitals in a game'. As for a man looking at another man who was naked (for example, while swimming): that was not a mortal sin, unless there was some danger involved 'because of a strong propensity to sodomy', or a risk of scandal because of the status of the man thus observed—for example, if he were a bishop.[58]

This psychologizing tendency in the treatment of sexual desire, which arose from the subtle analysis of human action and volition developed in the scholastic tradition, and, most probably, from the practical exigencies of the confessional, deserves to be considered carefully. There is a strong tendency in the modern historical literature on these topics—derived, again, from Michel Foucault—to say that mediaeval and early modern concepts of sodomy, and of sodomites, were limited to the classification of behaviour in terms of acts alone. A fuller discussion of this issue will be reserved for a later place. But it is worth noting now that a purely act-based idea of sodomy would not capture all the aspects of the situation that were considered by these theological writers.

Of course, we may still wonder how closely the theories of the theologians mapped onto the self-understanding of the sinners themselves. Some of the more extreme theoretical stances adopted by these writers may perhaps have diverged quite widely from popular opinion. Bernardino of Siena thought that the rape of girls was a lesser sin in comparison with the sodomizing of adolescent boys; many of his contemporaries may have disagreed. Jean Benedicti dutifully followed the teaching of those patristic writers who had said that sodomy was much worse than incest. And the theologians of Salamanca ranked sodomy as a more serious sin than bestiality, on the grounds that a man who penetrated an animal was at least taking the active role (which in itself accorded with his masculine nature), whereas the passive partner in the sodomitical act was doing something much more unnatural.[59] We are entitled to wonder how widely some of these rigorist views were shared. But what is undeniable is that the official norms of sexual morality in this period, which were derived above all from the teachings of the Church, were profoundly hostile to all forms of male–male sexual relations.

IO

Law and punishment

It is not surprising that the fierce disapproval of sodomy in Christian theology was the dominant influence on legal theory and practice throughout Christendom. But what may seem rather surprising is the fact that for roughly the first thousand years after Christ, secular law paid very little attention to this offence, leaving it almost entirely to the Church to deal with.

The only exceptions to this, if one leaves aside two edicts decreed by the Visigothic rulers of Spain in the seventh century, were a small number of laws issued by Byzantine emperors.[1] From the fourth century we have two laws condemning some forms of male–male sexual relations, the first referring, whether metaphorically or not, to some kind of marriage between men, and the second decreeing death by burning for those who forced or sold men into prostitution. From the reign of Justinian in the sixth century we have not only the law already mentioned, which included the word 'nefandam', but also two edicts which used heightened rhetorical language to condemn male–male sex in very general terms. One said that famines, earthquakes and plagues were consequences of these crimes; the other alluded to the destruction of Sodom. Historians have debated whether these laws were ever generally enforced (one comments that 'the only well-known individuals punished under these laws were bishops'), though some think Justinian used them to target political opponents, or perhaps just to raise money in fines.[2] Nevertheless, the fact that they were preserved in the authoritative corpus of civil law documents meant that they could influence legal thinkers in Western Europe during the later Middle Ages (after the rediscovery of Roman law) and throughout the early modern period. A later Byzantine law code, the 'Ecloga' of the seventh-century emperors Leo III and Constantine V, added that people convicted of sexual offences should

Forbidden Desire in Early Modern Europe: Male–Male Sexual Relations, 1400–1750. Noel Malcolm, Oxford University Press.
© Noel Malcolm 2024. DOI: 10.1093/oso/9780198886334.003.0010

have their noses cut off, and sodomites should be put to the sword; but this text would be much less well known.[3]

So the main judge and enforcer of sexual morality in these matters, over a very long period, was the Church. (This may have been the case even in Constantinople: while Justinian's first edict called for punishments to be meted out by the prefect of the city, his second ordered citizens to confess the sin to the Patriarch and do penance.) In piecemeal fashion, the Church gradually accumulated a handful of decrees on this matter, issued by regional Councils, which would exert some influence on the development of canon law. The Council—or, more correctly, Synod—of Elvira, held in southern Spain at the beginning of the fourth century, decreed that priests should refuse communion to men who raped boys. One of the canons issued by the Council of Ancyra (modern Ankara, Turkey), held in 314, set out heavy penances for men who acted 'irrationally'; this may have been a term for bestiality, but mediaeval readers took it to refer to committing sodomy—and understandably so, as the wording specified an age threshold (20) below which the penance was milder, and also decreed more severe punishment for those who fell into this sin when they were already married.[4] Interpreted in this way, the canon influenced many of the mediaeval 'penitentials': typically they would use 20 as the age threshold, imposing fifteen years of penance on those below it and 20 or 25 years on those above it.[5] And it was the penitentials that guided Church practice for much of the mediaeval period; with the exception of one regional Spanish Council in 693, which decreed that clerics found guilty of sodomy should be deposed and exiled, and that lay Christians who did not do sufficient penance should be permanently excommunicated, there were no more legislative acts of that kind until the twelfth century.[6] Then, in 1120, at a Council convened at the Palestinian city of Nablus to strengthen the moral state of the Kingdom of Jerusalem, various decrees were issued against offences such as adultery, bigamy and having sex with Muslims; these included one which said that in cases of consensual sodomy both parties should be burnt, and another which allowed that those who confessed the offence before being prosecuted could be received back into the Church on performing the appropriate penance.[7] Two generations later, in 1179, the Third Lateran Council prescribed, as punishments for sodomy, degradation for clerics and excommunication for laymen. This would be the only decision of a Council cited in the corpus of canon law that specified a penalty for this sin.[8]

Over time, canon lawyers would develop the doctrine that sodomy was a *delictum mixti fori*, an offence coming under mixed jurisdiction, both ecclesiastical and secular.[9] In any case, the Church did not itself inflict physical or capital punishments; as we have seen, people condemned to those by ecclesiastical courts had to be relinquished—or 'relaxed', as the standard phrase put it—to the secular arm. Clerics would not usually be handed over in that way, however, and if they were apprehended by the secular power for this sort of crime they would often be passed to the Church authorities. Fears about sodomy (and a range of other sexual offences) among the clergy were, for obvious reasons, of especial concern to those authorities; solicitation in the confessional—though mostly of women—was always a worry, and scurrilous stories about sodomitical monks and friars contributed to the popular anticlericalism which would be manipulated so effectively by Protestant reformers. Not long after the Council of Trent, the Counter-Reformation Pope Pius V announced a new punitive regime to deal with clerical sodomites: in his 'constitution' *Cum primum Apostolatus* (1566) he decreed that if they were found guilty of 'the unspeakable crime against nature', they should not only be degraded of all their ecclesiastical offices, but also 'subjected to a similar penalty' to that meted out to laymen—which meant in effect that, having been tried in an ecclesiastical court, they must be handed over to the secular power for physical or capital punishment. Two years later, in his bull *Horrendum illud scelus* (1568) he confirmed this in even more emphatic terms. All priests and regular clerics 'exercising such a terrible crime' should be degraded by the ecclesiastical judge, and then 'immediately delivered to the secular power', to receive the standard punishment for lay people.[10]

There are relatively few cases, however, of clerics being given up for physical punishment in this way. And the impact (such as it was) of Pius's proscriptions was weakened within a generation by clerical writers who found legalistic ways of picking apart his wording. The great Spanish casuist Martín de Azpilcueta argued that when Pius referred to clerical sodomites as 'exercising [or 'practising'] such a terrible crime', this should be applied not to a cleric who just committed sodomy a few times, but 'only to those who exercise it through continuous use'—just as, in Roman law, to qualify as a merchant one had to be not just a person who did a mercantile deal once or twice, but rather 'he who does them so often that general opinion views him as one'. And he also argued (though without being able to produce any particular evidence from the wording of the bull) that it applied not to people who exercised any kind of 'sodomitical act', but only to those who habitually had 'sodomitical copulation'.[11] This point was quickly taken up by the French Franciscan theologian Jean Benedicti, who explained that while the category of sodomitical acts could include any form of 'pollution' with another person of the same sex, sodomitical copulation had to include anal penetration and ejaculation.[12] In this way the distinction between so-called 'imperfect' and 'perfect' sodomy (the latter in the sense of the Latin adjective *perfectus*, meaning completed, fully realized) was strengthened in the minds of his many readers. Azpilcueta's argument was also endorsed by an even more influential writer, the Spanish Jesuit and casuist Juan Azor (Azorius); in his version of it, first published in 1611 and frequently reprinted thereafter, a cleric who 'polluted' himself with another male person in any sexual activity that did not involve anal penetration would not be covered by the papal bull, because 'this pollution, although it is against nature, is not the sin of sodomy.' It is hard to escape the conclusion that Azor was merely improvising on Azpilcueta's theme without having seen the actual text of the bull, which had in fact referred in the most general terms to 'that [sex-ual] incontinence which is against nature'.[13] Nevertheless, this stands as an example of how the variability of the conceptual relationship between the category of 'sins against nature' and that of 'sodomy' could affect the way in which actual legislation was interpreted.

One person whose future depended on such interpretative decisions was the priest Melchor Armengol, Rector of Bot in Valencia, who was arrested by the Inquisition in 1613 and charged with having sex with boys. He vig-orously contested all the evidence against him, which included quite explicit statements by the boys themselves, in some cases specifying interfemoral intercourse, but also mentioning anal penetration. In the end he was willing to confess to non-penetrative sex, and set out his defence in the manner of a university disputation, larded with Latin terms:

> *Mollities* [non-penetrative same-sex acts] and sodomy agree where the emis-sion of semen with pleasure is concerned, which is the aim of lust, and this is the same in each of them. They differ in their mode, as *mollities* emits semen *omnino extra vas* ['entirely outside the vessel', sc. the anus], while sodomy does so *intra vas spurcissimum et nefandum* ['within the most filthy and unspeakable vessel']. And therefore the one is not a sub-category of the other, nor can attempts at one of them be called attempts at the other; rather, they are two different paths by which one can arrive at shameful carnal pleasure. And if the law calls them both sodomy, and calls their actions sodomitical, it does so *improprie et figurate* ['improperly and figuratively'], taking the name of the spe-cies 'sodomy' for the genus *'peccatum contra naturam'* ['sin against nature'], which has that name [sc. 'sodomy'] only if it is given to it by circumlocution, and that

brevitatis causa ['for the sake of brevity'], using the trope or figure of speech which rhetoricians call 'synecdoche'.

Although he maintained his innocence under torture, twice, he was finally sentenced to degradation from holy orders, three years in the galleys, and perpetual banishment. Whether his learned disquisition had saved him from an even harsher sentence is not clear.[14]

★ ★ ★

By the time that Pius V issued his special proscriptions of sodomitical clerics, the secular punishments to which he consigned them could be severe. But the legislators of Western European cities and kingdoms had taken on the task of regulating and punishing this offence only in the latter part of the Middle Ages. Whilst the general shift in this direction occurred in the second half of the thirteenth century, the earliest examples are to be found in Spain towards the end of the previous one, when law codes were issued for towns in territories recently conquered from Muslim rulers. Cuenca, for instance, acquired in 1190 a code which was later taken as a model by many other towns: influenced probably by the Visigothic legal tradition, it decreed death by fire for sodomites. This inaugurated an active tradition of anti-sodomitical law-making; royal charters issued subsequently to various Castilian towns specified castration for all convicted sodomites, followed in some cases by hanging, burning or bleeding to death. In the major collection of laws gathered under Alfonso X and known as the *Siete Partidas* (1256–65), castration was to be followed by death by stoning. And here the imprint of the new theological thinking about this sin was clearly visible in the text of the law, which referred to the fate of Sodom and Gomorrah, and condemned sodomy as 'contrary to nature'. (Its definition of the offence was vague, but male-only: 'the sin into which men fall when they lie with one another against nature, and against natural custom'.)[15] Death was decreed also in Valencia in 1261. The law code of Tortosa (to the south-west of Barcelona), drawn up in the 1270s, specified death by beheading, and said that anyone could seize a thief, heretic or sodomite if caught in the act; if the culprit resisted, he could be killed on the spot.[16]

The reference there to heretics strikes a familiar note. It is a remarkable fact that in the latter part of the thirteenth century many different jurisdictions introduced laws, often with severe punishments attached, against sodomy, having previously taken no formal notice of it at all; the theological campaign on that subject, which not only marshalled theoretical and biblical arguments but also harped on the perceived connection with heresy, seems to have been a major factor. A new popular mood had apparently developed, which saw sodomy not as a private sin to be dealt with through confession and penance, but as a heresy-like rebellion against God which might compromise the whole community. (Without this development, it would seem unlikely that the campaign mounted against the Knights Templar by the French King Philip the Fair in 1307—a campaign transparently motivated by a desire for their wealth, but sustained to a large extent by accusations of institutionalized heresy and sodomy—could ever have gained credence.)[17] In some Italian towns associations of pious laymen, known as confraternities, sprang up in the mid-thirteenth century, with the encouragement of the Church, dedicated to purging their communities of heresy and sodomy. And as we have seen, when the city of Augsburg brought in its new anti-sodomy law in 1276, it referred to sodomites by using the German word for 'heretic'.[18]

Many Italian cities introduced severe penalties in this period: banishment and the confiscation of all property in Siena in 1262 (a revision of this law in 1270 stipulated a heavy fine and, for those who failed to pay, hanging by the genitals), death by burning in Bologna (1288), and the same punishment in Perugia (1309).[19] In Orvieto there was a notable shift in treatment between 1295, when the penalty was a fine set at half the rate for the rape of a woman, and 1308, when sodomites were to be barred from all public office, and those who did not pay a substantial fine were to be paraded through the streets, holding a cord attached to their genitals—a form of public shaming that must have referred symbolically to the grotesque form of execution which was actually decreed in Siena.[20] While the Luccan statutes of 1308 called for a heavy fine and perpetual banishment, those of 1331 specified the death penalty for offenders over the age of eighteen.[21] In Florence the fragmentary surviving statutes of 1284 suggest that sodomy was punished by exile, but by 1325 the standard penalty for a man who had sodomized a boy was castration, and if anyone permitted his house to be used as a venue for sodomy, the house was to be burnt down. A new law in 1365 introduced death by burning, and also offered rewards to informers. Other towns, such as Ascoli Piceno, also offered such rewards, and in Bologna the law provided for burning not only the house used for such immoral purposes, but also its owner. (According to Bernardino of Siena, this actually happened in Bologna in 1423, when the papal legate there, Gabriele Condulmier, the future Pope Eugene IV, had three men and a house incinerated, and decreed that the house was not to be rebuilt for all eternity.)[22]

As we have seen, the death penalty continued to be applied in several Italian cities, such as Venice and Ferrara, throughout the fifteenth century; in Bologna judges turned from its use after the 1430s, and in Florence and Lucca unusually mild judicial regimes for sodomy were established, with spectacular statistical effects. But in Florence harsher penalties were reintroduced in 1527, and the even stricter law of 1542 decreed years of hard labour in the galleys for convicted sodomites, with death for those who offended thrice (or only twice, if they were passive adults).[23] Sometimes the corpse was burnt after the convicted man had been executed by some other method: in Rome, for example, eight of the eleven men arrested for involvement in alleged same-sex marriages in 1578 were hanged, and their bodies were then transported elsewhere for public incineration.[24] Generally, burning was held to be justified not only by the fate of Sodom and Gomorrah in Genesis, but also by a number of New Testament passages: 'he will burn up the chaff with unquenchable fire' (Matt. 3: 12), 'Every tree that bringeth not forth good fruit is hewn down, and cast into the fire' (Matt. 7: 19), 'the tares are gathered and burned in the fire' (Matt. 13: 40), and so on.[25] Being burnt at the stake was, as we have seen, a form of execution decreed in some cities, but various other forms of execution were also possible, beyond decapitation and hanging. In Venice in 1407 a cleric was placed in a cage in the Piazza San Marco, to supply a public spectacle as he starved to death (a method which neatly avoided the problem of striking a death blow at an ordained man); the same treatment was also meted out to priests in Bologna, though that city also burnt at least one priest to death.[26]

One interesting feature of many of these laws, offering some insight into how such male–male sexual relations were viewed more generally, was the treatment of the younger partner. The mediaeval penitentials had typically used a threshold age of 20, as we have seen. This may have been influenced by the canon of the Council of Ancyra which used that age, or by the nature of older–younger sexual relations of this kind which, as we have also seen, were differentiated in Mediterranean societies around the age-range of 18–20, when facial hair appeared. But more generally they may merely have responded to a problem that must have arisen quite often, that of assessing the degree of responsibility of a boy or adolescent who could have been coerced, or taken advantage of in some other way; a fixed age threshold would have been the simplest guide to work by in uncertain cases. Boys in their teens—or even younger than that—were obviously more liable to be exploited in view of their subordinate status (as schoolboys, apprentices, etc.), and indeed more likely to be physically overpowered. Twenty was not a standard threshold age in law. The basic age of legal responsibility in many parts of Europe was fourteen for boys, as it was the age at which, in canon law, they could get married; but different jurisdictions had different rules, and for some legal purposes the threshold of full adult competence could be as high as 25.

The Italian laws were also mostly age-differentiated, though some just provided generally for age to be taken into account: the Bolognese statutes of 1288, for example, said that the passive partner should also be burnt unless he had been the victim of force, or 'unless his age excuses him'.[27] Those that referred to specific ages typically gave eighteen as the main watershed, with fourteen as a subsidiary one below it; but the stipulations varied. The severe Florentine statute of 1325, for example, which decreed castration for a man who sodomized a boy, said that youths between the ages of fourteen and eighteen who consented to being sodomized should be fined 100 lire, while boys under fourteen should either be fined half that amount or be stripped naked and flogged through the streets. In particular cases the harshness of the penalty could go far beyond the provisions of the law. A fifteen-year-old, Giovanni di Giovanni, was found guilty in 1365 of being sodomized by many men, as a willing partner; he seems to have been regarded as a morally corrupting element, requiring exemplary punishment. The boy was led through the streets of Florence to the place of execution, just outside the Porta della Giustizia (a gate opened only on such occasions), and on the scaffold he was castrated, and then killed by having a hot iron rod inserted in his anus.[28]

That same year, a new law was passed under which anyone guilty of sodomy, whether active or passive, could be executed (though the judge could use his discretion, in accordance with the age as well as the 'quality and condition' of the convicted persons). However, an exception was made for passive sodomites under the age of eighteen, who could not be executed and might, in some cases, even be freed without punishment. Gradually, the spirit of those last provisions prevailed. In the following century, the 'Officers of the Night' became disinclined to prosecute youths or passive partners, and this reluctance was tacitly recognized by a new law in 1459 which made no mention of either category. Michael Rocke observes that, consequently, 'officials in effect stopped convicting boys up to eighteen and passives after the late 1450s.' (A small number of passives were condemned, but these were mostly over eighteen.)[29]

In Venice, from the 1440s onwards, judicial practice seems to have applied different penalties to the active and passive partners; passive boys had been treated leniently before then, but it was unusual to ground the distinction on activity versus passivity rather than on age, even though these two categorizations largely coincided in practice. Possibly a simple legal principle, that the initiator of a crime bore heavier responsibility, was at work here— even though, as Zeb Tortorici points out, the initiative may in some cases have come from the passive partner.[30] (On the other side of the Adriatic, the city-state of Dubrovnik, whose anti-sodomy legislation was modelled quite closely on that of Venice, diverged from Venetian practice, insisting that the death penalty applied equally to active and passive culprits.)[31] Such was the hostility in Venice towards passive adults, however, that in 1500 the death penalty was decreed for all passive men over 20 (with banishment for minors); and in 1516 the authorities went so far as to guarantee immunity to youths who denounced passive adult men. In 1557 there was even a case in which the willing passive man was sentenced to seven years' galley service, while his active partner received only five.[32]

In Lucca, as we have seen, when the death penalty for sodomy was introduced in the fourteenth century it applied only to men over eighteen; those below that age qualified for lesser punishments. The new statutes issued in 1539 included an elaborate age-differentiated tariff of penalties for this offence. Boys under fourteen would be punished at the discretion of the judge. Those between fourteen and eighteen would be beaten or whipped on the first conviction, with the addition of a prison sentence on their second. Men aged 18–30 would undergo both the prison sentence and a fine (both to be doubled on a second conviction); men between 30 and 50 would have double the sentence and double the fine, plus exposure in the pillory; and those over 50 would be executed. Umberto Grassi notes that the punishments actually imposed were milder: beatings, small fines, brief incarcerations and periods of banishment. But they still followed a pattern of age-gradation, increasing through the age groups 10–14, 14–18, and over eighteen (where, however, the same punishments continued up to 35).[33] A somewhat similar pattern applied in the city of Perugia, where new anti-sodomy laws, inspired by the preaching of Bernardino of Siena, were introduced in 1425. These specified three months' imprisonment for a consenting boy aged 12–15, a fine for an older youth, and either a heavy fine or death by burning for an adult.[34] And in Rome, where the statutes of 1580 decreed burning at the stake, judges used their discretion when dealing with younger offenders: in seventeenth-century cases involving juvenile gangs, the older boys were sentenced to death, while the younger ones underwent public flogging.[35] Judicial discretion might well lead to the execution of boys in cases where particular aggravating conditions applied: the Ferrarese records offer just one case of a 'young boy' being executed for sodomy, but he was 'burnt for having sodomized a young boy in a church on the night of Good Friday'—not just a moral crime, but an act of gross sacrilege too.[36]

★ ★ ★

Spanish rulers, having led the way in legislating against sodomy in the Middle Ages, kept up their uncompromising stance. In 1497 a formal edict, known as a *pragmática*, was issued by Queen Isabella of Castile and her husband, King Ferdinand of Aragon. This stressed, as the thirteenth-century *Siete partidas* had done, the idea that sodomy was an offence against the natural order, which would bring down plagues and other divine punishments; but it also put an emphasis on the damage done to society at large, asserting that 'because of this, nobility is lost, and the heart becomes cowardly'. Noting that previous laws had failed to eliminate sodomy, it decreed that the standards of legal proof should be lowered from the level required by normal criminal justice to that which applied to the offences of heresy and *lèse-majesté*. Prosecutions should take no account of rank or quality; the penalty was death by burning, plus the confiscation by the state of all goods and property. One notable provision of this edict was its statement that where it was not possible to prove that the act had been fully accomplished and 'perfect', it would be sufficient to show that 'acts very near and close to the accomplishment of it' had taken place—in which case, the punishment for 'perfect' sodomy would be equally applied.[37] Although the wording of this decree made even less effort than the *Siete partidas* to define the nature of sodomy, merely referring to it as 'the unspeakable crime against nature', these allusions to 'perfect' sodomy would have given a sufficient idea of the nature of the primary offence: anal penetration and emission. But the category of acts 'very near and close' to that seems to have become an ever-expanding one in the minds of the judges; in 1510 a man was executed in the western Castilian town of Plasencia for putting his hand down the trousers of a youth and inviting him to go to bed with him, and, as we have seen, in 1579 two teenaged boys were put to death in Seville for 'frolicking' in bed together and touching or manipulating each other's genitals.[38] As for the standards of proof: a further *pragmática* on the crime of sodomy, issued by Philip II in 1598, said that since the offence was 'because of its nature very difficult to prove', his judges should decree punishment 'even if the said crime has not been proved by witnesses, but rather by other procedures established and approved in law, from which sufficient proof could arise to permit the imposition of ordinary punishment'. And where witnesses were available, the normal rules that required multiple witnesses to an act were relaxed: three witnesses, each testifying as sole observer of a different act, would be sufficient to ensure conviction, and those witnesses could themselves have been participants in the acts.[39]

The severe punishment regime, with death as the norm, was kept up well into the seventeenth century. Mary Elizabeth Perry's account of the sodomy trials in late-sixteenth- and early-seventeenth century Seville states that while death sentences were applied to those who were seventeen or older, 'Sixteen-year-olds, for example, were sent to the galley, while younger boys who seemed to have been merely passive partners were whipped or sentenced to watch the burning of their adult partners.' Pedro de León, who ministered to the condemned sodomites in that city, noted that there was a presumption that the junior partner would receive some punishment; a rare exception involved some young boys sodomized by an abusive schoolmaster in 1588, who were let off free. However, in the same year he also recorded the case of a 56-year-old cleric who was found in bed with a 'young lad': both of them were burnt, even though the boy was 'of a very low age'.[40]

King Ferdinand's hatred of sodomy seems to have been deep-rooted. In 1503, when ordering city governments in Castile to send men who had been condemned to capital punishment to the galleys instead, he made a special exception for convicted sodomites. And two years later he wrote to the Church authorities in the Murcian city of Cartagena, telling them to revoke the permission they had given to the Inquisition to prosecute sodomites in their diocese; only the royal government, he explained, could impose the severe penalties that were necessary in such cases.[41] The Inquisition in Seville did try a group of sodomites in 1506, but in 1509 the Supreme Council of the Inquisition issued an order forbidding all its provincial tribunals from dealing with the offence, unless heresy was also involved; probably this action too was prompted by Ferdinand's strong views on the matter, though it also seems that the authorities in Rome at this time preferred the Inquisition to concentrate on theological matters.[42] The next time a serious effort was made by a local Inquisition to gain jurisdiction over sodomy was in 1524, when the Zaragoza tribunal arrested a prominent citizen, and suspected sodomite, who had been an outspoken critic of the Inquisition. This time the Supreme Council was supportive, the King (now the future Emperor Charles V) allowed his ambassador in Rome to make the case, and the Pope complied, issuing a breve which gave jurisdiction to the Inquisition tribunals on the Aragonese mainland, thus excluding Mallorca and Sicily.[43] This was a historic step; even the Roman Inquisition—which covered mainland Italy and Malta—did not have jurisdiction over this sin. (It would gain it in 1557, but would make very little use of it, formally declaring in 1600 that it did not prosecute such cases.)[44] The Zaragoza tribunal, having requested this power, did use it; Barcelona followed suit within a few years; by the later 1560s Zaragoza had also taken on itself to prosecute the sin of bestiality; but Valencia stood back, not attempting to try any form of sodomy until 1572.[45]

The main difference, in effect, between the Aragonese Inquisition trials and those held by the Castilian secular courts was, as we have seen, that the sentences were milder overall—though the Inquisition did send a minority of convicted sodomites to be executed, and a much larger number to do hard labour in the galleys. Not enough evidence survives from the secular courts of Sicily and Mallorca to furnish a proper comparison, but what we have does strongly suggest that execution was the norm in both places—in Mallorca, either by burning alive or by drowning, which was followed by the incineration of the corpse.[46] In most ways, however, a large divergence between the practice of the Inquisition and that of the Aragonese criminal courts was not to be expected, because the papal breve had instructed the Inquisitors to proceed in accordance with the secular law. One consequence of this could be of real benefit to the accused: whereas the Inquisition would normally conceal the identities of the accusers, in these cases that principle of anonymity was dropped, and the accused were often able to cross-examine hostile witnesses. Also to the advantage of the accused person, the Inquisition maintained its usual practice of granting him a lawyer appointed by the court.[47] (Convicted criminals benefited too from the high age of legal majority in the Aragonese Crown lands, which was 25: the death penalty would not be applied to anyone younger than that.)[48] A set of rules for sodomy trials drawn up for the Barcelona tribunal said that the accused must have knowledge of all elements of the trial, including every witness statement: if witnesses could not appear in person to ratify their statements because they lived a long way away, the accused could delegate an observer to go there and see the ratification performed. But on the other hand the Aragonese tribunals worked on the principle that one witness—who might have been a participant in the act—was sufficient to justify prosecution, which could involve the use of torture, though not sufficient to achieve a conviction if the accused continued to protest his innocence.[49]

Torture—which was employed not as a punishment but as an investigative device, when the accused was thought to be lying, withholding information or feigning madness—was certainly used by the Inquisition. One historian calculates that it was applied in roughly 30 per cent of cases heard at the Aragonese tribunals, a figure which can be corroborated by sampling the sodomy trials at the Barcelona tribunal in the period 1570–1600, where torture was used in 17 out of 60 cases (28.3 per cent).[50] In 1593 the Royal Council asked the Supreme Council of the Inquisition why the Zaragoza tribunal used torture, given that it was not normally applied by the Aragonese secular courts, and given also the fact that the papal breve required the Inquisition in Aragon to proceed in accordance with the secular laws. The reply was that the secular judges there had requested that the Inquisitors should be tacitly mandated to use it, because they themselves could not; it also noted that the Barcelona tribunal involved secular judges with the Inquisitors in both hearings and sentencings.[51] Where general Inquisition practice was concerned, that last detail represented another anomaly, matched only by the inclusion in Venetian territory—at the insistence of the government—of secular judges in the tribunals of the Inquisition. It illustrates the way in which, thanks to the breve of 1524 and perhaps also the papal bull of 1568 insisting on secular penalties for clerics, the notion that sodomy was a 'crime of mixed jurisdiction' could lead to a significant merging of secular and ecclesiastical justice where this particular offence was concerned.

★ ★ ★

In Portugal, as in Spain, harsh secular laws were in place long before the involvement of the Inquisition. By the mid-fourteenth century sodomy was regarded by Portuguese law as equivalent to lèse-majesté, being thought of apparently as a kind of rebellion against God. In the law-code known as the Ordenações Afonsinas, promulgated by King Alfonso V in 1446–54, it was described as a crime against nature and against God, to be punished by burning at the stake. In the Ordenações Manuelinas, a major codification of

Portuguese law issued by King Manuel I in 1512–21, the equivalence to *lèse-majesté* was reaffirmed, confiscation of the convicted man's estate and 'infamy'—loss of all social status for his family—were added as penalties, and punishments were prescribed for those who failed to report any cases that they were aware of. And the *Ordenações Filipinas* (1603) of King Philip III of Spain (Philip II of Portugal) decreed galley service for '*mollities* and shameful touching', but ended the infamy of the culprit's children, and allowed them to inherit his property.[52] By that stage, however, these cases were mostly being handled by the Inquisition.

Jurisdiction over sodomy passed to the Portuguese Inquisition several decades after it had been given to the Aragonese one. Since the offence was traditionally viewed as a *crimen mixti fori*, it had always been brought to ecclesiastical courts too; in the 1550s the Archbishop of Lisbon agreed that the Inquisition should take over from them, and in 1553 King John III formally permitted the Inquisition to judge such cases. Keen to suppress this vice, the King had already begun negotiations in Rome to persuade the Pope to authorize such a change. That request was finally granted in 1562, after John's death, when a papal breve gave the Inquisitor General in Portugal (Cardinal Henrique, brother of the late king) the power to proceed against suspected sodomites, even those who normally enjoyed legal immunities; and another breve, in 1574, granted the Inquisition that power over the regular clergy.[53] As in Spain, here too the assumption was that the Inquisitors would prosecute and sentence people in accordance with the secular laws: King John's decree of 1553 said that convicted sodomites should be condemned according to the *Ordenações*, and in 1568 Cardinal Henrique instructed the Coimbra tribunal that it must follow the laws of the kingdom.[54] Generally, this assignment of secular responsibilities to an ecclesiastical institution seems to have worked well, though there was some pressure from the secular authorities, especially during the period when Portugal was under Spanish rule. In 1611, for example, King Philip II of Portugal (Philip III of Spain) sent a letter to the Inquisition asking whether it was right that people convicted of sodomy only, not sodomy plus heresy, were relaxed to the secular power for punishment without the secular judges seeing all the trial documents (and thus being able to form their own view); the Inquisition defended its ground, insisting that this was the correct procedure under the terms of the papal breve.[55]

As we have seen, however, the death penalty required by the *Ordenações* was applied by the Inquisition in only 8 per cent of cases. Galley service was by far the most common punishment (42 per cent). In another 8 per cent of cases, a long period of incarceration was imposed; but the great majority of these concerned clerics who were sent to be locked up in distant monastic houses, which shows that the bull of Pius V, demanding that all convicted priests be handed over for punishment by the secular arm, was disregarded.[56] Sometimes, indeed, self-confessed sodomitical priests were spared confinement altogether. We have already encountered the 67-year-old priest who admitted to sex with his servants, both actively and passively, over a seven-year period (though he said that he had given up the practice thirteen years earlier); he was forbidden to undertake any ecclesiastical office or cure of souls, and was given strict penances to perform, but no punishment beyond that.[57]

We have also seen that the procedural principles of the Portuguese Inquisition were quite favourable to the accused, allowing all possible benefit of the doubt. Adolescents were treated leniently: in one seventeenth-century case, an eighteen-year-old was let off all physical punishment because he was a minor, and the Inquisitors also commented that 'according to the opinion of many Doctors of the Church', those who had been the passive partners should undergo less rigorous penalties. Furthermore, the rules required two separate consummated sexual acts to be proven for a conviction to be made; and the accused was allowed to present a written rebuttal of any claims made by witnesses or denouncers.[58] Lack of sufficient proof was one reason why 10 per cent of those accused of this crime were acquitted; the fact that the Inquisition normally absolved those who had been victims of force was another. But a further reason was the Inquisition's principle that it would convict only for 'perfect' sodomy. In its *Regimento* (rule-book), drawn up in 1613, it excluded all forms of *mollities* from its jurisdiction; in some cases these were taken into account as aggravating factors, especially if they involved so-called *conatos nefandos*, acts of attempted sodomy which had not reached consummation, but the more minor forms were left for confessors to deal with.[59] It is thus a striking fact that Portugal, unlike Spain, criminalized all forms of *mollities* in its secular laws, while at the same time the Portuguese Inquisition, unlike the Aragonese one, refused to judge them. Indeed, one might suspect that those two points are connected: committed in theory to trying and judging in accordance with those laws, the Portuguese Inquisition knew that strict enforcement was not really feasible where the more minor infractions were concerned. But because the dividing-line which it sought to apply had been generally conceptualized in terms of 'perfect' versus 'imperfect' sodomy, it was left with the often problematic task of proving that both penetration and emission had occurred. Since the easiest form of proof was confession to the court, one might then expect the Inquisitors to have become particularly dependent on torture; but that was not the case. It has been calculated that torture was applied to only 15 per cent of those accused of sodomy at the Portuguese tribunals.[60]

★ ★ ★

One final aspect of these judicial and punitive regimes deserves comment: the degree to which they sought publicity. It is at first sight strange that a sin which was widely regarded as 'unspeakable', or, to be precise, not to be spoken about—so much so, that even experienced preachers, trusted to guide the morals of their communities, were advised not to discuss it at all—was the subject of judicial procedures that ended with the public spectacle of an execution. Only two categories of people might generally expect to escape that fate: priests, who were bundled off into remote monasteries, and nobles, whose trials were generally cloaked in greater secrecy, and whose sentences very rarely called for their deaths. Otherwise, when death sentences were issued, public execution was the norm, usually at a place reserved for that purpose just outside the city walls. This was a basic feature of mediaeval and early modern societies; and the point of the spectacle was not simply to act as a deterrent, but also to make a symbolic statement of an emotionally compelling kind, illustrating the purification of the community and the upholding of the divine moral order.[61]

The symbolic stakes were raised even higher by the *autos-da-fé* which were organized by the Spanish and Portuguese Inquisitions. At these grand public ceremonies, typically held in town squares, large numbers of people who had been processed by the Inquisition were paraded before the public, and then divided between those who were 'reconciled', to be given penances and other forms of punishment, and those who were condemned to death; the nature of their offences, together with their sentences, was publicly declared. This whole system had grown up around the central activity of the Inquisition, which was concerned with heresy (and especially, in Iberia, with the phenomenon of converted Jews relapsing into their former faith); the intensive mobilization of religious feelings among the ordinary population, on these occasions, was all conducted on that basis.[62] So it is a little hard to judge how the convicted sodomites, who would have been a small percentage of those paraded at a typical *auto-da-fé*, would have been fitted into these occasions. One historian has written that in Spain (as opposed to Portugal) 'the inquisitorial rules forbade the public reading of sentences regarding sodomites, most certainly so as not to offend those who were present and to avoid polluting the air.'[63] But the evidence for this is rather mixed. It is true that in Toledo, for example (where the Inquisition did not deal with sodomy), sentences were publicly proclaimed for 'Judaizing', crypto-Islamic practices and bigamy, but meted out behind closed doors for crimes against the Inquisition itself, and also for blasphemous statements; so the rationale for secrecy was readily available.[64] Yet on the other hand, Cristian Berco quotes a letter written by Inquisitors in Valencia to the Supreme Council in 1625, saying how important it was to present convicted sodomites at an *auto-da-fé*, because public shame was the most powerful deterrent of all: 'We believe that, given the character of the common people, were they to know that they will not suffer the affront of the Inquisition taking them out in public, they would gain greater audacity and ease in committing such crimes.'[65]

Certainly the secular authorities believed in the minatory effect of public punishment. When the mulatto Jerónimo Ponce and the slave Domingo López were both convicted of acts of sodomy within the prison of the Casa de Contratación in Seville, their joint sentence, issued in 1603, decreed that 'they should be conveyed by the usual route through the public streets of this city... and in the usual place and district of this city there should be erected two stakes, and they should be tied to those and garrotted until they die a natural death, and then their bodies should be burnt in flames of fire until they turn to dust and ashes so that their memory may perish.'[66] The notion of 'memory' invoked in that concluding phrase was concerned essentially with the memorialization—such as a gravestone—that could attend a final resting place. The procession through the streets, on the other hand, and the very public execution, were very definitely designed to ensure that the fate of convicted sodomites would be imprinted on the memory of the whole community. Seventeen years later the King of Spain (and of Portugal) would write to the Portuguese Inquisitor General, demanding constant vigilance and punitive action against both sodomites and necromancers, 'so that the public demonstration of the punishment of the guilty may preserve others [from committing such offences]'.[67] For memory of the punishment to have such an effect, it was necessary that there be public knowledge of the crime.

11

Literary works

Religion and law were powerful influences on the values of these societies. They moulded behaviour, not just by setting up external disincentives in this world or the next, but by helping to form people's beliefs
and attitudes. The cultural products of these societies also played a role here,
and perhaps in some ways a more complex one: they could reinforce those
norms, but some of the methods they used in doing so—comedy, satire,
social description—could modulate the ways in which people thought
about sodomitical behaviour, prompting forms of admission or acknowledgement. (Humour, in particular, was an instrument with ambiguous
effects, capable of co-opting the reader in enjoyment as well as—or even
instead of—disapproval.) In very rare cases they could even give expression
to some of the views and feelings of the sodomites themselves. But, more
commonly, they can also yield valuable evidence of how same-sex relations
were perceived.

In the Iberian peninsula, references to sodomy in literary works were
infrequent, and the comments made were very negative in tone. Fairly typical was the brief allusion to it in the major poetic treatise, the *Espill* (1460),
by the Valencian poet and physician Jaume Roig: 'the unspeakable, stinking,
horrible, strong leprosy of sodomy, a sin which is very worthy of both
earthly fire and hell fire, for the soul and the body'.[1] Other allusions in
Valencian literature are very rare. A general study of erotic poetry in the
Spanish Golden Age finds occasional references to sodomy, made for burlesque or insulting purposes, projecting the negative view of male–male
sexual relations which was 'dominant, and almost completely exclusive'; and
specialists looking for traces of same-sex relations in early modern Spanish
literature have gleaned a very slender harvest—beyond the small number of
satirical references, and a few mentions of Ganymede in classicizing works,
just a very limited range of possible oblique allusions, with absolutely no

Forbidden Desire in Early Modern Europe: Male–Male Sexual Relations, 1400–1750. Noel Malcolm, Oxford University Press.
© Noel Malcolm 2024. DOI: 10.1093/oso/9780198886334.003.0011

positive expressions of male same-sex desire.[2] The best-known author to make use of this theme was Francisco de Quevedo, writing in the first half of the seventeenth century; his three satirical epitaphs on dead sodomites, one of whom he pointedly identified as an Italian, are portraits of moral evil, tinged with physical disgust.[3]

One example which diverges, if only slightly, from this pattern can be found in a humorous collection published in Valencia in 1519. It is a brief, comic-fantastic tale, by an anonymous author, which hinges on an accidental act of sodomy. A cow-herd who was suffering from pains in his loins and flanks undid his clothes, lay on his back on a flat rock, and massaged himself with butter, giving himself an erection in the process. Meanwhile a demon was flying overhead, on his way to tempt a saintly hermit; seeing the cow-herd and thinking that he was 'inflamed with lust', he decided to alight on him and carry him off to Hell while he was in a state of mortal sin. Landing badly, however, he found himself impaled on the man's erection; and the cow-herd held him there, refusing to let him go while he summoned his fierce dogs. They then chased the demon back to Hell, 'where the miserable demon has been mending his arse until this day'.[4] Here, while the connections between acts against nature, mortal sin, infernal punishment and the Devil were basically upheld, the man in the story gained a sort of comic prestige for having mastered the demon in such a crude manner, inflicting humiliation as well as harm; the joke could not possibly work the other way round, with the cow-herd as the passive partner. In this way there was at least a glancing recognition of the hierarchy of sexual roles that prevailed in same-sex encounters. Possibly, too, some element of the humour here depended on a sense of the patently unlikely nature of the narrator's explanation of why the man was lying there, exposed and erect, in the first place; the story had to gain the reader's complicity in a rather absurd fib about what a man might actually be doing when found in such a position.

Generally, though, as there are so few references to sodomy in the literature of the period, these works have little to offer us in terms of supplementary information about how sodomites behaved, or were perceived as behaving. But there is one intriguing passage in a well-known treatise, composed in the 1430s and printed in 1498, by a Castilian author known as the Archpriest of Talavera: the *Corbacho*, alternatively entitled *Reprobación del amor mundano*. The work is hard to judge as social commentary, as it largely consists of extreme moral-religious denunciations of human lust in general, and women in particular; but this passage, which occurs in a discussion of hypocrites and pseudo-devout people, seems to contain an element of observation, however exaggerated. In the category of licentious friars, the Archpriest declares, there are some who fall into two types. The first sort devote themselves to sex, and 'want to have men, with whom to perform their vile act, committing it, as men, with them'—in other words, taking the active role. The second sort 'are like women in their acts [sc. passive], and like young women in their disordered appetites, and they desire men more ardently than prostitutes do'. He is reluctant to say anything more about their 'abominable deeds and sodomitical acts', because even to talk about the subject is to offend God. But he adds a further comment: many of them 'hate women, they spit on them, and some will not eat any food they prepare, nor wear any linen washed by them, nor sleep in a bed which they have made up. If you talk to them about women, they say "Lord, turn away your wrath!", permitting themselves to speak and act like that out of feigned virtue. And then they go amongst the boys, kissing them, caressing them, and giving them jewels, money, and little things suitable for their age.'[5] While the aversion to women described here seems, like many things in this text, hugely exaggerated, the charge of special hypocrisy is nicely made: here are friars pretending to be extra-zealous in their adherence to clerical celibacy when they are really exhibiting a strong sexual preference of a different kind. The idea that some sodomites had a physical aversion to women recurred in one of Quevedo's sodomite epitaphs, where he wrote that 'no cunt ever saw him erect.'[6] Some Italian writers, as we shall see, would make much more of this.

* * *

The default attitude in Italian literary culture was, again, one of strong disapproval. Dante placed sodomites in the third sub-circle of his seventh circle of Hell. Before reaching that level, his guide, Vergil, explained the rationale for grouping this sin with atheism and blasphemy as a form of assault on God and His creation: 'It is possible to do violence to the Deity, denying Him in one's heart and blaspheming against him, and scorning nature and its goodness.' (Where scorning nature was concerned, Vergil linked together the sins of 'Sodom and Cahors', the latter city being proverbial for usury; this expressed the standard view that it was unnatural to make money from money, as opposed to making it from labour and natural goods.)[7] The few references to sodomy in Boccaccio's *Decameron*, written in the early 1350s, are thoroughly negative. One story is about a venerable but innocent-minded friar being deceived by a shamelessly wicked man, Ser Ciappelletto, whose deathbed confession, humble and pious to an absurd degree, admits to only the most trivial of sins; the friar then has him buried in his convent, and encourages people to regard him as a saint. Boccaccio's description of the man's evil life is quite comprehensive: he has forged legal documents, borne false witness, murdered, blasphemed, indulged in gluttony, drinking and gambling, never been to church, and, moreover, 'he delighted in sex contrary to nature more than any other deplorable man.' Another story involves a virtuous Jewish merchant who is thinking of converting to Christianity, and travels to Rome in order to see what life is like at the very heart of Christendom. He quickly discovers that 'the Pope and the cardinals and the other prelates and all the members of the court' were 'all committing sins of lust of the most disgraceful kind, not only in the natural way but also sodomitically, without being at all restrained by remorse or shame'.[8]

Such hostile attitudes remained standard; as we have seen, when Mercurino Ranzo wrote his Latin drama *De falso hypocrita* for the students of Pavia in 1437, he made the sodomitical sacristan lustful and predatory as well as hypocritical, ending the play with the man's total humiliation.[9] A comic *novella* by the Bolognese humanist Giovanni Sabadino degli Arienti, written in 1478 and first printed in 1483, ends similarly with the denunci-ation of a lustful cleric. When an exceptionally good-looking novice priest has been dressed as a girl by his friends (for a prank), the Prior of the Augustinian friars is greatly smitten and invites 'her' to his cell, only to dis-cover, when he has thrown her onto his bed, that she is a man—whereupon he says that his desire is not at all reduced by that detail. The novice priest makes a strongly condemnatory speech ('How worthy you are of eternal vituperation!' and so on), the group of friends broadcast the story as widely as they can, and the Prior is expelled from his friary amid total shame and obloquy.[10] Even Benvenuto Cellini—or perhaps one should say, for reasons already discussed, especially Benvenuto Cellini—wrote about sodomy in strongly negative terms. Describing Luigi Pulci, a talented and 'extraordin-arily beautiful', but dissolute, young man from Florence whom he had befriended in Rome, he mentioned that the young man had acquired a patron called Giovanni. However, 'Giovanni's love for him turned out to be dirty rather than virtuous; for every day you could see that he was giving that young man different clothes of velvet and silk, and people knew that he had completely abandoned himself to wickedness...I had reproved him, telling him that he had given himself up as a prey to bestial vices, which one day would break his neck.'[11]

One distinct type that does emerge from several Renaissance Italian texts is the sodomite who has no sexual interest in women. Boccaccio's exemplar of wickedness, Ser Ciappelletto, 'was as fond of women as a dog is of the stick'. Another of his stories, set in Perugia, involves a rich man who got married 'rather to deceive others and counter the common opinion held about him by everyone in Perugia, than for any desire to marry'. His wife, who turns out to have a strong sexual appetite, complains: 'why did he take me as his wife, if women were not to his liking?' One evening, when her husband has gone out for dinner, she invites a handsome youth to the house; but the boy is discovered when the husband returns unexpectedly early. Defending herself against his remark that all women are people of the worst sort, she comments acerbically that 'you're as fond of us as a dog is of beatings'. The story has a comic ending (borrowed from an episode in Apuleius' *The Golden Ass*), in which the husband spends much of the night with the boy.[12]

Early in the following century, a comic Latin dialogue-poem, written probably in Pavia, also played on this theme. The 'Debate between Cavichiolus and his Wife' lets both parties speak their minds; and the husband's statements are especially frank. Before he got married, he says, 'no woman had ever disturbed my dreams. My prick had only ever been acquainted with golden boys; and it remains constant in the desire to live with them forever.' Waxing ever more rhetorical, he declares: 'the crow will turn white and the chicken turn into a swan, before my prick could ever enter the orifices as yet unknown to it—before my glorious prick could ever be aroused by your cunt... Only the Fates themselves will be able to alter my passions, unless death itself forestalls my vows.' The idea that this was a permanent preference or disposition could hardly be emphasized more strongly. As in the Boccaccio story—and very possibly under its influence—this work arrives at a kind of comic resolution: the husband says that if his wife is hungry for sex, she is welcome to make use of some of his boys.[13]

Also in this category is the protagonist of another *novella* by Sabadino degli Arienti: a hard-bitten, plain-talking Florentine seaman who, on a visit to Bologna, goes to a friar to say his confession. The friar asks him about sins of lust, and he says that he has never sinned with any woman; but when the friar then praises his chastity, he replies: 'You're wasting your time asking me about that, for this is the truth, and don't be surprised: I don't mean that women have failed to please me, but rather, it disgusts me even to look at them.' The friar then asks if he has sinned with the 'unspeakable vice against nature', and receives the answer: 'Yes; and I've committed that sin not so much for pleasure as to follow the Florentine motto, which in my days said "When you want to have fun, do it often with a boy."'[14]

Another text which presented a character of this kind was the full-length comedy *Il marescalco* ('The Stablemaster') by Pietro Aretino, published in 1533. The eponymous central character, stablemaster to the Duke of Mantua, is bombarded with rumours that his master has decreed that he must marry and has even chosen a wife for him. He resists this as long as he can, but is eventually obliged to go through a marriage ceremony with a mysterious young woman—who, despite her generally coy appearance, gives him a strong French kiss at the moment when he puts the ring on her finger. The joke is then revealed: the bride is the Duke's page-boy in disguise. The stablemaster is so put upon throughout the play that he cannot fail to gain a measure of sympathy from the audience; yet while it is true that his most negative outbursts are directed specifically at wives, not women in general, it is also obvious that he feels no sexual desire for women at all. Less obvious, but unmistakeably present in the text, are hints that he has sex with his own young servant, Giannico. When, referring to the servant boy, he says impatiently to a neighbour 'Pox take him!', Giannico pertly responds: 'It'll be your fault if it does.' Urging him to marry, his old nurse tells him to leave his 'wicked ways' ('What wicked ways?', he asks; 'You know what', she replies); and when the bride is revealed to be a boy at the end of the play, his neighbour says: 'You're not so reluctant now, are you?'[15] It would be an exaggeration to call this work, as one modern scholar does, 'a play sympathetic to masculine love'.[16] But by focusing on familiar tropes about the alleged disadvantages of marriage—female extravagance, controlling behaviour, infidelity, etc.—rather than on the undesirability of sex with women, and by pushing the stablemaster's sodomitical activities to the outer margins of the story, Aretino did avoid the requirement for a more directly condemnatory treatment of the man.[17] (That he personally would have felt less condemnatory than most people seems clear. While staying in Mantua in 1527 he fell in love, at the age of 35, with a woman, and wrote a poem declaring that 'Isabella Sforza has converted Aretino from being a sodomite, as he was from birth'—a miracle, he said, beyond even the powers of St Francis. The conversion was less than total, however; living in Venice in 1530,

he was reported to have a *bardassa* or catamite in his house, and other catamites seem to have followed in subsequent years.)[18]

Exclusively male-oriented sodomites make their appearance as a known
but distinctly untypical phenomenon in the literature of the time, just as
they did, it seems, among the real-life sodomites of these societies. The
standard view, that a man who had sex with male youths would also have
sex with women, was supported by most of the classical texts dealing with
sexual behaviour that began to exercise a strong influence on Italian writers
during this period—above all, the bawdy erotic or satirical poetry of
Catullus and Martial. Two fifteenth-century poets stand out for their
unusually vivid and daring ventures into this genre. The Sicilian humanist
Antonio Beccadelli spent time as a young man in Florence, Padua and Siena,
before writing his collection of mostly obscene Latin poems, *Hermaphroditus*,
which he began to circulate in 1425–6, in a version dedicated to Cosimo de’
Medici. As the title suggests, the verses are concerned with sex with males
as well as sex with females (though poems of the latter type predominate
overall); the tone ranges from defiant celebration to scoffing satire, from the
scathing to the disgusting. A brief quotation from the modern American
translation may suffice to give the flavour of the work. Warning a friend
about ‘Quintius, a Foul and Ugly Boy’, he writes: ‘Your cock will just lie
there shriveled for ever, | the minute you plant kisses on him. | Go far away
from here, Quintius, you dirty, stinking brothel… Who can count the number of members your gaping asshole has swallowed?’[19] Although the poems
are primarily shaped by classical models—Martial in particular—there are
some contemporary references, including the line ‘You’re a Tuscan, and
cock delights the Tuscan people.’ But what is particularly revealing of contemporary attitudes is the reaction to the collection as it rapidly circulated
in manuscript copies. Beccadelli’s literary skill was widely admired; the
famous humanist Poggio Bracciolini praised him for writing about ‘topics
so immodest and so ridiculous in a manner so charming and well put
together’. But he went on to warn him that such a work was tolerable only
as a youthful excess, and that he should now turn to more serious matters,
‘so that an impure life is not inferred from the obscenity of your book’—
adding that some aspects of pagan Roman writing were ‘not allowed to us
who are Christians’. Other reactions were much more hostile. A Franciscan
from Milan circulated fierce attacks on Beccadelli; Bernadino of Siena
organized public burnings of *Hermaphroditus*; and Pope Eugene IV (who, as
we have seen, had previously insisted on the incineration of three men and

a house in Bologna) threatened to excommunicate anyone who read it. Beccadelli eventually capitulated, writing a craven recantation in 1435.[20]

The other fifteenth-century poet who cultivated this style of Latin verse, also with great skill, was Pacifico Massimi. Born in Ascoli Piceno in 1406— and thus twelve years younger than Beccadelli—he spent time in Perugia, Rome, Lucca and Florence; and it was in the Tuscan capital that his collection of poems, *Hecatelegium*, was printed in 1489. (So this example of youthful excess was published by an octogenarian; Massimi would die in 1506, his centenary year.)[21] In these poems, the objects of sexual desire range from women—especially prostitutes—to male youths, and the first-person speaker expresses an ethos of indiscriminate hedonism, concentrating on physical pleasures and dismissing stories of Heaven and Hell as fables. When he boasts of the size of his erection, he says that one girl complained that it was painfully large; when he exults in the number of orgasms he can achieve in succession, he writes that the boys who visit him at night all know the power of his penis. But while gross exaggeration is clearly a literary device here, there are quite a few details (more, overall, than in Beccadelli's work) that supply a sense of contemporary *actualité*—such as the claim that he would often go to the bridges over the Arno to look for women to have sex with.[22]

Some of the poems relating to same-sex relations make points that match quite closely the information drawn by Michael Rocke from fifteenth-century Florentine sources. For example, the speaker here reproves a young man who already has facial hair but still offers himself as the passive partner: if he does not mend his ways, he will end up by losing his life. Gifts to boys, in gratitude for sex, are—in moderation—good practice; but he warns a friend that boys are greedy, and that parents eager for such gifts will even pimp their sons. 'If you hand over gifts, the fathers, and the mothers too, will become procurers and will make up the bed for you.' As for boys who seek payments rather than presents (the distinction being important in principle, though perhaps not so very clear in practice): these are vicious, and should be avoided. In a poem entitled 'To a Catamite', he urges the youth to give him what he wants for free, as it is 'such a small thing', and complains bitterly that 'you dare, sordid boy, to demand money with your hand held out'; he also warns that those who perform for payment will be sought out by practitioners of deviant sex, such as the 'fellator'. His final advice to the boy, who is trading on his looks, is that he should remember that beauty fades; and he adds that 'what you are, I too was; I was the envied hope—don't mock—of a thousand prayers', thus indicating, in his own life story, the classic progression from desired boy to desiring adult.[23]

One of Massimi's most sharply worded poems is about such a mercenary youth, who is evidently eager to have him as a customer. 'Often he greets me, and often he smiles at me and gestures with his fingers; now he follows me, now he walks in front of me.' What he wants, says Massimi, or rather his poetic persona, is not hard to guess, because one day he saw money in my hands, and 'I have a reputation for always giving presents to young catamites.' But I wouldn't have sex with this boy unless he were paying me, because he is so extremely unattractive, with stick-legs like a cicada and a dried-up body like a skeleton. 'It's true, I admit, that I often bugger boys, and I shan't deny it. But I eat only the best quality poultry: the boy should be juicy, plump, hot and white-skinned, and he must have fire in his arse.' With lines such as these, it is not surprising that, for all the admiration Massimi gained from connoisseurs of Latin poetry, his work too met with hostile reactions. The extreme rarity of copies of the printed edition suggests that most were destroyed; and in 1501 Machiavelli received a letter from a friend in Rome which said that if Massimi did not enjoy the protection of a cardinal, he would by now have been burnt at the stake.[24]

These two examples of writers mimicking the Roman poets' first-person references to sodomitical activity are as exceptional, in fifteenth-century Italy, as they are striking. They raise the larger question of how Renaissance humanists dealt with the frequent references to male–male sex and love in classical sources—not just the bawdily explicit works of this kind, but the much wider range of representations, from Greek myths about the loves of the gods to the idealizing theories of the Platonic dialogues or the passionate declaration of love for the beautiful Alexis in Vergil's second Eclogue. There were many things here that could cause embarrassment to early modern Christian scholars, who, accordingly, adopted a variety of tactics for dealing with them. The simplest method where particular passages were concerned was to suppress them. In early fifteenth-century translations from Greek into Latin, such as that of Plato's dialogue *Phaedrus* by Leonardo Bruni, or that of Diogenes Laertius' *Lives and Opinions of the Eminent Philosophers* by Ambrogio Traversari (a scholar-theologian who also served Pope Eugene IV as a trusted diplomat), passages suggesting paederasty were censored; in some sixteenth-century commentaries on Catullus, 'words, verses, and sometimes whole fragments of the text were removed'. Other forms of adaptation were possible: when the humanist scholar Guarino of

Verona translated into Latin the love poems attributed to Plato, he simply changed the gender of the love-object from male to female.[25] Where the offending text was left intact, its venom could be drawn by subjecting it to elaborate interpretation. An influential example of this was given by Erasmus in his educational treatise *De ratione studii*, where he showed how to teach Vergil's second Eclogue to a class of students: the lecturer should expound the classical principle that true friendship requires equality between the friends, in order to let them see that this depiction of passionate but unrequited love between an older shepherd and a younger city boy was a moral cautionary tale about the sort of inadequate relationship that should be avoided.[26]

The most general strategy, however, was to refine away any elements of apparent physicality in the classical references to 'masculine love'; this could be done either by taking physical beauty as something that pointed beyond itself, leading onwards and upwards to higher spiritual or intellectual qualities, or simply by treating the physical element as an allegory or metaphor. Authority for both approaches could be found in the classical sources themselves. The myth of Ganymede, for example—on the face of it, a story of Zeus seizing a beautiful boy because he desired him—was desexualized by Xenophon: 'it was not for his body but for his soul that he was elevated by Zeus to Olympus...So he is called Ganymede not because of his physical attractions, but because of his sweetness of thought.'[27] Humanists seized on this line of argument: Cristoforo Landino, writing in 1481, explained that Ganymede represented the contemplative soul, lifted up by divine grace, while his friend Marsilio Ficino put forward a Neoplatonist interpretation, in which the story represents the love of beauty raising the soul towards God. Sixteenth-century emblem books, full of morally and theologically improving images, developed this line further; one, produced by Achille Bocchi in 1555, had a picture of Ganymede being taken up by the eagle, with the motto 'True pleasure is found in the knowledge and worship of God.'[28]

Marsilio Ficino's commentary on Plato's *Symposium*, written in 1469 and published in 1484, was a particularly influential text. Ficino distinguished between heavenly love and earthly love; the former involved intellectual and spiritual development, while the latter led to sex and procreation. The proper appreciation of human beauty, as opposed to crude desire for another body, could lead the human mind to higher things, as beauty was an expression of the divine in God's creation. Central to Ficino's argument was the

Platonic defence of the love of an older man for a younger one: what the man really loved was the youth's mind, which he sought to develop. And, he explained, men of this kind, who cultivate heavenly love, 'naturally love men more than women and those nearly adults rather than children', because males had more mental ability than females, and youths approaching adulthood had more than boys.[29] The relative disdain for sexual love expressed by Ficino and his sixteenth-century followers helped to legitimize his prioritizing of the love (by men) of male youths, as a man's love for a woman was always likely to be tainted by sexual desire. For that reason—as well as for the purpose of defending his argument against an obvious accusation—he commented especially harshly on male–male sex, that 'nefarious crime, which Plato bitterly condemns, in his *Laws*, as a type of murder'.[30]

The obvious accusation, however, was not to be fended off so easily. It had an intellectual pedigree of its own: in a fiercely anti-Platonic text of 1455, the Greek scholar George of Trebizond, an admirer of Aristotle, had directly accused Plato of sodomy.[31] And in any case, in a society where sex between men and male youths was a well-known phenomenon, there would always be people who reacted with scepticism to high-minded claims about pure motives. Commenting on Plato's statement that the beautiful young man Alcibiades would spend the night in bed with Socrates and get up in the morning as chaste as if he had slept in his father's bed, a character in Baldassare Castiglione's famous book *Il cortegiano* (1528) drily observed: 'The bed, and the night, were indeed a strange place and time for admiring that pure beauty which Socrates is said to have loved without any improper desire—he who especially loved the beauty of the soul more than that of the body, but in boys, not in old men, although the latter are more wise.'[32]

That some Italian humanists became vulnerable to accusations of palliating or promoting or indeed committing sodomy is clear. The development of the 'high' theory of Socratic love by particular scholars was one factor; the general involvement of humanists in the world of classical texts, which contained so many references to male–male sex as well as male–male love, was another; and the cultural trope which viewed schoolmasters and tutors with suspicion may also have played its part. One humanist who found himself subject to such accusations was Pomponio Leto, a scholar from southern Italy who established himself as a teacher of Latin rhetoric in Rome in 1465. He quickly gathered there a group of scholars and littérateurs, which became the first Roman Academy. But soon afterwards Pope Pius II dismissed a number of Latin scholars (whom he suspected of disloyalty) from his Curia, and before long his hostility was directed at the Academy too. In 1468, when Leto was working as a tutor in Venice, the Pope demanded his extradition to Rome; the Venetian authorities agreed, describing him as subject to a 'clear suspicion of sodomy', but the charges brought against him in Rome were heresy, impiety and (most improbably of all) conspiracy to murder Pius. One historian concludes that the trial was clearly held 'for political reasons'.[33]

A long document survives, written by Leto in his own defence, and it includes his response to the accusation of sodomy. He explains that this was based only on some passages in letters he had written to friends in Rome, where he praised the two teenaged boys from patrician families whom he was tutoring in Venice. 'I treated them as my sons, which is the duty of a tutor; I was fed by their food, I was sheltered in their house, and I slept in their bed.' (That last detail may surprise modern readers, but it was perfectly normal practice for a tutor in this period.) He continued: 'In two letters I did praise them, with good reason, both for their natural endowments, that is, their beauty, and for their talent, that is, in their literary studies, and for their hard work.' And he explained that where their beauty was concerned, he followed the example of Socrates. 'For he held up a mirror to handsome youths, telling them: "where nature has given you such a gift, act in such a way that your deeds and writings do not make you seem shameful." And to the ugly ones he used to say: "where nature has denied you beauty, make sure that you have a beautiful mind." '[34] Modern research has discovered two short poems in manuscript, attributed to Leto, in the style of obscene classical poetry relating to male–male sex; these could have been stylistic exercises. It also notes that some members of his intellectual and social circle had interests that would now be described as homoerotic; but the pupil of Leto's who wrote a treatise on love (Paolo Pompilio, *De vera et probabili amore*) insisted that Socratic love was entirely virtuous.[35] Overall, there is no proper evidence to substantiate the charge of sodomy against Pomponio Leto.

Some modern scholars have argued for a deep and intrinsic connection between male–male eroticism and the historical phenomenon of humanism. The argument is a weak one, with little to support it beyond the three elementary factors already mentioned: the theory of Socratic love, immersion in classical texts, and the cultural trope about teachers. Certainly the classic presentation of this argument, by Leonard Barkan, rests on a very thin textual basis. Much emphasis is put on the idea that Dante consigned his old teacher, the scholar Brunetto Latini (or Latino; 1220–94), to Hell for the sin of sodomy. But many writers have argued against that interpretation of Latini's offence; and even if it were correct, this would be just one opinion about one mediaeval intellectual, not a comment on the entire later phenomenon of Renaissance humanism, of which Dante was necessarily ignorant.[36] Again, Barkan highlights a line in a poem by Ariosto of c.1524, which says that few humanists (*umanisti*) are without the vice of Sodom and Gomorrah. The claim is made that this is 'the first proper usage of the term *umanista*' in Italian, and that 'Ariosto is designating in a new way a term for scholar-and-poet'; Ariosto's usage is thus 'definitional', and its significance is that 'the defining context for this new man is homoerotic.'[37] However, the term *humanista* had been current in Latin since the previous century; Ariosto was not the first to use it in Italian; his poem is about finding someone who could teach his son classical Greek; and it is, in any case, a satire.[38] Barkan's larger argument is not lacking in theoretical ambition. 'The notions of unnaturalness that surround sodomy and pederasty...lend themselves so directly to troping that they become the means whereby a culture thinks in figural terms. By an act of transumption—of moving across—the sexual can then be equated with the intellectual, particularly since similar anxieties are associated with the "new" humanist pursuits and since the two activities have a direct cultural connection.'[39] Considered in this way, the procedure of 'moving across' from one category to another via figural thinking becomes remarkably easy to perform; one might just as well say that there was a deep connection between sodomy and warfare in this period, because there were anxieties about new methods of fighting, and soldiers were connected with sodomitical activity.

Instead of constructing such large-scale, essentialist claims about the nature of humanism, it is more useful to look at the specific cultural venues where some literary production touching on sodomitical themes took place: the academies. These, in Renaissance Italy, were not 'academic' institutions in the modern sense. Even the earliest examples, such as Leto's Roman one, were essentially social gatherings of like-minded men with intellectual or literary interests, not formal institutions of research and teaching. (Ficino's so-called Platonic Academy in Florence should be excluded here as a historical chimera, though he certainly had a circle of friends and a large number of pupils, among whom some of his ideas were shared.)[40] But as the vogue developed in many Italian cities over the next few generations, academies became societies or clubs of educated men, and especially young men, who met to enjoy food, drink, conversation and various kinds of literary exercises and performances. Without being polemically secular, they very much sidestepped the influence of the Church on intellectual life; and, being devoted to conviviality, social as well as intellectual, they had plenty of room for elements of hedonism. Some historians emphasize the fact that these were male-only, 'homosocial' institutions. They certainly were; but that fact in itself did not imply any special tendency towards the homoerotic, as the same was true of almost every other form of social organization that men took part in—guilds, confraternities, city militias, etc.—outside the home.

Nevertheless, it is probably not a coincidence that the two most daring and explicit texts referring to sodomy that survive from sixteenth- and seventeenth-century Italy were both products of these milieux. Antonio Vignali, author of *La cazzaria* (an invented abstract noun, from *cazzo*, the slang word for penis), was one of the group of Sienese literati who founded an academy in their city in 1525. The custom had already developed of giving these bodies facetious names; this one was called the Academy of the Intronati, meaning people stunned, dazed or deafened. Each member also took a pseudonym; Vignali's was 'Arsiccio', meaning scorched or singed. And the text he wrote took the form of a didactic dialogue in which Arsiccio instructed a younger member of the Academy, 'Sodo' ('solid'—but perhaps with an implicit reference to sodomy), in matters pertaining to sexual intercourse. The humour is partly parodic, as the scabrous subject-matter is handled in an archly intellectual way, with *quaestiones* imitating the style of a textbook of natural philosophy: 'Why are Women's Arses not Hairy?', and so on. In the second half of the dialogue a different kind of humour takes over, as Vignali satirizes recent developments in Sienese city politics, telling the allegorical story of a conflict between the Cocks, the Cunts, the Arseholes and the Balls.[41]

The underlying argument of the first half, where Arsiccio plays his didactic role, is that *bugerare* (to bugger) is better than *chiavare* or *fotere* (to fuck, i.e. to penetrate vaginally). One element of this is a sense of distaste for some aspects of the female body, an attitude sometimes expressed in strongly misogynistic terms. However, this does not mean that he is recommending male–male sex as opposed to male–female; the text's primary concern is with anal sex with women. The buggery of males is a relatively minor subset here, albeit one which Arsiccio includes with equanimity. Whenever it is mentioned, male–male sex is simply treated as a familiar feature of sexual life. Berating his younger interlocutor for his ignorance at the beginning of

the dialogue, for example, and at the same time raising the curious theoretical question of why the testicles remain outside the orifice that is being
penetrated, he exclaims: 'What the devil have you been doing poking
around the asshole if you haven't learned anything about it? What use has it
been to you to have fucked and to have been buggered so often if you
haven't even contrived to learn at the very least why no one's balls have ever
once entered your ass and you've never put yours in anyone from the front
or behind?'[42] With its outspoken sexual references, as well as its casual but
fierce anticlericalism—Arsiccio explains that the Church has prohibited
buggery only so that friars can monopolize the practice themselves—this
was self-evidently a text to be shared only within a trusted private circle.
Nevertheless, a version of it was somehow passed to a printer, and two separate editions, undated but probably from the 1530s, are known. Yet each
survives in only a single copy, and another sixteenth-century edition, once
reported to exist, is not extant. However surreptitiously this work was circulated in print, the guardians of public morality seem to have eliminated
its physical presence almost entirely.[43]

   The other sexually explicit work which emerged from this sort of social
and intellectual context has already been mentioned: Antonio Rocco's
Alcibiade, composed in Venice probably around the year 1630. Like La cazzaria, this text takes the form of a dialogue. Unlike that work, it is exclusively concerned with male–male sex. The two speakers are a tutor and his
handsome adolescent pupil, and the dialogue is itself the method used by
the former to seduce the latter, as the teacher counters and dispels, one by
one, all the objections put to him by the reluctant boy. Rocco was a member
of the Academy of the Incogniti ('the unknown'), a body founded in 1630
which brought together a number of more or less free-thinking individuals;
the presence of such an intellectual tendency is in itself unsurprising, given
that Venice had a lively publishing industry and a proud tradition of quasi-
independence from Rome, but what is a little surprising is that Rocco was
himself a Capuchin friar. Having studied at the University of Padua, a
stronghold of Renaissance naturalism, he gave lectures on philosophy at the
Benedictine monastery on the island of San Giorgio Maggiore, taught that
subject to large numbers of noble Venetian youths, and was also a teacher of
rhetoric in the city.[44]

   Rocco's text is a rich compendium of pro-sodomitical arguments, several
of which were already in circulation, but some of which he may have been
the first, in early modern Europe, to develop in writing. The tutor explains

that Cupid does not distinguish on grounds of sex; the desire for boys is natural, and indeed it is nature that makes boys resemble girls in their beauty. Our inclinations are 'given to us by nature and by God'. The traditional description of sodomy as 'against nature' arose only because the word 'nature' was also used to refer to the vagina. Boys derive pleasure from the stimulation of their anuses (a physiological explanation is offered for this), and if some are reluctant to be sodomized, it is only because of 'the habit of fear which they have imbibed from people who, by laws or other means, persuade them that it is shameful and a sin'.[45] Resorting to a familiar line of argument, he points out that sex with boys has been permitted by other nations, including some of the most civilized: the Persians, the Indians, and above all the Greeks. So why was it prohibited in the Bible? The answer takes a common free-thinking argument of the time, namely, that clever legislators claimed divine authority when framing laws for their own political purposes, and builds on it in a simple but original way. During their long journey through the wilderness, the people of Israel stopped having male–female sex because the women had become so ugly, so the men resorted to boys instead; fearing that the population would die out, Moses then forbade that practice. But even so, the cautionary tale Moses invented about Sodom and Gomorrah focused on sins such as impiety, cruelty and, above all, violence. 'So what was punished was violence, not pleasure; cruelty, not love; inhumanity, not embraces.'[46]

As that account of the Israelites shows, there is an element of misogyny in the tutor's argument; this becomes clearer when he not only claims that women seek despotic power over men, but also says that their menstrual fluid is a source of infection, which is why prostitutes should be avoided. On marriage, his view is that having sex only with one person is too dull, and entails a loss of freedom. But he concedes that many men do 'incline more to women than to boys', admitting that 'the beauty and grace of boys disappears at the end of their boyhood, lasting longer in a woman.' And it is worth noting that none of his criticisms of women, whether psychological or medical, necessarily implies that he himself would not take pleasure in penetrating a female sexual partner.[47] Nevertheless, there was more than enough here to scandalize censors and readers. That Rocco himself was involved in the printing of this work seems very unlikely; it was probably sent to the press by one of his friends in 1651, roughly 20 years after its composition. Two editions survive, dated 1652 and with false imprints, but each is extant in only a handful of copies.[48] Once again, with a text of such explicitness, there was a huge difference between what could be shared with an intimate circle of friends and what could safely be issued to the general public.

★ ★ ★

Aside from these two outspoken works, there are some other literary productions, also associated with the exuberant intellectual world of the Italian academies, that play on sodomitical themes. But the way that they do so is quite different, exploiting suggestivity, comic ambiguity and elaborate or outrageous *doubles entendres*. The key figure here was the poet Francesco Berni, who was born in Tuscany (near Pistoia) in 1497, was educated probably in Florence, and became especially active as a writer in Rome in the years between his arrival there in 1517 and the sack of the city by Habsburg troops in 1527. His passionate Latin poem about a plague-stricken boy, and his humorous Italian poem expressing the wish that some benefactor would give him a boy to 'guide', have already been mentioned; it seems that his sexual inclinations were not a secret, and indeed it is likely that they were the reason for his sudden removal from Rome and confinement in a distant monastery for several months in 1523.[49] But Berni developed ingenious ways of sailing close to the wind. The genre which he made his own was the *capitolo*, a mock-encomium in the vernacular, praising an apparently humdrum object. To the casual reader these poems were whimsical exercises, inconsequential and, in places, almost verging on nonsense. To readers in the know, however, they were brilliant concatenations of *doubles entendres* and sexually suggestive images—the sex in question being quite often male–male, but also male–female.

Several of these poems were about foodstuffs. Berni's encomium of eels, for example, comments on the animal's ability to penetrate narrow passages: 'it enters wherever it wants to, as it wishes, and comes out again . . . | it glides through by force and moves on, | however much one grabs and grips it with one's hand.'[50] His poem in praise of peaches plays on their unspoken resemblance to boys' buttocks: 'O fruit blessed of all others, | good to eat at the front, in the middle and at the back [or: 'behind'], | but good at the front and perfect from behind! . . . | Peaches used to be the food of prelates, | but, because everyone likes tasty morsels, | the appetite for peaches is now shared even by friars', and so on.[51] At the start of the poem, Berni has referred to a whole range of erotically symbolic fruits: apples (meaning buttocks), pears (penises), plums (vaginas), cherries (the anus) and melons (buttocks again); his argument implies that he values peaches most highly of all. In response to this, Francesco Maria Molza, one of his friends and a fellow member of the academy of the 'Vignaiuoli' (vine-dressers), composed an equivalent mock-encomium of the fig—a more familiar stand-in for the female pudenda.[52]

Others too took up the genre. During the 1540s the Florentine artist Agnolo Bronzino composed several similar poems; these circulated in manuscript, but a handful were printed in a collection in 1555. His *capitolo* on the paintbrush (penis) alluded to a variety of sexual acts; his poem in praise of the frying-pan (buttocks) explained that it could make decapitated eels spring back to life. An encomium to conditions on board a galley was not too difficult to decode: of a man driven mad by the love of women, Bronzino writes that 'once on board the galley, he has no need for any other cure for this disease. A man recovers immediately with a teeny-weeny bit of quick rocking.'[53] But some elements of the code were more systematic and at the same time more cryptic. When Bronzino states that boiled and roast meat are never mixed together on a galley, this relates to a general scheme of metaphors for two different forms of sex: humidity is associated with vaginal intercourse, and dryness with anal. Similarly, Berni's list of fruits refers to ones which, he says, can be eaten dry or fresh.[54]

At first sight, this may look like a scheme invented by Berni and merely developed a little further by one of his imitators. But in a masterly work of literary scholarship, Jean Toscan has demonstrated that Berni was tapping into a much larger system of allusive language which had developed over a long period in Florentine culture. It is to be found in the exuberant carnival songs of the late fifteenth and early sixteenth centuries, and also in the famous nonsense poetry of Burchiello (1404–49).[55] Some elements of this language are present in two long satires, composed in Florence in 1407 and 1412, which criticize sodomites. And in the previous century we find a small but distinctive trace of it in Boccaccio: when the sexually unsatisfied young wife resolves to take a lover, she says to herself (referring to her sodomitical husband): 'This miserable man abandons me in order, in his vicious way, to go walking on pattens where it's dry; so I shall find a way of bringing someone else on board ship for the rainy weather.'[56] As this example shows, the basic binary of wet/dry could be extended in all sorts of ways: rainy weather versus drought, travel by sea versus travel by land, and so on. Many other opposing pairs could also be brought into play: 'modern-style' for sodomy and 'old-style' for vaginal sex; 'light' versus 'dark', or 'south' versus 'north', for vaginal versus anal. With an acknowledgement of official norms, 'good' and 'bad', or 'truth' and 'lies', were also used to mean normal and sodomitical sex respectively. But the overall treatment of those who indulged in the latter kind was, for anyone who could interpret the terms correctly, hardly condemnatory. Indeed, among the words that referred to an active sodomite were *gagliardo* ('strong') and *destro* ('dextrous').[57]

What makes this whole phenomenon so unusual is that it flourished in a genre which belonged to popular culture: the lively, self-consciously transgressive carnival song. Whilst the songs that have come down to us were of course composed by individual authors, those poets were drawing on popular themes, and were always writing to amuse the populace—though whether all the *doubles entendres* were understood by all members of that audience may still be doubted. The editor of the only major printed collection (of 1559), Grazzini, was irked when one fussy contributor complained about the way his poems had been printed: 'But damn it,' he wrote to a friend, 'they're only carnival songs, plebeian, popular works; and as you've said, the worse condition you put them in, the better—and the more they please.'[58] That collection contains one suggestive composition after another: a drinking song which plays on the names of two taverns in Florence, the Fig and the Hole, for example, or a song about *calcio* (football) which advises putting the youths in front and the men just behind them. Some allusions to male–male sex are fairly clearly present, but it is important to understand that overall, both in this collection and in the language of innuendo studied by Toscan, buggery is just as much male–female as male–male—perhaps more so. Commenting on the 'Florentine carnival's obsession with sodomy', the modern editor of these songs insists that they do not simply represent a carnivalesque liberation from the usual norms (though they certainly do that). 'The invitation to male–male sodomy turns out to be sporadic, and always subsumed or implicit within a [sexually] undifferentiated sodomitical desire.'[59]

Berni was thus picking up on a broad existing tradition when he wrote his *capitoli*. Even in his hands, this type of poetry never became narrowly concerned with male–male sex. But glancing allusions to such sexual acts, in keeping with the generally transgressive spirit of the genre, remained common; they can be found, for example, as late as 1567 in a Florentine madrigal comedy based on 'the chattering of the women at the well'.[60] One talented imitator of Berni would, by dabbling briefly in this style, cause long-term damage to his own reputation: Giovanni della Casa (1503–56), an upper-class Florentine who began his career as a talented littérateur and ended it as an archbishop and papal nuncio. His mock-encomium of the oven was an ingeniously Berniesque work, with a predominantly male–female sexual meaning, referring to the insertion of loaves—my loaf is rather 'tiny', the poet regrets—and to the long wooden shovels that are used to place them deep inside the oven. Although, in the system of *doubles entendres*, the term 'oven' might suggest extreme dryness, and therefore anal sex, the oven here stood primarily for the vagina.[61] But this *capitolo* did include a few passages of a different kind. Some referred to the anal penetration of women: 'he who practises this marvellous profession [sc. of putting loaves in ovens] well knows where they have hidden a certain little oven at the back'; and some alluded to male–male buggery: 'there's a certain wicked bishop, I'm told, who, because he sometimes wants to be given bread in a hurry, always keeps some behind him—his servant keeps it in his breeches.'[62]

Years later, these playful sallies would catch up with their author. In 1548, when della Casa was papal nuncio in Venice, he was in charge of the prosecution of a Catholic bishop and former papal diplomat, Pietro Paolo Vergerio, who was suspected (correctly) of Protestant tendencies. Vergerio fled to Switzerland in the following year, and began to publish fiercely anti-Catholic tracts. The first of these contained comments on an Index of Prohibited Books which had just been issued by della Casa; and it ended with a very personal attack, accusing the nuncio of having himself published a book containing 'praises of sodomy'. The charge was gleefully taken up by Protestant polemicists, and soon the Protestant world became convinced that a Catholic archbishop had composed—in that capacity—an entire treatise entitled *De laudibus sodomiae*, 'In Praise of Sodomy'.[63] Understanding that offence was the best form of defence, Catholic polemicists then developed counter-charges of their own: Calvin was accused by an estranged follower of having been in danger of execution for sodomy as a young man, and his successor in Geneva, Theodore Beza, was denounced as a sodomite on the basis of some youthful poetic exercises, Latin love poems addressed to a young man as well as a young woman.[64] In this way allegedly sodomitical literary expressions, deliberately removed from their immediate context, were put to use as ammunition in the culture wars of the Reformation and Counter-Reformation.

The Berniesque style of poetry seems to have been protected—just—from outright censorship by the fact that an innocent meaning could be found at the surface level of the text. Another kind of vernacular production in this period had a more authentic, though still sometimes questionable, claim to innocence: poems addressed by a man to a male object of love, often celebrating the loved one's physical beauty. The most famous writer of this kind of poetry was the artist Michelangelo, but there were several others in sixteenth-century Italy: Antonio Brocardo (d. 1531); Benedetto Varchi (1503–65); Francesco Beccuti (1509–53) and Cesare Caporali (1531–1601). All except Varchi circulated their poems in manuscript only, but this was not because of any shocking sexual explicitness in their writings; Varchi himself was quite typical in never referring to any greater act of intimacy than kissing (though he did describe that in quite vivid terms). The strongest cultural influences moulding these writings were the Platonic theory of love, the classical bucolic love poetry typified by Vergil's second Eclogue, and the very stylized tradition of passionate but chaste love poems derived from Petrarch. The impression that these poets were not simply engaging in literary exercises is derived partly from what is known of their biographies— though it should be noted that all of them, with the possible exception of Michelangelo, had sex with women. Varchi is known to have been in love with a ten-year-old boy, Lorenzo Lenzi, and to have maintained a very close friendship with him for the rest of his life, in addition to forming a later attachment with a fourteen-year-old, Giulio della Stufa; Beccuti became enamoured of a nineteen-year-old youth, Francesco Bigazzini, and remained so for four years. Michelangelo's feelings for Tommaso Cavalieri (who was 23 when they met) were clearly very strong, though possibly entirely chaste, and it is noteworthy that when he was gathering a small collection of his poems for possible publication in 1545, he changed the gender of the love-object in several places from 'he' to 'she'. (The same operation would be performed quite systematically by his great-nephew in 1625, when preparing Michelangelo's poetry for publication.) That degree of caution may be indicative of how the stricter kinds of moral and social sensitivity operated; certainly there were readers who looked on this sort of celebration of male youths with disapproval. The author Girolamo Muzio, a poet but also something of a Counter-Reformation warrior, wrote to a friend in 1573 to complain about Varchi's poems in praise of the young Giulio della Stufa: 'this business of constantly talking about his eyes, forehead, cheeks and lips seems to me to have nothing healthy about it, nor does that large kiss have anything chaste about it, let the Platonists say what they like.' Nevertheless, poems of this kind were in principle avowable, protected as they were by an accepted set of cultural conventions. They had very little in common with the provocative naughtiness of Berni's work, even though one of these poets, Beccuti, did also turn his hand to the Berniesque style in a poem which was daringly entitled 'In Praise of Paederasty'—followed, however, by a corrective poem in the same manner, 'Against Paederasty'.[65]

The final example of skilled literary production, the obscene poetry of Curzio Marignolli (1563–1606), had a very different character again. Born to a patrician Florentine family, Marignolli led a dissolute life, squandering his patrimony; according to one report he was prosecuted in Spain for being a 'wicked lover', meaning probably a sodomite but possibly an adulterer. His poetry, almost all of it satirical to some extent, and a significant part of it explicitly sexual, circulated in manuscript in Florence. The influence of Berni and the carnival tradition is discernible here and there, but the obscene poems are much closer in spirit to those of Beccadelli and Massimi in the previous century—though Marignolli is writing in vivid colloquial Italian, not in the Latin of Martial and Catullus. Several of the poems refer directly to sodomy; one alludes to masturbation; one boasts of having fellated innumerable men; one fantasizes about lifting the shirt of 'my beautiful, pretty Adonis' to uncover his naked buttocks.[66] A narrative poem describes a visit to the poet's home (or, strictly speaking, to that of his poetic persona) by a servant boy, sent by a friend to recover a lantern which he had left there. The poet offered to give the boy not only the lantern but also a 'candle'— no need for elaborately coded allusions here—and soon had him on his bed. 'And there, having unbuckled | his trousers, without any noise | I pushed a full hand's breadth of cock into his arse | and stayed there a long time | getting so much pleasure; and at the moment of dawn | he wanted me to do it two more times.' The extreme explicitness of this sort of writing no doubt helped it to find private readers; but there is no reason to think that they would have been people with exclusively male–male sexual interests. Several poems refer to experiences with female prostitutes; and whilst these are easily describable as misogynistic, they do assume that vaginal and anal sex provide similar pleasures, conveying a typically Florentine sense of the equivalence of *potta* ('cunt') and *culo* ('arse')—where the latter could easily belong to the same body as the former. Characteristic here is a sonnet which begins by exclaiming against the poet's penis for wishing to enter a prostitute's cunt that has been visited by everyone, and ends with a reference to buggering her instead.[67]

Beyond these literary compositions, there are two works which are more simply classifiable as pornography. The earlier of these is a text which was

known to exist by 1577, when it was ascribed to Aretino; it is a dialogue
between two women, Giulia and Maddalena, one of whom tells the story of
her sexual initiation and later career as a courtesan. Male–female sex is thus
the subject-matter of the book, but two sodomitical episodes are briefly
recounted. First the courtesan describes how, as a girl, she witnessed two
teenaged boys buggering each other; then she recounts an experience from
her professional life in Rome, when a rich banker, pointedly described as
Florentine, arranged to be present when a handsome sixteen-year-old boy
came to her house for sex. What followed involved three different kinds of
triple coupling, with the banker buggering her in two of them and being
buggered by the boy—the only male–male sexual act on this occasion—in
one of them.[68] This text certainly has similarities with Aretino's most famous
pornographic work, the *Ragionamenti* (another dialogue between two
women about sex), though whether it is an authentic composition by him
which pre-dates that one, as its modern editor suggests, or a later effort by
an imitator, is not clear. (If the latter, it may have drawn some inspiration not
only from Aretino's writings but also from a scandalous biography of him
published in 1538, which described his own three-way couplings with his
catamite and the catamite's wife.)[69]

The other pornographic text, which has an almost entirely male–male
content, dates probably from the second half of the seventeenth century: it
is an attempt at a continuation of Rocco's *Alcibiade*, with the dialogue now
just recounting a series of sexual encounters—including less common forms
of sexual activity such as fellatio. This work survives, however, only in a
single manuscript copy.[70] In modern Europe, the genre of pornography—
meaning here writing that was aimed primarily at arousing sexual excitement in the reader, and which did so by breaking the normal taboos on
descriptions of sexual acts—developed in the sixteenth and seventeenth
centuries, first in Italy, with Aretino playing a leading role, and then also in
France; it met, and/or generated, a popular demand, and editions multi-
plied. Yet the presence of same-sex descriptions within this genre is almost
vanishingly small. The continuation of *Alcibiade* was, it seems, never widely
circulated. The dialogue between Giulia and Maddalena was eventually
issued in print, first perhaps in c.1650 and then by the famous Dutch publisher Elzevir in 1660. In that way, two rather incidental passages describing
male–male sexual acts did pass into broader circulation; but there is no sign
of any author or publisher trying to imitate this sort of sexual description
until the mid-eighteenth century, when John Cleland inserted a brief epi-

sode, involving a voyeuristic experience very similar to Giulia's, in his *Memoirs of a Woman of Pleasure,* better known as *Fanny Hill.*[71]

To conclude: where early modern literary references to sodomy are concerned, there is a striking difference between Iberia and Italy, which must surely reflect a more general disparity in attitudes between those two territories. And yet, in the Italian case, the harvest is still a very thin one. The number of relevant writings can only seem tiny when set against the huge efflorescence of literary production that took place in many parts of Renaissance Italy; and the main reason for the rarity of these texts is obvious. There were real risks involved. Of the most outspoken texts, those by Beccadelli and Massimi were openly published (the former in manuscript before the advent of printing, the latter in print) by their authors, for the delectation of highly educated readers of Latin, but before long both were subject to suppression. Vignali's work was printed under a false imprint, not by him, and Rocco's appears to have been published without the author's permission. Even the Platonizing and thoroughly chaste-seeming works of the sixteenth-century poets were, with only one exception, never printed; and although that fact in itself would be unremarkable, as manuscript circulation was normal for much literary production in this period, the changing of gender from male to female in Michelangelo's case does seem to strike a cautionary note. Only the carnivalesque and Berniesque tradition was able to resonate, it seems, with a larger public, though its popularity was very much rooted in a specifically Florentine culture. The connections between a number of these writers and their local academies does suggest the existence of a kind of cultural niche in which the risqué topic of sodomy might well have been handled more freely, behind closed doors. (The self-styled 'academy' of the abbate Volpino in Naples seems to have been more like a club devoted to pleasure and sex; yet it did produce one humorous text, a mock-decree about anal sex with women.)[72] Very possibly there were other literary performances, playing on sodomitical themes, which were produced in such circles but have not come down to us. Yet the reason why such materials have not survived must go beyond the usual causes of attrition of manuscript evidence: they could be very risky things to write, own or share.

★ ★ ★

After this brief survey of literary productions, it might be supposed that an equivalent account could, or should, be given of sodomitical elements in the visual arts. The material for such a treatment is, however, extremely sparse.

Hostile, condemnatory treatments of sodomy do occur in the religious art of the early Renaissance. Giotto's fresco of the Last Judgment, painted in 1303–5, shows a man—probably to be identified as a sodomite—being turned on a spit which has been driven through his anus. There is a similar scene, involving two sodomitical men, in the Campo Santo in Pisa, painted by Buonamico Buffalmacco in the 1330s or early 1340s. And the idea recurs in Taddeo di Bartolo's fresco of the Last Judgment, in San Gimignano, executed some time between 1393 and 1413: a man labelled *sotomitto* ('sodomite') lies on hot coals, with a metal rod inserted through his anus and emerging from his mouth, and the tip of the rod is close to the lips of a youth who is sitting next to him, labelled *cativo* ('wicked').[73] But such depictions were, overall, quite rare—understandably so, in a religious culture which warned preachers against even mentioning sodomy in their sermons.

Art historians who have hunted for allusions to such sexual relationships have come up with only a very small tally of examples. Ambrogio Lorenzetti's fresco *The Effects of Bad Government* in the town hall in Siena, painted in the late 1330s, includes two young men placed close together; the older of the two has one hand on the younger one's shoulder, and points downwards with the other hand, possibly to his companion's genitals. Given the theme of the fresco—a general breakdown of political, social and moral order—it seems very possible that this depicts an invitation to sodomy.[74] A painting of the Presentation of the Virgin (c.1465) by Fra Carnevale includes some small figures in the background exemplifying pagan immorality; among them are two men standing with their legs pressed together, one with his arm round the other as the other chucks him under the chin—a recognized sign of amorous or sexual interest. A predella painted by Ercole de' Roberti in the early 1470s presents various figures culpably ignoring the miracles of St Vincent Ferrer; these include an older man and a youth standing together, arms intertwined, with the man's hand on a sword-handle which is sticking up suggestively between his legs.[75]

As for more positive representations of male–male sexual relations: there appear to be no unequivocal examples of these among the paintings of the period. Even the artist Giovanni Antonio Bazzi (1477–1549)—who acquired, and seems to have accepted quite happily, the nickname 'Sodoma', going so far as to sign some of this paintings with that name—did not produce any clear representations of such a kind. At most, it is proposed that we can find in his fresco *The Wedding of Alexander and Roxana* (1517) a visual suggestion of the interest of Alexander the Great in both male youths and women. But the placing in the foreground there, on the other side of Alexander from the bride to whom he is turning, of Alexander's intimate friend Hephaestion together with the god of marriage, Hymenaeus, was dictated by the classical text which Bazzi was following quite closely; and it was the god whom he presented as a beautiful and near-naked young man, not the companion.[76]

A remarkable painting by Domenico Cresti, known as Passignano (1559–1638), *Bathers at San Niccolò* (1600), shows multiple men and boys, clad only in their underwear, swimming and playing games in the river Arno, with some sitting on the banks. When it was sold at Sotheby's, New York, in 2017, the catalogue entry described it as 'perhaps the most important artistic example of homoerotic art of the late Mannerist period'. Michael Rocke refers to its 'homoerotic atmosphere', citing the painting in connection with a case in the Florentine archive where a boy said that he had been sodomized many times by the older male who gave him swimming lessons in the Arno.[77] Yet in order to depict recognizably a couple who engaged in male–male sexual relations, it would have been necessary for one of them to be below, and the other above, the threshold age. Two couples are shown quite prominently in Passignano's painting, but in each case both members of the couple are visibly above that threshold; so while it is true that in one of these cases a man gazes up with a loving expression at his companion, it must seem unlikely that a sexual meaning was intended.

Art historians who do not constantly bear in mind the age-differentiation of Italian Renaissance sodomy are liable to fall into anachronistic interpretations. Patricia Rubin's recent book on the male posterior in Renaissance art presents as homoerotic various depictions of fully adult bodies, which would not have been regarded as desirable by adult male viewers (beyond a very small minority of untypical ones—and their feelings would not have been taken into account by any artist).[78] Those who see such sexual significances in the work of the pioneering Baroque artist Caravaggio, on the other hand, can at least point to several paintings of youths within the relevant age-range. Some of these works may seem homoerotic to present-day sensibilities; modern writers apparently find it easy to assume that where the youth is looking directly at the viewer, his gaze is 'erotically provocative', even if in some cases it might better be described as calm and superciliously enigmatic. However, the most influential study to emphasize homoeroticism in Caravaggio, by Donald Posner, was both highly subjective and anachronistic, and its approach is now largely discredited. Posner sought to strengthen his argument by adducing evidence that Caravaggio himself was 'homosexual', and that he painted to please a 'homosexual' patron, but the evidence for those claims is very insubstantial.[79] Overall, the task of interpreting these paintings remains problematic; but in any case they form only a minor element in Caravaggio's oeuvre.

Paintings—and, for the wider market, prints—designed at least in part to arouse the sexual interest of the male viewer were not uncommon; but these involved male–female sex, with the female body as the object of desire.[80] Cases of male bodies being presented in that way, with the intention of stimulating male desire, are much harder to identify. Of course it cannot be ruled out that some paintings had unintended homoerotic effects. An early biography of Lodovico Cardi (known as Cigoli; 1559–1613) offers an anecdote about his *Sacrifice of Isaac* (now in the Galleria Palatina, Florence), suggesting somewhat obscurely that a visitor to the residence of the Cardinal who had commissioned it was moved to inappropriate feelings by the depiction of the near-naked boy. He was then reproved by the Cardinal, who evidently had no misgivings about the work and blamed sinful reactions on sinful viewers.[81] But such a story is quite exceptional.

Of the innumerable paintings of St Sebastian produced in this period, many do depict a beautiful near-naked male body. A modern art historian singles out as specimens of homoeroticism one such work by Sodoma, which he describes as full of 'latent sado-masochism', and one by Guido Reni (1575–1642); yet in order to characterize these as homoerotic he resorts not to any evidence from the artists' own period, but rather to the reactions of John Addington Symonds, Oscar Wilde and Yukio Mishima.[82] Some people in Renaissance Italy certainly did see such works as capable of stimulating sexual desire, but that was in women, not in men: Vasari tells the story of such a painting of St Sebastian by Fra Bartolommeo, which was removed from display in a church when confessors discovered that it was provoking lustful thoughts in some of their female parishioners.[83] It is true that in some cases—though only a small minority—the saint, as portrayed in the picture, did come within the age-range that was understood to be capable of provoking same-sex desire.[84] Yet these were devotional paintings, commissioned by churches, religious orders, confraternities and pious patrons, and of all the agencies for enforcing the general taboo against sodomy, organized religion was the strongest. It seems that, for the great majority of people, this sort of male physical beauty could be contemplated without any association arising in the viewer's mind with sodomitical desire.[85]

There was probably more scope for sexually transgressive art where drawings were concerned. Generally speaking, they had a more informal status as art works, and could be kept out of sight in cabinets and albums. One drawing attributed to Giulio Romano (1499–1546) shows a near-naked Apollo with a naked male youth, possibly Hyacinthus, on his knee; the god reaches round the boy to touch his genitals.[86] Among the small group of erotically suggestive drawings by Parmigianino (1503–40) is a rather indistinct sketch of two standing men, where both have erections (though one of those has been mostly rubbed out, subsequently) and one is handling the erection of the other.[87] Much less explicit, but still perhaps suggestive, was a drawing by Michelangelo (of which a copy survives), depicting Ganymede being carried up to heaven by the eagle. The boy faces the viewer with his naked body splayed out, while the giant eagle holds him from behind; one modern writer has described this as 'an image of anal penetration', though an art historian has argued that such an interpretation is anatomically inaccurate as well as psychologically implausible.[88] A drawing by Francesco Salviati (1510–63) has three naked male figures grouped closely together, with the youngest of them apparently an object of desire on the part of the older two—though there is much that is unclear about what is really going on.[89] That there was a category of erotic drawings that were kept for private delectation is clear from other evidence. A pen-and-ink drawing by Pietro Testa (1611–50), for example, graphically depicts Venus gripped from behind by the god Pan; he is buggering her, while manipulating her genitals, and to one side of them Cupid is also masturbating.[90] However, not many drawings in this category have survived, and among them works of male–male eroticism are extremely rare.

12

Western Mediterranean attitudes

It is not easy to gather all the evidence relating to Western Mediterranean sodomy discussed hitherto—the forms of actual practice, the theological and legal norms, the cultural values and representations—into a single coherent pattern. One major background condition remains fairly constant: the official norms, formalized from the latter part of the Middle Ages onwards, were severely hostile. In the late thirteenth and early fourteenth centuries there was a quite rapid transition in many societies towards savage penal regimes, including castration and other kinds of mutilation, and typically specifying the death penalty. As we have seen, in the course of the fifteenth century the application of these draconian measures was toned down in most jurisdictions (though not, at that time, in Venice). Nevertheless, capital punishment remained on the statute book, and was still applied in Iberia and parts of Italy well into the seventeenth century. And when *autos-da-fé* and/or public executions did occur, crowds gathered to look on with satisfaction; as the Valencian Inquisitors explained in 1625, the strong element of public shame was an essential part of the rationale of these punishments.[1]

On the other hand, we have evidence, especially but not only from Italy, suggesting that the presence of sodomy in some of these societies must have been common knowledge, accepted more or less positively by the men who were participants in it (who, in some places, were not few), and apparently tolerated—whether as a neutral matter, or as a negative phenomenon which was unfortunately just part of ordinary life—by a significant part of the rest of the population. The investigation into the sexual scandal at the Venetian bailate in 1588 generated, in effect, an unusual survey of the attitudes of a large group of men: as we have seen, some were strongly disapproving, while

Forbidden Desire in Early Modern Europe: Male–Male Sexual Relations, 1400–1750. Noel Malcolm, Oxford University Press.
© Noel Malcolm 2024. DOI: 10.1093/oso/9780198886334.003.0012

some treated the matter with levity, but even the disapproving ones seem to have tolerated the affair for some time without reporting it. Cristian Berco notes a general sense, in the Crown lands of Aragon, that it was a feature of everyday life; in Sicily Nicola Pizzolato finds 'widespread tolerance at the level of the ordinary population'; surveying the evidence from seventeenth-century Rome, Marina Baldassari describes sodomy as something broadly accepted, especially by the lower classes, as a feature of quotidian life; by the early seventeenth century Nicholas Davidson finds 'a pervasive social toler-ance' in Venice.[2] The situation described by Jean-Jacques Bouchard in Naples, where young men habitually stood at street corners waiting to be picked up for sex, could not have existed in any society where ordinary people felt spurred into activism by the official norms. As for Florence: while the authorities were sufficiently embarrassed by the situation there, in the fifteenth century, to go to the trouble of setting up a special magistracy to deal with it, they knew that their only chance of managing the problem was if they brought the tariff of punishments down to a level that came perilously close to non-deterrence. Florence was the only place where there were quite open expressions of pro-sodomitical opinions, from the official who said, after the fall of Savonarola in 1498, 'Thank God, now we can sodomize!', to the group of young men who, raiding the government palace in 1512 in support of a Medici coup, demanded that all convicted sodomites who had been exiled or deprived of office should be reinstated.[3] And it seems to have been the only place where references to sodomy, oblique and jokey but really not condemnatory, were commonly made in popular poems and songs.

How do we explain this apparent contradiction between public vilifica-tion and everyday tolerance? The simplest thing to say—so simple that it would surely be hard to disprove—is that each of these societies contained a range of opinions and attitudes where male–male sex was concerned. While people with very hostile views would happily flock to public punish-ments in order to spit and jeer at convicted sodomites, others might stay at home. And conversely, when rowdy men chanted semi-obscene carnival songs, their more disapproving neighbours would choose not to take part. From which it would seem to follow that the severity of the actual treat-ment of sodomites would have varied in accordance with the amount of social and institutional power held by those who had the more negative views. But merely to offer this elementary, schematic account is to raise further questions about the basis of those opinions and attitudes, about the grounds on which the condemnatory and tolerant views differed, and even about what underlying assumptions they may have had in common.

The wave of fierce anti-sodomitical feeling which spread through these societies in the later Middle Ages was generated by theological concerns: above all, by the strong association with heresy, and the idea (making the connection with heresy) that such an 'unnatural' sin was peculiarly abhorrent because it rebelled against God and His ordered creation. A key point was the assumption that heresy, and this sort of accompanying moral disorder, had a collective significance, not just a private one; the whole community was threatened. The Church's large-scale campaigns against heretics were all based on such a supposition, and it was apparently easy to fit a sexual disorder into that model. As the fifteenth-century theologian Antoninus of Florence put it, sodomy 'infects others, because one person devoted to this vice is sufficient to infect an entire city'.[4] The Church itself was also a community, and the existence of sodomitical priests was one reason why popes and bishops became particularly concerned with the heinous nature of this sin (though not the only one—sensitivity to the charge of hypocrisy could only grow in a period when the moral authority of the Church was increasingly infiltrating the bedrooms of ordinary Christians). Thus the Church authorities ramped up the seriousness of sodomy, and gave it a collective significance which ensured that it entered the secular statute books.

Having elevated sodomy to such an extent in the hierarchy of evil, theologians could hardly resile from that position, even if they had had any particular reason for wanting to do so. But at some point, in practice— though this is hard to document—the association of sodomy with heresy, which had been the main motor of the argument, fell apart and was quietly discarded. That should have weakened the rationale for collective enforcement; and perhaps it did, over time, and subliminally. Yet the idea that the presence of sodomy might provoke a terrible divine judgement on the entire community remained, as we have seen, quite strong. In 1519 a Franciscan gave a sermon in the cathedral in Valencia, saying that pestilences and other ills currently suffered by the city were God's punishment for the sin of sodomy, which had been brought there by merchants from elsewhere, whereupon a large crowd left the church to hunt for the culprits; they hauled four foreign merchants before a judge, who immediately sent them to be burnt.[5] While that is an extreme case, involving outsiders (who were much easier to stigmatize than local men), it does give a sense of how a rather quotidian sin could become, for many people, an object of fear and hatred when presented in a certain way in certain circumstances. But moral panics, of course, provide evidence only of what was psychologically possible, not of what was normal.

Another theological principle with collective implications was the idea that the propagation of the human race was a divinely imposed duty. It was stated twice in the Book of Genesis: immediately after the creation of mankind (1: 28: 'Be fruitful, and multiply'), and after the Flood (9: 1: 'Be fruitful, and multiply, and replenish the earth'). Mediaeval theologians had emphasized this obligation, invoking it to argue that sodomites were in effect rebelling against God.[6] After the huge population losses caused by the Black Death in the mid-fourteenth century, this duty to replenish the earth was a theme which must have resonated especially strongly; one historian suggests that it was the main reason for the severity of anti-sodomy legislation in that period, even though, as we have seen, the most brutal punishments had been introduced before the plague struck.[7] At all events, a preoccupation with demographic loss was clearly present for several generations after the Black Death. 'Aren't you aware', demanded Bernardino of Siena in Florence in 1424, inveighing against the sin of sodomy, 'that this is the reason why you have lost half of your population in the last 25 years? Tuscany has fewer people than any country in the world, only because of this vice.'[8] In fact, this nexus of ideas had already formed the basis of public policy in Florence, in response to notably sluggish growth in the region (and even, in the 1390s and 1400s, a decline).[9] Since 1403 the government had brought in a range of measures to turn men away from sodomy and promote population growth; these included establishing a public brothel (to give young men an alternative to boys, thereby developing their interest in male–female sex), as well as setting up a dowry fund for young women, and trying—in the end, unsuccessfully—to pass a law banning men from public office if they remained unmarried after the age of 30.[10] By the sixteenth century, when the Italian states and most other parts of Western Europe enjoyed strong population growth, these demographic worries must have faded away; this change too may have contributed to a general reduction of anxiety where sodomy was concerned, allowing it to be seen more in terms of private behaviour. However, the underlying argument about procreative sex being encouraged by God (within Christian marriage), and unprocreative sex being contrary to His will, remained a structural principle of all moral theology on these matters. The language of 'natural' versus 'unnatural' or 'against nature' was deeply embedded in people's minds, and continued to frame their expressions of hostility to sodomy, regardless of whether they were thinking in specifically demographic terms.

While considerations of collective purity lost some of their force, and arguments aimed at collective growth gradually withered, the sin of sodomy remained (unlike, say, the sin of solitary masturbation) a social practice with social implications. Codes of behaviour, relating especially to the ideal of proper masculinity, governed sexual as well as social conduct; they helped to form a sense of an overall social order, which, while it was not theoretically comparable to the cosmic order of God's creation, formed what may well have felt like an unchanging framework for people's lives. That early modern societies were ordered in strongly hierarchical ways has always been clear. But one of the concerns of modern historians of sexual behaviour has been to show that there was also a sexual hierarchy, in which same-sex activity had its own accepted place, and to suggest that such activity became seriously objectionable only when it clashed with the social order. The essential argument here is that an adult man had to penetrate, and not be penetrated; penetrating was a proper act of masculinity, because it involved taking the dominant role. In that respect, it did not matter whether the person penetrated was a boy or a woman—both categories being intrinsically inferior to that of the adult male. But domination and superiority/inferiority were also more general social categories, and this could add another dimension to the situation: it was permissible, in this scheme of things, for a master to penetrate his servant, or for a free man to penetrate a slave, but not vice-versa, even if the servant or slave was an adult and the master or free man was a youth. On this basis, Cristian Berco has argued that popular disapproval of sodomites arose when the sexual hierarchy clashed with the more general social one: cases where slaves were found to have sodomized Christian youths, for example, or almost any cases involving foreigners, who lacked an established place in the local social hierarchy.[11]

It is certainly true, though not surprising, that perceived infractions of the normal rules of social status could act as aggravating factors, adding to the hostility with which some people looked at cases of same-sex relations. We have already encountered the case of Dr Gaspar González de Sosa, canon of the cathedral at Sucre in Bolivia, who took a poor boy from prison and installed him in his house as a servant; what shocked the witnesses was not just that he was keeping the boy for sexual purposes, but that, in defiance of normal social rules, the servant joined his master at the table and shared his food.[12] Similarly, when Luiz Delgado lavished his affection on a sixteen-year-old boy in the Brazilian town of Salvador, neighbours were scandalized by the fact that he dressed the boy in expensive clothes befitting someone of higher social status.[13] But there are plenty of cases—the great majority, indeed—where, in the absence of any such aggravating factors, the hostility of witnesses to the mere fact of same-sex activity was sufficient to prompt an investigation. And where the trials of foreigners at the Aragonese tribunals are concerned, we have already seen that although it is very likely that such people were objects of greater suspicion, the disproportion between Italians and Frenchmen runs significantly counter to Berco's explanation.[14]

It is also true, and even less surprising, that people of high social status fared better in most judicial processes. Not only did they receive lighter punishments, but they were much less likely to be brought to trial in the first place. When accusations against noblemen were put to the Portuguese Inquisition, they were often censored or suppressed; special permission was needed in order to proceed in such cases, and it seems that the punishments had also to be approved. In 1596, for example, the Council of the Inquisition wrote to the King for advice on how to deal with a nobleman who had been convicted of sodomy, on the basis of statements by seven of his sexual partners, by the tribunal in Goa; in their letter, the members of the Council also insisted rather defensively that the tribunal had followed the correct procedure before putting on trial a 'person of quality'.[15] At the Aragonese tribunals, trials of noblemen were rare. One of these cases, in 1572, involved Pedro Luis Galcerán de Borja, stepbrother of the Duke of Gandía; despite the evidence of several of his pages, he was eventually absolved, and went on to be appointed Viceroy of Catalonia.[16] The higher the person's status, the less likely he was to be tried at all, not only because of the embarrassment that this would cause to the social and political order more generally, but also because he could use his power and influence to obstruct an investigation or prevent a prosecution. High-ranking sodomites, especially in the more feudal societies, had both a greater opportunity to satisfy their desires, surrounded as they were by servants and pages, and a greater sense of impunity as they did so. Social hierarchy and sexual hierarchy could thus be effortlessly combined as the master freely sodomized his servants; but it is worth noticing also the corollary of this, which is that if a grandee wished sometimes to invert the sexual order and take the passive role—as in the case of Ponç Hug in Catalonia, or Dom Felipe de Moura in Portugal—his high status would normally have protected him from the obloquy that might otherwise have followed.[17]

Whatever they involved, the sexual exploits of the masters of large households were unlikely to remain secret. Rumours of such activities combined with stories from classical texts about heroes and emperors (Alexander, Caesar, etc.) to form another cultural trope: an association of sodomy with great men and rulers. In 1654 a Dalmatian friar, prosecuted in Venice for a range of offences including sexual assaults on novices, was quoted as saying that 'buggery is the tasty morsel of princes, not the food of riff-raff and common people.'[18] Daringly, Benvenuto Cellini turned this trope to his advantage when his rival, Baccio Bandinelli, denounced him as a 'great sodomite' in front of the Duke of Tuscany. 'If only God willed', Cellini exclaimed, 'that I should know how to practise such a noble art, as we read that Jupiter made use of it with Ganymede in Paradise, and here on earth it is practised by the greatest emperors and the greatest kings of the world. I am a low and humble little man, who wouldn't have the ability or the knowledge to involve myself in such a wonderful thing.'[19] According to Cellini, this witty response provoked raucous laughter, even from the Duke himself; but the story, if true, suggests that Cellini was sailing very close to the wind, even though he did of course imply that these high-ranking men would always adopt, like Jupiter, the active role.

To return to the question of hierarchy and domination: it is obviously true that there was an essential disparity built into the whole phenomenon we have been considering, in all but the untypical cases, since these sexual relations were normally age-differentiated. And it is also true that in many cases—especially the non-consensual ones—power relations were also at work, as masters took advantage of servants, workmen exploited apprentices, and so on. Yet the strongest version of the 'domination' theory goes much further than that. What it offers is not an empirical observation on the sexual behaviour of these people, or on the social contexts in which it took place, but rather an analysis—indeed, an explanation—of the sexual desire itself. Adult men, it is argued, desired to have sex with boys, and with women too, because the sexual act was an act of domination, and both of those categories were seen as suitable objects for dominative behaviour because they were inferior.

This approach conforms to a Foucauldian view of human culture and behaviour, in which almost anything—including, famously, knowledge itself—can be reduced to a question of power-relations. But it is not obvious that it fits the human experience which it offers to explain here. A passive adult man, who wanted to be sodomized by another adult, would no doubt have been seen as failing, disgracefully, to meet a necessary standard of masculinity. Since that meant that he was regarded as womanly and inferior, the theory would suggest that he might therefore have become desirable. Yet the evidence tends to show that most other men would have felt no desire for him at all: the comparison made by the tutor in *Alcibiade* was with eating meat from a stinking billy-goat. (One could push the theory even further. In a world of competitive masculinity, what could express a higher, more satisfying degree of dominative power than dominating another adult male, by sodomizing him? Such treatment may occasionally have been inflicted on defeated enemies, as an extreme humiliation, but there is no sign whatsoever of adult men being seen as desirable in this way.)[20] Again, where sexual relations existed between a teenaged boy and an adult ten years older than him, the former would clearly be inferior to the latter; but what changed when the boy reached the threshold age, somewhere between eighteen and 20, was not the degree of inferiority but the physical nature of the boy. Had the desire been simply for an opportunity to exercise domination, it is not clear why that opportunity would have been perceived as disappearing in such a case, when every aspect of the power-relation remained the same. What this suggests is that this sexual desire had a real object—a human body of a certain kind—outside the desirer; it was not just aimed in a rather solipsistic way at reinforcing, for the desirer, a certain sense of himself.

At this point we have arrived at the most basic, and perhaps the most difficult, task that confronts any historian of these matters: trying to understand the thoughts and feelings of an early modern man who, although he would eventually confine his sexual attentions to women only, regarded boys as desirable too, and may have acted on that desire during the earlier part of his adulthood. What was he thinking, and how was he feeling, when he looked desiringly a boy, and how did that differ, if at all, from the equivalent thoughts and feelings about a girl or a woman? One standard answer to this question is that there was no significant difference at all: men just experienced undifferentiated desire, and the biological sex of the desired object was a merely contingent detail. What distinguished sodomites from other men was simply the fact that the others employed self-control to confine the actual exercise of this general desire to sexual intercourse with women. (Enea Silvio Piccolomini, Pope Pius II, writing in c.1460, described

the notorious *condottiere* Sigismondo Malatesta as 'so unbridled in his lust
that he violated both his daughters and his sons-in-law'—as if just the same
lust, if sufficiently intensified, could lead first to incest and then to sodomy.)[21] It is possible to find some support for this idea in the moral theology
of the period, where all sexual sins were seen as instances of (generic) lust;
and Rafael Carrasco has argued that some of the explanations offered by
men prosecuted by the Inquisition confirm this view, as they blamed their
actions on the (generic) appetites of the flesh. He concludes that 'The sodomite was a creature of lust, a slave of sensual appetites, but of some appetites that did not differ qualitatively or essentially from those which were
stimulated by nature in all men generally.'[22] This approach also chimes with
some much more modern assumptions, held by those who view present-
day categories such as homosexuality and heterosexuality as nothing more
than social constructs. If the dividing-lines that separate these categories are
artificial impositions, it may be thought that some kind of pure, undifferentiated desire can be located beneath them, psychologically, and prior to
them, historically. Yet at the same time we have to note that neither the
moral theology of the period, nor the modern theory which sees any
homosexual/heterosexual division as artificial, can in itself account for the
fact that the desire felt by the great majority of these men did differentiate
sharply against adults of the same sex. Insofar as it could be described as
neutral, it was neutral only between women and boys, not between female
and male.[23]

An alternative view would regard these men as using boys as substitutes
for girls or women—or, in more general terms, would suppose that the
desire for boys was a sort of extension or diversion of the more basic desire
for specifically female sexual partners. Some support for this may be derived
from the fact that the physiological theories of the period, drawing on statements by Aristotle, supposed that boys had to some extent a feminine constitution, producing feminine characteristics, until the age of 18–20, when
their constitution was altered by the full development of masculine heat in
the body—the point being not that people's sexual feelings were dictated by
such theories, but that certain theories could seem plausible in a society
where certain more general attitudes were held.[24] In the article on 'Socratic
Love' in his *Dictionnaire philosophique*, Voltaire argued that the usual kind of
male–male desire was really just an erroneous form of male–female desire.
'Often a young boy, thanks to his fresh complexion, striking beauty and
gentle glance, resembles a beautiful girl for two or three years. If one loves

him, it is because nature makes a mistake: one pays homage to the fair sex by going after that which shares its beautiful characteristics, and when that resemblance evaporates with age, the misapprehension ceases.'[25] Although the invocation of cognitive error here seems very simplistic, there is much evidence from the early modern period that can be used to support the general idea that male–male desire was felt to be secondary to, and somehow derived or extended from, male–female. Some of it should be treated with caution, however. The mere fact that people used language and terminology drawn from male–female sexual relations in order to describe male–male ones—saying that a man was using a youth in bed 'as a woman', keeping him 'as a wife', and so on—is hardly decisive; not only was this the standard mode of description where sex was concerned in these societies, but it may in many cases have offered a way of sharpening the sense of criticism and disapproval (on the grounds that it was demeaning for any male, even a young one, to take a female role). More positive evidence is needed than that.

Some can be found in the ways in which men discussed the boys they regarded as beautiful. That they did so at all is already a potentially significant fact; had their interest focused simply on the sensations to be gained from penetrative sex with a boy (with or without the extra psychological element of dominating an inferior), they might have thought that any boy would do. But, as we have seen, the idea of young male physical beauty did play a role. When the papal lawyer Cardinal De Luca discussed male–male desire, he referred to 'that urge or indeed natural instinct which commonly arises towards good-looking boys'; and when the Jesuit Giovanni Domenico Ottonelli dealt with this issue, he cited St Basil's advice that 'chaste men' should avoid 'looking freely at the beauty of boys'.[26] Basil's text, a treatise on monastic asceticism, was written in the fourth century, but was still regarded as relevant in early modern Europe. 'It is frequently the case with young men', it declared, 'that even when rigorous self-restraint is exercised, the glowing complexion of youth still blooms forth and becomes a source of desire to those around them. If, therefore, anyone is youthful and physically beautiful, let him keep his attractiveness hidden until his appearance reaches a suitable state.'[27]

When early modern writers described good-looking boys, the terms they used were drawn from a standard repertoire that existed primarily to describe female beauty: coral lips, pearly teeth, ivory skin, and so on. Of course allowance should be made for a kind of cultural inertia, whereby authors lazily carried over the same categories from one context to another; the so-called 'blazon' of the features of a beautiful face was always a very stylized literary exercise (though, as Girolamo Muzio complained about the poems of Benedetto Varchi, not so stylized as to eliminate any sense of actual desire).[28] Yet even Antonio Rocco, whose opening portrayal of the handsome schoolboy Alcibiade in his text forms the longest and most detailed physical description of a sexually desirable youth in the Italian literature of the entire period, provided little more than an elaborate blazon drawn from the common stock of images and similes used for beautiful women.[29] In any case, however one chooses to judge these literary performances, the basic fact remains that the time at which a young man's looks became properly masculine (with facial hair, developed musculature, etc.), that is, fully differentiated from a feminine appearance, was precisely the time when he ceased to be seen as desirable by the great majority of older men.

That beautiful male youths looked like girls was the standard view. It was affirmed in many accounts, real or fictional, of such youths being mistaken for young women if they put on female dress. In the *novella* by Sabadino degli Arienti mentioned in the previous chapter, the sixteen-year-old novice priest fools everyone—including, fatefully, the Prior of the Augustinian friary—when he is dressed as a woman; significantly, he is described at the outset, before changing clothes, as possessing such beauty that he is like 'an extremely beautiful girl'.[30] Comic plays also made use of the interchangeability of youthful male and female looks. The bride chosen for Aretino's Stablemaster, who turns out to be the Duke of Mantua's page, is one example, but sometimes this conceit plays a more integral role in the plot. For example, the most famous production of the Academy of the 'Intronati' of Siena (of which Vignali was a member) was a play, written in 1538, entitled *Gl'ingannati*, 'The Deceived'. Its story concerns a brother and sister, separated as children; the brother has just returned to his home town after a long absence and is not recognized, while his sister, to avoid being married off to an old merchant, has put on male clothes and enrolled as the servant of the man she loves. When the old merchant sees the brother in the street, he assumes that it is his intended fiancée in masculine dress; and part of the humour of this scene consists in the way that the old merchant, scandalized though he is, warms to the beauty of the young man.[31]

Literary fiction is not the only source of relevant evidence here. In his autobiography, Benvenuto Cellini recounts having played a prank similar to the one in the Sabadino degli Arienti story, when he was invited to a dinner by a group of artist friends in Rome. They had told him to bring a female guest; he dressed up a sixteen-year-old Spanish boy, the son of a neighbour, and took him along instead. He describes the boy as 'beautiful, with a marvellous complexion', and delights in relating how the other men were stunned by the extraordinary beauty of this mysterious woman. And he also mentions that when the women who were present eventually realized that the mystery guest was male, they shouted at him 'with the sort of insulting words that are commonly applied to beautiful boys' (meaning that they called him a catamite); the reason why such abuse was directed at good-looking boys was, evidently, that they were the ones most likely to attract male admirers.[32]

★ ★ ★

It is difficult to know how exactly to categorize these aesthetic–psychological–sexual attitudes, though it seems reasonable to conclude that there was, broadly speaking, a carry-over process, in which the feelings men had when sexually attracted to women were transferred to male youths. Another, very different, type of transference and/or sharing concerned an actual form of sexual behaviour: anal penetration. It has already been noted that the references to this in the Florentine carnival tradition are by no means male–male only; the penetration of women in this way was a frequent theme. Lorenzo de' Medici, an accomplished poet who sometimes dabbled in the carnivalesque style, even wrote a humorous poem recounting the dialogue that took place between a wife and her husband while he was buggering her. ('It troubled his wife | that he was playing a certain game | which she could not see; | So she said: "Change position." | The husband just said: | "I want to follow my own method; | I don't want to go a different way, | unless I hear a better reason', and so on.)[33] The Florentine 'Office of the Night' seems to have been rather slow to take an interest in this offence: between 1478 and 1492 it was informed of thirteen cases but made only one conviction. Over the following decade, however, it looked at 109 cases and convicted 37 men. Some of these cases involved prostitutes, and there were further convictions of that kind in the early sixteenth century.[34] (It may be relevant here to recall that the main reason why the Florentine authorities had favoured the creation of brothels at the beginning of the century was precisely to divert young men away from sodomy.) The Venetian authorities also took action against prostitutes who permitted or encouraged this sort of sex: a document of 1470 referring to a prostitute who had escaped from gaol specified that she had been convicted of sod-omitical sex; a decree of 1496 referred to 'people, both male and female, who pimp boys and women for the vice of sodomy'; and in 1500 they took action against a prostitute for 'holding a school of sodomy, for men with women, in her house'.[35] There were also two cases, during the same period, of madams keeping girls under the age of twelve specifically for sex of this kind.[36]

Should we conclude that these cases indicate a kind of carry-over into male–female sex of what was primarily a form of male–male activity? In seeming support of that view, there is the evidence of decrees in both Florence and Venice prohibiting prostitutes from having masculine haircuts and wearing male dress, apparently to attract men who liked having sex with male youths. In Florence, 24 prostitutes were punished for such behav-iour between 1476 and 1506. A certain amount of this evidence may be set aside: we should possibly discount two of those cases that occurred during the Carnival, when all kinds of dressing-up could occur, and we should certainly not count the provision of the Venetian decree of 1480 which forbade women to wear false beards—a practice which might have facili-tated passing unnoticed through the streets to an illicit sexual rendezvous of a more normal kind, but which could not possibly have been aimed at sodomitically-inclined men.[37] Yet even after these adjustments, most of the evidence remains; and it is fortified both by a complaint by Bernardino of Siena, in one of his Florentine sermons of 1424, about prostitutes wearing male clothes, and by a record from Mallorca in 1455, describing the punish-ment of a woman who had adopted a male haircut and masculine headgear 'in order to provoke men to sin'.[38] In addition, some of the men tried for male–male sodomy were described as having wanted to penetrate women anally too. During the prosecution of Pietro Rasori in Bologna in 1474, his wife testified that she had left him eight years previously 'because she was badly treated by him as he brought boys into the house and abused them...and she was very often asked by Pietro to consent to anal sex'. Filipe de Moura, the Portuguese military commander processed by the Inquisition in Lisbon in 1644, confessed also to several affairs with women in which he had persuaded them to submit to anal penetration, either exclusively or in addition to regular intercourse.[39]

But on the other hand it would be rash to assume that the whole phe-nomenon of men sodomizing women was driven essentially by those who, like Pietro Rasori, had a definite preference for male–male sodomy. We have no reason to think that those prostitutes who did accept or encourage anal sex were all trying to look like boys; and even the ones who did adopt some element of a boyish appearance were surely not aiming at men who strongly preferred male–male sex, as their female identity was always evident. Most likely they were just signalling their availability for a form of sex that was within the range of possibilities for most men. In Aretino's *Ragionamenti*, a courtesan recounts how she gulled one of her admirers out of large sums of money by making him give her expensive clothes for the Carnival. He was present when she tried on the luxurious male stockings he had paid for, whereupon, as she put it, 'I let him have me as if I were a boy.'[40] The admirer was otherwise interested only in regular sex with her; so this detail seems to indicate that sodomy was, so to speak, just an accepted additional option; appearing male in some way may have worked as a trigger to suggest it, but there is nothing here to imply that the man had to think of the woman as a boy in order to be sexually interested in her. Analysing the evidence from Florence, Michael Rocke comments much more broadly: 'A wide variety of cases of heterosexual sodomy came before the courts, including men with female servants, sodomitical rapes by gangs of young men, and anal and oral sex between spouses, sometimes for the stated purpose of avoiding pregnancy.'[41]

Male–female sodomy is, perhaps understandably, not a subject that has attracted much attention from historians. The most valuable account is given in Jean Toscan's study of Florentine coded language; and what emerges from his research is that the practice was very widespread in Tuscany and elsewhere in Italy, enjoying much public acceptance. Men resorted to it when their wives were menstruating (the carnivalesque language has references to rainy days), and more generally for purposes of birth control. It was also common practice on the many occasions—Fridays and Saturdays, which were fasting days, and also the whole of Lent—when sex was forbidden by the Church; and there were other times, such as the torrid 'dog days' of the summer, and full moons, when popular belief warned against vaginal intercourse. Proverbial wisdom even advised that men should not have regular sex with women during the three hottest months of the year, June, July and August.[42] (This last detail provides the essential background to one of the most outlandish propaganda claims made by Protestant writers in the sixteenth century: that Pope Sixtus IV had granted, at the request of a Genoese cardinal, permission for the cardinal's entire household to sodomize boys during those three months.)[43] In Aretino's *Ragionamenti*, many of the lubricious stories involve men sodomizing women, though this form of intercourse is always secondary to the regular kind.[44] That the practice of male–female sodomy was thought to be widespread is also suggested by the mock-proclamation issued by the so-called academy led by the abbate Volpino in late-sixteenth-century Naples. It began by saying that it was drawn up in response to the complaints of so many women's miserable vulvas, 'making their case against all the phalluses for having perverted the rules', that is, for having penetrated the women's anuses instead. It said that the vulvas had provided good reasons, including both their own 'perpetual heat' (sexual desire) and the need for procreation; and so it decreed that henceforth the buggery of women should be limited to the times when they were menstruating.[45]

If the practice of male–female anal sex was so widespread, it might be asked why such cases are not much more frequent in the trial documents. Certainly they crop up much less in Spain: Rafael Carrasco found only a handful in the records of the Inquisition in Valencia. However, as he points out, most women, especially married ones, would have been very reluctant to bring such matters to the attention of a court.[46] Nor would the testimony of a sole witness—in this case, the woman—have sufficed for a conviction. Studying the limited evidence from Seville, Mary Elizabeth Perry suggests that male–female sodomy was simply not taken so seriously as an offence.[47] It is possible that the practice was rather less prevalent in Iberia than it was in Italy: in one case heard by the Coimbra tribunal in Portugal, the accused man, who was Italian, had explained (to a woman who rebuffed his request) that 'men in his country were accustomed to do that a lot.'[48] But even in Italy the trial statistics seem very low for a practice which, according to Toscan's evidence, was extremely common. Again, the explanation would seem to be a combination of two things: personal shame, on the part of the woman, at the thought of having such private matters aired in court, and a general belief that the practice, despite the religious condemnation it incurred, was not seriously wrong. Guido Ruggiero notes that when such spousal cases did come to court in fifteenth-century Venice, the husband was almost always acquitted.[49] (An apparent counter-example comes from a different jurisdiction, Ferrara, in 1454, where a man was described in the judicial records as 'a wicked sodomite, who did it with his wife, and was impaled and then burnt'; but here we should probably assume that the treatment of his wife was a supplementary detail added to a standard charge of sodomy.)[50]

The idea that male–female sodomy was a less serious offence gained sup-port from an unlikely quarter: the great Catholic moral theologian Martín de Azpilcueta. He argued that a husband who began sex with his wife anally, but with the intention of ending vaginally, was guilty of a form of 'illicit touching', but was not required to confess to the sin of sodomy; this implied that the anal penetration itself was only a venial sin, not a mortal one. Another Spanish theologian, the Cordovan Jesuit Tomas Maria Sánchez, strongly disagreed with this argument, as he did with Azpilcueta's claim that for a man to sodomize his own wife was less sinful than sodomizing some other woman.[51] (Strangely, in 1611, nine years after the first publication of Sánchez's work, the booksellers of Paris were forbidden to sell it, because its discussion of sodomy was thought to be scandalous; it seems to have been his summarizing of Azpilcueta's arguments—in order to reject them—that made the work so problematic.)[52]

But people did not need to read elaborate treatises in order to gain the idea that male–female sodomy was relatively excusable. The Sicilian Inquisition tried many men—for their heretical statements, not for actual sodomizing—who defended the practice. In 1586 a merchant was given a heavy fine for saying that St Peter had sodomized his wife; and in the same year an artisan was whipped for telling his wife that this form of sex was not sinful, 'even if it was done on the high altar at Rome'.[53] Others who denied that the act was a sin included several priests. One of them told a married couple that it was permissible while the woman was pregnant; a doctor of laws said the same; and Fra Pacifico La Ficarra asserted not only that male–female sex of this kind was not a sin, but also that having sex with boys was 'holy and just'.[54] Several men were prosecuted for repeating what was apparently a common saying in Sicily: that Adam had sodomized Eve, and that the instruction not to eat the apple had in fact referred to this kind of sexual act. William Monter takes this as an expression of a condemnatory view, but the evidence suggests that, for some at least, it was a way of describ-ing male–female sodomy as just part of the human condition. Sometimes the point about God's prohibition was entirely omitted. A 30-year-old Sicilian surgeon, prosecuted in Barcelona in 1597–8 for sodomy and heresy, was reported as having said: 'Didn't Adam, our first father, do it to his wife from behind?', and that 'if God had not created the arsehole, one would not take pleasure from it, but God did create it so that one could enjoy oneself and make use of it.'[55] These lines of argument could thus cover male–female and male–male sodomy equally. In 1618 a Sicilian cleric claimed that sodomy was only a venial sin, and boasted that he had sodomized boys; thirteen years earlier, a Lombard, resident in Sicily, was exiled from the island for ten years for having said that 'he did not regard it as a sin, because it was permitted by nature (meaning the sin against nature), responding in this way several times'.[56]

Given that Sicily, where these ideas were expressed, and Florence, where popular culture made light of the issue, were two places where male–male sodomy seems to have been particularly common, it might be tempting to assume that the relative acceptance of male–female sodomy was caused by the presence of the male–male variety. But on balance it is surely more likely that the influence worked in the opposite direction. Where this kind of male–female sex was part of the culture, practised because of widely held popular views about the need to avoid vaginal sex at various times, and also as a method of birth control, it must have been a more general phenomenon, present in the behaviour of many men who never had sexual dealings with boys. And in that case it would surely have had a normalizing function where the whole idea of anal sex was concerned. In a society where male–female sodomy is viewed as taboo by the general population, the act of penetrating a boy will seem to belong to a very different category from male–female sex; it will probably arouse a stronger sense of deviancy, and it is possible that in such a sexual culture the man who seeks sex with a boy will experience his own desire as very different in kind from desire for sex with a woman. Yet all the evidence we have been considering from early modern Western Mediterranean societies suggests that most of the men who indulged in sex with boys did not feel any sharp differentiation of that kind.

★ ★ ★

Most, but not all. As we have seen, there were also quite a few untypical cases, falling into categories that did not fit the general pattern. The most untypical of all were the passive adult males, a category which may not have been commonly encountered, but which was widely known about, as it so disgracefully violated the code of 'normal' sodomitical behaviour. Where the active sodomites were concerned, it is clear that, while the age distribution fell away rapidly above the age of 30, some 'inveterate sodomites' carried on into their 60s or beyond. Michael Rocke's analysis of the rich Florentine evidence shows that men of this kind above the age of 40 were much less likely to be married.[57] Among the small number of these men who did take wives, we cannot tell whether sexual desire for a woman—as opposed to economic motives, family pressures, respect for convention or a sheer tactic of camouflage—played the key role; but it seems reasonable to assume that the category of inveterate sodomites over 40 did significantly overlap with the category (another, or perhaps largely the same, untypical group) of men who did not desire women, having sexual feelings only for boys. These men were, as was illustrated in the previous chapter, a distinctive and culturally recognized type. And finally there were the men who developed very strong feelings of affection for boys; these may have overlapped to a significant extent with the ones who desired boys only.

There were thus four, or three, or at the very least two categories of men who, while they engaged willingly in forms of male–male sex, did not range freely between having regular sex with women, sodomizing them, and sodomizing boys. To reduce it to two: they were the passive adults on the one hand, and on the other hand the men whose interest, whether purely sexual or emotional too, was directed exclusively, or primarily, or unceasingly, at male youths.

The first of these was seen as the most deviant of all; yet at the same time it was the category for which the most 'natural' explanation was available. Drawing on the *Problems* (a text wrongly but traditionally attributed to Aristotle), which contained a full discussion of the question, 'Why is it that some [male] persons find pleasure in submitting to [penetrative] sexual intercourse?', medical writers had developed a physiological theory to account for this puzzling phenomenon. According to the Paduan physician Pietro d'Abano, whose commentary on the *Problems* was written in 1302, the cause was in many cases a congenital defect. Either the passage which conveyed semen to the penis was blocked, terminating at the anus instead, and causing pleasure to be felt only there; or there were passages to both destinations, permitting pleasure in both places. D'Abano did also accept that the explanation in some cases could be moral and psychological: a vicious disposition or habit.[58] This alternative view was present in the pseudo-Aristotelian account, and its authority was particularly strengthened by the Persian writer Ibn Sina (Avicenna), whose great treatise the *Canon of Medicine* had been translated into Latin in the twelfth century: in oposition to the physical theories, Ibn Sina strongly emphasized the role of habit and character. Nevertheless, the two types of explanation were commonly run in parallel in the Western medical tradition, with the psychological one never fully displacing the physiological one. And as Joan Cadden has written, 'there was broad agreement that those whose disposition was innate did represent a fixed category of the human male', so that this was 'a recognized natural phenomenon'.[59] Drawing on other ancient sources, Renaissance writers developed an even fuller account of the specific characteristics of passive males, and of the physical causes of those features. In a treatise written in c.1500, the physiologist and physiognomer Bartolomeo della Rocca, known as Cocles, included a whole chapter on the *cinaedus* or catamite, not only using that term for boys who wanted to be sodomized, but also commenting that 'I have observed this passion in many "boys" 40, 50, 60, 65, and 70 years old.' These males, he observed, had special physical characteristics, derived from an innate imbalance in their constitution: 'such people have soft flesh, fine throats, effeminate and often slender legs, large soft ankles, pale faces, and quarrelsome dispositions, and many other signs.'[60] One might therefore expect that this whole line of explanation would have exculpated passive males to a significant extent: after all, how could any person be blamed for behaviour caused by a congenital abnormality? But it seems that, thanks to the availability of the alternative, moral-psychological theory, and to the general revulsion at such sexual conduct by adult men, tolerance on those 'natural' grounds was seldom applied.

For the active sodomites, on the other hand, some kind of exculpation framed in terms of 'nature' was available, and was sometimes invoked, at least by the sodomites themselves. One of the basic ambiguities that arose over the concept of nature—as used by all the theologians and moralists who condemned sodomy as *contra naturam*—was to do with the level of description: did it concern nature in general, or the nature of the individual sodomite? That the point had been current for a long time is suggested by the fact that one of the heretical propositions condemned by the Bishop of Paris in 1277 was the claim that 'the sin against nature...although it is against the nature of the species, is not, however, against the nature of the individual.'[61] This idea was used as the central conceit of a comic *novella* published in 1554 by the popular Piedmontese writer (and Dominican friar) Matteo Bandello. The story concerns a Roman poet, originally from Naples, who is described as having many 'huge vices', chief of which was that 'the meat of young goats always pleased him far more than any other food he could be given, and so it was his supreme delight to walk on pattens where it's dry'. (Note here both the goat metaphor used by Antonio Rocco in *Alcibiade*, and the carnivalesque phrase for sodomy which first appeared in Boccaccio.) When the poet was seriously ill, a pious elderly friar was sent to hear his confession; the friar asked if he had ever sinned against nature, and he replied firmly in the negative. At the prompting of the poet's wife, who insisted that he was an inveterate sodomite, the question was asked again, and again answered in the same way. Only at the third attempt did the friar receive the following response: 'Ho ho, reverend father, you didn't know how to question me. To enjoy myself with boys is more natural to me than eating and drinking is to a man, and you asked me if I sinned against nature!'[62]

This kind of argument focused on the 'nature' of a sodomite who was different from the normal run of men, having a distinct preference for boys. (After his last conversation with the poet's wife, the friar tells him: 'I am assured that you are a thousand times more eager for boys than goats are for salt.')[63] But there were also arguments from nature that could apply to sodomy more generally. The tutor in Antonio Rocco's dialogue insists that several species of animals perform same-sex acts. He also formulates a much more general theological argument: adopting the standard comparison between God's creation and a clock, he explains that 'our inclinations are counterweights given to us by nature and by God, so whoever follows them is not straying from the principles of his own being, nor is he acting against his maker.'[64] Here Rocco was expressing, in rather formal terms, an attitude which seems to have been much more widespread. We have already seen that the Lombard man condemned to exile from Sicily described sodomy as 'permitted by nature', and therefore not a sin. In 1559 a cantor at the cathedral in Toledo was accused, at the Zaragoza tribunal of the Inquisition, of saying that male–male sex was not against nature. At an Inquisition trial in Naples in 1594, a man was described as keeping a beardless boy for sex, and saying 'that it was a natural thing, and that if he'd been able to get a dispensation, he would have taken him as his wife'.[65] Some people insisted that as the sexual drive itself was natural, acting upon it was therefore natural—even necessary. In the early fourteenth century Arnaud de Verniolles, who seduced several youths in his small town in south-western France, explained his actions by saying that if he went for too long without having sex with a woman or a boy, he felt ill. In 1580 a priest in the Peruvian city of Cuzco was charged with having told people that sex was a human necessity, and that if one did not have the opportunity to do it with a woman, 'it should be done in your hand, or in an arse'. A Camaldolese monk from Vicenza, tried by the Venetian Inquisition in 1707, had allegedly denied that sodomy was a sin, explaining that 'these were natural things, done for natural pleasure'.[66]

The idea that a sexual act could be seen as morally neutral, to be described in merely physical terms, was expressed in 1596 by a Frenchman in Lisbon, accused of soliciting another man for improper sexual acts: he said that mutual masturbation was not a sin 'since it was equivalent to blowing your nose on someone'. Going one step further, in 1628 a priest in Venice allegedly said that it was wrong to forbid anal sex, given that God had obviously designed the anus in such a way that it could be a source of pleasure. The same idea, as we have seen, was expressed by the Sicilian surgeon in Barcelona in 1597–8 who said that God created the anus 'so that one could enjoy oneself and make use of it.' And in 1596 a very similar point was made by an eighteen-year-old in Mallorca, who said that the sin committed by men who visited prostitutes was caused by God, who had created the women's vaginas. (Since it was also mentioned at his Inquisition trial that he had confessed to many acts of sodomy, we may guess that he did not apply this argument only to male–female sex.)[67]

Renaissance naturalism has already been mentioned briefly in relation to the intellectual background to Antonio Rocco. It involved an implicitly non-Christian or even anti-Christian worldview, which tended to substitute this-worldly motivations and pleasures for other-worldly ones, as it denied that the immortality of the soul, and thus also rewards and punishments after death, were knowable by nature. Whether this view played a significant role in propagating the 'natural' defence of sodomitical sex is hard to judge, given that that line of defence commonly took nature as embodying the intentions of God, its creator. In a few particular cases, including that of Rocco, it is possible to make the connection. One rather spectacular earlier example of an apparent link with radical naturalism is the case of Fra Francesco Calcagno, a former monk who was tried on charges of heresy and blasphemy by the Venetian Inquisition in 1550. Among his alleged offences, the records stated that 'he has said that a beautiful arse is his altar, his Mass, his host, chalice and paten; and again, that he would sooner worship a beautiful boy, by having sex with him, than he would worship God.' As if that was not enough, he had also declared, allegedly, 'that there never was any Christ, and that the person whom people call Christ was a carnal man, and that he often had sex with St John, and that he kept him as his catamite'. In addition, he had told one witness that it was 'mad' to believe the Holy Scriptures, which were no more worthy of belief than Ovid's *Metamorphoses*, and that the authors of those Scriptures were 'people of the devil, who did it in order to keep people in a state of fear and to govern the world as they wished'. 'Often', said the witness, 'he quoted that verse of Lucretius, *Primus in orbe deos fecit timor* ['it was fear that first made gods in the world'].' As for the teachings of the Church: 'people were mindless, and in those matters the common people believed what they were told, while the great ones believed what he believed, namely, that there is no God, and no Heaven, and the simple truth is that when the body is dead, the soul is dead, and everything is ruled by chance.'[68] Under interrogation, Calcagno denied having said much of this, or claimed not to remember the conversations, and insisted that the comments about boys had been jokes; but he admitted that he might have said 'that Christ was a man like other men, and that St John was his catamite'. And when questioned further about his remark that a beautiful arse was his God, his explanation was that he had read those words 'in a book called *La cazzaria*', which a friend had lent him.[69]

The Epicurean cosmology, the Lucretian tag about the origins of religion in fear, and the Machiavellian notion that rulers fabricated or manipulated religion for political ends (an idea which appeared also in Antonio Rocco's treatment of Moses): these all seem to signal an intellectual background to Calcagno's attitude to sodomy. But it would probably be a mistake to treat this rashly exuberant hedonist as following an agenda derived from the study of philosophical works. Almost every element here can be found in the sort of popular irreligion that existed among ordinary, uneducated people in this period. To give just a few examples: in 1571 a man from Ischia was denounced to the Inquisition in Naples for denying the existence of Heaven and Hell, and scornfully declaring that after death the soul 'goes into a pig's arse'. In the latter decades of the sixteenth century the Sicilian tribunal of the Inquisition punished people for saying that 'there is no God, no Heaven and no Hell', and that the soul died with the body. A proclamation issued by the Toledo tribunal of the Inquisition in the late sixteenth century contained a whole list of popular errors and heretical beliefs: it condemned those who said 'that there is no heaven for the good nor hell for the bad...or that have said heretical blasphemies like "I do not believe"...or who denied her [Mary's] virginity saying that Our Lady the Virgin Mary was not a virgin before, during or after giving birth, or that she did not conceive by the Holy Spirit...that simple fornication...is not a sin, or that...the soul of man is no more than a breath, and that blood is the soul'. In the same period the Cuenca tribunal encountered the common belief that there was no life after death (a woolcomber, brought before it, explained that he had pondered the resurrection of the dead and come to the conclusion that it was simply not believable). And the tendency to think about divine matters in regrettably human terms was not at all uncommon: in 1568 the 21-year-old María de Cardenas, daughter of a shepherd in Villanueva de Alcardete, said that 'God did it to Our Lady like her father [did] to her mother', and 'persisted in believing that God had known Our Lady carnally'.[70]

As for the blasphemous claim about a sexual relationship between Jesus and St John: this too was present in popular culture. It was an idea which could have occurred to anyone who had read or heard certain passages in St John's Gospel, where John is referred to several times as the disciple 'whom Jesus loved'. The final chapter also describes John as leaning on Jesus's breast at the Last Supper, and it was quite common for paintings of that scene to show him as a young man doing just that, in a pose expressing intimacy and affection.[71] Possibly the sexual interpretation was reinforced also, unintentionally, by pious writers who allegorized the ascent of Ganymede into heaven, comparing him to St John; but popular irreligion hardly needed support of such a recondite kind. The sexual allegation circulated widely, from sixteenth-century Naples (where a man in the Inquisition gaol described Christ as a 'great bugger') to early-seventeenth-century Venice (where a priest was denounced for saying, among other things, that Jesus sodomized John), to late-seventeenth-century Brazil: in 1685 the Brazilian poet Gregório de Mattos was accused of having said that 'Jesus Christ our Redeemer was a sodomite.'[72] When Bernardino of Siena explained in a sermon of 1424 that Jesus did not say anything against sodomy because 'in his time there were no sodomites' (a reference to the legend that they had all been eliminated when he was born), he seems to have been reacting against a line of argument which defended sodomy on the grounds that Jesus had never condemned it—which might, again, have connected with the idea that he had a personal preference for it. In the eastern Italian city of Macerata in 1722 three Carmelite friars, forcing a boy to submit to them sexually, assured him that Christ approved of sodomy.[73]

Similar blasphemies extended the focus beyond Jesus himself. Another case from seventeenth-century Brazil involved a man accused of saying publicly that 'Christ Our Lord's Apostles had been sodomites.' In 1609 a Spanish priest in the Yucatán Peninsula was denounced not only for sodomy and oral sex, but for telling people that St Peter and the Apostles had all practised fellatio. In 1585 the Mallorcan Inquisition investigated a 20-year-old man who had recounted a comic story about Jesus and St Peter travelling together. At one point, Peter took his donkey into a stable to bugger it; Jesus asked what he was doing, and he said he was making a nail for the donkey's shoe; whereupon Jesus said, 'Peter, you are so close to its arse, you are nailing it'—using a slang term for sexual penetration. (Under interrogation, the man—whose own acts of sodomy were also adduced as an aggravating factor—said that he had heard someone tell this story, and, with remarkable ingenuousness, he claimed that he thought it was true.)[74] In Naples in 1567 a priest, accused of saying that sodomy was not a sin, had allegedly said that the circular shape of the Host (in the Mass) symbolized the arsehole, and that sodomy was common among saints. Eleven years later, also in Naples, another priest was denounced for stating that God was a sodomite; and nine years after that, a man was prosecuted by the Venetian Inquisition for saying that God sodomized the angels.[75] In the same period, a man was punished by the Sicilian Inquisition for saying that the burning of St Lawrence (who was martyred on a gridiron) was a punishment for buggery. In 1722 a weaver in Rome was charged with saying that St Paul disapproved of men who did not bugger their wives.[76]

These examples cover a whole range of attitudes, from aggressive blasphemy (of the sort that simply tries to find the worst thing to say—for example, calling the Virgin Mary a whore)—to insouciant humour, to—possibly—some element of sincere belief. Not all of the people who made such remarks, therefore, were necessarily expressing a subversively positive view of sodomy. But another element of popular irreligion (or, if that is too strong a term, resistance to Catholic teachings) involved widespread disbelief in some of the norms of sexual behaviour propagated by the Church. Above all, it was quite commonly believed that simple fornication, sex between an unmarried man and an unmarried woman, was not a sin. This view, which we have already seen included in the Toledo Inquisition's list of popular errors, crops up frequently in the records: five people confessed to having said it at an *auto-da-fé* in Granada in 1574, for example, and two were punished for expressing this opinion in Mallorca in the 1580s.[77] Nor was this merely a theoretical position; several modern studies of sexual behaviour in early modern Spain have shown that general standards in these matters fell, in practice, a long way below the requirements of the Counter-Reformation Church.[78] If such moral laxity enjoyed a degree of social tolerance where male–female sex was concerned, it seems possible that, to some lesser extent, a kind of tolerance was also extended to the male–male variety, at least by some elements in the general population. But it required only one or two of the other members of the population—the intolerant ones—to make a denunciation; and such people, evidently, were not few.

13

Ottoman religion,
law and culture

After looking at the religious and legal norms relating to sodomy, and the cultural representations of it, in the Western Mediterranean, it is worth considering their equivalents in the Ottoman world. For although the basic phenomenon of age-differentiated male–male sexual relations was the same in both cases, it was, so to speak, modulated in different ways. These differences will help us to form a final judgement on how prejudicially sodomy in the 'East' was represented by observers from the 'West'.

The prime foundation of all normative thinking in Islam was, of course, the Koran. It contains one general statement which, although it uses slightly veiled language, has always been understood to refer to male–male sex: 'If two men among you commit indecency punish them both' (4: 16).[1] Otherwise, most of its pronouncements on this subject are formulated as references to the experience of Lot among the people of the city of Sodom (referred to in the Koran as the people of Lot). 'Remember the words of Lot, who said to his people: "Will you persist in these indecent acts which no other nation has committed before you? You lust after men instead of women. Truly, you are a degenerate people"' (7: 81–2); 'Their compatriot Lot said to them: "Will you not have fear of Allah?... Will you fornicate with males and leave your wives, whom Allah has created for you? Surely you are great transgressors"' (26: 165); and so on.[2] Altogether there are seven references to the story of Lot and the people of Sodom in the Koran. The Arabic words for 'sodomy', liwāṭ, and 'sodomite', lūṭī, are drawn from the phrase, 'the act of the people of Lot (Lūṭ)'. And despite the potentially broad variety of sexual acts that might be suggested by those rather general references to indecency and lust, the semantic range of these terms in Arabic is quite specific: liwāṭ refers only to anal penetration, and lūṭī to the person

Forbidden Desire in Early Modern Europe: Male–Male Sexual Relations, 1400–1750. Noel Malcolm, Oxford University Press.
© Noel Malcolm 2024. DOI: 10.1093/oso/9780198886334.003.0013

who commits that act. But while these Koranic passages clearly imply penetration of a male, Muslim jurists would later use the term for male–female sodomy too.[3]

Overall, then, the Koran's attitude towards male–male penetrative acts of this kind was certainly condemnatory. The only qualification that might be added is that the first quotation given above, 'If two men among you commit indecency punish them both', continues as follows: 'If they repent and mend their ways, let them be. Allah is forgiving and merciful.'[4] Some scholars have pointed out that whereas the Koran specifies fierce punishments for some moral offences (those guilty of male–female fornication or adultery, for example, are to receive 100 lashes), no particular penalty is stipulated for sodomy; this, they suggest, implies a relatively lenient attitude.[5] But what concerns us here is not how the sacred text of Islam might be interpreted but how it actually was understood by Muslim exegetes, and leniency played little or no role in that story. In addition, all the ḥadīths (traditional reports of the sayings and deeds of Muhammad) concerning sodomy were strongly hostile: for example, 'If sodomites become common, God, the Glorious and Exalted, will wash his hands of mankind and not care in which abyss they perish.' A ḥadīth included in some authoritative collections, though not in the two most authoritative of all, said: 'those whom you find committing the act of the people of Lot, kill the active and the passive partner.'[6] Similar in some ways to the ḥadīths were the akhbār (plural of khabar, meaning report or news), traditional sayings, and accounts of the Prophet, attributed to early pious Muslims; these too were condemnatory, often demanding the death penalty, and one recurrent theme was that sodomites would be resurrected as pigs or monkeys.[7] The ninth-century Baghdadi scholar Ibn Abī al-Dunyā recorded the saying that 'If there were one who might fittingly be stoned twice, he would be the sodomite'—as opposed to the perpetrators of other sexual crimes, for whom one lethal stoning was sufficient.[8]

However, when some of the anti-sodomitical sayings focused on the danger posed by sodomy, they seem to have taken for granted that the temptation to commit it might be strong. Ibn Abī al-Dunyā also reported one early Muslim as saying that 'I have less fear for a pious young man from a ravening beast than from a beardless boy who sits with him.' And in his treatise attacking musical entertainment, he cited another early saying: 'Do not sit with young boy singers, for their appearance is like that of women. They are an even greater temptation than young virgin girls.'[9] The famous Persian jurist, theologian and mystic Al-Ghazali (c.1058–1111) argued that 'anyone whose heart is affected by the beauty of a boy, even to the extent that he can perceive any difference between him and a bearded man, is forbidden to look at him at all.' He also quoted a man of the *salaf* (the first three generations of Muslims) who said that there were three types of sodomite: 'those who look, those who touch, and those who do the act'.[10]

Such attitudes may have seemed to set up a tension, or perhaps a slippery slope, between feeling attracted to a beautiful boy (something to which almost any man, apparently, could be prone), and committing the act of sodomy. And this in turn raised questions about the Koran's promise that in Paradise men would be served by beautiful male youths. 'They [sc. the faithful] will pass from hand to hand a cup inspiring no idle talk, no sinful urge; there shall wait on them young boys of their own as fair as virgin pearls' (52: 23–4); 'They shall recline on jewelled couches face to face, and there shall wait on them immortal youths with bowls and ewers and a cup of purest wine… And theirs shall be the dark-eyed houris, chaste as hidden pearls: a guerdon for their deeds' (56: 17–18).[11] Although the Koran makes no actual reference to sexual intercourse in Paradise, Islamic tradition tended to assume that the 'houris', beautiful young virgin women, were granted to the faithful for that purpose; so it could be asked whether the immortal youths might play a similar role. In the eleventh century two learned scholars had a debate on the issue of paradisal sodomy. One argued that committing *liwāṭ* was intrinsically wrong and vicious, but the other said that it was prohibited in this world for two specific reasons, neither of which would apply in Paradise: the problem of non-procreative sex leading to depopulation, which would be irrelevant as there would be no births anyway; and the need to avoid being polluted by excrement, which would disappear, as the faithful in Paradise would not excrete. (The argument about depopulation was a standard one in the Islamic tradition.)[12] The opinion that there might be sodomy in Paradise certainly did not prevail; its rejection was, in the end, overwhelming. Yet it is of interest to see that for one thinker at least, removing those two specific objections would leave the way clear for men not only to desire boys sexually, but also to act on that desire. Also interesting is the way the argument concerning depopulation was set out in a Shiite tradition which attributed to Ali (the cousin and son-in-law of the Prophet) the saying: 'If carnal penetration of a boy were permitted, men would dispense with women, and this would lead to the disruption of procreation.'[13]

As Khaled El-Rouayheb has shown, the general view in early modern Islamic culture was that for a man to be attracted to a beautiful boy was not in itself sinful, but that to act on that attraction by sodomizing the boy was a grave sin. Chaste love was therefore permitted. Indeed, some regarded the restraint of the chaste lover as a great achievement, the greatness of which was in proportion to the strength of the love. There was even a *ḥadīth* which reported Muhammad as saying: 'He who loves and is chaste [variants add: 'and conceals his secret'] and then dies, dies a martyr.' And although rigorists objected to this view, they may have represented only a minority opinion in the early modern period. 'Falling in love with a boy', El-Rouayheb observes, 'was widely considered to be an involuntary act, and as such outside the scope of religious condemnation. Many, perhaps most, religious scholars were prepared to concede that a person who died from unconsummated love for a boy could earn the status of a martyr (*shahīd*), which would guarantee him a place in heaven.'[14]

The issue of passionate love will come up again when we consider the literary culture of the early modern Muslim world. But here, in a discussion of religious norms and principles, there is another phenomenon— overlapping culturally with that to a significant extent, but distinguishable in principle—which needs to be addressed: the cult of contemplating young male beauty. This was a practice, known as *naẓar* or 'gazing', with a long history; it seems to have been well established by the first half of the tenth century, when the famous rabbi Saadya Gaon, then resident in Iraq, wrote an oblique but strong condemnation of it.[15] The theological justification of *naẓar* was formulated most clearly by the Andalusian mystic Muḥyī al-Dīn ibn 'Arabī (d. 1240), who argued that God was the only reality; His various attributes, denoted by divine names such as 'the Merciful', 'the Compassionate', 'the Beautiful', were manifested in the phenomenal world, which meant that with the right sort of understanding the believer could appreciate aspects of God's creation as expressions of God's own nature. Beauty, seen in this way, was always divine beauty, and the contemplation of it could lead the believer closer to God.[16] This vision of the relation between God and the world had been developed particularly within the Sufi tradition; and since sexual asceticism (including celibacy) was widely cultivated in classical Sufism, the distinction between gazing contemplatively at beautiful boys and lusting after them may have seemed, to many, a thoroughly tenable one.[17] From an early stage, however, opponents of this view accused it of committing a gross theological error: *ḥulūl*, meaning belief in the indwelling or incarnation of God in one of His creatures. This was an error that could lead to idolatry.[18] And of course there was always a simpler criticism to be made, a form of argumentation, so to speak, below the belt: practitioners of *nazar* were nothing more than lustful sodomites, inventing a bogus pretext for getting handsome male youths into their clutches. Scholars and jurists from the Hanbalite school—the tradition out of which Wahhabism would later develop—were prominent in making this argument; they were also especially keen to emphasize *hadīth*s and sayings which condemned sodomy and warned of the dangers posed by even the presence of a beautiful boy.[19]

The fact that the 'gazing' was directed in practice only at boys, and not at beautiful women (despite the agreement by some writers, including Ibn 'Arabī, that beauty was equally present in them), might in theory be explained by the relative unavailability of the latter.[20] Yet it is also clear that within this culture this special interest in beautiful boys did connect, in many ways, with feelings and behaviour involved in male–male relationships of a very this-worldly kind. The sort of infatuation that led a man to abase himself before an arrogant boy who was playing the role of *beau garçon sans merci*, for example, is well known to us from poems and stories; it too, apparently, could be incorporated into the practice of *nazar*. As Annemarie Schimmel puts it, mystics saw in the admired boy (who, she notes, was ideally fourteen years old), 'a *shahīd*, a witness of God's eternal beauty... which induced them to call him often an idol... the idol was meant to represent Divine Beauty, *jamāl*, and at the same time God's *jalāl*, His Majesty [connoting terrible power]. The beloved thus becomes a perfect mirror of the seemingly contrasting attitudes of God, attracting the lover by his radiant beauty, but submitting him to unending affliction by the manifestations of his whims or his outright cruelty.'[21]

In the early modern period, the charge of straightforward sexual vice and hypocrisy was very commonly made by anti-Sufi writers. A tract by Sinān al-Dīn al-Amāsi, written in the second half of the sixteenth century, exclaims: 'they [sc. Sufis] brag about it, and blame those who do not possess a beardless youth[, saying]: "You do not practise *liwāt* and you do not drink wine, so you are an unrefined Sufi"... Many of them do not marry women, and instead use boys, saying "we do not have to support them as we do women". They give them names such as "travel wife" or "bed boy"... You may see many in our times claiming to be learned *ulema* [experts in Islamic law and doctrine], sitting at the head of a court, and yet taking pride in their young companions... Some of them look for the prettiest youths and buy them.'[22] The idea that members of the Sufi orders—all-male confraternities, which met in their own lodges for social and religious purposes—were particularly inclined to sodomy was a cultural trope, on a par with Western stereotypes about monks and friars.[23] Many accounts of the Islamic world by West European travellers echoed this opinion, though on the basis of much more limited knowledge. Some of these observers were particularly struck by the *qalandars*, bizarre-looking wandering holy men, often half-naked, whose behaviour could range from ascetic self-mutilation to antinomian sexual indulgence. But while these figures may have had a disproportionate influence on the Western imagination where 'dervishes'—i.e. Sufis—were concerned, they were really quite tangential to Sufism proper, representing probably an importation of Indian religious practices.[24] In contrast to them, the major Sufi orders were fully integrated into society, and their behaviour could therefore be expected to align with general social tendencies (including regrettably sinful ones), rather than involving deliberately shocking breaches of rules for antinomian purposes. The standard anti-Sufi view in these societies was that the dervishes simply used their position and opportunities to practise a common vice. The French Capuchin missionary Michel Febvre, who lived for many years in the Ottoman Middle East, becoming fluent in Arabic, Persian and Kurdish, and getting to know many Sufis personally, wrote in the 1670s: 'Above all, they [sc. members of Sufi orders] are strongly inclined to carnal vices, and to sins against nature. For sodomy and other abominable deeds, which decency forbids me to name, are so common among them that they have become habitual, and they commit them without any pang of conscience.'[25] There were many Ottoman Muslims who agreed.

And yet, despite all the vulnerability to such accusations that the practice of boy-gazing inevitably caused, eminent Sufis continued to defend it. Khaled El-Rouayheb discusses the example of 'Abd al-Ghanī al-Nābulusī (1641–1731), a highly respected Damascene scholar who wrote works of jurisprudence and Koranic commentary, among many other things. He composed an entire treatise in defence of the pure love of beardless boys, adducing various theological arguments. He noted, for instance, that some of the companions of the Prophet were beardless youths; he invoked the references in the Koran to God ordering the angels to prostrate themselves before Adam, and in that connection he referred also to a tradition which said that Adam was created as a beardless boy. As El-Rouayheb points out, al-Nābulusī was always 'eager to distinguish the mystical love he defended from illicit lust, let alone sodomy'.[26]

★ ★ ★

The sexual acts which flowed from illicit lust were illicit in the fullest sense: contrary to law. Islamic law was based on the Koran and the *sunnah* (sayings and actions of the Prophet, as recorded by the *hadīths*), but like any system of law it depended on reasoning—about similar cases, underlying principles, and so on. And where sodomy was concerned, the lack of specificity in the Koran, as noted above, left some room for reasoned arguments to proceed to differing conclusions. One key point on which opinions diverged was the question of whether sodomy was to be included in the concept of *zinā*—a term sometimes translated as 'fornication', but with the more general meaning 'illicit sexual relations between a man and a woman'. This was important because *zinā* belonged to a small group of special offences, such as unbelief, murder and drunkenness, which were seen as transgressing the rights of God, not just the rights of human beings. Such crimes belonged to the category *hudūd*, meaning that God had revealed specific penalties for them. Out of the four historic schools of law in Sunnite Islam, three did view sodomy as essentially a form of *zinā*, and did call for very strict penalties. (Their reasonings still diverged, however: Shafi'ites demanded the stoning to death of the active male, if a married man, but not of the passive one; Hanbalites decreed the stoning of married men; Malikites would stone both partners unconditionally.) But the contrary approach was taken by the Hanafites; and although the other schools of law did operate in some parts of the Ottoman Empire, it was the Hanafite school that predominated, as it was officially accepted by the Ottoman sultans. Hanafites argued that *zinā* referred only to illicit vaginal sex, from which it followed that sodomy had no specified punishment in the Koran; this meant that it must fall into the category of *jināyāt*, regular crimes, not special offences against God. They noted that various early traditions did refer to companions of the Prophet meting out severe punishments of different kinds, including death by burning or being thrown off a high building; but the conclusion they drew from this was that the precise nature of the penalty lay within the discretion of the judge. And, to maintain a proper distinction between offences against humans and offences against God, it was normal practice to punish one of the former less severely: if the penalty was whipping, the number of lashes had to be lower than the lowest number prescribed for one of the latter

offences. Hanafite jurists did commonly recommend whipping or imprisonment as the punishment for sodomy, with the possibility of a death sentence only for frequent offenders. Where other forms of male–male sexual
activity were concerned, not involving anal penetration, the Hanafites proposed discretionary punishment at the level appropriate for a minor sin; and
on this point the other three schools agreed with them.[27]

Trials in courts of shariah law tended to be simpler affairs than their
counterparts in Western Christendom. Unless the perpetrator of an offence
confessed voluntarily, everything depended on the witnesses—not only on the
statements they made, but on the status they held as individuals. Witnesses
had to be Muslim free men of good character. To convict anyone of a sexual
crime of this nature, it was necessary for them to have observed the act itself
as eye-witnesses; hearsay evidence was ruled out entirely, and merely to have
seen telltale signs of movement under a blanket, for example, or to have
heard sounds, however unmistakeable, would not suffice. All the witnesses
had to appear before the judge and denounce the act immediately. If they
did not, they were obliged to keep silent. For the Hanafite school only two
witnesses were needed, whereas the other three schools, regarding sodomy
as *zinā*, accepted the Koranic requirement of four witnesses for such an
offence. The unlikelihood of two, let alone four, men directly witnessing
the act of penetration was a point which did not escape the attention of the
jurists; but, as Khaled El-Rouayheb has pointed out, some of them expressed
positive contentment with this, on the grounds that God did not want the
sins of his people to be exposed unless they were gross and frequent. Arno
Schmitt similarly draws attention to the influence of a number of commonly quoted *ḥadīth*s, which condemned spying on one's neighbours or
gossiping about them.[28]

For subjects of the Ottoman Empire, shariah law was not the only legal
framework of their lives. They were governed by the Sultan's own law-code,
the *kanun*, which was a sort of compound of shariah law, customary law and
sultanic decrees. Where sexual offences of all kinds were concerned, the
penalties imposed by this code were much more lenient: for sodomy, they
consisted mostly of fines. According to the *kanun* of Süleyman the
Magnificent, a married man was to be fined, according to his wealth,
between 40 and 300 *akçe*s (a small silver coin, and standard unit of account),
while the equivalent tariff for an unmarried man ranged from 30 to 100. If
a boy above the age of puberty (roughly, the mid-teens) had yielded to
penetration by a man, the judge was to order a beating for him and collect

a fine of one *akçe* for each stroke; 'and if he is not of age, his father shall be chastised [sc. beaten] because he has not guarded [him], but no fine shall be collected'. If young boys performed sexual acts with one another, a fine of 30 *akçe*s was to be levied from each—meaning, in practice, from the boy's father—but no beating was imposed. (For a man who had sodomized his wife, a serious but unspecified beating was prescribed, with a fine of one *akçe* per stroke—a sort of adult counterpart to the punishment for a post-pubertal passive boy.)[29]

These financial penalties were more than symbolic, but not at all severe. The *akçe* contained 0.7 g of silver until the mid-1580s, when the currency began to be debased; by 1600 this had brought it down to 0.3 g. In the 1590s a Janissary on garrison duty was paid up to seven *akçe*s per day (c.2,500 a year), while a judge could be paid 80 per day (c.29,000 a year).[30] In 1576 a convert from Islam called Gil, who was originally from North Africa, appeared before the Lisbon Inquisition on a charge of sodomy. When he was asked about such behaviour in his homeland, he said that he had often engaged in it there, 'because in his land the only punishment was to be arrested and then freed after making a payment'.[31]

An important difference between shariah law and the *kanun* was that the latter dispensed with the strict requirements for eye-witnesses: indeed, it made possible conviction on what Dror Ze'evi has called 'flimsy circumstantial grounds'. There was thus a kind of complementary relationship between the two legal systems. In theory, whenever the strict requirements of the sacred law could be satisfied, that law was to be applied, with its more severe penalties. The sultanic law-code would function as a back-up: it would deal with the less proveable cases, applying a lower standard of evidence, but also imposing much less serious punishments.[32] Yet in reality the requirements of shariah law were almost never met, and prosecutions under the *kanun* were also rare; in eighteenth-century Istanbul, for example, charges would be brought only in egregious cases involving force, while consensual sodomy was simply ignored. A detailed study of sexual offences in eighteenth-century Aleppo comments on the rarity of sodomy cases in the shariah court records (where just three are mentioned, only two of which were punished), and suggests that one reason for this was 'the popularity of the practice, which, although frowned upon, was pervasive socially'.[33]

To conclude: while sodomy was very definitely an offence in both these systems of law, that fact could generate very little effect in terms of deterrence.

On the one side, the chance of being convicted was extremely small; on the other, the likelihood of being prosecuted was quite low, and, if a conviction followed, the punishment was typically just a fine. (What is more, from the late sixteenth century onwards the fine was a diminishing one in real terms, as the law specified a fixed number of *akçes*, the value of which was eroded by recurrent debasements of the coinage.) Either or both of these flaws in the system were noticed by Western observers and writers. As early as the mid-thirteenth century, the polemical theologian Ramon Martí argued that although Islam condemned sodomy, the absurd requirement of four witnesses meant that, in reality, it encouraged the practice. Theodore Spandounes, the Greek author who had been brought up in the Ottoman Balkans and wrote his account of the Ottoman system in the early sixteenth century, said that while Muhammad had denounced sodomites, the fine they were made to pay was feeble. In the middle of that century the French scholar and traveller Guillaume Postel claimed that the fine was only six *akçes*. A report on the Ottomans by the Ragusan diplomat Francesco Gondola (Franjo Gundulić) in 1574 observed that they were 'lustful, and in the most perverse way, even though their law decrees that they should be punished, together with the passive partner, by being thrown from the highest tower in the city; but a degree of circumstantial proof is required which is almost impossible'. And in the 1670s the experienced missionary Michel Febvre wrote that punishments for sexual crimes against nature were almost never carried out, and that this fact had the effect of increasing the number of offences.[34] When Christian writers implied that such evidence demonstrated a deliberate encouragement of sodomy, their argument was entirely prejudicial. No judge, in a court of either sacred or sultanic law, would have entertained any such purpose. But the lack of any major deterrent effect was a reality, not something invented by Western commentators; and it seems that the leniency of the secular law did reflect a general sense of relative tolerance among the population.

★ ★ ★

In a previous chapter we looked at literary expressions and representations of male–male sexual desire in Western Mediterranean societies. The evidence from Iberia was extremely limited, and entirely negative. Italy yielded a larger quantity of texts, and some of the more daring ones among them did take on the task of expressing sodomitical desire directly. Yet, overall, this was a very small and rather disparate assortment of materials, not at all typical of the major literary genres of the time, existing often in a kind of semi-obscurity, and sometimes subjected to active censorship. The contrast with the literary culture of the mediaeval and early modern Islamic world could hardly be greater.

Descriptions of the physical charms of beautiful boys, expressions of love for such youths, and references not only to the desire to have sex with them but also to the accomplishment of that desire: all of these were common. Beautiful women were also described, and the desire for them expressed, but homoeroticism was not a subsidiary theme in this type of literature—it was the predominant one. And while this is true of the Arabic literature of most of the Middle Ages and the early modern period (where one modern scholar has referred to 'the saturation of literature with homoerotic sentiment'), it is even more true of the Ottoman Turkish *divan* poetry, short lyric poems gathered in popular collections, which developed under Persian and Arabic influence from the late thirteenth century to the end of the eighteenth.[35]

The earliest stages of this development have not been well charted. One scholar detects elements of homoeroticism in pre-Islamic Arabic texts, but there is little trace of these themes in the writings of the first century of Islam; another refers to 'the sudden appearance of pederasty as a literary theme in early Abbasid poetry'—that is, after the commencement of the Abbasid caliphate in AD 750.[36] One of the greatest erotic poets in Arabic, Abū Nuwās, was born a few years after that date, and would spend the latter part of his life in the newly founded city (and cultural centre) of Baghdad, dying there in c.816. He developed a literary style known as *mujūn*, a hard-to-translate term which implied licentiousness, coarseness and frivolity; the leading modern expert, Zoltan Szombathy, characterizes its essential principles as 'on the one hand a decided disregard for the usual norms of honourable behaviour...and on the other a jestful, tongue-in-cheek attitude'.[37] Much of the effect of this writing came from the shamelessly explicit way in which it presented—typically in the first person—the breaking of taboos, and for this reason sodomy was one of its favourite themes. As Szombathy puts it, 'Given the ubiquity of homosexual affairs in the greatest cities of the mediaeval Middle East, the difference between an ordinary man pursuing sex with adolescent boys and a libertine doing the same was not the habit itself, but the deliberate lack of discretion on the part of the libertine.' Of course, the use of the first person did not necessarily involve making truthful statements about the poet; the desire to shock and entertain was the main thing, and the ethos of *mujūn* could encourage gross exaggeration or sheer invention. But those who have studied Abū Nuwās are generally convinced that when he declared a distinct preference for sex with boys, he was not inventing.[38] In one of his poems he wrote:

> This woman reproaches me for my choice of a boy as beautiful as an antelope;
> And she says I deprive myself of the delights of relationships with fine young girls.
> However, I say to her: 'You know nothing; the likes of me will never be duped with nonsense.
> 'Am I to choose the sea over firm land, and fish over a gazelle of the desert?'[39]

Such veiled language was untypical of Abū Nuwās, even if the transgressive meaning was clear. One of his usual shock tactics was explicitness, and another was a deliberate playing on religious beliefs and images.

> Sit down in every tavern, where wine and lovemaking are offered...
> When the month of the fast [sc. Ramadan] comes, make out like you are sick.
> And if you are asked: 'Is pederasty permitted at this time?'
> Say: 'Of course!'[40]

He was even prepared to break the ultimate sexual taboo, presenting himself as a passive sodomite, in a poem addressed to, of all people, an imam:

> Oh Sulayman, sing to me
> and give me a cup of wine...
> Give me a cup of distraction
> from the Muezzin's call.
> Give me wine to drink publicly
> and bugger and fuck me now'[41]

And not only did he turn elements of his religion to ribald purposes (for example, using the meaning of *islam*, 'submission', to argue that Jewish, Christian and Zoroastrian boys must let him penetrate them); he also expressed outright disbelief in the existence of an afterlife.[42]

Through the poetry of Abū Nuwās we glimpse a culture of male–male sexual behaviour which was already fully established. He refers, for example, to boy prostitutes; he says that while the *hamam* is a good place for looking at youths, the tavern is better, as there you can make a boy drunk in order to have sex with him; and he emphasizes the importance of beardlessness, saying that when facial hair begins to grow on a young man's cheek he turns into an ape.[43] Abū Nuwās was presumably not the first writer to give literary expression to elements of this flourishing culture; he seems to have found an audience that was already primed to be appreciative of this sort of material. He was frequently quoted and imitated.

Sexual explicitness was cultivated not only in this kind of poetry, but also in a range of prose works which parodically adopted the forms of learned dissertations or even sermons. The prolific ninth-century scholar al-Jāḥiẓ (who was himself no libertine) wrote a work assessing the rival claims of male–male and male–female sex; his younger contemporary Abū l-Anbas al-Ṣaymarī composed a treatise entitled 'Book of the Superiority of Arse-Lovers to Cunt-Lovers and Sodomizers to Womanizers' (in addition to full-length works on lesbianism, male prostitution and masturbation); the Persian-born poet and physician Abū l-Faraj 'Alī b. Hindū, who died in the early eleventh century, produced an epistle 'Mediating between Fornicators and Sodomizers'.[44] In the words of one modern scholar, 'Erotological hand-books were written on the sizes of the holes of boys and women, with volumes more devoted to the shape and beauty of male and female buttocks and to the sexual activity that seems to have been most popular, anal inter-course with boys and women.'[45] Nor was this interest in male–male sex confined to works of deliberate coarseness, bawdy humour or parodic ingenuity. There was no comic intent on the part of the author of the *Qābūsnāme*, an eleventh-century Persian 'mirror of princes' text, when he recommended having sex with women in the winter and boys in the summer.[46]

Central to the literary culture of this entire period, from the early part of the Abbasid dynasty to the first three centuries of Ottoman rule, was the writing of love poetry, typically in the form of the *ghazal* (Turkish: *gazel*). This was a roughly sonnet-length poem of rhyming couplets expressing the feelings—physical admiration, devotion, hopelessness, and so on—of the lover towards his beloved. *Ghazals* could be tests of the poet's ingenuity in the use of symbolism and allusive language; yet at the same time they typic-ally worked with a standard stock of metaphors and similes for the beautiful features of the loved one, who had a face like the moon, teeth like pearls, and so on. Because much of this standard imagery could be applied indis-criminately to boys or women (as with the blazon of beauty in Western European poetry), prudish modern editors have felt able to claim that these works were mostly about the latter; but as Khaled El-Rouayheb points out, references to things that unmistakeably indicate the masculine nature of the beloved, such as his name, his occupation, his being encountered in the mosque or the *hamam*, and above all the eventual growth of his 'beard-down', prove the falsity of that argument.[47] Similarly, the fact that spiritual references were sometimes also woven into the text, especially by writers influenced by the Sufi tradition, has led some modern interpreters to claim that the genre was essentially devotional; but this too is misleading. Most *ghazal*s were love poems, and most concerned beloved boys; typically they were chaste (though passionate) in tone, but they could also refer to erotic physical acts of various kinds.

The genre spread rapidly throughout the Islamic world. In Muslim Andalusia—where homoerotic poetry, again, predominated—it influenced a number of Hebrew poets, who developed their own imitation of the *ghazal*, called the *ṣevi*. One of the first examples, by the eleventh-century writer Yiṣḥaq ben Mar-Saul, exclaims: 'Lovely of eyes like David, | he has slain me like Uriah. | He has enflamed my passions | and consumed my heart with fire'; his younger contemporary Solomon Ibn Gabirol (born c.1021) wrote about the beloved's first beard-down: 'Say to him whose hair embraces his cheek: | how can noon embrace the morning!'; and Moses Ibn Ezra (1055–c.1135/40), perhaps the greatest Jewish poet of Spain, composed the lines: 'Night and day I was only with him. | I undressed him, and he undressed me; | I sucked his lips and he sucked mine.'[48]

In the Arabic- and Turkish-speaking lands, poetry of this kind was written throughout the late-mediaeval and early modern period. It was supplemented by other genres and forms. One was the *wasf*, a short epigram on the beauty of a boy or woman; a fifteenth-century collection of these contains more than 2,500 examples, almost all of them about boys.[49] Another genre which became very popular among Ottoman Turkish writers from the sixteenth century onwards was the *şehrengiz*, an extended poem listing and describing the beautiful young people of a particular town. The word 'people' is used here because there is one work in this form which lists beautiful women (including a number of prostitutes); but otherwise all known examples, of which there were at least 60 by the middle of the seventeenth century, were about handsome male youths. Probably the *şehrengiz* was derived from a Persian genre which went back at least to the early twelfth century; its development interacted with a growing taste among Turkish readers for collections of *gazel*s about young craftsmen, shop-boys and apprentices.[50] And beyond these there were other kinds of work that depended on bawdy humour, such as the compilation, in prose and verse, of comic-erotic stories and observations by the poet Deli Birader (known as Gazālī), written for the entertainment of a prince in c.1500, which contained a substantial chapter about sex with boys.[51] The spirit of

mujūn lived on. When the poet Sa'yi left his côterie of friends in Istanbul
for the city of Edirne in the mid-sixteenth century, he sent them a high-
flown poetic epistle:

> What news, oh east wind, how are things in the world?
> Are Istanbul and Galata still as lovely?...
> Do the pure-born still flow like water towards Molla's Bath?...
> Do lovers still recite adorned *gazels* about the beautiful ones?'[52]

From the poet Sani he received the following reply:

> If you're wondering, descriptions of your verses
>   are still written
> On the walls and door of the privy
>   in the Molla's Bathhouse...
>
> If only he'd come and get tipsy
>   we'd bugger him, they say.
> For you, friends have their cocks ready in hand,
>   the heads wet with spit...
>
> Both prince and pander are distraught
>   since you left.
> Come and be the filling between layers
>   of pederast and catamite.[53]

★ ★ ★

It is now possible to draw together some of the threads of the argument
where the overall differences between 'East' and 'West' are concerned. The
religious norms were fundamentally very similar. Both Christianity and
Islam were set firmly against sodomy. In some ways there may have been a
little more room for variations of opinion on the Islamic side: some *hadīths*
might be accepted by rigorists, and rejected by others. But that would make
little difference overall. On a question which was both theological and legal
(though those two categories are generally hard to distinguish in Islam),
namely, whether sodomy was condemned in the Koran as an offence against
humans or as an offence directly against God, there was a real divergence of
views between different Muslim jurists. But that too would not affect the
essential position.

In one way Christianity's disapproval was more far-reaching: it developed
a more elaborate moral–theological scheme to describe 'sins against nature',
including such things as masturbation; and while there was scope for

conceptual confusion between these and sodomy in the narrow sense, there was general agreement that they were all mortal sins. The two seventeen-year-old boys who were executed in Seville for mutual masturbation would not have met any such fate in the Muslim world, not just because of different legal arrangements, but because the religious and moral disapproval of their actions by all those around them, including the authorities, would have been much less intense.[54]

The other significant difference between the two religions is that one of them could support, over many centuries, a tradition which regarded 'gazing' at young male beauty as a genuinely devotional act. True, this was not part of what is often called 'official' Islam, the Islam of the mosque and the madrasa; but the Sufi orders should certainly not be thought of as fringe phenomena, as they penetrated most parts of Muslim society and had a huge influence on ordinary religious life. It is very hard to imagine such devotional 'gazing' being promoted by any form of organized Christianity in the West. The closest equivalent would be the teaching of the small number of Italian humanists who consciously revived the Neoplatonic doctrine of beauty and love. (This resemblance is probably not coincidental, given that the Sufi doctrine, at least as it was formalized by writers such as Ibn 'Arabī, seems to have had its roots in Platonic and Neoplatonic philosophy.) At best, those Italians represented a very minor phenomenon of élite lay culture, quite extraneous to the Church.

Turning to legal norms, we find a more marked difference between the two sides. After sodomy became viewed by Christian theologians as a collective issue, apparently because of the supposed connection with heresy, there was an expectation that the secular power would apply severe physical punishments, including death. The legal procedures that were involved, including some ecclesiastical ones adapted to secular law, were calibrated at a level that made conviction possible, and many were indeed convicted. In principle Islam, with its assumption that the principles of religion must at the same time be the principles of law, had also required heavy legal penalties; but the procedures it stipulated in the courts of shariah law made conviction much less likely. The penalties imposed by Ottoman sultanic law, on the other hand, were so light as to be barely deterrent. The closest equivalent to the sultanic tariff of fines is the light-handed regime of the Florentine 'Office of the Night'. But Florence was exceptional; and there was still a significant difference between the two cases. The Florentine authorities, badgered by the clergy and troubled by their own consciences, regarded the presence in their society of any form of sodomy—including the consensual kind—as a serious problem; it was only because they thought it serious that they went to the trouble of creating such a magistrature and lightening the penalties in order to encourage denunciations and confessions. Nothing like that is visible on the Ottoman side, where social attitudes were much more easy-going.

The greatest difference between the two sides, however, is visible at the level of culture. The contrast with Iberian and Italian literary production has already been noted; those Western literatures could not begin to match the degree of homoerotic feeling that permeated the writings of Ottoman Arab and Turkish authors. Of course, if we are to treat this fact as evidence, we should approach it with some care. In his carefully measured judgement on the Ottoman Arabic materials, Khaled El-Rouayheb notes that literary conventions have their own force: for any given writer, the fact that he composed a poem in a homoerotic genre will not necessarily mean that he was expressing his personal feelings. But, he points out, if a whole culture accepts and enjoys such genres, that must tell us something about the underlying social reality.[55] El-Rouayheb's perspective at this point is that of a historian using literature as evidence of actual conduct. In any complex matter of human behaviour, however, the same things may be both consequences and causes; the widespread cultural celebration of homoeroticism was surely not only a reflection of the social reality, but also a stimulus to it. In the early modern Ottoman Empire the pursuit of boys, often with feelings of passion and devotion, was woven into patterns of male social life and conviviality. As Walter Andrews and Mehmet Kalpaklı have shown, the writing and reciting of homoerotic poetry was also an intrinsic part of that milieu where the more educated men were concerned. (This was not just an élite phenomenon. The Scottish traveller William Lithgow commented generally on the Ottomans' songs about 'Lovers, whom they openly name in their rimes, without rebuke or shame'; Jean Thévenot noted that the vice of sodomy was so unashamedly acknowledged that 'all their songs are about nothing other than these infamous loves, or wine.')[56] In Florence, men certainly existed who felt passionately attached to particular boys; but they appear only rarely in the records. They had no publicly acceptable way of expressing those feelings, or of hearing them expressed by others. In Ottoman society, almost the reverse was the case: the practice was culturally validated, to the point where one might well suspect that some men adopted the role of love-poet, or indeed lover, when their heart was not really in it. There was a cult of love, as well as a practice of sex. The former was partly sustained by literary culture; and that culture was a stimulus not only to the same-sex behaviour, whether Platonic or physical, but to the degree of avowability with which it could be conducted.

This last point, about the openness of the behaviour, brings us back to the issue of the reports by Western—especially, Western Mediterranean—observers. We have seen that there are good reasons for suspecting the presence of prejudice in their accounts; yet, as we have also seen, even when one has made full allowance for that, they cannot be accused overall of inventing the phenomenon they described. So should we just say that they—at least, the ones from the Western Mediterranean—were being hypocritical? To some extent, depending on the strength and nature of the disapproval expressed by particular writers, the answer must be yes. But that answer does not suffice. The interactions of religious norms, legal norms and cultural expressions were genuinely different on the two sides; a single form of underlying sexual behaviour was, so to speak, differently modulated. This had real effects, and the observers were not wrong to remark on them.

It is very common to find, in a given society, some disjunction between norms and practice. To take an obvious example: many societies have strongly reprobated fornication, while tolerating prostitution. Where early modern attitudes to sodomy were concerned, the differences between the two parts of the Mediterranean involved both norms and actual conduct. On the one hand the Western norms had taken, in effect, a harsher line; while this widened the gap between norms and practice in the Western Mediterranean societies, it also put pressure on the practitioners to behave less openly. And on the other hand, while the Eastern norms were less severe in the way they operated, the disjunction between norms and practice there was more noticeable because the sexual practices could afford to be more visible, enjoying as they did some cultural legitimation. Where actual sexual conduct was concerned, discretion was needed on both sides; but the need was greater in the 'West', while more openness was possible in the 'East'.

And this prompts a final thought about the so-called renegades, very many of whom had Western Mediterranean origins. Recognizing the Mediterranean pattern of same-sex relations as a whole makes it possible to offer a simpler and better explanation of the alleged link between their sodomy and their conversion to Islam. De Nicolay's comment on the renegades of Algiers was that they were 'above all, many from Spain, Italy and Provence, the islands and coasts of the Mediterranean, all addicted to lewdness, sodomy, theft, and all other detestable vices'.[57] Most had been slaves before they converted. Salomon Schweigger, Stefan Gerlach's successor as chaplain at the Imperial embassy in Istanbul, remarked about the inhabitants of the slave *bagno* there that 'they are addicted to all vices; but especially the Spaniards and Italians do shameful acts against nature, as is their custom'; Reinhold Lubenau, apothecary to the Imperial ambassador in the late 1580s, said it was the Italians in the *bagno* who enacted 'horrible vice and sodomitical behaviour with one another'.[58] (Note that it is Southern Europeans—not Northerners, who were also present—who are singled out in these descriptions.) In many cases, it seems, for a renegade to be a sodomite was not to display some new vice occasioned by Islam or by the abandonment of Western life; rather, it was to continue with a previous form of behaviour (acquired in the Western Mediterranean), merely doing so with a sense of greater freedom from constraint.

If Gregorio the barber had succeeded in escaping from the bailate and converting to Islam, he too might have followed that pattern, enjoying that greater liberty. Gianesino, as a native resident of Galata—a place both Ottoman and cosmopolitan, described by the sixteenth-century Turkish poet Laṭīfī as 'the greatest tavern in the world, famous for its wine and its beauties, and reputed to be a place of debauchery'—may have enjoyed it to a large extent already.[59] But the *bailo* felt that a cultural distinction of real importance was at stake, and it was his decision that prevailed.

14

Northern Europe: broad patterns

Until this point, our attention has being focused almost exclusively on the territories of the Mediterranean region. All the evidence confirms that the predominant model of male–male sexual behaviour was essentially the same throughout that whole area. Northern Europe—or, to be precise, the northern part of Western Christian Europe—has been left, hitherto, on one side. And there are good reasons for that. It is not just that the evidence from the North is, before the eighteenth century, much less full, both quantitatively and qualitatively, though that is certainly the case (and, as we shall see, carries its own significance). It is that this evidence, when analysed properly, points towards a very different conclusion. Male–male sexual relations in the North have a different history; and while the forms of behaviour exhibited there may have overlapped in some ways with those of the South, there were major dissimilarities. The pan-Mediterranean pattern was not pan-European.

A few modern historians have commented in passing on some aspects of this differentiation, when discussing a particular country or period; but the scale and nature of the divergence between North and South have never been properly addressed. And the voices of those few who have dissented, if only in part, have been drowned out by a large and confident orthodoxy. Very little serious work had been done on male–male sexual relations in Northern Europe until Alan Bray produced his path-breaking study, *Homosexuality in Renaissance England*, in 1982. In it he commented on the surprising paucity of direct evidence from the period before 1700, such as records of English sodomy trials—a fact which many social historians have subsequently confirmed. His explanation was that there were few trials because the population generally accepted that male–male sex was a common

Forbidden Desire in Early Modern Europe: Male–Male Sexual Relations, 1400–1750. Noel Malcolm, Oxford University Press.
© Noel Malcolm 2024. DOI: 10.1093/oso/9780198886334.003.0014

feature of life; people would be denounced and prosecuted only if they had broken some higher-level rules of social order—for example, using violence or offending against social hierarchy. But what evidence was there that male–male sex really was such a feature of everyday life? How were these men actually behaving, and how can we know about their behaviour? These questions were not answered at all adequately; those who sympathized for whatever reason with Bray's basic assumption that male–male sexual relations were common, and commonly accepted, were left facing a gap which seemed hard to fill.

So when, over the next decade and a half, there appeared a number of scholarly studies of sodomy in early modern Mediterranean societies—from the relevant chapter of Guido Ruggiero's *The Boundaries of Eros* (1985) to Michael Rocke's outstanding *Forbidden Friendships* (1996)—the flow of new information seemed like an answer to a prayer. It was no longer quite so necessary, perhaps not even necessary at all, to substantiate a claim about a Northern European society by finding evidence from that society itself. Instead, it was sufficient, apparently, to refer to the wealth of evidence from Florence, and to use the situation in that part of Southern Europe as a template which could conveniently be lowered onto the Northern European case. And so the lack of convincing evidence that sexual behaviour in London was just like sexual behaviour in Florence was not a problem; or at least it ceased to be seen as a problem, as historians assumed that the Florentine evidence would do the job just as well.

This approach was then subsumed under a larger argument. One of the points on which it could be argued that practitioners of sodomy in early modern England resembled their Italian counterparts was the idea that they desired, indifferently, both boys and women. (Some English evidence—for example, statements by Restoration rakes—was put forward in favour of this, though, as we shall see, it needs careful scrutiny.) But for the period from the late 1690s to the 1720s there was quite a rich body of English documentation, including, at long last, a good number of trial records, which led Bray and other historians to conclude that a different kind of sexual conduct was appearing at that time: this involved men whose sexual interest was primarily or exclusively focused on other males, very much including adult men. And it seemed to exhibit other features too, including consciously effeminate behaviour, and private social gatherings of like-minded men, where a sense of common identity might be expressed and developed. Other evidence from the early eighteenth century, in France and the Netherlands, was quite similar. And so the larger historical claim was formed: whereas male–male sexual relations before c.1700 were quite unlike modern homosexuality, as they conformed to the Florentine model, something recognizably close to modern homosexuality emerged in these Northern European societies around that time.

This more ambitious argument has attracted dissent, though the dissenters have remained a small and rather neglected minority. Some of the most cogent objections have come from Rictor Norton, a scholar who has studied the early-eighteenth-century English evidence with great care, reaching some different conclusions. But even for readers without Norton's specialist knowledge, there were what looked like worrying weaknesses in the argument. No particular causes had been identified that would account for this major historic change. And the extraordinary suddenness of it—the emergence of a whole new form of sexual behaviour and personality within a couple of decades—was also entirely unexplained. These points were well made by those few historians who expressed dissenting judgements. But those who defended the argument were also committed to another rather puzzling proposition. What they regarded as a pan-European pattern—i.e. what has been identified in this book as the Mediterranean one—disappeared quite rapidly, they said, in Northern Europe, but only there; apparently it continued more or less undisturbed for at least a couple of centuries in Southern Europe. This problem too was never properly examined, even by their critics. The idea that sexual behaviour in the North had been essentially the same as in the South remained the working assumption of almost everyone in the field. It is to that assumption, for the period before 1700, that we should now turn.

★ ★ ★

Trial statistics, as we have seen, cannot be used for comparative purposes with any degree of precision. There are too many variables between different societies and legal regimes, too many dificulties in trying to calibrate the varying degrees of policing of different parts of a given population (urban versus rural, for example), and too many unknowns about the factors that may have promoted, or reduced, the impulse to denounce and prosecute. Only the most broad-brush comparisons are possible, and they will be at their least unreliable when they concern sheer orders of magnitude. It is on that basis that we should look at the contrast between the statistics from Mediterranean societies and those from Northern Europe.

The huge figures for Florence and Lucca must be largely set aside here, as we know that they were generated by special judicial regimes which had no equivalents elsewhere. Other cities and territories provide more typical statistics. To recapitulate: in Venice, 264 sodomy cases were tried in the fifteenth century, involving 498 individuals, and in the early sixteenth century the frequency of such trials rose to more than five per year. In Rome, one of the courts that dealt with this offence—the records of the other main court, unfortunately, do not survive—held at least 47 sodomy trials in the period 1560–85. In Seville, 71 men are known to have been executed for sodomy in 1567–1616 (which suggests that a significantly larger number of men and boys were tried); in Valencia, 107 trials were held in 1571–1600. In Barcelona there were 124 trials, involving 137 individuals, in 1540–1640.[1]

As for Northern Europe: in Denmark and Norway, taken together, only five cases (one of which, in 1628, concerned two members of a Scottish regiment) are known before 1700. The best documented involved an army captain who had abused his position, forcing some of his soldiers to submit to 'bodily intercourse in a sodomitical manner'.[2] Four pre-1700 cases of male–male sex are known in Sweden; of these, one concerned a boy who had apparently fellated an older youth in exchange for a knife, and another involved a ten-year-old who, on 'five separate occasions', had lain with a nine-year-old 'as with a woman'.[3] Two cases are known in Scotland before 1700.[4]

In fifteenth-century Regensburg, where quite detailed judicial records survive, only two sodomy cases are known.[5] Two sodomites were punished in Frankfurt in the entire period 1562–1696, and four in Nuremberg between 1594 and 1692.[6] In Bavaria three cases are known from the period 1363–1625; one of these concerned an Italian, Astorre Leoncelli, Master of the Horse to the Duke of Bavaria, who was executed in 1603 for having had sex with several male partners including a ten-year-old boy.[7] Between 1592 and 1700 the records of the Duchy of Württemberg provide just three cases.[8]

In Austria, a recent study of sodomy cases has found only three in the period 1581–1780, of which two were concerned with male–female sodomy and the third, which was male–male, occurred in the latter part of that period, in 1742.[9] In Switzerland, the records of the city and territory of Lucerne yield four executions for sodomy in 1530–1607. (This was a jurisdiction where such offences were taken very seriously: in 1489 two men were burnt at the stake for mutual masturbation.)[10] In Basel, if we exclude the group of Italian soldiers put on trial in 1474, there were roughly ten sodomy cases between 1399 and 1799.[11] For the city and canton of Zurich, one study has found five executions for sodomy in the fifteenth century, and eight in the sixteenth; another calculates that there were approximately 20 cases brought to trial in the period 1568–1668.[12] And in Geneva, a cosmopolitan trading city connected with the Mediterranean world, 60 men or boys were tried for sodomy in the period 1400–1650; of those, one was Greek, three were described as 'Turks', six were Italians and seventeen were French, some from France's Mediterranean provinces.[13]

In the city of Leiden, out of roughly 5,000 criminal sentences in the period 1533–1729, two were for male–male sex: one in 1645 and one in 1684.[14] In Amsterdam the records reveal just two convictions for sodomy in the sixteenth century, and combining Amsterdam, The Hague and Utrecht yields only 34 for the whole period 1400–1650 (33 if we subtract one offender who was Italian).[15] The detailed judicial records of the *ammanie* of Brussels, an administrative district extending far beyond the city itself and containing a large part of the duchy of Brabant, yield 26 convictions for sodomy in the fifteenth century, seven in the sixteenth, and none in the seventeenth.[16] Combining that territory with six of the other largest cities of the southern Netherlands—Bruges, Antwerp, Malines, Ghent, Ypres and Louvain—produces a higher total: in 1400–1700, 181 trials were held, with 305 people convicted (of whom 234 were executed).[17] Yet since the population involved was, at a rough estimate, between 250,000 and 300,000 for much of that period, the rate of prosecution was still much lower than in Venice or Seville.

Six of those towns, taken individually, had only modest rates of conviction: in fifteenth-century Ghent, for example, which was one of the largest cities in the region, fourteen men were executed for sodomy and seven cases ended with the payment of a fine.[18] The total for all seven cities in the early modern period is swollen by one exceptional case: half the convictions were in Bruges, where a vigorous anti-sodomy campaign occurred in the latter part of the fifteenth century, bringing the number of executions there to 73 during that century as a whole. In the whole period 1395–1515, the authorities in Bruges executed 90 people, while nine were flogged and three were fined. Admittedly, not all of the convictions were for sodomy in the narrow sense. A recent study of sodomy cases in both Bruges and Ghent estimates that up to 15 per cent of those convicted were women; it seems that, unusually, the magistrates hunted down practitioners of female–female sex. Some men or boys were punished—usually with a fine, or exile—for *mollities*, mutual masturbation. And up to eight of the men included in the overall total for the seven cities were from the Mediterranean region. Nevertheless, even after these adjustments have been made, the scale of the prosecutions in Bruges remains a puzzling phenomenon. The authorities seem to have been determined to convict, allowing very few acquittals in comparison with the treatment of such cases in Ghent. In 1475 they took it upon themselves to investigate an allegation that a man had had sex with another man 20 years earlier; the other man, who had been in his late teens at the time, was now prosecuted, convicted and executed. Marc Boone, the historian who first investigated this body of evidence, suggested that the municipal authorities were acting out of a politically motivated desire to show that they could manage their own affairs better than the dukes of Burgundy, their feudal overlords; but as Mariann Naessens has pointed out, exactly the same political attitude was present in Ghent, where no such anti-sodomy campaign occurred. She puts forward the possible explanation that sodomy really was more prevalent in Bruges, because of that city's close commercial contacts with Italy. But even if that claim is correct, it surely does not explain the fervency of the authorities' approach. For whatever reason, the city seems to have been undergoing a prolonged moral panic, of the kind that strengthens and exacerbates itself as it uncovers more evidence of what it fears.[19]

The case of France may be a more complex one, for the obvious reason that France was a country both Mediterranean and Northern European. It is also relatively poorly served by modern studies; the local archives of northern France have not been searched in any systematic way. An account of the criminal law and its applications in the period c.1350–c.1450 has found a few isolated sodomy cases—one in Tournai in 1385, for example, and one in Caen in 1452—but concludes that this crime was rare.[20] One chronicler wrote that many sodomites from Picardy were burnt at Lille, after being prosecuted by the Church, in the years 1457–60; the circumstances, and the actual numbers involved, are unknown.[21] As that statement reminds us, this was a *delictum mixti fori*, justiciable in ecclesiastical courts as well as secular ones. For the diocese of Troyes in north-eastern France, detailed records survive of the 'officiality' court (presided over by the official who represented the bishop) in the fifteenth century. The documentation covers many sexual offences, but does not yield a single case of sodomy.[22] A sixteenth-century Parisian chronicler noted two convictions for sodomy, in Blois in 1533 and in Lyon in 1534; in each case, however, the offender was

Italian.[23] According to one modern scholar, the officiality court of Senlis tried a priest in 1614 for the attempted seduction of a youth who was a novice monk; yet while the man was certainly accused of helping the boy to abscond from his monastery, there is no convincing evidence of any sexual activity, or even of a sexual motive.[24] When a major collection of law cases, Jean Papon's *Recueil d'arrests notables des cours souverains de France*, was published in 1565, it contained one case of female–female sex but no male–male sodomy at all; the revised and enlarged edition published in 1648 did mention four male–male cases, but one of these involved an Italian, burnt in Paris in 1584. The historian who has drawn attention to this source comments that sodomy cases were very rare, constituting 'a tiny fraction of the crimes relating to the family and to sexuality that were committed by French people in this period'.[25]

The only major body of evidence from the courts of northern France to have been analysed so far consists of the cases heard on appeal at the Parlement de Paris. This was the highest court for a huge area—mostly but not exclusively northern—with a population of 8–10 million, representing more than half of the French population. Verdicts involving capital punishment were the ones most likely to be appealed against, and sodomy was a capital offence. In the period 1540–1700, the Parlement dealt with appeals from 131 men convicted of sodomy. That seems a very small number for such a huge catchment area over such a large timescale. What is more, nearly thirty of these cases were from the southern half of France, and/or involved Italians. The most recent study of this evidence, by Tom Hamilton, comments that the magistrates of the Parlement 'rarely prosecuted anybody for sodomy at all'.[26]

Of all the territories of Northern Europe, England is the one best supplied not only with surviving documentation in the archives, but also with studies by modern historians. The offence of sodomy was not handled by the secular courts before the so-called Buggery Act of 1533, which for the first time made it a crime under statute law; so it is to the ecclesiastical courts that we must turn first. From the Consistory court of Rochester, the documents for most of 1347–8 and much of 1363–4 survive; they include 54 accusations of fornication and 23 defamation cases relating to adultery, but no mention of sodomy at all.[27] A study of the church courts in York from 1396 to 1489 has found roughly 400 cases of sexual offences, but sodomy was not among them.[28] An analysis of defamation cases from the Church courts of Wisbech, Durham and London in the late fifteenth century yields more than 100 cases, but none referring to sodomy.[29] From the bishop of London's Commissary court (the equivalent of a French 'officiality' court) over the period 1470–1516, we have records of 21,000 people undergoing prosecution; out of that total, just one person was accused of sodomy, and one was tried for defaming a man by accusing him of it.[30] An account of the sexual culture of late mediaeval London notes that 'Homosexual relations are almost entirely absent from the late medieval English documentary record.'[31] A study of all courts in Kent for 1460–1560 has found not a single prosecution for sodomy; and the same is reported of a study of the ecclesiastical courts of Herefordshire and Worcestershire.[32]

After 1533 sodomy cases were tried by the secular authorities—either at the Quarter Sessions or, more typically, at the county Assizes, as the statute had made it a capital offence. The records of these, from the reign of Queen Elizabeth I onwards, survive for many counties, and those for a number of Home Counties in the sixteenth and seventeenth centuries have been published. In the reigns of Elizabeth and James I (1559–1625) Kent had two cases; Surrey had two, Sussex had one, Hertfordshire had one, and Essex, with a population of c.100,000, had no cases at all.[33] Middlesex and the City of London had a special institution, with its own policing officers and judicial regime: the Bridewell Hospital. Set up in 1553, with a charter which instructed it to seach for all 'ydell [sc. idle] ruffians and taverne haunters, vagabonds, beggars and all persons of yll name and fame', it functioned as a court of justice, a venue for physical punishments such as floggings, a prison, and a house of correction involving hard labour. More than half of those processed by it were vagrants, but the rest were mostly brought in for sexual offences. Its workload was heavy: between September 1600 and August 1601 at least 300 and possibly up to 1,000 men and women were punished there for fornication, adultery and prostitution.[34] Yet in all its surviving court books, which cover most of the period from 1559 to 1610, it is possible to locate only a maximum of four sodomy cases—such as that of 'Adrian petite servt of James de grewe frencheman', who was accused in April 1561 of 'most fylthy buggery w[t] a boye', and was sentenced to be whipped. (The name, with the comment on his master, indicates that he was French, and the sentence suggests that he was probably not an adult.)[35]

As for defamation cases during this period: Alexandra Shepard's study of the Vice-Chancellor's court at Cambridge in the period 1560–1640 has found just two that involved accusations of sodomy; Shepard comments on the great rarity of such cases, compared with the many slanders referring to fornication and adultery.[36] And Laura Gowing's analysis of more than 1,600 defamation cases in London, in the period 1572–1640, reveals not a single reference to sodomitical behaviour.[37] Martin Ingram's wide-ranging study of sexual crimes in this period calls the 'paucity' of such evidence 'striking', commenting that 'there is no doubt that cases were extremely uncommon.' Ingram adds: 'The paucity of slander suits featuring accusations of buggery or sodomy, in London as elsewhere, is especially telling. Even in the most heated slanging matches in alehouses or on the open streets, it would seem that people did not raise accusations of same-sex acts or predilections… Prosecutions were perhaps more likely to occur in higher ecclesiastical courts, but even so, they were rare.'[38] There is a clear contrast here with the situation in Italy, where an analysis of libels in Rome in the period 1565–1666 finds typical examples such as 'I cite you before the Tribunal of the Capitol as a most solemn bugger', or the mock-inscription for a tombstone: 'the sodomite Broccholo lies here | Reader, flee, his spirit has the same tastes.'[39]

Beyond these statistics from the law courts, there is one other body of evidence, from pre-1700 England, of a more or less quantitative kind: the findings of the monastic visitations of 1535–6, where some accusations of sodomy were reported. One historian, taking a small and very untypical sample of this evidence, has extrapolated to claim that at least one quarter of all Englishmen engaged in male–male sex—a calculation which, he claims, 'supports the more certain Florentine figures'.[40] However, the findings of these visitations have to be approached with great care. They were hugely prejudicial exercises, designed very deliberately to discredit monasticism. (For example, after the new Injunctions had forbidden all contact with women, monks could be recorded as guilty of sexual incontinence for having any such contacts at all, including talking to two women at the monastery gate, or even taking a nun's confession through a grated window.) In cases where individual monks were absent, they could be recorded as guilty of offences merely on the basis of accusations by others—a procedure which a normal episcopal visitation would never have adopted.[41] Half-way through the entire process, the definition of sodomy was altered to include masturbation; and the entire 'Northern Visitation' seems to have recorded accusations as facts (regardless of whether the accused were absent or not), making little or no effort to validate them. Even so, without the masturbation cases the men accused of sodomy, in the usual sense, formed only 1.1 per cent of the monastic population in the Norwich Visitation and 1.3 per cent in the

Northern one—a far remove from 25 per cent or more.[42] The prejudicial procedure meant that in many of these cases the charge was not validated by confession or by any kind of proper judicial process, so it seems reasonable to assume that some of these accusations may have been malicious. Nevertheless, the fact that they were made shows that sodomy was not felt to be simply unspeakable or unthinkable. And this can only underline the significance of the almost total lack of cases involving defamation for sodomy, among the general population, in the courts.

★ ★ ★

This brief survey of statistics from non-Mediterranean territories—Germany, Austria, Switzerland, northern France, the Netherlands, Scandinavia, England and Scotland—has yielded a fairly consistent contrast with the figures from Italy and Iberia. Modern historians, committed almost unanimously to a one-size-fits-all application of the Florentine model, have not considered this evidence in the round. But some studies of northern societies have acknowledged a significant difference at the quantitative level, and have put forward, if only in passing, possible explanations for it.

In his first discussion of this issue after the publication of Michael Rocke's book, Randolph Trumbach wrote that the Florentine pattern 'probably also existed in northwestern Europe, but the records there are not so good as those for southern Europe...But the paucity of prosecutions does not demonstrate that there was very little sodomy. Instead it is likely that the severity of the law's punishment—death—made for few denunciations in a society that was not wholeheartedly committed to the Christian standard of sexual behavior.'[43] The last part of that comment may perhaps be disregarded; a society did not need to be uniformly censorious to generate denunciations for sexual offences, and the high level of prosecutions for other sexual crimes in early modern England (not only at times when the Puritan movement was strong) shows that a sufficient willingness to see offenders prosecuted was always present. Nor does it seem very plausible that the death penalty should have raised such an insuperable obstacle in people's minds, when it was commonly applied to a wide range of felonies. In particular, it was the standard penalty meted out for bestiality; and, as we shall see, there were many more prosecutions for that offence than for sodomy in early modern England. But in any case, capital punishment for sodomy was introduced only in 1533, and the paucity of evidence from the ecclesiastical courts long precedes that date.

The situation in other parts of Northern Europe was broadly similar. Throughout the Holy Roman Empire, the criminal code known as the 'Carolina' (in full: the 'Constitutio criminalis Carolina', or criminal law-code of Charles V), which decreed capital punishment for sodomy, operated from 1532. It built on earlier codes, such as that of Bamberg of 1507, which, combining aspects of customary and Roman law, had stipulated the same; and, as we have seen, the death penalty had routinely been applied in the Netherlands (and also Switzerland) during the previous century.[44] The standard treatise on criminal law in the Burgundian territories of the Netherlands, composed in c.1510 by Philippe Wielant, was summarizing existing practice when it said that male–male sex was punishable by death.[45] In Sweden sodomy was dealt with by the Church courts until the sixteenth century, but became a criminal offence by 1608, when Karl IX's law-code made it a capital crime.[46] In some parts of northern France the traditional punishment seems to have been milder—Breton customary law had imposed a fine—but by the sixteenth century capital punishment was the norm.[47] One aspect of the punitive regime which could vary from jurisdiction to jurisdiction was the treatment of passive partners, and of boys. In fifteenth- and early-sixteenth-century Bruges, boys were executed too; in Antwerp, while most active partners were burnt, passive ones could be flogged or banished; in seventeenth-century Basel a boy under the age of fourteen received milder punishment (even if he had been the active partner); in France an influential jurist, Jean de Coras, wrote in 1610 that the passive partner should be treated more leniently because the act might have taken place against his will.[48]

However, while death was indeed the standard prescribed penalty in most of Northern Europe, this fact can hardly be used to explain a difference in the rate of prosecution between that region and the Mediterranean territories, since, as we have already seen, it was standard in those places too. Jonas Roelens contrasts north-western Europe, where the death penalty was common, with Italy, where he claims that sodomy was punished mostly by fines. However, he refers only to Florence (an exceptional jurisdiction) and Venice (where the figures for sodomy trials were in fact high in the period, up to the 1530s, when execution and mutilation were routine punishments); and he does not mention places such as Rome, where the death penalty was applied well into the seventeenth century, or indeed any of the Iberian jurisdictions.[49] It is true that the use made of the death sentence by judges in Southern Europe went into a gradual decline, starting in some places earlier than in others. But where direct comparisons can be made—between, for example, England and Seville in the late sixteenth century—the idea that the existence of the death penalty inhibited people from bringing sodomites to trial is clearly unsustainable.

Another explanation of the paucity of English evidence, put forward by Kenneth Borris, is that English courts, unlike Southern European ones, did not make use of torture. This, it is supposed, led to fewer confessions in England, and the prospect of fewer confessions led to fewer prosecutions. The basic difference here was a genuine one: in England torture was generally reserved for the gravest political cases, such as sedition and treason (though in the Elizabethan period it was sometimes used for the investigation of serious felonies too).[50] There is no known example of an English sodomy case in which torture was applied. In Southern Europe torture was used: as we have seen, it featured in approximately 30 per cent of sodomy trials conducted by the Aragonese Inquisition, and roughly 15 per cent of those held by the Portuguese one.[51] It is not clear how decisive a factor it was; the great majority of suspects escaped this treatment, but of course the knowledge that they could be tortured may have had some influence on their willingness to confess to the crime. However, England was something of a special case, as most other jurisdictions in Northern Europe did employ torture. It was especially common in the German lands, where the Carolina laid down detailed rules for its use. Indeed, it seems to have been more frequent there than in the Mediterranean countries; one classic modern study describes torture as 'almost the first and only resort of the German investigating magistrate'.[52] In Geneva it was common, possibly more so than in Iberia: of twelve sodomy trials in the period 1535–64, it was applied in five and eschewed in three, while the records do not show whether it was used or not in the other four.[53] In Sweden it was employed in bestiality cases, which suggests that it would have been available for use on people accused of sodomy.[54] And in France, while torture was applied much less routinely than in the German lands, the rate of its use in sodomy cases approximated quite closely to that of the Aragonese Inquisition: of the 131 convicted sodomites brought to the Parlement de Paris, 40 were interrogated under torture.[55]

Other explanations put forward for what has been regarded as English exceptionalism are no more convincing. It has been argued, for example, that few cases were prosecuted because the English law required proof of something that was generally unprovable, namely, the fact that penetration and ejaculation had taken place, and that 'the increasing precision of the legal definition of sodomy—as, essentially, anal penetration—left all other kinds of male–male sexual activity...outside the scope of juridical detection.'[56] Yet, as we have seen, this was the concept of 'perfect sodomy' that also applied in the tribunals of the Portuguese Inquisition, where hundreds of men were prosecuted and convicted. It is true that the 'Buggery Act', which referred simply to 'the detestable and abominable vice of buggery committed with mankind or beast', did not criminalize other forms of sexual behaviour. But this did not entirely exclude the prosecution of other offences, outside the scope of the Act: the Bridewell court would have punished male prostitution, if it had found any cases, and in 1628 it did take action against a man called Jeremy Farrer who was found 'abusing himselfe on the fast day in St Faith's church' in 'a sodomiticall manner' (note the traditional assumption that masturbation belonged to the general category of sodomy) and admitted having done the same 'in other churches for the space of a yeare'.[57] Nor is it convincing to claim that the procedures of English common law made conviction especially difficult. The requirement of two witnesses was in line with the rules that applied in several European jurisdictions; on the other hand the provision by the tribunals of the Aragonese Inquisition of a defence lawyer to the accused was a privilege of which arrested Englishmen could only dream.[58]

In the case of Holland and the other United Provinces of the northern Netherlands, it has been suggested that much of the documentation of pre-1700 sodomy trials has gone missing, as a result of either accidental loss or deliberate suppression. There is some evidence that records of these trials were kept separately, which would support this hypothesis—though the survival of 34 such records from Amsterdam, The Hague and Utrecht before 1650 shows that the loss was not systematic.[59] Nevertheless, even if the Dutch documentation is deficient in this way, that fact can have only a small effect on our interpretation of the whole pattern of evidence from Northern European territories, where the paucity of sodomy trials is striking in many judicial archives where there is no reason to suspect that such losses have occurred.

This raises, however, a larger question about attitudes towards the publicizing of these offences; might a fear of publicity (which, some thought, could put ideas into people's heads) have made the authorities reluctant to prosecute, thus significantly reducing the number of sodomy trials? That some people did think like this is clear. In Cologne in 1484, when the authorities were told by the pastor of one of the churches that there were many sodomites in the city, they consulted theologians, who advised them to adopt a policy of total silence on the subject; and when they questioned a range of pastors and confessors, one of those made the same recommendation. (Note, however, that this was a minority view among those clerics, and that the authorities had gone ahead with their investigation against the theologians' advice.)[60] In his wide-ranging study of the German lands, Helmut Puff has noted evidence of a desire, which seems to have grown during the sixteenth century, to avoid unnecessary publicity: a shift towards more veiled language by judges after the middle of that century, the use of a coded reference to sodomy by court clerks (though the code was not hard to crack), and more generally a 'rhetoric of disgust and a politics of silence'.[61] And yet the trials continued, and there is no evidence of any jurisdiction adopting a general policy of not bringing such cases to court. The city authorities in Hamburg did hold one secret sodomy trial in 1657, and twelve years earlier efforts had been made to keep another such trial secret in Frankfurt. But such cases were very unusual; after the previous conviction for sodomy in Frankfurt, in 1598, the offender had been put in the pillory to serve as a public example.[62] Overall, the dilemma which, as we have seen, was present in Southern Europe—the undesirability of spreading ideas about the 'unspeakable' sin, versus the need to reinforce public moral values by making its punishment known—seems to have been felt equally in Northern Europe; and while particular responses to it could veer one way or the other, no systematic difference between North and South emerges from the evidence.

Another general claim that has sometimes been made is that the number of sodomy trials in England (or elsewhere) is low because cases of consensual sex were not brought to court.[63] In absolute terms, this claim is not correct. At the Bishop of Lincoln's court in 1529, for example, a 40-year-old man from Kirby Bellars, in Leicestershire, admitted that he had twice committed sodomy with a married man from the same village; the other man also confessed to those two acts (one in bed, the other while standing), and said that his partner had also fondled his genitals on several different occasions.[64] At the Maidstone Assizes in 1645, Henry Gibbs of Ashford, a 40-year-old grocer, and William Phillpott, a 50-year-old oatmeal-maker, were put on trial for sodomy with each other, and both were found guilty. The former was hanged, while the latter was sentenced to be hanged but then reprieved; while the reason for leniency is not recorded, it is hard to imagine that a 50-year-old man would have been the unwilling victim of a successful sexual assault.[65] Likewise, many of the cases recorded in the German lands involved fully consensual sex between two adults.[66]

In relative terms, on the other hand, it must surely be correct to say that consensual cases were less likely to be brought to court than non-consensual ones. This was not because the general population had a benignly tolerant view of such mutually accepted sexual acts, but because the cases at the other end of the spectrum, involving serious coercion, rape and physical damage, were much more likely to motivate people to call for prosecutions. And that was especially true where young boys were concerned—so long as they were sufficiently in contact with their parents, or with other adults willing to protect their interests. (In several European jurisdictions individuals could launch a criminal prosecution, paying for its costs, and in some legal systems civil litigation was possible, which also came at a price; a majority of the French trials were civil cases, typically brought by parents of the victim. And in sixteenth-century Rome, cases involving force were mostly brought by the victims, or by individuals acting on their behalf. The historian who has examined these Roman trials observes that cases of consensual sodomy were also prosecuted, but were probably under-represented.)[67] The general argument put forward by Alan Bray, and repeated by many subsequent writers, that sodomy became a matter of concern only when the commission of it breached rules of social order, states at best a partial truth: while the use of violence would indeed make a sodomy case more concerning, it is not correct to suggest that the sin or crime of sodomy was in itself of no concern. Nor is this invoking of social order adequate to explain the treatment of some other sexual offences. Simple fornication by unmarried men and women, which was constantly denounced to the ecclesiastical courts, hardly posed any threat to social order as such; children born to unmarried mothers may have been seen as a socially undesirable phenomenon, which also brought disgrace upon the women and their families, but consensual fornication did not threaten order in the way that rape did—or adultery, with its challenge to the husband's authority and its threat to his blood line. Acts of bestiality, committed usually by solitary men in barns or remote fields, did not threaten the social order at all; yet in England they were prosecuted much more frequently than sodomy.

* * *

It is worth pausing to make the comparison between prosecutions for these two offences, sodomy and bestiality, as it tends to confirm that there was a general difference between Northern and Southern Europe. In almost every Northern European jurisdiction, the figures for bestiality were much higher. The most extreme case was Sweden. In the kingdom of Sweden, excluding Finland, 546 prosecutions for bestiality were reported to the Royal Superior Courts in the period 1635–1714; adding the period up to 1754 brings the total to 1,500. It has also been calculated that between 1620 and 1778 up to 700 people were executed for this offence.[68] In Scotland, where two sodomy trials are known before 1700, a partial search of the records for prosecutions for bestiality has yielded 77 cases between 1570 and 1734.[69] The English evidence also exhibits a strong imbalance. In Essex, where no one was tried for sodomy between 1559 and 1625, there were eleven trials for bestiality; in Hertfordshire between 1575 and 1602 there were four for bestiality but no prosecutions for sodomy; in Kent between 1559 and 1603 there were ten for bestiality and two for sodomy.[70] Susanne Hehenberger's study of so-called sodomy cases in Austria between 1581 and 1780 finds one involving male–male sexual relations (probably mutual masturbation), two cases of male–female sex, and 50 which were for bestiality. Similarly, in eighteenth-century Brandenburg-Prussia, the great majority of so-called sodomy trials concerned men having sex with animals: between 1700 and 1730 there were 29 cases specifying the sodomizing of an animal, five clearly involving male–male sex, and two cases where no details were given beyond the word 'sodomy' itself, which was used for both.[71] The records of the Basel criminal courts, in the period 1399–1799, contain four or five cases of male–male sex and 46 cases of bestiality.[72]

In sixteenth-century Zurich there were eighteen investigations for sodomy, leading to eight executions, while the number of people executed for bestiality was 56; Lucerne saw twelve sodomy investigations during that century, leading to five executions, but in the period 1530–1607 there were 36 prosecutions for bestiality, with 31 men sentenced to death.[73] In the canton of Fribourg, from the fifteenth century to the seventeenth, one case of sodomy was recorded, and 32 of bestiality.[74] In the German-speaking area of Lorraine (the north-eastern part of the duchy), a study of the criminal trial records for the late-sixteenth and early-seventeenth centuries yields fourteen convictions for so-called sodomy. Ten of these were clearly for bestiality, with in some cases the record specifying also that the animal itself was burnt; one case referred to both bestiality and sodomy, which suggests that the latter offence was with another man or boy; but the other cases simply referred to sodomy or 'sodomitical sins', which may well have meant sex with animals.[75]

A study of fourteenth- and fifteenth-century France comments that bestiality cases were more frequent than sodomy ones in the north of the country—contrasting this with the situation further to the south, in the Rhône Valley, where sodomy was more frequent—but does not give specific figures.[76] The number of bestiality cases brought on appeal to the Parlement de Paris, which covered part of southern France too, was almost identical to that of sodomy cases in the period 1564–1639: 104 of the former, and 107 of the latter.[77] These figures may illustrate once again the mixed nature of the French evidence, but in the absence of a detailed geographical breakdown they cannot be interpreted further. Otherwise, there are only two jurisdictions where the evidence, for the period before 1700, points the other way. In Geneva, of 74 men tried for so-called sodomy between 1444 and 1789, nine were actually accused of bestiality.[78] Even if we subtract all the people from the Mediterranean region, who were more strongly represented among the cases of male–male sex, the disparity is still striking. And the records of the *ammanie* of Brussels also go against the trend: in the fifteenth and sixteenth centuries we find only two men tried for bestiality, versus 33 convicted of sodomy.[79] The reasons for the divergence of Geneva and Brussels are not at all apparent. But the overall pattern is so consistent that it can hardly be undermined by two exceptions of this sort.

Since all early modern societies, other than city-states of the most narrowly delimited kind, were mostly agricultural, one might expect the statistical predominance of bestiality cases to have been more or less universal. (It would be wrong, however, to assume that the perpetrators all worked on the land. A study of 47 bestiality cases in eighteenth-century France has found that only fifteen of the men were peasants, farm labourers, shepherds and vineyard-workers; there were five servants, four merchants, one cobbler, one soldier, and people from a variety of other walks of life.)[80] Yet the evidence from Southern Europe disproves that expectation. At the Évora tribunal of the Portuguese Inquisition in the period 1533–1668 there were 45 investigations of sodomy, and five of bestiality.[81] In eighteenth-century Seville the same pattern is clear: between 1740 and 1799 there were 27 prosecutions for sodomy, and seven for bestiality.[82] In the three mainland territories of the Crown of Aragon, sodomy cases brought to the Inquisition significantly outnumbered bestiality cases: of the four main categories of sexual offences tried there (sodomy, bestiality, bigamy and solicitation), sodomy represented

38 per cent of the total, and bestiality 27 per cent. William Monter has commented that 'in the kingdom of Aragon, prosecutions for bestiality were far outnumbered by prosecutions for homosexual acts, with the exception of the sheep-raising area of Saragossa, where prosecutions for bestiality and homosexuality were more equal in number, although with a clear dominance for bestiality.'[83] Rafael Carrasco calculates that at the Valencian tribunal in the period 1565–1785, just 85 people were prosecuted for bestiality—roughly one third of the total for sodomy. The disparity was greater in the period after 1655, when there were 50 sodomy cases but only three involving bestiality. Carrasco warns against assuming that popular attitudes were more tolerant towards those who committed sexual acts with animals; such people were, he notes, harassed and hunted down 'with incredible aggression'.[84] Instead of positing, on the basis of no evidence at all, some special tolerance of bestiality in Southern Europe, it surely makes more sense to accept the conclusion to which the entire pattern of evidence clearly points: that sodomy was more frequent in the South, and less common in the North.

★ ★ ★

To return to Northern Europe: one aspect of some of the sodomy cases which has caught the attention of modern historians is the time-lag between members of the community becoming aware of the offender's activities and the eventual launching of a prosecution. There were cases in France, Germany and the southern Netherlands where it took several years for gossip to reach the level of *fama* (public reputation) or *clamor* (public outcry).[85] Here it is necessary to understand that in traditional legal systems *fama* had been both a technical term and an important criterion for action: in the ecclesiastical courts it had functioned not only as a basic justification for prosecution, requiring multiple witnesses of good standing, but also as a threshold condition for a process known as 'compurgation', where someone who was the object of such public criticism went to court to swear to his or her innocence. According to the great fourteenth-century jurist Bartolus, *fama* took at least three years to develop. In the criminal justice systems of Italian city-states, *publica fama* provided a justification for investigating and prosecuting someone, and in specified conditions it could even be a basis for conviction.[86] Most sodomy prosecutions did not take place on this basis, as they involved particular acts to which specific witnesses might testify. But the idea that a general reputation for ill-doing took a long time to build up was deeply rooted in the legal culture; and in some cases individuals would feel uneasy about reporting what they had seen or experienced in the absence of some sort of corroborating background of similar testimonies. In a sodomy trial in Somerset in 1622, one witness explained why he had previously kept quiet about an incident which had taken place fourteen years earlier: 'he spake not thereof unto anyone ever since until about a week last past, and thinks he should [sc. would] never have spoken thereof, but that now of late he heard diverse others charge him with facts of the like kind.'[87]

More generally, we should not be greatly surprised by the idea that some men's transgressive sexual conduct may have been common knowledge in the community for some time before any prosecution was launched; any individual was typically located within a network of close family, extended kin, professional colleagues and social companions, which might offer some degrees of social protection, both by tugging at the bonds of loyalty and by inhibiting potential critics from incurring larger enmities. As Christine Reinle has pointed out, in this sort of social context reluctance to act against an offender should not be confused with tolerance of the offence itself.[88] Reinle's comment arises in a discussion of the issue of sodomy in late-mediaeval Europe generally, both Northern and Southern; and indeed it is hard to see why such an inhibiting factor should have operated any more strongly in the former region than in the latter. It may go some way towards explaining the general attitudes which several modern historians, discussing Southern Europe, have portrayed as acceptance or tolerance—though some of the cultural evidence (the Florentine carnival songs, for example) suggests that there may have been something closer to actual tolerance in some of those Western Mediterranean societies.

Likewise, there was nothing peculiarly Northern about being reluctant to denounce offenders who had a high birth status or a position of social authority. One rather vivid example of this concerns the Lutheran pastor of the village of Nordheim, near Heilbronn in Württemberg, who appeared in court in 1689. Witness after witness came forward to attest to his previous actions. One woman described how her husband had been subjected to his unwanted attentions five years earlier: the pastor had kissed him, put his tongue in his mouth, and reached with his hand into his trousers. A former mayor of the village, aged 46, said that the pastor had frequently asked him for sex, and that when his request was denied he had masturbated in front of him; a sixteen-year-old boy said he had invited him to his house, taken out his own penis and put it in the boy's hand; a 30-year-old man said the pastor had approached him for sex frequently over the previous twelve years. The court's investigations revealed a total of sixteen males, from an eight-year-old boy to adults in their 40s, with whom he had had, or tried to have, sexual contacts. And yet the pastor himself was not on trial; he had foolishly launched a defamation case against one of his parishioners. It seems that the dignity of his office, and perhaps the feeling that the authorities would close ranks on his behalf, had—in addition, probably, to sheer embarrassment—stayed their hands. (In the event, the judges did decide against instituting a criminal trial, for fear of scandal, but they degraded the pastor from his office and sentenced him to six years' incarceration in a fortress.)[89] There are plenty of examples of sodomitical clergymen in Southern Europe—albeit with more age-differentiated victims of their attentions—whose flocks were similarly long-suffering, no doubt for the same reasons.

In short: while it must be true that the number of people brought to trial for sodomy was only a fraction of the number of actual sodomites in any given jurisdiction, it is very difficult to find any reason for this, applicable in Northern Europe, that would not have been applicable in the South. In the general population, some people may have been more censorious and some less; but that was the case in every society, and there is no reason to think that Northern Europeans were more uncensorious overall. As for the basis of those hostile feelings: the strong condemnation of sodomy by Christian theologians had roots going back into the Middle Ages, and dominated all thinking on this subject in every part of Europe.

Did the Reformation make a significant difference, causing Northern European societies to be more inclined to disregard this offence? Trying to explain the general difference between North and South on that basis would be a hopeless task. The paucity of English evidence is just as clear in the fifteenth century as in the sixteenth and seventeenth; the picture in post-Reformation Germany is the same in Protestant and Catholic territories; northern France, a Catholic society, resembles the Netherlands and the Protestant cantons of Switzerland; and so on. Northern rulers did not go soft on sodomy after the Reformation; in England and Scandinavia they introduced severe legislation, demanding capital punishment. Generally speaking, Protestants legislating for morality were more inclined than Catholics to turn their attention to the strict provisions of the Mosaic law; the Swedish anti-sodomy law of 1608 clearly had Leviticus in mind when it said that 'Thou shalt not lie with man as with a woman' and decreed that both partners must be executed.[90]

As we have seen, stigmatizing sodomy had become part of Protestant culture from Martin Luther onwards, as the issue was put to work in anti-Catholic polemics—Luther's jibes about sodomy at the papal court, Vergerio's attack on Archbishop della Casa, the absurd but widely credited accusation that a pope had authorized sodomy in the three hottest months of the year, and so on. In theory, such a polemical stance could have had the effect of making Protestant authorities keen to cover up the existence of this particular sin in their own populations. But there is no evidence of that as a distinctively Protestant practice; the occasional expressions of concern about the risk of granting publicity to such an offence were on a par with those in other European societies, including Catholic ones. Among people motivated by Protestant zeal, the need to build a godly community—and therefore to root out such sinfulness as actively as possible—took absolute priority. On this subject Calvin himself argued for exemplary public punishment.[91] And on the other hand the confessional culture wars had produced a body of Catholic anti-sodomy polemics against Protestants, with personal accusations against Beza and indeed against Calvin himself.[92] On that basis, one could just as well argue that Catholic authorities felt motivated to cover up sodomy in their own societies, for fear that Catholics would be seen as participating in a Protestant vice.

One consequence of those Protestant–Catholic polemical exchanges is that when we read a Lutheran or Reformed author saying that sodomy was much more common in Italy than in Germany, we have to regard it as a statement animated, to some extent, by prejudice. But that does not necessarily mean that the statement was untrue. When the seventeenth-century Lutheran Benedikt Carpzov observed that sodomy cases were rare in the German lands, he was writing as a jurist with decades of experience as a judge; it may also be relevant that he had spent many months in Italy as a young man, learning Italian and living in Venice, Rome and Naples.[93] Neither confessional nor national prejudice, however, can account for the statement in the middle of the previous century by the Italian philosopher and physician Girolamo Cardano that sodomy was completely monstrous in Germany, but 'less so in Italy'.[94]

15

Northern Europe: forms of sexual behaviour

The previous chapter looked at some of the broad, *prima facie* evidence that Northern Europe differed from the Mediterranean territories in these matters. Now we should consider the more qualitative issues involved; for what a wide range of evidence suggests is that the nature of the male–male sexual behaviour itself diverged significantly from the Mediterranean model. And there are also reasons for thinking that it was less visible in the Northern societies—which may suggest not only that it was a lesser phenomenon quantitatively, but also that it was, so to speak, less integrated into common patterns of male behaviour.

At the heart of the Mediterranean pattern of male–male sexual relations was age-differentiation. To summarize again: adult men took the active role; boys were passive. The transition from boy to man occurred typically in the age-range 18–20, and the key marker that signalled it was the development of facial hair. Up to that time, any boy above the age of nine or ten could be seen as desirable; but thereafter he could not be desired, except by a very small and untypical minority of men. Adult males who still wanted to take the passive role were also exceptional, attracting opprobrium and disdain. Finally, the men who desired boys and acted on that desire were predominantly in their early adulthood. This type of behaviour declined fairly rapidly beyond the age of 30, and those who persisted in it in later decades seem mostly to have belonged to a category, the inveterate sodomites, that was also very untypical.

The Northern European records do furnish many examples of men having sex with boys. This fact should not surprise us, given the nature of these early modern societies. Many children were drawn at an early stage into the world of work, as agricultural labourers, domestic servants, shop-boys,

Forbidden Desire in Early Modern Europe: Male–Male Sexual Relations, 1400–1750. Noel Malcolm, Oxford University Press.
© Noel Malcolm 2024. DOI: 10.1093/oso/9780198886334.003.0015

apprentices, pages, and so on. A majority of boys left home at some point in their teens. In England, fourteen was the average age for beginning an apprenticeship (though it was higher in London, and lower in small provincial towns); the typical age for entering agricultural service was between thirteen and fifteen. The numbers involved were very large: every year in early-seventeenth-century London roughly 3,000 boys began their apprenticeships, and in the whole country household servants were present in between a quarter and a third of all homes.[1] These were, by modern standards, very hierarchical societies, in which masters exercised power over those under them, especially if the latter were young; and the nature of this employment often meant that the boys were living, as well as working, under the master's roof, removed from the direct protection of their parents. In addition there were many children who had been orphaned, or had left their parents or been abandoned by them. They could join the significant underclass of vagrants and beggars: a study of vagrants in England has found that in the period 1570–1622, 43 per cent of them were under the age of sixteen, and 67 per cent were under 21.[2] We have already encountered the sexual exploitation of apprentices and street-boys in Italy, where similar conditions applied.[3] Indeed, this relative availability of boys was a feature of every early modern European society. It meant that these were by far the easiest targets for sexual advances. Yet at the same time their youth and vulnerability also meant that if those advances were made with violence, causing extreme distress or physical harm, parents or other responsible adults were more strongly motivated to have recourse to the law. For both these reasons, one would expect such cases to be well represented in the records.

Where the English evidence is concerned, we should probably put to one side the cases recorded in the monastic visitations of 1535–6. The majority of these did involve adults allegedly sodomizing youths; but even if the findings of these visitations could be accepted as reliable (which they cannot), we would still be well advised to doubt the typicality of the sex-lives of monks, with their easy access to choristers, schoolboys and teenaged novices in a largely all-male context. Other judicial records, relating to a much wider range of people, yield a better picture of sexual behaviour in early modern English society. Existing studies yield 22 cases of men prosecuted for sodomy in England between 1390 and 1650 where their partner's or victim's age-status—meaning not necessarily the precise age, but whether the person was a boy or an adult—was recorded; this evidence is drawn from a range of courts, both ecclesiastical and secular, and may be treated as a random sample, as the way in which it has been gathered is not susceptible to any particular bias where the question of age-status is concerned. Subtracting one (a man from Spanish territory, called Domingo Drago— probably a freed slave, as he was described as black) and adding seven other similarly recorded cases involving judicial or quasi-judicial processes (an Englishman tried in Ireland, four defamation cases, an Oxford Fellow expelled from his college, a clergyman deprived of his living) gives 28 adults. Of these, eighteen were accused of sex with boys and fourteen of sex with men, while four, double-counted here, were accused of both; so 50 per cent of these adults were thought to have had or sought sex with other adults.[4] The particular percentage figure here is not important, as with such a small sample just a few cases added to one category or the other would change it significantly; what matters is the order of magnitude. In Florence, if we exclude a transitional age-range of nineteen to 22, the cases of adults sodomized by adults came to just over 1 per cent.[5] Thus if we found fourteen such cases there, we would expect them to be accompanied by nearly 1,400 cases of men having sex with boys.

The German and Swiss evidence is quite similar, but suggests that, if anything, men seeking or having sex with other men were the absolute majority. Again there is no large-scale database that could furnish a statistical analysis comparable to the one provided by Michael Rocke. However, if we look at all the cases discussed by Helmut Puff in his wide-ranging study, and select the ones where age-status is clear from the evidence, we arrive at the following figures: 25 men whose sexual partner (actual or desired) was another man; sixteen for whom it was a boy; and four—again, double-counted here—who sought or had sex with both men and boys.[6] That means that 68 per cent of these adults were, or were thought to be, interested in performing sexual acts with other adult males. The sample here is still very small, but since these cases are cited by Puff to illustrate a wide range of behaviours, social attitudes, legal procedures, etc., there is again no reason to think that their selection would have been affected by a bias towards one category rather than another. Certainly the evidence from Basel, very limited though it is, can only strengthen the impression that men seeking men formed a majority: of all the cases involving adults prosecuted for sodomy, four were for adult–adult sex, one concerned an adult who took the passive role with a boy, and only one involved a boy being sodomized by an adult.[7] The cases that arose in late-seventeenth-century Zurich, where the authorities vigorously prosecuted sodomy, apparently offer no dominant pattern: the historian who has investigated them reports that while some involved employers exploiting employees, and some arose from experimentation between two youths, there were also adult–adult cases, some of which took the form of long-lasting relationships.[8] The limited evidence of sodomy cases in the Netherlands before 1700 has not been made available for this kind of analysis; but one scholar who has studied it observes that, in the period before 1675, while some cases were age-differentiated, a number were simply described as involving men with men.[9]

One detail worth noting is that in these two small and very approximate surveys of evidence from England and from Germany and Switzerland, more than 10 per cent of the cases involved sex with both men and boys. (Note also that the evidence in most of the other cases is not sufficient to show that those men confined themselves to either men or boys; typically, it just relates to a particular accusation, which involved one category or the other. So this percentage may in reality have been higher.) We have already encountered one example of this kind of free-ranging sexual desire: the Lutheran pastor from Nordheim, who pestered a whole gamut of his male parishioners, from small boys to middle-aged men.[10] Another such case was brought to trial in Somerset in 1622, when George Dowdeney, a village innkeeper in his 40s, was charged with a sexual assault on the son of one of his neighbours. The boy's father testified that fourteen years earlier he himself had shared a bed with this man when they were travelling together, and that Dowdeney had grabbed his genitals, kissed him and tried to sodomize him. The local blacksmith had undergone a similar experience of attempted sodomy, and said that on many occasions Dowdeney had thrust his hand into the blacksmith's breeches and suggested 'that they might go to some private place to the end Dowdeney might bugger him'. For good measure, he had also invited the blacksmith to watch him buggering a sow.[11]

Where age-patterns are concerned, as on other issues, France offers a mixed picture. In just 23 of the Parlement de Paris cases the age of the person in the passive role was recorded: the great majority were under 20, but six were 20 or above. Even if we allow that some of these may have been in a transitional age-range, this suggests that the percentage of passive adults was significantly higher than in Florence. Rather more striking is the pattern of ages of the men or youths accused of taking the active role. Out of 61 people, thirteen were in their teens, but only sixteen were between 20 and 30; no fewer than 32 were over the age of 30, of whom eighteen were over 50. Altogether, more than 40 per cent of the active partners were over 40.[12] By Florentine standards, this means that 'inveterate' sodomites were hugely over-represented; equally, it suggests that we are not looking at the sort of Mediterranean life-cycle in which active sodomy was predominantly the pursuit of men in their first decade of adulthood. Some modern studies, acquiescing in the idea that the Florentine model was universal, have tended to blur these distinctions. For example, the earliest known sodomy case recorded in the police archives in Paris, dating from 1666, concerns a 72-year-old man who made sexual advances to a fifteen-year-old boy, and was found to have pestered other youths in previous years. The study which presents this evidence describes these ages as fitting the general model of age-differentiation, even though such an elderly man would have been highly untypical in Florence.[13] The same comment is passed there on the notorious Parisian case of Jacques Chausson and Jacques Paulmier, alias Fabri, who had been burnt at the stake five years earlier for sodomy and blasphemy. Their ages were given as 43 and 36 respectively, and they had been convicted of a sexual assault on a teenaged boy. Those ages would differentiate them somewhat, perhaps not decisively, from typical sodomites in Florence; but it is very misleading to describe them as fitting the standard Florentine pattern, given that these two adults had also had sex with each other, alternating the active and passive roles—something almost unknown, for this age-category, in Italy.[14]

Even in cases where there was a clear difference in age between two partners (or between the man and the person he desired or attempted to have sex with), this did not always accord with the Mediterranean pattern. A well-documented case survives from 1651: it was heard in the court of the Archbishop of Cambrai, as the accused, Jean Verré, was a parish priest. He had pestered a whole range of men for sex, both priests and laymen, often taking their hands and putting them in his breeches; when he invited men to spend the night in his bed, he tried to masturbate them, and in some cases made apparent his desire to sodomize them (though no witness was willing to state that he had succeeded). But where the records cite the ages of these men, they are mostly in their 20s, and one is described as 27 or 28.[15] So while Verré may well have been sexually attracted to men younger than himself, the situation here was quite different from that in Southern Europe, where the desirability of a male youth normally evaporated when he grew facial hair. There is a telling anecdote in the memoirs of Giovanni Battista Primi Visconti, who lived the first part of his life in his native Varallo (in Piedmont), before moving to the court of Louis XIV in 1672, at the age of 24.

There he was soon befriended by the marquis de la Vallière, who was six years older. When the marquis propositioned him for sex (quoting a version of Scaliger's *bon mot*: 'in Spain the monks do it; in France, the great men; in Italy, everybody'), he did his best to decline politely. As he put it in his memoirs, 'I replied humorously that such an idea was far from my mind, and that I was 25 years old and had a beard. He replied that Frenchmen of good taste paid no attention either to age or to hair; in short, it was quite a hard task for me to get out of the situation.'[16] Roughly three decades later, in 1704, a Parisian man explained to the police that the reason why he was acting as a pimp for young men was that now he had reached the age of 30, he himself was no longer succeeding in attracting older men for money.[17] It seems that while there was some premium on youthful appearance, the Mediterranean threshold age simply did not apply.

The relatively high proportion of cases of adult–adult sex in Northern European societies indicates, obviously enough, that there was also a higher proportion of men who were willing to take the passive role. One rather spectacular example was Louis Joseph de Bourbon, duc de Vendôme, one of the greatest of Louis XIV's generals, whose sexual interest in men was well known. Where a satirical song, preserved in a manuscript collection, referred to him as 'the best bugger in the world', an annotation explained that he was a *bardache* rather than a *bougre*. 'For the great pleasure of this Duke was to have himself buggered, and for that purpose he made use of servants and peasants, for want of more refined practitioners.' Knowing his tastes, the peasants who lived around his country house 'took care to stand along his path when he went hunting, because he often took them aside into the woods to have himself fucked, and gave each one a *pistole* [a substantial gold coin worth ten *livres*] as the price of his labour'.[18] Cases from Northern Europe of men inducing their young servants to have sex with them tend to be treated by modern historians as confirming the existence of the standard pattern of age-differentiation; but nothing could be further from the truth if the older man was the one being sodomized.

While passive adults seem to have been relatively more common among the known sodomites in these societies, the same is true of those adults who were willing to take either the passive or the active role. Two men were convicted of engaging in such reciprocal sex in Strasbourg in 1400; one was executed, but the other had managed to flee the city.[19] One of the two known cases in Regensburg, from 1471, involved a merchant who had first sodomized another man, a skinner, and on their next meeting had invited the skinner to sodomize him.[20] A case tried in Münster in 1536 concerned a man from Brabant who had settled in the nearby village of Hamm, where he apparently worked as a doctor; the investigation revealed not only that he had been sodomized repeatedly there, but also that when he had lived in Rome, four years earlier, he had had sex in both the passive and the active roles.[21] In Geneva, the evidence which emerged at the trial of two men who were convicted and executed in 1562 shows that they were 'a long-standing couple' who had 'taken active and passive roles in turn'.[22] Similarly, two Franciscans from a friary in Bruges, put on trial in 1578, were found to have had a sexual relationship extending over 20 years, in which each would penetrate the other.[23] Henri de Bourbon, prince de Condé (1588–1646), who was notorious for his liking for male youths, was said also to have taken both the active and the passive role. In his great compilation of anecdotes and biographical materials, Tallement des Réaux told the story of a Venetian nobleman who had been delighted to learn that this prince would succeed to the throne in the event of the deaths of Louis XIII and his brother: in that case, said the noble, ' "I would be able to boast that I had fucked the greatest king in Christendom." For he said that he and the prince had fucked each other by turns in Venice.'[24]

★ ★ ★

Tallement's account of Condé's sexual tastes focused, however, on a rather different theme. He described how one of his own acquaintances, when a fifteen-year-old schoolboy, had been picked up by the prince and invited into his chamber. Condé inquired of the boy whether he had friends at school with whom he could enjoy some mutual stimulation, and then put his hand into the boy's trousers and asked him whether he masturbated; finally he took out his own penis and got the boy to masturbate him. Overall, Tallement's judgement on the prince was that 'I wouldn't want to say that he was altogether a bugger, but he was a great masturbator.'[25] The relative frequency with which mutual masturbation crops up in the Northern European evidence, in contrast to that from Mediterranean societies, is quite striking. The case of the two men burnt for mutual masturbation in Lucerne in 1489 has already been mentioned. One of the earliest German cases, from Bavaria in 1378, concerned a man who confessed to masturbation and mutual masturbation with a student and three or four other men. In 1533 Conrat Mühlibach, a 26-year-old weaver from a village near the Swiss city of St Gallen, was tried for mutual masturbation: the charge stated that 'each had taken the other's male member in his hand, and then each had milked the other to the point of ejaculation.' Having confessed that he had been introduced to this practice by another boy when he was eleven or twelve, and had performed it with many other boys ever since, he was duly found guilty and burnt at the stake.[26]

In 1541 the well-known Protestant cleric Werner Steiner, successor to Zwingli in Zurich, was tried for an episode which had taken place 23 years earlier, when he was in his 20s. While sharing his bed with a farm labourer of roughly the same age, he had offered to teach the other man the pleasures of masturbation (which, he assured him, were as great as those of sex with a woman). Under questioning from the court, Steiner explained that he had acquired this vice while travelling as a student in France: first he had had an encounter with a Frenchman who 'tried to manipulate his male member', and then, in Paris, he had been initiated into this practice—which, his account implied, was at least sometimes a mutual one.[27] Mutual masturbation is also recorded in the Netherlands in this period: in Middelburg in 1561 and 1568, men who had engaged in it were sentenced to one year's galley service, and elsewhere prison sentences were applied.[28] Generally, what seems to have been distinctive about this practice in Northern Europe is that it was viewed by its participants as an end in itself, a self-sufficient sexual act; whereas in the rare cases that emerge from the Mediterranean evidence, it was apparently either a *pis-aller* substitute for penetrative sex, or a prelude to it.

We can easily conclude that a rather different kind of sexual psychology lay behind this practice, though it may be hard to characterize it in anything more than general terms. The basic pattern in Southern Europe involved a man taking his own pleasure from the body of a youth; if the youth himself gained physical pleasure from the act, that was, so to speak, a side-effect, and if the man took any additional trouble to stimulate the youth, the main purpose of that was to facilitate the man's own enjoyment by making the youth more compliant. But mutual touching of the genitals and masturbation, especially between adult men, surely proceeded on a different basis: each man was stimulated by the other's genitals, especially by the other's sexual excitement, and what mattered was the shared maleness of the two—not the differentiation of them into two categories (of which, in Southern Europe, only one category would be understood to be motivated by sexual desire for the other).

Something of this psychology may also have been present in the practice of initiating—or at least trying to initiate—sexual contact by grasping another man's genitals, or taking the other man's hand and thrusting it into one's own breeches. This practice, again, surfaces much more often in the Northern European evidence. We have already encountered it in the cases of George Dowdeney in Somerset, the pastor of Nordheim in Württemberg, Jean Verré in Cambrai, and the prince de Condé in Paris. The authorities in Basel heard complaints in 1416 about a Dominican who had pestered several young men in the friary there; one of those, a layman who worked in the bakery, said that the friar had called him over to a secluded spot in the garden and ordered him 'to take out his penis so that he could see it'. When he hesitated, the friar grabbed at his penis, 'which was still in his breeches'.[29] In Bruges in 1470, a man accused of grabbing another man's genitals in a tavern admitted, under torture, that he had done this to other men in the public bathhouses many times (but denied that he had ever had sexual inter-course with them). In the only sodomy-related defamation case heard at the London Commissary court in the period 1470–1516, one woman had insulted another by saying that that woman's husband lunged at priests between the legs.[30] Other examples, from the Zurich archives, include a man tried in 1537 who admitted that he had grasped at another man's geni-tals but insisted that he had been acting 'in jest' while drunk; a man inter-rogated there in 1547 who said, somewhat implausibly, that 'if he had grabbed other men's private parts it was to assess the state of their health'; and a father of three, on trial in 1592, who was accused of grasping at other men's genitals and, in some cases, having engaged in mutual masturbation, over a period of 20 years.[31] The rich Florentine archive supplies only very rare instances of this practice; and it is probably significant that the two specific examples given by Rocke both involved inveterate sodomites, whose behav-iour generally seems to have diverged from the norm.[32]

★ ★ ★

One other possible difference between North and South relates to men actually meeting in groups for sexual purposes. A previous chapter con-sidered the possibility of this in Mediterranean societies; the evidence was very slight, when set against the overall wealth of documentation from Italy and Iberia, and it seemed likely that some of the prosecutions of multiple suspects, which have sometimes been offered as proof of such a phenomenon, were caused by the unravelling of small networks—for example, of men happening to share the favours of a particular boy who had now started to give evidence to the authorities. The strongest reason for thinking that group meetings would have been extremely untypical was the simple fact that the great majority of adult men in Mediterranean societies felt no interest at all in having sexual relations with other adult men. In the North, among those who did engage in male–male sex, that limitation did not apply (or applied to a much smaller extent), and while the problem of interpreting multiple prosecutions does also arise with the Northern European evidence, there are cases where some sort of group sex may well have taken place. That seems to have been the implication of the trial, in Augsburg in 1381, of five men—two monks, two laymen under religious vows, and a peasant—for committing sodomy 'with one another'; and in 1409 another group of five—two chaplains, a priest, a friar and an artisan—were convicted there on the same charge. The two men who were burnt at the stake in Lucerne in 1489 were part of a group of three (the third, a Benedictine monk, escaped the death penalty) who, as the trial record put it, had 'rubbed their penises against one another until they ejaculated'. Somewhat less clear is the evidence, from Augsburg in the early 1530s, of a 'circle of men who…had sex with each other'; nine men were directly involved, and a senior patrician was also implicated.[33] In Geneva in 1610, when the authorities arrested a prominent citizen, Pierre Canal, on a charge of spying for the Duke of Savoy, they also rounded up nine of his known friends and associates because they knew that he was in the habit of inviting those men, as a group, to dinner at his house; it soon became clear, through their interrogations, that they had all been going there not for treasonable intelligence-sharing but for sex.[34]

One tantalizing piece of evidence concerns a group of men meeting in London in the early 1630s. The Puritan artisan Nehemiah Wallington (1598–1658) wrote the following entry in one of his notebooks:

> in Southwarke there were [about sixten *deleted*] [maried *inserted*] men of good estate that lived in the sinne of Buggeri and were sworen brothers to it they lived in this sin about seven yeeres the time they committed this sinne it was one [sc. on] the sabath day in sarmon time this came to light by a man that lay on his death bed who sent for the Minister and said to him that he could not dy before he had revealed his mind, and that the divell stood to fetch him away for he was one of that companie.[35]

The entry is not dated, and the notebook in which it was written was not arranged in chronological order; but what was surely the same episode was referred to in a polemical pamphlet printed probably at the Jesuit College of Saint-Omer, in France, in 1633:

> In the year *1632* there was discouered in *London* a Society of certain *Sodomites*, to the number of fourty, or fifty; all of them being earnest and hoat [sc. hot] *Puritans*, who had their common appointed Meeting-place, for their abominable Impiety: Of which number diuers of them (and such as were of good temporall estates and meanes) were apprehended, and the rest instantly fled.[36]

The pamphlet supplies no more information; its author, B. C., who has not been identified, seizes on what must have been a news item (presumably the source, directly or indirectly, of Wallington's information) to argue that the doctrines of the Puritans 'do euen iustify *Sin*', before recycling some familiar material connecting sodomy and Protestantism, such as Beza's male–male love-poem and the story, spread by a disgruntled ex-follower of Calvin, that the founder of Calvinism was a sodomite. But it does claim that this group of London sodomites constituted 'a peculiar *Society* or *Body*, hauing a common designed place for their publike meetings'; and Wallington's note also makes that point. Again, the pamphlet says that these men were 'in state competent, and some of very good meanes', which chimes with Wallington's description of them as 'men of good estate'; but where the number of individuals involved is concerned, the difference between the two accounts is large, and the polemical pamphlet obviously had reasons for exaggeration.[37] (Another divergence between the two, which is explicable on the same basis, involves B. C.'s claim that all these men were Puritans; Wallington's circumstantial detail that they held their gatherings on 'the sabath day in sarmon time' makes that seem very unlikely.) If any such mass arrest did take place, however, whether of sixteen men or of a larger number, the record of it seems not to have survived. There are no references to it either in the Middlesex Sessions of the Peace registers for 1629–33, or in the surviving indictments at the Surrey Assizes in Southwark between 1631 and 1634 (though the series is unfortunately incomplete) or in Croydon in 1633.[38] Nevertheless, although such a regular 'society' would certainly have been unusual, the meetings in Geneva a little more than 20 years earlier serve to make this episode more credible; and, as we shall see, within less than a century there would be many gatherings of such a kind in London itself.

★ ★ ★

From the early-eighteenth-century evidence, we know that the designated houses or inns where those meetings took place were not male brothels, and had very little in common with such establishments; the fairly detailed documentation that has come down to us shows, in the words of Rictor Norton, that male prostitution was 'not widespread enough to provoke public comment, nor did it involve a network of pimps and male whore-houses'.[39] It is worth considering briefly here the issue of prostitution in Northern Europe in the period before 1700, a subject on which some of the English scholarship has made very exaggerated claims. As we have seen, male prostitution is quite well attested in Southern Europe: some boys will-ingly had sex for money, some were individually pimped, some slaves were bought to be hired out sexually, and certain inns were well-known venues where boys could be found for paid sex. A few houses of ill repute in Florence may have performed some of the functions of a male brothel, but there is no evidence from any of those societies of an established brothel in the full sense of the term.[40] In Northern Europe the evidence is much more scanty, but there is just enough to show that some individuals did prostitute themselves for money.

The earliest case is very striking, but also highly untypical. In 1394 a man named John Rykener, 'calling himself Eleanor', was arrested in a London street after dark. He was dressed as a woman, and another man had approached him for sex; Rykener had asked him for money, and they had entered a nearby 'stall' to perform the act. Under interrogation Rykener explained that he had learned his trade from a female prostitute, and that another woman, who pimped her own daughter, had used him to play a trick on some of the daughter's clients: the young woman would be sup-plied to them in an unlit bedroom for sex, and in the morning, after she had slipped away, they would be presented with Rykener in female dress and told that they had had sex with this man—presumably, for purposes of blackmail. Earlier that year he had spent some time living as a woman in Oxford, where he had frequently engaged in sodomy with three students; given his female persona, we may assume that he took the passive role. He had also worked as a tapster in an inn in nearby Burford, where he had had sex with three friars and six other men. One of the friars had given him a golden ring; three of the other men had given him, respectively, a shilling, 20 pence, and two shillings. (These were presumably cumulative totals rep-resenting many sexual encounters: in 1390 a labourer might have earned eighteen pence, i.e. one shilling and sixpence, in a week.)[41]

Although the transvestism must make that case an extremely untypical one, it does show that men selling their sexual services to other men were not an unknown phenomenon. And yet the later evidence of such prostitution, in England, is almost non-existent. As we have seen, the surviving records of the Bridewell court do not include any cases of male prostitution at all, even though that was exactly the sort of behaviour that it would have dealt with. That some individuals may have supplied sex for money should certainly not be ruled out; it would be surprising if this never occurred. Yet we have only glancing literary references to such behaviour, such as the reference to a man enjoying a 'prostitute boy' in Donne's first Satire (c.1593), and a description in a poem by Thomas Middleton (c.1599) of an attractive, feminine-looking youth encountered in the street, who gave the impression of being available for sex, possibly for money—though this is not very directly stated—but turned out to be a 'Cheating youth'.[42] In the literary culture that was richly proliferating in this period, and which has been intensively studied by modern scholars, the tally of such references is very slight. It is impossible to agree with Alan Bray's statement that 'the literary evidence shows how common homosexual prostitution was'; what it does tend to show—so far as literary evidence can demonstrate such things, which may depend significantly on the type of literature involved—is quite the opposite.[43]

In other parts of Northern Europe the evidence is also thin. Franz von Alsten, the man who was sodomized by a circle of men in a village near Münster in the 1530s, mentioned in court that he had been paid eight shillings by his most regular partner, and had been offered a couple of silver coins by a man who propositioned him; but he seems generally to have been a willing participant anyway, with or without payment, and could not be described as someone who earned his living as a prostitute.[44] Pierre Canal, the prominent citizen of Geneva arrested in 1610, who had held dinners for groups of sodomites in his house, confessed under torture 'that he had been passive and active with numerous men and that he had given and received money in exchange for sex'.[45] Yet he was certainly not living as a prostitute; this evidence shows that some kinds of transactional sex could involve payment, but leaves open the question of whether any of the other individuals involved were engaged in prostitution as a way of life.

In France there is only minimal evidence of ordinary male prostitution in the first half of the seventeenth century. One of the accusations made against the poet Théophile de Viau, who was put on trial in 1623, was that he used to eat and drink at a disreputable tavern in Paris, where young men were available; the implication of that charge (which Théophile denied, so far as the young men were concerned) was not entirely clear, but may have involved male prostitution.[46] Definite evidence of boys or young men prostituting themselves appears only later. The man who told the Parisian police in 1704 that he had become a pimp because he could no longer attract paying customers himself had obviously been working as a male prostitute in the 1690s. In 1702 another police report had described him as a 25- or 26-year-old, 'with an attractive face', who invited numerous young men to his lodgings where 'he prostitutes himself to all the young people who come to find him in his bed'; a search of his papers revealed that he had been carrying on this 'abominable commerce' for many years, and that one of his clients was the comte de Tallard, a lieutenant-general in the French army.[47] And in 1703 another police report discussed the case of a man who, 'having spent his youth in disgraceful sodomy, prostituted young men'.[48] Clearly that behaviour had been going on for some time.

It is in the second half of the seventeenth century that evidence emerges of French procurers who 'traded' in boys or young men. This could involve hiring them out for individual sexual encounters, but they might also be supplied on a long-term basis to men of sufficient social standing who could keep them, often as 'lackeys' (laquais, personal servants), in their households. Two of the charges against Jacques Chausson and Jacques Paulmier, who were tried and executed in Paris in 1661, involved activities of this kind. One witness reported that Chausson had brought 'a very beautiful young boy' to his lodgings, and that thereafter a well-dressed man, identified as the marquis du Bellay, made regular visits there, when Chausson would close the door 'and one would hear the said boy crying out and sobbing'. Chausson confessed that he had then sold the boy to the marquis for 50 gold louis, and said that, having been taken off to the marquis's country residence, the boy was now his 'chief valet of the bedroom'. A similar fate had befallen a fourteen-year-old boy, who had been abducted, held against his will, and then sold to the baron de Bellefore.[49] There seems to have been a growing market for this kind of human commodity. Between 1673 and 1683 Louis XIV's brother, the duc d'Orléans—whose own interest in young men was notorious—employed an unscrupulous maître d'hôtel, described by the duc's indignant wife as follows: 'he was an atheist and a sodomite; he kept a school of them, and sold boys like horses. He would go to the pit of the Opera to clinch his deals.'[50]

In 1701 a Parisian police report described what had happened to some seventeen- and eighteen-year-old boys who had been reported missing. A man called Neel (said to be of Irish origin: perhaps Neill) had 'seduced' them, and then, 'having used them for the most criminal purposes on his own account, had sold them to his friend the sieur de la Guillaumie, and to some other criminals who have been engaged in this infamous business for a long time'.[51] And in the following year a 24-year-old man called Lebel, described as 'a good-looking youth', was questioned by the Paris police after he had been found in 'a place where every day you see young boys coming in with people of quality, and even monks'. He told the police that he had been 'debauched' by an older man when he was just ten (in 1688). That man had been one of a group of three who frequently invited young boys to a tavern, or to their lodgings, in order to seduce them. 'As they have no financial means', he explained, 'and live only on the proceeds of this business, they deliver the youths they have debauched to people who pay them well, and they share the price between them.' He went on to name eleven other men—six of them clergymen—who were currently engaged in this sort of trade. One of them, a M. Leroux, ran a sort of sexual employ-ment agency: 'he sends handsome lackeys to lords in the provinces, on demand, arranging here in Paris their conditions of employment.'[52] All this evidence suggests that such practices were well established in Paris by the final decades of the seventeenth century. There seems to be no factual docu-mentation of them in London at that time. But it is noteworthy that in a play by Thomas Durfey, published in 1682, when the beautiful young hero-ine has disguised herself as a boy, one character comments: 'The Youth may come to preferment in time; for to my knowledge there's many a *Noble Peer* in this Country would give 100 Guineys for such a Page.' (The hero, to whom she has attached herself, responds: 'Let 'em be damn'd; I love him for his Virtues.')[53]

To return to England: the lack of clear documentary evidence of male prostitution in the sixteenth and seventeenth centuries has not deterred some writers from asserting that it was common—or even from positing the existence of male brothels. That last claim was put forward by Alan Bray on the basis of two texts. One was a poem by John Marston, published in 1598, which referred to 'male stewes'; but this was a work of grotesquely exaggerated satire. The passage where that phrase occurs comes after a description of a man so debauched that, having abandoned his regular whore, he has now turned to 'his *Ganimede*, | His perfum'd shee-goate, smooth kembd & high fed. | At Hogsdon now his monstrous lust he feasts, | For there he keepes a baudy-house of beasts.' Finally, giving up both 'faire *Cynedian* boyes' and 'Veluet cap'd Goates, duch Mares', he falls back on 'the

Cynick friction'—solitary masturbation.[54] If we are to treat this flight of fancy as documentary evidence, we should also be arguing that it was standard practice to keep a collection of animals for sexual purposes. Bray's dependence on this poetic source is particularly surprising, given that he himself issued a warning—which will be quoted in the next chapter—against treating the works of such writers as if they were reliable descriptions of actual contemporary behaviour.

The other text was a brief passage in a work by Clement Walker, a cantankerous lawyer who, after being purged from the Long Parliament in 1648, became such an outspoken critic of the parliamentary regime that he was eventually committed to the Tower of London on a charge of high treason. The passage comes in the work which helped to bring on that charge, *Anarchia anglicana*, published in 1649. In the course of an attack on the senior politician Sir Henry Mildmay, who was a member of the Council of State, he wrote that Mildmay had tried to seduce a citizen's wife in Cheapside, and then added: 'but more of this I will not speak, lest his wife beat him, and give an ill example to other women, to the prejudice of our other new States men, and their new erected Sodomes and Spintries at the Mulbury-garden at St *Iames's*.'[55] Bray glosses this as a reference to 'several newly built homosexual brothels in London'; but such an interpretation is simply unviable. First, the context of this remark is entirely concerned with male–female sex, the implication being that the wives of other politicians might be encouraged to beat their husbands, who are indulging in sex with other women at the Mulberry Garden. As we shall see, the term 'Sodom' was used for sexual sins generally (and indeed for a range of other sins). The Latin word *spintria*, a term of uncertain signification occurring in a few passages in Tacitus and Suetonius, referred to some sort of perverse sexual performance or the person performing it. The use of it in English was so rare that it had not acquired a clear, fixed meaning. For some people it may have had a primarily male–male connotation, though it was also used in Renaissance Italy for a kind of pornographic medal depicting male–female sex; but it did not refer to a brothel.[56] Secondly, although the phrase 'newly erected' might suggest the construction of actual buildings, it cannot have that meaning here, for the simple reason that the Mulberry Garden was a park-like space (located where the western part of Buckingham Palace now stands), beyond the limit of the Westminster conurbation, with no nearby buildings whatsoever other than the noble residence of Goring House. Other evidence, from John Evelyn and Edmund Ludlow, shows that this garden was open to the public, as a place of recreation, between 1653 and 1660, and Walker's reference to it indicates that that development had taken place no later than 1649.[57] In Restoration London the name of the garden was applied to another area a little to the east, adjoining St James's Park; a famous poem by Rochester from the early 1670s indicates that the latter was used then as a place of sexual assignations and encounters ('*Foot-Men*, fine *Fops*, do here arrive, | And here promiscuously they swive').[58] So the simplest reading of Walker's comment is that such behaviour, involving individuals meeting individuals, was newly established—or, at least, rumoured to be so—in the Mulberry Garden in 1649. If he definitely intended the word 'spintries' to have a male–male meaning, that may have been just a rhetorical addition to his more general reference to sexual vice; but even if, as seems unlikely, he meant it as a description of real sodomitical encounters, this had nothing to do with the creation of brothels.

The risk has been taken here of belabouring this point, because it offers an example of how a very speculative and implausible claim can be taken up by subsequent writers, whose broader arguments it seems to support. The existence of these brothels is now well established in the modern scholarly literature. One literary historian, for example, confidently states that 'Seventeenth-century London clearly supported several male brothels', citing John Marston, Clement Walker, Donne's phrase about a 'prostitute boy' (which implies nothing about brothels), and a further literary reference, by Michael Drayton, to 'Malekind Stewes' ('He looks like one for the prepostrous sinne, | Put by the wicked and rebellious Iewes, | To be a Pathique in a Malekind Stewes'—this comment, in a fantastic satirical-allegorical poem, alludes to temple prostitution in the Old Testament and has nothing to do with seventeenth-century London). The same scholar goes on to assert that 'male brothels seem to have been condemned but not suppressed in the Stuart period'; presumably Walker's remark is the only basis for that claim, as the note to it supplies no other evidence, mentioning only Rykener's case in the 1390s and two modern scholars who, far from supplying further evidence, have commented on the striking lack of it in subsequent centuries.[59] These claims are put to work as part of a larger argument: the supposed prevalence of male prostitution, to the point where it allegedly included the known and apparently tolerated presence of male brothels, is used to reinforce a 'homoerotic' interpretation of a body of literary works. Yet the basis of the claims themselves, if one puts aside the brief remark by Clement Walker, consists only of a tiny quantity of literary references, one of which

did not relate to contemporary England at all. In the work of some modern
literary scholars there is sometimes a circular pattern of argument, in which
literary evidence, however slight, is taken as establishing a historical reality,
and that claimed historical reality is then taken as providing guidance on
how to interpret literary evidence. To this and some related problems we
shall return in a later chapter.

16

Northern Europe: contexts of sexual life

Just as the conditions which made youths—apprentices, servants, etc.—sexually exploitable were essentially the same across the whole of Western Europe, so too most of the other social and institutional contexts where the system of power-relations could have the effect of facilitating sodomy, as discussed in previous chapters, were no less present in Northern Europe: the Church, schools, ships, military units, noble households and so on. The one institution which was almost entirely absent in the North was that of slavery; small numbers of Muslim slaves, captured in the Habsburg–Ottoman wars, were scattered around the German lands, but there are no particular known instances of such men or youths being sexually coerced or exploited because of their subordinate status. (One of the very few autobiographical narratives by such people does contain a sexually suggestive episode, but of a rather different character. Osman ağa of Timişoara, an Ottoman cavalryman captured by the Austrians at the age of seventeen in 1688, was required one evening to share a narrow bed with a slightly younger Austrian boy, who, to his great surprise, took off all his clothes and told Osman to do the same. The boy then 'asked me about the morally degrading practices of the Turks, which he had heard about, and wanted me to teach him how it was done'. But Osman, who always presents himself to the reader as a pious Muslim, insists that he maintained strict self-control, 'even though I was very aroused at times'. He does comment that 'If a shameless person had been in my place, he would have felt such strong desire that he would not have been able to restrain himself, as the boy was attractive.')[1] Evidence of same-sex relations inside prisons is also lacking for the period before 1700 (there are two Swedish cases from 1734 and 1735), but there seems to be no deeper reason for that than the paucity of evidence overall.[2]

Forbidden Desire in Early Modern Europe: Male–Male Sexual Relations, 1400–1750. Noel Malcolm, Oxford University Press.
© Noel Malcolm 2024. DOI: 10.1093/oso/9780198886334.003.0016

The Church was certainly an institution in which sodomites could find a home. We have already encountered sodomitical friars in Bruges and Burford, priests and monks in the German lands, an eminent Swiss cleric, a French priest and a sexually voracious Lutheran pastor; and even though the records of the English monastic visitations must be treated with great caution, it is reasonable to suppose that not all of the accusations there were false. One of the handful of men prosecuted for sodomy at the Home Counties Assizes was a 'clerk' (meaning probably a clergyman), Matthew Heaton of East Grinstead, accused in 1580 of sodomizing a boy; and in 1643 a vicar was ejected from his parish (Arlington, in Sussex) for having 'divers times attempted to commit buggery with Nathaniel Brown, Samuel Andrews and Robert Williams, his parishioners'.[3] In 1667 Samuel Pepys recorded that a scandal had arisen concerning the Bishop of Rochester: his enemies were spreading the story 'of his being given to boys and of his putting his hand into a gentleman (who now comes to bear evidence against him) his codpiece while they were at table together'.[4] Pepys seems to have shared the view that these were calumnies; but the senior clergy in France during the latter part of the seventeenth century offered several examples of notoriously sodomitical prelates, including the Cardinal de Bouillon (son of the duc de Bouillon and nephew of the maréchal de Turenne) and Hyacinthe Serroni, Archbishop of Albi, who was said to have been passionately in love with the young man whom he appointed as his secretary.[5]

Where schoolteachers are concerned, the Northern European evidence is very patchy. Helmut Puff's wide-ranging study yields only one teacher who was actually prosecuted for sodomy, a member of the Augsburg group in the early 1530s—and he was charged with having sex with other adults, not with the boys in his care. Otherwise Puff mentions two allegations: a libel of c.1506 against the humanist Jakob Wimpfeling, claiming that he lusted after his male students, and a statement in a letter of 1507 that the magician Georg Faustus had been forced out of a previous job as a schoolmaster when it became known that he was sodomizing the boys.[6] A Czech schoolmaster is known to have been executed in 1590, at the little town of Žehušice, to the east of Prague, for molesting his pupils.[7] In the Netherlands, a teacher in Arnhem was accused of sodomizing his students in 1576, and a private tutor in Leiden, Litius Wielant, was put on trial in 1654 for the same offence. (Wielant's case was a curious one: a former monk from Germany, he was said to have encouraged his two pupils to plot against their widowed mother in order to get their inheritance, and it was even claimed that he had bought them pistols so that they could kill their guardian. The evidence against him on the charge of sodomy, however, consisted only of a statement by the housemaid. He protested his innocence eloquently and consistently, and in a letter to the authorities, written in his prison cell, he complained that he had lost his good name, so that 'henceforth, for the rest of my life, I shall be regarded as unworthy of all the public employments to which, previously, I could honourably aspire: professor, pastor, rector, and so on.')[8]

In France a number of cases involving teachers are known, though the overall totals are not high. Tom Hamilton's analysis of the 132 men accused of sodomy in the Parlement de Paris between 1540 and 1700 specifies fourteen schoolmasters, alongside 26 artisans and 24 clergymen. (The other known categories were as follows: fourteen office-holders, fourteen servants, fourteen labourers, five merchants and three noblemen.) He notes that clerics and schoolteachers predominated in the period 1650–80, when the appeals 'clustered around cases that generated some degree of public outrage'; so during the century before that, their numbers had been distinctly low.[9]

One of the earlier cases, which attracted some public attention, involved Nicolas Dadon, a regent of the Collège du Cardinal Lemoine at the University of Paris. It was normal for Dadon to have two, three or four boys sleeping in his chamber; but in 1586 the parents of one of these, an eleven-year-old, accused him of inviting the boy into his bed and sodomizing him. Defending himself, Dadon said that in the past 'several children had gone to bed with him, and he had never lapsed in this way'. But a surgeon confirmed that the boy had been penetrated anally, and the regent was sentenced to death.[10] Bed-sharing of this kind, when pupils lodged with their teacher, or indeed when a private tutor lived in the family home, was normal in all parts of Europe; and the general opportunities for sexual exploitation that were enjoyed by men exercising pedagogical authority over boys were no doubt universal as well. The surprising thing, therefore, is not that schoolmasters and tutors appear in the records of accusations and trials for sodomy, but that they feature there as seldom as they do—even allowing for the almost certain fact that the number of recorded cases was a fraction of the number of actual ones. In a previous discussion of this issue in Southern Europe, it was suggested that in Mediterranean societies most people would have expected an adult man surrounded by boys to be capable of wanting to have sex with them—an expectation of which the teachers themselves would have been very conscious, in a way that encouraged self-restraint.

If the argument of this book is correct, such a consideration would not have applied in Northern Europe. Here the explanation of the relative infrequency of such cases is surely a simpler one: in these societies, sodomy was just infrequent anyway.

One would gain a very different impression from reading Alan Bray's comments on these matters. In England, he wrote, 'there is evidence that homosexuality was institutionalised not only at the universities but also in grammar schools and even in the village schools.' The evidence he offers for this is very slight. He offers just two examples of schoolmasters: Nicholas Udall, the headmaster of Eton, who apparently confessed to having committed buggery with one of his pupils in 1541, and the master of a village school in Essex in 1594, who was said to have engaged in 'beastly behaviour amongst his scholars', teaching them 'all manner of bawdry'. (The nature of the latter's offence is quite unclear; as he was called before an ecclesiastical court, it is highly unlikely that it was sodomy.)[11]

For the universities, Bray confines himself to quoting passages from two satirical poems. The earlier of these, the satire by John Marston which has already been quoted, denounces the sodomitical tendencies of English Jesuits, returning under cover from their Continental seminaries and 'Tainting our towns and hopeful academies' with their unnatural lusts. This was hardly a general comment on the English universities, whose employment of such foreign-trained undercover Catholics was minimal or non-existent. The later satire, a poem of uncertain authorship composed in c.1615, does inveigh against tutors at the universities poisoning their pupils with the 'infection' of sodomy; but this forms part of an exorbitantly phrased denunciation of the whole of English society ('In Academie, country, citty, Courte, | Infinite are defiled with this spurt [sc. sport, in the sense of sexual play]').[12] What makes Bray's dependence on such evidence all the more surprising is the fact that earlier in the same chapter he had strongly warned against treating such literary texts as historical testimony. The problem with such writings, he observed, was that 'when one looks closely at them it becomes apparent just how little they are the stuff of social life and how much the product of purely political or literary influences.' He concluded: 'the satirists' portrayal of homosexuality...is not a convincing source for social history.'[13]

In an attempt to bolster Bray's case, one could add the very small number of other surviving references to sodomitic, or allegedly sodomitic, English schoolmasters. Lawrence Willington, of Rotherhithe, was prosecuted in 1613 for sodomy with three boys, each aged ten or thereabouts, two of whom he was accused of molesting in the Rotherhithe school house.[14] Anthony Death, headmaster of Oundle School, was accused in 1625 of inviting 'the most pretty and amorous boys' to see him in private, where—in the words of four boys, at least two of them in the age-range 13–16, who testified against him—'he used towards them sorry, wanton behaviour.' There is also a report in a printed newsletter of 1655 that 'there was the last Assizes at *Lincoln* a Schoolmaster hanged for Buggering one of his Schollars.'[15]

One well-documented case from a university can be added too: that of Richard Edmund, a young Fellow of Merton College, Oxford, who was investigated for a variety of moral offences by the College authorities in 1492. Among them was this specific charge: 'that you encouraged and pro-voked various and diverse youths to the sin against nature, and that you miserably misused them, or at least some of them, in that sin at various times, to the extreme peril of your soul, and to the immense scandal and considerable infamy of our College'. First he denied the other accusations but pleaded guilty to this one; then he withdrew his guilty plea; finally he was condemned to be expelled.[16] One example may prove little (though this is the only clear example we have); but the reaction of the authorities here does suggest that such sexual activities were not passed over in com-placent silence. Two later defamation cases at Cambridge show that sexual abuse of pupils by tutors there was certainly conceivable (though that in itself has never been in doubt); but in one of them, in 1589, the pupils admitted that theirs was a malicious prosecution, and in the other, in 1611, the case was dropped—apparently for tangential reasons—so no verdict is available.[17]

To strengthen Bray's case further, one might be tempted also to cite the recollections of Augustine Baker, the Welsh Benedictine who studied at Oxford in the early 1590s. During his time at Broadgates Hall (later incorp-orated into Pembroke College), he wrote, he had found extreme 'vicious-ness' there, of the kind referred to by St Paul in Romans 1:26–7; and 20 years later, when he lodged briefly in Oxford, his landlady complained of this vice among the scholars. In the account he gave of his school days, at Christ's Hospital, he referred also to a master who had been guilty of this sin. But, speculating that the man was a Cambridge graduate, he immediately went on to say that this demonstrated that 'the greatest corruption, in our land, as to such abominable vice (besides that of fornication and drinking) cometh from the two universities of England, which the enemy of mankind hath extremely corrupted in these daies of heresy.' Elsewhere in the same text he blithely informed his readers that during the idyllic period preceding the Reformation, people did not commit fornication or adultery, 'much lesse other yet more abominable sins of the flesh, that heresy brought in'. As Alan Stewart has pointed out, this whole text was so strongly shaped by a religio-polemical motive that 'As historical "evidence", the value of Baker's *Memorials* is highly questionable.'[18]

The issue is not whether sodomy ever took place in English schools and universities, but whether it was frequent there—or even whether it was, in Bray's surprising phrase, 'institutionalised'. Bray's key point, an application of his more general argument about the ubiquity of sodomy causing its invisibility, was that the mild treatment given to those accused or convicted of sodomy demonstrates that its presence in the educational system was generally accepted: 'The limited effect which complaints... had is revealing of how deep-rooted the institution [sc. of sodomy] was.'[19] Yet this claim is based only on the two cases of schoolmasters mentioned above. One of them, as we have seen, was very probably not accused of sodomy; his case went to an ecclesiastical court. For reasons which are unknown, he did not come to court to answer the charge, which means that all other relevant details are unknown too. Such evidence does not supply a strong basis for general claims about leniency or acceptance. Nicholas Udall's case is more puzzling, and the puzzles begin with the fact that it was heard in the first instance by the Privy Council—where the indictment had been primarily concerned with Udall's complicity with a former pupil, Thomas Cheney, and another Eton scholar, in a robbery. When questioned about 'the sayd fact & other felonious trespasses wherof he was suspected', Udall apparently confessed 'that he did com[m]itt buggery w^t the sayd Cheney sundry times heretofore'.[20] The most likely explanation, both of the involvement of the Privy Council and of the further interest in his relations with his former pupil, is that Thomas Cheney was a close relative of one of the Privy Councillors, Sir Thomas Wriothesley; and this in turn may explain why Udall was only imprisoned, and not given the more publicity-generating sentence of hanging. There are also signs that he had powerful patrons, and perhaps some connections at the royal court. Udall's case is simply too unusual, and too unclear, for it to be the basis of any general theory about institutionalization. And in any case, his offence was certainly treated as a crime, punished by ejection from his headmastership as well as incarceration; it is strange that Bray should take those facts as 'indicative of the degree to which homosexuality was effectively tolerated in the educational system'.[21]

★ ★ ★

Among other walks of life where conditions may have favoured the practice of sodomy were soldiering and seafaring. Some early modern countries on the Atlantic side of Europe did use convict rowers in the sixteenth century, but there was nothing really equivalent, in scale and nature, to the *bagni* of the Mediterranean. For the period before 1700 the tally of known cases of sodomy on board English ships is low. Sometimes the trial and sentencing took place at sea, though this was less common on merchant ships, few of whose captains were given a royal commission with power over life and death. Such cases of judgment *en voyage* include that of Thomas Ogle, steward of one of the vessels that took part in Francis Drake's West Indian voyage of 1585–6, who was executed for buggering two boys; and a coxswain hanged for sodomizing the purser's boy on an East India Company ship in 1609.[22] A handful of cases were brought to the High Court of Admiralty in London: one in 1608, where the age of the alleged victim was not stated; one in the early or mid-1630s, where a sailor was accused of sodomizing three boys; two quite separate cases in 1638, each involving a man and a boy (where both men were sentenced to be hanged, but after a year's imprisonment were reprieved by the King); and one in 1661, where a fourteen-year-old boy made an accusation against a naval chaplain. But these are the only known cases at that court in the seventeenth century.[23] One modern writer, again developing the Bray thesis, has claimed that such evidence demonstrates that cases had to involve 'more than ordinary buggery or sodomy for them to be considered important'; yet all of these cases were quite ordinary, involving no special disruption of 'social order' beyond the perceived threat to proper order and discipline on board ship.[24] From 1661 onwards, naval regulations incorporated the wording 'If any Person belonging to the Fleet shall commit Buggery or Sodomy, he shall be punished with Death'.[25] But this offence, which had been a serious felony in English law since 1533, had evidently been punishable long before 1661 where activities on board ship were concerned; and the standard language used by the court in its indictments suggests that sodomy did not need to be accompanied by any special socially disruptive acts or circumstances in order to attract fierce disapproval. In the first half of the century there was a regular Latin formula: 'most wickedly and feloniously, and against the order of nature, he feloniously committed and perpetrated that detestable and abominable crime of sodomy—in English, "of buggery"—which is not to be named among humans.' And by 1661 this had become 'he committed and perpetrated that detestable and abominable sin of sodomy—in English, "of buggery"— which is not to be named among Christians, feloniously, wickedly and diabolically, and against the order of nature, to the great displeasure of Almighty God and to the dishonour of the entire human race, breaching the peace of our said lord, the King.'[26]

Given the hierarchical power-relations that existed on board ship, it is not surprising that the great majority of these cases concerned the exploitation of boys by adult men. But not every instance of sodomitical behaviour took that form. In 1655 a printed London newsletter reported that 'two Youths' had been brought as prisoners from the fleet to be tried 'for most horrid Buggery with each other, who were first discovered to five young godly Youths of the ships, that... revealed it to the officers, and two more were sent up for that filthy Crime a while before'.[27] And in one case, from 1679, the surviving evidence (which is frustratingly slight) appears to suggest that sodomy took place between a number of men. In February of that year the Governor of Jamaica reported that 'A fortnight since five men of His Majesty's Ship Jersey were tried for sodomy, and four found guilty and sentenced to die, whereof I suffered but one to be executed, viz., Francis Dilly, who appeared to be the chief ringleader. The other three I have pardoned, white men being scarce with us.'[28]

One prominent case involving a naval officer took place in late-seventeenth-century London, though in an entirely civilian context. It involved an attempt by Captain Edward Rigby, commander of the warship HMS *Dragon*, to have sex with William Minton, a nineteen-year-old boy. On 5 November 1698, '*Minton* standing in St. *James's* Park [which was by now a well-known place for sexual contacts] to see the Fireworks, *Rigby* stood by him, and took him by the hand, and squeez'd it; put his Privy Member Erected into *Minton's* Hand; kist him, and put his Tongue into *Minton's* Mouth, who being much astonish'd at these Actions went from him'; Rigby caught up with the boy and persuaded him to meet him in a tavern two days later, but—according to the earliest printed account of the trial—the boy went to the authorities and arranged a trap. At the tavern, Rigby took Minton to a private room and repeated his rather crude seduction routine: '*Rigby* ... kist him, took him by the Hand, put his Tongue into *Mintons* Mouth, and thrust *Mintons* Hand into his (*Rigby*) Breeches, saying, *He had raised his Lust to the highest degree.*' Making some further efforts to persuade the boy, he 'spake most Blasphemous words' (it has been suggested that these included the traditional claim about Jesus and St John) 'and said, *That the French King did it, and the* Czar *of* Muscovy *made* Alexander, *a Carpenter, a Prince for that purpose,* and affirmed, *He had seen the Czar of* Muscovy *through a hole at Sea, lye with Prince Alexander*'. Having pulled down Minton's breeches, he was on the point of sodomizing him when the boy gave the pre-arranged alarm, and a constable rushed in from the adjoining room.[29] Rigby escaped the death penalty, no doubt because actual penetration had not occurred, but the sentence he received was nevertheless a severe one: three sessions in the pillory, a colossal fine (£1,000) and a year's imprisonment.[30]

Evidence from other Northern European countries is also very scanty. For the Dutch, the greatest continuous seafaring enterprise in this period was their United East India Company, the 'Vereenigde Oostindische Compagnie' or VOC, which generated a large quantity of documentation. But cases of sodomy on shipboard appear there very infrequently in the seventeenth century. One prosecution which attracted great interest because of the status of the convicted man was that of Joost Schouten, a high official and member of the Council of the Indies—and former judge—who was executed for sodomy in Batavia (modern Jakarta) in 1644. He confessed to a number of partners over the previous seven years, in acts of sodomy where he had always taken the passive role. One had been a boatswain's mate, on board a ship sailing from Malacca to Acheh in the Indonesian archipelago, another was a boatswain, who was also executed, and another had been a captain. Seafarers may have been over-represented among his sexual contacts (of whom the total of named individuals came to nineteen, though rumour had it that there were many more), given the major role they played in the operations of the VOC in the East Indies, where Schouten was stationed; but this evidence does at least show that some sodomy was committed by such men, while also indicating that it was not necessarily age-differentiated.[31] Two years later, three youths were convicted of sodomy and sentenced to flogging on a VOC ship returning from the Indies to Holland. And at another trial in Batavia in 1647, a ship's captain and a young boy were both sentenced to death for sodomy—though whether the boy was a member of his crew, or a local resident, is not clear.[32] But these are virtually the only relevant cases in the seventeenth-century records.[33] And if suitable documentation exists for France, another maritime power of the Atlantic side of Europe, it has not yet been researched or published. Only evidence of a rather indirect kind is available for this period, such as an order issued by the secretary of the Navy, Jean-Baptiste de Colbert, in the late 1680s, demanding that the authorities at the port of Brest put a stop to the activities of the naval officers there, who, the King had been told, were engaged in the abominable practice of sodomy.[34]

Cases involving soldiers are also few and far between. To a large extent this probably reflects the fact that military authorities tended to dispense their own justice, leaving no trace in the ordinary administrative records. But still the paucity of evidence is quite striking; and in one case, at least, it suggests that male–male sex was not at all 'institutionalized' within the relevant military unit. A trial in mid-sixteenth-century Zurich revealed that when it had become known that a Swiss mercenary had had sex with a boy while his platoon was serving in northern Italy, an 'outcry' (*Geschrei*) had arisen among his colleagues, who expelled him from the platoon.[35] This presents a strong contrast with the picture of Italian military life that emerged from the prosecution of the group of so-called Lombard soldiers in Basel in 1474, where several testified to having been sodomized when young, and to having engaged in active sodomy thereafter.[36] In Slovakia in 1603, during the Habsburg–Ottoman war, a Czech or Austrian *Rittermeister* (cavalry officer) called Aslborn was tried for sodomy by the military authorities in the field; the death sentence meted out to him shows that this offence was taken seriously, though it must also be noted that the judicial proceedings were started by Aslborn himself, when he foolishly accused another officer of defaming him. That other officer had been moved to raise the topic with Aslborn by a conversation with Aslborn's young page, who was a victim of his sexual assaults. It seems that Aslborn was not expecting the commander of the army to summon the page immediately and question him, 'whereupon the page gave him the answer that just a few days earlier he [Aslborn] had committed such an assault on him'; and thereafter other victims of the *Rittermeister's* sexual attentions were also produced. Aslborn managed to flee the camp before the verdict was given, but he was captured and executed shortly afterwards.[37] A Polish officer, serving in the Netherlands in 1684, was accused of sexually exploiting his young servant and a junior soldier; he contested the accusation strenuously, and was eventually acquitted.[38]

Two military cases from this period in Scandinavia have been mentioned briefly already: one involving a Scottish officer and a younger man from his regiment, and the case of a captain in the army of the Danish–Norwegian kingdom. The latter came under investigation in 1673–4 after several of his men accused him of forcing himself on them; the authorities concluded that he had been taking advantage of his men in this way over a period of several years.[39] As with other abuses of officerly power, it was much easier for a group of soldiers than for a lone individual to gather sufficient confidence to report the offence. But if we move forward a little into the eighteenth century, another, perhaps deeper, reason emerges, which tells us something about the sort of limited understanding of male–male sexual behaviour that may have been quite common in these societies. In Sweden in 1719 an investigation was held into a Captain Johan von Hoen, who was the object of complaints and accusations by seventeen of his men (and one servant); he was found guilty, and banished from the country. On many occasions he had put his hand into a soldier's trousers and told the soldier to do the same to him; usually he was seeking to perform mutual masturbation, but sometimes he attempted interfemoral sex. This behaviour had gone on for years. The men had mostly reacted with unease and distaste: typical statements by some of them, summarized in the court records, included 'he had not understood what this was meant to imply', 'he felt uneasy', and 'he understood that something was wrong.' The drummer, while extricating himself from the captain's grasp, had asked him what this was supposed to mean, and what he wanted from him. Another soldier said that he felt fearful but assumed that the captain was just engaging in some sort of foolish play. Apparently it was only when a number of soldiers compared their experiences that a clearer idea emerged of the sodomitical nature of these actions.[40] Such evidence is hardly compatible with the claim, by some modern historians, that the reason why same-sex activities were seldom reported was that they were generally understood and accepted.

An even more striking example of limited comprehension comes from another Swedish case, just four years earlier; it happened to involve two soldiers, though otherwise there was no particularly military aspect to it. Over several years, a dragoon and a corporal had enjoyed sexual relations; these had begun when they were sharing a bed, and the corporal had tried to grab the dragoon's genitals. That advance had been resisted at the time, but soon afterwards the dragoon, remembering stories he had been told about women who dressed as men and volunteered for the army (a rare but genuine phenomenon at the time), had convinced himself that the corporal was in fact a woman in disguise—even though the corporal was married.

On that basis he then had sexual relations with the corporal many times, receiving kisses and caresses in bed while engaging, face to face, in what was presumably interfemoral sex. (The corporal never allowed him actually to see his genitals.)[41] This is not so much a story about military life, as an illustration of what could happen in a society where male sexual desire for other males was not a very widely understood phenomenon.

★ ★ ★

There are several known examples of senior French officers whose sexual interest in young men was well known: the duc de Vendôme (who took the passive role) and the prince de Condé (who may have taken both roles) have already been mentioned, and also the comte de Tallard. In the latter part of the seventeenth century there were other well-known examples, including the marquis de La Feuillade, the marquis de Courcillon and the duc de Villars.[42] As that roll-call of titles suggests, this phenomenon cannot be separated from the more general one of the practice of male–male sex by members of the nobility and the privileged upper class. Some general factors have already been noted in Southern Europe: the reluctance of courts and tribunals to indict such people; their own ability to block or face down any attempts to prosecute them; the likelihood that any sentences, if applied, would be light; and the general sense of relative impunity with which some of them, accordingly, conducted their personal lives—in addition to the fact that, as landowners and/or employers, they could select potential sexual partners from a range of men or youths whose deference to their will might be assumed. All these factors could apply in Northern Europe too, though in varying ways in different societies. The overall result was that while the number of nobles and patricians appearing in the trial documents was very limited, other sources suggest that, at least in the seventeenth century, male–male sexual relations were more visible, and perhaps more common, in the upper strata of some of these societies.

One of the earliest cases concerned an Alsatian nobleman, Richard Puller von Hohenburg, who was arraigned in 1463, on the prompting of another nobleman, and deprived of several of his landholdings. (Already this detail raises a more general point about nobles when proceedings were taken against them, which is that there were often other major interests, economic or political or dynastic, at stake.) The rival nobleman said he had become suspicious when he saw one of Puller's servants wearing fine clothes unsuited to his status; under questioning, the servant admitted that the sexual interest shown in him by his master had given him an opportunity for blackmail. No formal trial for sodomy took place, however, perhaps partly because Puller had arranged for one key witness to be drowned. Arrested again in 1474, he was released two years later in return for confessing to sodomy, giving up his lands, and agreeing to be incarcerated in a monastery (a promise he immediately broke). Seeking Swiss help for his campaign to recover his possessions, he briefly convinced the authorities in Zurich to support him, until they found that he was having sex with another servant—and, as he confessed under torture, had had sexual relations with a number of other men. He was finally burnt at the stake in Zurich in 1482.[43]

Political factors seem to have played the main role in the case of Walter, Lord Hungerford, who was condemned by act of attainder in July 1540. He died on the scaffold alongside his patron, Thomas Cromwell—whose execution was very much a political act. Hungerford was accused of committing 'the abominable vice of buggery with Wm. Maister, Thos. Smith, and other his servants', but another accusation was that he had employed a wise woman or witch to 'conjure and show how long the King should live', and one report soon after his death stated that he had been 'attainted of sodomy, of having forced his own daughter, and having practised magic and invocation of devils'.[44] What was meant to be proof of depravity looks much more like evidence of an utter determination on the part of the authorities to convict.

Politics, involving fierce aristocratic rivalry as well as some manoeuvring between religio-political factions, was also at work in the case of Edward de Vere, 17th Earl of Oxford, against whom some quite detailed accusations of sodomy were made in 1580—though in this case the matter never came to a trial. At a time of strong political divisions at court, Oxford had denounced three Catholics with whom he had previously been associated, and they in turn drew up detailed lists of charges against him. Again the range of accusations was very wide, including blasphemous atheism, treason, sodomy, bestiality and necromancy. Some of the blasphemies attributed to him (for example, that the Trinity was a 'fable', that the Bible was made by humans to keep people in obedience, that there was no life after death 'and that the rest was diviseid but to make vs afrayd') have quite a formulaic feeling to them, fitting the standard portrait of a Renaissance Italian atheist. However, enough circumstantial details were supplied of Oxford's sexual exploitation of pages and young servants—including an Italian boy whom he had spotted singing in a choir in Venice, aged fifteen, and had quickly recruited to his personal service—to make the charge of sodomy seem plausible at least. But there was apparently no appetite to prosecute a high-ranking nobleman for same-sexual relations, and since he was able to weather the brief political storm, these matters were taken no further.[45]

The second actual trial of an English nobleman on a charge of sodomy, and the last for a very long time, concerned Mervin Touchet, Lord Audley, 2nd Earl of Castlehaven, who was convicted by a jury of his peers and executed in 1631. The allegations of sodomy involved the Earl's dealings with three, or possibly four, household servants; one was described as a page, but most, or perhaps all, were young adults, two of them clearly of marriageable age. It was claimed that the Earl had engaged in mutual masturbation with one man, and sodomized or attempted to sodomize two others. One of those, an Irishman called Florence or Lawrence Fitzpatrick, testified that Castlehaven had summoned him to his bed, 'where hee [sc. Castlehaven] Buggered him, & spent his seed vpon him, but did not penitrate his body, & that the same Fitz Patrick did ye like againe to his lord'.[46] Yet if these had been his only offences, he might never have been brought to trial. For at the heart of the case were his alleged actions in encouraging his servants to rape his wife, and his attempt to persuade one of them to have sex with his daughter-in-law, with the promise that he would convey a rich inheritance to any resulting child. Those issues—plus the fact that he had favoured one of his servants with huge gifts—formed the basis on which his son had initiated the legal process, by making a formal complaint to the Privy Council. On those matters, which were summarized in a charge of rape, he was convicted almost unanimously. The conviction for sodomy passed only by a slender majority, as it was very doubtful whether the accepted legal definition, which required penetration, had been satisfied in this case. (In his final appeal to the court, Castlehaven said that the kind of buggery attributed to him by the witnesses did not qualify for the death penalty under the law; the judges then told him that 'the words of the Statute made no distinction of Buggery, & that Buggery Generally was punishable by death, though there was not a penitration, vpon which resolution the Lord Audley seemed much amazed'.) The whole trial lasted only one day, and Castlehaven was executed three weeks later.[47]

A case involving a Bavarian nobleman two decades later resembles that of Castlehaven in one significant respect: it too would surely not have reached the point of a judicial investigation without the intervention of a family member. In 1649 Philipp von Pappenheim asked the Imperial court in

Vienna to deprive his elder brother, Caspar Gottfried, of the hereditary position of Imperial Marshal and transfer it to him instead, arguing that Caspar Gottfried's irreligious and immoral actions—habitual sodomy—rendered him unsuited to such a high office. The court set up a high-level commission to investigate. It found that Caspar Gottfried, who was then aged 58, had indeed been involved in male–male sexual activities over many years. His targets were young servants, pages, and male youths of all kinds, including even the eighteen-year-old son of the mayor of Pappenheim; his agents would invite them to his private rooms, where he would kiss them, take off his clothes, and ask them to do the same. Sometimes he engaged in fellatio, but he also told one boy that he wanted to have sex with him 'the way they do it in Spain and Italy' (meaning, presumably, anally). Another youth was told that there was no need to mention this to his confessor, as it was not a sin, merely 'fun and games'. The commission also found that he had raised up some of his long-term favourites in improper ways, showering them with rich gifts, expensive clothes, and so on, and sharing both his bed and his coach with them. Caspar Gottfried von Pappenheim was put under house arrest, but died just before the commission was due to issue its final judgment. No doubt he would have been stripped of his hereditary office, and disgraced in other ways; but we can reasonably doubt whether the death sentence would have been passed on a nobleman of his standing.[48]

In France, as we have seen, the cases of just three nobles were heard by the Parlement de Paris in the entire period 1540–1700. The upper nobility were more or less beyond the reach of the law in these matters: generally, those among them who wished to engage in male–male sex could do so. To the aristocratic military commanders mentioned above, the names of quite a few other high-ranking noblemen of seventeenth-century France can be added; although the total of these men may have been only a small fraction of the nobility as a whole, many of them were prominent enough for their behaviour to be observed and commented on.[49] In the last quarter of the seventeenth century, among the younger members of the aristocracy who gathered around the royal court, a self-consciously 'libertine' ethos developed, where young blades would vie with one another to display their devil-may-care attitude towards the ordinary codes of moral and religious life. (Primi Visconti recalled the son of the duc de Vitry exclaiming, after a dinner with the princes de Vendôme, 'Let's see which of us can blaspheme the best!')[50] The kinds of behaviour this led to included drunken rampages, sacrilege and the sexual abuse of women; male–male sex seldom features in the accounts, no doubt because it did not fit the 'macho' values which such men typically espoused when gathered in groups. But there is one story, emerging from this culture, which seems to depict a very self-consciously organized system of same-sexual behaviour.

In the early summer of 1682 a prince of the House of Bourbon, then aged eighteen, was expelled from the court and ordered to live in confinement at Chantilly. Soon afterwards the ambassador of the Elector of Brandenburg in Paris reported that 'the debauchery of the young lords at Versailles is a reason why several more members of that group have been sent away from there, having been accused of wicked plans to commit sodomy'; and he added that members of the group had been on the point of corrupting another member of the royal family, Louis de Bourbon, comte de Vermandois, a son of the King (born illegitimate but later legitimized), who was only fourteen.[51] One memoirist, who himself frequented the court, wrote that at the beginning of June the King ordered 'the exile of a large number of eminent people accused of Ultramontane [sc. Italian, sc. sodomitical] debauchery'. Giving what seems to have been a very well-informed list, he named eleven individuals, plus the two young royals—the younger of whom, he claimed, was already 'very much involved in these debauches'.[52]

Much more detail was later supplied by a text known as *La France devenue italienne* ('France Turned Italian [sc. sodomitical]'), which was printed in a collection of works by the popular memoirist Roger de Bussy-Rabutin and became widely attributed to him. According to this work, a small 'cabal' of nobles with sodomitical interests, wishing to make their activities less public, had decided to set up a self-styled 'order' or 'confraternity', which could meet in private conclaves. Three initial organizers were named, of whom one, Bernard de Longueval, marquis de Manicamp, was 47, another, Antoine Charles, duc de Gramont, was 41, and the third, Gabriel de Cassagnet, chevalier de Tilladet, a Knight of Malta, was born probably in the 1640s, so might have been in his late 30s. A fourth, Antoine, marquis de Biran, aged 25, was then added; the only other member mentioned by name was Camille d'Hostun de La Baume, comte de Tallard, who was 20.[53]

The text printed the set of formal rules which, it said, the organizers drew up for their sexual confraternity. In mock-solemn, innuendo-laden language—which, on the surface, imitated the regulations of religious orders such as the Knights of Malta—it decreed that the members would, in a spirit of strict chastity, have nothing to do with women (though they could be given permission to marry and procreate for dynastic purposes); that young novices would enter the order and be subjected 'to the rigours of the novitiate' until they started to grow facial hair; that the four Grand Priors of the order would have the right to try out the suitability of each new recruit; and so on.[54] Modern historians have taken this as a genuine historical document. Yet the text which presented this alleged constitution was in fact written by Gatien de Courtilz de Sandras, a prolific novelist and journalist who is best known today for his fictionalized version of the memoirs of the musketeer d'Artagnan. By 1684, when the text was originally published (with the title *Les Intrigues amoureuses de la cour de France*) under a false imprint in Holland, he had gone to live in that country, where he was able to produce scurrilous works outside the reach of the French authorities. The text was one of a number of satirical pamphlets he composed, designed to titillate the public with scandalous stories while at the same time tending to discredit the world of the court. Other historical sources, such as the two mentioned above, do confirm that men regarded as belonging to some sort of group of sodomites at court, including some with the highest social connections, were accused of same-sex 'debauchery' in 1682; de Courtilz de Sandras evidently picked up on that, and on the story of the two young royals, which he also wove into his account. But it seems that he was working on the basis of quite distant gossip, and perhaps filling in the details as he pleased; apart from the two young princes, only one of the five men mentioned in his account (the chevalier de Tilladet) appears in the detailed list supplied by the memoirist. As for the 'confraternity': in the complete absence of any corroborating evidence, it would be rash to assume—as so many historians have—that such a formal organization ever existed, even as a parodic *jeu d'esprit*. The rules of this alleged confraternity are written with a sly ingenuity which accords well with de Courtilz de Sandras's own literary imagination; and indeed the detail about facial hair may reflect more an inherited literary trope than the realities of same-sexual desire in this particular society, of which he may have had no direct experience at all.[55]

If, as seems to have been the case, same-sex relations did flourish, relatively speaking, at the French court during this period (even though the point of the 'confraternity' story was that those nobles were trying to make their activities more secret, to avoid Louis XIV's well-known disapproval), one key reason must have been that the King's brother, Philippe, duc d'Orléans—known by his formal title of 'Monsieur'—was notoriously addicted to male–male sex, and had a number of men suited to that purpose in his circle. His greatest favourite, a man with whom he was closely associ-ated for 30 years, was Philippe de Lorraine-Armagnac, who was just three years younger than him; one modern historian has described him as 'seduc-tive, brutal and completely unscrupulous'.[56] Another sodomite to whom he gave positions of trust was Antoine Coëffier de Ruzé, marquis d'Effiat, who was one or two years older than Monsieur. These and other associates of the duc had sexual relations with him, and helped to supply him with good-looking young men; but all the evidence shows that Monsieur took the passive role, predominantly or exclusively.[57]

Much of what we know about this circle surrounding him comes from the letters of his long-suffering second wife, Elisabeth-Charlotte of the Palatinate, known as Madame Palatine. While some modern scholars suspect that she became rather obsessed with the subject of sodomy (one describes her as someone 'who, angered at her husband's homosexuality, was willing to regard the phenomenon as universal'; another calls her 'ever ready to uncover male and female homosexuality in every corner'), there can be lit-tle doubt about the overall validity of her observations, at least about people with whom she came into frequent contact.[58] In one of her letters from 1689, for example, she described her unsuccessful effort to dissuade her husband from appointing as governor of their young son the marquis d'Effiat, of whom she remarked that 'there is no greater sodomite than he in the whole of France.' More generally she observed: 'What prince is there, indeed, who loves his wife exclusively and does not have something else on the side, whether mistresses or *mignons* [male favourites]?' Sodomy, she wrote in 1699, was 'fashionable' at court; and two years later her comment on it was that 'They regard it as just an amusement. They hide it as much as they can to avoid scandalizing the common people, but they speak about it openly among people of quality.'[59]

★ ★ ★

Early modern courts were important arenas for politics—a special kind of politics where personal relations played the essential role. Almost everyone was striving, naturally enough, for advantage, and every kind of personal quality might be put to work to achieve that end; conversely, those who were raised up to high favour could easily become the objects of malicious gossip about the methods they had used. Since the highest favour was dis-pensed by the monarch, it is not surprising that, in almost every case where a king was accused of sodomy, political resentment against his favourite or

favourites was the key factor. That is obviously true where Edward II
(r. 1308–27) was concerned: it was his raising of the knight Piers Gaveston
above the established nobility that first stimulated the hostility of the barons
and earls. Probably it gave rise to the accusation of sodomy; but that charge
cannot be securely documented in Edward's lifetime, and seems to have
developed only after his death—the evidence that he was a sodomite is in
fact vanishingly slight.[60] Resentment against a highly promoted favourite
was certainly the central concern when such accusations were made—
contemporaneously—against another fourteenth-century monarch, Magnus
Eriksson (Magnus IV of Sweden and Magnus VII of Norway). Because of
his interest in the handsome nobleman Bengt Algotsson, whom he made
duke of Finland and Halland, he was nicknamed 'Smek' (kiss, caress); and in
1356, after a noble revolt, he had to banish Bengt from Sweden.[61] Again,
there is no actual evidence of sexual relations. But it seems that after the
widely publicized accusations against the Knights Templar in 1307–11, and
the extraordinary attempts, under blatant political pressure, to try Pope
Boniface VIII posthumously, in 1310–11, on a set of charges which included
sodomy, the use of this sexual accusation as a political weapon had become
well established.[62]

   That genie, once out of the bottle, could not be confined to it again. And
its application to royal favourites was easily made, partly because a favourite
was typically younger than the monarch who was his patron and promoter,
but mainly because favourites were objects of great resentment anyway.
From the king's point of view, it was an essential feature of such a person
that he owed his position entirely to the king's favour, and could therefore
be expected to direct all his loyalty towards his royal patron. That is why the
favourite was almost always promoted far above his own initial social status,
leapfrogging members of the upper aristocracy whose loyalty to the King
was not absolute, as they belonged to established power-networks with
interests of their own. Discussing accusations of sodomy against such kings
and their favourites, some modern historians have invoked Alan Bray's idea
that sodomy became objectionable only when it was accompanied by a
breach of the social order—in this case, the raising of an individual far above
his 'proper' status. But to apply that principle to all these cases of kings and
their favourites is to assume that sodomy was taking place; it is to suppose
that the alleged sexual relations were genuine and well known, and that the
change in the favourite's status merely acted as the trigger for talking openly
about them, as opposed to letting them pass in indulgent silence. This is a

curious position for historians to take in cases where there is simply no evidence to corroborate the existence of those sexual relations in the first place. In such cases, a much less question-begging explanation is easily available: that the entire accusation—the substance of it, not just the fact that it was voiced—was a product of the fierce resentment which the elevation of the favourite had caused (plus, very commonly, some further reasons for political hostility to the monarch).

In the best-known case of a sixteenth-century ruler being subjected to such allegations, that of King Henri III of France, such personal resentment certainly played a role—above all, where Anne de Joyeuse was concerned. The son of a provincial nobleman, and nine years younger than the King, Anne was promoted rapidly in the royal household and then married off, at the age of 21, to the Queen's half-sister; thereupon he was given the title 'duc de Joyeuse' and declared to have precedence over all the peers of France. Yet the hostility this engendered was only one of the factors contributing to scurrilous accusations against the King. Joyeuse belonged to a whole group of young courtiers favoured by Henri. They were known as his *mignons*, a word which had fairly neutral, non-sexual connotations to begin with—'companions', 'favourites'—but, during the course of his reign, began to be used as a term of abuse. As the diarist Pierre de l'Estoile put it in 1576, they became hateful to the population 'as much for their ways which were jesting and haughty as for their paint [make-up] and effeminate and unchaste apparel...Their occupations are gambling, blaspheming... fornicating and following the King everywhere.' We may note that the only sexual accusation here was about general dissoluteness, involving 'fornicating' (with women); these young men's fastidious interest in their fashionable clothing and physical appearance was judged to be effeminate, but, as we shall see, that was not necessarily thought to have implications for same-sex behaviour. What caused those potential implications to be expressed, in scandalous poems and songs, was the larger political context, where several factors were at work: the fierce hostilities towards Henri that had been stirred up by the French Wars of Religion; the machinations of his brother, who strove to present himself as a much more 'manly' figure, a true man of action; and the embarrassing failure of Henri and his wife to produce an heir, despite all his well-publicized attempts to do so. Nowhere in the records of his reign do we find any clear evidence that he indulged in sexual relations with his *mignons*. But it is a fact of political history that the accusations were made and circulated, and thus also a fact of social and cultural history that a broad public, in France and beyond, was exposed to the idea that that was what might be going on between a king and any attractive young man whom he favoured.[63]

By the time James VI of Scotland came to the English throne as James I in 1603, the term 'minion' had entered the English language. On the face of it, James was an unlikely object for charges of same-sex relations; far from being a louche sensualist, he was a notably bookish man with a keen interest in theology, whose treatise on regal and moral behaviour, written in the form of a letter of advice to his son, had already condemned sodomy as a crime that should never be pardoned.[64] What has led some historians to describe him as a sodomite or 'homosexual' is, above all, the fact that he openly displayed very strong affection for two younger men who became his successive favourites. The first, Robert Carr, was the son of a Scottish laird; as such, he would probably have incurred resentment from English aristocrats anyway, even without his rapid promotion to the rank of Earl of Somerset and to the role of the King's most trusted counsellor. The second, George Villiers, from a gentry family in Leicestershire, rose just as rapidly and even higher, being created Earl of Buckingham in 1617 and Duke of Buckingham in 1623. And having classified James sexually on the basis of his relations with those two younger men, some historians have not hesitated to assert that his relationship with Esmé Stuart, Lord d'Aubigny—the man, 24 years older than James, who became a father-figure to him when he was a boy—was sexual too (plus, for good measure, his relations with two other men, one younger and one older, who were close to him during the follow-ing years). Michael Young, for example, quotes a report by an English agent at the Scottish court, written when James was thirteen years old and d'Aubigny (the future Duke of Lennox) was 37: James was 'in such love with him, as in the open sight of the people, oftentimes he will clasp him about the neck with his arms and kiss him', and swiftly concludes that 'it is reasonable to believe that he had his first sexual experience with Lennox.'[65]

But are such conclusions, based on such descriptions of physical behav-iour, reasonable? There was nothing necessarily sexual about kissing. For centuries kissing, embracing, eating from the same dish and sharing the same bed had all been understood as ways of expressing, and strengthening, a bond between two men.[66] And if embracing and kissing could be accepted ways of expressing closeness and affection between two adults, we should surely allow them to have been performed non-sexually by a boy. It is true that, at his English court, James's displays of affection towards his favourites seemed unusually demonstrative: one courtier, describing his treatment of the young Robert Carr, wrote that James 'leaneth on his arm, pinches his cheek, [and] smoothes his ruffled garment'. (Others noticed that he tended to lean on other men, because of a weakness in his legs; using this and a range of other evidence, including his tendency to 'fiddle' with his hands, a medical historian has diagnosed him as suffering from mild cerebral palsy.)[67] Observers found this behaviour odd, and the degree of attentiveness—deference, even—that he showed to his favourites struck them as unbecoming in a king; yet there is no contemporaneous evidence of any courtier alleging that he performed sexual acts with them.[68]

Certainly the King himself thought he had nothing to be ashamed of, as he expressed his affection for his favourites openly and emphatically. According to a report by the Spanish Ambassador, James told the members of his Privy Council that he loved George Villiers 'more than all other men and more than all who were there present'. Such a statement is noteworthy, not just because it could not have failed to offend them, but because it implied that the kind of love involved was qualitatively the same; that, indeed, is the reason why they were offended, as he was referring not to sexual passion but to the kind of amity, involving trust, honour, and a wish for the other's well-being, which they had the right to expect from him. According to the same report, he also told them that just as 'Christ had his John', so 'he had his George'—again, invoking the model of a leader who loved all his followers, but one most of all, while emphasizing in addition that his love for his favourite was entirely pure.[69]

Long after James's death, a few disgruntled ex-courtiers, and/or bitter enemies of the Stuarts, did claim or insinuate that his interest in his favourites had been sexual. During his reign, however, such allegations were extremely rare; one modern study, by Robert Shephard, notes that they were much less common than rumours about the sex life of Queen Elizabeth had been, and that they do not feature in the substantial number of slanders against James that were reported to the authorities. There are just two dated examples, both from 1622: a passage in an anonymous polemical pamphlet, and a comment recorded in the private diary, written in code, of a Puritan law student.[70] The context of both was the heated political debate—to which the pamphlet was an outspoken contribution—about James's refusal to go to war in defence of his son-in-law, the Elector Palatine, who was viewed by Puritans as fighting for the survival of Protestantism in Europe. And the subtext was that Villiers, in particular, was leading the King astray by advocating a policy of diplomatic negotiation with Spain. The same concern is audible in one other text which also makes sexual allegations, an undated poem which circulated in manuscript copies. With lines such as 'Thou wilt be pleased great God to save | My soveraigne from a Ganymed | Whose whorish breath hath powre to lead | His excellence which way it list', this presented the influence of James's handsome favourite as undesir-. able because of its political consequences; it also called on God to protect the monarch 'From Spanish treaties that may wound | Our countries peace or Gospels sound'.[71]

'How can we account for the relative paucity of rumours and gossip about James's homosexuality?', Shephard asks. His answer is that 'by far the most likely' explanation is that 'most of James's contemporaries did not see his behaviour towards his favourites as signifying a sexual relationship between them.'[72] In the almost complete absence of evidence of such a sexual view being taken by others, historians have depended instead on statements and expressions found in some of James's own personal corres- pondence with his favourites. These need to be properly interpreted, how- ever, without importing anachronistic modern assumptions. When Michael Young cites an angry letter from James to Robert Carr which complains of 'your long creeping back and withdrawing yourself from lying in my cham- ber, notwithstanding my many hundred times earnestly soliciting you to the contrary', he writes: 'these words would appear to make nonsense of Maurice Lee Jr's contention that the king was "simply not much interested in physical sex at all". What purpose did James have for "many hundred times earnestly soliciting" Somerset to lie in his chamber if it was not for sex?'[73] David Bergeron, similarly, claims that that letter expresses 'homoerotic desire'; he also cites a letter from Villiers to the King, referring to an occa- sion on which, when they slept in the same room, 'the bed's head could not be found between the master and his dog' (meaning, apparently, that he had been promoted from the truckle bed at the foot of the King's own bed to joining James in the latter), and calls this 'a probable sexual encounter'.[74]

Yet bed-sharing, as has been mentioned already, was common in this period at every level of society. In family homes, brothers shared with broth- ers; schoolboys and students shared with one another and/or their tutors; servants with servants; masters with servants; lodgers at inns with other lodgers; and so on. Practical necessity was not the only reason. This was also a social convention, experienced as possessing real value. As Sasha Handley explains, 'sleeping beside the right kind of person could affirm or enhance a friendship by sharing close physical contact, an intimate conversation and a bond of trust.' For people of high social status, inviting another person to share their bed was a way of dispensing honour as well as reinforcing trust. 'The sovereign's bedfellows were invested with the most profound confidences in the hours between retiring to bed and falling asleep. Kings and queens unburdened their most secret thoughts and fears to trusted bedfellows who were charged with providing physical security and emotional felicity as darkness fell.'[75] Indeed, the principle that to invite someone to one's bed was to grant an honour or privilege extended far down the social scale. There are many examples of this: an older male might honour a younger in this way, a tutor could reward a boy, or an officer a junior soldier, and the same principle applied when an official at a French monastery asked a local peasant to let his—the peasant's—son spend the night with him.[76] It is simply unhistorical to suppose that when one man joined another in his bed—or even, in Young's interpretation of the letter to Carr, was present in his bedchamber—this must have been for sexual purposes.

Noting the absence of direct evidence for a claim is, of course, not the same thing as disproving it. But if indirect evidence is to be used in a case such as this, the proposed inferences from it need to be drawn in accordance with the cultural practice of the period. The fact that James told Villiers 'George I love thee dearly' and 'never one loved another moore then I doe thee' does not merit Young's comment that 'While there is no overt mention of sex in these expressions, they do seem sexually charged.' Young's argument about James I depends on modern assumptions; and even then, it has to undergo what might be called a process of rhetorical self-reinforcement in order to reach its conclusion, progressing from the initial observation that 'King James loved other males, but did he have sex with them? It must be admitted at the outset that we cannot answer this question with absolute certainty' to the final declaration that 'he did have sex with his favourites, and it is nonsense to deny it.'[77] This is a style of argumention encountered more often among those who write about sodomy in literary history—to which we shall now turn.

17

Northern Europe:
literary works

Cultural representations of sodomy in Southern Europe were discussed in Chapter 11. As we saw, in Iberia references to it were very infrequent and—with one marginal exception, a bawdy tale about a peasant and a devil—thoroughly negative. In Italy some attempts were made to express sodomitical desire in literary forms, but these were very rare and, if published, subject to vigorous suppression. Several authors did compose a kind of love poetry that celebrated the beauty and charm of a young male, without making any reference to sodomy; some produced humorous verses which alluded to sodomy, but under the cover of innuendos and *doubles entendres*. And from a range of writings, particularly comic stories, it is possible to gather a number of descriptions of sodomites and their behaviour, especially ones with a strong aversion to having sex with women. Taken together, all of this evidence has the effect of confirming and supplementing the picture of male–male sexual relations in Italian society supplied to us by other sources—even though, when set against the huge quantity of literature produced in Italy between 1400 and 1700, it amounts to only a very minor phenomenon within the literary realm.

In Northern Europe the quantity of such materials is even smaller. With one arguable exception, representations of sodomites seem to be absent from late-mediaeval English literature. In the words of one scholar, 'It is hard to avoid the conclusion that sodomy, as either social practice or ideological construct, was a minor presence in Chaucer's cultural world. So far as I know, there is no recognizable representation of sodomy or what we might call the "sodomitical personality" in the literature of the time—with the possible exception, of course, of the Pardoner.' (The hints at deviant sexual behaviour in the Pardoner's Tale are, however, intriguingly indirect, to the

Forbidden Desire in Early Modern Europe: Male–Male Sexual Relations, 1400–1750. Noel Malcolm, Oxford University Press.
© Noel Malcolm 2024. DOI: 10.1093/oso/9780198886334.003.0017

puzzlement of modern commentators.)[1] A study of masculinity in late-mediaeval England notes that male–male sexual relations are largely absent from the sources, and adds: 'Nor was Middle English literature fond of the theme; it did not exploit it either for horror or humor, yet another difference from the Italian situation.'[2] And the German lands in the Middle Ages present a very similar picture; Brigitte Spreitzer has commented on 'the almost total absence of the theme of homosexuality in mediaeval German-language literature'. One exceptional work tends to prove the rule: written in the first half of the thirteenth century by the Austrian court poet known as Der Stricker, it is a moral-didactic poem on the subject of sodomy, entirely devoted to denouncing it.[3]

Theological works and moral treatises did of course deal from time to time with sodomy, especially if they were going through sins systematically. Ruth Mazo Karras notes references to it in several mediaeval English texts of that kind, but she also observes that it was never treated in detail, and that the overall impression given by these sources is of 'a remarkable lack of concern with sodomy'; whilst it was categorized as the most grave form of lechery, discussions of that whole class of sins concentrated overwhelmingly on fornication and adultery.[4] A study of northern French sermons in the period 1350–1520 comments, similarly, that both sodomy and bestiality were of only minor concern to the preachers in comparison with other sexual sins.[5] And when sermons in Northern Europe did refer to the sin of sodomy, it is remarkable how little their descriptions of it seem to have owed to any direct knowledge of it as a social reality—in striking contrast to the sermons of Italian preachers such as Bernardino of Siena, with their references to boys dressing up to attract customers, parents pimping their sons, and so on. Helmut Puff offers one apparent exception to this rule, the sermons given by Johann Geiler von Kaisersberg, who preached in Strasbourg in the late fifteenth and early sixteenth centuries (and, as we have previously seen, showed an unusual willingness to address this 'unspeakable' topic). Yet the evidence that he was describing a known *actualité* is still rather thin; Puff cites, for example, the fact that he distinguished between those who 'florenced' and those who let themselves be florenced by others, which seems a rather elementary distinction to make.[6]

The strongest piece of apparent evidence is Geiler's statement that if a man remained in the sin of sodomy beyond the age of 33, he would never be able to reform himself. On the face of it, this looks like a piece of social reportage, and also seems to confirm the presence of the Mediterranean pattern of same-sex relations, where the 'inveterate' sodomites were seen as particularly problematic. Yet this was a standard trope which had been in circulation for a long time: it was stated in the *Malleus maleficarum* in 1486, and had previously been used by Bernardino of Siena in sermons of 1424 and 1425. Bernardino might well have thought that this age-limit accorded with the social reality he observed; but its origin was purely theological, signifying (as the *Malleus* explicitly said) the age of Christ at the time of his death. The trope itself can be traced back at least as far as the writings of the thirteenth-century Flemish Dominican Thomas of Cantimpré, who had explained that since Jesus taught humans virtue throughout his life, those who resisted such teaching for a longer period were irredeemable. (He did add a little *actualité*-based comment of his own, saying that he had known octogenarians and centenarians who were 'enmeshed' in the sin of sodomy; but the specific age-limit he gave was clearly not arrived at on an empirical basis.)[7]

The lack of real social observation remained a feature of the Northern European sermon literature for a very long time. In England, a huge number of sermons survive from the late-sixteenth and seventeenth centuries. Some refer to Sodom; some, indeed, make foreboding comparisons between Sodom and England or London; but specific references to male–male sex are very rare. When reading such works, we have to bear in mind that the biblical city of Sodom was used as a general exemplar of a society mired in sin; as obdurate sinners destroyed by God, the Sodomites were often contrasted with the people of Nineveh, who repented. So the term might just imply sinfulness in general; or if it did refer to sexual sins, it could connote the entire range of them. (In the Elizabethan comedy *Misogonus* one character exclaims: 'darst thou kepe company with another mans wife thou abhominable sodomit?')[8] Also present in the minds of preachers and their congregations were the words of Ezekiel 16: 49, 'Behold, this was the iniquity of thy sister Sodom, pride, fulness of bread, and abundance of idleness was in her and in her daughters, neither did she strengthen the hand of the poor and needy', which supplied the classic list of four anti-social sins: pride, gluttony, sloth and uncharitableness or covetousness. So there was plenty to discuss under the heading of 'Sodom', without having to dwell at any length on same-sex relations—which was just as well, as most preachers had almost nothing to say on that subject.

A few examples of this may suffice. In 1593 Adam Hill preached a 'Paul's Cross' sermon—typically a bracing jeremiad, addressed to a huge crowd of 'godly' people in the churchyard of St Paul's Cathedral in London—on

Genesis 18: 20–2, 'Because the cry of Sodom and Gomorrah is great...'. He began by explaining that London was just like Sodom, full of heinous sins. The worst was the idolatry of the Papists, which he discussed at some length; next came blasphemy, then profaning the sabbath, and then murder. Only on page 24 of the printed edition did he finally get to 'Sodometrie also and vnnatural lust', which 'crieth to God for vengeance & punishment'. The only example he gave was that of the monks accused of sodomy nearly 60 years earlier in Henry VIII's visitations; then he moved quickly on to the monks' sins of fornication with women, and then to whoredom in general, followed by oppression of the poor, atheism and excessive pride in one's own apparel.[9] When Robert Milles gave his Paul's Cross sermon on the same topic in 1611, he began by asking what the sins of Sodom were, and turned immediately to Ezekiel for the answer. Lengthy declamations on those four sins then followed, with only the most glancing reference to same-sex relations near the end of the sermon: 'For lust and secret whore-dome, like *Salomons* harlot wiping our lips, as though all were well: Wee with *Iudah* discry our selues and filthinesse...nay, the horrible and name-lesse sinne of *Sodome* hath poisoned some.'[10]

John Harris's sermon on the destruction of Sodom, given to the House of Commons in February 1629, also used Ezekiel's categorization. He did go on to discuss male–male sex (which he called 'Masculine beastiality'), as part of his account of the sins of the biblical Sodomites, devoting several lines to excoriating it: 'A sinne, none but a Diuell, come out of Hell in the likenesse of a man, dares to commit: a sinne, enough to defile the tongue that talkes of it...'. When he turned, in the latter part of the sermon, to the 'application' of his biblical text to the society around him, he was able to offer many present-day examples of particular sins, such as idleness among vagabonds, and gluttony and covetousness among courtiers, lawyers and the gentry. Had he been able to make similar observations on 'masculine beasti-ality', he would no doubt have done so. But this, he said, was the one sin of the biblical Sodomites that was lacking from his own society:

> If I had a Catalogue of the number of Sodomes sinnes, and a relation of their will and greedinesse to commit them, and were tasked to compare ours with theirs, I beleeue for quantity and manner, wee are neare euen with them: Indeed, *Peccatum nefandum,* that sin not fit to be named, the high hand of God hath kept out of our Countrey, and euer may it remaine a stranger, otherwise I cannot set my thoughts to worke, to muse of any sinne that I doe not finde acted in abominable manner.[11]

This was surely not an example of the syndrome of complacency that afflicted some early modern Europeans when they insisted that sodomy was a vice of other societies, but, thank God, not of their own. Preachers of this kind were committed to the very opposite of complacency. England's fate was in the balance: would God blast it for its manifest sins, or could its people be persuaded to repent in time? A sin as grave as sodomy, if observed among those people, would have been placed by such a preacher emphatically before their eyes. But that did not happen—not, we may assume, because sodomy did not exist at all, but because evidence of it was so barely visible that it could be genuinely overlooked.[12]

Some modern scholars, apparently unaware of the reflex way in which the verse from Ezekiel functioned in the minds of early modern authors, have supposed that those who invoked its set of four sins were engaging in some sort of analysis of the nature and conditions of sodomy (in its narrow sense) within their own society. For example, when Sir Edward Coke composed the short chapter on buggery in his law treatise, he added the sentence 'The Sodomites came to this abomination by four means, *viz.* by pride, excess of diet, idlenesse, and contempt of the poor'; but his argument made no further use of that observation, which was just a routine nod in the direction of the biblical text.[13] A literary historian comments that 'Sodomites, Coke implies, are haughty, fat, lazy, and snobbish—and they are apt to be caught up by foreign fashions... sodomy is an aristocratic vice, a temptation especially appealing to men who have nothing better to do'; a social historian writes that 'Sir Edward Coke was only repeating a commonplace when he located the seeds of sodomy in arrogance, idleness, and gluttony. Rape and sodomy, contemporaries argued, were by-products of greed and egoism.'[14] This is to give the impression that an author such as Coke was analysing a form of sexual behaviour in his society and carefully tracing its contemporary causes; but he was doing no such thing. Again, a modern literary critic cites a complaint, made against a London minister in 1613, that the minister had slandered his parishioners by saying in a sermon that 'We have some sodamites in the parishe which do abound in pride, fullnes of bread idlenes not strengtheninge the hand of the needye... their sinnes are greater than the sinnes of Sodome and Gomorrhe they contemne or refuse the sacraments and service of God but do they thincke to escape the vengeance of God', and argues that such evidence 'will help to illustrate the "proximate" relation of same-sex behavior to social disorder'. This interpretation is then put to work as confirmation of Alan Bray's theory that sodomy was objected to only when it was accompanied by offences against social order.[15] Yet the minister was merely using the biblical text as a standard point of reference for thoroughgoing sinfulness; nothing in his words implied any particular concern with same-sex behaviour.

Sermons were not the only works that castigated contemporary society from a religious point of view. In England in this period, moralizing treatises poured from the presses. One of the most famous was *The Anatomie of Abuses*, published in 1583 by Philip Stubbes. Bewailing the moral laxity of English society, Stubbes offered vivid descriptions of all kinds of excesses, from fashionable hats ('pearking up like a sphere, or shafte of a steeple, standing a quarter of a yarde above the crowne of their heades') to church-ales (strong ales brewed by the parish, which make people 'as drunke as apes, and as blockish as beasts') to the village game of football (which 'may rather be called…a bloody and murthering practice, then a felowly sporte or pastime').[16] Yet he did not include a single sentence about the practice of same-sex relations in England. He did refer to Sodom, but described it as having been 'consumed with fire and brimstone from heaven for the sin of whordom, adulterie, and fornication'; denouncing popular feasts and festivals, he referred to people spending days on end 'in drunkennesse, whordome, gluttony, and other filthie sodomiticall excercyses'. Sodom, as applied here to the English population, signified sins of the flesh in general, and sexual sins in particular, but the sex involved was between men and women. In his lengthy discussion of fornication he told the story of an ostentatiously pious man who had bailed a notorious prostitute from Bridewell and then taken her home for sex, explaining rather gleefully that 'Whylest these two members of the devil were playing the vile sodomits together in his chamber…it pleased God, even in his wrath, to strike these two persons dead in a moment.' For Stubbes, to play the sodomite was simply to engage in illicit sex.[17] (As we shall see, he used the same phrase when discussing immoral behaviour in connection with the London theatres, in a passage which modern historians have consistently misread.)

Divinely ordained deaths of that kind, and other such signs of God's judgement, were matters of intense popular interest. Writers gathered whole collections of these providential events for the edification of the public, and the more local and actual the material was, the better suited it would be to their instructive purpose. The best-known example was a work first published in 1597, Thomas Beard's *The Theatre of Gods Judgement*; it was subsequently expanded with more providential examples, reaching a fifth edition in 1648. In its chapter on 'Gods Judgements upon Adulterers' that edition gives a whole series of recent English examples: 'Not long since, here in our own Countrey, a Noblemans servant...'; 'Another in Hertfordshire about Barkway, having the company of a harlot in a Wood, was also surprised by the judgement of God...'; 'We read also of a Chirurgeon...', and so on. But in the chapter entitled 'Of effeminate Persons, Sodomites, and other such like Monsters' the only examples given are Sardanapalus and two Roman emperors (illustrating effeminacy; the former is described as living among his whores), the people of Sodom and Gomorrah, 'divers Bishops of Rome', della Casa, and the monks of the city of Tours during the reign of Charlemagne.[18] This lack of contemporary local material contrasted strongly with the frequent references to sodomy found in the writings of travellers who had been to Italy, North Africa and the Levant.

In the English literary culture of this period, vivid representations of sodomites did exist, as we have seen: they formed part of the repertoire of a small number of satirists who, basing their work in varying degrees on classical models (especially the satires of Juvenal and Horace, and the epigrams of Martial), offered extravagant depictions of immoral types. Alan Bray's sensible advice about not taking such texts as contemporary social reportage has already been quoted. Nor should we exaggerate the frequency or scale of these sodomitic references. One literary critic writes that 'The prevalence of homoerotic allusions within [English] Renaissance satires is easily documented', and offers four instances; a few more might be added, but 'prevalence' seems a strong word to use for a total which may barely exceed single figures, where most of the allusions amount to only a few lines in much larger bodies of text.[19] Of course some of these satirists may have had actual examples of sodomitical behaviour somewhere in their minds; but their inspiration seems to have been much more literary than observational, adhering to standard tropes and formulae. One of these has already been encountered: the sexual progression from whore to catamite to animal (typically a goat—goats being traditional symbols of lechery). John Marston's pairing of Ganymede and goat was matched by John Donne: 'beauty they in boyes and beasts do finde'; 'Who loves Whores, who boyes, and who goats'. And both were followed by Ben Jonson in his satirical epigram 'On Sir Voluptuous Beast': 'Telling the motions of each petticote, | And how his GANIMEDE mov'd, and how his goate'. That these imagined sodomites were roués and voluptuaries, with sufficient money and leisure to pursue their sexual tastes, was also a rather formulaic feature, hardly justifying the significance which some literary historians have attributed to it. (One, for example, writes that 'Only in satire, with its insistent attention to the social surface of human experience, does social class become important...in depicting sodomy. Sodomy, for certain of the satirists at least, is an aristocratic vice.')[20] And it is worth asking whether the concentration on 'boys'— in a society where, as we know, sodomites might also desire men—was not to a large extent a product of literary tradition, deriving especially from the Roman world.

The terms 'Ganymede' and 'catamite', which crop up from time to time in the writings of this period, also have a rather high-flown, literary quality to them. Henry Cockeram thought it necessary to give the meaning of the latter ('A boy which is vsed for buggery') in his dictionary of 'hard English words'.[21] But there was a simpler English word which certainly could be used to mean a male youth who allowed himself to be sodomized: 'ingle'. John Florio's great Italian–English dictionary resorted to it several times, for example explicating *bardascia* as 'a bardash, a buggering boy, an ingle', and *catamito* as 'a ganimed, an ingle, a boie hired to sinne against nature'.[22] The word is puzzling, however, not just because its etymology is completely obscure, nor because it seems to have entered the language quite suddenly in the 1590s, but because it clearly had a broader range of meanings. The verb 'to ingle' could mean to embrace, cuddle, attract or inveigle—actions (performed by women as well as men) which might be related to sexual intercourse but were not at all confined to it.[23] The noun could refer to a serving-boy, or more generally to someone who acted as an obsequious servant, or to a man who behaved sycophantically towards another man, or went out of his way to serve that man's interests, or cultivated him assiduously.[24] In Ben Jonson's *Every Man in His Humor* a character uses the word and then immediately glosses it as meaning 'retainer', someone who 'follows' an important person in the hope of gaining something from his service. And in one mid-seventeenth-century text, the term refers to a woman who has been recruited to act as a man's accomplice or assistant.[25]

Elsewhere Jonson uses the word more generally. In his comedy *The Case is Altered*, one character greets his friends and acquaintances with the words 'welcome sweet Ingle' and 'Sirrah *Ingle*'; he refers to one of these in particular as 'my Ingle', meaning perhaps his particular friend, but without any apparent sexual connotation. This usage chimes with that of another play from the same period, Thomas Dekker's *Satiro-mastix*, where one character greets the poet Horace (a satirical version of Jonson himself) as 'my sweet ningle', and describes him thereafter, in his presence, as 'mine Ingle'.[26] Overall, examples of the word being used in its narrowly sexual sense—catamite or 'buggering boy'—are outnumbered by cases which are ambiguous, or general, or clearly not sexual at all.

One particular usage is worth looking at in more detail: the application of 'ingle' to boy actors in the theatre. In the prelude to Jonson's *Cynthia's Revels*, one of these boys explains that the playwright does not closely monitor their performance, correcting every small mistake, 'as some *Author* would, if he had such fine *Ingles* as we'. A few years later Thomas Dekker, complaining of the lack of literary patrons, described 'Nobody' as 'The now-onely-onely-Supper-maker to Enghles & Plaiers-Boyes'.[27] In Jonson's *Poetaster*, when Tucca, a military man with a pronounced hostility towards the world of the theatre, has encouraged his two young servants or pages to declaim a variety of speeches to a professional actor, the actor asks if he can hire them from him for a week, and receives the very negative response: 'No you *mangonizing* slaue, I will not part from 'hem: you'll sell 'hem for Enghles' (where 'mangonizing' means trading dishonestly, especially in slaves, but 'slave', as addressed to the actor, is just a term of abuse). Here the word just signifies a boy actor; but earlier in the play, when Ovid's ill-tempered father was under the impression that his son was writing for the theatre, he had exclaimed: 'What? shal I haue my son a Stager now? an Enghle for Players? a Gull? a Rooke? a Shot-clog? to make suppers, and bee laught at?'[28] There the implication of 'an Enghle for Players' seems to have been that Ovid junior, by seeking to act for the benefit of the players (becoming a supper-maker, the role of a benefactor as described by Dekker; the term 'shot-clog' referred to an otherwise unwelcome guest whose presence at the meal was tolerated because he paid the bill), would be in effect subservient to them, and thus like a boy actor vis-à-vis the adult ones. But whatever the precise nuance of this expression, it seems clear that 'ingle' could function as a general term for boy actors, without implying that they were being sodomized; indeed, it is hardly likely that one of them would have been presented as happily referring to 'such fine *Ingles* as we' if that had been a necessary implication.

There is a reason why this point needs to be emphasized. Literary historians searching for homoeroticism and same-sex innuendo have focused on the Elizabethan and Jacobean theatre as a hotbed of such sexually transgressive behaviour. It may not be unreasonable to suppose that, insofar as the sexual exploitation of boys did take place in early modern English society, it

could have found congenial conditions in the theatrical companies. These
were all-male groups where adults were in frequent contact with boys, and
where at least some of the boys had been chosen for their good looks—a
desideratum when playing romantic and tragic heroines. What is more, the
theatres on the south bank of the Thames were located in a kind of red light
district, close to taverns, brothels, venues for bear-baiting, and other places
of low entertainment; the playhouses themselves had a reputation for
attracting prostitutes, who touted for business in the theatre pits.[29] Yet
although some element of sexual banter might well have taken place within
these companies, evidence of actual sexual exploitation is extremely hard to
find.[30] One modern scholar confidently describes this world as 'a theatrical
economy that included boys for sale'; but no example of prostitution is
given, other than Tucca's remark 'you'll sell 'hem for Enghles'. (That can
hardly be used as direct evidence of English practice, as Tucca is a character
in a play which, although it satirizes some aspects of contemporary English
literary culture, is set in ancient Rome; and the phrase refers in any case to
the sale of slaves, not to pimping.) The same writer offers three texts from
the period 1604–9 that allegedly play on the sexual desire of men for boy
actors; but one involves two adult men briefly exchanging bawdy remarks,
and the others have no necessarily sexual implications at all. For good measure she also cites a much later description of the actor Stephen Hammerton
as 'at first a most noted and beautiful Woman Actor', commenting that this
shows he was a 'love object', on the grounds that '"noting" leads to desire'—
though whether it does or not must surely depend on other factors which
she has taken entirely for granted.[31]

   The *locus classicus* to which most historians and literary critics have turned
when associating the Elizabethan stage with sodomy is the passage, briefly
mentioned above, in Philip Stubbes's *Anatomie of Abuses*:

> marke the flocking and running to theatres...to see playes and enterludes;
> where such wanton gestures, such bawdy speaches, such laughing and fleering,
> such kissing and bussing, such clipping and culling, such winckinge and
> glancinge of wanton eyes, and the like is used as is wonderfull to behold.
> Th[e]n, these goodly pageants being done, every mate sorts to his mate, every
> one brings another homeward of their way very freendly, and in their secret
> conclaves (covertly) they play the Sodomits, or worse. And these be the fruits
> of playes and enterluds for the most part.[32]

Yet, as we have seen, 'playing the Sodomites' was a phrase used by Stubbes
for male–female sex—something which should have been obvious to

readers, not only from his previous use of it, but from the whole sense of this passage, which describes people being sexually aroused by the spectacle of suggestive male–female behaviour on the stage. Nor was this point original or unusual. It had already been made by Stephen Gosson in his *Schoole of Abuse*, where he portrayed the theatres as places where 'euery wanton and his Paramour, euery man and his Mistresse, euery John and his Joan, euery knaue and his queane, are there first acquainted & cheapen the Merchandise in that place, which they pay for elsewhere as they can agree', and in his *Playes Confuted*, where he described how the representation of sexual behaviour on the stage could arouse lustful feelings in the audience.[33]

To explain how enactments of male–female sexual attraction could have caused allegedly sodomitical desire in many of the male members of the audience, literary historians have placed almost all their emphasis on the fact that the female parts in these plays were performed by boys. Here they can at least invoke some arguments that were made at the time. The people who made them were moralizing Protestants; their main concern was with the idea of males appearing in female clothing. And this would have offended them whether or not they thought it provoked sexual desire, because it seemed to violate a clear injunction set out in Deuteronomy 22: 5: 'The woman shall not wear that which pertaineth unto a man, neither shall a man put on a woman's garment: for all that do so are abomination unto the Lord thy God.' That text was fundamental to the argument of the Oxford academic John Rainolds, whose correspondence with two opponents on the issue of male youths playing women bore fruit in his influential treatise of 1599, *Th'Overthrow of Stage-Playes*. Rainolds did argue that such performances could raise unnatural—i.e. male–male—lust in some members of the audience, but he also had another line of attack relating to sexual psychology: he quoted a passage from the theologian Dionysius Carthusianus, saying that when a man puts on a woman's clothes it 'doeth vehemently touch and move him with the remembrance and imagination of a woman: and the imagination of a thing desirable doth stirr up the desire'.[34] Like any good rhetorician, he was assembling all the points that could be made in support of his case. Modern literary historians usually single out the issue of unnatural lust, as if it were driving the entire argument; it was an important element of the case he made, but it was also—as he explained in his correspondence in the early 1590s with William Gager, his first opponent—quite a limited one. Gager objected to his claim that the mere act of dressing a male in female clothing could 'kindle sparkes of lust in vncleane affections', and insisted that most men would not experience any such feelings. In response, Rainolds explained that he had been referring only to a particular category of men: 'I saide not, in all mens affections, but in some; not in sanctified, but in vncleane...For my speech was generall, that the cladding of youthes in such attire is an occasion of drawing & provoking corruptlie minded men to most heinous wickednes, & therefore should be wiselie cutt off by the faithfull.'[35]

The strongest version of the argument from Deuteronomy was presented by the political and religious polemicist William Prynne in his large-scale treatise *Histrio-mastix* of 1633. One part of Prynne's argument was the idea that sodomites in the classical world had made their catamites adopt a female appearance in order to put their own unnatural desire in a better light, by making it seem more natural. This would seem to imply that most men, on looking at apparently feminine figures, were liable to feel the 'natural' type of desire. Prynne's indignant description, not only of the fact of male actors wearing female costumes, but also of the kinds of sexual behaviour they then enacted on the stage, suggests that the arousal of 'natural' lust was one major element of what he disapproved of. Yet he also feared that some would be led to masturbation or sodomy:

> this putting on of womans array (especially to act a lascivious, amorous, whorish, Love-sicke Play upon the Stage[)], must needs be sinfull, yea abom-inable; *because it not onely excites many adulterous filthy lusts, both in the Actors and Spectators; and drawes them on both to contemplative and actuall lewdnesse*...which is evill; but likewise *instigates them to selfe-pollution, (a sinne for which* Onan *was destroyed:) and to that unnaturall Sodomiticall sinne of uncleanesse, to which the rep-robate* Gentiles *were given over;* (a sinne *not once to be named,* much lesse then practised *among Christians*).[36]

To support this last claim about the theatre encouraging people to commit sodomy, he cited a number of classical and patristic passages; the one mod-ern text he referred to—inaugurating the long tradition of misinterpret-ation as he did so—was Stubbes's *Anatomie of Abuses*. But he then added: 'together with *some moderne examples of such, who have beene desperately enamored with Players Boyes thus clad in womans apparell, so farre as to sollicite them by words, by Letters, even actually to abuse them*', to which he appended the note: 'This I have heard credibly reported of a Schollar of *Bayliol* Colledge, and I doubt not but it may be verified of divers others.'[37] Had he possessed more evidence than that, he would surely have included it in this dense treatise of more than 1,000 pages.

Some literary historians have taken this line of argumentation, which was developed by a small number of polemicists, as definitive, even though a large part of the culture clearly did not agree with it. Stephen Orgel has claimed that 'the deepest fear in antitheatrical tracts' is of 'an undifferentiated sexuality, a sexuality that does not distinguish men from women and reduces men to women'; but Rainolds distinguished clearly enough between those who were attracted to boys and those who were not.[38] Another form of differentiation that most playgoers probably found easy to make was between the actor and the character he played. Lady Mary Wroth, describing a man who was unmoved by a woman's charms, wrote that he was 'no further wrought [sc. worked upon], then if he had seen a delicate play-boy acte a loving womans part, and knowing him a Boy, lik'd onely his action'. And in his defence of acting Thomas Heywood, while agreeing that it was wrong to disguise a boy as a girl in real life for any 'sinister intent', exclaimed: 'But to see our [sc. the theatres'] youths attired in the habit of women, who knowes not what their intents be? who cannot distinguish them by their names, assuredly, knowing they are but to represent such a Lady, at such a time appoynted?[39] The use of boys to play women was an accepted convention. Its basic justification lay in the idea that the use of adult women would have been too sexually provoking (given the nature of the sexual desire felt by almost all men), leading to a merging of the functions of actress and prostitute. And why use teenaged boys rather than adult men? The answer is obvious enough: boys bore more of a physical resemblance to women, as they had smooth-skinned faces, less developed musculature and, importantly, voices which had not yet broken. It is quite extraordinary that Stephen Orgel should put that question and propose, as his general answer, that 'boys were, like women—but unlike men—acknowledged objects of sexual attraction for men.'[40]

In his classic study of these issues, Michael Shapiro points out that there were many ways in which inventive authors could play with disjunction between boy actor and female character. It could be reduced to a minimum, allowing male spectators to become absorbed in an erotic situation; and if it were made more obvious, that might sometimes have been for the delectation of female members of the audience (whose interests literary historians have tended to overlook). Overall, he notes, 'there is no evidence of a coterie of male spectators whose primary interest in the representation of women by play-boys was homoerotic.'[41] But, given the long tradition—derived via Italian Renaissance dramatists from Roman comedy—of plots in which a female character goes disguised as a male one, there were many opportunities for exploiting the tensions that could arise between being, acting, and, so to speak, acting acting. Comic effects could certainly arise, though on balance it is remarkable how seldom they were exploited for any kind of male–male sexual innuendo. Shapiro's thorough researches have yielded just a handful of plays where, in his opinion, a male–male sexual implication is touched on, however briefly. Yet even these cases are questionable. For example, when a man in John Fletcher's *The Honest Man's Fortune* is told (falsely) that his faithful page is a woman in disguise, and says 'It may be so, and yet we have lain together, | But by my troth I never found her Lady', he surely means only that he has had the page as a bedfellow without noticing any of the giveaway features of a female body; this does not mean, *pace* Shapiro, that he has had 'homosexual relations' with the page. Similarly, in Heywood's *The Four Prentices of London*, when a knight learns that the page who has shared his bed really is a woman (indeed, a princess), and exclaims, 'she hath beene my bedfellow | A yeare and more, yet had I not the grace', this surely signifies that while he had engaged in the normal practice of bed-sharing, he had not had the pleasure of discovering that she was a woman; she herself had previously said that she was embarrassed by this sort of intimacy, which again would be unsurprising in a woman, and can hardly justify Shapiro's suggestion that she was being 'used sexually' as a boy. And in Shirley's *The Grateful Servant*, when the Duke of Savoy utters a soliloquy about an unusually good-looking page (who is in fact a princess in disguise), 'Our hot Italian doth affect these boys | For sin; I've no such flame, and yet methought | He did appear most lovely; nay, in his absence, | I cherish his idea; but I must | Exclude him while he hath but soft impression…', Shapiro may be right to say that the Duke is made to 'worry about his sexual inclinations'; but this is a way of emphasizing the feminine—in fact, genuinely female—beauty of the person in question, as well as the authentically non-sodomitical nature of the Duke's sexual feelings. The worrying occurs precisely because such a feeling for a boy is unaccustomed and seems wrong—being something, indeed, characteristic of a 'hot Italian'.[42]

It has been necessary to dwell on these matters, because the idea that the London stage was a prominent arena for the representation of male–male sexual desire has become almost an orthodoxy in the historical literature. Randolph Trumbach has written that 'The most sympathetic discussion of sexual relations between males in the seventeenth century appeared in the plays of the London stage, and a good deal of the opposition to the theatres by the Puritans was inspired by this tolerance.' Drawing on Shapiro's work, he notes that roughly 74 plays involved girls (played by boys) disguising themselves as boys; and since he contends that sodomy was, in all the situations that followed, an element which 'could never be entirely displaced', he concludes that a significant percentage of all the plays performed in London were at least partly sodomitical in content. In some of these plays, he even claims, 'Boy actors are represented as the sexual companions of the adult actors who are their masters.'[43] It is hard to think of any evidence that would begin to justify such a statement, beyond the tiny handful of references to 'ingles', the meanings of which have already been discussed.

★ ★ ★

If we turn instead to actual representations—or even expressions—of male–male sexual feelings, it is possible to identify a very small number of texts, in pre-Restoration England, that qualify. The scarcity of these is particularly striking, given that, from the early sixteenth century onwards, humanist educational practice had stocked the minds of literate English people with classical texts, many of which contained explicit same-sexual material. Generally, readers could not fail to understand the literal meaning of those texts. In some cases, the sort of moralizing interpretation recommended by Erasmus could be attempted, and stories from classical mythology might be rendered pure and high-minded by Neoplatonic allegorizing; but such techniques could hardly be applied to the sexually explicit verses of Martial or Catullus. For dealing with these, one common technique was gender-switching. An Elizabethan translation of Martial's Epigram IX.25, which refers to ogling a handsome servant or slave-boy, turns 'your sweet servant, Hyllus' into 'thy wife'; among seventeenth-century translations of Anacreon, 'Thomas Stanley's versions…regularly make the poems refer to women, while Cowley's are sometimes completely sexless.' As one modern critic has observed, 'most of the many imitations or adaptations of homoerotic classical literature discreetly de-eroticized or heterosexualized their sources.'[44]

Too direct a representation of Greek or Roman sexual realities would have induced strong feelings of awkwardness. But on the other hand, the fact that classical allusions were easily available (and, especially in the case of stories about gods and heroes, formed the raw material of so much modern cultural production of a highly respectable kind) offered a convenient solution to what would otherwise have been an awkward problem: the problem, for those who did wish to refer to same-sex relations, of finding some way of doing so that could be culturally acceptable. The few references that were made tended to apply this method—and nowhere more so than in the writings of Christopher Marlowe, the only major author to have introduced material with clear male–male sexual implications into several of his works. In Marlowe's *Edward II* (1594), for example, while there are various indications that the King's love for his favourite Piers Gaveston is a disordered passion—including the fact that it has supplanted his love for the Queen, and the open use of the term 'minion'—the strongest suggestions of a sexual relationship come from invoking some of the famous classical pairings of man and youth, including Hercules and Hylas, Jupiter and Ganymede, Alexander and Hephaestion.[45]

Telling a classical story, or following a classical genre, could also supply the opportunity and the means for introducing an element of homoeroticism. Perhaps the strongest example of this is the lengthy passage in Marlowe's *Hero and Leander* (1598) where the handsome young Leander, swimming naked across the Hellespont, attracts the interest of the sea-god Neptune, who begins to play erotically with his body:

> He clapt his plumpe cheekes, with his tresses playd,
> And smiling wantonly, his love bewrayd.
> He watcht his armes, and as they opend wide,
> At every stroke, betwixt them would he slide,
> And steale a kisse, and then run out and daunce,
> And as he turnd, cast many a lustfull glaunce,
> And throw him gawdie toies to please his eie,
> And dive into the water, and there prie
> Upon his brest, his thighs, and everie lim,
> And up againe, and close beside him swim,
> And talke of love: *Leander* made replie,
> You are deceav'd, I am no woman I.
> Thereat smilde *Neptune*...[46]

And so on. In a similar exploitation of classical myth—this time, Ovid's account of Apollo and Hyacinthus—one of the Eclogues by the poet Lewis Machin (1607) also supplied a kind of erotic description that could hardly have been presented within a realistic, contemporary English setting:

> But *Phebus* heart did pant and leape with joy,
> When he beheld that sweete delicious boy.
> [...]
> And then he kist him, and the boy then blusht,
> That blushing coulour, so became his face

That *Phebus* kist againe, and thought it grace
To touch his lips, such pleasure *Phebus* felt,
That in an amarous deaw his heart did melt.[47]

Something of the same ethos was offered by the minor poet Richard Barnfield, whose *The Affectionate Sheapheard* (1594) imitated Vergil in expressing the infatuation of a shepherd, Daphnis, with a beautiful boy called Ganymede. Here the shepherd idolizes the boy's beauty, pleading for kisses and embraces and nights spent in his arms. The tone, though intensely passionate, is ostensibly concerned with admiration and tender affection rather than actual sexual conquest; but here and there what look like suggestive elements of bawdy are semi-visible. (For example, he tells Ganymede that if he wants to go shooting at little birds—he specifies 'the Thrustle-cocke and Sparrow'—'I haue a fine bowe, and an yuorie arrow: | And if thou misse, yet meate thou shalt [not] lacke, | Ile hang a bag and bottle at thy backe'.)[48] In the preface to his next volume, published in the following year, Barnfield referred rather defensively to *The Affectionate Sheapheard*, complaining that some people had interpreted it 'otherwise then (in truth) I meant, touching the subiect therof to wit, the loue of a Shepheard to a boy'. What they had criticized in it—presumably, its sexual content—was 'a fault, the which I will not excuse, because I neuer made', for the whole composition had been 'nothing else, but an imitation of *Virgill*, in the second Eglogue of *Alexis*'.[49] But those readers had probably not misread it. Barnfield's work seems to belong to a small cluster of texts, written in the 1590s, which, partly under Marlowe's influence and mostly making use of classical themes, experimented with explicitly physical descriptions of erotic intimacy between males. The experiment was not a public success, as Barnfield's comment shows; and another of these texts, Michael Drayton's *Peirs Gaveston Earle of Cornwall* (1594), which contained lines such as 'his loue-sick lippes at every kissing qualme, | Cling to my lippes...' and 'Such our imbraces when our sporte begins, | Lapt in our armes, like *Ledas* louely Twins', was reissued by Drayton in 1605 in a revised edition from which such material had been rigorously excised.[50]

It might be tempting to include, in that cluster of homoerotic poetic works of the 1590s, Shakespeare's *Sonnets*, the majority of which were probably written during the period 1594–6. In a few places, they may even contain some echoes of Barnfield's poetry.[51] Yet the whole character of Shakespeare's work is very different. Yes, the beauty of the beloved young man is celebrated, and the love which is expressed for him is deep and powerful; but where Barnfield just evokes the sorts of feelings that will reach fulfilment in acts of physical intimacy (probably including penetrative sex), Shakespeare—or his poetic persona—takes this emotional situation as the starting-point for a series of elaborate meditations on age, youth, time, hope, regret, self-love, self-abnegation, possession, loss and so on, running these themes through complex systems of metaphor drawn from all aspects of life. There are many different aspects to his feelings for the youth, but the one aspect he explicitly eschews is the desire to perform sexual acts with him. In Sonnet 20, one of the most important in the sequence, he begins by saying that the youth has the beauty of a woman—a beauty which 'steals men's eyes and women's souls amazeth'. He continues:

> And for a woman wert thou first created,
> Till Nature as she wrought thee fell a-doting,
> And by addition me of thee defeated,
> By adding one thing to my purpose nothing.
> But since she pricked thee out for women's pleasure,
> Mine be thy love, and thy love's use their treasure.[52]

(The 'one thing' added is the youth's penis, jokingly alluded to also in 'pricked thee out'; the last line says that he demands only the youth's pure love, not the acts of the youth as a physical lover, which will be reserved for the benefit of women.)[53] Shakespeare shared the general assumption of Renaissance writers—Southern and Northern European—that the beauty of a male youth was similar in kind to that of a woman; Marlowe made use of this, when presenting Leander as saying 'You are deceav'd, I am no woman I.' But Marlowe's Neptune lusted after Leander in the full knowledge that he was a boy: his 'prying' upon 'his brest, his thighes, and everie lim' surely included in its inspection the one particular 'lim' which distinguished him from a girl. For Shakespeare's persona, on the other hand, the mere fact of the youth's being male settles the matter: one might say that the youth's possession of a penis operates, for this adult, like a young man's possession of facial hair in the culture of Southern Europe, eliminating the desire for sexual acts. Not adulthood but maleness itself is, in this case, the determining factor.

★ ★ ★

English literary culture before the second half of the seventeenth century offers no examples of the sort of scabrous, sexually explicit poetry on same-sex themes that had been produced, at least by a few writers, in Italy. But something similar did emerge in the early seventeenth century in France. Whether there is any direct connection here is hard to say, but it may be significant that the last important Italian writer in that style, Curzio Marignolli, spent several of his final years in France, dying in Paris in 1606.[54] For the most famous poem in the new French tradition of caustic sexual explicitness, a sonnet by Théophile de Viau published in 1622, is highly Marignolliesque in both theme and treatment:

> Philis, everything is fucked, I am dying of syphilis;
> It is exerting all its power against me:
> My cock lowers its head and has no vigour
> [...]
> Philis, I got this disease from having fucked you.
> God, I repent of having led such a bad life;
> And if your wrath does not kill me this time,
> I vow that henceforth I shall fuck only in the arse.[55]

'Philis' here was a female prostitute, and the final line played on what seems to have been a widely held and long-lasting belief that whereas having sex with such women carried a strong risk of venereal disease, sodomizing a man or boy did not.[56] This was an example of what a modern critic has called Théophile's 'cabaret poetry'—*cabaret* being the contemporary term for a tavern where groups of men would socialize and drink for hours on end. It is not among the most typical ones; the majority of his comic-erotic compositions were about male–female sex only, and some were quite short poems in simple quatrains.[57] (That format, so well adapted to memorizing and oral transmission, may have derived from a popular tradition of satirical oral poetry, which seems to have run from the late sixteenth century to the end of the seventeenth and beyond.)[58] Fatefully, however, this scabrous sonnet became the most famous thing he wrote, as it was used as a central piece of evidence when he was prosecuted in Paris, first in his absence in 1623 and then in person in 1623–5, for obscenity and sodomy. In vain did he argue that 'writing verses about sodomy does not make a man guilty of actually doing it; to be a poet and to be a paederast are two different things.'[59] He died in 1626, aged just 36, his health having been broken by the two years he spent in atrocious prison conditions.

The crackdown on de Viau had been largely the consequence of an initiative by a Jesuit priest, François Garasse, who had been preparing a huge polemical treatise against what he called the *beaux esprits*—meaning, roughly speaking, those who expressed fashionable irreligious views. He thus had other targets in his sights; and he was all the while conducting a larger campaign to reconfigure religious debates in a way that would embarrass or marginalize those who did not line up with the Jesuit position.[60] But for his purposes it was highly convenient that he could associate Théophile (whose more serious poems did in places seem to express somewhat heterodox philosophical beliefs) with the gross sin of sodomy, as he was trying to build up a composite picture of 'libertinism', combining intellectual, spiritual and moral corruption.[61] Historians like to distinguish between *libertinisme* and *libertinage*, seeing the former as an intellectual phenomenon, while the latter was a social and cultural one involving deliberate norm-breaking. Yet although there was much that was artificial, indeed purely prejudicial, about Garasse's argument, his sense that there might be a link between heterodox religious belief and sexual immorality was not completely far-fetched. As we have seen, Renaissance naturalism had supplied a line of argument which could be used in defence of so-called deviant or immoral sex: the genitals and anus, and the pleasures derived from them, were natural; God was the creator of nature; He could thus be presumed to have intended or authorized these natural effects; and in any case a good God would not create human beings with desires that were evil.[62] Whether consciously or subliminally, such ideas did find an audience within French culture during the first half of the seventeenth century.

Libertine forms of thought and expression, including jocular, explicit references to sex (both male–female and male–male) lived on after Théophile's death. Indeed, some of the handful of writers who continued to produce such poetry had been members of his circle. One, Denis Sanguin de Saint-Pavin (c.1595–1670), was apparently known as the 'King of Sodom'; among the poems attributed to him in manuscript is one that begins: 'Today, when Calista | Caught me with her young brother, | She reproached me angrily, | Saying that she, like him, had an arse...'. Another, expressing his attitude to life, says that 'without restraining my desires | I devote myself entirely to pleasures.'[63] Also in this tradition, though a little too young to have known Théophile personally, was Claude de Chouvigny, baron de Blot l'Eglise (1605–55), who exclaimed in one of his poems, 'I am a dyed-in-the-wool bugger'; another verse by him, entitled 'The Arse', declares that 'All our moral teachers have forbidden it, | But a wiser author | Says that it is for the benefit of the individual | And the cunt is for the benefit of the species.'[64] Attention-grabbing though such verses are, however, they circulated only in manuscript, or through private recitation. This minor literary phenomenon faltered as the individual poets who practised it died or ceased to write; it did not generate any lasting poetic tradition. But the values that were at least partly expressed through it—of hedonistic psychology, *carpe diem* pleasure-taking, casual irreligion, carefree humour and *épatez les bourgeois* provocation—lived on, supplying a libertine ethos which appealed not only, as we have seen, to some members of the French nobility in the latter part of the century, but also to a number of upper-class Englishmen in the same period.

Restoration England offered suitable conditions for an element of libertinism to flourish in the higher reaches of society. Attempts to police sexual morality could now be associated with the Interregnum regime, which, in a statute of 1650, had decreed the death penalty for adultery and a prison sentence for fornication; the word 'puritanical' was gaining some of its modern connotations. There were many men from noble and gentry families who had spent years leading quite private lives, often in exile, where they had been less constrained by the framework of Church, state and provincial society which would have moulded their behaviour in normal conditions in England. And in reaction to the sort of severe divine-command morality that had been discredited, in their eyes, by the religious radicals of the previous two decades, some of them were attracted by a new ethos of self-interest, grounded on nature and loosely associated with the philosophy of Hobbes.[65] The concept of 'libertine' behaviour became a recognized part of the culture, at least in London, where such men could socialize with one another. In Thomas Shadwell's play *The Libertine* (1675), an adaptation of the legend of Don Juan, the central character is described by his servant as follows: 'He owns no Deity, but his voluptuous appetite, whose satisfaction he will compass by Murders, Rapes, Treasons, or ought else.' In Don John's own words, 'There's nothing good or ill, but as it seems to each man's natural appetite, if they will consent freely.' Yet it is noteworthy that when Shadwell put together this portrait of an ultra-libertine, he did not include the slightest hint of male–male sexual behaviour. To the (male) servant of a household where he has wrought sexual havoc during his brief visit, Don John says: 'I know your Family has a great respect for me, for I have lain with every one in it, but thee and thy Master.'[66]

Of the known individuals identified with libertine or rakish behaviour in Restoration England, only a small handful seem to have been associated with the practice of sodomy: these included the free-thinker Lord Vaughan and the poets Sir Charles Sedley and John Wilmot, Earl of Rochester. Of Vaughan's sexual conduct almost nothing is known, other than what is said in an anonymous satirical poem, which mentions both him and Sir Charles: '*Sidley* has fuck't a thousand Arses | And so has Vaughan as well as he.'[67] Despite the claim made in the first of those two statements, there is little evidence of sodomy in the known facts of Sedley's life, nor would one guess such a thing from his writings—though he was certainly both a man of pleasure and, together with his friends Rochester and Charles Sackville, Lord Buckhurst, someone who was not afraid of defying conventional opinion. He features routinely in accounts of Restoration sodomy because of a notorious public performance which took place in London in 1663, when he was 24 years old. Samuel Pepys learned about Sedley's escapade, and his subsequent trial, from two friends at dinner; they told him that Sedley had appeared on the balcony of an eating-house in Covent Garden 'and showed his nakedness—acting all the postures of lust and buggery that could be imagined'. At some point in the subsequent conversation, Pepys's dining companions told him 'that buggery is now almost grown as common among our gallants as in Italy, and that the very pages of the town begin to complain of their masters for it'. He immediately added, however: 'But blessed be God, I do not to this day know what is the meaning of this sin, nor which is the agent nor which the patient'—which would be a surprising statement by such a man of the world, unless it simply meant that he was not sure whether someone described as a 'bugger' was the active or passive partner.[68] The concentration by modern historians on the 'buggery' element of Sedley's performance may, however, be misleading. Pepys himself devoted more attention to other aspects: 'abusing of scripture and, as it were, from thence preaching a Mountebanke sermon from that pulpitt, saying that there he hath to sell such a pouder as should make all the cunts in town run after him'. Another report did not mention the miming of buggery at all. It explained that Sedley, Sackville and another friend, when thoroughly drunk, 'went into the balcony looking into the street, put downe their breeches, and shit into the street; stripped themselves naked (they say). Sir Charles Sedley, being the most eager, preached blasphemy to the people. And thereupon a riot raised.'[69]

This story illustrates the *épatez les bourgeois* mentality that was present in the minds of a small number of Restoration libertines. If Sedley did somehow mime an act of male–male buggery (as opposed to male–female sex) or male–male fellatio (as opposed to female–male fellatio, or male–female cunnilinctus) he did so in order to shock. Modern historians have tended to enlist such Restoration rakes in their account of 'normal' sodomy in pre-1700 England, on the assumption that if they buggered boys and also had sex with women, they were simply representing a continuation of the standard pattern of sexual behaviour (the pattern, that is, which this book identifies as Mediterranean and not Northern European). But as Michael Young points out, when criticizing the version of this argument presented by Tim Hitchcock: 'Hitchcock repeats the familiar refrain that "the classic image of the seventeenth-century libertine as having a catamite on one arm and a whore on the other expresses clearly the extent to which bisexuality was the norm". In fact, it shows precisely the opposite. Libertines do not demonstrate norms; they *violate* norms.'[70]

The only one of these libertines to deal explicitly with male–male sex in his writings was Rochester. Of his desire to shock there can be no doubt, though in his case one senses not just a shallow wish to gain attention—present though that may have been—but a deeply negative view of human nature and the human condition. Same-sex acts are only a minor theme within the range of sexually explicit descriptions in his verse, but they are striking when they do appear. For modern readers, maintaining the distinction between Rochester and his poetic persona is always difficult, because we know that for years he did lead a very 'debauched' life. Whether his debauchery regularly included male–male sex is, admittedly, far from clear; there is one passage in a letter from Rochester to his friend Henry Savile in Paris, commending in sexually suggestive terms 'this pretty fool the bearer', a young Frenchman who had served as Rochester's valet; and in an earlier letter to Savile Rochester had described himself as 'a tired bugger'.[71] But the references to sodomy in the poems tend to be, as Paul Hammond has observed, 'perfunctory', making the reader wonder whether the poet really is 'interested in sexual relations between men'.[72] The misogynistic 'song' which begins 'Love a Woman! Th'rt an Ass' explains that to 'drudge' in a woman's body is a dull activity, aimed at producing children for the benefit of one's old age, and ends with the following two stanzas:

> Farewell *Woman*! I entend
>   Henceforth every Night to sitt
> With my lewd well natur'd Freind
>   Drinking to engender witt.

> Then give me health, wealth, Mirth, and wine,
>   And, if buizy love intrenches
> There's a sweet soft Page of mine
>   Can doe the Trick worth Forty wenches.[73]

This certainly expresses a willingness to sodomize a page. But its central conceit is that mental procreation—engendering wit—with a friend is better than the physical variety; busy love, i.e. the physical sexual urge, is just an afterthought, not one of the four major goods mentioned in the previous line, but a distraction, albeit one that can be pleasantly satisfied in an alternative way.

Rochester's phrase 'a sweet soft Page' may seem to evoke an element of more traditional eroticism between an adult man and a youth—traditional, that is, in a classically derived literary culture. Yet other references to male–male sex in his writings are hard to judge. In 'The Disabled Debauchee', verses spoken by a raddled veteran of vice, the speaker refers to 'fucking' a 'well-look'd Linkboy'; the term 'linkboy' was a generic phrase for a lantern-carrier, with 'boy' denoting his status as a servant, not his age.[74] In 'The Imperfect Enjoyment', when the speaker bewails the inability of his penis to recover from a premature ejaculation, he boasts (in the wording of Harold Love's edition) that in the past, 'Stiffly Resolv'd t'would Carelesly invade | Woman, nor Man, nor ought its fury stayd— | Where ere it pierc'd a Cunt it found or made'. Love admits that the manuscript tradition is thoroughly ambiguous, and notes that several of the manuscripts have either 'or man' or 'or Boy'. Regardless of whether 'nor' or 'or' is correct, the clear implication of the third line is that the male body could also be 'pierc'd'; and the fact that 'man' was preferred to 'Boy' by some contemporary copyists may itself be significant.[75] But any attempt to analyse such texts as evidence of Rochester's own sexual practice is probably misguided: the more correct reading is likely to be the more outrageous one, since causing outrage was part of his poetic purpose.

The most outrageous literary production of all in this period, the burlesque drama *Sodom and Gomorrah* (or *Sodom: Or, The Quintessence of Debauchery*), has until fairly recently been attributed to Rochester, though the arguments in favour of doing so have never been strong; modern scholarship points instead to the involvement of two minor writers, Thomas Jordan and Christopher Fishbourne. This play—which was clearly never intended to be acted—was written in the late 1670s and survives in a number of manuscripts, attempts to print it in the following decade having been suppressed.[76] Comical and intensely pornographic, the drama is set at the court of King Bolloxinian, who, weary of sex with his Queen, Cuntigratia, not only announces that he will devote himself to sodomy instead, but issues a proclamation allowing the entire population to do so too. But although there are recurrent references to buggery, the play focuses mainly on the women of the court—Queen Cuntigratia, Princess Swivia, and maids of honour named Fuckadilla, Cunticula and Clitoris—and on the complaints they make, the lascivious desires they express, and the experiences they graphically describe. The only sex acted out on stage is male–female too, in a dumb-show of oral and vaginal sex committed by six naked men and six naked women, and in a scene where Swivia initiates her younger brother, Pricket, in the pleasures of sexual intercourse. The play ends after Bolloxinian's medical adviser informs him that, as a result of his decree, the entire population is sickening and dying; the King remains defiant to the end, Don Juan-like, as fire and brimstone rain down upon him.[77] In all this phantasmagoria of obscenity and absurdity, there seems to be only one definite contemporary reference, when the royal decree permitting buggery is described as an 'indulgence', and Bolloxinian says: 'Let Conscience haue itts force of liberty. | I do proclaim that Buggery may be vsd | O're all the land so C[un]t be not abus'd'—an allusion to Charles II's Declaration of Indulgence of 1672. Beyond that, however, the play has no application to Charles, and attempts to identify individual characters with members of his family and court are entirely unconvincing.[78] The authors' main concern is to stretch the bounds of literary parody, titillating and shocking as they do so; and while they draw on many aspects, real or imagined, of contemporary male–female sexual behaviour, there is no attempt to portray anything of the actual psychology or experience of male–male sex as it existed in the world around them.

★ ★ ★

That male–male sex did take place in Restoration London is not in doubt. As we shall see in a subsequent chapter, once an active campaign of vigilante policing got under way at the turn of the century, a significant amount of evidence of such sexual activity quickly began to emerge, revealing a kind of social underworld that must have been already in place well before 1700. But the main point made in this chapter has been that sodomy did not play anything more than a very marginal role in the cultural products of this period. And the reason for that was surely a simple one: even if authors had wanted to explore the representation of sodomy, they could not have expected such a theme to resonate with their audience in the way that it did for readers of comic *novelle* or humorous poems in Italy.

One might gain a very different impression from the works of modern literary historians who have gone in search of male–male sexual signifi-cances in early modern English writings, and have returned with what is presented as an abundant harvest. Several factors have been at work here, including the influence of Alan Bray's theory that sodomy was ubiquitous in early modern England. This can lead to strange misunderstandings. One modern literary historian cites, as a suggestive example of what he calls 'intensely affective male relationships', a passage from Josias Bodley's Latin description of his travels through Ireland in 1602–3: in the morning, when servants came into the room where the men had been sharing a bed and began to light the fire, 'we all awoke, and greeted one another (as the cus-tom is among the well educated): but among our party there were some who greeted their companions the back way, which was not—to my way of thinking—very decent, although some say that it is good for the loins; but nothing is amiss which is not taken amiss.'[79] It must be doubted whether, in the absence of Bray's claim, it would have occurred to anyone to see a sod-omitical significance, or even an 'intensely affective' one, in this simple description of men farting.

Another factor, already discussed, is the tendency to assume that if certain practices typically have a sexual meaning today, such as men sharing a bed or kissing, they must always have had that meaning. In Thomas Middleton's play *Michaelmas Term* (written probably in 1605), the scheming London draper Quasimodo targets a naïve young country gentleman, Richard Easy, who has just come to town, and forms an elaborate plan to defraud him of his lands. He instructs his servant to pose as a gentleman and insinuate him-self into Easy's company, becoming his most trusted friend while at the same time leading him into debt ('Train him to every wasteful sin, that he | May quickly need health, but especially money'). Quasimodo's instructions to the servant end with the lines: 'Drink drunk with him, creep into bed with him, | Kiss him and undo him, my sweet spirit.' The servant does become the intimate friend of Easy, who praises him later in the play as 'such a good, free-hearted, honest, affable kind of gentleman'; to a third party Easy has no hesitation in explaining that 'we lie together', and at a later stage another character, surprised that Easy does not know the whereabouts of the friend for whom he has stood surety for a large sum of money, says 'you're his bedfellow'.[80] These were normal signs of close trust and personal affection in Elizabethan and Jacobean society, with no sexual significance.[81] But to a modern literary critic the relations between the two men must have involved 'sexuality', and the methods used by the servant to gain Easy's trust are 'explicitly homoerotic'.[82]

The use of the term 'homoerotic', in that instance, does at least conform to its normal meaning: in modern English, 'homoerotic' relates to sexual feelings towards people of the same sex. Yet the same writer refers elsewhere to the 'pervasiveness' of 'nonsodomitical or nonsubversive homoerotic relations in early modern England', which—even when one allows for the exaggerations of the Bray thesis—must imply something much broader.[83] In the hands of many modern literary and cultural historians, the meaning of this term has been diluted and extended to the point where almost any kind of positive affective relationship between two people of the same sex may apparently qualify as 'homoerotic'. (One contributing factor here has been the influential argument of Eve Kosofsky Sedgwick which posits 'the potential unbrokenness of a continuum between homosocial and homosexual', and then uses the phrase 'male homosocial desire' for the whole continuum. Critics operating with a simplified version of this theory might naturally make several assumptions: first that 'homoerotic' is the middle term between homosocial and homosexual; secondly that the point of the continuum model is to suggest that everything described by it is qualitatively the same; and thirdly that 'homoeroticism' may characterize that underlying quality rather better than the puzzling phrase 'homosocial desire'.)[84]

A study of the English prose romances of the Renaissance period, for example, notes at first that 'explicitly homoerotic or perilously sodomitical episodes are conspicuously absent from romances', but quickly goes on to say that homoeroticism is 'inscribed' in them: there is a range of ways in which 'male–male desire' is manifested, including 'passion, intimacy (enabled by touch, embrace, wish to share time and space away from the gaze of other characters, secretly), oaths of loyalty', and so on. All this amounts, apparently, to 'a nongenital form of bonding between men, whose purpose is to solidify, not subvert, the very fabric of the nationalist Protestant English state'; what is achieved thereby is 'the representation of homoeroticism as nonthreatening'.[85] It can easily be agreed that there is no sense, in these prose romances, of any scandalous sexual meaning being conveyed. But this writer's assumption appears to be that signs of affection which lack any clear sexual significance can nevertheless be described as implicitly homoerotic; and so, if the term 'homoerotic' is allowed its normal meaning, the underlying idea seems to be that all forms of affection between men are implicitly sexual. If Renaissance writers really had shared that peculiarly modern way of thinking, then it might well be reasonable to claim that in these cases they had found clever ways of making homoeroticism 'nonthreatening'. But it is simpler, and much more historical, to suppose that their representations were non-threatening because—among other reasons—they were not representations of homoeroticism at all.

The ways in which close male friendship was expressed in the early modern period can surprise modern readers. When Shakespeare's Coriolanus refers to 'Friends now fast sworn, | Whose double bosoms seem to wear one heart, | Whose hours, whose bed, whose meal and exercise, | Are still together, who twin as 'twere, in love | Unseparable', he is simply describing the strongest form of friendship, which he contrasts with those at the opposite extreme who live in 'bitterest enmity'.[86] In his essay 'On Friendship', Michel de Montaigne gave a famous description of this kind of male friendship (after dismissing the male–male sexual relations of the ancient Greeks as 'abhorrent'); his concept of soul-sharing drew on classical sources, especially Plato, but he was also trying to capture the nature of the relationship he himself had experienced with his closest friend, Étienne de La Boëtie. 'In the friendship which I am talking about', he wrote, 'souls are mingled and confounded in so universal a blending that they efface the seam which joins them together so that it cannot be found. If you press me to say why I loved him, I feel that it can only be expressed by replying: "Because it was him: because it was me."' He added that such friends were like 'one soul in bodies twain…so they can neither lend nor give anything to each other'.[87]

Similarly, Sir Thomas Browne celebrated the ideal of 'one soule in two bodies' in his *Religio medici* (first published in 1643): 'I love my friende before my selfe…when I am from him, I am dead till I bee with him; when I am with him, I am not satisfied, but would still be nearer him; united soules are not satisfied with embraces, but desire each to be truely the other, which being impossible, their desires are infinite, and must proceed without a possibility of satisfaction.'[88] Alan Sinfield cites this passage and comments: 'How might two friends be truly each other, *beyond embracing*? What would *satisfaction*, without which we must proceed, be like? Browne is saying that friends cannot do what husbands and wives do. Sodomy (or should we say sexual love?) is shadowing friendship.'[89] While the use of rhetorical questions renders Sinfield's argument somewhat opaque, the suggestion seems to be that even if such friendship is contrasted here with sexual desire, that contrast itself indicates an inevitable tension between the two, such that the friendship is constantly fending off sodomy and thereby, however negatively, invoking the idea of it. Yet the passage, in its context, is not making any sexual reference at all; it has no concern with what husbands and wives do in bed. It simply says that when two such perfect friends are together, neither the fact of being in each other's company nor even a physical hug can satisfy their desire, which is real, for a total uniting of souls, which is impossible.

One of the best correctives to the tendencies described here was actually offered by Alan Bray in his last book, *The Friend*, where he argued that the task of the historian is 'to let the past speak in its own terms, not to appropriate it to those of the contemporary world', adding that 'The inability to conceive of relationships in other than sexual terms says something of contemporary poverty.' If the terms in which strong friendship was described seem strange to us, he argued, that is because they belonged to a quite formalized system of conduct and expression: 'The language of love between men that one sees in the English Renaissance is simply that: a language and a convention. It could be heartfelt, it could be hollow ...'.[90] Modern literary historians, however, are often inclined to take the language itself as a sort of free-floating medium in which sexual meanings can be found, regardless of how those differ from the primary meaning, in its context, of the passage they are discussing. An example may help to illustrate this.

In *All for Love* (1677), John Dryden's version of the story of Antony and Cleopatra, a character called Dolabella is introduced in Act III. He had been Antony's most beloved friend, until he (Dolabella) had fallen in love with Cleopatra, which caused Antony's jealousy and the estrangement of the two men. But Antony still warms to the thought of their former friendship, describing it as follows:

> He lov'd me too,
> I was his Soul; he liv'd not but in me:
> We were so clos'd within each others brests,
> The rivets were not found that join'd us first.
> That does not reach us yet: we were so mixt,
> As meeting streams, both to our selves were lost;
> We were one mass; we could not give or take,
> But from the same; for he was I, I he.[91]

Readers will easily recognize here a slightly adapted version of that classic passage from Montaigne's essay on friendship. The fluid metaphor of 'mingled and confounded in...blending' is preserved as 'mixt | As meeting streams'; the concept of a 'seam', which joins two things together, has been nicely strengthened to 'rivets'; the phrase about giving or taking is borrowed from Montaigne's later comment; and the final six words have switched Montaigne's meaning while retaining the cadence with its lapidary juxtaposition. But the literary historian George Haggerty interprets these lines very differently, seeing them as expressing sexual feeling 'in almost blatant terms'. He draws attention to the phrases about rivets and streams, and the expression 'We were one mass', and comments: 'all these images stress physicality, fluidity, and bodily identification in a way that belies any simple "friendship" interpretation; *even if* the attempts to dissolve the distinction between the two individuals here *could be read as metaphorical* [my italics], the tenor of these tropes amounts to more than spiritual affection.' (The precise line of argument is not spelt out, but seems to involve connecting rivets with erect penises, streams with semen, and 'one mass' with two sexually conjoined bodies.) Haggerty concludes that this is a 'sexualized male relation', announcing more generally that 'Restoration tragedy is a largely untapped source for the acculturation of sodomitical relations.'[92]

The ways in which early modern writers used metaphors were, in one sense, more straightforward than those available to their Romantic and post-Romantic counterparts (for whom the much more open-ended concept of 'images' was developed): a metaphor was something that could be cashed into its meaning, in a way that made sense locally within the text. But in another sense their approach to metaphor can sometimes strike modern readers as extraordinarily bold, since they were capable of transferring a metaphor into its meaning without feeling that the meaning was in any way contaminated (so to speak) by the connotations of the metaphorical term itself. In one of John Donne's most famous devotional poems, 'Holy Sonnet 14', the poet tells God that although he loves Him, he is 'betrothed unto your enemy' (Satan), and can be saved only by God's violent intervention: 'Take me to you, imprison me, for I | Except you'enthrall me, never shall be free, | Nor ever chaste, except you ravish me.'[93] The metaphor of being imprisoned and enthralled translates into being taken entirely within God's power; and the metaphor of being ravished translates—after the previous reference to becoming a bride of the Devil—into being subjected in an overpowering way to union with God. Modern readers are likely to feel that that final metaphor can never altogether lose its sexual connotation; and on that basis they may assume that Donne was expressing homoerotic feelings about yielding to some kind of male sexual conquest. That, presumably, is why this poem features in a modern anthology entitled *Same-Sex Desire in Early Modern England* (alongside other deeply devotional poems by George Herbert, Richard Crashaw and Thomas Traherne).[94] Yet it is inconceivable that any of Donne's contemporaries would have understood it in such a way.

One important factor here was the familiarity of devout Bible readers with the Song of Songs; its sensual language—beginning with 'Let him kiss me with the kisses of his mouth'—had long been thoroughly theologized, with its strong statements of physical desire translated into strong statements of spiritual yearning.[95] Thus it was that the pious Puritan minister Samuel Rogers could write in his diary 'oh when will I see him, when shall I lye in the embraces of Jesus Christ; when will he kisse mee with the kisses of his mouth, amongst those that excell in virtue', and the leading Independent Francis Rous could celebrate, in his *Misticall Marriage*, the idea of the 'chamber within us, and bed of love in that chamber, wherein Christ meets the soule'.[96]

It is at least understandable that modern readers should perceive a sexual implication in such forms of writing, given the strongly sensual nature of the terms of the metaphors used. But some literary historians do not require even that level of apparent justification for finding sexual significance in a text; they are capable of conjuring it up on the basis of little more than word association. A striking example is given in one of the most prominent works of modern literary–cultural history on this topic, Jonathan Goldberg's widely acclaimed *Sodometries*. Goldberg devotes a chapter to William Bradford, the Puritan who sailed to New England on the *Mayflower*, helped to set up the Plymouth Colony, and was the leading figure there until his death in 1657. In his journal, a work known as *Of Plymouth Plantation* which is one of the most important texts of the early colonial period, Bradford comments briefly on the case of a teenaged boy who was convicted and executed in 1642 for buggering animals, and also refers, in passing and rather obliquely, to a person who 'had made some sodomitical attempts upon another'. In a general comment on that year, Bradford mentioned fornication and adultery and added that 'even sodomy and buggery (things fearful to name) have broken forth in this land oftener than once.' Goldberg takes these minor references as a starting-point for an investigation into the allegedly deep significance of sodomy in Bradford's mind. He jumps back to 1629, to another text, reproduced in Bradford's work but not written by him: a letter to him penned by Charles Gott in Salem, describing how he and the members of his community had chosen a minister and a religious teacher for their Church. In the full text of that letter, Gott explained that whilst they were satisfied that each of the two men had an inward calling, the procedure followed in Salem ensured that those men also had

> an outward calling which was from the people, when a company of believers are joined together in covenant to walk together in all the ways of God. And every member (being men) are to have a free voice in the choice of their officers, etc. Now, we being persuaded that these two men were so qualified as the Apostle speaks to Timothy, where he says 'a bishop must be blameless, sober, apt to teach, etc.', I think I may say, as the eunuch said unto Philip, 'What should let from being baptized, seeing there was water?' and he believed.[97]

(The first reference is to 1 Tim. 3: 1–3; the second is to Acts 8: 36–7, where the Apostle Philip journeys with an Ethiopian eunuch and persuades him to believe in Christ. When they reach a pond or stream, the eunuch says 'See, here is water; what doth hinder me to be baptized?', and Philip replies 'if thou believeth with all thine heart, thou mayest.')

Goldberg quotes from that passage in Gott's letter very selectively, citing only the phrases 'every member (being men) are to have a free voice' and 'I may say, as the eunuch said'. He then comments as follows:

> as the eunuch, he locates himself, dismembering the members and severing the 'natural' bond to women in order to make 'free' male members—free to have relations with each other that are nominally desexualized and are resexualized, nominally, in the very words on the page, in their being exchanges, member to member. The sexuality that flows at such moments in the representation of the ideal male community suggests how close sodomy is to this discourse and why, when sodomy 'broke forth', as Bradford puts it—when it became visible—it was violently repudiated. The fundamental nonrecognition in Bradford's text, I would argue, is the proximity of the ties that bind these men together and the possibility of literally enacting them.[98]

Innocent readers dependent on Goldberg, who has not paused to explain the reference to the eunuch in the Acts of the Apostles, might perhaps imagine that New England Puritans could not write about the 'members' of their religious community without thinking at some deep level about male genitalia and sex, and that if they wrote about those members making a 'free' choice they must also be thinking, at a deep level, about the freedom to make sexual 'exchanges' (whatever that might mean, if literally enacted). This is a method of reading texts which enables some modern literary or cultural historians to see in those texts exactly what they want to find. Indeed, they are guaranteed to do so, as they have projected it onto the texts themselves.

18

European colonial societies

In several previous chapters, mention has been made of sodomy cases that took place in colonies, both in the Americas and in Asia. Such cases have been treated hitherto as sources of supplementary details, adding to the stock of information about the practices and mentalities of the home societies from which the colonists came. But it is worth looking a little more closely at these extra-European societies; the forms of sexual behaviour that took place within them may raise other issues, especially about relations between Europeans and native inhabitants. And at the very least, these far-flung offshoots of West European cultures offer a further opportunity to consider the divergences between the different parts of Europe itself.

A great deal of modern academic research has focused on identifying and analysing all possible evidence of same-sex relations in the North American colonies during the first century of English settlement. The tally of cases which we now possess is probably close to complete, so far as the available documentation is concerned. Indeed, efforts to identify such cases have even gone beyond the evidence, seeing such sexual activity where none existed. One standard compilation of documents begins by quoting from a passage in a description of Virginia published in 1612, describing the plight of the early colonists in June 1607 when the ships which had brought them there departed for England:

> within tenne daies scarse ten amongst vs coulde either goe [sc. walk], or well stand, such extreame weaknes and sicknes oppressed vs. And thereat none need marvaile, if they consider the cause and reason, which was this; whilest the ships staied, our allowance was somewhat bettered, by a daily proportion of bisket which the sailers would pilfer to sell, giue or exchange with vs, for mony, saxefras, furres, or loue. But when they departed, there remained neither taverne, beere-house nor place of relife but the common kettell.[1]

Forbidden Desire in Early Modern Europe: Male–Male Sexual Relations, 1400–1750. Noel Malcolm, Oxford University Press.
© Noel Malcolm 2024. DOI: 10.1093/oso/9780198886334.003.0018

The compiler, Jonathan Ned Katz, argues that the word 'love' there meant 'sexual favors' or 'what are now usually called "homosexual" contacts', on the grounds that 'it was unlikely that seventeenth-century English sailors would have traded stolen biscuit for the settlers' affection'; and he concludes that 'The casualness of the reference to the exchange of "love" for biscuit suggests that such life and death barters were common knowledge among some seventeenth-century Englishmen.'[2] But 'love' in this passage had its perfectly normal meaning of gratitude for an act of charity (as preserved in modern usage when something is described as not obtainable 'for love or money'). The three terms in the previous clause set out the three possibilities of sale, gift, or exchange; and the corresponding terms have merely been shuffled slightly out of order: sale for money, exchange for sassafras and furs, and charitable giving for love. It is hard to understand how a modern scholar could seriously imagine that a narrative of this kind, written in the first person and printed as publicity material for the settlement of Virginia, could have alluded so casually to male–male sexual relations.[3]

Where records of actual sodomy are concerned, the evidence from early modern British North America is slight. In 1624 a ship's captain was tried and executed in Virginia for coercively buggering his steward; the latter, referred to in some of the testimony as a 'boy', was 29 years old—a reminder that the term 'boy' often denoted status rather than age.[4] Thereafter, no definite, undisputed cases are known in that colony during the rest of the century, though there is one ambiguously worded record—discussed below—which, although commonly taken to refer to a male–female offence, does more probably relate to a sodomitical assault. Other instances of sodomy may of course have occurred without reaching the attention of the authorities; it seems reasonable to suppose this, not only because the same was surely the case in England, but also because the gender balance in the Chesapeake Bay colonies (Virginia and Maryland) during their early development was heavily skewed, with four or five Englishmen to every Englishwoman and very little access to native women or, in the early decades, to female slaves.[5] (This factor, leading to an element of 'situational' same-sex activity, would have been one of the distinctive features of those early colonial societies where relations with native women were generally unavailable.) In New England—where the gender balance was much better, with perhaps six men to every four women—just two men were executed for sodomy, or related offences, in the seventeenth century. William Plaine was arrested for 'unclean practices' and hanged at New Haven in 1646, accused of having 'committed sodomy with two persons in England' and of having 'corrupted a great part of the youth of Guilford [i.e. the colony of New Haven]' by masturbating with them. It was alleged that, in an apparent aggravation of his offence, 'to some who questioned the lawfulness of such a filthy practice, he did insinuate seeds of atheism, questioning whether there were a God, etc.'; a later summary of his case would simply state that he was hanged for corrupting boys, and it seems that his main offence was introducing youths to mutual masturbation.[6] Nine years later, in the same town, John Knight was convicted of a 'sodomitical attempt' on a teen-aged boy.[7]

That both these executions took place in New Haven may not be a coin-cidence, as the authorities in that particular colony—which had been founded by a group of 'intensely rigorous Puritans'—had a more expansive notion of what might qualify as 'sodomitical' and worthy of capital punish-ment.[8] When they drew up their law-code in 1655 they included in the definition of sodomy not only female–female sex and the anal penetration of women, but also the vaginal penetration of girls before puberty. (That last point reflected the old tendency to conflate sodomy with the broader category of sins against nature, meaning in this case non-procreative sex.) Masturbation 'in the sight of others . . . corrupting or tempting others to do the like, which tends to the sin of sodomy' was also punishable by death. Elsewhere, the laws of the Plymouth, Massachusetts, Connecticut and New Hampshire colonies simply quoted the verse from Leviticus which decreed death for any man who 'lyeth with mankind', while Rhode Island cited the equivalent verse from the First Epistle to the Romans.[9] But although these biblical texts provided a satisfying sense of religious certainty, they did not supply the actual criteria that were needed for putting such a law into practice. What exactly was to count as 'lying with'? In 1642 the authorities in Massachusetts wrote to ministers and magistrates throughout the northern colonies, asking for their advice on 'whether touching and rubbing, to the point of ejaculation, is sodomy punishable by death'. A majority of the replies seem to have followed the narrower view of the English legal tradition, which saw penetration as a necessary element of sodomy. But one minister, John Rayner, argued that 'full intention and bold attempting' should receive the same punishment as the act itself, and that the practice of 'touching and rubbing' might be seen as equivalent to penetration in cases where it had been indulged in frequently over a long period.[10]

If these details give the impression that the authorities in New England were preoccupied with sodomy, the impression is misleading. In reality they encountered this offence very rarely. Hence, indeed, their definitional uncertainties when it—or something resembling it—arose; as Thomas Shepard (minister at Cambridge, Massachusetts) wrote to John Winthrop later in 1642, 'in discussing these questions we generally walk in untrodden paths.'[11] Yet they were certainly preoccupied with sin in general. A central element in the rhetoric of the 'Great Migration' during the 1620s and 1630s was the claim that it was necessary for godly people to leave England, which was a cesspit of sin and corruption, before God in His righteous anger destroyed it, just as he had eliminated Sodom and Gomorrah. The worst thing that could happen to the 'city upon a hill' which the colonists set up in the New World was that it might turn into another Sodom (in the general sense, that is, of a society sunk in sinfulness), and this was a source of anxiety throughout the century.[12]

The old stereotypes of ascetic Puritans disapproving of all the pleasures of the flesh have long been abandoned by historians; partly but not only because of their hostility to the celibacy of the Catholic priesthood, Puritan preachers could in fact show 'a frank and comforting acceptance of practical sexuality', so long as it was expressed within marriage.[13] But they did feel particularly concerned by the presence of 'filthy lusts'—tending towards fornication, adultery, and any kind of sexual sin against nature—in both the individual and the community. In his autobiography Thomas Shepard described how, as a teenaged student at Emmanuel College, Cambridge, in the late 1610s, 'I was once or twise dead drunke; & liued in vnnaturall vncleanesses not to be named, & in speculatiue wantonnes, & filthines, w[ith] all sorts of p[er]sons w[hich] pleased my eye (yet still restraynd fro[m] the grosse act of whoordom...).'[14] Alan Bray assumed that the 'vnnaturall vncleanesses' here were acts of sodomy; but the rest of the sentence portrays the young Shepard ogling at women and fantasizing about them, which suggests that his unnatural uncleannesses consisted most probably of masturbation.[15] However, the diary of Michael Wigglesworth, who taught at Harvard as a young man during the 1650s, does describe feelings which the diarist himself identified as involving same-sex desire: it refers to 'unnatural filthy lust' and 'Such filthy lust flowing from my fond affection to my pupils whiles in their presence...that I confess myself an object of Gods loathing as my sin is of my own; and pray God make it no more to me'.[16]

The ordinary population, of course, did not consist entirely of such godly folk, engaged in spiritual self-questioning to the point of self-laceration. But people of that kind filled many of the public offices, and helped to set the tone. Given the project of building a spiritual community, there was much emphasis in Puritan New England on an ethos of edification, brotherly attention, and 'watchfulness'. It has been argued that the physical arrangement of the early settlements facilitated watchfulness in a literal sense, with the clustering of dwellings around the meeting house.[17] In an entry for 1642, William Bradford commented despondently on the presence of fornication and adultery in his society, adding, as we have seen, that 'even sodomy and buggery (things fearful to name) have broken forth in this land oftener than once.' He asked himself why these grave sins were so frequent. Their apparent frequency was, we may suspect, largely relative to his expectations, but it is true that, given the small size of the New England population—c.23,000 in 1650, rising to c.90,000 by 1700—the ratio of known sodomy-related cases to total population exceeded that of the Home Counties in this period.[18] (It was also greater than that in Virginia and Maryland, which had a numerically similar population. Nor did those colonies lack the machinery for policing sexual morality: from 1634 Virginia had an efficient network of county courts, to which people were presented for offences such as fornication and adultery, and although those courts did not try major felonies such as sodomy, their officials and sheriffs did help to apprehend people suspected of such crimes.)[19] In answer to his own question, Bradford gave as one reason the fact that the population was so closely monitored that the sins were more easily detected there than in ungodly England: it was not that there were 'more evils in this kind', merely that 'they are here more discovered and seen and made public by due search, inquisition and due punishment; for the churches look narrowly to their members, and the magistrates over all, more strictly than in other places.'[20]

Such remarks suggest that, if the Bray thesis about the ubiquity of sodomy is implausible in the case of England, it is even less likely to be true when applied to this colonial society. Indeed, one modern historian of New England has commented, on the basis of the paucity of the court records, that 'homosexual behavior was virtually unknown in everyday life'; he describes both sodomy and bestiality as 'probably extremely rare practices... so uncommon as to be statistically insignificant', arguing that the vast majority of the people had 'internalized the taboos' against both.[21] His critics have pointed out, on the other hand, that we cannot assume that every instance of sodomitical behaviour was taken to court.[22] Some known or suspected cases might have failed to satisfy the legal requirements of evidence; and the court records themselves are sometimes fragmentary, or at best summary. But from the very small body of existing documentation of sodomy-related offences (beyond the two cases already mentioned, there were just nine others involving inhabitants of New England in the seventeenth century), one gets the impression that even relatively minor instances of same-sex behaviour could attract attention and disapproval.[23]

In 1641, for example, a resident of Plymouth Colony was presented for 'uncleane carriages towards men that he hath lyen withall'. Sodomy was not mentioned, and the phrasing of the indictment probably means that he had groped at his bedfellows; Richard Godbeer comments that the case 'does not appear to have proceeded further, suggesting that the testimony available against him was too flimsy to substantiate even a crime of lesser degree'. In 1658 an inhabitant of Middlesex, Massachusetts, was accused of 'sodomiticall uncleanes'; again the phrasing was approximate, and the charge was taken no further.[24] At Plymouth in 1636, John Allexander and Thomas Roberts were found guilty of 'lude behaviour and uncleane carriage wone w[th] another, by often spendinge their seede one vpon another' (implying either mutual masturbation or reciprocal interfemoral sex); it was said that Allexander was 'form[er]ly notoriously guilty that way' and sought to 'allure others therevnto'. He was whipped, branded and banished; Roberts, a servant or apprentice, was whipped and forbidden ever to own land in the colony.[25] One modern historian, Robert Oaks, comments: 'If Alexander was so notorious, why had he not been prosecuted before? Perhaps the authorities were willing to overlook homosexuality unless it became too obvious, an attitude not unlike that of twentieth-century America.'[26] The answer to that question, probably, is that in using the phrase 'notoriously guilty' the court was invoking the legal concept of public fame, which could be used to strengthen the case for the prosecution; the word 'formerly' suggested some distance in time, so perhaps this alluded to an earlier episode when, while the witnesses who could have guaranteed a conviction were lacking, Allexander had received a formal admonition.

Similar issues have been highlighted by historians studying one of the best-documented cases from this period, the trial of the 59-year-old Nicholas Sension in Windsor, Connecticut, in 1677. This man, a respected and relatively wealthy citizen of the town, had been pestering younger men and youths over many years. One 47-year-old witness said that 20 years earlier, when he and Sension were both serving on the town watch, Sension had invited him back to his house and had tried to sodomize him as he slept; another, aged 38, said that nineteen years earlier he had gone to Sension's hay-barn to sleep, only to find, just as he was about to nod off, that Sension had undone his breeches and 'with his mouth and nose rubd about my breech'. The central business of the trial concerned Sension's treatment of two young male servants. Nathaniel Pond, whom he had taken into his service when he was a young orphan, had complained to his (Pond's) elder brother about his master's advances: Sension 'did often in an unseemly manner make attempts tending to Sodomye, soe that he was forced by violence to throw him of from him... his attempts were so violent & constant that he found it difficult worke to keepe him off.' The brother negotiated with Sension to release Nathaniel from his service, but then Nathaniel relented and agreed to stay on; however, by the time of the trial, he had left to become a soldier, and had then met his death. The other servant, Daniel Saxton, had similar complaints about sexual advances; he had left Sension's service, and when he talked to others about his experiences, Sension sued him for defamation. It was the evidence which emerged from that process that led to the prosecution of Sension for sodomy.[27]

Richard Godbeer notes that on two previous occasions, in the 1640s and the 1660s, the town elders had investigated Sension for such activities and reprimanded him. He concludes that those elders had a 'live-and-let-live attitude', and that 'the community as a whole seems to have been remarkably tolerant of Sension's behavior.' That this citizen's standing in the community would have made the authorities more circumspect about tackling him in public can easily be imagined; yet the fact remains that they did tell him twice, more privately, to mend his ways. Even when his full history was exposed at his public trial, only one person claimed that Sension had actually committed sodomy. All the other evidence related to lesser acts, or merely attempted ones, and since two witnesses were needed for a conviction, the charge of actual sodomy failed. He was found guilty only on the lesser count of attempted sodomy, and his entire estate was placed in bond, to be forfeited if he relapsed into such behaviour.[28] In a society which took due process of law seriously, some may have felt on the previous occasions that there was no point in bringing legal proceedings if the available evidence was insufficient to convict; and of course it may only have been the holding of the actual trial that brought out of the woodwork enough further individual testimonies to build up a strong case even on the lesser charge. This may not have been the hyper-vigilant moral community of the Puritan ideal, but terms such as 'live-and-let-live' and 'tolerant' probably give a misleading impression.

The evidence of sodomy in the other European colonies of North America during the seventeenth century is also sparse. In the Dutch 'New Netherland' colony, before its conquest by the English in 1664, four cases are known. 'Jan Creoli, a negro' was executed for sodomizing a ten-year-old boy in 1646; a Dutch merchant, accused of sexually molesting two boys in 1647, drowned early in the following year when trying to cross the frozen Hudson River after escaping from detention; a soldier from Prague was investigated on a charge of attempted sodomy in 1658; and another soldier, from Brussels, was executed in 1660 for having forcibly sodomized his servant boy.[29] Although the sample is small to the point of statistical insignificance, one may sense in these last two cases the intrusion of a certain kind of military sexual ethos, deriving from the male world of the company and the barracks, which was normally less subject to the scrutiny of the civil authorities. Similarly, in the Canadian colony of 'New France' the only known sodomy cases both involved military men. In 1648 a soldier was convicted of that offence and sentenced to death; at a second trial (demanded by the Jesuits, who opposed the death penalty) he was condemned to galley service, and that sentence was then dropped on condition that he serve as the colony's executioner. In 1691 a lieutenant in a company of marines, based in Montreal, admitted to having tried to 'debauch several men'; two of those who served under him were also prosecuted for allowing him to have sex with them 'over a period of time'. The officer was fined and banished from the colony, while the men were given prison sentences of two and three years.[30]

No other sodomy cases are known in New France in the period up to its conquest by the British in 1759. Statistically this is not very surprising, as the European population of the colony was small—rising from just over 3,000 at the time of the first French census in 1665–6 to 55,000 by the time of the last one in 1754. That sodomitical acts were believed to take place is suggested by a decree of the Bishop of Quebec in 1690, instructing confessors to be less lax in granting absolution for grave sins such as magic, sodomy, bestiality and incest; four years later, the power of absolution for sodomy and bestiality would be reserved to the bishop alone. Commenting on the contrast between this indirect but positive evidence and the virtual absence of sodomy cases from the judicial records, Patrice Carriveau emphasizes the geographical dispersion of the population, which weakened the grip of the civil authorities over daily life; generally, he ascribes the lack of known cases to 'the strong self-regulation of colonial society, characterized by its rural way of life, where the family unit is at the centre of social regulation, and where reprehensible acts are not drawn to the attention of officials to such an extent'.[31] These may have been features of a certain kind of settler colonial society more generally; as we shall see, such comments have also been made about the rural society of colonial Brazil.

That the conditions of rural life played a role, similarly, in obscuring evidence of same-sex relations in the British North American colonies during the eighteenth century must also be likely. In 1806 the Swiss-American Albert Gallatin, who was then Secretary of the Treasury, said to a friend that the 'Grecian Vice' was 'common among the Indians as well as among the back Woodsmen'—the latter being the most rural settlers of all.[32] Yet even the urban society of British North America generated only a very small tally of records of same-sex activity during the eighteenth century. In an intriguing defamation case (intriguing because the result of it is not known), a citizen of Bath, North Carolina, said that two brothers in 1718 had maliciously accused him of seeking to sodomize them; he said that this had brought him into 'great Disgrace, Trouble, Shame, Scandal, Injury, Scorn, [and] hatred amongst his Neighbors', as well as 'very Great and apparent Dangers of Prosecution'.[33] One man is known to have been convicted of sodomy, and of 'inciting others' to commit it, in Savannah, Georgia, in 1734; he was sentenced to be given 300 lashes under the town gallows.[34] In Massachusetts three sodomy cases were heard in the Superior Court during the eighteenth century, but only one of the accused was executed: a black slave who was convicted in 1712 of 'forcible Buggery' (the victim being a girl aged 13–14), and whose master happened to be one of the chief justices of the colony. The other two cases, in 1714 and 1740, involved a white servant and a gentleman respectively. Both were accused of using force, against an 'Infant boy' and a thirteen-year-old boy respectively, but their cases were dropped, perhaps because of the high standards of proof required in capital cases.[35] Also in Massachusetts, a member of the First Church of the small town of Marblehead was suspended from communion there in 1732 because of his 'long series of uncleanness with mankind', but restored six years later when he had convinced the membership that he was a reformed character.[36]

A more complex case arose in New London, Connecticut, concerning a Baptist minister, Stephen Gorton. In 1726 he was indicted at the county court there for having 'lasciviously behaved himself towards sundry men, endeavouring to commit sodomy with them', but the charge was dismissed for lack of evidence. Thirty years later, however, he was suspended from his position at the Baptist church of New London because of his 'unchaste behaviour with his fellow men when in bed with them'; and in 1757 the General Meeting of Baptist Churches declared that Gorton's 'offensive and unchaste behaviour, frequently repeated for a long space of time', showed that he had 'an inward disposition . . . towards the actual commission of a sin of so black and dark a dye'. They recommended that he absent himself from the Lord's Supper for several months and devote himself to 'true humiliation' and reformation.[37] The wording of the General Meeting's declaration suggests that the behaviour, while unseemly and evidently sexual in nature, had not reached the threshold—'actual commission'—required for prosecution in the secular courts. Once again, it is clear that judicial processes were not the only available means of regulating behaviour.

Other evidence from the British colonies in North America during the eighteenth century is mostly lacking. It may be true that the appetite of ordinary people for launching prosecutions that might end in capital punishment was waning during this period. But the paucity of the evidence, for a population which had surpassed one million by 1750, is still quite striking. Clare Lyons's study of Philadelphia during that century describes it as the most cosmopolitan city in British North America; she also notes that from the 1740s onwards many readers there were able to learn salacious details about the behaviour of sodomites in London from the popular publication *Select Trials*, which circulated widely—so relevant knowledge certainly existed. Yet she has found no evidence of criminal prosecutions for sodomy, nor even any trace of such accusations in the disciplinary records of the Presbyterian churches, during the entire century. Nor, apparently, was anyone executed for sodomy in the whole of Pennsylvania in that period, though some were hanged for bestiality.[38] It is hard to escape the conclusion that sodomy was just not a widespread phenomenon in this society.

★ ★ ★

The nature of the colonial system imposed on Central and South America by Spain and Portugal differed so greatly from that of the North American colonies that straightforward comparisons between them are seldom possible. Yet, where sodomy is concerned, the evidence clearly shows that this phenomenon was more common in the colonies of the two Southern European powers.

This is not a consequence of the better survival of judicial records—still less of the greater thoroughness of the Inquisition, which in fact had very little direct jurisdiction over sodomy in the Spanish colonial territories. As we have seen, in Spain itself that jurisdiction belonged to the Inquisition only in the mainland dominions of the Crown of Aragon. The secular law which prevailed generally in the Spanish American colonies was that of the Crown of Castile; so it was the secular courts that mostly dealt with sodomy cases. The Aragonese Inquisition was responsible for the tribunals of Mexico and Lima (both from 1569), as well as the Colombian city of Cartagena de Indias (from 1610); but it lacked general jurisdiction over this offence. In Mexico it could prosecute only the sorts of cases that involved heresy (for example, saying that sodomy was not a sin) or the abuse of a sacrament (such as solicitation during confession); the same was true in Lima, where otherwise it dealt only with sodomy perpetrated by ecclesiastics; and at the Cartagena Inquisition—which, in any case, heard only four sodomy cases before 1745—the issue tended to surface during the prosecution of another offence, such as witchcraft.[39]

For the Portuguese colonial territories in America and Africa, the situation was in principle much simpler, as they came under the jurisdiction of the Lisbon tribunal of the Inquisition. So in Brazil there was no local tribunal; people accused of relevant offences could be sent to Lisbon, and many were. Between the early 1590s and the late 1610s, there were also visitations by senior officials of the Inquisition to Bahia and Pernambuco. But an Inquisition conducting only sporadic visitations of particular areas, with, until the end of the seventeenth century, only the most minimal network of familiars on the ground, could not have the same degree of power in monitoring sexual behaviour as existed in Portugal itself.[40]

The general patterns of same-sex behaviour in these Iberian colonies corresponded quite closely to the ones in the colonists' European homelands; and although we do not possess the sort of quantitative evidence that would make proper comparisons possible, it seems that the incidence of sodomy was broadly similar too. At a theoretical level, one could expect the conquistadors, and the early officials and settlers, to have been more intolerant of sodomy, because its perceived prevalence among the native people was sometimes cited as a justification for conquest. The hard-line theorist Juan Ginés de Sepúlveda declared, for example, that a population which did not regard sodomy as a sin was ignoring basic principles of natural law, so that 'the Christians would be fully justified in destroying it for its unspeakable crimes and barbarities.'[41] But this view about the justification of conquest was contested at the time, most famously by the theologian Francisco de Vitoria; and in any case it would be naïve to assume that lines of legal and theological argument developed by intellectuals in Spain were fully internalized by conquistadors and officials on the ground, who were perfectly capable of conquering territory, enslaving people and extracting wealth without depending on such theoretical pretexts.[42]

It is true that many of the early accounts of the conquest mention disapprovingly the signs of male–male sexual activity encountered by the conquistadors in the local population. It is also true that this theme was sometimes used, long after the conquest, not only to assert the moral superiority of the Christian Europeans but also to give a providential explanation of their rule: in 1585 a preacher in Lima declared in his sermon that 'because of this [sc. sodomy] ... God destroys kingdoms and nations. Let it be known that the reason why God has allowed that you, the Indians, should be so afflicted and vexed by other nations is because of this vice sodomy that your ancestors had, and many among you still have.'[43] As for the conquistadors themselves, there are just two known instances of sodomy being punished among their forces, both from the early 1530s: the case of two sailors who had served on land under Captain Nikolaus von Federmann, who were sent back to Cadiz and executed there; and that of five Italian soldiers—of whom at least one was from Florence—involved in the conquest of Venezuela under Alonso de Herrera, who were all garrotted, and their bodies reduced to ashes.[44] Strong moral disapproval may have been involved, alongside a concern for military discipline. But there is no reason to think that any essential connection between the conquest and the extirpation of sodomy was made at the time, let alone institutionalized thereafter. (Certainly the Portuguese authorities, both before and during the period of Spanish rule over Portugal, did not make any such connection: if they had done so, they would surely not have adopted the practice of exiling convicted sodomites from Portugal to Brazil.)[45]

If anything, the evidence relating to sodomy in these Iberian colonial societies suggests that people felt able to act with greater impunity than would have been the case in Barcelona, Seville or Lisbon. We have already encountered cases of prominent figures whose sexual attachments were poorly concealed: men such as Doctor Gaspar González de Sosa, canon of the cathedral at Sucre (Bolivia), who recruited a young sexual partner from a prison and installed him as a pampered servant in his house. In southern Peru Juan Ponce de León, who enjoyed high social status because he was descended from one of the founders of the city of Huamanga, would accost male Indians in the street, or visit their villages in the neighbouring valley, asking them for sex.[46] A little less openly, the cobbler André de Freitas Lessa, living in the Brazilian city of Olinda in the 1590s, attracted many boys to his house and workshop, where he gave them food and drink and encouraged them to have sex with one another; some of the sexual activity took place also at the home of another adult, where one of the youths worked as a servant.[47] Such practices could not have remained secret for long.

The most notorious example was Diogo Botelho, who served as Governor-General of Brazil from 1602 to 1607. According to one of his former pages, who gave detailed testimony to the Inquisition's visitation in 1618, Botelho had held same-sex orgies in the governor's palace in Salvador (the historic city of Bahia, then serving as the administrative centre), to which he invited officials, servants, pages and others; he had participated in the sodomy 'both actively and passively', and had taken further pleasure as a voyeur.[48] By its very nature, this was an extreme case. Yet even if some of the younger participants were co-opted against their will, this evidence tends to suggest the existence of some kind of community of like-minded men, whose activities were emboldened by such patronage. Less openly, there may have been other small communities or groups in other colonial towns: as we have seen, there was a group of at least ten men in Potosí and Sucre (in the then Viceroyalty of Peru) who took part in a 'rotation of sexual couples' in the 1590s.[49] Ronaldo Vainfas, who has studied the Brazilian evidence, insists that there was nothing like a sodomitical subculture; any such phenomenon was precluded by geographical dispersion and 'the very low level of urbanization that characterized Brazil from the sixteenth to the eighteenth centuries'.[50] The term 'subculture', however, may raise more questions than it answers. (An attempt will be made, below, to respond to some of them.)[51] Overall, it looks as if individuals with an interest in sodomy were no less able to meet potential partners and fellow sodomites in these colonial settlements than they would have been in towns of similar size in their European homelands—or even, possibly, more able.

As for those sodomites who were dispersed in the countryside, it would be wrong to think that their isolation had a generally dampening effect on their sexual activity. For some, it seems rather to have enhanced the sense of

relative impunity. This is most obvious in the case of sodomy-inclined plantation owners with large numbers of male slaves; as we have already seen,
the Brazilian visitations of the early seventeenth century brought to light
several men of that sort, such as the owner of 30 black slaves who was 'notorious' for sodomizing them.[52] The psychology of impunity was greatly reinforced here, of course, by the nature of the power exercised by a slave-owner;
but in other, lesser ways the nature of a colonial society of this kind could
also strengthen a person's sense of hierarchical power in relation to other
groups. Servants, if transported thousands of miles from their homes and
families, may have felt more dependent on their masters. The native population, even when not reduced to formal subjection (as it was, by enslavement,
in some of the Spanish mining territories during the initial colonial period),
had a generally inferior position with much less power to defend itself
against exploitation of any kind. And from an early stage the products of
interracial marriages, especially after African slaves had become a significant
presence in the population, began to be seen as occupying places on a
descending scale of caste-like status.

The place of the indigenous people—'Indians' in the terminology of
the time—in this scheme of things requires special attention. Even after the
demographic devastation caused by European diseases, they formed the
overwhelming majority of the population; so on merely statistical grounds
one would expect them to have featured in some of the sodomy cases. But
there were more specific reasons than that. A characteristic remark was
made by a 31-year-old Franciscan friar who appeared before the Lima
Inquisition in 1597. Having admitted that he had sodomized 'many innocent novice friars', he also confessed that previously, in Mexico, he had done
the same to four local boys who worked for the convent of Tarímbaro,
'because they were young boys, and, as Indians, gente facil [easy people—
where 'easy' has the sense of 'compliant']'.[53] The man from the city of
Huamanga mentioned above, Juan Ponce de León, had taken a similar view
of adult Indians, entering their villages and casually offering money to
induce men to sodomize him. In one case he offered payment merely to see
a man's genitals, but his approaches were not always so tentative or complai-
sant; he grabbed the hand of another man, who had rejected his proposition,
and thrust it into his own breeches.[54] Reading such evidence, one gets the
impression that for this individual too the Indians generally were, or could
at least be treated as, a gente facil. And a similar attitude may well have been
held by a Dominican who was tried by the secular authorities in Santa Fe

in 1551. He had persuaded the local people to help him to build a friary, to which he could recruit young Indians and *mestizos* (people of mixed Spanish and Indian descent); as the prosecution showed, he had forced the boys in his charge, who were aged between nine and twelve, to submit to sodomy, and had threatened them with whipping or death if they told anyone.[55] Such tactics towards defenceless boys were not unknown in Spain, Portugal and Italy, of course; but this Spaniard may well have felt that their status here, as fully or partly indigenous, rendered them even less likely to be defended. The improbability of such people initiating legal processes was an important factor. As late as 1793, a priest in Mexico who confessed to having solicited 32 men said that he had always singled out 'rustic and obscure people, with whom there was the least risk that they would denounce him'.[56]

However, it would be wrong to suppose that the involvement of Indians in male–male sexual activities was always the consequence of exploitation. In the early 1590s the visitation of Bahia was informed about an Indian called Joane who committed sodomy 'with many others, acting as a female, particularly with the Indian Constantino with whom he lived as if they were man and woman'.[57] A rural Mexican case from 1604, studied in detail by Zeb Tortorici, arose initially because two indigenous men, aged 20 and approximately 25, were seen copulating in a *temascal* or steam bath. Under questioning, the elder of the two said that he had first committed sodomy four years earlier with another Indian, and that this had taken place in the company of two other indigenous men. He also implicated a local baker (indigenous, again), who was in his mid-30s and lived with another man; the baker's home apparently served as a meeting-place for Indians who sought sex with other men. By the end of the trial, a total of thirteen indigenous males had been named as sodomites, six of whom were actually prosecuted.[58]

Exclusively indigenous cases do not feature prominently in the records, for the simple reason that the authorities concentrated most of their attention on the Iberian settler community; but the cases they considered could easily include non-coercive sexual relations with indigenous men. Juan Ponce de León, in the city of Huamanga, certainly found some willing partners among those Indians whom he had approached for sex. In 1595 the visitation of Pernambuco convicted a 30-year-old 'old Christian', Baltazar da Lomba, of committing sodomy 'a great number of times in different places with many men, he, the accused, being always the passive one'; many of his partners had been young Indians from the village of Guaramané,

whom he had invited to sodomize him.[59] It has been calculated that of the
165 individuals from Brazil incriminated by the Inquisition, 46 per cent were
Europeans, 25 per cent were blacks, 14 per cent were Indians, and another
14 per cent were of mixed race (*mestiços* and *mamelucos*, who were of
European-Amerindian descent, and *mulatos*, whose origins were partly black).[60]
While the authorities were less interested in those non-European categories,
however, they were more inclined to issue harsh punishments to such lower-
status people. Out of the 45 Europeans convicted of sodomy in the Viceroyalty
of Peru, only six were executed, with three condemned to galley service; of
the ten non-Europeans, five were executed, and two sent to the galleys.[61]

One of the scholars most familiar with the Brazilian evidence, Ronaldo
Vainfas, argues that male–male sexual relations in that country benefited
from a degree of tolerance because they were accepted practices among the
Indians (and also among some of the Africans brought there as slaves).[62] This
raises a much larger question, which has been seriously contested: how
widespread was such sexual behaviour among the indigenous peoples of the
Americas in the pre-Columbian period? Many early accounts by Iberian
writers witness to the presence of same-sex practices among a very broad
range of native civilizations, cultures and tribes. Given the fact, mentioned
above, that Spanish theorists occasionally cited sodomy as a justification for
conquest, and the more general prejudice of incoming Christians against
'heathen' peoples, plus the large degree of incomprehension that accompanied the initial encounters between very different cultures, it has been
tempting for some modern writers to assume that such accounts of sodomitical practices should be dismissed as ideologically motivated constructs
rather than actual descriptions. But the evidence, overall, is much too exten-
sive, and too consistent, to be explained away. It is found in a wide range of
sources—not just comments by invading military men or passing travellers,
but accounts by people who spent prolonged periods living in these societies during the first century of colonial rule.[63] That many of these early
references to sodomy were tinged with prejudice is true, and it is also true
that ulterior purposes, religious or political, were often at work when
authors gave special emphasis to such behaviour. But none of that can alter
the fact that, in the words of one leading historian, 'At the time of the conquest, same-sex eroticism existed in many, perhaps all, of the indigenous
societies of Latin America.'[64]

A particular focus of modern scholarly attention has been the figure of
the so-called *berdache*, meaning in this context a male who had been selected

during childhood for a more or less formalized lifelong cross-gender role, in which he/she would adopt many elements of female behaviour (including, typically but not always, female dress) and submit to being used sexually by a man. This phenomenon extended well beyond the Iberian-conquered territories; as late as the 1880s, *berdaches* could be found among the Crow, Sioux, Shoshoni and other peoples of the northern plains, as far north as Oregon and the Dakotas. Richard Trexler has commented, with very little exaggeration, that 'one would be hard put to identify one tribe in today's Latin America, or in the hemisphere as a whole, without the berdache having been part of its historical social organization.'[65]

A similar kind of cross-gender or 'third gender' figure was also found in some parts of Africa. In southern Angola the *kimbanda* was, until quite recently, regarded as a man who had been 'possessed since childhood by a spirit of the female sex'; he/she would dress like a woman, do women's work and undergo marriage to a man. Reports of this phenomenon can be found in the writings of the early Portuguese travellers and settlers in Angola. During the first visitation of the Brazilian region of Bahia by the Lisbon Inquisition, a black slave called Francisco Manicongo or Congo was denounced for seeking the passive role in sodomy, and also for refusing to wear the male clothing which his master gave him. His accuser, who had travelled in Africa, described the costume of 'the black sodomites who play the passive, womanly role in sodomy, and who are called *jinbandaa* in the language of Angola and the Congo', and said that Francisco wore 'a loin-cloth girded up in just the same way as the passive sodomites wear it in the Congo'. (Ronaldo Vainfas also notes what may have been a similar case in Lisbon 40 years earlier: a fully adult but beardless man from Benin, called Antônio, who went out at night in female dress, competing with the local prostitutes.)[66] Given the wide range of African populations and cultures from which slaves were drawn, all generalizations about these early African-Brazilians must remain very tentative. But it is evidently possible that some of these people brought with them attitudes towards forms of male–male sex that differed significantly from the official values of Iberian society. In her study of sodomy prosecutions in Cartagena, where Africans formed the majority of the accused, Carolina Giraldo Botero suggests that some had indeed maintained homoerotic practices or attitudes first acquired in their homelands.[67]

If we accept that in many, probably most, of these Latin American societies there was a significant element of same-sex practice operating as a background condition in the native population, this may lead us to suspect that the general attitudes of ordinary members of the settler population—excluding, that is, the religious and civil authorities—were in some ways softened thereby. Luiz Mott's argument that colonial insecurities stimulated an intensification of machismo, leading to greater 'homophobia', is not well supported by documentary evidence in this early modern period, and surely requires qualification for the modern one: public machismo is certainly not incompatible with private homoeroticism, though it does of course have the effect of strengthening the taboo against adopting the passive role. (A study of courts martial in the nineteenth- and early-twentieth-century Brazilian armed forces confirms this, showing that there was a considerable degree of tolerance for those who engaged in male–male sex as the active partner.)[68] But a significant extra element of the story in the Latin American case is the fact that, as Richard Trexler has pointed out, there is no evidence of any sense of revulsion at the passive role in the traditions of these native societies.[69]

It is likely that this factor, combined with the *berdache* tradition, played a part in producing a form of social and sexual behaviour that went well beyond the normal confines of Southern European same-sex activity. In 1657–8 the authorities in Mexico City found themselves investigating an unusually wide-ranging network of sodomites. The whole process began when a witness reported seeing a *mulato*, Juan de la Vega, having sex with another man; when the magistrate later forced his way into Vega's lodgings, he found him with four other males (at least one of whom was a young boy), all naked. Lengthy interrogations produced lists of further names, and much information—highly unwelcome to the authorities—about a flourishing underworld of same-sex contacts and meetings. Vega himself adopted feminine manners, prepared food and washed clothes like a woman, trimmed his clothing with womanly ribbons and kerchiefs, and addressed boys as 'my sweetheart' or 'my love'; he had the female nickname 'La Cotita' (a word for an effeminate sodomite). A similar, but older, figure was Juan de Correa, known as 'La Estampa' ('the print'—so called allegedly after a fine lady who had lived in the city, but perhaps after a popular print of a beautiful woman); now in his 70s, he confessed to having been a sodomite since he was seven years old, and said that he still considered himself a beautiful young girl. He organized parties for like-minded people in his house, and boasted that he had imparted his sexual skills to many men and boys. Others hosted similar revels, at which they would be addressed by female names; the men would dance, 'and they presented each to the others as gifts'. Most or all of the participants would then engage in sodomy.[70]

In late 1658 fourteen of these men were convicted and burnt at the stake; a boy, too young to be executed, was heavily flogged and condemned to work in the mines; others remained under questioning, and a very long list of other suspects was compiled, for arrest and investigation. The total came to 123 individuals. An analysis by Serge Gruzinski shows that 33 were Indians, 29 *mestizos* (plus one *castizo*, i.e. half-*mestizo* and half-Spanish), 28 Spanish (plus one Portuguese), nineteen *mulatos* and ten blacks. This was a very mixed group, mostly from the lower-middle and lower social strata; of those whose occupation was given, nearly a third did artisanal work such as tailoring and shoemaking; just under a quarter were servants or slaves, while a little over 10 per cent were students. Only eight men took on gender-crossing identities, wearing female dress and/or using female nicknames; three of these were *mestizos*, two were Spaniards, and the other three were Indian, black and *mulato* respectively. (Gruzinski points out that as only one of the eight was an Indian, we cannot assume a simple line of filiation here from a continuing *berdache* tradition among the indigenous population; but some elements of that tradition may have undergone quite a broad diffusion within this increasingly mixed society during the nearly 140 years since the conquest.) And it was also a very urban group, with 83 individuals from Mexico City itself, and 37 from the nearby town of Puebla.[71] Theorists writing about the idea of a sodomitical 'subculture' have usually stressed that such a thing can emerge only in an urban society. In this case, the evidence suggests that such a thing had well and truly emerged.[72]

★ ★ ★

The evidence of sodomy committed by Europeans in southern and south-east Asia during this period is limited. The most spectacular case recorded by the Inquisition in Goa has already been mentioned: that of the Portuguese priest João da Costa, sacristan of the Santa Casa de Misericórdia there, whose confessions, first in 1666 and then in 1671, revealed a total of 49 boys with whom he had attempted or committed sexual acts. Some of the boys were slaves, or servants, or sons of servants; several were from the local Indian population.[73] Modern historiography is particularly sensitive, in colonial contexts, to the racial dimension of such sexual exploitation; yet in this case the priest's predatory activities seem to have been quite indiscriminate, with the key factor being his ability to exercise power, whatever the modality it made use of—age, social status and religious authority being the most obvious.

A similar impression is given by some of the evidence from the Dutch trading posts and settlements in the East Indies. Records survive of at least eight death sentences arising from sodomy trials in the Indonesian archipelago, and in Malacca and Ceylon, during the seventeenth century. Two of these involved 'Mardijkers', descendants of manumitted slaves in Batavia (modern Jakarta), who were of south Indian origin, and usually Portuguese-speaking: in 1643 a young Dutch sailor was convicted of sodomy with Bento de Sal, a Mardijker, and in 1652 another trial focused on sexual relations between a 40-year-old Dane and five 'black' boys—'black' being a term commonly used for these relatively dark-skinned people.[74] There seems to have been no difference between the treatment of these cases and that of other sodomy cases which involved only Europeans. Trials conducted by the VOC (Dutch East India Company) in the eighteenth century, several of them relating to episodes on board ship, also suggest a close equivalence between interracial and intra-European cases, where the key factor for the active sodomite seeking sex with youths was not colour but power—colour being, in some circumstances, just the concomitant of a powerless status. In 1747 the bookkeeper Willem Bax was accused of molesting two teenaged slaves, of unstated racial origin (one complained that Bax had 'twice stuck his finger into his anus, which made it necessary for him to cry out from the pain and hurt'); this case was closely paralleled by one in the following year, when another man was convicted of sodomizing two boys on board ship, one of whom was a Dutch fifteen-year-old from Amsterdam.[75] The racial intermingling, both at sea and on land, was such that the initiative for sodomy could sometimes come from the non-European side. A complicated case heard at Batavia in 1735 revolved around a disputed episode which had occurred when two men were sleeping on a ship: Isaack Hendris Marcelis, from the southern Dutch city of Venlo, accused Golami, from Bengal, of attempted sodomy, while Golami accused Marcelis of having stolen his money. In a case of 1748, five young male Europeans accused two Asians of pestering them for sex—allegedly the Asian men had offered the gift of a knife in return for their compliance. And in 1779 a sixteen-year-old Dutch boy was found to have been given money, in return for sex, by a Chinese man.[76] (Same-sex relations initiated by Chinese men had previously been noted by the Spanish authorities in the Philippines. In 1588 they arrested fourteen or fifteen of them for this offence,

executing two and flogging the others; the accused explained that 'the practice was quite common among men in China.')[77]

It is difficult to generalize about patterns of behaviour in these Dutch
colonial societies, as the total number of known cases is quite small. (We
should note that during the seventeenth and eighteenth centuries at least
4,700 ships went out from the Netherlands to the East Indies, carrying
approximately one million people—though many of them did not survive
there for long.)[78] Peter Boomgaard has put forward several reasons for suspecting that the incidence of sodomy may nevertheless have been somewhat greater there than in the Netherlands. Some men with a preference
for male–male sex might have been motivated to move to such distant territories that were less socially controlled; they might have believed—in
some cases correctly—that such sexual behaviour was more accepted in
those native societies; and the port cities where they settled usually had a
strong gender imbalance, caused not only by the mostly male Europeans but
also by the migration into those cities of local workers.[79] One case (to
return to the South American world) which might fit the first of those
reasons is that of Mathijs de Goijer, quartermaster of the Dutch garrison in
Surinam. At his trial in 1731, when he was 41 years old, he confessed that he
had been introduced to sodomy nine years earlier when he was living in
Amsterdam. In Surinam he had approached at least five men for sex; these
were mostly in their 30s, and it seems likely that one did become a willing
sexual partner, as he was condemned to death together with de Goijer.[80]
These men were all Dutch; it is possible that men seeking boys would have
been more likely to turn to the native population, where the difference in
social and economic power could have combined, to their advantage, with
the difference in age. But again the body of evidence is not large enough to
substantiate this clearly.

One of the factors mentioned by Boomgaard is that all those who went
to the Dutch settlements in the East Indies had to undergo lengthy voyages
by sea, spending months in a virtually all-male environment. Mariners were
also a major presence among the transient populations of the ports, where
trade involved not just the major shipments to Europe, but much carrying
of goods between different places in the South China Sea and Indian Ocean.
The sexual culture on board ship was, for obvious reasons, rather different
from that in the towns and villages of the home society. Records survive of
sodomy trials held at the court of Cape Town, a necessary staging post for
all the VOC ships which travelled between the Netherlands and the East

Indies; this was the only place where, in the middle of a voyage, sodomy cases could be dealt with by an official judicial body. No fewer than 44 such trials were held in the eighteenth century, the majority of them between 1750 and 1775; many involved the molesting of boys, servants and young slaves. Acts of sodomy between members of those categories also took place: in 1729 two Indian slaves were sentenced to death for sodomy, and in 1733 two more, who were described as young, were condemned to be flogged and sent back to Asia. But one more factor emerges from this body of evidence, which further enhances the difference between the world of the mariners and that of ordinary life in Holland. A significant number of these sailors were from Mediterranean countries: 'Vincent Stavace' (probably 'Starace') from Naples, 'Constantijn Joan van Constantinopel', 'Anthonij van Malta', and so on.[81] The world of the VOC brought together not just Europeans and Asians, but also people from the differing sexual cultures of Northern and Southern Europe.

★ ★ ★

Much care is needed when considering the racial element in these colonial sexual encounters. Sometimes, as we have seen, race was probably just an accompanying aspect of a difference in social status or power relations; any menial servant or young boy might have been exploited in the same way, regardless of ethnic origin or skin colour. And for some of the participants in these male–male relations, it seems that sex could level the playing field—in a game which could be played from both sides. In the European colonies of this period, the question of racial prejudice in sexual matters is in any case a complex one. Sex and miscegenation with native women were the norm for Portuguese male settlers in India, Africa and Brazil. The Portuguese authorities in India positively encouraged interracial unions; the Dutch gave bonuses to employees who married Asian brides; and in 1687 the English East India company also offered to give a special payment for every child born to an English soldier and a native woman at Madras.[82] In Virginia in the 1640s and 1650s, cases of interracial fornication were punished on exactly the same basis as cases involving a white man and a white woman. But attitudes were changing, and in 1662 a statute was passed in that colony, decreeing that a 'christian' man or woman who committed fornication with, respectively, a black woman or man would pay twice the usual fine.[83] 'Christian' was a term commonly used to distinguish whites from blacks, on the assumption that blacks were generally heathens; how to assess the relative weights of religious and racial motives in these issues is just one of the questions that render the whole historical topic so complex.

An intriguing case, which has divided historians, surfaces briefly in the Virginian records in 1630. Our entire knowledge of it is derived from the following entry: 'Hugh Davis to be soundly whipped, before an assembly of Negroes and others for abusing himself to the dishonor of God and shame of Christians, by defiling his body in lying with a Negro; which fault he is to acknowledge next Sabbath day.' Some writers have assumed that the 'Negro' here was a black female slave, and that the severely condemnatory language was motivated by racial disapproval as well as a sense of social propriety. However, Alan Scot Willis has used a range of persuasive arguments to suggest that the 'Negro' here was male: he cites, for example, the echoing of the language of 1 Corinthians 6: 9, where 'abusers of themselves with mankind' means sodomites; the use of 'Negro' and not, as was common in contemporary writings, 'Negress', 'Negro woman', 'Negro wench', etc.; the numerical rarity of black women in Virginia at this time; and the other evidence of a lack of prejudice against interracial unions.[84] The phrases about 'the dishonor of God' and the 'shame of Christians' were standard condemnations of the sin of sodomy, and would no doubt have been used regardless of the race of the other person involved. Yet in a lengthy and otherwise scrupulous discussion of the case, Willis passes over two aspects of the evidence. The first is the fact that there is no mention of punishment for the 'Negro' himself; this strongly suggests that Hugh Davis's partner, or rather victim, was a young boy. And the second is the very unusual stipulation that Davis was to be whipped 'before an assembly of Negroes and others'. The most likely explanation is that, in committing a sexual assault on a defenceless boy (and perhaps inflicting physical harm as he did so), he had caused outrage among a large number of adult slaves; assembling them to witness the flogging was a way of satisfying their righteous anger. While the authorities and slave-owners may well have had self-interested motives for taking that action, the evidence gives us no reason to think that in their eyes the gravity of a sexual assault on a boy was diminished by the fact that the boy was black. Whether it was so diminished in the mind of Hugh Davis when he committed the act cannot now be known; but the key point for him may well have been simply the sense of greater impunity which he felt when acting towards someone of slave status.

(In the subsequent history of black slavery in the English colonies, the sexual exploitation of slaves is one of many deeply repugnant aspects of the story. But although such exploitation of black male slaves by white men must surely have occurred, the evidence of it in the early modern period is very slight. In an article devoted to the sexual exploitation of male slaves, Thomas Foster concentrates mostly on exploitative forms of male–female sex, offering just one clear instance of male–male activity from before the nineteenth century: a passing mention in the diary of an eighteenth-century Jamaican planter. The contrast with Iberian slavery is quite striking; at least part of the explanation for that must surely lie in the broad difference between Northern and Southern European sexual mores.)[85]

Finally, there is one well-documented case from the operations of the English East India Company in the seventeenth century, where questions about the significance of race and religion may also be asked. In April 1649 the *Faulcon*, a Company ship, was returning from Mocha, at the entrance to the Red Sea, to Surat, on the coast of Gujarat. Its English crew was supplemented by a number of Indian Muslim 'lascars' (sailors) and 'peons' (manual workers). One of the officers, Henry Gary, was informed 'by his man Sydy Jameem' that 'Abdull Rhyme [Abdul Rahim, Abdarrahim], an Hindostan Peon had Committed Sodomy with the Carpenters boy'; Gary told the captain, who put both suspects in irons and called a 'Councell' the following day to investigate 'this abhominable crime, both before God, and man'. Seven of the Indians were questioned, and their testimony was presented in a formal document, written first in Persian and then translated into English. Abdul Rahim had confessed to several of them, asking for their advice: he feared that, since three English crew members had witnessed the offence (or rather, some indirect signs of it), he would be executed by the captain. He told one man that he would abscond as soon as they reached land, and he gave to another of his colleagues the ten dollars he possessed, saying 'Brother what euere becomes of me deliuer these things vnto my Wiffe.'[86]

To one of these men, Abdul Rahim insisted that 'the Boy inticed him to perform the Act'; to another he claimed, similarly, that 'vpon a Satturday night a Boy called him downe betwixt decks, with whome he had committed the act of Sodomy.' But the attitudes of his compatriots were, by their own account, very disapproving. Two said that after hearing him confess to this crime, they refused to eat with him. One strongly reproved him, 'saying that Musslemen [sc. Muslims] ought not to commit such Acts'; another, 'Hodgee Ibrahim an Hindostan Lasskare' ('Haji' being the honorific title of a Muslim who has made the pilgrimage to Mecca), called him a 'baise rouge [sc. base rogue]...adding that amongst the Persians he had heard it had bin often done; But neuer amongst their Hindostan people; nor did he euer know it done in any Ship that euer he was in before, saying withall, could you not stay till you came to Sroakine, where you might haue had Woomen eynough.' The three English quasi-witnesses described the circumstantial evidence they had seen: for example, Nicholas Griffen, the ship-caulker, said that late in the evening he 'saw Rhyme betwixt two bales with the Carpenters Boy vnder him, who being demanded what he did theire, replyed he came for his pillow', when Griffen, his suspicions aroused, came back a little later, 'Rhyme was gon vp and the Boy was crying.' Under questioning, Abdul Rahim answered quite directly, saying in English 'That after some passages of dalliance betwixt ye Carpenters Boy and him, he plainely Committed the Act of Sodomy with him, putting (they are his owne words) his Prick in his Arse.' And finally the boy, John Durrant, who was aged sixteen, gave a somewhat fuller account. After leaving Surat, he said, Abdul Rahim had 'continually importund him to lye with him'. One evening he 'came to him, and putting his Yarde in his hand, cry'd belay, belay, and presently vpon that (there being a hole in his Britches behinde), he the said Rhyme thrust his Yarde to his Arse, when he askt him what he ment, he replyd what will you not belay belay, and therevpon told him that he had noe mony, But had some Duttyes [sc. *dhotis*, lengths of cloth used as sarongs] out of which he would giue him foure or fiue peeces, if he would consent.' Durrant said no then, but 'after wards by this means, and his dayly sollicitations, and impor- tunities, when he found him alone, sume times putting his Yarde in his hand, and at other times giueing him raysins, he obtayned at last his bestiall designes.'[87]

The captain and his 'Councell' clearly decided that the boy was complicit enough to deserve punishment. They also thought that Abdul Rahim mer- ited execution, but this could not be carried out, as he was a subject of 'the King of India' (the Mughal Emperor). So both received the same punish- ment: first 40 lashes, then 20 on the next day, then ten lashes to be repeated twice a week, with each flogging followed by a washing down in salt water to increase the pain. The sentence on John Durrant referred in passing to 'the dishonour of our nation and our Christian profession', and indeed of God, bewailing the fact that he had committed 'soe vile an act with an Heathen'.[88] But to engage in sodomy was automatically seen as dishonouring

God, Christianity and one's Christian society, regardless of the religious affiliation of the other participant in the act. Modern historians may be tempted to read too much significance into that last brief phrase—or, for that matter, into the racial difference between the two culprits, to which the sentence made no direct reference at all.

19

England after 1700

The opening pages of Chapter 14, above, discussed the large-scale argument about the development of modern homosexuality which has almost completely prevailed in the recent historical literature. According to this view, everything changed, or began to change, around the year 1700. As this chapter will be devoted to looking at the evidence from the first half of the eighteenth century, it will be useful to bear in mind the claims made by that standard argument. It can be summarized more fully here, using the words of the historian who has been by far its most influential exponent, Randolph Trumbach.

'Europeans before 1700', Trumbach declares, 'presumed that all males desired both women and adolescent boys.' Indeed, that presumption was no mere speculation; it was a statement of fact. 'In the Renaissance, all men desired both women and boys, and a substantial majority of men (if not all) acted at some point in life on their desire for boys', although unfortunately 'It is not possible to prove statistically for England the existence of this sodomitically acting majority.'[1] However, there then occurred 'a profound shift...in the conceptualization and practice of male homosexual behavior in the late seventeenth and early eighteenth centuries'. The timing of this is not entirely certain, but, for such a tectonic social change, it can be located within a remarkably short span of years: it began to emerge in north-western Europe in the 1690s, and by the first decade of the eighteenth century it was already apparent that 'a new kind of sodomite had appeared...These new sodomites were the first European men who might reasonably be called "homosexuals".' So the year 1700 can conveniently stand as the symbolic starting-point; and 'it is only after that year that the use of the model of the gay minority, with its subculture and its roles, becomes appropriate in the study of Western societies.'[2] Much time would elapse, however, before this new form of behaviour became pan-European. It first appeared in 'England,

Forbidden Desire in Early Modern Europe: Male–Male Sexual Relations, 1400–1750. Noel Malcolm, Oxford University Press.
© Noel Malcolm 2024. DOI: 10.1093/oso/9780198886334.003.0019

France and the Dutch Republic', becoming 'fully established by 1750' in those countries; it then became visible in central Europe by 1800, 'but it did not arrive in southern and eastern Europe much before 1900.'[3]

The most basic and defining feature of these new sodomites was that they wanted sex 'entirely with males'. This in itself represented a profound change. (Rafael Carrasco's evidence that some pre-1700 Valencian sodomites had a strong preference for young males, rather than women, is dismissed with the somewhat casuistical comment that 'the men who preferred boys to women only knew this because they had slept with both.') And this development was accompanied by another deep shift in attitude: many or most of these new sodomites desired adult men. Admittedly, 'Half of them still desired to have sexual relations with adolescents. But most adolescents no longer shared these desires, and their seduction therefore became extremely problematical.' As that comment indicates, if only in passing, yet another important change was taking place, or had recently taken place: male adolescents, who before 1700 had apparently been content (or even desirous) to take their allotted role in sodomitic sex, were 'no longer' willing to do so. And there was another major change, which further intensified the predicament in which these new sodomites found themselves: 'at the same moment it began to be felt that it was impossible for the average, normal male to feel any sexual desire for another male of any age or condition. To be masculine was to experience sexual desire only for women.'[4]

Was that the reason why these new sodomites adopted feminine manners, behaviour, and sometimes dress? The argument at this point suffers from some uncertainties. It is said that they sought sexual partners both outside their own category, among the men who could now be described as heterosexual (for which purpose, trying to resemble women might have seemed a natural strategy), and within their own community: these sodomites 'either seduced males from the majority who were not effeminate and thereby ran the risks of arrest and punishment, or of blackmail; or they safely had relations with each other inside a protective subculture'. It is also suggested that effeminacy was a classificatory concept imposed contemptuously by the heterosexual majority, which adopted 'the presumption that all men who engage in sexual relations with other men are effeminate members of a third or intermediate gender, who surrender their rights to be treated as dominant males, and are exposed instead to a merited contempt as a species of male whore'. In this new sexual regime, 'it seems to make little difference whether a man takes the active or the passive role, or whether his partner is an adult male or a boy—any sexual desire by one male for another leads to categorization as an effeminate sodomite.'[5]

In an early study, Trumbach pointed out that in their actual behaviour 'the majority of sodomites could not have been effeminate, let alone transvestite.' Subsequently, however, he has described the new sodomites as 'markedly effeminate men'; he has claimed that after 1700 'Adult males who desired males were socialized to be sexually passive and effeminate'; and he has defined the type as follows: such a person was 'an effeminate adult man who desired to have sex only with men or boys. His speech and gait were similar to a woman's.'[6] Elsewhere he has argued that these sodomites, probably, 'were able to put on and discard their effeminacy at will'. But what has remained constant is the idea that their sexual conduct placed them in a new gender category. In north-western Europe 'almost all the men arrested after 1700 for homosexual behavior could reasonably be described as members of a third gender.' This meant that these sodomites, regardless of what they wore, now occupied essentially the place held by the transvestite male or *berdache* in non-European societies. True, they suffered from the disadvantage that, unlike those traditional transvestites, they were not viewed as legitimate sexual partners by the general male population; nevertheless, 'the sodomite and the transvestite do not differ in the degree to which they become women.'[7] And, illegitimate partners though they were, these new European sodomites did succeed in attracting members of the heterosexual male majority who were willing to have sex with them; although their most uninhibited sexual behaviour took place within their own subculture, with other members of their own minority, the practice of 'cruising' in public places such as parks or latrines 'allowed sodomites to have sexual encounters with men who were not sodomites'.[8] This seems to imply that another major change had taken place: some of the men who belonged to the properly 'masculine' majority, who before 1700 would happily have sodomized boys but would have regarded other men as completely undesirable, were now willing to sodomize adult males.

At the same time, within the enclosed world of the new sodomites, the apparent association between effeminacy and sexual passivity did not in any way dictate sexual positions: many of these men were happy to take the active, penetrative role. (This marks a major divergence from the non-European *berdache* model.) Indeed, they had sex 'perhaps mainly' with one another. Commenting on a case from London in 1726, involving a man with a female nickname who first asked to be active and then offered to be passive, Trumbach writes: 'It is likely that by 1726 such sexual versatility was widespread among all sodomites.' Elsewhere he asserts, more definitely, that 'after 1700 most adult sodomites were both active and passive.'[9] So here we witness yet another fundamental change: sodomites had become willing to swap and reciprocate between the roles of penetrated and penetrator. That, in itself, would be a significant change of pattern, given Trumbach's general assumption that before 1700 all of Europe resembled Florence in these matters. But it becomes even more striking, when set against the assumption that these sodomites had adopted a new kind of identity which shifted their gender in the direction of much more womanly behaviour.

This whole account thus involves no fewer than six large changes in sexual mentality and behaviour happening more or less simultaneously. Some of them, of course, can be regarded as interrelated; but it seems impossible to tie all of them together by means of necessary connections. Indeed, some of these developments appear to be in tension one with another: the new stress on 'normal' masculinity rejecting any kind of sexual desire for males, for example, contrasts with the new phenomenon of men who did not belong to the sodomite minority willingly penetrating adult males who did. The overall pattern of change is hard to make sense of in the abstract, even before one attempts the task of reconciling it with the empirical evidence. As for the even more fundamental task of explaining why these developments occurred, Trumbach has been able to offer only the most broad generalizations about newly emerging gender roles within the family, involving greater 'equality between men and women'; and, perhaps because those might just as well turn out to be concomitant features of the same larger, unexplained, change in sexual psychology, his final judgement on the emergence of modern homosexuality is that 'No one at the present moment has any satisfactory explanation as to why this transformation occurred.'[10] Still, it should be said that Randolph Trumbach has been both a pioneering figure in this field over many years, and someone who has not shied away from trying to set this story in a much larger context, chronological and geographical; for that at least he should be given credit.[11]

Although not every aspect of Trumbach's argument has met with equal enthusiasm, the central claim has been very widely accepted, not only by British and American historians but by continental European ones too.[12] Negative criticism of the theory has come from a small number of writers. Some—such as Joseph Cady, who gave it the dismissive label 'new-inventionism'—are specialists in the period before 1700 who have been able to show that some of the things called distinctively 'modern' by Trumbach were also present at that time.[13] Others have disagreed with Trumbach about the interpretation of the eighteenth-century evidence, the most important of them being Rictor Norton, who has made a detailed study of the English case. The contrary points Norton makes about effeminacy and 'third-gender' behaviour will be considered below. But his more general reasons for rejecting the idea that a new kind of same-sex behaviour suddenly appeared around 1700 in England, France and the United Provinces can be stated here at the outset. He accepts that a wealth of detailed evidence emerges from those three societies in the period 1700–40, on a different scale from anything previously available there. However, he notes that the sodomitical subculture revealed by that evidence was not something just taking its first tentative steps; it is clear that, by the first decade of the century, 'all of its characteristic features are already fully formed.' Nor, he points out, did it undergo any significant further development during the rest of the century. The idea that such an elaborate social phenomenon could have been 'fully grown at birth' is, as he gently puts it, 'unlikely'. It follows that 'around 1700 the British gay subculture was *discovered and revealed* in the public prints: it was not "born", it was *exposed*.' And the natural explanation for this is that there were major changes in the methods and activities by which such evidence was generated: 'The "shift" is not a shift in homosexual "role", but a shift in prosecution practices.' A new kind of sodomite did not rapidly emerge; an existing kind was made much more visible by new techniques of surveillance and control.[14]

★ ★ ★

In England, the key development was the formation of self-styled 'Societies for the Reformation of Manners' after the change of regime in 1688. The first of these was set up in Tower Hamlets, in the East End of London, in 1690, when a group of churchwardens, constables and local residents agreed to meet once a month 'to consult and resolve upon the best methods for putting the laws in execution against houses of lewdness and debauchery and also against drunkenness swearing and cursing and profanation of the Lord's day'. As that wording shows, the primary emphasis was on the suppression of ordinary brothels. The Tower Hamlets society publicized its work, encouraging others to create similar organizations. By 1694 there were sixteen of these in London, and with their help the Tower Hamlets group extended its own activities across the city, playing the dominant role

where the detection of sexual crimes was concerned, while the others concentrated more on such offences as Sunday trading. The Societies for the
Reformation of Manners ('SRMs') mostly operated through the existing
legal procedures; their main contributions were that they ran a network of
informers, and had salaried agents who assisted the local constables. (They
also raised money through their subscriptions to cover the costs of prosecutions; for many years this included trials for sodomy in cases uncovered by
their agents, though in 1726 they persuaded the government to cover the
expenses of those.) But they also worked hard at consciousness-raising, and
one of their methods might be seen as a new kind of moral policing: from
1694 onwards the original SRM published an annual *Black Roll* or *Black
List*, giving the names and crimes of all the people it had prosecuted for
brothel-keeping, pimping and prostitution during the previous twelve
months. (Up to 1700, the totals came to an average of 791 per year.) This
whole movement clearly struck a chord with a significant element of the
population; by the early eighteenth century many such societies had been
set up in other cities, counties and provincial towns, as well as in Edinburgh,
Dublin, Jamaica and Boston.[15]

The scale of the SRMs' activities in London was extraordinary. In 1728
they were able to boast that in the previous 30 years they had prosecuted
94,322 offenders for disorderly practices, drunkenness, gaming houses and
other forms of moral delinquency; during the latter part of that period they
had been bringing nearly 2,000 prosecutions for sexual offences every
year.[16] Only a tiny fraction of these involved same-sex activities; yet the
cumulative effect of the SRMs' pursuit of sodomy cases was significant, not
least because of their policy of publicizing such sins in order to induce
shame, disgust and greater vigilance. (This was probably their most important achievement where sodomy was concerned; many of the cases heard in
the courts were not directly managed by them.) Their first publicity coup
concerned the trial of Captain Rigby in 1698. Whether by chance or not,
the teenaged boy who was the object of Rigby's sexual advances was a servant in the household of a man who was a close associate of the Reverend
Thomas Bray, one of the leading lights of the SRM movement; with the
help of a supportive Justice of the Peace, Bray helped to arrange the circumstances in which Rigby could be arrested in flagrante, and he also organized
the prosecution in court.[17] Partly because of Rigby's defiant behaviour, both
in court and at the pillory, the case was widely discussed. A broadside produced immediately after the trial offered a description of his sexual

approaches to the boy which was so prurient in tone that modern scholars have suspected it of pornographic intent; yet, as Rictor Norton has pointed out, the details given there were accurately copied from the trial documents. To the benefit of the SRMs, such salacious material did attract the attention of a wide circle of readers. One enterprising publisher cashed in on the new popular interest in sodomy by producing a version of the trial records of the Earl of Castlehaven.[18]

Evidently the SRMs were pleased with the impact their intervention had achieved; they had gained the scalp of one prominent same-sex offender, and felt able to issue more general threats against others. An anonymous pamphlet by one of their members, published in 1702, addressed the sodomites as follows: 'to your shame, many of your *Names* and *Places* of Abode are known: and tho' they are at present conceal'd, to see whether you will reform; some way may be taken to publish you to the World, that your *Scandalous Company* may be shun'd by all that regard their Reputation, if ye persist in your inhumane Filthiness. For your *Scandalous Haunts* are also known, and will (we hope) be visited by such as may bring your Crimes to just Punishment.'[19] In the following year, the annual report of the SRM could proudly announce that 'since the trial and punishment of the sea captain [sc. Rigby] ... three persons, by the diligence of a society for Reformation, were found guilty of sodomy ... at Maidstone, and were accordingly executed.'[20] It is worth noting, however, that executions were relatively rare; at the Old Bailey, for example, 21 out of the 29 men prosecuted between 1700 and 1750 did not receive a death sentence.[21] Only when there was proof that penetration had taken place could the death penalty follow; this set a high legal threshold, and, as we shall see, arrests prompted by the vigilante methods of the SRMs would normally take place well before the stage of actual sexual intercourse. Accordingly, in the period between the Rigby trial and the 1720s a new offence emerged in the courts, 'attempted sodomy' or 'assault with intent' (where 'assault' was a technical term, not necessarily implying any use of physical force); this was a misdemeanour rather than a felony, and so could be punished with lesser penalties such as standing in the pillory, imprisonment and fines. The judge had wide discretion where sentencing for a misdemeanour was concerned, and the possibility of a pardon did not arise.[22]

Saying that the sodomites' 'Scandalous Haunts' were known was not an empty boast. Before long, members of the SRMs were patrolling some of the public places that were frequented by sodomites looking for sexual partners. A broadside published in 1707, giving brief details of eight men recently prosecuted and convicted in London, offers some idea of the *modus operandi*. The first case it mentioned concerned Thomas Lane, who had been a soldier for 'many Years'. He had approached Richard Hemmings and Samuel Baker on London Bridge: 'He came to Mr. *Hemmings*, and pulling out his Nakedness offer'd to put it into his Hand, and withal unbutton'd the Evidence's [sc. Hemmings's] Breeches, and put his Hand in there'; Hemmings 'bore with' this because his colleague, Baker, had told him that 'the Prisoner was such a kind of Person, and therefore design'd to apprehend him, which they did'. Six days earlier, Hemmings and another activist, Thomas Jones, had caught another sodomite, a young porter called William Huggins, in another busy public place, the Royal Exchange. They explained to the court that 'walking upon *Change*, with design to detect such wicked Persons; they were sate upon one of the Benches, and the Prisoner came to them severally, and offer'd to put his hand into their Breeches, pulling out his Nakedness at the same time; upon which they apprehended him.'[23] These are some of the best-documented examples from 1707. The actual judicial records are mostly missing, but Rictor Norton has estimated, on the basis of other sources such as newspaper reports, that the SRM campaign led to the arrest of more than 40 men in the space of ten days.[24]

Apart from London Bridge and the Exchange, other popular locations included St James's Park (especially Birdcage Walk, which runs along the southern side of it), Lincoln's Inn Fields (where there was a 'bog-house' or public latrine), and an area of Moorfields, just to the north of the City walls, where one path or lane became known as 'The Sodomites' Walk'.[25] It was at the last of these that another SRM activist, Thomas Newton, helped to arrange the arrest of William Brown in 1726. In the words of Newton's statement to the judge at the Old Bailey:

Willis and *Stevenson* the Constables having a Warrant to apprehend Sodomites, I went with them to an Ale house in Moorfields, where we agreed that I should go out, and pick one up, and they'd wait at a proper Distance. There's a Walk in the upper *Moorfields*...I knew this to be a Place that Sodomites frequented, and was well acquainted with the Methods they took in picking one another up.—So I takes a Turn that Way, and leaning over the Wall, The prisoner passes by, and looks at me and at a little Distance from me, he stands up against the Wall as if he was making Water, then he moves higher and higher to where I stood till he came close to me.—*Tis a fine Night* says he, *Aye*, says I *so it is* Then he takes me by the Hand, and (I shewing no dislike) he guides it to his Breeches, and puts his Privities into it. I held him fast, and call'd out to my Companions, who coming up we carry'd him to the Watch-house.[26]

From this and other similar evidence one learns that a kind of standardized choreography had developed, by means of which one sodomite could indicate his interest to another. There was probably nothing radically new about this. The final, clinching gesture, involving the hand of one man being placed in the breeches of another, or on his exposed penis, had long been a standard one in Northern Europe; it featured, for example, in the case of the Somerset villager George Dowdeney in 1622, who had repeatedly thrust his hand into the breeches of the local blacksmith.[27] That a place such as St James's Park, or the areas adjoining it, could be used for casual encounters leading to sex was suggested by Clement Walker in 1649, graphically described by Lord Rochester in the early 1670s, and illustrated by the case of Captain Rigby in 1689.[28] It is also a simple fact—somewhat neglected by many writers on this aspect of early modern sodomy—that many, probably most, of the notorious public spaces were also places where female prostitutes plied their trade.[29] The sodomites' methods of attracting attention and signalling interest may well have been adapted from more traditional techniques used in male–female, and indeed female–male, interactions. Certainly the act of grabbing at the other person's genitals was something done both by female prostitutes to their prospective clients and vice versa ('Gropecunt Lane' is recorded as the name of a street, typically where prostitution took place, in more than 20 English towns); some men 'even took out their private member and laid it in women's hands'.[30]

However, as time went by, greater subtlety and discretion may have been needed where these male–male approaches were concerned. Among other things, the burgeoning publicity given to crimes of sodomy or attempted sodomy enabled a new sort of profitable crime to flourish: blackmailing the sodomites. During the eighteenth century the Old Bailey dealt with roughly 50 such cases. Sometimes the threat of exposure for sodomy was a completely spurious tactic, used by robbers and highwaymen: in one case in 1722, the victim of a robbery, just off the Mall in London, was told that if he cried out for help his assailant would claim that he had been making sodomitical advances. (As the victim testified, 'I cry'd out Murder, and two Soldiers coming up, he told them I was a *Sodomite*. They ask'd him *How he knew that?* and he answer'd *Why[,] don't you see my hand in his Breeches?*— a response which serves to show that the methods of the SRM activists had by now attained general cultural recognition.)[31] On the other hand, as Rictor Norton has argued, many of the blackmail cases probably arose from genuine sexual advances made by the person who was then blackmailed; the man who took advantage of him may sometimes have been a 'hustler' who found this a more profitable course of action, just as female prostitutes who were offering sex sometimes stole gentlemen's watches.[32] These risks added to the danger posed by the SRM activists, whose tactics could go well beyond those of vigilante observers, turning them into positive *agents provocateurs*. It is not surprising that some sodomites preferred to meet in private, or at least semi-private, gatherings behind closed doors—though even this did not save them from the attentions of the investigators.

Before turning to those social venues, it is worth considering the age pattern of the English cases in this period. All the examples of attempted sodomy given above, other than the Rigby case, involved adult men making approaches to other men. This could hardly have been otherwise when the recipients of those advances were adults working for the SRMs, since for understandable reasons these guardians of morality were reluctant to use boys for such purposes. (The use of a teenager to facilitate the arrest of Captain Rigby had been an exception, apparently brought about by Rigby's initial propositioning of him.) Even without these active entrapment operations, it is likely that in a general climate of greater vigilance, with neighbours and passers-by encouraged to come forward as witnesses, the proportion of cases based on consensual sexual relations between adults would have risen, as those activities had previously been more likely to be neglected, for a range of reasons, than the more pressing cases involving sexual assaults on young children and adolescents. A statistical analysis of the early-eighteenth-century accusations is not available. But it is clear that opportunistic attempts continued to be made on boys, and that these followed quite a traditional pattern.[33] One day in April 1722, John Meeson, a delivery boy, was accosted in the street by a man called John Dicks, who persuaded him to go for a drink in an ale-house. There, as Meeson later testified, 'when he had made me almost fuddled, he buss'd [sc. kissed] me, put his Hand into my Breeches, and took my Hand and put it into his Breeches.' Dicks led him to several more ale-houses, plying him with ale and gin, until, having taken a private room at one of these (where a witness could 'hear him kiss the Boy, and call him his *Dear*, and his *Jewel*, and his *precious little Rogue*'), he was able to undress the semi-conscious boy and sodomize him.[34] One year later, in March, a fifteen-year-old was similarly approached, at night, by a man in Wood Street in the City of London. 'When we came to the Cross-keys', the boy testified, 'he run [*sic*] me up against the Gate, call'd me his Dear and his Precious, and unbutton'd my

Breeches, and acted several indecent things.' (Invited to join him in a tavern, the boy refused; and when the man repeated his attempts on the following night, the boy's father and two other men were able to apprehend him.)[35]

Nothing in such cases requires us to posit a 'new' type of sodomite; and at the same time it is notable that the hand-in-breeches technique was used with both boys and men. The mentality of those employing this technique seems essentially the same in both cases. With boys, allowance was made for their presumed inexperience or incomprehension: extra elements of behaviour could include initial friendly conversation, drinking together in a tavern—to develop some psychological rapport, as well as to let the alcohol erode inhibitions and resistance—and expressions of tenderness, which may not have been merely cynical ploys in some cases. Also, of course, a man approaching a boy was expecting the latter to take the passive role, which was not always the case when approaching another adult. Unsurprisingly, sodomy cases in the Navy consisted mostly of men inducing or forcing boys to submit to their sexual advances, as had previously been the case. (The frequency of naval prosecutions increased in the early eighteenth century, with twelve cases, leading to six death sentences, between 1703 and 1710. This may well reflect the heightened interest in this offence in society generally; but the quantity of such cases tended anyway to rise in times of war, both because the Navy itself expanded in numbers then, and because the authorities saw sodomy as linked to indiscipline. During the Seven Years War (1756–63), similarly, there would be eleven courts martial for sodomy and a lesser number of other known cases that did not go to trial; the leading authority on the history of the Navy summarizes this as 'a very insignificant total; a score or so of known instances, over a period of nearly nine years during which at least a hundred thousand individuals must have served in the Navy'.)[36] Overall, there is nothing in this whole pattern of eighteenth-century behaviour that could not have taken place in the previous century, or the one before that.

★ ★ ★

Such a claim would seem less easy to make where the gatherings of sodomites behind closed doors are concerned. This phenomenon emerges gradually in the surviving evidence. In 1699 brief reference was made to a 'gang' of sodomites who had been rounded up in Windsor; it was said that they had formed a 'beast-like confederacy among themselves for exercising this unnatural offence'.[37] That is a suggestive detail, but we should bear in mind that hostile opinion was always quick to portray the objects of its fears in terms of secret sects, conspiracies or organized gangs. A broadside published in 1709 explained that despite the recent exposures and prosecutions of sodomites, 'several Knots, and Gangs of them, still Associate themselves together'. A convicted soldier, before his recent execution, had given the authorities information about them, including 'the Houses they met at'; apparently as a result of that, nine of these men had now been arrested, some of them at a brandy-shop in Jermyn Street, and it was hoped that 'the whole Knot of them will now be detected, to the great Satisfaction of all honest People.'[38]

It was in that same year, 1709, that the journalist and satirical writer Ned Ward published an account of 'a particular Gang of *Sodomitical* Wretches, in this Town [sc. London], who call themselves the *Mollies*'; he described them as meeting every night in a certain tavern, where they would 'mimick a female Gossiping', adopting womanly voices, gestures and manners. Some of this consisted of parodic performances (with, on one occasion at least, a man in female dress pretending to go into labour and give birth to a wooden doll); but they also imitated 'the Indecencies of lewd Women', in order to incite sexual feelings. Later in the evening they would 'enter upon their Beastly Obscenities, and [take] infamous Liberties with one another'. Ward announced that 'they continu'd their odious Society for some Years, till their Sodomitical Practices were happily discover'd by...some of the Under-Agents to the *Reforming-Society*'; but his assumption that this was a one-off problem, now successfully dealt with, was quite mistaken.[39] By the 1720s the phenomenon was much more widely attested, and it has been estimated that during that decade nearly 20 'molly houses' came under investigation.[40]

The term 'molly' seems to have emerged in just this period; the earliest example in the *Oxford English Dictionary* of its use in this sense is from another text by Ned Ward, of 1708, referring to 'one of those Ridiculous Imitators of the Female Sex, called Mollies'. Historians have supposed that it was derived from the Latin *mollis*, meaning soft or delicate; this may seem plausible because that is the word used in the Latin Vulgate translation of the Bible for the Greek *malakos*, which, translated as 'effeminate' in the Authorized Version, features in St Paul's denunciation of both the 'effemin-ate' and the 'abusers of themselves with mankind'. *Mollis* certainly did have that connotation in moral theology, as it was the root of the abstract noun *mollities*, used for non-penetrative same-sex acts. However, the word 'molly' owed its rapid emergence to popular usage, not to Latinate culture or theological debate. The woman's name 'Molly', a version of Mary, had been widely used in late-seventeenth-century songs, ballads and plays as a generic term for a lower-class young woman—as in, for example, the ballad *Dolly and Molly: Or, The Two Country Damosels Fortunes at London*.[41] (Having quickly acquired associations with low life and prostitution, it survives in the modern expression 'a gangster's moll'.) Given Ned Ward's statement, cited above, that it was the sodomites 'who call themselves the *Mollies*', and given also the evidence of their general use of female nicknames among themselves, quite often including the name 'Molly' or 'Moll', this is surely the most likely derivation.

Ward's brief description of the goings-on among the mollies is confirmed by several other sources, including testimonies presented at trials. The typical molly house was a pub or tavern; some would have just a private room where the mollies would meet, but several were entirely devoted to this type of customer. At least 30 might be gathered there on an evening, especially on a Sunday night, drinking, singing bawdy songs, and dancing. The most notorious molly house was run by a woman known as 'Mother Clap' (Clap being her actual surname) in Holborn. It gained its notoriety when a police raid in February 1726 rounded up no fewer than 40 of its clients; three of these would later be convicted of sodomy and executed. An agent of the SRM who had infiltrated the molly house described one of his previous visits there as follows:

> I found between 40 and 50 Men making Love to one another, as they called it. Sometimes they would sit one on another's Laps, kissing in a lewd Manner, and using their Hands indecently. Then they would get up, Dance and make Curtsies, and mimick the voices of women. *O, Fie, Sir!—Pray, Sir.—Dear Sir. Lord, how can you serve me so?—I swear I'll cry out.—You're a wicked Devil—And you're a bold Face.—Eh ye little dear Toad! Come, buss!*—Then they'd hug, and play, and toy, and go out by Couples into another Room on the same Floor, to be marry'd, as they call'd it.

That last detail—where being 'marry'd' was just a jocular euphemism for sex, not a reference to a mock-ceremony—is confirmed by descriptions of other molly houses containing a 'Marrying Room' or 'Chapel' with a large bed in it.[42] Mock-weddings did occasionally take place, however. One example in 1728 involved two men who seem to have been regular sexual partners, as they had previously been put in the pillory together; the bridesmaids were a street robber who offered sex to men for the purpose of blackmailing them, and an occasional transvestite known as 'the Princess Seraphina'.[43]

For obvious reasons, efforts were made to keep these activities secret. New entrants to the group were typically introduced by existing members. (However, that does not mean that a fully club-like ethos prevailed, with members all known to one another: a young Dutchman who had attended a molly house in London in the mid-1720s later testified to a Dutch court that he had had sex there several times with 'people unknown to him, who had used him from behind'.)[44] Most probably, fears of word getting out were the main reason why boys were not involved; and this has the effect of heavily skewing the resulting evidence towards adult–adult sex. One of the youngest people to attend a molly house, Ned Courtney, was only eighteen years old, but it would have been assumed that he had his own reasons for not divulging the secret, as he was engaged in male pros- titution—an activity which, although it did occur in some of these places, did not characterize most of what went on there. Testifying in another trial, Courtney described how a proprietor of a molly house had said to him: 'there's a Country Gentleman of my Acquaintance, just come to Town, and if you'll give him a Wedding-Night, he'll pay you very hand- somely.'[45] Despite the impression given by that remark, however, these gatherings were not patronized by gentlemen; the typical clientele con- sisted of men from the lower-middling classes, such as tradesmen, shop- keepers and artisans. During the day, these were 'normal' people, going about their ordinary business in an unremarkable, and unremarked, way. They were not a visible minority.

This raises the question of the nature and purpose of their effeminate behaviour. For Randolph Trumbach that was their defining feature, with transvestism the strongest manifestation of it. He admits that 'mollies who cross-dressed were probably always a minority', contrasting them with 'the larger number who were effeminate in gesture, movement, and speech'.[46] One might assume from such comments that these people were consciously adopting female manners, or even dress, as a way of life. Yet almost all the evidence relates to their behaviour when they were safely enclosed within the molly house. There is only one well-attested example of a man who sometimes wore female dress, and was known by his female nickname, among the general community: the so-called Princess Seraphina, who was briefly mentioned above. His real name was John Cooper, and detailed information about him survives because he imprudently took a man to court in 1732 for stealing his (male) clothes; the man counter-charged, say- ing that Cooper 'laid his Privy parts in my hand, and offered to bugger me...he gave me his Cloaths to let him commit Sodomy with me'. One witness, the landlady of a local pub, said that she had seen Cooper 'several times in Women's Cloaths', and that 'She takes great Delight in Balls and Masquerades, and always chuses to appear at them in a Female Dress, that she may have the Satisfaction of dancing with fine Gentlemen...I never heard that she had any other Name than the Princess Seraphina.'[47]

That reference to balls and masquerades is significant; for 'midnight masquerades' had become a hugely popular form of public recreation in London from 1717 onwards. Held originally at the Haymarket Theatre, but later extended to large-scale events in public gardens, these were fancy-dress balls, with drinking, dancing and gambling, which went on until dawn. Men could dress as women, or in other extravagant costumes, and women could wear breeches; masks could be worn, and moralists were soon arguing, with some justification, that these events were occasions for lascivious behaviour and debauchery.[48] Some mollies apparently enjoyed reproducing the atmosphere of the masquerade within the molly house: a raid on one such house in 1725 found nearly 40 men dressed in 'Masquerade Habits'—most but, significantly, not all of the costumes being female.[49] Without the influence of the masquerade, an institution popular with men and women generally, much of what now strikes historians as flamboyant cross-dressing by mollies might never have occurred. It seems likely, for example, that the Princess Seraphina was able to get into the habit of borrowing items of clothing from women he knew, and then occasionally wearing them locally, thanks to this culturally recognized and accepted phenomenon.

Yet the fact remains that mannerisms of feminine speech and behaviour were commonly adopted in the molly house, and that female nicknames were used there too, for a significant number of the regular participants: Miss Kitten, Moll Irons, Flying Horse Moll, Pomegranate Molly, Dip-Candle Mary, Aunt England, Orange Deb, Nurse Mitchell, Susan Guzzle, Miss Sweet Lips, Green-Pea Moll, Plump Nelly, and so on. As Rictor Norton has emphasized, there was no correlation between having a female nickname and taking the passive role in sex. Nor did some of these men seem at all feminine in a physical sense: Fanny Murray was described as 'an athletic Bargeman', Lucy Cooper was 'an Herculean Coal-heaver', and so on.[50] Convincingly, Norton argues that the prime purpose of all this humorous game-playing was internal to the group. The nicknames, like the effeminate behaviour more generally, helped to 'cement relations within a tightly-knit community', as well as contributing to the atmosphere of 'vigorous and lusty bonhomie'. A shared sense of identity must indeed have been strengthened thereby, but what this involved was, Norton emphasizes, 'self-identification *as a molly—not as a woman*'; and to take on the molly identity, during the hours they spent in the molly house, was precisely to join in a role-playing game, where perhaps the most important ingredient of the role was the persona of a female prostitute, rather than that of a woman in general.[51]

This element appealed, one may assume, not only because it authorized saucy dialogue and shameless behaviour, but also because it allowed the mollies to take the derogatory language used against them by the general population ('he-whores', etc.) and, among themselves, turn it back in defiance—a familiar syndrome among denigrated minorities. The curious phenomenon of the mock-birth (mentioned several times in accounts of the molly houses) involving a wooden doll or in one case a Cheshire cheese, may also have been an example of this syndrome. In a Gloucestershire village in 1716, when word spread that a local farmer had sodomized a young agricultural worker, the villagers held what they called a 'Mock Groaning', at which the sodomized young man himself, dressed in a petti-coat, apron and head scarf, gave birth to a straw baby; the new-born child, paraded outside the farmer's house, was then baptized as 'George Buggarer', taking its surname from its father.[52] This would have been a form of rural 'rough justice' or public shaming, occasionally inflicted on known or sus-pected sodomites; incomers from the countryside might have introduced it to the molly house and adapted it there, for the amusement of their companions.

To sum up: Randolph Trumbach's interpretation, in which effeminacy and transvestism take the central role and thereby indicate the rapid devel-opment of a deep-level gender shift, is not at all convincing. Cross-dressing was a very rare phenomenon, outside the context of the masquerades (or the symbolic use of a few female accoutrements in the occasional mock-birth or mock-wedding); effeminacy belonged largely to game-like behav-iour within the molly house, extending very little into ordinary life. In the trial records relating to would-be same-sex encounters in streets, parks and other public places, there are hardly any references to effeminate speech or manners at all, and no particular reasons for thinking that the men arrested for those offences had ever set foot in a molly house.[53] The phenomenon of the molly house seems, in any case, to have been confined to London. One historian who has made a detailed study of sodomy trials in Bristol and the counties of south-western England has commented: 'The evidence available from provincial England, in which not a single molly house has been verified, suggests... that far from parading deviance overtly in feminine manners, speech or dress, the majority of men who attracted attention as suspected sodomites presented an unremarkable face to the world.'[54] The peculiar characteristics of behaviour inside the molly houses are of course of great interest, but there is no reason to suppose that this evidence opens a window through which we can see a whole new way of being a sodomite in society at large. The window opens only into the molly house itself: it was a specific institution which had its own development, flourishing, and decline, just as the masquerade did in roughly the same period.

Just how and why the phenomenon of the molly house faded away is not known in any detail. From the outset there had been some resistance to the work of the SRMs where ordinary sexual offences were concerned. Their 'outstandingly draconian' crackdown on mollies in the mid-1720s may have gone too far; one of the men convicted after the raid on Mother Clap's house in 1726 came close to being pardoned, on the apparently disinterested intervention of three aristocrats, and only a determined effort by the Bishop of London secured his execution.[55] By the next decade the SRMs were outstaying their public welcome, having attracted widespread disapproval of their sometimes corrupt methods, and in 1738 they were officially disbanded. One might reasonably suppose that the decline in evidence of the existence of molly houses after that date was due simply to the absence of those evidence-gatherers; yet in the years around 1740 the whole system of policing in London was greatly strengthened, with a salaried night watch, more constables, and more Justices of the Peace. While some of the molly houses may have continued to function, their heyday, as Rictor Norton puts it, was at an end: over time they seem to have been 'superseded by more organized prostitution and even male brothels on the one hand, and by public cruising grounds on the other'.[56] In Bristol—where the SRM had also been very active—prosecutions for sodomy continued during the rest of the century, but at a much lower rate after the 1730s: of the 55 indictments made between 1730 and 1800, 40 per cent (22) were issued in the years 1730–9 alone.[57]

In recent historical treatments of these matters, the misplaced or exaggerated emphasis on effeminacy and cross-dressing has generated a great deal of discussion of how effeminate men were thought of and represented, in the hope that this might provide a kind of cultural genealogy of the eighteenth-century sodomite. Much ink has been spilt on how or whether the figure of 'the fop' turned into or merged with the figure of 'the molly'—a development which would have been highly unlikely in real terms, given that fops were fine gentlemen and mollies were artisans, butchers, porters and so on.[58] That satirists found 'effeminacy' a perennially useful target is clear; and because the range of characteristics viewed as effeminate was quite large and varied over time, it may always be possible to make some extended connections where literary representations are concerned. But a significant difference remains between satire and documentation.

Broadly speaking, the term 'effeminate' had always been used to mean 'unmanly'. No notion of a shift in sexual orientation was necessarily involved; even a positive sense of a shift in gender need hardly have been intended, since an underlying set of binary assumptions implied automatically that to become less like a man was to become more like a woman. Hence, for example, the role of the idea of effeminacy in politically motivated rhetoric against rulers who did not go to war. Some behaviour characterized as effeminate did involve taking on what was seen as a greater resemblance to women, the classic example being an excessive interest in fine clothes. Yet this did not necessarily imply a change in one's sexual preferences; it was easily supposed that to be finely dressed, with greater than usual attention to personal hygiene, and to have fine manners, were ways of making a man more attractive to women and more welcome in their company—where flirtation and, ultimately, seduction could follow. For a man to spend too much of his time with women was by definition effeminate, even if it was motivated by sexual interest in them, as it took him away from his proper, manly business. However, the long-term movement away from traditional military values as definitive of maleness in ordinary life, and the steady application of the civilizing process to rough masculine manners, did leave writers and moralists with the task of defining the correct degree of refinement that was compatible with being a proper gentleman; satire against effeminacy, from the fops of the Restoration stage to the 'Macaroni' of late-eighteenth-century prints, was one way of doing that, by identifying and stigmatizing excess.[59] During the same period, the increased public attention given to sodomites ensured that they too were objects of satire; and sodomy was seen as intrinsically unmanly, and therefore effeminate, regardless of whether it was accompanied by speech or gestures imitating women. There was of course some interaction and overlap between these different lines of satirical development (the scornful treatment of John, Lord

Hervey by Alexander Pope and other writers being one prominent example).[60] But it would be a mistake to look for a single, unified history of effeminacy as such; and, as we have seen, even if such a history existed, it would not give us anything like a key to the actual behaviour of early-eighteenth-century English sodomites.

20

France and the Netherlands
after 1700

In the case of France—or rather, specifically, of Paris—our knowledge of sodomitical practices expands greatly after the end of the seventeenth century, just as it does in the English case, and for a very similar reason: a change in policing practices generated a much larger quantity of evidence. Under Louis XIV's reforming minister Colbert, a new 'lieutenancy of police' for the city of Paris had been set up in 1667, with a range of powers and duties that included protecting public order and public health, and supplying reports about various aspects of life in the capital. It also had its own judicial power, as a magistracy. Since it answered not to the municipal authorities but directly to a minister of the King, it met with some local institutional resistance at first, especially from the Parlement de Paris (which was essentially a judicial body), and thus took time to establish itself. The most effective of the early *lieutenants de police* was Marc-René d'Argenson, who held the position from 1697 to 1718. He established a network of *commissaires* and *inspecteurs* throughout the city, and sought to strengthen the legitimacy of their operations by putting more emphasis on policing moral disorders of the kind that offended respectable citizens; his preferred methods included the surveillance of places such as theatres, where immoral acts might occur.[1]

From 1698 until 1749, reports survive from the patrols which were sent out in the evenings to monitor, and intervene in, the activities of sodomites in public places. The police used young men as bait; known as *mouches* ('flies'), these could be individuals who had themselves been arrested for sodomy and had then been 'turned' to work as agents and informers. Most of what we know about male–male sex in Paris in this period comes from these reports or from the subsequent questioning of the men who were arrested. The venues were the predictable ones: streets in certain parts of

Forbidden Desire in Early Modern Europe: Male–Male Sexual Relations, 1400–1750. Noel Malcolm, Oxford University Press.
© Noel Malcolm 2024. DOI: 10.1093/oso/9780198886334.003.0020

town, the river embankments, the *boulevards* or ramparts of the old city walls, and especially the parks and gardens. The royal gardens—those of the Tuileries, Luxembourg and Palais-Royal—were particularly popular. Traditionally they had been outside the jurisdiction of the city watch; arrests could not take place there, so the *mouche* had to accompany the suspect beyond the garden's boundaries. (By the mid-1720s, however, the police had overcome this legal obstacle, and were making arrests on the spot.) Those places were in any case preferred by many sodomites because the rougher-looking Parisians were excluded from them; a better class of potential clientele was therefore to be found there, including nobles, master craftsmen, students and servants of the well-to-do.[2]

During the daytime, men who swam naked in the Seine (and were ogled by women as well as men) could be picked up when they emerged onto the river bank. In the gardens, where much 'cruising' went on in the evenings, a common technique for making sexual contact involved standing in view of another man and pretending to urinate, thereby displaying one's erect penis. Other methods included offering a pinch of tobacco: in June 1724 a 24-year-old lackey called Dupuis did this to a *mouche*, before exposing his penis and saying that he was sure he would like it more than tobacco. In July 1727 a report stated that René Desprez, a 28-year-old mathematics teacher, 'walked round me several times, gave me a bump with his elbow, and made a sign with his handkerchief that I should follow him'. There seems to have been a whole repertoire of signals of this kind; the dossier on an infantry captain arrested in the Tuileries gardens in April 1725 noted that 'he assures us that this is his first time, yet he knows all the sodomites' manoeuvres'.[3] Many men resorted almost immediately to 'grabbing' behaviour. This was particularly common in the well-known cruising grounds: typically, the *mouche* would sit on a park bench and wait for another man to sit next to him, and in those circumstances it was common for the man to assume that the *mouche* was already sexually aroused. In February 1725, for example, a priest accosted his target in the Tuileries gardens, 'wishing him good evening and asking, without any further formality, whether he had an erection, and wanting to put his hand in his breeches'; three months later, in the same place, a man first pretended to urinate, and then approached the *mouche*, 'to whom he said that he had an erection, and wanted to put his hand in his breeches to see if he did too'.[4]

An explicit proposition to have sex would usually follow. Reading large numbers of these reports, one is struck by how little of the behaviour could be described in any narrow sense as predatory; mutual interest and desire were generally assumed. (In one case in 1724, a military officer simply told a man that he wanted to bugger him and then, with the help of two companions, seized him and held him firm while he performed the act; but that was quite exceptional.)[5] It was quite common for the man making the proposition to ask the other person what his preference was. In July 1724, again in the Tuileries gardens, the abbé Garaine asked if the *mouche* liked to sodomize or to be sodomized, adding that a few days earlier a young man had ejaculated between his thighs, and that 'for his part, he liked variety, doing it sometimes this way and sometimes that.'[6] Overall, the number who offered to be either active or passive was exceeded, but only slightly, by the number who definitely sought the active role, while those who wanted merely to be passive were a relatively small minority; there were also some who offered to perform fellatio, and several who sought nothing more than mutual masturbation.[7] In many cases the proposal was to perform the act in the park or garden itself, if conditions were dark enough; but quite often— especially at the colder times of year—a trip was suggested to a tavern or a *cabaret* (where meals, as well as drink, were served, and rooms could be hired). In the former cases, from the mid-1720s onwards, the police would usually intervene before any penetrative sex took place; in the latter, they would typically arrest the man as he accompanied the *mouche* out of the park gates. Given that the informer's testimony could not really be questioned, many men were arrested on the basis of their reported conversation with him; occasionally, people could be hauled off just for being in a well-known cruising place in the hours of sexual activity—which was seen as sufficient proof that they were *de ce caractère-là*, 'of that type'.[8]

Quite a few of these men made comments to the *mouche* which demonstrated that they were conscious of having a distinctive sexual orientation. A 35-year-old man (who turned out to be married), striking up a conversation in October 1723, said that he enjoyed 'all the pleasures of sodomy', and that 'he did not like women at all, saying that he knew several young men who were of this taste'; in May 1727 a 45-year-old servant (who offered to perform whatever act the *mouche* preferred) said that 'he had never had any inclination other than that [sc. for male–male sex], that he had never liked women, and that he found even their their company wearisome'.[9] Occasional remarks alluded to a world of sexual activity between like-minded men which took place beyond the parks and river-banks. In October 1723 a lace merchant described a recent visit with a page to a *cabaret*, 'where the waiter who served them turned out to have the same taste; he [the lace merchant] did it to the page and the page did it to the waiter, all three at the same time'. In June 1724 a 24-year-old lackey called Dupuis explained that less than a week earlier he had been in a group assembled by the duc de Villars-Brancas, including 'six of the most strapping buggers in Paris', and that after all six of them had sodomized the duc, the duc had then sodomized him.[10]

Dupuis also mentioned that he had recently buggered the duc de Richelieu three times, receiving a total of three gold louis. One 28-year-old former lackey, arrested in the Tuileries gardens in July 1723, tried to recruit the young man he spoke to for a dinner with the marquis de Tressay on the following evening, where he promised that a fee of one gold louis could be earned (to be shared between the two of them); he could also introduce him to 'a German prince, who was very generous'.[11] But while that last case involved active procuring, there are no signs of organized prostitution taking place in the regular cruising grounds themselves. Payment was requested or offered quite frequently, but on a very ad hoc basis. One soldier, cruising in the Tuileries gardens in September 1723, said that he was ready to perform any act 'so long as there is money to be earned', but did not state a price. In some cases in 1725 where a man sought to sodomize the *mouche*, a coin worth 26 sous was offered in advance; in another case, to overcome reluctance, a 40-sous coin was handed over. (40 sous was equivalent to roughly 1 shilling and 8 pence in English money, at a time when an agricultural labourer in England might earn 1 shilling per day.) Yet there was little sense of a regular tariff; the wealthier the man, the more he might offer. That cruising soldier in 1723 said 'that a few days earlier he had done it to a man of quality who gave him 7 livres and 10 sous [150 sous in total], but that this sort of encounter was rare'; the marquis de Grave, in August 1727, offered the extraordinary sum of 2 gold louis to sodomize the *mouche*. At that time one gold louis was worth just over one pound sterling, i.e. 20 shillings.[12]

A significant number of men from the upper classes—though not from the very highest ranks of the aristocracy—feature directly in these records. Between February and April 1725, for example, the police arrested two marquis, two comtes and a *chevalier* or knight. Some would be looking for sex there and then, but others would just be searching for sexual partners to take back to their own residences. The comte d'Autry, for example, told a sixteen-year-old boy (not a *mouche*) in the Tuileries gardens that his coach was waiting at the gates, and that 'on the way home he would do it to him, tomorrow he would do it to him in the mouth, and the day after in the arse', with a promised payment of one gold louis to be handed over in the coach. He also explained that until recently he had had a young man whom he sodomized regularly for one gold louis each time, and now offered the same deal to the boy.[13] However serious the offence committed or proposed by such high-born men, it was normal practice for the police to let them off with a warning. Most seem to have reacted with calm self-confidence; but the *chevalier* de Janson, caught almost *in flagrante*, attacked one of the policemen 'with several blows' before his sword was taken off him, 'and threatened the said M. Haymier [the senior police officer] with having him dismissed from his position, adding further that he wanted to fuck in the middle of the Tuileries gardens without anyone daring to stop him'.[14]

The range of social backgrounds of the men arrested by the police was a large one, extending downwards from noblemen, *bourgeois* and clergymen to menial servants. Thierry Pastorello has analysed the police documents relating to 335 eighteenth-century sodomites in Paris whose professions are stated: 46 per cent were artisans, tradesmen and workmen, 21 per cent were servants, and 19 per cent clergymen. Michel Rey's study of people arrested in particular years between 1723 and 1749 yields a similar proportion of artisans and tradesmen (48 per cent), and of servants (26 per cent), plus the figure of 14 per cent for members of the nobility and gentry.[15] Their ages were not always recorded, but some of Rey's sample years give us the following details. In 1723, out of 25 men with known ages, one was under 20, eight were between 20 and 29, and sixteen were older; in 1737–8, out of 45 men, twelve were under 20, fourteen were between 20 and 29, and nineteen were older. And Thierry Pastorello's analysis of 216 men whose ages are given finds that 52 per cent were between ten and 29, while 48 per cent were aged 30 or above.[16] The use of young men as *mouches* in these police operations may introduce a slight bias where the youngest category of offender—typically, a teenager offering sex for money—is concerned, as the *mouche* was perhaps more likely to be sought out by an older man than by a young one (though a fair number of approaches by young men are recorded in the 1737–8 statistics).[17] But the general pattern, where the adults are concerned, is consistent with the evidence from the period before 1700 in France, where the large proportion of sodomites above the age of 30 was in contrast to that in the Florentine statistics.[18] And in any case, as we have seen, there was no necessary connection between seniority and seeking the active role.

Under the provisions of the criminal law, sodomy was a serious offence, alongside such felonies as sacrilege, counterfeiting and sedition. Even though most of these arrests took place before the sexual act could be committed, and with only one key witness to what the man had done or proposed, there were some cases that could have been sent to the courts; but that hardly ever happened. D'Argenson and his successors preferred to exercise their own judicial powers, and the punitive regime they operated was a relatively light one—so much so that one historian has referred to d'Argenson's 'policy of discreet paternalism'. While the most serious offenders might be deported to the colonies or enlisted in the army, brief prison sentences, of between a week and a few months, were much more common; the sentence could be as long as two years, but on the other hand some men would be let off with only a warning, so long as they supplied the police with information about their activities and the other sodomites they knew, and promised not to frequent the cruising grounds again.[19] The long-term sentences were served in the Bicêtre, a notorious prison-hospital (and former fortress), where conditions were dire; some sodomites were consigned there not by the police but by *lettres de cachet*, unappealable decrees against individuals, issued by the King and signed by his minister at the request of relatives or colleagues of the offenders who just wanted them out of the way.[20]

Only very rarely, therefore, did sodomy cases proceed to the criminal court, where the death penalty could be imposed. The most notorious case was that of Étienne-Benjamin Deschauffours, who was arrested in the summer of 1725, aged 36. From his own admissions under interrogation, and from the evidence of a wide range of witnesses, it became clear that for many years he had been active as a procurer, supplying boys and young men to satisfy the desires of gentlemen and nobles—a type of business which, as we have seen, was already well established in the latter part of the seventeenth century.[21] Deschauffours's methods, however, were extreme even by the standards of the most unscrupulous practitioners of that trade. One seven-year-old boy was kidnapped in the street, in broad daylight, and sold to an Italian clergyman; a fourteen-year-old was raped by Deschauffours and three other men, before being sold to a Polish nobleman for 35 gold louis; a sixteen-year-old, who had been sent to Deschauffours's apartment merely to deliver a watch, was given a glass of wine laced with opium and then raped by him and two others; and a boy aged ten or eleven, taken by force to his apartment, was beaten so badly—to stop him crying for help—that he later died. Deschauffours frequently picked up street urchins for sex;

he also sodomized one of his two servants (a young adult) regularly, which the servant reluctantly accepted on condition that he was allowed to sodomize many of the boys. All this had been going on for years; evidently it had supplied Deschauffours with a good income, as he dressed in fine clothes and posed as a nobleman, under a false title. Among his clientele there were many genuine members of the nobility, including a significant number of Italians. Most wanted boys, but one of the witnesses at the trial was a big, strong young man, to whom Deschauffours had explained that he had a client who would pay good money to be sodomized by him.[22]

One historian has suggested that the decision was taken to make an example of Deschauffours because of some recent scandals, in 1722 and 1724, involving sodomy at court; his trial and death sentence would instil fear in the minds of many noblemen who had had dealings with him.[23] Certainly his execution was designed to have a public impact: printed placards were posted in the streets of Paris, announcing that he would be burnt alive in the place de Grève, and his ashes scattered to the winds, for the crime of sodomy (without mentioning the details of kidnapping and murder).[24] A well-informed diarist noted in his journal that René Hérault, the *lieutenant de police*, decided to make an example of Deschauffours 'as it was not possible to punish all those who were named [sc. in the interrogations and trial], because that would cause too much of an uproar'. Interestingly, he added that the extra publicity generated by the punishment of multiple culprits would have another negative effect: it would 'shed light on this crime and make it more frequent, whereas most of the common people don't even know what it is'.[25] It was indeed rare for the police, who liked to monitor and control the sodomites in semi-obscurity, to aim at publicity in this way. During the eighteenth century there were only nine formal trials of sodomites in Paris, and just five of those concluded with the death penalty; but in four of those five cases, the conviction was not only for sodomy but also for a capital crime such as murder or rape. The fifth case, in 1750, arose merely because two workmen, one aged c.21 and the other perhaps as old as 40, were found committing sodomy in the street after dark. (The older of the two had simply approached the younger and asked him to bugger him.) The fact that those men were sentenced to be strangled and their bodies burnt in the place de Grève was highly anomalous, as theirs was a routine offence, unrelated to wider social circles and with no further incriminating factors; yet although their execution was public, the nature of the charge on which they had been convicted was not divulged to the spectators.[26] Perhaps the treatment of them related to some temporary moral panic, or some intra-jurisdictional conflict, among the authorities, the details of which have not survived. Whereas the multiple crimes committed by Deschauffours were so gross that, once established, they could have led to no other sentence than death.

From evidence presented at the Deschauffours trial, and from almost all the cases involving members of the upper classes arrested in the parks and gardens, it is clear that the assumption of relative impunity held by the French nobility continued to operate. Moderately well-informed Frenchmen also continued to assume that sodomy was primarily a vice of the upper classes. The diarist who commented on the trial noted that Deschauffours had plied his trade mostly among the nobility and the prosperous *bourgeoisie*, 'since, generally speaking, that [sc. sodomy] is not a pastime of the *petit bourgeois*'.[27] Although his claim was surely true about the great majority of that class (as it would have been about the great majority of any particular social class), the idea that these lesser folk were proportionately rare among the sodomites is—as we have already seen, from the analyses of professions mentioned above—disproved by the general evidence of the Parisian police reports. To some extent, indeed, they had their own sodomitical milieu. For while noblemen could try their luck with servants and shopkeepers among the trees in the royal gardens, there was also a certain amount of socializing among sodomites in taverns, and this was a world into which upper-class men did not enter. These social gatherings in Paris are less well evidenced than their London counterparts, as the taverns were not raided by the police; but enough information emerges to suggest some quite striking similarities with the molly houses. Reports from 1748 suggested that there were at least eight *cabarets* and taverns where groups of between fifteen and 30 men would meet to eat, drink, sing, dance and have sex, sometimes in a special room set aside for that purpose. One informant, describing such a gathering of 20 men in the previous year, said that eventually 'they all had sex with one another, either in the *cabaret* or after they had left it.'[28]

Two of the reports from 1748 indicate an even closer parallel with the molly houses. An informant who said that he had been seven or eight times to gatherings in different taverns noted that 'at the said assemblies there were some who mimicked women's manners.' Another report explained that 'some of them put napkins on their heads and imitate women, making affected gestures and curtsying as they do; when some new young man comes along, they call him the bride and, when this happens, he becomes the object of everyone's attentions.'[29] Even though it was only 'some' of the participants who engaged in this behaviour, it had an effect on the tone of the whole occasion; there is a report of one recruit, a painter, who left one of these gatherings because he found it tiresome, and wished that these people would behave as men.[30] However, there was no special French term for such people, corresponding to 'molly'. Some modern accounts fix on the phrase *gens* (or *chevaliers*) *de la manchette*, 'people (or knights) of the cuff', which features occasionally in the police reports; its origins are quite obscure, and there is no definite evidence that it referred to any kind of flamboyant dress. But when it first appeared in the records, in the first half of the 1720s, it was just a general term for 'sodomites', and it does not seem to have acquired any more specialized meaning thereafter.[31]

Game-playing of a similar but more elaborate kind, containing an element of gender-switching, was described in the testimony of two men— lackeys, aged 29 and 34—questioned by d'Argenson in 1706. Together, they had held what they called 'pleasure parties' or '*cabaret* parties', to which other young men were invited. A mock-ceremony of welcome or initiation had apparently taken place, at which the younger of the two organizers, nick-named 'Madam General' or 'the Grand Master', made each new entrant swear loyalty to the group, and gave him a female name. Because of those titles, d'Argenson assumed that they had set up some kind of 'order', though they refused to accept that word, referring to it only as a society. Perhaps d'Argenson had at the back of his mind the story of the aristocratic mock-religious order of the early 1680s, as described by de Courtilz de Sandras; possibly the two organizers did so too, despite their protestations. But as Gary Ferguson has pointed out, a more likely model was the kind of trade brotherhood for journeymen known as *compagnonnage*, which similarly involved titled officers, oaths of loyalty, the granting of nicknames and communal drinking in taverns. As for the feminine element: under questioning, it was explained that the older of the two had been given a female name by local women during the previous year's carnival, when the two men, dressed as women, had sold baked apples in the street. Both men then added that the use of female names came also from going to a ball, where 'everyone dressed differently and took names that suited their masquerade costumes.'[32]

The mock-organization run by those two men, whatever it was exactly, was very untypical; none of the later accounts of gatherings in taverns mentions anything similar. But the reference to carnivals and fancy-dress balls does help to show—again, in parallel with the English case—that the surrounding culture had created a taste and an opportunity for a kind of gender-crossing game-playing, which could then be adapted, within the closed group of sodomites, to more sexually suggestive meanings. Here too there is no reason to think that the nicknames and mannerisms used in these 'assemblies' demonstrate the emergence of a whole new kind of sodomite in daily life. At most, as Michel Rey has observed, a few of the men who went cruising for sex in the evenings wore rouge, or had tied some ribbons to their clothes; that seems more like discreet signalling than the adoption of a different gender.[33] The vast majority of the men searching for casual sex—who outnumbered the attendants at the gatherings in taverns by a very large margin—displayed no effeminate behaviour at all. And meanwhile, elsewhere in the evidence so carefully assembled by the Paris police, we find accounts of sexual relations which were much less transitory: a man who had been living for six months with a clergyman, for example, pretending to be his cousin, or two lackeys who were described as having slept together every night for two years. In the words of the report: 'They were unable to fall asleep without having mutually touched each other and without having performed infamous acts. It was even almost always necessary for Duquesnel to have his arm extended along the headboard, under Dumaine's head. Without that Dumaine could not rest.'[34]

★ ★ ★

The Netherlands is the third country where, for the first half of the eighteenth century, we have a much larger quantity of evidence of sodomitical activity. In this case the reason was not a vigilante campaign or a new kind of official policing, but an apparently contingent sequence of events. One chance arrest in Utrecht in 1730 led to the interrogation of a well-travelled and extremely promiscuous sodomite, whose identification of previous partners set off more investigations in a kind of chain reaction; as news of these cases spread it caused a sudden surge of popular concern, which itself led to the exposing of more cases. What all these discoveries revealed was the existence of a well-established sodomitical world within Dutch society. And this functioned in ways very similar to the world of the sodomites in London and Paris: it had its own cruising places and methods of recognition, as well as its own forms of socializing in taverns and houses.

Clearly these phenomena had been developing over quite a long time. Some of the confessions obtained in the wave of trials of 1730–1 referred to events many years earlier; one of the first men to be arrested in Utrecht, for example, described a 'society' to which he had belonged in 1710, which had met once a week for mutual masturbation. And although the judicial records are relatively thin before 1730, they contain enough evidence to show that many of the practices which began to come to light in that year were already current from at least the late seventeenth century onwards. A trial in Rotterdam in the early 1680s involved a group of three men who sodomized one another; the eldest of them, aged 56, had solicited men for sex in a public lavatory. At another trial, in Amsterdam in 1689, four men in their early 20s were prosecuted for similar acts of solicitation—which they had then used for blackmailing purposes—in a latrine and at the city's cornmarket. It was noted that they had a way of signalling interest to another man by stepping on his foot.[35] In 1702, when a male prostitute and blackmailer was tried at the Court of Holland in The Hague, he described several other standard signs, including tugging at another man's arm, urinating as he watched, or simply tapping on the back of one's own extended hand with the palm of the other hand. (Later evidence would add the common practice of two men lightly bumping into each other as they passed.) Going for a walk in the city's woodland holding a handkerchief was another method; and later evidence confirms that those woods, like the parks and gardens of London and Paris, were regular venues for sexual encounters.[36] A blackmailer arrested in 1715 in Amsterdam referred to common meeting-places for sodomites in that city, Rotterdam and The Hague; two years later, in Rotterdam, a man was charged with soliciting other men in a latrine.[37]

As much later evidence would show, the use of public lavatories for this purpose was widespread in the Netherlands—more so, seemingly, than in Paris or London, though the 'bog-houses' of Lincoln's Inn Fields, the Temple and the Savoy do feature in the English evidence. The encounters in latrines were generally between one adult and another, although the man accused in Rotterdam in 1717 said that it was so dark there that he could not tell whether he was making his approach to an adult or a youth.[38] Obviously the main advantages of these venues were the degree of privacy, the male-only clientele, and the fact that there was a reasonable pretext for making one's genitals visible to others, and looking at theirs. It was suggested in a previous chapter that the practice of two men taking an interest in each other's genitals, which was at work in the phenomenon of 'grabbing' and hand-placing, rested on a different psychological basis from that of the great majority of adult sodomites pursuing boys in Florence (who had no concern with the boys' genitals, and in most cases would not have expected the boys to be interested in theirs).[39] The standard modern historical view, as formulated by Randolph Trumbach, would take this evidence from the early eighteenth century as confirming that a major change had taken place after 1700. But in fact there was no change here in Northern Europe, where the use of public lavatories for same-sex purposes—just like the touching and grabbing behaviour—had a long previous history. In 1400 two adults were prosecuted in Strasbourg for repeated acts of mutual masturbation, the first of which had taken place in a public lavatory; two of the men arrested for sodomy in Regensburg in 1471 had had sex in the latrine of the Augustinian friary there; the latrine of the Franciscan Friary in Hamm was similarly used in 1536; several of the sodomy cases tried in Zurich in the late seventeenth century involved encounters in lavatories.[40] The prominence of such venues in the later Dutch evidence might be explained, at least in part, by the simple fact that the well-managed cities of the seventeenth- and eighteenth-century Netherlands had more of these public facilities.

The wave of prosecutions of 1730–1 began in January 1730 with the arrest of two sodomites, a 52-year-old man and a nineteen-year-old, who had been caught *in flagrante* one evening inside the tower of Utrecht's cathedral. When interrogated, the man explained that he had engaged in mutual masturbation and sodomy—sometimes taking the passive role with a younger man—with a number of partners over the years. One of them, a tailor now aged 25, named some recent partners of his own, several of whom were in turn brought in for questioning.[41] And it was one of those, a 22-year-old called Zacharias Wilsma, whose evidence would have a transformative effect. His direct testimony to the Utrecht magistrates enabled them to draw up a list of no fewer than 144 of his own sexual contacts, both in that city and in a variety of other places in the Netherlands. In May 1730 they sent out letters to the magistrates in eight other towns, and to two military courts, giving the names of sodomites who had been thus identified. What had begun as a minor local investigation was now quickly turning into a nation-wide campaign.[42]

Zacharias Wilsma was born in Leeuwaarden in 1707, the son (possibly the orphan child) of a soldier. By his own account he was introduced to male–male sex at the age of fifteen, when a servant he knew, who was three years older, invited him to bugger him. On that person's recommendation he got a job as a servant in Zwolle, and then went to Breda, where he found several men who wanted to masturbate with him or sodomize him, sometimes giving him money for it. In 1726, aged nineteen, Wilsma moved to The Hague.

He made contact there with a man in his early 50s, Jacobus Backer or Bakker, who ran a business supplying servants, both male and female, to employers. But that was not his only source of income. The more amenable young men seeking work would stay in Backer's house, where he would have sex with them in lieu of charging them rent, and also introduce other men who would pay to have sex with them. He was thus running, on the side, an informal quasi-brothel, involving a network of sodomites of his acquaintance. (When the law finally caught up with him, he would be sentenced to death not only for sodomy, but also for letting his house be used for it, and for making 'immoral earnings'.)[43]

And that was the reason why Wilsma went to see him. He had heard all about the sodomitical world of The Hague, including the role of Backer, from a young soldier, a drummer called Frederick Gurck, whom he had met and had sex with earlier in 1726 in Breda. Gurck had portrayed The Hague as a sexual paradise: he claimed that during a visit there lasting two weeks he had been buggered at least 100 times, and had had at least 30 sexual partners. Most of this had been accomplished by cruising in public places; sometimes he had dressed in female clothes, and on at least one occasion he had robbed the man who, convinced that he was a woman, had picked him up. But he had also been regularly sodomized by Jacobus Backer while staying in his house.[44] When Wilsma went to live with Backer, he too was required to satisfy his voracious sexual appetite, as the older man buggered him, fellated him and masturbated with him. Backer also introduced other men to Wilsma for sex; they were from a range of backgrounds, but included some members of the upper classes, such as the baron van Meeuwen and another man called Backer (Jacob Cornelis Backer), who held the high office of seneschal of the town of Buren.[45] It was the inclusion of such names in the extracts from Wilsma's evidence sent to the authorities in The Hague that helped to convince them that the whole issue required in-depth investigation. (Note however that when the magistrates in Amsterdam, who were similarly alarmed, consulted three eminent lawyers on the treatment of sodomites, the reply they received included the correct statement that, under the Criminal Ordinances of 1570, judges were advised to make allowance for the social status of the accused.)[46]

The repercussions of Wilsma's testimony were huge. In July 1730 the Court of Holland and Zeeland issued, after many days of debate, a *plakkaat* or decree against sodomy, which was widely circulated. Investigations sprang up in many other towns, some of them as a direct consequence of Wilsma's confessions; because he had referred (inaccurately, as it turned out) to an official from Groningen with whom he had had sex several times in The Hague, the authorities of the former city began searching for sodomites, and soon found five of them.[47] Much worse was to follow in the little village of Faan, eight miles to the west of Groningen. In April 1731 an anonymous letter was sent to Rudolf de Mepsche, the magistrate who resided there and whose judicial and administrative powers extended to the whole surrounding district of Oosterdeel-Langewold. The letter denounced a local farmer's son, aged 20, for sodomy; that young man was quickly arrested, and within a few days de Mepsche had six suspects, aged between thirteen and 21, locked up in the cow-shed next to his house. A 39-year-old man, apparently named by some of those young people, was then brought in for questioning, and after what seems to have been severe torture he produced a list of no fewer than 30 men and youths. Many of these seemed such unlikely candidates for the charge of sodomy that critics of de Mepsche argued that the tortured man had been reduced to a complete mental collapse by the time he named them. But new waves of arrests followed, with houses in Faan requisitioned to function as prisons, and torture was more widely applied. It seems that de Mepsche was, to some extent, settling old scores, as at least six of his local rivals and opponents were among the accused. Although some evidence was brought to light of sexual experimentation between some of the youths, there were no plausible signs of the kind of sinister network that was gestured at in de Mepsche's heated denunciations. In any case much of the evidence was thoroughly unreliable, having been extracted under torture; two of the accused died from the treatment they received. His judicial power prevailed, however, and on 24 September he presided over the public execution of no fewer than 21 men and boys, including one fifteen-year-old and two sixteen-year-olds. Some sense of the outrage this caused among the local population can be gained from the fact that he had requested from the authorities a military detachment of 300 men to keep order on the day.[48] This mass execution was almost the last and certainly the worst effect of the chain reaction set off by the testimony of Zacharias Wilsma.

Most of the details vouchsafed by Wilsma and by other incriminated men in Utrecht, The Hague and elsewhere related to life in the towns, not the villages. The Netherlands had a relatively dense urban network, with much communication and migration between the towns, so it is not surprising that quite a consistent picture of sodomitical life emerges from trials held in different cities. Beyond the 'cruising' already discussed (the use of this term derived from the Dutch nautical verb *kruysen* or *kruisen*—one sodomite explained that he often went to the Voorhout, an avenue in The Hague, 'which that sort of people refer to as the cruising route'), there was also some socializing indoors.[49] Mention has already been made of the masturbation society in Utrecht, 'which', as one confession put it, 'came together once a week, in one another's houses, where each handled the others in a shameful way'.[50] One of the first suspects to be questioned in Utrecht referred to gatherings in the house of a tobacco merchant where twelve men would masturbate together; in Leeuwaarden the authorities learned about the existence of an inn where between six and ten men would meet for non-penetrative sexual play. Masturbation, whether in pairs or in larger groups, was evidently a popular pastime among the Dutch sodomites; one man, executed in Amsterdam in 1730, supplied a list of the men he had masturbated with, which filled seven pages.[51] In principle there was nothing novel about this phenomenon in the Northern European lands. As we have seen, mutual masturbation had been practised as an end in itself for several centuries in the German lands (Helmut Puff calls it 'the sexual practice that men adopted most frequently'), and there is also some evidence from those territories of adult men meeting in groups for sexual purposes.[52] But it seems likely that such meetings, in Dutch towns, had increased in scale and degree of confidence from the latter part of the seventeenth century onwards.

In several cities there were inns or taverns where sodomites congregated. One in Utrecht had a back room, to which men could retire; one in Amsterdam operated on two floors, serving a general clientele below and sodomites upstairs, where the rooms contained beds. For such inns, as well as for private houses such as Jacob Backer's, a special term developed, at least in The Hague: *lolhuizen*, possibly meaning 'fun houses' (though the derivation is quite uncertain). These could function as venues for prostitution of a more or less informal kind, or just as reliable places where male–male sex could take place. Some customers would ask the proprietor if he had any agreeable young men to offer, but others would turn up with a man they had just met while cruising, and better-off customers might bring their own servants.[53] Those conditions suggest that there was less of an enclosed, club-like atmosphere of self-conscious identity-sharing than in the molly houses or the gatherings in the Parisian *cabarets*. Nevertheless, the court documents do show that there were some elements of a distinctive subculture among sodomites generally, such as a shared linguistic code (*vlaggeman* for a sodomite, *vlag* being a slang term for 'penis'; going *een glas wyn drinken*, 'to drink a glass of wine', for going to a private place to have sex). Other terms for a sodomite included *cousijn*, *neef* and *nicht*; all meant 'cousin', while the last two meant male and female cousin (or nephew and niece) respectively.[54]

The use of *nicht* has been highlighted by historians keen to find signs of effeminacy and third-gender identification in the Dutch evidence. There are some traces—though rather faint ones—of the kind of game-playing that took place in London and Paris. Theo van der Meer has come across a few examples of female nicknames, though these are mostly from later in the century. When arrested in 1730, the landlord of the two-level inn in Amsterdam was described as speaking *op sijn jan mijsjes*—roughly, 'as little Miss Johnny'; much has been made of this, even though, in the mass of evidence from 1730–1, no other definite reference to effeminate speech has been found.[55] As for cross-dressing: it may be significant that when law officers searched the upstairs part of that inn in Amsterdam, they found a chest containing women's hats and aprons. And yet, while that is a suggestive detail, the only clear reference to such behaviour in a *lolhuis* comes from the evidence against just one man in The Hague, who was said to have been seen in one of those inns with a male companion in female dress. There are very rare references to men cruising in women's clothes; but the best attested examples, Frederick Gurck in the 1720s and a similar practitioner, Gabriel de Berger, in 1702, were clearly doing this as an occasional tactic for purposes of robbery and/or blackmail, not as a way of expressing a new gender identity.[56] Overall, two factors may explain the contrast between the Dutch and English evidence here: the Netherlands had not succumbed in the same way to the general fashion for masquerades; and, while cross-dressing in the molly house was very much a way of expressing the sense of membership of that group as it met behind closed doors, the greater openness of the *lolhuis* reduced the scope for such 'membership only' activities.

An interesting fact that emerges from the Dutch evidence is that some of these men in the Netherlands were well aware of the nature of sodomitical life in England. Gabriel de Berger described to a friend how the English sodomites signalled to one another, and urged him to go with him to England, where they could have a prosperous life—on the basis, presumably, of blackmail and robbery. One of the people prosecuted in The Hague in 1730, Dirk van Wanrooij, who was then aged 30, described how he had worked as a servant in London in 1725–6, where he was able to go to special houses to have sex with men; he had left England in a hurry after the arrest and execution of some of his friends. In June 1730 an Irish newspaper stated that several Dutch sodomites, who had fled their country, had been arrested for sexual solicitation in St James's Park in London. From that year, there is a detailed report of a young Dutchman being sentenced to the pillory in London: a man testified that the Dutchman had seen him urinating in an alley and had 'caught hold of my Privities, and clap'd my Hand to his'; seized by that man, the Dutchman cried out 'My Dear, my Dear, first time, first time.' (The English were well informed about the apparent outbreak of sodomy in the Netherlands: at least 2,000 articles relating to it appeared in British newspapers during 1730–1.) One of the more prominent suspects in the Netherlands, Jacob Cornelis Backer, seneschal of Buren, escaped just in time and went into permanent exile in England or Ireland.[57]

Altogether, it has been estimated that during 1730–2 roughly 400 Dutchmen fled their homes, many of them travelling abroad, to avoid prosecution. In the territory of Holland alone, 166 out of the 232 known trials took place *in absentia*. A total of 174 men and youths were arrested in the Netherlands; 98 were executed, and many of the others received sentences of flogging or banishment.[58] The authorities continued to act against suspected sodomites, or people involved in sodomy-related blackmail: after 1732 there were 265 prosecutions in Amsterdam, The Hague and Utrecht during the rest of the century, though many of them were conducted *in absentia* and some resulted in acquittals. Exile or flogging was the typical punishment for those who were arrested and convicted. Included in the total of 265 are the prosecutions caused by one other major wave of anti-sodomite concern which swept the nation in 1764, when 78 individuals were indicted.[59] But nothing as severe as the national moral panic of 1730–1 ever happened again.

★ ★ ★

In other parts of Northern Europe the evidence of sodomy is sparser, and the signs of a distinct subculture with its own forms of socializing are faint or non-existent. Late-seventeenth-century Zurich does seem to have had something like a moral panic of its own, albeit one which was less intensive and more extended over time. Between 1669 and 1719 roughly 100 sodomy cases, deriving from the city itself and the entire territory of the canton, were heard; the degree of official concern is reflected in the fact that several of the cases dealt with in the 1680s related to sexual acts performed in previous decades, as far back as the 1630s. In all the evidence that emerged, there are no signs of anything resembling molly houses or *lolhuizen*. But on the other hand baths, inns and latrines do feature as venues for sexual encounters; and a baker from the town of Winterthur, tried for sodomy in 1678, named a total of eighteen partners there, which may suggest the existence of some kind of circle of like-minded men.[60] In Hamburg, where roughly fourteen cases are known in the eighteenth century, the contrast with London, Paris and the Netherlands is also strong. Jakob Michelsen's study concludes that the sources reveal 'no establishments particularly frequented by sodomites, and no definite meeting-places such as green open spaces, public lavatories or particular churches'. However, he does also note a case from 1760 in which between 20 and 24 men were implicated; at the heart of that case was an individual who operated as a procurer, so it seems that there was quite a large circle of men who made use of his services as he supplied willing soldiers and servants to some of the city's merchants and artisans.[61] Where Berlin is concerned, some historians have argued for the existence of a well-established sodomitical subculture by the late eighteenth century. The evidence for this has been drawn entirely from a book published anonymously in 1782, which referred not only to social gatherings of *warme Brüder* ('warm brethren') but also to specialized brothels stocked with teenaged boys; however, more recent scholarship has dismissed that work as entirely fictitious.[62] And in Stockholm, the very limited evidence from the eighteenth century offers no signs of a socializing subculture at all.[63]

Scandinavia had, in any case, nothing like the dense urban network of the Netherlands, and no cities remotely approaching London or Paris in size. The overall rarity of sodomy trials probably reflects, as has been argued above, a generally low level of sodomitical activity in the population. But in this period another factor came into play: unlike their counterparts in the Netherlands and England, the authorities seem to have adopted a deliberate policy of avoiding publicity for this offence. When a new criminal code was issued for Sweden and Finland in 1734, it contained no explicit reference to sodomy at all. Although one historian has argued that this just reflected an easy-going attitude ('The law was generally based, after all, on a rather pragmatic view of sexuality in society; the sexual crimes that were punished were those that could give rise to offspring'), it is much more likely that an active fear of publicity was work—a fear which, while it may have been stimulated by news of the recent English and Dutch prosecutions, clearly had a longer history.[64] At a meeting in 1699 of the Law Committee, which advised the King, one member had suggested including provisions for sodomy, whereupon another replied that 'it seems inadvisable to mention sodomitic sins; rather it would be better to pass over them in silence as if unaware; should it go so far that such acts are committed, then due punishment should be meted out.' In a case of 1713, the sentence imposed on a man found guilty of attempted sodomy was a flogging behind closed doors and a secret acquittal on the charge of sodomy, to be followed by three years' hard labour; an army captain accused by his soldiers in 1719 was subjected to a confidential investigation, and eventually sent into exile on a foreign ship so that the news of his crime would not spread via Swedish sailors.[65] Denmark seems to have followed a similar policy in this period. In one case in Jutland in 1744, where a local Lutheran minister had denounced two men for sodomy, the trial was held in secret, and the judge criticized the minister for not having dealt with the matter by admonishing the culprits privately.[66]

The issue of the possible dangers of publicizing sodomy was an old one. As we have seen, it had exercised minds in other parts of the continent too. In Northern Europe it was never entirely settled; arguments on both sides could be heard. The traditional view was expressed, for example, by the Dutch Calvinist preacher Jacobus Hondius in 1679, when he wrote that the sin of sodomy should be 'treated with the utmost circumspection, so that no one should be aware that it can take place'; similarly, Daniel Defoe—another stern moralist—reacted in 1707 to newspaper reports of the prosecution of sodomites by saying that they should be 'sent expressly out of the World, as secretly and privately, as may consist with Justice and the Laws'.[67] This was a very different attitude from that of the SRMs, or of the authorities in Amsterdam who, in June 1730, proclaimed the sentences of execution against four sodomites from the balcony of the town hall and, after the men were killed, put their bodies on public display before throwing them in the river.[68]

One of the basic points made by the pro-secrecy moralists, which looms much larger in Northern European debates than in Southern European ones, was the claim that many people would simply not know what sodomy was unless they were told about it. As we have seen, a Parisian lawyer, commenting on the Deschauffours case in 1726, wrote that multiple public punishments would 'shed light on this crime and make it more frequent, whereas most of the common people don't even know what it is'.[69] Similarly, a senior official said to the Senate of Hamburg during a discussion of a sodomy case in 1750 that publicizing the crime would mean that 'a mass of

people, especially young ones, would be brought from a state of blessed
ignorance, in which they know nothing more about sodomy than the word
itself, to a harmful state of knowledge.'[70] We have already encountered
some evidence of such ignorance: in Sweden, for example, the semi-
incomprehension of soldiers molested by their captain, or the innocence of
another soldier who had sex with his colleague in the belief that the latter
was a woman.[71] Some of the accused in the Dutch trials—especially, as the
Hamburg official said, young ones—had little sense that what they had
done was a sin or a crime. Several of the people who confessed at Faan in
1731 did so quite freely at first, as they did not think the offence was serious.
A sixteen-year-old, tried in Cape Town in 1736, admitted that he had been
introduced to sodomy by his brother in the Netherlands, and told his inter-
rogators that he could see nothing wrong with it. A fifteen-year-old boy
who admitted to letting a man sodomize him on a VOC ship in 1748 said
that 'if he had only known that this crime was so filthy and unnatural, he
would never have let his body be tainted with it', explaining that, instead, he
had been 'entirely ignorant of it'.[72] A boy corrupted by Deschauffours who
eventually talked to a priest about his experience was shocked to learn that
sodomy was a grave sin and a serious criminal offence.[73] Similarly, the
Dutchman Dirk van Wanrooij, describing how he had been regularly sodomized by a schoolmaster in 1715–16, when he was aged 14–15, explained
that he 'did not complain to his parents, because he thought there was nothing wrong with it'.[74] Within any particular community there would certainly have been some people who had a clear idea of the nature and
heinousness of this sin, but even among adults there may have been some
whose understanding was somewhat hazy, until they read graphic details in
the newspapers. In cases where long-standing behaviour was described by
witnesses in the community, it may have been only in retrospect that some
of the accumulated details acquired their full significance (at least, to some
of those who had recounted the details). As we shall see, it was not uncommon in these societies to refer to sodomites as 'that sort of people'; some of
those who used such phrases may have had a clearer idea than others of
what that sort of people actually did, while some other people may simply
have lacked the ability to categorize their neighbours in that way. The evidence, both of understanding and of disapproval, is mixed, most probably
because the reality itself was mixed too.

On the other hand, once popular hostility was aroused, it could be
powerful—perhaps because, to many people, such sexual practices seemed

so outlandish once they were recognized and explained. As Rictor Norton has described, men who were convicted of attempted sodomy and sentenced to stand in the pillory could find themselves 'at the centre of an orgy of brutality and mass hysteria', as filth and refuse, and also stones, were hurled at them by the crowd; in 1763 one young man died of the injuries he received in this way. Norton also notes that extortioners, who had threatened to denounce people as sodomites unless they were paid for their silence, were similarly treated.[75] Allowance should be made for the fact that this was a form of participatory public entertainment, where those who enjoyed inflicting suffering could do so with the added satisfaction of knowing that their actions were endorsed by the authorities.

In a society where some people, at least, could grow up without internalizing any strong sense that sodomy was a sin or crime, it was perhaps possible to carry through into adulthood a 'default' attitude which saw such sexual activity as unproblematic unless proven otherwise. William Brown, who was arrested in the 'Sodomites' Walk' in 1726 after approaching the *agent provocateur* Thomas Newton, said to the constables: 'I think there's no Crime in making what use I please of my own Body.'[76] Some men, though sufficiently aware of the taboo against penetrative sodomy, had not absorbed any sense of the wrongness of other kinds of same-sex activity. The Swedish army captain who had pestered his men for mutual masturbation or interfemoral sex told the investigators that he did not think such actions were sinful, and seemed to lack any clear idea that a criminal offence might be involved. In 1756 a carpenter on a British naval vessel, accused of soliciting mutual masturbation with two midshipmen, had told them that 'there was no Sin in the Action.'[77] Similar remarks about sodomy itself do occasionally surface in the earlier evidence from Southern Europe, as we have seen; but in some cases those comments were tinged with defiant anticlericalism, while in others they may have been expressions of a kind of presumptive acceptance of common practice. Both of those factors seem less present in the Northern European societies.

Those who sought to defend their predilection for sodomy could reach for a variety of arguments. The Dutch preacher Andreas Klink, tried in 1757–9 for pawing at servants or guests who shared his bed, explained that such behaviour 'belonged to his nature', because his father had been away when his mother was pregnant with him, and the strong desire she had consequently felt for the company of a man had been 'inherited' by him. In any case, he said, whatever he had done in bed happened while he was asleep, and must have been caused by his dreams. But his attempts at self-justification went further than that: when one object of his advances told him that the sin he was committing was incompatible with being a God-fearing man, he had countered with the example of King David and his love for Jonathan.[78] Educated people offered a variety of biblically related arguments. In 1732 another Dutch preacher was said to have proposed that the ban on sodomy in Leviticus should be treated in the same way as the many other Levitical prohibitions which were no longer seen as binding; it had applied only to the people of Israel. A lawyer tried at The Hague in 1749 had claimed that the city of Sodom was destroyed not for same-sex behaviour but because of the range of other sins specified in Ezekiel; this was apparently just one of the reasons he gave for thinking that sodomy was not a sin.[79] And according to the Princess Palatine, writing from Versailles in 1701, some of the sodomites at court, who did not reject the authority of the Bible, got round the Levitical proscription by arguing that sodomy 'was a sin only for so long as the world was not yet populated'.[80]

Some intellectuals were prepared to mount explicit defences of sodomy. In 1732 the Piedmontese anticlerical writer Alberto Radicati, count of Passerano, who had gone into exile in England, published a treatise denying the wrongness of suicide which, in passing, also defended sodomy against those who would prohibit it on moral or religious grounds. Moral notions, he argued, cannot be innate, given that the ideas of different societies vary so greatly on theft, adultery, sodomy and other issues; the ancient Cretans venerated sodomy, and 'In the Empire of China, Adultery and Sodomy are tolerated, in the Men, by the Laws both Divine and Human.' No sooner had this book been published in London than the author, translator and printer were all taken into custody.[81] In Paris the free-thinking—indeed, openly atheistic—playwright and scholar Nicolas Boindin (who died in 1751) was sufficiently prudent not to put his opinions on religious morality into print, but he did express them freely when holding court at the Café Procope. 'Put aside the Holy Scripture and [Sodom and] Gomorrah,' he said, 'and you'll see that sodomy contains no more evil than the sin of Onan [sc. masturbation]. If this act were contrary to nature, it would be condemned by all those nations for whom the voice of nature [sc. reason] makes itself audible; however, it is condemned only by Christians.'[82]

A similar argument was advanced by the Englishman Thomas Cannon in his treatise *Ancient and Modern Pederasty Investigated and Exemplify'd*, a text which—astonishingly, given its nature—was actually printed in London in

1749, though swift action by the authorities led to the destruction of all the copies. While Cannon fled into exile, the printer was seized by the authorities; his arrest was beneficial to historians, as recent research by Hal Gladfelder has discovered a lengthy indictment of him in which many pages of the original text are quoted. Cannon's work began by commenting, with ironic pseudo-piety, that the 'Demolition of Pederasty' was one of the 'Unspeakable Benefits which redound to the World from the Christian Religion', and marvelling at the fact that 'curst Pederasts advance, that Boy-love ever was the top Refinement of most enlighten'd Ages; or, never in Supreme Degree prevail'd where liberal Knowledge had not fix'd his Seat, and banish'd crampsoul Prejudice.' Later in the text, he revived a traditional response to the argument from 'unnaturalness': 'Unnatural Desire is a Contradiction in Terms; downright Nonsense. Desire is an amatory Impulse of the inmost human Parts: Are not they, however constructed, and consequently impelling, Nature?... The Pleasure, all Beauty gives, is even of Necessity follow'd by Desire.' He also rejected the argument, which preyed on some eighteenth-century minds as it had done in the late Middle Ages, that sodomy would lead to depopulation. More unusual was his point that in all animals the male of the species is more beautiful than the female; despite his concentration in this text on 'Boy-love', he extended this observation to adult men—thus going well beyond the bounds of Southern European thinking about these matters. This was combined with outspokenly misogynistic remarks about the inferior psychology of women; and, to cap it all, he also included some rhapsodic and more or less pornographic descriptions of the pleasures of sex with boys.[83] It is hard to believe that a text containing such objectionable elements, if it had ever been allowed to circulate, would have done much to advance Cannon's cause.

Later in the century some Enlightenment thinkers, especially in France, did include more or less open defences of sodomy in their works. The standard arguments—that such areas of morality were culturally relative, that sodomy had coexisted with virtue and wisdom among the ancient Greeks, that the passions are natural or indeed that nothing that actually happens in the physical world can be unnatural—were developed by writers such as Helvétius and Diderot. The political author and participant in the Revolution the comte de Mirabeau (son of the economist of that title) revived Plato's theory of instinctive human desire, in which primaeval male–female, male–male and female–female joint entities had been split, leaving each half to seek its original companion: 'certain males, split from other males, have preserved an exclusive taste for their own sex.'[84] A few thinkers even argued that sodomy should be decriminalized. Condorcet did so on the grounds that it did not violate the rights of any human beings (although, as he thought it had a bad effect on the social order generally, he believed that it should be kept under control by public opprobrium—a view expressed also by Voltaire towards the end of his life); and Jeremy Bentham, who addressed this issue in a series of manuscript writings from the 1770s to the 1810s, concluded that he could find 'no reason for punishing it at all: much less for punishing it with the degree of severity with which it has been commonly punished'. In all these writers, hostility to the imposition of moral codes by organized religion was a strong underlying attitude. As Bentham put it: 'If then merely out of regard to population it were right that paeder-asts should be burnt alive, monks ought to be roasted alive by a slow fire.'[85]

One modern account of these matters points to a strand of radical Enlightenment theorizing which aimed at an 'erotic revolution, entailing a whole new culture of desire, voluptuousness, and pleasure'.[86] That such a line of thought can be identified in a small number of writers (some of them widely read, but some less well known, or confiding their thoughts only to unpublished manuscripts) may be true, but it poses the question of whether their thinking had any significant influence on society at large. Simple generalizations about eighteenth-century Europe being gradually transformed by the spread of Enlightenment values are not sustainable in this case. Mainstream Enlightenment thinkers such as Montesquieu con-tinued to view sodomy as 'unnatural' in a normative sense, and therefore as something to be restrained or repressed by government; indeed, a new type of justification for the punishment of sodomy was developed, based on its perceived weakening of society and the state.[87] It is certainly true that by the last decade of the century the treatment of sodomites was much less severe than it had been in its early years, with fewer prosecutions and, in some jurisdictions, the complete abandonment of the death penalty. Yet even in the one case where we could expect radical Enlightenment argumentation to have played the key role—that of the new Penal Code passed by the French Constituent Assembly in 1791—it is far from clear that it did; a modern study concludes that the legislators' omission of sodomy from the Code was 'simply a fortuitous and unforeseen consequence of their secu-larization of criminal law', as the offence, still connected in legal minds with blasphemy, heresy, sacrilege and witchcraft, was just automatically discarded with those other religious crimes.[88]

A growing distaste for applying the death penalty is visible in several societies. By the 1730s the punitive zeal of the SRMs had come to seem distasteful to many English people, and the execution of two ordinary workers found committing sodomy in the street in Paris in 1750 caused a wave of disquiet in France. There was a gradual accumulation of legal and governmental experience that tended towards a less savage treatment of such offences. In 1746 King Frederick II of Prussia wrote, in a letter to one of his senior officials about a man convicted of bestiality, that he normally commuted the death sentence in these cases to hard labour. Such miscreants, he explained, were ignorant common people, who knew little of religion; and many around them would be more scandalized than edified by seeing such a person executed. At the same time, he recommended that the convicted man should be visited by a religious minister.[89] There was thus no radical secularization at work here, but there may have been a shift towards treating some offences as matters for private religious instruction and improvement rather than as triggers for the descent of the full weight of the law. In that same year, 1746, the marquis de Vauvenargues published his *Maximes*, one of which said: 'that which does no harm to society is not to be dealt with by its judicial system'—a principle which, while not denying religious morality, required it to operate within its own domain.[90] Even that most unsecular of bodies, the Portuguese Inquisition, seems to have been moving in a similar direction. In the words of David Higgs, 'In the later eighteenth century in Portugal sodomy or homoerotic practices were prosecuted rarely by the Inquisition save in cases of child abuse, or sexual solicitation of male penitents by priests. Lay adults were left alone, or merely warned to mend their ways.' And indeed the tally of prosecutions there had been declining for some time: only 22 sodomites were sentenced in the eighteenth century, as opposed to 247 in the seventeenth.[91] The great waves of prosecutions and executions in England and the Netherlands seem, when looked at in this larger perspective, to have been temporary exceptions to some much deeper trends.

21

Conclusion: from sodomy to homosexuality

The time has come to address the larger issues raised by this account of same-sex relations in early modern Europe. Just before doing so, however, we should consider some of the limitations of the material studied here. The geographical coverage has been necessarily uneven; while the Mediterranean region and north-western Europe have been discussed in some detail, almost nothing has been said about sodomy in the Orthodox Slav world during this period, for the simple reason that very little research has been carried out on that subject. The best available treatment is a short section of a more general book by Eva Levin; it relies heavily on the texts of the Orthodox penitentials which, stemming from the Byzantine tradition, exhibit broad similarities from the Balkans to Russia. There are always uncertainties involved in extrapolating from the prohibitions of moral theology to actual practice; nevertheless, this sort of evidence does give some sense of the social and sexual world which the priests and their flocks inhabited. (As the great Slavic scholar Konstantin Jireček wrote, commenting on a report that St Sava, head of the Serbian Orthodox Church in the early thirteenth century, begged his flock with tears in his eyes not to engage in adultery, bestiality or sodomy: 'he would not have done that without a reason'.)[1] But more concrete evidence of actual behaviour is in short supply.

As Levin explains, sodomy was strongly reprobated in the Slavic penitential codes, which saw it as a sin against nature. At the same time, however, distinctions were drawn which suggest a certain pastoral familiarity with the varieties of male–male sexual activity: mutual masturbation and inter-femoral sex were given much lighter penances, and the relative degrees of responsibility of men and boys were also taken into account. Priests were advised 'to determine the age of the offender, the number of times he

Forbidden Desire in Early Modern Europe: Male–Male Sexual Relations, 1400–1750. Noel Malcolm, Oxford University Press.
© Noel Malcolm 2024. DOI: 10.1093/oso/9780198886334.003.0021

participated in intercourse, his marital status, his willingness, and the role he played. The usual leniency for young people under thirty held for homosexual relations... Two or three youthful homosexual experiments were viewed as a minor violation.' Passive partners who had been coerced would be treated much more moderately, and boys under twelve could be absolved without penance. Such details conjure up a very age-differentiated pattern of sexual behaviour; but at the same time there were authors who specified that 'the worst possible case involved two homosexual partners alternating active and passive roles, so that both parties were equally guilty.' There was also a specified penance for kissing another man with lust, set slightly higher than the equivalent for kissing a woman. And the fact that some priests objected to men shaving their beards, on the grounds that it made them woman-like and thus potentially the objects of lust, may be significant, as the objection was to such a practice by men of any age, not just by teenagers delaying the onset of fully visible masculinity.[2]

Occasional accounts by visitors to Russia testify to the presence of sodomy there. The poet George Turberville, who accompanied an English envoy to Moscow in 1568–9, produced a grim description of the life of the Russian peasants or *muzhiks*, portraying them as filthy, drunken idolaters who also practised this vice:

> Perhaps the Mausick [sc. *muzhik*] hath
> a gay and gallant wife:
> To serue his beastly lust yet he
> will leade a bowgards [sc. bugger's] life.
> The monster more desires
> a boy within his bed
> Then any wench, such filthy sinne
> ensues a drunken head.[3]

The German scholar Adam Olearius, who travelled through Russia as secretary to a diplomatic envoy in the 1630s, reported that 'some are addicted to the vile depravity we call sodomy; and not only with boys...but also with men and horses. Such antics provide matter for conversation at their carouses. People caught in such obscene acts are not severely punished. Tavern musicians often sing of such loathsome things, too, in the open streets, while some show them to young people in puppet shows.'[4] Samuel Collins, who spent the years 1659–66 in Moscow as personal physician to Tsar Alexei I, commented on the alleged sexual preferences of the Tsar's father-in-law, Ilya Danilovich Miloslavsky: he wrote that Alexei, 'perceiving

Eliah too kind to some of his handsome Tartar and Polish slaves... urged him (being an old Widdower) either to marry or to refrain the Court. For the Russians highly extoll marriage, partly to people their Territories, and partly to prevent Sodomy and Buggery, to which they are naturally inclined, nor is it punished there with Death.'[5] And in the bizarre case, investigated in 1715, of two Swedish soldiers, one of whom had persuaded the other to think that he was really a woman, that soldier testified that he had spent time as a prisoner in Russia, and that the Russian officers used to bugger boys; the Swedish court concluded that he had been corrupted there.[6] Such testimony is suggestive; but in the absence of corroborating evidence from within the culture itself, it is impossible to estimate how common sodomitical behaviour was, or how far it corresponded to either the Mediterranean pattern or the north-western European one.

Another limitation of the materials for this study is that there is relatively little information about the Western Mediterranean lands in the eighteenth century. The prosecution of sodomites in Spain and Portugal did continue; the number of cases was much lower than in the previous two centuries, but that probably reflects a shift in attitudes and policies.[7] There was certainly no major change in the nature of the sexual behaviour that came to light in those eighteenth-century trials. For areas where the Inquisition was not responsible for prosecuting sodomy, including almost the whole of Italy, the records of the ordinary criminal justice system have not been searched for evidence, so the available body of knowledge is very slight, consisting primarily of Inquisition cases involving heretical statements about the non-sinfulness of sodomy—which were typically made by men, especially ecclesiastics, to the youths they sodomized. (A modern study notes such cases from Rome and eight other cities from the eighteenth century, including that of the friars of Macerata in 1722—already mentioned—where three friars had sodomized a number of boys, sometimes meeting together to enjoy the same boy in turn.)[8] The only jurisdiction to have been studied properly is Venice, where Tommaso Scaramella has conducted a detailed analysis of sodomy cases in the period 1681–1789. He has found 153 cases in the judicial records, 128 of them post-1700. Roughly 10 per cent concerned male–female sodomy; 12 per cent may have involved consenting adult men; in 19 per cent of cases, the details are unknown; but by far the largest element, amounting to 48 per cent, did involve men having sex with boys. If we distribute the 19 per cent proportionally to the other categories, and subtract the male–female cases, the age-differentiated cases emerge as 70 per cent of the same-sex total. The frequency of such trials was less than it had been in the earlier period studied by Guido Ruggiero, and the nature of the punishments meted out was also much milder.[9]

Occasional comments by travellers and writers support the idea that age-differentiated male–male sex remained embedded in the culture. When Giacomo Casanova visited Ancona in 1744, for example, a youth called Petronio offered to work for him as his servant (and, when given a tip for doing an errand, responded by kissing Casanova fully on the lips). 'This Petronio', he wrote, 'was a real catamite, by profession. This is not unusual in the strange country of Italy [Casanova was writing for French readers], where intolerance on this subject is neither deranged, as it is in England, nor ferocious, as it is in Spain.'[10] Discussing social life in Rome in 1787, the Milanese adventurer and diplomat Giuseppe Gorani described the cult of good-looking teenaged male actors in the theatres, where women were still played by boys. There was much gossip, he wrote, about the love affairs between these actors and their patrons, and he explained—again, to French readers—that 'this predilection, which is known and avowed, is almost universal; they call it "the noble sin" or "the refined sin".' He was keen to emphasize, also, that prelates and cardinals were prominent among the suitors of these handsome boys.[11] It would in any case be surprising if the practice of paederastic sex had suddenly died away in eighteenth-century Italy, not only because it had been so thoroughly established there over at least several hundreds of years, but also because its availability would still be attracting northern European writers and artists to the Italian peninsula, from Venice to Capri, in the nineteenth and early twentieth centuries.[12]

As for the Ottoman world after 1700: there is abundant evidence that the sexual and cultural practices described earlier in this book continued for a long time. Khaled El-Rouayheb's work discusses the whole period from 1500 to 1800, and the essential nature of the evidence is qualitatively the same throughout. At one point, for example, he quotes lyrical descriptions of boys at the moment when 'beard-down' first appeared on their cheeks ('I was infatuated with the honey-lipped when he was beardless...', etc.), drawn from fourteen poets whose dates of death range from 1699 to 1780; elsewhere he cites a number of eighteenth-century historical and biographical writers who celebrated the charms of famously beautiful youths in Damascus, Aleppo and Cairo.[13] Abdul-Karim Rafeq's study of sexual mores in Damascus draws on evidence from the 1720s to the 1760s, confirming that the courting of boys by men was 'widespread and socially accepted'.[14] Comments by European travellers who visited the region in the late eighteenth and early nineteenth centuries indicate that the old pattern of same-sex behaviour still applied. One of them, the naturalist Charles-Nicolas-Sigisbert de Sonnini, who spent more than a year (1777–8) in Egypt, noted that the vice of sodomy was 'widespread' in that country: 'the rich man, like the poor, is infected with it. And whereas in cooler climates it has the effect of being exclusive, here, on the contrary, it is combined with a desire for women'—a comment which, coming from someone born and brought up in north-eastern France, clearly highlights a perceived divergence from Northern European practice.[15] According to El-Rouayheb, it was only between the mid-nineteenth century and the early twentieth that the 'prevalent tolerance of the passionate love of boys' faded away, thanks at least partly to the influence of Western European attitudes. And in some parts of the Arabic-speaking Mediterranean world, the old pattern of age-differentiated sex seems to have continued well into the late twentieth century.[16]

★ ★ ★

In 1976 the French theorist Michel Foucault published the first instalment of a projected multi-volume history of sexuality, in which he contrasted the modern 'homosexual' with the pre-modern 'sodomite'. As he aimed to show, homosexuality—understood not just in terms of the performance of certain sexual acts, or even the tendency to perform them, but rather as a distinctive way of being a person—was a purely modern phenomenon. Its emergence, Foucault argued, was inseparably linked to the development of new ways of categorizing people which arose in late-nineteenth-century medical and legal discourse, and thus related ultimately (according to his larger theory about culture and power) to the newly evolving ways in which state power sought to control its subjects. The category of 'homosexuality' was moulded by hidden power-structures; so too were the lives of the homosexuals, who now inhabited and embodied that category.[17] Indeed, the whole notion of a person having a 'sexuality', whether homo- or hetero-, was also a product of this relatively late stage of socio-political history. Before that major shift occurred, there had been sexual acts and sexual behaviours of various kinds, but not sexualities in the proper sense. And so, where male–male sex was concerned, Foucault set out the following distinction.

Sodomy, as it appears in the old codes of civil or canon law, was a category of forbidden acts; the person who committed those acts was just the juridical subject of them. The homosexual of the nineteenth century became a kind of person: a past, a history and a childhood, a character, a way of life...Nothing in his entire being escapes his sexuality. It is everywhere in him, underlying all his ways of behaving...It is consubstantial with him, not so much as a habitual sin but more as a distinct nature...The sodomite was someone who committed a sin; the homosexual is now a species.[18]

Over time, those words came to have a very large influence on the way in which historians approached this entire subject-matter. It became common practice to organize all large-scale historical treatment of it around a quest for the 'origins' of modern homosexuality. Looking for origins is not an invalid kind of historical enquiry, but when such a search takes over an entire field it can have a distorting effect, privileging some aspects of the evidence and downplaying others—which is why it has been avoided in this book. And there is another problem. All forms of complex human social behaviour have their historical origins, or at least their development over time up to the point where they became recognizably what they are now; but that earlier history typically involves gradual and multiple processes of change. To frame the question from the outset in terms of a radical contrast between the modern phenomenon and its pre-modern alternative is to set up expectations of finding a turning point, a transformation or even an 'invention', which, because of its suddenness and specificity, may be assumed to have had essentially a single cause. In Foucault's theory, the cause was the formation of a new kind of medical–legal discourse in the late nineteenth century. In the work of some subsequent writers influenced by him, the transformation (around the year 1700) has been presumed to have been both sudden and far-reaching, but no adequate causal explanation has ever been offered.

Another major effect of Foucault's claim has been to make historians think in terms of a clear distinction between sexual acts and sexual identity: the acts were things that the pre-modern sodomite did, while the identity constitutes what the modern homosexual is. In a simple version of Foucault's theory, adopted by some of his followers, the pre-modern sodomite could not even have anything like a disposition to commit those acts—the category could refer only to the acts themselves, and could not begin to characterize the actor. Foucault himself, as we have just seen, referred to 'habitual sin'; and it has been argued by one of his defenders that there is some room in his theory for pre-modern orientations or inclinations, even though he said almost nothing about them.[19] Yet the basic act/identity contrast is built into his account, at least at the level of categorizations by religious, legal and other forms of 'discourse', and cannot be wished away.

The main reason why this distinction has loomed so large in the historical literature is that in the years after Foucault wrote, all the research that was published on early modern Mediterranean sodomites seemed to confirm its validity and importance. And this was not just because so many of those studies were founded on the records of trials and judicial procedures, which are act-centred by their very nature—though that probably did have a reinforcing effect. Rather, the primacy of acts over identity seemed to be built into the whole nature of the pre-modern sexual behaviour itself. If, as Michael Rocke demonstrated, most of the Florentine men who had penetrative sex with boys during their early adulthood were also happy to have sex with women, and soon settled down to a life of marital sex with no more same-sex activities at all, what had distinguished them from other men was not any special identity but merely the fact that they took the opportunity of performing male–male sexual acts and other men did not.

While accepting this overall scheme, however, historians did make a major revision to Foucault's argument: as we have seen, they pushed the turning-point back to the beginning of the eighteenth century. The main reason for doing so was that in the large body of evidence from Northern Europe in the early part of that century there were clear signs of sodomites being referred to as a distinctive kind of people, in a way that went beyond identifying them just as performers of certain acts. William Huggins, the young porter arrested in 1707 for making an approach to an SRM activist at the Royal Exchange, offered the rather lame-sounding defence that 'he had hear'd there were such sort of Persons in the World, and he had a mind to try.'[20] As early as 1702 female witnesses in The Hague were referring to a house used by 'those people', and in the Dutch trials of 1730–1 one finds a range of phrases including 'such people', 'one of those people' and 'of that sort'. The usage was common to both the disapproving outsiders and the interested insiders: Zacharias Wilsma once asked Jacobus Backer, about a man they had gone to visit in Delft, 'Is he also one of those people?'[21] And in Paris, as we have seen, the police would arrest men, if found in the regular cruising-grounds, merely on suspicion that they were 'of that type'.[22]

Some of these early-eighteenth-century sodomites were quite clear in their own minds that they had a strong or exclusive sexual preference: a

38-year-old French servant arrested in 1724, for example, who, while explaining that he was happy to be either active or passive with another man, insisted 'that he didn't like women, that he had done nothing but fool around with men since his youth, that this pleasure was in his blood', or the 50-year-old (sieur de Ste Colombe), found masturbating in a park, who told the *mouche* that he had always felt sexual desire for men only.[23] A Dutchman in his 80s, questioned in 1730, said that he had never wanted to have sex with a woman, and that his only delight was looking at men and touching their genitals. And in Zurich in 1695 a rural minister, brought in for interrogation, explained that in the nine years since his marriage he had never had sex with his wife; he formed emotional attachments to adolescent farm-boys, whom he would invite to share his bed when his wife was away, but he said that his pleasure came only from touching their genitals. As he put it, he had a weak constitution which made him unable to produce children. He called this his 'nature'; he did not know why it was different from that of other men, and wondered whether he could change it.[24]

Whether all the men who came within the category 'that sort of people' or 'of that type' would have expressed such a strong, even exclusive, sexual preference is a more open question. Even a cursory look at the evidence will suggest that there were different degrees or kinds of possible identity. Some were more specific, some more general; some were more individual-focused (like that of the puzzled rural minister), and some more linked to participation in a social world. Large and unnecessary difficulties have been created by fixating on the most fully developed concept of modern homosexual identity, and then sending historians off to search for it in previous epochs—a quest which was always unlikely to succeed. At its most ambitious, the modern idea of sexuality rests on the principle formulated by the pioneering writer on sex Richard von Krafft-Ebing in the 1880s: 'a person's mental individuality, especially in its ethical, aesthetic and social feelings and endeavours, is mostly determined by the nature and manner of his sexual feeling.'[25] Even though arguments could be made for associating this kind of deep-rooted and far-reaching sexuality with a few earlier sodomites, such as the art historian Johann Joachim Winckelmann (1717–68) or the novelist and aesthete William Beckford (1760–1844), the assumptions that are bound up in it seem to belong much more to the world of Oscar Wilde (and beyond); there can be little point in using such a concept of sexual identity as the criterion for judging whether sodomites in past societies had any sense of identity at all.[26]

Instead of trying to impose one absolute and anachronistic concept of identity, therefore, we should open our minds to the more limited and particular identities that were referred to and thought about, and embodied in some people's lives, during the earlier periods. And for this purpose it will suffice to take 'identity' as involving any notion of a specific kind of sodomitical person, as opposed to someone who just happened to commit sodomitical acts.

One type which has attracted some scholarly attention is that of the passive adult male. As we have seen, European medical writers from Pietro d'Abano onwards had claimed that such people had a distinct physical constitution, and physiognomists had described the visible indications of it: 'soft flesh, fine throats, effeminate and often slender legs, large soft ankles, pale faces', and so on. In Joan Cadden's words, the consensus view was that this was 'a fixed category of the human male'.[27] Renaissance theorists could draw on a number of classical sources to develop their accounts of this type: not only the pseudo-Aristotelian *Problems*, but also the medical writer Caelius Aurelianus and the astrological authorities Ptolemy and Firmicus Maternus, who described the specific alignments of the planets that would cause a man to have this peculiar nature.[28] Another important source was the work of the Persian philosopher and medical writer Ibn Sina; and that had been just one contribution to an on-going debate in the Muslim world about the causes and treatment of *ubnah*—the condition of the *ma'būn*, who was always seen as a distinct type of man.[29]

That category clearly overlapped with another set of men, who consciously adopted female manners or dress as part of a general pattern of sexual behaviour centred on attracting other men in the hope of being sodomized by them. The comments of the late-sixteenth-century natural philosopher Giovanni Battista Della Porta have already been noted: in a specific discussion of effeminate men, he described one he had seen in Naples as 'more womanly than the women themselves: he spoke like a woman, and always called himself "she"'.[30] Other observers may have shared the use of the term 'effeminate men' in this sense (even though effeminacy could be understood quite differently in that period); but there was nothing like a fully theorized category, of the kind that had developed in medical writings on passive males. The significance of this evidence, rather, is that the individuals described in this way obviously had a form of sexual identity which went far beyond the mere commission of sexual acts. Examples of such people have already been given, including the Valencian friar Pedro

Pizarro, nicknamed by his colleagues 'la Pizarra', and the Mexican *mulato* Juan de la Vega, who adopted feminine manners, did women's work and called himself 'la Cotita'.[31] Within the great mass of evidence from before 1700, however, such cases are extremely rare; and even after that year, such gender-switching as a way of life (as opposed to a role-playing game in special circumstances) was still very uncommon.

The same is true of habitual transvestism, where the evidence is so sparse that it is hard to generalize at all on the basis of it—beyond the fact that here too a form of self-identifying was involved which clearly went beyond the level of mere sexual acts. In most of the very few known cases, this was associated with prostitution. Thus in 1354 a young man called Rolandinus (or 'Rolandina') Ronchaia was burnt in Venice for having spent several years working as a prostitute in female dress; John (or 'Eleanor') Rykener, 40 years later, plied his trade while living as a woman; and Antônio from Benin, in mid-sixteenth-century Lisbon, wore female clothing when going out to prostitute himself in the evenings.[32] It is less clear, however, whether this was a factor in the case of a boy arrested in Venice in 1641, who, 'pretending to be a girl, frequented the churches using female clothes, gestures and manners', and was condemned, after a period of imprisonment, to mutilation of the nose, ears and lips.[33]

A much more commonly encountered category was that of the habitual or persistent active sodomite. From a very early stage, the Church penitentials distinguished between those who had committed one act of sodomy and those who did it habitually.[34] A guide for confessors, written in c.1000 and attributed to Burchard of Worms, said that the penitent sodomite should be required to say whether this was a habitual sin; in the late sixteenth century the Portuguese Inquisition would emphasize, as a justification for more severe punishment, the fact that the accused was 'habituated' to sodomy. (And, in the same period, the great canonist Azpilcueta would try to get occasionally sodomitical priests off the hook of a papal bull by claiming that it referred only to those who were habitual sodomites.)[35] As we have seen, from the thirteenth century to the fifteenth, moralists and preachers warned that if a man could not be made to stop committing sodomy by the age of 30 or 33, he would be irredeemable; while the particular choice of age was theologically determined, the overall claim may well have rested on experience.[36] And in the tradition of medical theorizing just mentioned, physiological explanations alternated with psychological ones, in which habituation played an important role.

It might be argued that according to these ways of thinking, habit was just a mechanism for producing a multiplication of acts, so that invoking it would not involve any real change to the underlying act-based view. Yet, as we have also seen, early modern moral theologians developed quite a sophisticated theory of intentionality to analyse the psychology of such sins. Tommaso de Vio's statement that 'the sodomite is motivated by a person of the improper sex', and his idea that for a man to indulge in a sexual fantasy or 'lingering delectation' about another man was to commit the sin of sodomy, implied a very different understanding of the nature of a sodomite, clearly not based on acts alone. Or, at least, a very different understanding of the nature of some sodomites—and those would presumptively have been the regular and persistent ones. The Florentine records brought to light a number of men, known as 'inveterate' sodomites, who continued to commit this offence long after the age at which most men abandoned it; in Lucca the legal regime specified heavier punishments for such over-age offenders. And as Michael Rocke has noted, the great majority of the Florentine men in this category were unmarried.[37] What all this evidence indicates is the existence, which was quite widely understood (at least in Southern Europe), of men who were characterized by a distinctive orientation of sexual desire.

This was attested to by many writers. Bernardino of Siena, warning his flock that if they let their young sons go out into the streets unsupervised they would fall prey to the sodomites, exclaimed: 'Send your girls out instead, who aren't in any danger at all if you let them out among such people' (a rhetorical exaggeration, no doubt, but still a useful corrective to the modern theory about universally undifferentiated desire in this period— and also a noteworthy use of the phrase 'such people'). 'The sodomite', he declared in another sermon, 'hates women.'[38] Several literary representations of such men have already been cited: for example, the two characters in Boccaccio who are 'as fond of women as a dog is of the stick', the man in the fifteenth-century Latin poem who declares that 'no woman had ever disturbed my dreams', or Pietro Aretino's put-upon Stablemaster.[39] The strong emphasis on misogyny in these cases was perhaps a kind of literary heightening; among actual individuals of this type, there may well have been a much wider range of attitudes, from hostility to indifference to non-sexual affection. We cannot tell where to place on that spectrum the several sodomites who told the Lima Inquisition that they had no interest in women, or the landowner and civil servant Sir Anthony Ashley, who was described in anonymous manuscript of the 1620s as someone 'who never loved any but Boyes'.[40] And in some cases the preference for male–male sex, while definite, may not have been exclusive.

What muddles the issue, of course, is the fact that while the term 'sodomite' was used, in Southern Europe, for men of this kind who had a positive sexual inclination towards boys, its application was at the same time much broader. It was also used for the larger number of men who did have sex with youths but who, as all the evidence suggests, were at least equally interested in male–female sex and would turn to it exclusively before long. Those other men, indeed, are the prime exemplars of an acts-based version of sodomitical behaviour. So when we find a man described as a sodomite, it is not always clear whether this refers to someone with a special orientation, or just to someone who commits sodomitical acts. Marina Baldassari writes that in the seventeenth-century Roman criminal courts, 'the term *sodomizzatore* ['sodomizer'] specified a person who was known for his particular "inclination" for boys'; but in some of the individual cases it would be hard to say which of those two categories the man belonged to.[41] Nor is it always clear what people meant to imply when they referred to themselves as sodomites. But at least some men—contrary to Jonathan Goldberg's claim (summarizing Bray) that it is 'virtually impossible to believe that anyone might self-identify as a sodomite' in the Renaissance period—did exactly that.[42] When the chaplain at Basel Cathedral, Johannes Stocker, accused of seducing a choirboy in 1475, was obliged to put his signature to the sentence which condemned him, he defiantly added the words *presbiter et sodomita*, 'priest and sodomite'. The early-sixteenth-century artist Bazzi was content to sign paintings with his nickname, 'Sodoma'; Anthony Bacon allegedly told his page that 'there's nothing wrong with being a bugger and a sodomite'; and the baron de Blot was happy to proclaim in one of his poems that 'I am a dyed-in-the-wool bugger'. Most strikingly of all, Pietro Aretino declared in one of his that he was born a sodomite—and it is certain that he was referring there to a special sexual orientation, as the purpose of the poem was to celebrate the miraculous fact that he had just now been converted to the pleasures of sex with women.[43]

Another category of person that cannot be adequately captured by the 'acts' model consists of the males who fell in love with other males. This usually involved men infatuated with boys, though there are rare cases, as we have seen, involving strong emotional attachment as well as sex between people of more or less the same age.[44] Again, there was no standard category to be invoked when describing such people; most of the descriptions, which are by hostile observers, just express scandalized disapproval, tinged occasionally with ridicule. But the behaviour of the besotted sodomite—including, in the rarest cases, the writing of love-letters—is enough to show that something more than the mere performance of sexual acts was involved.

The categories mentioned above have been drawn mostly from the Southern European evidence. In fact they correspond quite closely to the forms of sexual behaviour previously identified as present but untypical in the Western Mediterranean societies; those contrasted with the typical pattern of same-sex activity, which we can reasonably describe as more or less acts-based. In Northern Europe there was no such 'default' pattern. Men had sex with boys, or with other men, or with boys and men; some men were active, some passive, and some reciprocal; and a significant number seem to have felt a sexual interest in the masculinity of their partners (or hoped-for partners), as shown by the touching of genitals and the common practice of mutual masturbation. Evidence of how such people were categorized at the time is sparse, beyond the terms for 'sodomite' that were used in indictments and reports of trials. Yet the nature of some of these practices does suggest that the men involved would have had some sense of having a particular sexual orientation—as, for example, with the long-lasting reciprocal relationships between adults recorded in Geneva in 1562 and in Bruges in 1578.[45] Generally speaking, it would seem easiest for a man performing same-sex acts to remain free of identity implications in cases where his activity resembled most closely that of a man having sex with a woman. The Mediterranean model, where the man takes the active role and penetrates only a 'beardless' boy, satisfies that requirement. But men in early modern Northern Europe who penetrated other adult men, or took the passive role themselves, or found sexual pleasure in handling other men's genitals, were surely more likely to be conscious of diverging from the normal pattern. And if they felt strongly motivated, over a long period, to engage in such behaviour, they would surely have experienced a sense of difference from most other men. Like that rural minister from the Canton of Zurich, they might have pondered the fact that they had a special constitution or 'nature', even if they had no adequate way of describing or explaining it.

★ ★ ★

The other fixation of recent scholarship, when trying to identify the origins or advent of modern homosexuality, has been with the concept of a 'subculture'. On some accounts, this is inextricably linked with the concept of identity, as the latter is thought to depend on a sense of membership of the former. As one theorist has put it: 'homosexual and heterosexual *identity and consciousness* are modern realities. These identities are not inherent in the individual. In order to be gay, for example, more than individual inclinations (however we might conceive of those) or homosexual activity is required; entire ranges of social attitudes and the construction of particular cultures, subcultures, and social relations are first necessary.'[46] To investigate the truth of that statement about modern homosexuality would fall beyond the scope of this book. But regardless of whether modern homosexual identity is closely, or only loosely, tied up with the existence of a subculture, it is entirely reasonable to ask questions about the sorts of subculture that may have existed among same-sex practitioners in the early modern period. What is not reasonable is to frame the whole enquiry in terms of a search for a special type of subculture that meets peculiarly modern criteria. Once again, we need to be open to the existence of subcultures of various different levels or kinds, as they appear in the historical evidence.

To start at the simplest level of practicality: for same-sex activity to occur, two people must meet, and this will happen in some sort of social context. In fifteenth-century Florence, it seems that a man could simply go out into the streets in the evening to find a boy who might be coerceable, or persuadable, or positively willing. There was some shared knowledge of rather basic behavioural codes—the most distinctive behaviour involving grabbing a boy's hat and demanding sex as the price for its return. There were also known venues, such as the fields just outside the city gates, for performing the sexual act. Certain streets and districts, containing notorious taverns, feature prominently in the evidence; and inns and taverns could also be used as places for sex. But we should remember that much of this activity mapped, behaviourally and spatially, onto existing patterns of male–female sex: those districts contained brothels, the inns could also host female prostitutes, and even the hat-grabbing game may have been derived from those prostitutes' regular practice.[47] So if we are to call this set of social practices a subculture, it will be in only a very rudimentary sense of the term. It involved no sense of membership, and what made it distinctive, beyond the fact that not every man engaged in it, was simply the fact that the sexual act itself transgressed religious and legal norms—which meant that tactics of concealment would sometimes be required. In some Italian and Iberian cities there were certainly male prostitutes and procurers, and therefore also clients of their services. If we were looking only at female prostitutes in the same societies, we might hesitate to say that the men who made use of them belonged to a special prostitution subculture; the claim may seem a little more plausible where male prostitutes were concerned, but the men who formed the clientele might not have felt that the difference between the two cases was a large one.

The term 'subculture' can be used for the shared practices and values of almost any subsection of society whose members interact in specific ways: ballroom dancers, Pentecostalists, and so on. But when reading historical works that refer to a subculture of homosexuals or sodomites, one often senses that the prefix 'sub-' is taken to connote some kind of underground existence.[48] The reasons for this are entirely understandable. The game of hunting for sex on the streets of Florence may have been played with unusual openness, and if Bouchard's description of early-seventeenth-century Naples is to be believed, the youths who stood on street corners waiting to be picked up were making little effort at concealing their purpose; nevertheless, in many other places more cautious behaviour would have been needed. Pedro de León, the Jesuit who ministered to condemned sodomites in late-sixteenth-century Seville, was convinced that such people communicated in a special way: 'they recognize one another by touch, and when one of them touches another one's hand he knows, by means of a certain sign that he makes, whether he is in on the deal, and whether he can make bold with him or not; they sense and perceive one another's thoughts as if they could read them, both in the very way they speak and walk, and in other movements they make'.[49] Even though secret handshakes are often thought to be the stuff of conspiracy theories, we should bear in mind that this priest had probably had more in-depth conversations with avowed sodomites than any other moralist of the time; his account may well have over-generalized from a few cases, but it cannot be simply dismissed. Possibly some kind of similar signalling was involved in the behaviour of the mercenary boy castigated by Pacifico Massimi in one of his Latin poems: 'Often he greets me, and often he smiles at me and gestures with his fingers; now he follows me, now he walks in front of me.'[50]

However, there are no other descriptions of this kind of encrypted behaviour—allowing communication between the insiders in the presence of uncomprehending outsiders—until we come to the gestural language of the early-eighteenth-century cruising grounds of Northern Europe. Less elaborate forms of guarded behaviour were probably more common. In Northern European societies there was a long history, as we have seen, of men using latrines as places where sexual approaches could be made; what protected them there was the element of plausible deniability, in a place where there was an innocent reason for exposing their genitals. More generally, however, when one reads the many accounts of Northern Europeans grabbing and groping at other men, one gets the impression that they would try this with strangers, without the use of any preliminary signalling at all. Perhaps in many cases coded behaviour to communicate their purpose was not needed, because the incomprehension of uninterested men could be taken for granted: the action would be viewed as a strange kind of inappropriate game-playing, not a direct invitation to mutual masturbation or sodomy.[51] Overall, there is little evidence in any part of Europe of a developed subcultural system governing such sexual encounters in public places until the practice of cruising began to be noticed towards the end of the seventeenth century. And there too, the behaviour was calqued upon an already thriving practice of male–female encounters in public parks and gardens. It could well be argued that in London, the key change was not the arrival of a special 'subculture' of male–male signalling, but the previous establishment of places such as St James's Park as venues for male–female pick-ups and sexual acts.

More promising signs of a subculture emerge from the evidence of men meeting in groups, typically indoors, for sex and/or for socializing. In a previous chapter it was noted that some of the claims in the modern historical literature about groups of sodomites in Southern Europe have to be treated with caution. The arrest of a number of men at the same time does not necessarily mean that they were having sex together; it may just represent the rapid unravelling of a chain or network of contacts. (And although it may be tempting to think that a network implies a subculture, that assumption too should be questioned—unless, once again, the notion of a subculture is to be used in a quite minimal sense. If a boy named three men who had sex with him, and two of those men each named two other boys, that might constitute a 'network' of eight individuals, but without implying that the network as such had played any formative role at all.) As we have seen, a small number of genuine groups can be identified. Most striking was the group of eleven mainly Iberian men in Rome in 1578, who socialized together and had sex in several permutations of couples. There was also the self-styled 'Academy' of the abbate Volpino in Naples in 1591, members of which engaged in parodic sexual games; and the group of four adults found having sex together in a private garden in Madrid in 1655.[52] To those we might add the group of sodomitical men in Lisbon described by a witness to the Inquisition there in 1643: 'all of these men continued to meet in the house of João Mendonça, and when they are there they talk of these filthinesses, saying that such a queer [*bobija*] takes pleasure of this *bobija*, and that so-and-so was good in his time.'[53]

In view of the sheer quantity of evidence from the Western Mediterranean, however, that is still a very small total. The simplest explanation of this must be that among those who engaged in same-sex activities there, the great majority were adult men who had no sexual interest at all in other adult men. Most of the participants in the groups just mentioned were, evidently or probably, members of the small minority of untypical practitioners. It is quite possible that a shared sense of their own untypicality motivated them to come together in these ways. Members of the sodomitical majority, practising 'normal' age-differentiated sex with boys, would not have had that motive; they would have felt little interest in discussing their same-sex activities with other men; and to form a club-like group with a membership that included boys, whose sense of confidentiality could not be trusted, would in any case have been a risky venture.[54] So although the particular groups just referred to clearly have some of the characteristics that would justify the use of the term 'subculture', what we see here appears to represent a very patchy phenomenon of mini-subcultures, representing anomalies within the larger world of same-sex practitioners in these Mediterranean countries. Even if we allow that other such groupings may have flourished without leaving a trace in the historical record, it would still seem unjustified to talk, on this basis, about a general sodomitical subculture in these societies.

The available evidence suggests, however, that one quasi-Iberian case of this kind was on a much larger scale: the world of the sodomitical house-parties held in Mexico City in the 1650s. As we have seen, there were several venues and regular organizers; the socializing included music and dancing (followed by sex); and the participants actually identified by the authorities came to 123 individuals, which suggests that the real total could have been much larger. Most were adults, but some boys were also included.[55] It seems that, while the Spanish had brought with them the regular, age-differentiated pattern of same-sex behaviour, this had supervened on other, local traditions, including the use of *berdache* boys or men, and the general lack of any taboo where the passive role was concerned. The result was a society with a more fluid set of same-sex practices, and perhaps one in which the strict prohibitions of Christian moral theology had still not been fully internalized.

These factors, combined with the opportunities for gathering like-minded people that arose in a large city, made possible the development of a kind of subculture, with adult sodomites seeking fun in one another's company, that could not have happened on such a scale in Iberia or Italy at the time.

In Northern Europe, on the other hand, there was no dominant pattern of age-differentiation to inhibit adult sodomites from gathering together. The real inhibiting factor, it seems, was just the relative scarcity of sodomites in the society as a whole. So the phenomenon was again very patchy, albeit for a different reason. Details have already been given of small groups of men acting together, in some cases for the purpose of mutual masturbation, especially in the German lands. Beyond that, there are the intriguing references to two larger and more organized groups, one meeting for dinner and sex at the house of Pierre Canal in Geneva in 1610, the other gathering every Sunday at a house in London 20-odd years later.[56] Did the second of these resemble the 'society' of men who, in Utrecht in 1710, were meeting once a week for mutual masturbation?[57] While the evidence does not permit any definite answer to that question, the possibility seems a reasonable one. Attempts at club-like sodomitical socializing would have been highly risky affairs in both places until the general relaxation of public morality in the latter part of the seventeenth century. But thereafter all the conditions were in place for the development of a subcultural life of that kind: men with a sexual interest in other men; sufficient numbers of them, in a large city (London, Paris) or urban network (the interconnected cities of Holland); and a policing and judicial regime which was sufficiently hostile to motivate them to meet behind closed doors, but not so oppressive—until the English and Dutch crackdowns took place—as to make even those meetings hazardous. The efflorescence of this subculture, which must have developed in the second half of the seventeenth century, but which became visible only in the early eighteenth, would have represented a significant change in the conditions and opportunities of quite a large number of men. But that does not mean that it endowed them with a whole new sense of identity—a quasi-modern homosexual identity—as they went about their daily lives; that claim, which misinterprets the limited evidence of effeminate and 'third-gender' behaviour (building it up into a principle of identity with which, one suspects, some modern homosexuals might well disagree), remains unconvincing.

To conclude: this subculture was probably a more developed and carefree version of a form of socializing that had a longer history; it did not create the sort of new, full-blown identity that has been attributed to it; and the idea that identity as such must depend on membership of a subculture is unnecessarily limiting, given that there is sufficient evidence to suggest the presence, in earlier centuries, of rudimentary but definite same-sex identities of various kinds.

* * *

The standard theory—as it has become—has not gone entirely unchallenged. Criticisms and alternative views have been put forward, though they have not prevailed. The simplest alternative is to say that we do not need to look for the historical emergence of homosexuality, because homosexuals, in one form or another, have always been with us. This was the approach of John Boswell, whose major work on the mediaeval period appeared when the new orthodoxy was in its infancy; he had no hesitation about referring to 'gay people' in the Middle Ages, who, he argued, would naturally form a gay subculture or culture if the appropriate conditions—urbanization, and public tolerance—applied. Reading the works of pioneering historians such as Boswell, who were also gay activists, one senses something resembling the mentality of the patriotic historians of newly formed nations, who are keen to show that the distinct people whose story they tell did not just come into existence recently; rather, it had a long and proud history. (Or, in a variant of that approach, a long and tragic history as an oppressed minority, which can now serve to inspire both sympathy and defiance.) This way of looking at the history of homosexuality set Boswell at odds with the followers of Foucault, who dismissed it as a specimen of 'essentialism'. A lengthy and largely fruitless argument ensued between 'essentialists' and 'constructionists'; the fruitlessness was intensified by the tendency of each side to take the most extreme version of the other's argument as typifying it. Fortunately we now have enough historical evidence to shape our interpretations, without having to submit them in advance to aprioristic theorizing of this kind.

In any case, most historians have operated in practice in the rather indeterminate middle ground of this debate. Boswell's category of 'gay people' was, despite its self-consciously modern adjective, a broad one, which admitted historical variation. As he himself wrote, in a later reflection on the controversy engendered by his book: 'I would no longer characterize the constructionist–essentialist controversy as a "debate" in any strict sense: one of its ironies is that no one involved in it actually identifies him- or herself as an "essentialist", although constructionists ... sometimes so label other

writers.'[58] No so-called essentialist had claimed that people's sexual behaviour was uninfluenced by the assumptions and practices of the society in
which they lived. And on the other hand, few constructionists took the
extreme view that people's most basic sexual desires were nothing more
than social constructs. The moderate constructionist position had been set
out as early as 1977 by Lawrence Stone, when he wrote that humans, like
other animals, do have a sexual drive, but 'the abnormal size and development of man's cerebral cortex means that the sexual drive is stimulated or
controlled by cultural norms and learned experience. Despite appearances,
human sex takes place mostly in the head.'[59] Anyone inhabiting this middle
ground, under whichever label, might want to reject Boswell's use of the
word 'gay' as anachronistic, feeling that modern homosexuality does differ
significantly from its pre-modern antecedents, but without rejecting his
view that some sort (or sorts) of same-sex-oriented identity did exist in pre-
modern times. Yet the issue of whether the move towards a modern form
of homosexuality was so transformational that it involved a deep and rapid
qualitative change remains a historical question; what has become the modern orthodoxy has answered it with a resounding 'yes', and most historians
have fallen into line with that.

Those who have objected to it have mostly done so for a range of particular reasons. Some have pointed to the mediaeval medical and scientific
tradition, with its classification of the passive sodomite as a distinct type,
presenting this as disproof of the general claim about sodomy being an acts-
based category before 1700. Others, for example, have noted the existence
of a recognizable type of effeminate sodomite in the Hispanic world long
before the 1700 watershed. Historians have also drawn attention to the
exclusively male-oriented sodomites described by Boccaccio and others.[60]
All these points, and more, have been valid in themselves; but they have not
dislodged the orthodox argument. And the reason for that is very simple:
that orthodoxy makes use of the mass of evidence put forward by Rocke,
Carrasco, Ruggiero and other investigators of the early modern Mediterranean
world, evidence which does display acts-based same-sex relations in the
great majority of cases. These objections, on the other hand, bring forward
examples from the minority of untypical cases. They cannot disprove the
general claim, unless it has been made so absolutely—as it has, by some
writers—as to exclude even the possibility of such exceptions. We shall
never make sense of the evidence unless we begin by distinguishing between
the typical and the untypical cases in these Southern European societies.

At the same time, we also need to recognize that the untypical ones fall into a number of distinct categories, such as the passive adult and the inveterate active sodomite, which may have had little in common. When the orthodox theory posits the appearance of a single new kind of person, the modern homosexual, around 1700, it displays a unifying, totalizing tendency which in itself seems very questionable. There are no good reasons why those who highlight the pre-1700 exceptions to acts-based sexual behaviour should adopt that same tendency themselves.

As for the Northern European societies: here one finds no general cultural evidence of a 'normal' life-pattern in which a man would happily sodomize beardless boys when he was a young adult, before settling down into a life of exclusively male–female sex; the mere fact that some cases did involve men and boys does not suffice to show that the Mediterranean pattern was at work. And among the variety of individuals that appear in the Northern evidence, one finds examples of virtually all the untypical categories in the Southern European societies: passive adults, reciprocal adults, effeminate men, inveterate active adults, men infatuated with boys, and so on. Again, there are significant differences between most of these categories; what unites them is the bare fact that they all involve sexual desire for another male.

It is possible, now, to put forward an overall interpretation of the European evidence, located somewhere in the theoretical middle ground mentioned above. To keep at bay the risk of anachronism, let us continue to avoid using the word 'homosexual' as a general historical term. Instead, let us just use the invented term 'same-sexual' to refer to any male whose sexual desire was exclusively or primarily for another male (while bearing in mind that the desire could take different forms and lead to different behaviours). And conversely, let us use 'other-sexual' for those males who preferred, primarily or exclusively, sex with females. Let us take as a working assumption the idea that in each of these European societies there was a small percentage of males who were same-sexuals. (This assumption is made without adopting any position on the question of why they had such a preference; it is sufficient for our purposes that the existence of such people is confirmed by historical evidence.) In all of these societies, religious and legal norms were set strongly against putting such desires into practice; those norms were reinforced by social disapproval, and may well have been internalized by many same-sexuals, in a way that limited or entirely precluded their acting upon their desires. And among those who did act, some would have found

ways of doing so without attracting attention—or, at least, the kind of attention that would lead to prosecution. So the actual total of people appearing
in the legal records, or in other sources available to historians, would be very
limited indeed; it would be a fraction of a fraction of the small percentage
of same-sexuals in that society. This model fits the available evidence from
Northern Europe.

It would perhaps have matched the Southern European evidence too, if
that evidence had contained only the cases that have been identified here as
untypical. But in these societies the small percentage of same-sexuals was
able to shelter, so to speak, within a larger quantity of other-sexuals who,
during part of their life-pattern, were happy to sodomize boys. This created
a very different set of conditions. The degree of (grudging) acceptance of
same-sex behaviour in the society at large was probably higher here, even if
that has to be off-set against the fact that in Northern Europe there were
people who would barely recognize the signs of same-sex behaviour in the
first place. In Italy in particular, the broader phenomenon of men having sex
with youths generated rather more cultural visibility for male–male sex
overall; within the range of literary references to it some room could be
found for representations of the untypical kinds, such as Boccaccio's exclusive sodomites. In some places, Florence being the prime example, same-
sexuals would have found it relatively easy to act on their desires—and the
more closely those desires were aligned with the prevailing pattern, the
easier it would have been. Men who fell in love with boys came closest,
attracting only disapproval or ridicule for the nature of their passion. Possibly
some same-sexual men who would have been happy to sodomize young
men above the watershed age of 20 adjusted their desires, consciously or
subconsciously, to fit the standard practice. On the other hand, those whose
desires were in conflict with that standard pattern may have felt even more
stigmatized, as a minority transgressing the principles not just of the majority but also of the larger minority. Even if the percentage of same-sexuals
who were able to act on their desires was greater here than in Northern
Europe, we should not forget that, outside the specially lenient regimes of
Florence and Lucca, such actions could always incur savage penalties.

★ ★ ★

If we accept this way of looking at the evidence, the question about the
emergence of modern homosexuality becomes altogether less problematic
and less demanding. The forerunners of modern homosexuals were the

same-sexuals who existed generally in Northern Europe (so far as one can talk about a general population which was so small and limited), and whose existence in Southern Europe was in effect camouflaged by a much larger body of other-sexuals engaging in same-sex acts. Seen in this light, the fact that the 'emergence' narrative has focused so thoroughly on Northern Europe becomes much less surprising. These forerunners were not the same as nineteenth- or twentieth-century homosexuals, but they would most probably be connected with them by lines of filiation and gradual development over time, as social behaviours and psychological types evolved. Even the lively subculture which appears so strikingly in the early-eighteenth-century evidence was surely a product of such a process of development; the suddenness of its appearance in the records no doubt reflects, as Rictor Norton says, only a sudden change in the methods of evidence-gathering. Thanks mainly to urbanization, quantitative growth could also affect qualitative change. But again we should guard against the tendency to squeeze the evidence into the mould of a single narrative. There were various different kinds of early modern sodomites. To this day, many observers would say that there are different kinds of modern homosexual; so one might expect the lines of filiation to form quite a tangled skein. One of the effects of the 'discourse' of homosexuality, as it was developed in the late nineteenth century and thereafter, was to impose a single category on what was surely a more multifarious human reality. But that, again, is an issue which lies beyond the scope of this book.

Looking at the historical evidence in this way also shifts the burden of explanation. The Foucauldian view was that 'sexuality' as such was invented or constructed at a late stage; so before it existed, there was just an open field of sexual possibilities. Within that field, behaviour might have been influenced or directed by power-relations more generally (penetrator exerting power over penetrated, and so on), but human beings had not taken on any sort of sexual identity which defined them. In a curious way, this strong version of constructionism rested on something that looks rather like essentialism: humans are all *essentially* free-floating in their potential sexual behaviour, unless and until a sexuality is imposed upon them. To historians influenced by the Foucauldian approach, the acts-based Mediterranean pattern seemed to confirm this as a historical insight: for men to penetrate both women and boys indifferently was a kind of natural, initial state of affairs, so that the only thing which needed to be explained was how a different system of behaviour had supervened. If the arguments set out above are correct, however, this state of affairs in the Mediterranean world is just as much in need of explanation, and perhaps more so. Same-sexuals, as they are called here, existed everywhere in early modern Europe; the acts-based, age-differentiated pattern of sexual behaviour did not.

Almost everyone who looks at this pattern in the early modern period begins to wonder sooner or later whether it is to be traced back all the way to Ancient Greece. Several have affirmed that it is, though only in the most general terms. Rafael Carrasco refers to 'a certain pagan atavism', derived from 'the great culture of the old Mediterranean'; Michael Rocke describes the age-differentiated system as 'an ancient institution in the Mediterranean region', which seems to have 'persisted strongly throughout this area during the medieval and early modern periods'.[61] David Halperin, a classical scholar as well as a theorist of homosexuality, writes that 'Possible evidence for an age-structured, role-specific, hierarchical pattern of sexual relations among males can be found in the Mediterranean basin as early as the Bronze Age civilizations of Minoan Crete... and as late as the Renaissance cities of Italy in the fourteenth and fifteenth centuries.'[62] Some mediaevalists have concurred: Mathew Kuefler argues that 'there is every indication that the ancient pattern of pederasty continued as the dominant paradigm for homoeroticism throughout the Middle Ages', while Marlisa den Hartog argues for a continuous tradition in Italy going back to ancient Rome.[63]

The strongest similarity lies in the main criterion used for age-differentiation: the advent of facial hair. The ancient Greek sources use the terms 'beardless' and 'recently bearded'; it was considered shocking for an adult man to court a young man with a beard. There was, however, a transitional period: facial hair began to appear at the age of roughly eighteen and a half, yielding a 'shaveable' beard by roughly 20½.[64] In Rome the full beard was expected in the 20th year; as Craig Williams puts it, 'just as in the Greek textual tradition, the arrival of a full beard often appears in Roman texts as a distinct signifier: at this point a boy is no longer a boy but a man and thus no longer generally desirable to other men.' In accordance with this, there was also a general taboo, in both places, against taking the role of a passive adult.[65]

On the other hand, there were significant differences between these classical same-sex relations and the ones we find in the early modern Mediterranean. While practices varied between different ancient Greek societies, the overall context was a process of socialization. In some places, such as Crete and Sparta, there was quite a formal system of mentoring and bonding between a young adult and a youth; sex seems to have formed part of this, but the main purpose was the induction of the youth—especially one from the ruling class—into adult civic and military roles. In the best-documented system, that of Athens, there was a cult of competitive admiration for handsome boys, but those boys were sexually off-limits until the age of eighteen, and the penalty for raping one was death. So the window of opportunity for sexual relations was narrow, lasting roughly two years. (The appearance of beard-down on the cheek of the beloved, commemorated by Arab poets as a poignant signal that the boy's desirability would soon begin to fade, was thus taken by these Greeks as the initial green light.) In Rome the lower age limit for sex was around twelve, and there were no complex social conventions involved—just one firm social rule, which was that freeborn citizens were out of bounds.[66]

It is far from clear whether the Roman system can be correctly described as merely a simplified version of the Greek one—or at least of some earlier system closer in kind to that of the Greeks. But it must be the case that if there was continuity between these ancient patterns of sexual behaviour and those of the mediaeval and early modern Mediterranean, even more simplification took place, eliminating socially stratified codes and significances, and reducing the behaviour almost entirely to sex. To make a strong case for historical continuity one would need much more evidence than is available; there is, however, just enough to make it seem a plausible assumption. St Basil, writing in the fourth century, warned against the inevitable desire felt by adult men for attractive boys, as we have seen. Near the end of that century, St John Chrysostom penned a fiery sermon against sodomy, on which Stephen Morris comments as follows: 'He seems to attach no blame to the active partners, as they are never mentioned in the homily. It is the classical Roman abhorrence of sexual penetration that we find in Chrysostom's text; presumably the man who does the penetrating is acting in accord with nature's dictates and thus is blameless.' A work known as the 'Sayings of the Desert Fathers', compiled for monastic communities in the fifth century, includes the injunction that 'beardless youths should not be accepted'; the writings of the Egyptian monastic leader Shenoute of Atripe (d. 465) contain denunciations of paederastic liaisons between older and younger monks. Salvian of Marseille, also in the fifth century, criticized men who engaged in paederasty and specifically mentioned the many boys who followed the army.[67] The poet Luxorius, writing in or near Carthage in the early sixth century, penned three poems reviling adult men who took the passive role. A brief Coptic inscription of the seventh or eighth century refers disapprovingly to effeminate young men.[68] In ninth-century Byzantium, poems in the classical genre of 'paederastic epigrams' were still being collected and read. Morris notes rules excluding beardless boys from the monasteries of Mount Athos in the tenth and eleventh centuries, and comments generally that the assumption that men would seek sex with boys was 'as true of medieval Byzantium as it was of the fourth-century desert'.[69]

The survival of a simplified version of ancient paederasty in the Byzantine world may be the key to the appearance of something similar in the world of Islam; for the first and most important phase in the huge territorial expansion of the Muslim Arabs was the conquest of the Byzantine provinces of Syria and Egypt in the period between 634 and 642. These were populous regions, with a well-developed culture entrenched in large cities; in many respects one would expect that culture to have had a greater effect on the conquerors than vice versa. Arno Schmitt has gone so far as to say that the Arab conquests did not alter what he calls the hellenistic culture which existed there, and that Mecca, Medina and Arabia were themselves gradually hellenized, as converts to Islam brought their culture with them.[70] There are, admittedly, some gaps in the chronology of the evidence here. As we have seen, the strong presence of homoeroticism in Arab literary culture begins only with the Abbasid dynasty, after the mid-eighth century; the textual record before that is very slight, even though it is clear from the writings of Abū Nuwās, produced near the end of that century, that the social world of male–male sex was already fully developed. Another imponderable is the question of whether the Arabs found something similar to the Greek–Byzantine sexual culture in the territories of Sassanian Persia when they conquered them. And there are larger questions about the possible transmission of what has here been called the Mediterranean pattern of same-sex relations, via Muslim culture, to territories further to the east. But these too lie beyond the scope of this investigation.

★ ★ ★

In addition to continuity from the ancient world, there is one other basic factor which may be relevant to the Mediterranean pattern of same-sex relations in the early modern period: the relative unavailability of women. The point here is not to offer an explanation at the individual level. It is not suggested that when any given Mediterranean sodomite sought sex with a boy, he was doing so only because he could not find a woman to have sex with at that time; no doubt he was following, at least to some extent, a pattern of social behaviour which had become established in its own right. The point is rather to look at a possible structural reason for that pattern itself. And whatever form that reason takes, it must involve something that differed significantly between the Mediterranean region and the north-western European one.

As it happens, such a reason is available: a difference in marriage patterns, which for several decades has been an object of study by demographic historians. In 1965 the statistician John Hajnal argued that the age-patterns of marriage had long differed between northern or north-western Europe and the eastern and southern parts of the continent.[71] The claims he made about eastern Europe need not concern us here; it is the contrast between the north or north-west and the Mediterranean region that is relevant to the history of sodomy, and that contrast has been broadly confirmed by subsequent research.

For our purposes the central consideration is the size of the gap between the ages at which women and men got married. Studies of societies in Iberia, southern France, Tuscany, Malta and Sicily, in periods from the seventeenth century to the nineteenth, have yielded marriage ages in the range of 18–20 for women and 25–29 for men.[72] Some earlier evidence offers an even greater age-gap. One of the strongest examples of the Mediterranean pattern is supplied by fifteenth-century Florence, where girls were married at seventeen or eighteen, while men waited until they were 30 or 31. The general view there, from the fourteenth century to the sixteenth, was that the man should be between 25 and 35, while a girl should be married in her teens, with the age of 20 as her 'last chance'.[73] In Renaissance Venice, eighteen was the standard age for girls, with men at least twelve years older; according to a mid-sixteenth-century treatise, the wiser sort said that the bride should be in the age-range 16–20, and the groom between 30 and 35, but others recommended eighteen for her and 36 for him.[74] Part of the reason for the high age of marriage for men was that in this mercantile and artisanal society they were expected to have already established themselves financially, so that they could set up their own home when they married. (In the merchant city-state of Dubrovnik the average age of betrothal for men in the fifteenth century was 33, with their brides typically aged eighteen.)[75] Women in the urban labouring classes, or in peasant economies, might delay marriage until their early 20s, possibly because they had to earn their own dowries.[76] A study of a village in the diocese of Parma in the second half of the seventeenth century gives an average age of 25½ for women; but as the men were typically 33, there was still a significant gap.[77] The key point is that for a young adult male in these societies, there would be many years during which the majority of the female members of his age cohort, and indeed of cohorts well below him, were *hors de concours* where sex was concerned.

In early modern England the typical age of marriage for a man was in the mid- or later 20s, with the woman only a little below that, at one, two or three years younger. In rural parishes in the seventeenth century, the median age for the man was between 24 and 26, and that for the woman was between 22 and 25.[78] A study of three villages in different parts of Germany, covering the seventeenth and eighteenth centuries, finds that rural men would wed between 27 and 28½, with their spouses averaging between 24½ and 27, while urban men were just under 26, and their brides roughly three years younger, at a little over 22½.[79] With many Northern European women waiting until their mid-20s, there was a larger proportion of single women in the adult population; and that figure was increased by a significant number of women who never married. (The general estimate is that nearly one quarter of the population, male and female, did not marry; this is the other fundamental difference between the northern and Mediterranean patterns.)[80] As a consequence, the total numbers of single women were remarkably high, especially in the towns. In late-mediaeval Coventry, Rheims and Zurich, such women made up more than 40 per cent of the adult female population. The English poll tax data for 1377 suggest that in the population at large, nearly a third of all women aged fourteen or over were single. In the Tuscan town of Prato in 1372, on the other hand, only 1.5 per cent of lay women reached the age of 30 without ever being married.[81]

The psychology of sexual relations must have been affected by these factors. In Northern European societies, with more unmarried women earning their livings outside the home, there were more regular opportunities for contact between the sexes; male apprentices and servants in fifteenth-century London could go looking for future wives on market days and in the local taverns. In sixteenth- and seventeenth-century England, it was also possible for young women to take the initiative in courting men.[82] What proportion of marriages were the products simply of mutual choice is hard to say, but it seems to have been high. Evidence from York in the fourteenth and fifteenth centuries suggests that the majority of first marriages there were 'companionate', something both reflected in and strengthened by the closeness in age between the two people: out of a sample of 47 couples, eleven were actually of the same age, with ten having the husband older by between one and five years.[83] And with companionate marriage to look forward to, both parties in a courtship might well have been aiming from an early stage at a combination of sex and affection.

Such a combination could have been achieved in Southern European marriages too, of course, but there are reasons for thinking that it was probably rarer. The fourteenth-century Tuscan merchant Paolo da Certaldo, in his advice book on good conduct, set out a common view: 'A woman is a very empty-headed and easily influenced thing, so when she is without her husband she is in great danger. So, if you have women in your home, keep them close to you, as much as you can; return home frequently, look after your affairs, and keep the women in fear and trembling all the time.'[84] The nature of the 'great danger' was known to all. Adultery, in the words of the fifteenth-century Florentine humanist Matteo Palmieri, was 'the supreme disgrace to decency, it effaces honour, destroys union, renders paternity uncertain, [and] heaps infamy on families'.[85] Women who gave birth to illegitimate children brought disgrace on their menfolk; so a girl was guarded by her father until she could be married, and then guarded again by her husband—whose resemblance to a paternal figure could have been more than merely notional, when he was her senior by up to fifteen years.

Fynes Moryson, who visited Italy in the 1590s, noted that 'It is the fashion of *Italy*, that onely men, and the Masters of the family, goe into the market and buy victuals, for seruants are neuer sent to that purpose, much lesse weomen, which if they be chast, rather are locked vp at home, as it were in prison.'[86] Historians and anthropologists are nowadays much more chary than they used to be about invoking general Mediterranean codes of shame or honour or machismo; but where the 'lock up your daughters' or 'lock up your wives' syndrome is concerned, the similarities between a range of cultures in the region are hard to miss. Commenting on acts of solicitation by lecherous priests in early modern Spain, Stephen Haliczer notes that the confessional gave them a unique opportunity to bypass 'the extreme restrictions placed on the freedom of all kinds of women to move through the streets, visit their neighbors, admit strangers to the house, or even attend church', which were grounded on 'the ubiquitous fear of loss of family honor through a lack of sexual purity among women'. One case he cites, from the late seventeenth century, involved a 31-year-old woman who was (very unusually) single, and lived a secluded life with her parents in the family home; they forbade her even to go into the nearby village. Having been the victim of a serious case of solicitation, she waited six years, until both parents had died, before reporting it to the authorities.[87]

For young adult men in these societies the unavailability of women for sexual purposes was of course only relative, not absolute. There were women whose work took them outside the home; and some better-off families had female domestic servants, who, as the Spanish evidence suggests, were frequently targeted for sex by the men of the household.[88] (Note, however, that such servants were much less common in these Southern European societies than they were in Northern Europe, where it was part of the normal life-cycle for a woman to be a domestic servant in the years before her marriage.)[89] And there were prostitutes. Their services were not expensive; the price in a fifteenth-century French brothel was between an eighth and a tenth of a journeyman's salary. General social norms opposed the use of prostitutes by married men, but permitted it for the unmarried; the stricter religious norms which prohibited all such fornication were not much enforced until the second half of the sixteenth century, when rulers began to shut down the official, municipally organized brothels, in a sequence of policy shifts running from a royal decree in France in 1561 to one in Spain in 1623.[90] In Florence, one of the arguments used in defence of officially tolerated prostitution was that if it did not exist, more men would turn not only to adultery but also to sodomy.[91] As we know, however, its existence did not succeed in preventing the latter in that city. At the simplest level, many young men may have preferred a form of sexual satisfaction which was free to one which came at a price, however small. Also, after the advent of 'the pox' in the late fifteenth century, many viewed female prostitutes as likely carriers of the disease; some may have subscribed to the surprisingly long-lasting popular belief that it was impossible to catch it from sodomizing a boy. And beyond these factors, there was an established social practice of seeking sex with male youths, into which young adults could easily be drawn—very easily, we may surmise, if they had been induced to take the passive role when they were youths themselves. Michael Rocke's argument that in the Florentine case this sort of same-sex behaviour was woven into the social practices of young urban males is well grounded, though we should be wary of extrapolating from Florence to other Western Mediterranean cities where the practice of male–male sex had to be a much more discreet affair.

The Florentine evidence does show a strong correlation between the age at which men married (c.30) and the age at which their sexual relations with boys entered, statistically, into a significant decline. This in itself is striking *prima facie* evidence of a link between sodomy and the marriage pattern. But it is also possible to speculate about a more general psychological connection at a deeper level. Men who were expected to have sex only with prostitutes in their first decade of adulthood, and then to have it with a much younger woman in what might quite often have been a non-companionate marriage, may perhaps have gained an attitude to sex generally that was merely transactional—notwithstanding all the ideals of romantic love to which the more literate ones were exposed through the works of Dante, Petrarch, Ariosto and others. This is not to say that such transactionality was uncommon in Northern Europe. But if, as seems likely, there was less of an alternative to it in the quotidian life of the Western Mediterranean world, that could perhaps have made it a little easier for many individuals to embark on 'acts-based' sodomy as a form of sexual behaviour. This point is suggested here, however, only as one possible factor in the background. And even the general point about marriage ages is surely not a simple explanation of the whole phenomenon of Mediterranean sodomy. In some ways it is the north-western European marriage pattern that is the unusual case (especially where the high percentage of never-married people is concerned). The later marriage and larger age-gap of Southern Europe may well be found in societies elsewhere which did not exhibit the same pattern of sodomitical behaviour. But it seems reasonable to suppose that where a long tradition of such behaviour existed, stemming probably from the ancient world, that tradition was more likely to be preserved and practised in a society of this kind.

★ ★ ★

If we turn, finally, to the Muslim societies on the eastern and southern shores of the Mediterranean, we find a broadly similar pattern there too. Detailed evidence of marriage-ages for this period, however, is hardly available. In eighteenth-century Palestine women were generally married off at an early age; 18 per cent of marriage contracts in Nablus were for girls even before puberty. A study of eighteenth-century Aleppo has found that while girls were married at 14–17, men would wed 'at an older age in order to prepare themselves for the financial burdens of married life'. In nineteenth-century Istanbul, the age of first marriage for women was relatively high, from 20 to 23, but the man would typically be around the age of 30. Among ethnic Turks in mid-nineteenth-century Bulgaria, the average ages of first marriage were between 27½ and 30 for men, and between 18½ and 19½ for women.[92] Leslie Peirce notes that women in early modern Ottoman society were normally married soon after puberty, in order that the awakening of their sexual desire would take place within the marriage; Walter Andrews and Mehmet Kalpaklı refer to the 'customary late marriage' of men as a factor which contributed to sodomitical behaviour.[93] In his study of early modern Ottoman Jews, whose way of life was close to that of the surrounding society, Yaron Ben-Naeh notes that 'many of the young girls were wedded at a very young age', whereas most of the young men 'had to wait ten, fifteen, or even twenty years to wed'.[94] Khaled El-Rouayheb, on the other hand, argues on the basis of several eighteenth- and nineteenth-century sources that early marriage was common for men too.[95]

One clear similarity between the Ottoman world and the Western Mediterranean, at any rate, was the desire to keep female family members under careful sexual supervision. The role of the father as guardian of his daughters was strongly supported in Islamic law; while opinions differed about the desirability of consulting a daughter about her proposed husband and gaining her consent (with some scholars definitely recommending this), the general principle was that the father could marry off a daughter who was *bikr* (virgin, unmarried) without consulting her at all. Once she was married, although a woman did have some rights to seek divorce that were not available in Western Christian society, the general ethos required her to live a modest life so far as possible within the home. The famous sixteenth-century Mufti of Istanbul Ebu's Su'ud explained that, even though this was not a direct application of Islamic law, it was important for a woman to be *muhaddere*, of honourable reputation, and that the way to achieve this was to avoid letting herself be seen by any males outside her immediate family.[96] Men had to police the behaviour of their womenfolk; Paolo da Certaldo's view of their sexual flightiness was fully shared by Mustafa Ali of Gallipoli, who observed that 'Men's failure to concern themselves with the protection of women opens the way to each [woman] succumbing to her animal nature and following the desires of her own heart and to their interacting with outsiders, thereby rending the curtain of modesty and shamelessly shredding the veil of chastity.'[97]

Just as some mediaeval Italians thought that the way to reduce the incidence of sodomy was to supply more female prostitutes, so some Arabs blamed the former on a simple causal nexus: the polymathic Christian writer Qustā ibn Lūqā al-Ba'labakkī, who died in 912, observed that sodomy was a common practice mainly because of the inaccessibility of women.[98] Ben-Naeh's study of early modern Ottoman Jews describes the situation of not-yet-married men in such a society: 'Added to the fact that many of the young girls were wedded at a very young age, separation between the sexes and the rules of modesty made adultery or even pre-marital sex difficult. Jewish and non-Jewish bachelors who wished to have sexual liaisons had, therefore, two options. They would either seek out prostitutes (usually Christian), or they could vent their urges on young boys.'[99] That is surely a plausible description of at least some elements of the social reality at work there. Count Radicati, in his free-thinking tract of 1732, may have been basing his argument mostly on cultural stereotypes when he wrote that 'throughout the Dominions of the *Mahometans* and *Roman-Catholics*... where the Husbands are excessively jealous, the Men for Want of Women, addict themselves to the detestable practice of Sodomy'; but that does not mean that he was entirely wrong, if the Catholic societies he had in mind were Mediterranean ones. And it is worth noting the comment he immediately added: while it was true, as objectors would point out, 'that there are Sodomites also in *England* and *Holland*, tho' the Women there have a very great Liberty', it was important to understand that 'they are in very small Numbers in Comparison with those to be met with in the Countries I mentioned.'[100]

Nevertheless, to state this causal factor in such simple terms is to risk falling back to the level of merely individual choice, as if each sodomite within the Mediterranean pattern of same-sex relations was pursuing a boy, at any given moment, only because a woman was not available at that time. If that were the implication, the theory would be a very inadequate one; for there are many cases of Ottoman men who continued with this practice long after they were married—so many that it must seem unlikely that they all belonged to what has been described, in the discussion of Western Mediterranean societies above, as the untypical category of inveterate sodomites. Once again we come back to the main difference between the Eastern and Western Mediterranean where same-sex behaviour was concerned: in the former, the cult of young male beauty and the practice of seeking a 'beloved' (with or without sexual intercourse, but presumptively with) were much more strongly embedded in the culture, and thus visible both in literary productions and in masculine social behaviour. In these circumstances, unlike in the Western Mediterranean ones, men who lacked a 'companionate' emotional–sexual element in their lives might even have been prompted to seek it in precisely the sort of male–male sexual relationship which, though forbidden by religion, was broadly accepted by culture and society. (Again this point is tentative; but it is worth remembering the commonplace Ottoman observation, previously quoted, that a boy, unlike a woman, could supply not only sex but also companionship on a journey or a military campaign.)[101]

If not only the pursuit of boys for sex but also the cultivation of their company and the celebration of their beauty, practices sharpened by social competition and expressed in poetry and song, were forms of learned behaviour, then a rather paradoxical conclusion follows. Many of the men who engaged in this behaviour were other-sexuals whose attitude to male–male sexual intercourse itself was similar to that of their counterparts in Florence and other Western Mediterranean places—that is, it was transactional and acts-based, not endowing them with a distinctive sexual identity. And yet at the same time their learned behaviour gave them roles to play which went much further than that, endowing them with interests and values above and beyond the mere satisfaction of a sexual urge. So they had acquired, in an 'acts-based' way, some of the apparent attributes of an identity, comparable to that of the romantic boy-lover in Western Europe, even though they remained, so far as one can tell, other-sexuals who were doing no more than follow a social script. This may serve as a final reminder that, however neatly theorists and historians draw up their categories, the sheer complexity and creativity of human behaviour—above all, sexual behaviour—may still evade them.

Afterword

The origins of this book lie in a chance discovery. Years ago, when I was preparing a study of relations between the Venetian and Ottoman worlds in the sixteenth century, I was working through the reports from the *baili* in Istanbul, in the Venetian state archive, when I came across the document which is presented in the first chapter of this volume. It struck me as unusually interesting, so I took detailed notes, thinking that I might write about it one day. My research for what became a later book, on Western ideas about Islam and the Ottoman Empire in the early modern period, had also involved reading a great number of descriptions of Ottoman society by travellers, diplomats and others, in which sodomy was quite frequently mentioned; this gave me a larger context in which to explore the implications of the Venetian document. As I worked my way through the scholarly literature on early modern sodomy, it became clear to me that there were new things to be said on at least three major issues: the existence of a pan-Mediterranean pattern of sexual behaviour; the difference (notwithstanding that underlying identity) between 'East' and 'West' in the visibility of that behaviour, a difference which broadly validated the reports by Western observers; and the fact that the pan-Mediterranean pattern was not pan-European, as it was not replicated in Northern European societies. I wrote a substantial article setting out these points, and sent it to a leading historical journal.

The responses which, nine months later, I received from the journal's referees were more than puzzling; they were bewildering. In three out of the four reports, key elements of my argument were misrepresented or ignored; one writer had not even noticed that the piece contained many references to Ottoman sources, bizarrely asking why I had not mentioned any. On my basic argument about the difference between Southern and Northern Europe, one wrote: 'Argument that this is a pan-Mediterranean

Forbidden Desire in Early Modern Europe: Male–Male Sexual Relations, 1400–1750. Noel Malcolm, Oxford University Press.
© Noel Malcolm 2024. DOI: 10.1093/oso/9780198886334.003.0022

pattern but not a Northern European one sounds unlikely to me. Best to drop this claim.' In support of it, I had offered pages of evidence, both statistical and cultural; this writer put forward no reason for dismissing the claim other than its alleged unlikeliness. That kind of uninformed dogmatism prevailed in many of these comments, involving an almost blind deference to some of the familiar orthodoxies which I was seeking to challenge. And I had to assume that if it were true (as the editor assured me, though otherwise I would have found it hard to believe) that these were experts in the field, their expertise must have been limited to the history of one society or another, rendering them ill-equipped to consider the sorts of large-scale cross-cultural comparisons that I was making. Their comments also included many demands that I supply further evidence, even though I had reached the maximum word-limit of the journal. For all these reasons I began to think that I would do much better to write a book on the subject, in which I could substantiate my arguments in full and explore many other aspects of this whole phenomenon in early modern Europe; and although a cosmetically revised version of my article was later accepted for publication (I hereby acknowledge permission to re-use some material from it), I decided to persevere with that larger project. If readers, having reached this point, believe that that was worth doing, then in a curious way they have those dysfunctional journal referees to thank for it.

I tell this story in order to explain why it is that a historian who has worked in a range of fields in intellectual, cultural, political and international history, but has never previously written about the history of sexual behaviour, came to produce a whole book on the subject. When I entered this particular field I did so as an outsider, and I hope that means that I brought to it a fresh pair of eyes. I am well aware that there are scholars who have been working on these matters for decades, and it will be apparent that I have benefited hugely from their researches. Indeed, without the painstaking archival work of Ruggiero, Rocke, Grassi, Baldassari, Carrasco, Perry, Berco, Riera i Sans, Molina, Garza Carvajal, Tortorici, Mott, Vainfas, van der Meer, Boon, Puff, Hergemöller, Norton and many others, a book such as this could never have been written. A great many authors have contributed to the growth of knowledge and understanding in this field that has taken place in the last four decades or so. But on the larger interpretative issues they have tended over time to form—with some notable dissenting exceptions—a mutually reinforcing system of belief, which may seem hard to question from within.

Another, perhaps related, problem has been the role of what has to be called wishful thinking. Many examples have been given in this book, from Bray's basic assumption about the widespread nature of male–male sex in Renaissance England to the frequent cases of modern literary historians reading anachronistic sexual significances into early modern texts.[1] I have commented above, in passing, on the parallel with historians of so-called new nations, eager to find their own nationals in past epochs. The problems this attitude can give rise to are not only quantitative (recruiting individuals to whom this category should not be applied) but also qualitative, as it tends to project a relatively unchanging identity into the past. As the literary historian Jim Ellis has noted, 'gay studies depends to a certain extent on an investment in essentialism and identity politics for its very existence, both actual and intellectual.'[2] Some writers have even criticized the constructionist approach on the grounds that it may have an undesirable effect on modern identity politics; thus Bruce Smith has complained that, because of constructionism, 'sexual minorities ... are being denied the legitimacy of a history'.[3] Yet the socio-political consequences of adopting a particular method of interpreting the past should be just that—consequences, not causes. And while it is of course true that we all bring to the study of the past some prior assumptions about how to interpret human behaviour, nevertheless a central part of our role as historians is to keep questioning, testing and modifying those assumptions as we gradually learn more about the ways in which the past differs from the present. That process cannot benefit from being subordinated to present-day social or political requirements, however potentially beneficial those requirements might seem to be in contemporary terms. As Richard Trexler has said, there may be a 'price ... [that] researchers pay when they allow their own personal search for identity to determine their reading of the past'.[4]

This may make it sound as if the pressures of gay activism have been directed mainly in the 'essentialist' direction. But, if anything, it is the hardline constructionists who have been most clearly and openly driven by an agenda. Sometimes this has been explicitly political. Writing a few years after Foucault's account of sexuality was published, Robert Padgug declared that 'Through a better understanding of how capitalist societies developed, and are continuing to develop, the modern ideology of sexuality ... we will better understand the specific role it plays in legitimating contemporary society and in defusing class struggle, as well as its contradictory potentialities for undermining the capitalist system.'[5] Just over a decade later, David

Halperin published a study of sodomy in ancient Greece, *One Hundred Years of Homosexuality*, in which he trained the heavy artillery of Foucauldian theory on his target. As he later explained:

> My aim was not to champion the cause of a homosexual minority that might be imagined to have existed in every human society, for to do that would be merely to pay heterosexuality the backhanded (and undeserved) compliment of being the normal and natural condition for the majority of human beings in all times and places. My purpose in historicizing homosexuality was *to denaturize heterosexuality*, to deprive it of its claims to be considered a 'traditional value', and ultimately to destroy the self-evidence of the entire system on which the homophobic opposition between homosexuality and heterosexuality depended.[6]

Again, attacking current assumptions about heterosexuality in this way may or may not have beneficial consequences; but the desirability of those consequences is not something that should dictate a historian's handling of the past. As for the approach taken in this book: I can only say that I have come to this subject with no personal investment in it and no axe to grind, pursuing neither of the activist agendas just mentioned. I am not so naïve as to believe that that must make me a perfectly objective judge; but I have done my best to consider evidence as evidence, and theoretical schemes as things that should be treated as ways of making sense of that evidence, not as ways of bringing about desired changes in the present. If a note of scepticism has crept in here or there when discussing grand aprioristic theories about the past, that is simply because of their *a priori* nature. To be sceptical is, I believe, the 'default mode' which every historian has a duty to adopt.

★ ★ ★

One final point remains to be explained: the limitation of this study to male–male sexual relations, leaving aside female–female ones. My analysis of the male–male story has led me to agree with the moderate constructionist view (with which moderate essentialists may also concur) that there is a significant difference between modern homosexuality and the behaviours and mentalities discussed in this book. This is most obviously the case with the Mediterranean pattern; but the untypical Southern European sodomites, and those belonging to the general range of Northern European ones, do also seem to have differed in important ways from those people today who have a definite sense of what homosexuality is and identify with it— even though I believe that further research would most likely find processes of continuous development from what I have called the same-sexuals of the past to the homosexuals of the present. The assumption that there is a single basic category of 'homosexuality', such that any proper account of it must cover both men who have sex with men and women who have sex with women, is itself distinctively modern. As a historian of the early modern period, I cannot feel bound by it.

It is true that, as we have seen, some of the classificatory schemes set out by mediaeval theologians did include female–female sex among the 'sins against nature'. Sometimes that general category of sins was referred to broadly as sodomy, and sometimes not; some writers, having mentioned male–male sex, did then add a reference to the female–female sort, often in a kind of reflex acknowledgement of the verse in the Epistle to the Romans which mentioned both together, while others did not. If the textbook classifications of the period are to dictate how historians organize their material today, then histories should be written not of homosexuality but of sins against nature, as a category embracing male–male sex, female–female sex, bestiality, male–female anal sex, solitary masturbation and mutual masturbation. (Brief discussions of several of these topics have in fact been included here, but only because of their relevance to the actual subject-matter of this book, not simply because of their presence in those early classificatory schemes.) However, what matters most of all is not the theoretical listings in the textbooks of the time, but the actual assumptions that moulded the feelings and behaviour of people in these societies; and here the relation between male–male sex and female–female sex is much more tenuous, so far as the early modern period is concerned. I can see no evidence that males who had sex with other males—even in Northern Europe; still less in Southern Europe—felt any sort of similarity to, let alone commonality with, females who had sex with females.

That would probably have been true even if female–female sex had been widely noticed and commented upon. But reported cases were rare, and so too were literary representations based on observed realities.[7] It would be quite wrong to imagine that women who had sex with other women were always so neglected that they enjoyed, in effect, a 'free pass' in these societies; in some jurisdictions, especially in Northern Europe, women were convicted and even executed for such offences.[8] (The authorities in Southern Europe seem to have taken less interest; a few cases are recorded in Spain, but the Valencian Inquisition prosecuted none at all. Such cases were also very rare in Latin America, with the exception of Brazil, where the

Inquisition did process a number of women for same-sex acts.)[9] Nevertheless, the overall body of evidence that emerges from the archives is tiny in comparison with the surviving records of male–male sexual relations. And what we do know about female–female sex seems not to correlate in any significant way with the observable male–male patterns of behaviour; there is, for example, nothing equivalent to age-differentiation in Southern European societies, and the developmental steps in the male–male history, such as they are (the emergence of rudimentary forms of subculture, for example), do not have any clear counterparts on the female–female side. The history of sex between women in early modern Europe is an important subject, but it seems to have run its own course quite separately from that of male–male sex, and the mere fact that the two phenomena were linked in some legal or theological classifications does not suffice to turn those two different stories into a single one. Often, when reading general histories of 'homosexuality' which include this period, one finds that at the end of a chapter devoted almost entirely to the male–male evidence, a few brief paragraphs about women's relations with women have been rather dutifully appended. The intention to be inclusive may be a very good one in contemporary human terms, but the unintended effect is to create an impression of tokenism. That is one more reason why such an approach has not been attempted here.

★ ★ ★

I am very grateful to the staff of all the libraries and archives in which research for this book has been carried out. Some are named in the List of Manuscripts; to those I would add the Library of All Souls College, Oxford; Cambridge University Library; and the Library of the Warburg Institute, London. During the period of the Covid pandemic I also benefited from the generosity of various publishing houses, and other resources, that made their texts freely available online; I should like to express my thanks to them too. I am extremely grateful to a number of friends and colleagues who read chapters or sections of chapters of this book, and provided very helpful comments and suggestions: Colin Burrow, James Hankins, Peregrine Horden, Deni Kasa, Fitzroy Morrissey and Jacob Willer. Many thanks also to Uran Ferizi, for all his patient work as a reader. I am greatly indebted to Keith Thomas, who uncomplainingly took on the task of reading the entire work in typescript; for more than 50 years, his own work has set a gold standard when it comes to understanding the mentalities and behaviours of people from the early modern period, so it was deeply reassuring to know that this book passed his scrutiny. But finally my greatest debt of gratitude, as always, is to the Warden and Fellows of All Souls College, Oxford, for continuing to provide the perfect conditions in which to pursue scholarly research and writing.

Notes

CHAPTER I

1. On the *baili* and bailate see E. R. Dursteler, *Venetians in Constantinople: Nation, Identity and Coexistence in the Early Modern Mediterranean* (Baltimore, 2006), pp. 25–40; on the trainees see F. Lucchetta, 'La scuola dei "giovani di lingua" veneti nei secoli XVI e XVII', *Quaderni di studi arabi*, 7 (1989), pp. 19–40.

2. Matteca's services were strongly criticized in 1574 and 1592–3 (V. Lamansky, *Secrets d'état de Venise: documents, extraits, notices et études* (St Petersburg, 1884), pp. 102–5), yet he seems to have remained in Venetian employ throughout that period. A complicating detail was the fact that the bailate building was rented from Matteca's family: see B. Simon, 'Les Dépêches de Marin Cavalli Bayle à Constantinople, 1558–1560', École Pratique des Hautes Études, Paris, doctoral thesis (1985), 2 vols., i, p. 281.

3. E. Albèri, ed., *Relazioni degli ambasciatori veneti al Senato durante il secolo decimosesto*, ser. 3, *Relazioni dagli Stati Ottomani*, 3 vols. (Florence, 1840–55), ii, pp. 321–426, relazione of Lorenzo Bernardo (1592), at p. 417.

4. Ibid., i, pp. 251–322, relazione of Morosini (1585), at pp. 319–20.

5. Archivio di Stato, Venice (hereafter: 'ASV'), Capi del Consiglio dei Dieci, Dispacci (Lettere) di Ambasciatori (hereafter: 'CCD, DA'), busta 6 (Costantinopoli, 1581–99), item 99, letter of *bailo* Giovanni Moro, 10 Sept. 1588 (designated by Senate).

6. M. P. Pedani-Fabris, ed., *Relazioni di ambasciatori veneti al Senato*, xiv: *Costantinopoli: relazioni inedite (1512–1789)* (Padua, 1996), p. 392 ('ultimamente', 'di spirito molto vivo').

7. ASV, CCD, DA, busta 6, item 103, fo. [1r].

8. G. Colavizza, R. Cella and A. Bellavitis, 'Apprenticeship in Early Modern Venice' (2017): <https://www.researchgate.net/publication/318284139_Apprenticeship_in_Early_Modern_Venice>, pp. 12–13. On the guild, and the medical roles, see W. Eamon, 'Science and Medicine in Early Modern Venice', in E. R. Dursteler, ed., *A Companion to Venetian History, 1400–1797* (Leiden, 2013), pp. 701–41, at pp. 722–3.

9. ASV, CCD, DA, busta 6, item 99 ('hauendolo fatto riprendere, et ripreso ancor io stesso alcune uolte, in fine mi conuenne licentiarlo, come per innanzi gli haueuo protestato che farei, s'egli non mutasse uita, et costumi').

10. Ibid., item 100, fo. [1r] ('tutti quelli che mangiano al Tinello, perche si bas-
    ciauano alla finestra del camerino di esso m[esser] Gianesin, che stando nel
    tinello si poteuano uedere', 'no[n] sò, mà sò bene che tutti di casa diceuano che
    si faceuano uergogne l'un l'altro insieme', 'V. S. Ill.ma se lo può bene imagin-
    are', 'come se si negotiassero', 'no[n] sò, mà sono stati molte uolte serrati nel
    camerino, et tutti di casa lo han[n]o potuto uedere'). The last phrase presum-
    ably means that everyone could see that they were together in the room, not
    that they could see them performing sexual acts.

11. Ibid., item 100, fo. [1v] ('hò ueduto ch[e] giocauano insieme, et ch[e] si cor-
    reuano dietro', 'et tutti di casa'); item 101, fo. [1r] (silence).

12. Ibid., item 102, fo. [1r] (silk, gloves, cap); item 103, fo. [1v] (knife). Coins were
    also mentioned by one witness: ibid., 104, fo. [1r].

13. Ibid., item 101, fo. [1v] ('se fussero le forche preparate', 'no[n] è cosa, ch[e]
    no[n] facesse per lui').

14. Ibid., item 104, fo. [1r] ('haueria messo la uita per lui', 'il Barbiero fusse inam-
    orato in Gianesin, et Gianesin in lui').

15. Ibid., item 102, fo. [1r] ('si uagheggiauano insieme'); item 104, fo. [3r] ('dopò
    ch[e] V. S. Ill:ma commandò ch[e] no[n] douessero parlarsi insieme, si faceuano
    cenni trà loro, et se poteuano ritrouarsi in alcun luoco, ragionauano anco, mà
    come se[n]tiuano à uenire alcuno, si separauano').

16. Ibid., item 104, fo. [1r].

17. Ibid., item 102, fo. [1r] ('Gregorio si era offerto di dargli da negotiar, si [sic]
    hauesse uoluto accommodarlo del cauallo, et il Turco ricusò di farlo, dicendo di
    hauer sua moglie').

18. Ibid., item 104, fo. [1r] ('fatto poltronarie', 'potria esser co[n] M[esser]
    Marc'Ant:o Scalco, perch[e] andauano necess:o insieme, doue stauano le hore').

19. Ibid., item 102, fo. [1v]–item 103, fo. [1r] ('si uogliano bene, mà no[n] per
    pecato', 'no[n] hò altro, se no[n] ch[e] li hò uisti à basciarsi', 'doue no[n] si
    basciauano? in sala, in cucina, et al forno', 'io dormiuo co'l barbiero, et alcune
    notte è uenuto m[esser] Gianesin, mà io no[n] me ne accorgeuo seno[n] la
    matina, quando el si uoleua uestir', 'io mi trouauo da una banda, et teneuo
    poco luoco, et loro dormiuano dall'altra banda; me ne son anco accorto alcune
    uolte, ch'è uenuto la sera, et per q[ue]sto no[n] uoleuo più dormir là', 'sentiuo
    ch[e] ragionauano insieme, mà no[n] poteuo intender le parole; pareua anco
    ch[e] si basciassero, mà se facessero altro no lo posso dir certamente, ma se'l
    fusse una donna hauerei creduto, che si facessero quel seruitio insieme').

20. Ibid., item 104, fo. [5v] ('dirò il uero. Io l'ho amato grand:te, haueuo piacer di
    trouarmi con lui, et hò dormito più uolte seco', 'Io l'ho basciato, et ogn'uno
    crederia che fusse uero, mà però no[n] è così', 'Sig:ri nò', 'sig:ri sì co[n] m[esser]
    M. Antonio Scalco', 'due uolte, ch'egli me ne ricercò').

21. Ibid., item 99 ('perche fù egli persuaso à lasciarsi intender che si farebbe Turco,
    son andato differendo per ottener prima un commandamento di poterlo man-
    dar in ferri, accioche sotto questo, ò altro pretesto non mi fusse leuato dal
    Vassello', carver, Gianesino). Gianesino was restored to his position by the time

of Lorenzo Bernardo's return as acting *bailo* in 1591–2: Albèri, ed., *Relazioni*, ii, p. 417.

22. ASV, CCD, DA, busta 6, item 104, fos. [4v] ('no[n] sò ch[e] ui sia altra intrinsi-chezza, ch[e] quella che è trà noi altri'), [5r] ('andauano qualche uolta in cre-denza, et si correuano dietro burlando insieme').

23. Ibid., item 103, fo. [1r] ('tutti noi glielo habbiamo detto, et credo, ch[e] no[n] sia nessuno in casa, che non l'habbia auuertito').

24. Ibid., item 104, fo. [1v]. He also said that he had reproved both men 'four times, six times, but they replied each time that it was a false imputation' ('4, et 6 uolte, mà essi tal hora rispondeuano, ch[e] era una falsa imputat:^{ne}').

25. Ibid., item 103, fo. [1r] ('mi dauano la burla').

26. Ibid., item 103, fo. [1r] ('si andaua uantando p[er] Galatà di hauer negotiato il barbiero'); item 104, fos. [1v–2r] ('mi dimandò qual era il barbiero, ch[e] si diceua esser amato da Gianesin, et io comprendendo q[ue]llo ch'egli uolesse dire, gli mostrai un'altro seru:^{re}, il q[ua]le essendo brutto di faccia, si pose à rider, et [s'accade?] ch'io no[n] glie lo uolsi mostrare'). This last detail may suggest that Agudi's motive for wanting to see the attractive young barber derived from sexual interests of his own.

27. A notorious scandal involving sodomy did occur at the Venetian embassy in Rome in 1486; what made it serious, however, was not only the fact that the ambassador himself was one of the parties, but also the fact that he revealed diplomatic secrets to the boy, who then transmitted them to the Cardinal of Naples. See Anon. [G. Lorenzi], *Leggi e memorie venete sulla prostituzione fino alla caduta della republica* (Venice, 1870–2), pp. 238–9.

CHAPTER 2

1. Anon. [G. Lorenzi], *Leggi e memorie*, p. 235 ('ragatio christiano etatis satis adulte'); R. Canosa, *Storia di una grande paura: la sodomia a Firenze e a Venezia nel Quattrocento* (Milan, 1991), p. 125. The boy was whipped, imprisoned for one year, and then banished—punishments which, as we shall see, suggest that he was no older than his teens.

2. M. P. Pedani, *In nome del Gran Signore: inviati ottomani a Venezia dalla caduta di Costantinopoli alla guerra di Candia* (Venice, 1994), p. 84 ('un bel ragazzo').

3. K. Teply, 'Vom Loskauf osmanischer Gefangener aus dem Grossen Türkenkrieg, 1683–1699' *Südost-Forschungen*, 32 (1973), pp. 33–72, at p. 68.

4. T. van der Meer, *Sodoms zaad in Nederland: het ontstaan van homoseksualiteit in de vroegmoderne tijd* (Nijmegen, 1995), pp. 109–10 ('soekende hem op allerleij wijzen te persuadeeren, dat hij met hem nae Turkijen soude meede gaan met betuijging van de grote lieffde die hij voor hem had', 'grote force').

5. D. A. Coward, 'Attitudes to Homosexuality in Eighteenth-Century France', *Journal of European Studies*, 10, no. 40 (1980), pp. 231–55, at p. 244.

6. J. van der Does ['G. Dousa'], *De itinere suo constantinopolitano epistola* (Leiden, 1599), pp. 30–1 ('Eorum enim pulchritudo passim Co[n]stantinopoli felium

pullariaru[m] insidiis obnoxia: Quod etiam quidam Nobilis Polonus, cum Oratore sui Regis eò appulsus, expertus est, cuius fidei ac patrocinio ingenuae indolis ac formae puer concreditus harpaces plagiariorum manus effugere non potuit. In deuio aliquo Vrbis angiportu furtim abreptus, ac nescio quo terrarum asportatus').

7. A. Hill, *A Full and Just Account of the Present State of the Ottoman Empire in All its Branches* (London, 1709), pp. 80–1.

8. J. P. Laugier de Tassy, *Histoire du royaume d'Alger, avec l'état présent de son gouvernement* (Amsterdam, 1725), pp. 120–1 ('Il vit un jeune garçon nud, la chemise sur la tête, se défendant de son mieux. Il crût qu'on se rejouissoit autrement qu'on ne faisoit, & prétendit avoir part au plaisir. Il mit son demi-sabre à la main pour écarter les autres domestiques, & se saisit de celui qu'on vouloit fesser', 'nous... eumes bien de la peine à faire sortir le Turc, & à lui persuader que ce n'étoit pas ce qu'il pensoit'). Laugier de Tassy observed that generally the authorities in Algiers disapproved of beatings on bare buttocks as a punishment, because of the temptation that this would occasion.

9. T. P. Graf, *The Sultan's Renegades: Christian-European Converts to Islam and the Making of the Ottoman Elite, 1575–1610* (Oxford, 2017), pp. 84–5, 91–4, 99–101, 139–42; F. Seidel, *Denckwürdige Gesandtschafft an die Ottomanische Pforte* (Görlitz, 1711), pp. 11 ('in Eisen und Ketten'), 17–20 (raid).

10. N. de Nicolay, *Dans l'empire de Soliman le Magnifique*, ed. M.-C. Gomez-Géraud and S. Yérasimos (Paris, 1989), p. 65 ('tous adonnés à paillardise, sodomie, larcins et tous autres vices détestables'); A. de Sosa ['D. de Haedo'], *Topographia e historia general de Argel, repartida en cinco tratados* (Valladolid, 1612), fo. 35r ('por viuir a su placer, y encenagados en todo genero de luxuria, sodomia, y gula').

11. M. A. de Bunes Ibarra, *La imagen de los musulmanes y del Norte de África en la España de los siglos XVI y XVII: los caracteres de una hostilidad* (Madrid, 1989), p. 239.

12. A. Gonzalez-Raymond, *La Croix et le croissant: les inquisiteurs des îles face à l'Islam, 1550–1700* (Paris, 1992), p. 216 (Justiniano, Catalan). These accusations were made on the basis of statements by witnesses.

13. J. Riera i Sans, *Sodomites catalans: història i vida (segles XIII–XVIII)* (Barcelona, 2014), pp. 216–17 ('su amo le besava, retoçava y dormía con él... le servía de bardaxe y paciente, cometiendo con él el pecado de sodomía').

14. E. d'Aranda, *Relation de la captivité et liberté du sieur Emanuel d'Aranda, jadis esclave à Alger*, 3rd edn. (Brussels, 1666), p. 202 ('debauché par un Renié Portugais'). In this case, d'Aranda mentions also a monetary payment by the renegade to the boy.

15. L. Mott, 'Musulmani sodomiti in Portogallo e bardassi cristiani in Africa del Nord nei secoli dell'età moderna', in U. Grassi and G. Marcocci, eds., *Le trasgressioni della carne: il desiderio omosessuale nel mondo islamico e cristiano, secc. XII–XX* (Rome, 2015), pp. 155–86, at p. 180 ('tutti i rinnegati hanno il costume di possedere ragazzi al posto delle donne per i loro piaceri (*sensualidades*), e con loro praticano il peccato della sodomia e se ne vantano').

16. Laugier de Tassy, *Histoire du royaume d'Alger*, p. 87.

17. Ibid., p. 87.

18. J. ['G.'] Gracián de la Madre de Dios, *Tractado de la redempcion de captivos* (Rome, 1597), pp. 24–5 ('De los muchachos, y mozos desbarbados por marauilla se escapa alguno: porque a vn que sea vn Grumete, ò el mas baxo y pobre le compran los Turcos con excessiuo precio, para sus maldades, y de tan mal principio facil es la heregia', 'Especialmente que de ordinario lleuan pobrecillos, de los que seruian en Naos, ò guardauan pecoras en Corzega, que en su tierra ni tenian que comer, ni que vestir. Y quando se veen atauiados de seda, y con abundancia de manjares, y adorados del patron (cuyos esclauos son co[m]prados para malos fines) pareceles que es bien auenturanza renegar la fee Christiana, cuya doctrina aun no auian aprendido').

19. de Sosa, *Topographia*, fo. 9v ('dende muchachos los imponen sus amos en la vellaqueria de la sodomia, a que se aficionan luego').

20. See e.g. B. Bennassar and L. Bennassar, *Les Chrétiens d'Allah: l'histoire extraordinaire des renégats, XVIᵉ–XVIIᵉ siècles* (Paris, 1989), pp. 174, 278; Gonzalez-Raymond, *La Croix et le croissant*, p. 216; Mott, 'Musulmani sodomiti', p. 181; Riera i Sans, *Sodomites catalans*, pp. 216–17.

21. M. Masson, 'Barda, bardache et bredindin: la base "BRD" dans les langues romanes', *La Linguistique*, 51 (2015), pp. 41–88. For the early French usage see C. Courouve, *Vocabulaire de l'homosexualité masculine* (Paris, 1985), pp. 59–61. An alternative theory relates it to the Greek βαδάς ('catamite'), recorded by Hesychius in the 5th or 6th century AD: R. Conner, 'Les Molles et les chausses: Mapping the Isle of Hermaphrodites in Premodern France', in A. Livia and K. Hall, eds., *Queerly Phrased: Language, Gender, and Sexuality* (New York, 1997), pp. 127–46, at p. 133.

22. Riera i Sans, *Sodomites catalans*, p. 192 (Ponz: 'contra christianos', 'aunque por fuerza'); Gonzalez-Raymond, *La Croix et le croissant*, p. 216 (de Pedro).

23. A. [Abd el Hadi] ben Mansour, ed., *Alger, XVIᵉ–XVIIᵉ siècle: journal de Jean-Baptiste Gramaye, 'évêque d'Afrique'* (Paris, 1998), pp. 302–4 ('si qui liberalioris formae, ad nefarios vsus & horrenda nefandaque scelera domi concluduntur & continentur, & denique ad certissimam perniciem donum magno Turcae, eieusque officiatis mittuntur').

24. G. Turbet-Delof, *L'Afrique barbaresque dans la littérature française aux XVIᵉ et XVIIᵉ siècles* (Geneva, 1973), p. 96(n.).

25. Albèri, ed., *Relazioni*, iii, p. 224 (relazione of 1583: falling out).

26. Biblioteca Ambrosiana, Milan, MS Q 116 sup., fos. 136r–146v, [G. Barelli,] 'Relatione delle cose di Constantinopoli', at fo. 138r ('molto dedito al uitio nefando ha in delitie piu di / 300 / paggi', 'huomini uili & che non siano accasati & quanto piu sono uiciosi tanto piu li piace anzi tiene / 50 / sbarbati & piu per li apetiti di essi schiaui & crede che trattati in tal maniera non hauerano desiderio di fuggire').

27. de Sosa, *Topographia*, fo. 38v ('La sodomia se tiene... por honra, porque aquel es mas honrado, que sustenta mas garçones', 'que le sirua de cozinar, y de acompañar en la cama').

28. On St Pelagius and his cult see M. D. Jordan, *The Invention of Sodomy in Christian Theology* (Chicago, 1997), pp. 10–28.

29. M. Tanner, *Societatis Jesu apostolorum imitatrix*, part 1 (Prague, 1694), p. 841 (López: 'Juvenis castissimus', 'manibus & dentibus'); M. Herrero García, *Ideas de los españoles del siglo XVII* (Madrid, 1966), p. 545.

30. M. Febvre, *Theatre de la Turquie* (Paris, 1682), p. 267 ('un peché honteux & abominable'); interestingly, he wrote that the local Muslims also saw this as a miracle and, viewing the boy as a martyr, wished to bury him in their own cemetery.

31. A. M. de Turre, *Orbis seraphicus*, tome 2, part 2, ed. A. Chiappini (Quaracchi, 1945), p. 87a ('candidissimam conversationem').

32. V. Vratislav, *Prihody Wáclawa Wratislawa swobodného pána z Mitrovic*, ed. F. M. Pelzel (Prague, 1777), p. 199 ('pro mau Mladost snadne od nekterých Bassuw wzát, a poturčen budu. Nebot Turcy, á wzlasst Renegati, pewelmi nesslechetnj Sodomáj gsau, a mladj Lidé w Nebezpečenstwj welikem býwagj').

33. van der Does, *De itinere suo*, p. 30 ('hos septis aedium includunt, nec antequam mentum lanugine vestitum fuerit, exire permittunt').

34. Stadsarchief, Amsterdam, arch. 5075, inv. no. 378A (Jacob en Nicolaes Jacobs), fo. 267r–v ('bowen maten sehr groot peryckel is, Inn reysen van dese Land nach Constantinopolen, & andre pladtsen in turchÿen, voor allen menschen & Bowen al voor ankommend Jongclingen van ouderdom van 10 12 tot 18 & 20 Jahren', 'misbruÿcken te werden...spetialyck als de Jongens eenichsins schoon ofte Bevallych syn', 'In Turckyen is geboren, & lange Jaeren In Constantinopolen gewoond heeft'). The document is briefly summarized in E. M. Koen, 'Notarial Records Relating to the Portuguese Jews in Amsterdam up to 1639', *Studia Rosenthaliana*, 8 (1974), pp. 138–45, at p. 145.

35. M. G. Brennan, ed., *The Travel Diary of Robert Bargrave, Levant Merchant (1647–1656)* (London, 1999), p. 106.

36. J. a Sancto Felice, *Triumphus misericordiae, id est sacrum ordinis SSS. Trinitatis institutum redemptio captivorum* (Vienna, 1704), pp. 84–5.

37. J. Carlier de Pinon, *Voyage en orient*, ed. E. Blochet (Paris, 1920), p. 119 ('Sont aussy fort subjects au vice de Sodome, et plus les grans que le vulguaire, n'y ayant gueres un cappitaine quy n'ait un bardache ou davantaige').

38. T. Sherley, 'Discours of the Turkes', ed. E. Denison Ross, *Camden Miscellany* 16 (Camden ser. 3, vol. 52), item 2 (London, 1936), p. 2.

39. S. Gerlach, *Stephan Gerlachs dess Aeltern Tage-Buch*, ed. S. Gerlach (Frankfurt, 1674), p. 313 ('Er sagt...was die Türcken für grosse Schande / mit den Knaben treiben. Die sich aber selbsten dazu aussbutzen / und vor grosser Herren Häuser vorüber gehen / dass diese sie sehen sollen...Sie haben auch grossen Lohn').

40. J. de Villamont, *Les Voyages du Seigneur de Villamont*, 2nd edn. (Paris, 1596), fo. 233r ('ce n'est rien... au regard des Bardaches, qu'ils ont en leurs maiso[n]s, desquels ils sont plus jaloux que de leurs fem[m]es mesmes, & quand ils vont aux champs ou à la guerre, ils les meinent auec eux pour leur seruir de femmes').

41. Sir Henry Blount, *A Voyage into the Levant* (London, 1636), p. 14.

42. Hill, *Full and Just Account*, p. 80 (*pusht* was a Persian word for 'catamite').

43. T. Spandounes, *On the Origin of the Ottoman Emperors*, ed. and trans. D. M. Nicol (Cambridge, 1997), p. 130; L. Bassano, *Costumi et i modi particolari della vita de' Turchi*, ed. F. Babinger (Munich, 1963), p. 89 ('quella natione e machiata del vitio della Sodomia').

44. P. Rycaut, *The Present State of the Ottoman Empire* (London, 1668), pp. 31–3.

45. de Nicolay, *Dans l'empire*, p. 215 ('ainsi que les Turcs et toutes autres nations orientales, sont tellement adonnés au détestable péché contre nature, qu'ils ne le tiennent à honte ni vergogne'); H. J. Breuning, *Orientalische Reyss* (Strasbourg, 1612), p. 58 ('sein die Türcken grosse Sodomitae, welches Teuffelisch Laster bey Hohen und Niders Standes Personen gar gemein'), quoted in S. A. Falkner, '"Having It Off" with Fish, Camels, and Lads: Sodomitic Pleasures in German-Language *Turcica*', *JHS*, 13 (2004), pp. 401–27, at p. 412; J. Thévenot, *L'Empire du Grand Turc vu par un sujet de Louis XIV*, ed. F. Billacois (Paris, 1965), p. 165 ('ils sont grands sodomites...c'est un vice fort commun chez eux'). For other examples see D. Carnoy, *Représentations de l'Islam dans la France du XVIIᵉ siècle* (Paris, 1998), pp. 130–1, 266.

46. G. Sandys, *A Relation of a Journey Begun An: Dom: 1610* (London, 1621), p. 66.

47. M. Baudier, *Histoire generale de la religion des Turcs* (Paris, 1625), p. 142 ('ils sont descendus au vice abominables des Sodomites, & la pederastie; où l'amour des masles maistrise tellement leurs sens, qu'à la Cour du Grand Seigneur, & ailleurs, les Grands s'entretiennent en leurs plus serieux discours, de la beauté de leurs Ganymedes'); M. Baudier, *Histoire géneralle du serrail et de la cour du Grand Seigneur empereur des Turcs* (Paris, 1652 [1st publ. 1625]), p. 217 ('ils abandonnent leurs affections aux jeunes garçons...ils les caressent, & s'en seruent au lieu de femmes. Ce vice abominable est si ordinaire dans la Cour du Turc, qu'à peine y trouuera-t'on vn seul Bassa qui n'y soit malheureusement addonné').

CHAPTER 3

1. d'Aranda, *Relation de la captivité*, pp. 17–18 ('ne pouvoient sortir du logis, de crainte d'estre debauchez par les Turcs: car pour Alli Pegelin nostre Patron il avoit la reputation d'estre ennemy du peché abominable. Et il tenoit ces garçons par ostentation, comme en la Chrestienté les grands Seigneurs tiennent des Pages, Lacquais, & Estaffiers').

2. D. Galán, *Cautiverio y trabajos de Diego Galán, natural de Consuegra y vecino de Toledo, 1589 a 1600*, ed. M. Serrano y Sanz (Madrid, 1913), p. 9 ('comenzó á halagarme pasando la mano por el cabello, diciendo: no tengáis pena, gentil hombre, que no os harán mal'); A. Mas, *Les Turcs dans la littérature espagnole du siècle d'or*, 2 vols. (Paris, 1967), ii, p. 329 (modern scholar).

3. See e.g. A.-T. Khoury, *Polémique byzantine contre l'Islam (VIIIᵉ–XIIIᵉ s.)*, 2nd edn. (Leiden, 1972), pp. 92–3; J. V. Tolan, *Saracens: Islam in the Medieval European Imagination* (New York, 2002), pp. 93, 166, 237.

4. T. Bibliander, ed., *Machumetis Sarracenorum principis vita ac doctrina omnis, quae & Ismahelitarum lex, & Alcoranum dicitur*, 3 vols. (Basel, 1543), i, p. 17: 'Mulieres uobis subiectas penitus pro modo uestro, ubicunque uolueritis, parate', 'Violentius hic locus à nostris tortus est, quasi nefaria permittat, quu[m] adijciat, Deum timentes'). The word 'parate' here may have been an error for 'perarate'; cf. the quotation from Peter of Poitiers, cited in n. 5 below. The verse is 'your women are a tillage for you; so come unto your tillage as you wish' in the standard modern version by A. J. Arberry, *The Koran Interpreted* (Oxford, 1998), p. 31.

5. J. Kritzeck, *Peter the Venerable and Islam* (Princeton, NJ, 1964), pp. 215, 217 (citing the verse in a different wording from Robert of Ketton's, with 'perarate' for 'parate').

6. N. Daniel, *Islam and the West: The Making of an Image* (Edinburgh, 1962), pp. 6, 12, 142–3.

7. J. Boswell, *Christianity, Social Tolerance, and Homosexuality: Gay People in Western Europe from the Beginning of the Christian Era to the Fourteenth Century* (Chicago, 1980), pp. 279–80.

8. Daniel, *Islam and the West*, p. 143; for a later atrocity story of this kind see also K. van Eickels, 'Die Konstruktion des Anderen: (Homo)sexuelles Verhalten als Element des Sarazenenbildes zur Zeit der Kreuzzüge und die Beschlüsse des Konzils von Nablus 1120', in L. M. Thoma and S. Limbeck, eds., *'Die Sünde, der sich der tiuvel schamet in der helle': Homosexualität in der Kultur des Mittelalters und der frühen Neuzeit* (Ostflidern, 2009) pp. 43–68, at p. 55.

9. Daniel, *Islam and the West*, p. 144; on these 'effeminate men' see E. K. Rowson, 'Omoerotismo ed élite mamelucca tra Egitto e Siria nel tardo medievo', in U. Grassi and G. Marcocci, eds., *Le trasgressioni della carne: il desiderio omosessuale nel mondo islamico e cristiano, secc. XII–XX* (Rome, 2015), pp. 23–51, at p. 24.

10. A. de Espina, *Fortalitium fidei* (Lyon, 1487), sig. A6v ('concedit sodomiam tam cu[m] masculo qu[am] cum femina'). On the broader development of this theme see V. Lavenia, 'Tra eresia e crimine contro natura: sessualità, islamofobia e inquisizioni nell'Europa moderna', in U. Grassi and G. Marcocci, eds., *Le trasgressioni della carne: il desiderio omosessuale nel mondo islamico e cristiano, secc. XII–XX* (Rome, 2015), pp. 103–30, esp. pp. 108–22.

11. J. M. Mendoza Garrido, *Delincuencia y represión en la Castilla bajomedieval (los territorios castellano-manchegos)* (Granada, 1999), p. 422(n.).

12. R. García Cárcel, *Herejía y sociedad en el siglo XVI: la Inquisición en Valencia 1530–1609* (Barcelona, 1980), p. 289; C. Berco, *Jerarquías sexuales, estatus público: masculinidad, sodomía y sociedad en la España del Siglo de Oro*, trans. E. Cano Miguel (Valencia, 2009), p. 149. Note, however, that they were statistically under-represented as defendants, probably because many lived in rather enclosed self-policing communities which the Christian authorities could not really penetrate: see W. Monter, *Frontiers of Heresy: The Spanish Inquisition from the Basque Lands to Sicily* (Cambridge, 1990), p. 292.

13. L. Mott, 'Le Pouvoir inquisitorial et la répression de l'abominable péché de sodomie dans le monde luso-brésilien', in G. Audisio, ed., *Inquisition et pouvoir*

(Aix-en-Provence, 2004), pp. 203–18, at pp. 210–11. He later added that in his own country he had habitually sodomized boys.

14. Arquivo Nacional da Torre do Tombo, Lisbon, PT/TT/TSO-IL proc. 4026, fo. 18r–v.

15. P. Aznar Cardona, *Expulsion justificada de los moriscos españoles* (Huesca, 1612), fos. 97v, 99v; Lavenia, 'Tra eresia e crimine contro natura', pp. 127–8 (Bleda).

16. Boswell, *Christianity, Social Tolerance*, p. 52 (crusaders); D. F. Greenberg, *The Construction of Homosexuality* (Chicago, 1988), p. 295 (1376); Falkner, ' "Having It Off" ', p. 426, citing Anon., *Ausszug eynes Briefes, wie eyner so in der Türckey wonhafft, seynem freünd in dise land geschriben* (Nuremberg, 1526), sig. A3.

17. See W. Schleiner, 'Linguistic "Xenohomophobia" in Sixteenth-Century France: The Case of Henri Estienne', *The Sixteenth Century Journal*, 34 (2003), pp. 747–60, esp. p. 751.

18. van der Meer, *Sodoms zaad*, p. 162.

19. G. Ricci, *I Turchi alle porte* (Bologna, 2008), pp. 77–8 ('Fantasie sessuali', 'ansia della passività omosessuale, in quanto metafora di permeabilità religiosa e militare'); M. Wiesner-Hanks, *Christianity and Sexuality in the Early Modern World: Regulating Desire, Reforming Practice*, 2nd edn. (London, 2010), p. 108.

20. E. Said, *Orientalism*, 2nd edn. (London, 1995), pp. 60, 63, 95, 96.

21. N. Matar, *Turks, Moors, and Englishmen in the Age of Discovery* (New York, 1999), pp. 109, 112–13.

22. See N. Malcolm, *Useful Enemies: Islam and the Ottoman Empire in Western Political Thought, 1450–1750* (Oxford, 2019), *passim*.

23. On the reality of sodomy among the Amerindians, see p. 325.

24. Matar, *Turks, Moors, and Englishmen*, pp. 119, 125, 126.

25. For the account by Atkins (1622) see P. Hammond, *Figuring Sex between Men from Shakespeare to Rochester* (Oxford, 2002), pp. 25–6.

26. Matar, *Turks, Moors, and Englishmen*, p. 118; W. Lithgow, *The Totall Discourse of the Rare Adventures and Painefull Peregrinations of Long Nineteen Yeares Travayles from Scotland to the Most Famous Kingdomes in Europe, Asia and Affrica* (Glasgow, 1906), p. 323 ('I have seene at mid-day, in the very Market places, the Moores buggering these filthy Carrions, and without shame or punishment go freely away').

CHAPTER 4

1. K. El-Rouayheb, *Before Homosexuality in the Arab-Islamic World, 1500–1800* (Chicago, 2005), p. 79.

2. See e.g. W. G. Andrews and M. Kalpaklı, *The Age of Beloveds: Love and the Beloved in Early-Modern Ottoman and European Culture and Society* (Durham, NC, 2005), *passim*; İ. C. Schick, 'Three Genders, Two Sexualities: The Evidence of Ottoman Erotic Terminology', in A. Kreil, L. Torbero and S. Tolino, eds., *Sex and Desire in Muslim Cultures: Beyond Norms and Transgression from the Abbasids to the Present Day* (London, 2021), pp. 87–110.

3. A. al-Aqḥiṣārī, *Against Smoking: An Ottoman Manifesto*, trans. Y. Michot (Markfield, 2010), p. 21 (citing his treatise *Majālis al-abrār* ('The Councils of the Pious'), sect. 77).
4. El-Rouayheb, *Before Homosexuality*, pp. 25–32 (31: quotation); L. Peirce, 'Seniority, Sexuality, and Social Order: The Vocabulary of Gender in Early Modern Ottoman Society', in M. C. Zilfi, ed., *Women in the Ottoman Empire: Middle Eastern Women in the Early Modern Era* (Leiden, 1997), pp. 169–96, at p. 177 (*emred*). For more detailed evidence of the age at which beards developed, drawn from Western Europe, see pp. 46–7.
5. El-Rouayheb, *Before Homosexuality*, pp. 3–5, 53–6.
6. Pierce, 'Seniority, Sexuality, and Social Order', p. 178.
7. El-Rouayheb, *Before Homosexuality*, p. 117; cf. A. Bouhdiba, *La Sexualité en Islam* (Paris, 1975), pp. 46, 146; L. Berger, *Gesellschaft und Individuum in Damaskus, 1550–1791* (Würzburg, 2007), p. 242.
8. See above, p. 15.
9. D. Ze'evi, *Producing Desire: Changing Sexual Discourse in the Ottoman Middle East, 1500–1900* (Berkeley, CA, 2006), p. 92.
10. E. K. Rowson, 'The Categorization of Gender and Sexual Irregularity in Medieval Arabic Vice Lists', in J. Epstein and K. Straub, eds., *Body Guards: The Cultural Politics of Gender Ambiguity* (New York, 1991), pp. 50–79, at pp. 64–5; M. W. Dols, *Majnūn: The Madman in Medieval Islamic Society*, ed. D. E. Immisch (Oxford, 1992), pp. 95–8; El-Rouayheb, *Before Homosexuality*, pp. 19–20.
11. Y. Ben-Naeh, 'Moshko the Jew and his Gay Friends: Same-Sex Sexual Relations in Ottoman-Jewish Society', *Journal of Early Modern History*, 9 (2005), 79–105, at p. 95.
12. Rowson, 'Categorization of Gender and Sexual Irregularity', pp. 69–71. Some writers regarded the *mukhannath* as representing a completely separate category from that of the passive adult males; see the text of c.1500 by Deli Birader, in S. S. Kuru, 'A Sixteenth Century Scholar: Deli Birader and his *Dāfiʿ ʿü'l-ġumūm ve rāfiʿ ʿü'l-humūm*', Harvard University PhD dissertation (2000), pp. 138, 258, distinguishing *rencūrlar* (passive adults) from *muḥanneṣler*.
13. El-Rouayheb, *Before Homosexuality*, p. 32.
14. Z. Szombathy, *Mujūn: Libertinism in Mediaeval Muslim Society and Literature* (n.p., 2013), p. 11(n.).
15. R. Dankoff, *An Ottoman Mentality: The World of Evliya Çelebi* (Leiden, 2006), pp. 119–20.
16. Rowson, 'Categorization of Gender and Sexual Irregularity', p. 66.
17. See A. Schmitt, 'Appendix', in A. Schmitt and J. Sofer, eds., *Sexuality and Eroticism among Males in Moslem Societies* (Binghamton, NY, 1992), pp. 164–7; cf. the description of this by Deli Birader in Kuru, 'Sixteenth Century Scholar', pp. 202–3.
18. D. S. Brookes, ed. and trans., *The Ottoman Gentleman of the Sixteenth Century: Mustafa Ali's* Meva'idü'n-nefa'is fi kava'idi'l-mecalis, 'Tables of Delicacies Concerning the Rules of Social Gatherings' (Cambridge, MA, 2003), pp. 18–19.

19. Matar, *Turks, Moors and Englishmen*, pp. 118, 121–3; Ze'evi, *Producing Desire*, p. 153. Rycaut had at least one informant who had direct and intimate knowledge of conditions in the palace: the Polish renegade Ali Ufki (Wojciech or Albert Bobowski), who had been captured in his youth in a Tatar raid and taken to Istanbul, where he served for many years in the Imperial household as a musician and trainee page, later acting as the Sultan's Second Dragoman. See S. P. Anderson, *An English Consul in Turkey: Paul Rycaut at Smyrna, 1667–1678* (Oxford, 1989), p. 41; Cemal Behar, *Ali Ufki' ve mezmurlar* (Istanbul, 1990), esp. pp. 12–25; A. Berthier and S. Yerasimos, 'Introduction', in A. Bobovius, *Topkapi: relation du sérail du Grand Seigneur*, ed. A. Berthier and S. Yerasimos (Arles, 1999), pp. 9–22.

20. El-Rouayheb, *Before Homosexuality*, pp. 27–8 (playing off admirers, parents' complicity), 90 (power inversion); P. Sprachman, '*Le beau garçon sans merci*: The Homoerotic Tale in Arabic and Persian', in J. W. Wright and E. K. Rowson, eds., *Homoeroticism in Classical Arabic Literature* (New York, 1997), pp. 192–209; Berger, *Gesellschaft und Individuum*, pp. 240–54, esp. p. 250 (financial ruin). Andrews and Kalpaklı discuss gifts (*Age of Beloveds*, p. 95), noting also that a high-status beloved might present a gift to his lower-status lover; in this case the social-hierarchical convention trumped the usual amorous one.

21. Rowson, 'Categorization of Gender and Sexual Irregularity', p. 57 (al-Jurjānī); Szombathy, Mujūn, pp. 12(n.) (Baghdad), 149(n.) (al-Ṣaymarī).

22. Y. Tov Assis, 'Sexual Behaviour in Mediaeval Hispano-Jewish Society', in A. Rapoport-Albert and S. J. Zipperstein, eds., *Jewish History: Essays in Honour of Chimen Abramsky* (London, 1988), pp. 25–59, at p. 27 ('professionalized'); D. Eisenberg, 'Juan Ruiz's Heterosexual "Good Love"', in J. Blackmore and G. S. Hutcheson, eds., *Queer Iberia: Sexualities, Cultures, and Crossings from the Middle Ages to the Renaissance* (Durham, NC, 1999), pp. 250–74, at p. 256 (Seville).

23. Kuru, 'Sixteenth Century Scholar', pp. 143, 264.

24. Evliya Çelebi, *An Ottoman Traveller: Selections from the Book of Travels of Evliya Çelebi*, ed. and trans. R. Dankoff and S. Kim (London, 2010), pp. 20, 250, 394, 425; M. Sariyannis, 'Prostitution in Ottoman Istanbul, Late Sixteenth–Early Eighteenth Century', *Turcica*, 40 (2008), pp. 37–64, at pp. 55–6. *Boza* is a mildly alcoholic drink made of fermented millet.

25. Brookes, ed. and trans., *Ottoman Gentleman*, p. 131.

26. E. Boyar and K. Fleet, *A Social History of Ottoman Istanbul* (Cambridge, 2010), pp. 200–1; S. N. Erdoğan, *Sexual Life in Ottoman Society* (Istanbul, 1996), p. 77 (quotation).

27. Andrews and Kalpaklı, *Age of Beloveds*, pp. 157–9.

28. al-Aqḥiṣārī, *Against Smoking*, pp. 64–5.

29. El-Rouayheb, *Before Homosexuality*, p. 41 (quotation); A. Cohen, *The Guilds of Ottoman Jerusalem* (Leiden, 2001), pp. 55–6 ('beardless youngsters').

30. de Sosa, *Topographia*, fo. 38r ('publicos burdelas').

31. El-Rouayheb, *Before Homosexuality*, p. 42; Andrews and Kalpaklı, *Age of Beloveds*, p. 284 (quotation).

32. Kuru, 'Sixteenth Century Scholar', pp. 131, 249 (Deli Birader); N. Macaraig, *Çemberlitaş hamamı in Istanbul: The Biographical Memoir of a Turkish Bath* (Edinburgh, 2019), p. 133 (order).

33. K. Babayan, ' "In Spirit we Ate Each Other's Sorrow": Female Companionship in Seventeenth-Century Safavi Iran', in K. Babayan and A. Najmabadi, eds., *Islamicate Sexualities: Translations across Temporal Geographies of Desire* (Cambridge, MA, 2008), pp. 238–74, at p. 265. Another of the decrees, issued in the 1550s, forbade teenaged boys from shaving to delay the visible onset of adulthood.

34. El-Rouayheb, *Before Homosexuality*, p. 42.

35. Evliya Çelebi, *Ottoman Traveller*, pp. 41, 103–4.

36. Sariyannis, 'Prostitution in Ottoman Istanbul', p. 61. An apparently late-seventeenth-century text, *Dellaknâme-i dilküşâ* ('The Heart-Breaking Book of Masseurs'), describing several masseurs and listing the sexual services they provided, has been published by Murat Badakçı in his *Osmanlı'da seks: sarayda gece dersleri* (Istanbul, 1993), pp. 86–102. However, some of the descriptions involve forms of sexual behaviour which seem to relate much more to modern homosexuality than to Ottoman sexual relations (see the extracts translated in Erdoğan, *Sexual Life in Ottoman Society*, pp. 95–107). The sole manuscript belongs to the writer who published it, and has apparently not been examined by specialist scholars; until such examination takes place, the value of this text may remain uncertain.

37. Kuru, 'Sixteenth Century Scholar', pp. 67, 177; Andrews and Kalpaklı, *Age of Beloveds*, pp. 137–8.

38. Szombathy, Mujūn, p. 139.

39. M. Zilfi, 'The Kadizadelis: Discordant Revivalism in Seventeenth-Century Istanbul', *Journal of Near Eastern Studies*, 45 (1986), pp. 251–69, at p. 264.

40. A. Tietze, ed. and trans., *Muṣṭafā ʿĀlī's Description of Cairo of 1599* (Vienna, 1975), pp. 51–4.

41. Berger, *Gesellschaft und Individuum*, p. 252 ('scheint eine Neigung zu schönen Knaben als der Regelfall angesehen worden zu sein'); El-Rouayheb, *Before Homosexuality*, p. 21 (1606).

42. Brookes, ed. and trans., *Ottoman Gentleman*, p. 37.

43. Ben-Naeh, 'Moshko the Jew', pp. 101–2.

44. Brookes, ed. and trans., *Ottoman Gentleman*, pp. 28, 97.

45. Bouhdiba, *La Sexualité en Islam*, pp. 129–30 (Islamic law); Boyar and Fleet, *Social History*, pp. 202–3 (slave-dealers). Islam forbade owners to prostitute their slaves: see G. Veinstein, *Les Esclaves du Sultan chez les Ottomans: des mamelouks aux janissaires (XIVᵉ–XVIIᵉ siècles)* (Paris, 2020), p. 34.

46. M. Glünz, 'Das männliche Liebespaar in der persischen und türkischen Diwanlyrik', in T. Stemmler, ed., *Homoerotische Lyrik: 6. Kolloquium der Forschungsstelle für europäische Lyrik des Mittelalters* (Mannheim, 1992), pp. 119–28, at p. 121.

47. El-Rouayheb, *Before Homosexuality*, pp. 40 (quotation), 124 (examples of such scholars); cf. also the discussion of the views of the different legal schools on this

in A. Schmitt, '*Liwāṭ* im *Fiqh*: Männliche Homosexualität?', *Journal of Arabic and Islamic Studies*, 4 (2001–2), pp. 49–110, at pp. 72–90.

48. Evliya Çelebi, *Ottoman Traveller*, p. 62.

49. El-Rouayheb, *Before Homosexuality*, pp. 3, 6, 93; Berger, *Gesellschaft und Individuum*, p. 252 (gravitas); A.-K. Rafeq, 'Public Morality in the [*sic*] 18th Century Damascus', *Revue du monde musulman et de la Méditerranée* 55–6 (1990), pp. 180–96, at p. 187.

50. Schmitt, '*Liwāṭ* im *Fiqh*', pp. 108–9 ('Halbdunkel'); Peirce, 'Seniority, Sexuality, and Social Order', p. 175 (sexual congress).

51. Brookes, ed. and trans., *Ottoman Gentleman*, p. 109.

52. Ibid., p. 29.

CHAPTER 5

1. M. Rocke, *Forbidden Friendships: Homosexuality and Male Culture in Renaissance Florence* (New York, 1996), p. 60. Samuel Cohn has challenged Rocke's claims about the substantial proportion of the Florentine male population this represented, suggesting that that calculation has been inflated by repeat offenders and people from the countryside (review of Rocke, *Speculum*, 74 (1999), pp. 481–3); but even with these qualifications, the absolute numbers are still very striking.

2. U. Grassi, *L'Offizio sopra l'Onestà: il controllo della sodomia nella Lucca del cinquecento* (Milan, 2014; translated as *Bathhouses and Riverbanks: Sodomy in a Renaissance Republic* (Toronto, 2021)); M. Baldassari, *Bande giovanili e 'vizio nefando': violenza e sessualità nella Roma barocca* (Rome, 2005); P. H. Labalme, 'Sodomy and Venetian Justice in the Renaissance', *The Legal History Review*, 52 (1984), pp. 217–54; G. Ruggiero, *The Boundaries of Eros: Sex Crime and Sexuality in Renaissance Venice* (New York, 1985), pp. 109–45; G. Martini, *Il 'vitio nefando' nella Venezia del Seicento: aspetti sociali e repressione di giustizia* (Rome, 1988); N. S. Davidson, 'Sodomy in Early Modern Venice', in T. Betteridge, ed., *Sodomy in Early Modern Europe* (Manchester, 2002), pp. 65–81; U. Zuccarello, 'La sodomia al tribunale bolognese del Torrone tra XVI e XVII secolo', *Società e storia*, no. 87 (2000), pp. 37–51; T. Dean, 'Sodomy in Renaissance Bologna', *Renaissance Studies*, 31 (2016), pp. 426–43; cf. also Canosa, *Storia di una grande paura*.

3. See W. Monter, *Frontiers of Heresy: The Spanish Inquisition from the Basque Lands to Sicily* (Cambridge, 1990), pp. 276–99 (Sicily, Aragon); R. Rosselló, *L'homosexualitat a Mallorca a l'edat mitjana* (Felanitx, 1977); Riera i Sans, *Sodomites catalans* (Barcelona); R. Carrasco, *Inquisición y represión sexual en Valencia: historia de los sodomitas (1565–1786)* (Barcelona, 1985) (Valencia); C. Berco, *Jerarquías sexuales, estatus público: masculinidad, sodomía y sociedad en la España del Siglo de Oro*, trans. E. Cano Miguel (Valencia, 2009) (Aragon); M. E. Perry, 'The "Nefarious Sin" in Early Modern Seville', *JH*, 16 (1989), pp. 67–89; T. A. Mantecón Movellán, 'Los mocitos de Galindo: sexualidad *contra natura*, culturas proscritas y control

social en la edad moderna', in idem, ed., *Bajtín y la historia de la cultura popular: cuarenta años de debate* (Santander, 2008), pp. 209–39 (Seville); F. Garza Carvajal, *Butterflies will Burn: Prosecuting Sodomites in Early Modern Spain and Mexico* (Austin, TX, 2003) (Andalusia); L. Mott, *O sexo proibido: virgens, gays e escravos nas garras da Inquisição* (Campinas, 1988), and his 'Le Pouvoir inquisitorial et la répressions de l'abominable péché de sodomie dans le monde luso-brésilien', in Gabriel Audisio, ed., *Inquisition et pouvoir* (Aix-en-Provence, 2004), pp. 203–18 (Portugal); H. Johnson and F. A. Dutra, eds., *Pelo vaso traseiro: Sodomy and Sodomites in Luso-Brazilian History* (Tucson, AZ, 2006).

4. Rocke, *Forbidden Friendships*, pp. 96, 116–17, 243–5.
5. Grassi, *L'Offizio sopra l'Onestà*, pp. 79–81.
6. Dean, 'Sodomy in Renaissance Bologna', pp. 432–3 (15th century); Zuccarello, 'La sodomia al tribunale bolognese', p. 40 (16th, 17th centuries). Dean's research is thorough, but it seems that not all cases were recorded in the registers that survive: e.g. the several people arrested for sodomy at the University of Bologna in 1375 (see Benvenuto da Imola, *Comentum super Dantis Aldigherij Comoediam*, ed. J. P. Lacaita, 5 vols. (Florence, 1887), i, pp. 523–4).
7. P. Blastenbrei, *Kriminalität in Rom, 1560–1585* (Tübingen, 1995), p. 277; Baldassari, *Bande giovanili*, pp. 142–59.
8. N. Davidson, 'Sodomy in Early Modern Venice', p. 68 (5+ per year); Ruggiero, *Boundaries of Eros*, pp. 109–45 (reported cases), 117–18 (1467 law); E. Crouzet-Pavan, *'Sopra le acque salse': espaces, pouvoirs et société à Venise à la fin du Moyen Âge*, 2 vols. (Rome, 1992), ii, pp. 839–40 (1458: 'compagnie non convenientis etatis videlicet magnis cum parvis'); Anon. [G. Lorenzi], *Leggi e memorie*, pp. 81–2 (1496).
9. A. Rocco, *L'Alcibiade fanciullo a scola*, ed. L. Coci (Rome, 1988), p. 76.
10. Carrasco, *Inquisición y repression*, p. 111 ('La eterna pareja del hombre maduro y del adolescente hermoso atraviesa como un hilo de Ariana los procesos inquisitoriales').
11. Ibid., p. 222; Berco, *Jerarquías sexuales*, p. 38.
12. Cf. D. Higgs, 'The Historiography of Male–Male Love in Portugal, 1550–1800', in K. O'Donnell and M. O'Rourke, eds., *Queer Masculinities, 1550–1800: Siting Same-Sex Desire in the Early Modern World* (Basingstoke, 2006), pp. 37–57, at p. 38; I. M. R. Drumond ['Drummond'] Braga, 'Foreigners, Sodomy, and the Portuguese Inquisition', in H. Johnson and F. A. Dutra, eds., *Pelo vaso traseiro: Sodomy and Sodomites in Luso-Brazilian History* (Tucson, AZ, 2006), pp. 145–64, at p. 148 ('The partners of those who took the active role were usually younger'). For a range of cases see the essays in Johnson and Dutra's book, and Mott, *O sexo proibido*, pp. 75–129.
13. A. Vieira, 'Contributions to the Study of Daily Life and Sexuality on the Island of São Miguel in the Seventeenth Century: The Case of the Count of Vila Franca', in H. Johnson and F. A. Dutra, eds., *Pelo vaso traseiro: Sodomy and Sodomites in Luso-Brazilian History* (Tucson, AZ, 2006), pp. 105–44, at pp. 116–17, 126–9.

14. L. Lage da Gama Lima, 'Sodomia e pedofilia no século XVII: o proceso de João da Costa', in R. Vainfas, B. Feitler and L. Lage da Gama Lima, eds., *A Inquisição em xeque: temas, controvérsias, estudos de caso* (Rio de Janeiro, 2006), pp. 237–52.
15. Vieira, 'Contributions', pp. 117, 128–9.
16. E. Cunha de Azevedo Mea, *A Inquisição de Coimbra no século XVI: a instituição, os homens e a sociedade* (Porto, 1997), pp. 323–4 ('elle exercitou o pecado nefando de sodomia consumada por espaço de sete anos, cometendo o dito pecado com outros homens activa e passivamente agendo et patiendo, sendo incubo e subcubo', 'porque os complices erão seus criados que estavão em sua casa e o servião').
17. F. A. Dutra, 'Sodomy and the Portuguese Nobility: The Case of Dom Filipe de Moura and His Circle', in H. Johnson and F. A. Dutra, eds., *Pelo vaso traseiro: Sodomy and Sodomites in Luso-Brazilian History* (Tucson, AZ, 2006), pp. 165–94, at pp. 168–72.
18. D. Higgs, 'Tales of Two Carmelites: Inquisitorial Narratives from Portugal and Brazil', in P. Sigal, ed., *Infamous Desire: Male Homosexuality in Colonial Latin America* (Chicago, 2003), pp. 152–67, at pp. 153–5.
19. Rocke, *Forbidden Friendships*, p. 116.
20. H. Moller, 'The Accelerated Development of Youth: Beard Growth as a Biological Marker', *Comparative Studies in Society and History*, 29 (1987), pp. 748–62, at pp. 753–5 (up to 23); D. Biow, *On the Importance of Being an Individual in Renaissance Italy: Men, Their Professions, and Their Beards* (Philadelphia, 2015), p. 197 (17–18); Mott, 'Musulmani sodomiti', p. 163 (17).
21. Rocke, *Forbidden Friendships*, p. 100 (citing Francesco Maria Molza's 'Novella di Ridolfo fiorentino').
22. Baldassari, *Bande giovanili, passim*, esp. pp. 56, 67, 69.
23. F. Mormando, *The Preacher's Demons: Bernardino of Siena and the Social Underworld of Early Renaissance Italy* (Chicago, 1999), p. 115.
24. Berco, *Jerarquías sexuales*, p. 41.
25. G. D. Ottonelli, *Della christiana moderatione del theatro libro primo, detto la qualità delle Comedie*, 2nd edn. (Florence, 1655), p. 195.
26. G. B. De Luca, *Il dottor volgare, libro decimoquinto* (Rome, 1673), p. 322 ('vn certo stimolo quasi naturale').
27. Ibid., p. 322 ('Che però quando si verificasse quello di che in alcuni paesi si suole mormorare, e che appresso persone onorate, e puntuali pare impossibile à crederlo, cioè che la cosa fosse nell'opposto, e che la parte del paziente si facesse da persone d'età graue, e matura, no[n] già per questo stimolo, ouero per quell'istinto naturale, il quale si suol dare... verso i giouanetti di bell'aspetto, mà per una sensualità, la quale pare che abbia della bestialità, e di sporchezza troppo grande, in tal caso la pratica dourebbe essere al contrario, anzi con maggiore seuerità').
28. Rocco, *L'Alcibiade*, p. 75 ('L'età mutano specie e natura nei trastulli amorosi... si mangia delicato il capretto, che fatto becco è fetidissimo; ma quelli che a questi caproni attendono sono ribelli d'amore, sono bestie di ferino e corrotto senso').

29. Davidson, 'Sodomy in Early Modern Venice', p. 81(n. 49) (1500); Rocke, *Forbidden Friendships*, p. 104 (1516).
30. Berco, *Jerarquías sexuales*, p. 87 ('su propia perversión', 'irracional desorden', 'no satisfecho con la corrupción ajena procuró este oprobio en sí mismo').

CHAPTER 6

1. Carrasco, *Inquisición y represión*, p. 107 ('una separación radical entre la afectividad y el sexo').
2. Rocke, *Forbidden Friendships*, pp. 151–5. Cristian Berco's analysis of the Aragonese records yields a figure of 25% for public places; but—given the different catchment area in this case—most of these were in the countryside (*Jerarquías sexuales*, p. 57).
3. Baldassari, *Bande giovanili*, p. 63 (Rome); Dean, 'Sodomy in Renaissance Bologna', p. 433; Riera i Sans, *Sodomites catalans*, p. 432 (Barcelona); J. J. Alves Dias, 'Para uma abordagem do sexo proibido em Portugal, no século XVI', in *Inquisição: comunicações apresentadas ao 1.º Congresso Luso-Brasileiro sobre Inquisição realizado em Lisboa, de 17 a 20 de Fevereiro de 1987*, 2 vols. (Lisbon, 1989–90), i, pp. 151–9, at p. 157 (Lisbon).
4. Above, pp. 9, 26.
5. O. Niccoli, *Il seme della violenza: putti, fanciulli e mammoli nell'Italia tra Cinque e Seicento* (Rome, 1995), p. 187.
6. Blastenbrei, *Kriminalität in Rom*, p. 278; Rocke, *Forbidden Friendships*, p. 166. A *giulio* was a papal coin containing nearly 4 grams of silver; this would have been more than enough for the boy to live on for a week.
7. Rocco, *L'Alcibiade*, pp. 64–5 ('liberale e cortese', 'convenzione e mercede', 'sordida mercanzia').
8. Rocke, *Forbidden Friendships*, pp. 164–5.
9. F. Molina, 'La sodomía a bordo. Sexualidad y poder en la Carrera de Indias (siglos XVI–XVII)', *Revista de estudios marítimos y sociales*, 3:3 (2010), pp. 9–19, at pp. 16–17; Lage da Gama Lima, 'Sodomia e pedofilia', pp. 244, 248–9.
10. Rocke, *Forbidden Friendships*, p. 166.
11. Ibid., pp. 177–80.
12. Ibid., p. 165.
13. M. Hewlett, 'The French Connection: Syphilis and Sodomy in Late-Renaissance Lucca', in K. Siena, ed., *Sins of the Flesh: Responding to Sexual Disease in Early-Modern Europe* (Toronto, 2005), pp. 239–60, at pp. 253–4.
14. P. de León, *Grandeza y miseria en Andalucia: testimonio de una encrucijada historia (1578–1616)*, ed. P. Herrera Puga (Granada, 1981), pp. 438–9 ('bien famoso por el trato que tenía con los caballeros de buen parecer').
15. Monter, *Frontiers of Heresy*, p. 140; C. Berco, 'Social Control and its Limits: Sodomy, Local Sexual Economies, and Inquisitors during Spain's Golden Age', *The Sixteenth Century Journal*, 36 (2005), pp. 331–58, at p. 354.

16. M. E. Perry, *Gender and Disorder in Early Modern Seville* (Princeton, NJ, 1990), pp. 25–6.

17. Bernardino of Siena, *Le prediche volgari*, ed. C. Cannarozzi, 2 vols. (Pistoia, 1934), ii, p. 45 ('luoghi riposti ove si tiene pubrico [*sic*] bordello de' garzoni come di pubbliche meritrici').

18. Rocke, *Forbidden Friendships*, pp. 157–8 (denunciations), 160 (frequenting brothels), 228 (denunciations).

19. Ibid., p. 159; above, p. 44; N. Pizzolato, ' "Lo diavolo mi ingannao": la sodomia nelle campagne siciliane (1572–1664)', *Quaderni storici*, 122 (year 41, no. 2) (2006), pp. 449–80, at p. 479(n.) ('uomini barbati', 'giovani sbarbati').

20. Baldassari, *Bande giovanili*, pp. 55 ('per quanto intendo tutti gli hosti sono consapevoli di tal vitio et trovandone [gli osti] loro attività e guadagno per lo spaccio della robba alle suddete loro hosterie ci tengono la mano et ci danno quelle comodità che loro desiderano'), 73 (rooms set aside), 87 ('più volte mi ha cercato che io volessi andare in la osteria a farmi buggiarare').

21. a Sancto Felice, *Triumphus misericordiae*, p. 103 ('cubicula aliqua secretiora ad comedendum, quamvis sciant saepissimè requiri ad commodiorem usum Sodomiae'). The request added that they could not refuse without incurring loss of earnings, threats of beatings and other vexations. The response from Rome was that they were permitted to rent out such rooms, even if they thought they would probably be used for sodomy, so long as they did not positively intend them to be used for that purpose.

22. A. Roby, *La Prostitution au Moyen Âge: le commerce charnel en Midi toulousain du XIIIᵉ au XVIᵉ siècle* (Villemur-sur-Tarn, 2021), pp. 191–5.

23. Rocke, *Forbidden Friendships*, p. 203; Grassi, *L'Offizio sopra l'Onestà*, pp. 111–12.

24. Ruggiero, *Boundaries of Eros*, p. 138; cf. I. Bloch, *Die Prostitution*, 2 vols. (Berlin, 1912–25), i, p. 796, saying that barbers were in this regard the most frequently mentioned profession in the Venetian records.

25. Rocke, *Forbidden Friendships*, p. 138 (Florence); Grassi, *L'Offizio sopra l'Onestà*, p. 50 (Lucca); Carrasco, *Inquisición y represión*, p. 168 (Valencia). Cf. also Baldassari, *Bande giovanili*, p. 50.

26. Zuccarello, 'La sodomia al tribunale bolognese', pp. 37–44, esp. p. 38.

27. Perry, 'The "Nefarious Sin"', p. 82.

28. Rocke, *Forbidden Friendships*, p. 164; cf. p. 231, on an incident in 1521 when two boys were gang-raped by a captain and six soldiers. Dean notes a trial in Bologna in 1452 where it was stated that a boy had been sodomized by several soldiers in a Florentine troop: 'Sodomy in Renaissance Bologna', p. 434.

29. H. Puff, *Sodomy in Reformation Germany and Switzerland, 1400–1600* (Chicago, 2003), pp. 43–4; C. Sieber-Lehmann, *Spätmittelalterlicher Nationalismus: die Burgunderkriege am Oberrhein und in der Eidgenossenschaft* (Göttingen, 1995), pp. 144–9 (p. 148: 'Schauprozess').

30. A. Cicuta ['A. Adriano'], *Della disciplina militare del Capitano Alfonso Adriano* (Venice, 1566), p. 403 ('espulsa, & aspramente castigato chi l'usa').

31. R. C. Trexler, *Sex and Conquest: Gendered Violence, Political Order, and the European Conquest of the Americas* (Ithaca, NY, 1995), p. 53.

32. Ruggiero, *Boundaries of Eros*, p. 111 (and cf. pp. 134–5).

33. Archivio Segreto Vaticano, Vatican City, MS Misc., Arm. II, vol. 110, fos. 385r–399v, at fo. 390r–v ('i uitij enormi della bestemmia e sodomia, il quali sogliono regnare tanto fra galeotti come fra soldati', 'tutti li ragazzi di soldati').

34. Ibid., fos. 394r–396r ('molti altrj malj Xr[ist]ianj, che non sono ne marinarj, ne inferiorj officialj, con il mezzo del denaro, con gli detti giouani fanno cose abomineuolj', 'tanto uniuersale, che non solamente non si castiga ne si riprende, ma è tenuto per cosa di persone honorate', 'tanto dishonore al Christianesmo che si faccia come fanno i Turchi; che menano li giouani').

35. A. Barbero, *Lepanto: la battaglia dei tre imperi* (Rome, 2010), p. 385; cf. M. Rivero Rodríguez, *La batalla de Lepanto: cruzada, guerra santa e identidad confesional* (Madrid, 2008), p. 140.

36. S. Bono, *Schiavi musulmani nell'Italia moderna: galeotti, vu' cumprà, domestici* (Naples, 1999), pp. 375–6 (Italian ports); L. Mott, '*Justitia et misericórdia*: The Portuguese Inquisition and the Repression of the Nefarious Sin of Sodomy', in H. Johnson and F. A. Dutra, eds., *Pelo vaso traseiro: Sodomy and Sodomites in Luso-Brazilian History* (Tucson, AZ, 2006), pp. 63–104, at p. 87 (1585); Drumond Braga, 'Foreigners, Sodomy', p. 153 (1585).

37. A. Zysberg, *Les Galériens: vies et destins de 60,000 forçats sur les galères de France, 1680–1748* (Paris, 1987), pp. 161–2.

38. J.-J. Bouchard, *Journal*, ed. E. Kanceff, 2 vols. (Turin, 1976–7), i, pp. 81–2 ('de sorte qu'il ne se peche plus maintenant là dedans qu'en sodomie, mollesse, irrumation et autres pareilles tendresses'). (Technically, 'irrumation' referred not to the act of a fellator, but to that of a person who makes someone fellate him.)

39. Riera i Sans, *Sodomites catalans*, pp. 208–9.

40. Berco, *Jerarquías sexuales*, p. 100.

41. N. Pérez Cánovas, *Homosexualidad: homosexuales y uniones homosexuales en el Derecho español* (Granada, 1996), p. 12 ('no se haga lo que hoy día hacen los inquisidores, que condenan tan solamente a galeras a los reos de tan enorme delito... de lo que se siguen muchos inconvenientes que no se pueden explicar por la vileza y enormidad del crimen').

42. Garza Carvajal, *Butterflies will Burn*, pp. 91 ('younger mariners...'), 95 (burning), 106 ('many seamen...'), 113–17 (1566 case); Molina, 'La sodomia a bordo', 12 (ages of pages, grummets), 16 (1566 case).

43. See for example A. N. Gilbert, 'Buggery and the British Navy, 1700–1861', *Journal of Social History*, 10 (1976), pp. 72–98, at p. 87.

44. F. Bethencourt, *The Inquisition: A Global History, 1478–1834*, trans. J. Birrell (Cambridge, 2009), p. 276 (Inquisition sentence).

45. Higgs, 'Tales of Two Carmelites', p. 156.

46. Carrasco, *Inquisición y represión*, p. 22 ('los presos se pasaban las noches espiándose unos a otros').

47. Garza Carvajal, *Butterflies will Burn*, pp. 97–104, 193–4; see also F. Molina, *Cuando amar era pecado: sexualidad, poder e identidad entre los sodomitas coloniales (Virreinato del Perú, siglos XVI–XVII)* (La Paz, 2017), p. 97; Z. Tortorici, *Sins against Nature: Sex and Archives in Colonial New Spain* (Durham, NC, 2018), p. 109.

48. Bouchard, *Journal*, ii, pp. 377–8 (boy, 'lequel luy [referring to Bouchard] adoucit tant soit peu l'amertume et tristesse en laquelle il se treuvoit, *adeo homo a natura est ad voluptatem proclivis*'), 379 ('aussi bien souvent in the prison, le geolier introduisant pour de l'argent γαροες et γαροους, soit de dehors, ou de ceus et celles qui se trouvoint prisoniers'). Bouchard wrote some key terms, relating to sex, in Greek letters in his journal, to guard against prying eyes.

49. See Greenberg, *Construction of Homosexuality*, p. 286.

50. Mott, '*Justitia et misericórdia*', pp. 70 (Agostinho), 81 (João, António); L. Mott, 'My Pretty Boy: Love Letters from a Sodomite Friar, Lisbon (1690)', in H. Johnson and F. A. Dutra, eds., *Pelo vaso traseiro: Sodomy and Sodomites in Luso-Brazilian History* (Tucson, AZ, 2006), pp. 231–61, at pp. 236–51 (affair), 261 (Manoel; António, 33 partners).

51. Molina, *Cuando amar era pecado*, p. 75.

52. G. Romeo, *Amori proibiti: i concubini tra Chiesa e Inquisizione, Napoli 1563–1656* (Bari, 2008), pp. 107–9 ('bordello di bardasci'), 110, 229–32 ('confession'). For documents on the Volpino case see also P. Scaramella, *Le lettere della Congregazione del Sant'Ufficio ai Tribunali di Fede di Napoli, 1563–1625* (Trieste, 2002), pp. 120–4, 151–2, 158.

53. British Library, London, MS Add. 6877, report by Giovanni Francesco Graziani to Paul V, 1610, fos. 21v ('tal uolta caminaua alla presentia sua et di quelli che erano stati suoi cinedi ignudo p[er] camera co[n] la carne alterata, et che sentiua co[n]tento et gusto in farsi uedere et toccarsi carnalme[n]te in quella maniera'), 25v ('l'Idea di tutte le sceleratezze et che sia il piu pessimo huomo c'habbi il mondo'). The writer's claims have been taken as essentially truthful by one recent work, V. Frajese, *Une Histoire homosexuelle: Paolo Sarpi et la recherche de l'individu à Venise au XVIIᵉ siècle*, trans. J. Castiglione (Paris, 2022). But what Frajese offers as corroborative evidence consists, to a large extent, either of contingent social connections with a few Venetians who have been regarded as sodomitical, or of general elements in Sarpi's thought which involve dissimulation, religious scepticism and philosophical naturalism. Neither form of argument can constitute a positive reason for thinking that he was a sodomite himself.

54. S. Haliczer, *Sexuality in the Confessional: A Sacrament Profaned* (New York, 1996), pp. 107–9. On the general issue, but citing only cases of female victims, see also A. Sarrión Mora, *Sexualidad y confesión: la solicitación ante el Tribunal del Santo Oficio (siglos XVI–XIX)* (Madrid, 1994).

55. Molina, *Cuando amar era pecado*, p. 131 ('a ynstancias de este reo sacaba el muchacho sus partes verendas y este reo se las manoseaba').

56. Rocke, *Forbidden Friendships*, pp. 138–9.

57. Ruggiero, *Boundaries of Eros*, pp. 142–3.

58. Riera i Sans, *Sodomites catalans*, pp. 185 (1550), 256–9 (1590), 302 (1603), 318–19 (1607); for other cases see pp. 183–4, 324–6, 359–64, 371–3.

59. Carrasco, *Inquisición y represión*, pp. 140–1 ('[el] dicho reo…enseñaba a dichos muchachos a ser sodomitas, haciéndoles que se conociesen carnalmente, metiendo sus miembros genitales los unos a los otros y alternativamente por los óculos traseros, tomándoles el dicho reo sus miembros en las manos y poniéndolos en los óculos de los pacientes, haciendo a los agentes hacer fuerza hasta que los metiesen dentro', 'haciéndoles decir las oraciones cuando estaban en dichos actos torpes').

60. Mott, *'Justitia et misericórdia'*, p. 85.

61. G. Boccaccio, *Esposizioni sopra la Comedia di Dante*, ed. G. Padoan (Milan, 1965), p. 680 ('così a' disonesti come agli onesti comandamenti de' lor maestri').

62. Benvenuto da Imola, *Comentum*, i, p. 522 ('sunt otiosi, et habent materiam paratam, scilicet copiam puerorum').

63. V. Cian, 'Una lettera di Carlo Sigonio contro i pedanti', *Giornale storico della letteratura italiana*, 15 (1890), pp. 459–61, at pp. 460–1 ('tutti dal volgo notati sono dishonestissimamente peccare in lussuria, et non pur nella natural, ma eziandio nella sogdomitica').

64. A. Grazzini, *Le cene*, ed. G. B. Squarotti and E. Mazzali (Milan, 1989), p. 313 ('PER AVER FALSATO LA SODOMIA').

65. Labalme, 'Sodomy and Venetian Justice', pp. 228–9 (1496); Rocke, *Forbidden Friendships*, pp. 158–9 (Florentine laws); W. A. Rebhorn, *The Emperor of Men's Minds: Literature and the Renaissance Discourse of Rhetoric* (Ithaca, NY, 1995), p. 192 ('there is…').

66. Rocke, *Forbidden Friendships*, p. 140.

67. Bono, *Schiavi musulmani*, p. 35 (Italy); B. Bennassar, 'L'Esclavage des femmes en Europe à l'époque moderne', *Storia delle donne*, 5 (2009), pp. 131–46, at p. 132 (Spain, 50,000); A. Domínguez Ortiz, 'La esclavitud en Castilla durante la Edad Moderna', *Estudios de historia social de España*, 2 (1952), pp. 369–48, at p. 277 (Spain, 100,000); A. C. de C. M. Saunders, *A Social History of Black Slaves and Freedmen in Portugal, 1441–1555* (Cambridge, 1982), p. 59 (Portugal); G. Wettinger, *Slavery in the Islands of Malta and Gozo, ca. 1000–1812* (San Gwann, 2002), p. 33 (Malta); Zysberg, *Les Galériens*, pp. 62, 303 (French fleet).

68. A. Giuffredi, *Avvertimenti cristiani*, ed. L. Natoli (Palermo, 1896), p. 77 ('paggi o schiavotti').

69. Carrasco, *Inquisición y represión*, p. 14; D. Blumenthal, *Enemies and Familiars: Slavery and Mastery in Fifteenth-Century Valencia* (Ithaca, NY, 2009), pp. 89–91.

70. F. Carboni, *L'umanità negata: schiavi mori, turchi, neri, ebrei e padroni cristiani nella Sardegna del '500* (Cagliari, 2008), p. 63; Carboni also cites a case of a slave impregnated in this way in Sardinia in 1539 (p. 97). On the sexual exploitation of female slaves in these societies see also S. McKee, 'The Implications of Slave Women's Sexual Service in Late Medieval Italy', in M. E. Kabadayi and T. Reichardt, eds., *Unfreie Arbeit: ökonomische und kulturgeschichtliche Perspektiven* (Hildesheim, 2007), pp. 101–14; S. McKee, 'The Familiarity of Slaves in Medieval

and Early Modern Households', in S. Hanss and J. Schiel, eds., *Mediterranean Slavery Revisited (500–1800). Neue Perspektiven auf mediterrane Sklaverei (500–1800)* (Zurich, 2014), pp. 501–14, esp. pp. 505–8; R. M. Karras, *Unmarriages: Women, Men, and Sexual Unions in the Middle Ages* (Philadelphia, 2012), pp. 83–94.

71. Molina, *Cuando amar era pecado*, pp. 89–90.

72. R. Vainfas, 'The Nefarious and the Colony', in H. Johnson and F. A. Dutra, eds., *Pelo vaso traseiro: Sodomy and Sodomites in Luso-Brazilian History* (Tucson, AZ, 2006), pp. 337–67, at pp. 353–4.

73. R. Vainfas, *Trópico dos pecados: moral, sexualidade e Inquisição no Brasil* (Rio de Janeiro, 1989), p. 173; D. Higgs, 'Rio de Janeiro', in D. Higgs, ed., *Queer Sites: Gay Urban Histories since 1600* (London, 1999), pp. 138–63, at p. 139.

74. R. Barahona, *Sex Crimes, Honour, and the Law in Early Modern Spain: Vizcaya, 1528–1735* (Toronto, 2003), p. 81.

75. Vainfas, 'The Nefarious and the Colony', p. 342.

76. R. García Cárcel, *Herejía y sociedad en el siglo XVI: la Inquisición en Valencia 1530–1609* (Barcelona, 1980), p. 291.

77. R. Rosselló, ed., *Procés contra Ponç Hug Comte d'Empúries per pecat de sodomia* (Palma, 2003), pp. 37 ('és fama publica, que amb els seus domèstics que li ho consenteixen, exerceix aquest crim i afavoreix aquests pacients, però els qui el rebutgen, els vol mal i els despedeix'), 40 (whipped), *passim* (rubbing).

78. Baldassari, *Bande giovanili*, pp. 35–6.

79. Hewlett, 'French Connection', pp. 252–3.

80. Rocke, *Forbidden Friendships*, p. 163.

CHAPTER 7

1. Rocke, *Forbidden Friendships*, pp. 162–3 (anal injuries); Baldassari, *Bande giovanili*, p. 132 (Rome); above, p. 44 (Venice).

2. Ruggiero, *Boundaries of Eros*, pp. 114–16, 190(n.).

3. Carrasco, *Inquisición y represión*, p. 127; Carrasco also notes a different technique, involving the 'active' partner rubbing his erect penis against the belly of the passive one.

4. I. M. Drumond Braga, 'Pelo universo da sexualidade proibida: os Mouriscos portugueses e o pecado nefando de sodomia', *Revista lusófona de ciência das religiões*, 21 (2018), pp. 7–25, at p. 13 (and for typical examples of this claim see pp. 16, 21); Vainfas, *Trópico dos pecados*, pp. 263–4 ('Prisioneira de sua morfologia dos atos').

5. El-Rouayheb, *Before Homosexuality*, p. 138.

6. Rocke, *Forbidden Friendships*, pp. 28, 245.

7. Ibid., pp. 173–4 (and cf. p. 245). Ronaldo Vainfas notes the presence in the Brazilian records of several men in their 50s and 60s, up to one aged 70: 'The Nefarious and the Colony', p. 344.

8. Grassi, *L'Offizio sopra l'Onestà*, p. 41. As Grassi notes, however (pp. 42–3), the punishments actually inflicted were much milder than this.

9. Rocco, *L'Alcibiade*, p. 79 ('fanciulli coetani').

10. L. Mott, 'Crypto-Sodomites in Colonial Brazil', trans. S. Popat, in P. Sigal, ed., *Infamous Desire: Male Homosexuality in Colonial Latin America* (Chicago, 2003), pp. 168–96, at pp. 182–3; cf. also Vainfas, *Trópico dos pecados*, p. 170.

11. C. Seijas and J. Melchor Toledo, *Demencia nefanda: estudios sobre la homosexualidad en Guatemala del siglo XVII al XXI* (n.p., n.d.), pp. 77 ('meneando el cuerpo como quando están en acto carnal'), 84 ('dame un besito'). The case came to court not because of this alleged offence by the apprentice, but because his master had whipped him so savagely for it that the boy's mother litigated (successfully) both to have her son removed from that man's service and to obtain from him the costs of the boy's medical treatment.

12. Rocke, *Forbidden Friendships*, pp. 97–8.

13. Pizzolato, '"Lo diavolo mi ingannao"', pp. 465–8 (Sicily); Riera i Sans, *Sodomites catalans*, p. 386 ('dos o tres vezes...se havían conozido carnalmente por detrás, alternatibamente el uno al otro'): the offences had taken place during the previous 16 years, when they were aged c.45–c.61 and 20–36 respectively.

14. Davidson, 'Sodomy in Early Modern Venice', p. 70.

15. Above, pp. 46, 48; Mott, 'Crypto-Sodomites', pp. 183–9.

16. Rocke, *Forbidden Friendships*, p. 79. Rocke notes (p. 243) that he is the only passive adult in the records above the age of 26.

17. Davidson, 'Sodomy in Early Modern Venice', p. 70.

18. Vainfas, 'The Nefarious and the Colony', pp. 346–7; cf. also Vainfas, *Trópico dos pecados*, pp. 166–7. Lucas admitted to having had 99 previous sexual partners.

19. Carrasco, *Inquisición y represión*, p. 135 (Roca, 'Pedro' Pizarro); Berco, *Jerarquías sexuales*, p. 45 (Roca, 'Francisco' Pizarro).

20. G. B. Della Porta, *Della fisionomia dell'uomo*, ed. M. Cicognani (Parma, 1988), pp. 533–4 ('io ne viddi uno in Napoli di pochi peli in barba o quasi niuno; di piccola boca, di ciglia delicate e dritte...insomma con corpo e gesti di femina... era più femina che l'istesse femine; ragionava come femina, e si dava l'articolo femineo sempre...et il peggio era, che peggior d'una femina sopportava la nefanda Venere'). One modern writer has claimed that this is a description of a *femminiello*, a type of homosexual in modern Naples who adopts effeminate behaviour and may undergo a mock-marriage to a man: M. Bertuzzi, *I femminielli: il labile tra il sacro e l'umano*, 2nd edn. (Florence, 2018), p. 136. But otherwise no *femminielli* are mentioned in historical sources before the late 19th century; see M. Atlas, *Die Femminielli von Neapel: zur kulturellen Konstruktion von Transgender* (Frankfurt, 2010).

21. Alves Dias, 'Para uma abordagem do sexo proibido', pp. 157–8 ('bem barbado', 'Os famchonos são os pacientes e nunqua famchono com famchono pecão neste peccado'); on the term see Vainfas, *Trópico dos pecados*, p. 150 (effeminate; also masturbator); Johnson and Dutra, *Pelo vaso traseiro*, p. 475 (passive only). Possibly 'well bearded' just meant that he was well past the age at which he had begun to grow facial hair.

22. Carrasco, *Inquisición y represión*, p. 126.

23. Drumond Braga, 'Foreigners, Sodomy', pp. 152–3 (man with man); L. Mott, 'The Misadventures of a Portuguese Man in Seventeenth-Century Brazil', in H. Johnson and F. A. Dutra, eds., *Pelo vaso traseiro: Sodomy and Sodomites in Luso-Brazilian History* (Tucson, AZ, 2006), pp. 293–335, at p. 310 (not 'perfect'; man with boy); D. Higgs, 'Lisbon', in D. Higgs, ed., *Queer Sites: Gay Urban Histories since 1600* (London, 1999), pp. 112–37, at pp. 118–20 (men with boys).
24. Tortorici, *Sins against Nature*, pp. 186–7.
25. Rocke, *Forbidden Friendships*, pp. 93 (exceptions, 'apparently not...'), 94 ('a new...'), 129 ('older single...'), 285(n. 48) (83 and 18). Rocke finds that fellatio occurred in 12% of all cases, an extraordinarily high figure in comparison with the evidence from other Mediterranean societies. This is based (pp. 92–3) on taking all references to sodomy 'ex parte ante' (from the front) to mean fellatio; in one single case, the notary did explicate it in that way, but it is surely possible that it could also refer to face-to-face interfemoral intercourse—or even to face-to-face anal sex, which is clearly described by Deli Birader. See Kuru, 'Sixteenth Century Scholar', pp. 88 ('oġlanun ḫōca dudaḳların aġzına almış ayaḳların boynına ṣalmış'), 198 ('the teacher was sucking the boy's lips and had his legs over his shoulders'), and cf. the description of sexual positions on pp. 101, 210.
26. Drumond Braga, 'Foreigners, Sodomy', p. 150.
27. Higgs, 'Historiography of Male–Male Love', p. 41; see pp. 138–9.
28. de León, *Grandeza y miseria*, p. 399 ('tocamientos deshonestos', 'retozando', 'hablando palabras deshonestas'). They were members of a company of soldiers, and their captain was evidently concerned to strengthen military discipline; but he did so with the support of the Castilian court.
29. Ruggiero, *Boundaries of Eros*, p. 115.
30. L. Pérez, L. Muntaner and M. Colom, eds., *El Tribunal de la Inquisición en Mallorca: relación de causas de fe, 1578–1806*, i (Palma de Mallorca, 1986), pp. 269–72.
31. Carrasco, *Inquisición y represión*, p. 126 ('más ruidosas o agitadas').
32. Rocke, *Forbidden Friendships*, p. 129.
33. Arquivo Nacional da Torre do Tombo, Lisbon, PT/TT/TSO-IL proc. 5106, fo. 11v ('o peccado de molicies'); the sexual relations thus established continued, twice a week, for four years.
34. Baldassari, *Bande giovanili*, pp. 76–8 (Rome); Drumond Braga, 'Pelo universo da sexualidade proibida', pp. 20–1 (Lisbon).
35. Ruggiero, *Boundaries of Eros*, pp. 121, 124, 135, 193(n. 70).
36. Rocke, *Forbidden Friendships*, p. 188.
37. Molina, *Cuando amar era pecado*, p. 160 ('rotación de parejas sexuales'); N. Alonso Cortés, *La muerte del conde de Villamediana* (Valladolid, 1928), p. 94; Garza Carvajal, *Butterflies will Burn*, pp. 43, 220–1(n. 22).
38. Davidson, 'Sodomy in Early Modern Venice', p. 70. The word was also used by one Florentine writer; Rocke notes that it could be used for a political faction (*Forbidden Friendships*, p. 189).
39. J. de Barrionuevo, *Avisos de Jerónimo de Barrionuevo (1654–1658)*, ed. A. Paz y Miéla, 2 vols. (Madrid, 1892), i, pp. 215–16 ('acostados de dos en dos', 'para averiguar

más cómplices'); they were described as 'putos' (a general term for sodomites), and identified as a jeweller (a rich man, owner of the garden), a 'Genoese', a necklace-maker and a notary. The next newsletter (p. 222) named the jeweller as Agustin de la Paz.

40. See G. Marcocci, 'Matrimoni omosessuali nella Roma del tardo cinquecento: su un passo del "Journal" di Montaigne', *Quaderni storici*, n.s., no. 133, year 45 (2010), pp. 107–37; G. Ferguson, *Same-Sex Marriage in Renaissance Rome: Sexuality, Identity, and Community in Early Modern Europe* (Ithaca, NY, 2016). Most of these men were Spanish; Marco was Portuguese; Battista was described as 'Albanian', as he was from the territory known as 'Albania veneziana', but was from the Slav-speaking Paštrović tribe on the Montenegrin coast (on which see P. S. Šerović, 'Paštrovići, njihovo plemensko uredjenje i pomorska tradicija', *Godišnjak pomorskog muzeja u Kotoru*, 5 (1956), pp. 25–37).

41. Baldassari, *Bande giovanili*, p. 163.

42. Tortorici, *Sins against Nature*, p. 110.

43. Carrasco, *Inquisición y represión*, pp. 116–17 ('rarísimas excepciones'); Rocke, *Forbidden Friendships*, pp. 167–8.

44. Rocke, *Forbidden Friendships*, pp. 169–70.

45. Above, p. 4.

46. Molina, *Cuando amar era pecado*, pp. 101–2, 144–6 (Gaspar), 145 (Don Diego).

47. C. Giraldo Botero, *Deseo y represión. Homoeroticidad en la Nueva Granada (1559–1822)* (Bogotá, 2002), p. 32 ('habia hecho muchos excesos de sentimiento').

48. Mott, 'Misadventures of a Portuguese Man', pp. 302–9. For a fuller account of Delgado, see Mott, *O sexo proibido*, pp. 75–129.

49. See pp. 162–3.

50. F. Berni, *Poesie e prose*, ed. E. Chiòrboli (Geneva, 1934), pp. 195–7 ('De puero peste aegrotante', 'Debueram tecum stratis iacuisse sub isdem, | Et conferre tuis oribus ora mea; | His etiam saevo de vulnere dira venena | Exhaurire, et tecum inde perire simul', 'amans'); in a subsequent poem (p. 197) he sent word to his friends that the boy had recovered.

51. Ibid., pp. 69–71 ('Capitolo d'un ragazzo', 'Oh state cheti, egli è pur un trastullo | Aver un garzonetto che sia bello, | Da insegnarli dottrina e da condullo!').

52. B. Cellini, *La vita di Benvenuto Cellini, scritta da lui medesimo, nuovamente riscontrata sul codice Laurenziano*, ed. G. Guasti (Florence, 1890), p. 51 ('per aiuto avevo solo un fanciulletto, che con grandissime preghiere d'amici, mezzo contra la mia voglia, avevo preso per fattorino. Questo fanciullo era di età di quattordici anni incirca, aveva nome Paulino, ed era figliuolo di un cittadino romano, il quale viveva di sue entrate. Era questo Paulino il meglio creato, il più onesto ed il più bello figliuolo, che mai io vedessi alla vita mia; e per i sui onesti atti e costumi, e per la sua infinita bellezza, e per la grande amore che lui portava a me, avenne, che per queste cause io gli pose tanto amore, quanto in un petto di uno uomo rinchiuder si possa. Questo sviscerato amore fu causa, che per vedere io più sovente rasserenare quel maraviglioso viso, che per natura sua onesto e

maninconico si dimostrava, pure quando io pigliavo il mio cornetto, subito moveva un riso tanto onesto e tanto bello, che io non mi maraviglio punto di quelle pappolate che scrivono e'Greci degli Dei del Cielo: questo talvolta, essendo a quei tempi, gli arette fatti forse più uscire de'ganghere'); the editor notes an apparent lacuna in the text, filled here by the words added in square brackets.

53. M. A. Gallucci, 'Cellini's Trial for Sodomy: Power and Patronage at the Court of Cosimo I', in K. Eisenbichler, ed., *The Cultural Politics of Duke Cosimo I de' Medici* (Aldershot, 2001), pp. 37–46, at pp. 37 (sentence, commuted), 43 (career).

54. Carrasco, *Inquisición y represión*, p. 117 ('desnudos en la misma cama'). Both men were burnt at the stake.

55. L. Mott and A. Assunção, 'Love's Labors Lost: Five Letters from a Seventeenth-Century Portuguese Sodomite', in K. Gerard and G. Hekma, eds., *The Pursuit of Sodomy: Male Homosexuality in Renaissance and Enlightenment Europe* (Binghamton, NY, 1989), pp. 91–101, at p. 94.

56. Arquivo Nacional da Torre do Tombo, Lisbon, PT/TT/TSO-IL/026/0141 (Caderno 14° de nefandos), fo. 229r ('muitos e repetidos actos de Molicias').

57. Mott, 'My Pretty Boy', esp. pp. 240–7. Some confusion may have been caused by the fact that the older man's confession mentioned that, while the singer was still present in the monastery, they corresponded with each other by 'love letters, which the said chorister wrote to him, and some replies which he, the confessant, gave to him': Arquivo Nacional da Torre do Tombo, Lisbon, PT/TT/TSO-IL/026/0141 (Caderno 14° de nefandos), fo. 229r ('cartas de amores, que o dito corista lhe escreuia e por alguas ripostas que este declarante lhe daua'). Mott gives the full Portuguese texts of the surviving letters in the original version of his study, 'Meu menino lindo: cartas de amor de um Frade sodomita, Lisboa, 1690', *Luso-Brazilian Review*, 38:2 (2001), pp. 97–115, at pp. 102–8. Unfortunately the archival reference he gives for the letters (Caderno 14° de nefandos, fos. 228r–237v) refers only to the Inquisition record of the older man's confession; this does not contain the letters, though some folios appear to be missing from the numbered sequence.

CHAPTER 8

1. Herrero García, *Ideas de los Españoles*, pp. 349–51 (writers); A. L. Martín, 'Sodomitas, putos, doncellos y maricotes en algunos textos de Quevedo', *La Perinola*, 12 (2008), pp. 107–22, at pp. 110–11 (Quevedo).

2. J. Howell ['J. H.'], *Paroimiographia: Proverbs; Or, Old Sayed Sawes & Adages in English (or the Saxon Toung), Italian, French and Spanish* (London, 1659), 'Refranes, ò proverbios morales' (separately paginated), p. 26 ('Tres *Italianos, dos* Bugerones, el otro Ateista'); J. Dupuy and P. Dupuy, eds., *Scaligeriana, sive excerpta ex ore Josephi Scaligeri* (Geneva, 1666), p. 329 ('in Hispania fratres esse Bugerones... in Gallia magnos, in Italia omnes'); L. Bély, 'Homosexuelle Netzwerke am Hof

Ludwigs XIV.', in N. Domeier and C. Mühling, eds., *Homosexualität am Hof: Praktiken und Diskurse vom Mittelalter bis heute* (Frankfurt, 2020), pp. 101–18, at p. 103 (France); van der Meer, *Sodoms zaad*, p. 373 (Holland).

3. Berco, 'Social Control', p. 346.

4. Riera i Sans, *Sodomites catalans*, p. 233.

5. Mott, 'Le Pouvoir inquisitorial', p. 209 (imagination); Mott, 'Crypto-Sodomites', p. 173 (Inquisition, Minas Gerais).

6. H. Estienne, *Apologie pour Herodote, ou traité de la conformité des merveilles anciennes avec les modernes*, 2 vols. (The Hague, 1735), i, pp. 115–16; cf. R. E. Zorach, 'The Matter of Italy: Sodomy and the Scandal of Style in Sixteenth-Century France', *Journal of Medieval and Early Modern Studies*, 28 (1998), pp. 581–609, at pp. 586, 589; Schleiner, 'Linguistic "Xenohomophobia"', p. 751.

7. G. Williams, *A Dictionary of Sexual Language and Imagery in Shakespearean and Stuart Literature*, 3 vols. (London, 2001), ii, s.v. 'Italian fashion'; for literary examples see A. Bray, *Homosexuality in Renaissance England*, 2nd edn. (New York, 1995), p. 75; Hammond, *Figuring Sex between Men*, pp. 22, 38; H. G. Cocks, *Visions of Sodom: Religion, Homoerotic Desire, and the End of the World in England, c.1550–1850* (Chicago, 2017), p. 159; C. McFarlane, *The Sodomite in Fiction and Satire, 1660–1750* (New York, 1997), p. 79.

8. Puff, *Sodomy in Reformation Germany*, p. 13 and *passim*; G. Steinhausen, ed., *Briefwechsel Balthasar Paumgartners des jüngeren mit seiner Gattin Magdalena, geb. Behaim (1592–1598)* (Tübingen, 1895), p. 238 ('verprend um florendinischer unzucht').

9. van der Meer, *Sodoms zaad*, p. 382 (poem); L. J. Boon, *'Dien godlosen hoop van menschen'. Verfolging van homoseksuelen in de Republiek in de jaren dertig van de achttiende eeuw*, ed. I. Schöffer et al. (Amsterdam, 1997), pp. 22–3 (travel).

10. S. Limbeck, '"Ein seltzam wunder vnd monstrum, welches beide mannlichen vnd weiblichen geschlecht an sich hett": Tetralogie, Sodomie und Allegorese in der Medienkultur der frühen Neuzeit', in L. M. Thoma and Sven Limbeck, eds., *'Die Sünde, der sich der tiuvel schamet in der helle': Homosexualität in der Kultur des Mittelalters und der frühen Neuzeit* (Ostfildern, 2009), pp. 199–247, at pp. 233–4 ('Hermaphroditae, Androgyni, Cynedi, Pedicones et similia Monstra'); cf. also Puff, *Sodomy in Reformation Germany*, p. 138; G. Wassilowsky, 'Homosexualität am frühneuzeitlichen Hof des Papstes', in N. Domeier and C. Mühling, eds., *Homosexualität am Hof: Praktiken und Diskurse vom Mittelalter bis heute* (Frankfurt, 2020), pp. 79–99, at pp. 80–2.

11. D. Potter, *Der minnen loep*, ed. P. Leendertz, 4 vols. (Leiden, 1845–7), ii, p. 4, bk 3, ll. 98–9: 'Nochtan so doetmense alle daghe | In Ytalyen openbaer' (emphasizing again in ll. 100–5 their lack of shame); K. Stadtwald, *Roman Popes and German Patriots: Antipapalism in the Politics of the German Humanist Movement from Gregor Heimburg to Martin Luther* (Geneva, 1996), p. 61; Puff, *Sodomy in Reformation Germany*, pp. 117 (mercenary), 125 (Regensburg).

12. Riera i Sans, *Sodomites catalans*, p. 295 ('Mala casta italiana, que·ns ve a inficionar del que—glòria a Déu!—està neta Catalunya').

13. Puff, *Sodomy in Reformation Germany*, p. 130.

14. M. A. Penrose, *Masculinity and Queer Desire in Spanish Enlightenment Literature* (Farnham, 2014), p. 17.

15. Carrasco, *Inquisición y represión*, p. 217 (Valencia); Monter, *Frontiers of Heresy*, p. 291 (Barcelona: table, entries for 'Homosexuality').

16. Berco, *Jerarquías sexuales*, p. 153; Monter, *Frontiers of Heresy*, pp. 291 ('vastly over-represented'), 292 ('even in...').

17. Monter, *Frontiers of Heresy*, pp. 291–2.

18. Riera i Sans, *Sodomites catalans*, p. 413 ('¿De Nápoles soys? Si soys de Nápoles, no puede ser que no os haian fornicado, porque los napolitanos tienen grande fama de bujarrones', 'por burlas'); Berco, *Jerarquías sexuales*, p. 153. The man was sentenced to 50 lashes and perpetual banishment from Barcelona.

19. Carrasco, *Inquisición y represión*, p. 219 ('los testimonios de no pocos sodomitas españoles amantes de Italia, corroboran esta sospecha. Más de un viajero, eclesiástico, soldado o peregrino, que por varias razones habían residido en Génova, Roma, Nápoles o Venecia, admitieron sin rodeos en declaraciones no exentas de nostalgia, la facilidad de contactos homosexuales que habían hallado en la vieja Italia, contactos, por lo general, venales y con chicos muy jóvenes').

20. Perry, *Gender and Disorder*, p. 125.

21. Puff, *Sodomy in Reformation Germany*, p. 81; H. Puff, 'Nature on Trial: Acts "Against Nature" in the Law Courts of Early Modern Germany and Switzerland', in L. Daston and F. Vidal, eds., *The Moral Authority of Nature* (Chicago, 2004), pp. 232–53, at p. 235.

22. Rocke, *Forbidden Friendships*, pp. 60 (convicted), 115 (quotation); cf. also p. 433(n. 1) of the present work.

23. Rocke, *Forbidden Friendships*, pp. 63–4.

24. M. Wittkower and R. Wittkower, *Born Under Saturn* (New York, 1963), p. 169 (sermon by Fra Giordano, 1305); Mormando, *The Preacher's Demons*, p. 140 (Bernardino).

25. G. Savonarola, *Scelta di prediche e scritti di Fra Girolamo Savonarola*, ed. P. Villari and E. Casanova (Florence, 1898), p. 261 ('Tutti quelli del vizio della sodomia si partano!—oh! quanti se ne andrebbero via').

26. R. Derosas, 'Moralità e giustizia a Venezia nel '500–'600: gli esecutori contra la bestemmia', in G. Cozzi, ed., *Stato, società e giustizia nella repubblica veneta (sec. XV–XVIII)* (Rome, 1980), pp. 431–528, at p. 437.

27. Ruggiero, *Boundaries of Eros*, p. 137 (Venice); Dean, 'Sodomy in Renaissance Bologna', p. 434.

28. Grassi, *L'Offizio sopra l'Onestà*, pp. 40 (statistics, population), 41–2, 80–1, 166 (punishments); Hewlett, 'French Connection', p. 243.

29. Ruggiero, *Boundaries of Eros*, pp. 127–33 (1406 case); Davidson, 'Sodomy in Early Modern Venice', pp. 67–8 (Council, Collegium); B.-U. Hergemöller, 'Sodomiter: Erscheinungsformen und Kausalfaktoren des spätmittelalterlichen Kampfes gegen Homosexuelle', in B.-U. Hergemöller, ed., *Randgruppen der spätmittelalterlichen Gesellschaft*, 2nd edn. (Warendorf, 1994), pp. 361–403, at p. 378 (Collegium).

30. G. Scarabello, 'Devianza sessuale ed interventi di giustizia a Venezia nella prima metà del XVI secolo', in S. Bettini et al., *Tiziano e Venezia: convegno internazionale di studi, Venezia, 1976* (Vicenza, 1980), pp. 75–84, at p. 81(n.) (decapitation, burning); Canosa, *Storia di una grande paura*, pp. 108 (death or exile), 121 (nose), 145 (galleys); Martini, *Il 'vitio nefando'*, pp. 32 (passive adults), 69 (galleys); Labalme, 'Sodomy and Venetian Justice', pp. 235 (exile), 246 (branding, mutilation).

31. Ruggiero, *Boundaries of Eros*, p. 128 (15th century, noting that this total includes 34 cases of heterosexual sodomy); Davidson, 'Sodomy in Early Modern Venice', p. 68 (16th century).

32. Blastenbrei, *Kriminalität in Rom*, p. 277; Baldassari, *Bande giovanili*, pp. 118–19 (Cardinal Vicar), 131 (totals).

33. Dean, 'Sodomy in Renaissance Bologna', pp. 426–7.

34. W. Gundersheimer, 'Crime and Punishment in Ferrara, 1440–1500', in L. Martines, ed., *Violence and Civil Disorder in Italian Cities, 1200–1500* (Berkeley, CA, 1972), pp. 104–28, at pp. 110, 114. Note, however, that the city's official list of executed people for the period 1441–1577 specifies 10 executed for sodomy, of whom at least 3 were after 1500: S. M. Mazzi, *'Gente a cui si fa notte innanzi sera': esecuzioni capitali e potere nella Ferrara estense* (Rome, 2003), pp. 16, 18, 143, 145, 162. Many people were listed without their offences being mentioned, so the real total for this offence was very probably higher.

35. Dean, 'Sodomy in Renaissance Bologna', pp. 430, 436–8; see also the present work, pp. 130–1. The *strappado* was a form of torture in which the victim was lifted by a rope tied to his crossed wrists behind his back, and then suddenly dropped, which typically caused dislocation of the shoulders.

36. Dean, 'Sodomy in Renaissance Bologna', p. 426 (referring to P. Cherubini, 'Un fonte poco noto per la storia di Roma: i processi della curia del Campidoglio (sec. XV)', in L. Biancini et al., *Roma memoria e oblio* (Rome, 2001), pp. 157–82, at pp. 163–6).

37. S. Limbeck, '*Sacrista—Hypocrita—Sodomita*. Komödiantische Konstruktion sexueller Identität in Mercurino Ranzos *De falso hypocrita*', in A. Bihrer, S. Limbeck and P. G. Schmidt, eds., *Exil, Fremdheit und Ausgrenzung in Mittelalter und früher Neuzeit* (Würzburg, 2000), pp. 91–112, esp. pp. 99 ('Agas, te queso, suaue, ne propter tuum maximum genitale mihi posteriora perscindas'), 103 ('formosus'), 106 ('ages et patieris, utrum libuerit', 'Sine me prius sputo madefaciam').

38. F. Vanhemelryck, *De criminaliteit in de ammanie van Brussel van de Late Middeleeuwen, tot het einde van het Ancien Regime (1404–1789)* (Brussels, 1981), p. 159(n.) ('Et la cause de ceste piteuse advenue est comme aulcuns dient, le péchié de Sodome, de laquelle chose les femmes se sont plaintes et encore se plaindent à Dieu. Car ledit péchié et énorme crieme règne fort, pour le temps présent').

39. Bouchard, *Journal*, i, p. xx (8 months): ii, pp. 270–1 ('En somme, c'est aujourdhui la jeunesse la plus infame d'Italie que cette petite noblesse napolitaine, ne

s'addonant à autre emploi qu'à cet infame mestier qu'elle professe mesme pub-liquement, se tenant tout du long du jour aus carrefours des rues et dans les places pour attirer les chalants: et c'est le seul serieus exercise et plus honeste divertissement qu'elle aye. En quoi elle est tellement imitée et suivie si univer-sellement de tout le reste de la jeunesse, soit bourgeoise ou de dehors, des provinces du royaume, qui vient estudier en cette ville, que si Naples est sur-montée de Rome par la quantité de βουγρες, come sans doute elle est, tout le monde s'en meslant à Rome, et à Naples seulement les cavaliers, les philosophes et les docteur[s], les marchands, les artisans et le reste de la populace n'y estant pas bien fort enclins, Naples surpasse de bien loing Rome au nombre come en la beauté et bon marché des βαρδαχες. Je me suis estendu sur ces particularitez que j'ai sçeues par ouï dire à Naples, pour laisser à juger au lecteur lesquels ont raison des Romains et des Napolitains de s'accuser l'un l'autre de σοδομιε, en quoi je croi qu'ils ont raison et tort tout ensemble'). Whether Bouchard's knowledge of this phenomenon came only from what he had been 'told', and not from direct involvement, may be doubted, in view of his account of his experience in the Salerno gaol (above, pp. 59–60) One other entry in his journal made a Rome–Naples comparison: reporting a conversation with a physician in Rome, he wrote that boys who suffered from anal ulcerations attributable to frequent sodomy received free treatment (cutting and cauterizing) from sur-geons in Rome, without any punishment, whereas in Naples the treatment was preceded by 50 lashes (*Journal*, i, pp. 149–50).

40. Lithgow, *Totall Discourse*, p. 38.
41. Pizzolato, '"Lo diavolo mi ingannao"', pp. 450 (Monreale), 451, 476–7(n. 10) (executions); R. Canosa, *Sessualità e Inquisizione in Italia tra cinquecento e seicento* (Rome, 1994), p. 54 (decree).
42. G. Marrone, *La schiavitù nella società siciliana dell'età moderna* (Caltanissetta, 1972), p. 217 ('tocados deste mal').
43. Pizzolato, '"Lo diavolo mi ingannao"'.
44. On the role and status of familiars more generally see Bethencourt, *Inquisition*, pp. 74–80, 162–73.
45. Monter, *Frontiers of Heresy*, pp. 62–4 (familiars, statistic), 187 (quotation). The precise figure is of 1,572 familiars in 1575 (pp. 63, 64(n.22)). The hugely dispro-portionate figure of 12,000 given in H. G. Koenigsberger, *The Government of Sicily under Philip II of Spain: A Study in the Practice of Empire* (London, 1951), p. 163, is not documented; but Koenigsberger's account of the Inquisition (pp. 161–70) does give a good sense of the severe tensions that arose between its authority and that of the Viceroy.
46. García Cárcel, *Herejía y sociedad*, p. 206.
47. A. Fernandez, 'The Repression of Sexual Behavior by the Aragonese Inquisition between 1560 and 1700', *JHS*, 7 (1997), pp. 469–501, at p. 483 (691 trials); Berco, *Jerarquías sexuales*, p. 100 (626 sentenced). The higher figures given by some historians (e.g. Garza Carvajal, *Butterflies will Burn*, p. 71) include prosecutions for bestiality: see García Cárcel, *Herejía y sociedad*, p. 288.

48. Molina, *Cuando amar era pecado*, p. 59 (Zaragoza, Valencia); Riera i Sans, *Sodomites catalans*, pp. 192–295.

49. Molina, *Cuando amar era pecado*, p. 61; Riera i Sans, *Sodomites catalans, passim*.

50. Perry, ' "Nefarious Sin" ', p. 71.

51. F. J. Quintana Toret, 'De los delitos y las penas. La criminalidad en Málaga y su tierra durante los siglos de oro', *Estudis: revista de historia moderna*, 15 (1989), pp. 245–70, at pp. 252, 268. Unfortunately only the percentage figure is given.

52. F. Soyer, *Ambiguous Gender in Early Modern Spain and Portugal: Inquisitors, Doctors and the Transgression of Gender Norms* (Leiden, 2012), p. 32.

53. J. A. Solorzano Telechea, '*Fama publica*, Infamy and Defamation: Judicial Violence and Social Control of Crimes against Sexual Morals in Medieval Castile', *Journal of Medieval History*, 33 (2007), pp. 398–413, at pp. 400 (appeals rare), 408 (statistic).

54. J. M. Mendoza Garrido, *Delincuencia y represión en la Castilla bajomedieval (los territorios castellano-manchegos)* (Granada, 1999), pp. 423–5.

55. E. Villalba Pérez, *¿Pecadoras o delincuentes?: delito y género en la Corte (1580–1630)* (Madrid, 2004), pp. 251, 307 (statistic; I subtract one case involving a man and two women, and one case of bestiality), 251(n.) ('En este dicho año quemaron quatro hombres porque los cojieron en habitos de frayles y pecaron contra natura en el pecado nefando'); Carrasco, *Inquisición y represión*, p. 77.

56. I. Bazan Díaz, *Delincuencia y criminalidad en el Pais Vasco en la transición de la Edad Media a la moderna* (Vitoria-Gasteiz, 1995), pp. 345–8 (Basque Country); Solorzano Telechea, '*Fama publica*', pp. 410–11 ('llamas bibas de fuego fasta tanto que naturalmente muera').

57. d'Aranda, *Relation de la captivité*, p. 273 ('un Païs, où le peché abominable est incognu').

58. Bazan Díaz, *Delincuencia y criminalidad*, p. 348 (permission refused, heretical statement); A. Bombín Pérez, *La Inquisición en el País Vasco: el tribunal de Logroño, 1570–1610* (Bilbao, 1997), pp. 175–6 (1570s cases); see also Monter, *Frontiers of Heresy*, pp. 281 (1547), 284–5 (1570s).

59. Alves Dias, 'Para uma abordagem do sexo proibido', p. 152; Drumond Braga, 'Pelo Universo da Sexualidade Proibida', pp. 12–13.

60. Mea, *A Inquisição de Coimbra*, p. 327 ('em duvida, se não ha de presumir crime nem pecado; e que aquellas causas ou feitos que podem referir se a bem ou a mal, sempre se hão de interpretar in meliorem partem; em conformidade destas mesmas regras ha outra semelhante, a saber, que quando por algum respeito se ha de presumir mal, sempre de dous males se deve presumir o menor', 'quando entre ambos não ha parentesco ou outra rezão que o obrigasse a dormir juntos', 'assim enquanto não ouver cousa que obrige ao contrario, se deve presumir antes o pecado de mollicies ou outra qualquer pollução extraordinaria que não o crime de sodomia pois he mais grave e maior mal').

61. Mott, '*Justitia et misericórdia*', pp. 93 (reductions), 97 (sentences).

62. Ibid., pp. 64 (lists), 97 (totals); Mea, *A Inquisição de Coimbra*, pp. 322–3 (Coimbra).

63. Higgs, 'Lisbon', p. 116.
64. Wettinger, *Slavery in Malta and Gożo*, pp. 521 (quotation), 529–32 (cases).
65. Lithgow, *Totall Discourse*, p. 335.
66. B. Krekić, 'Abominandum crimen: Punishment of Homosexuals in Renaissance Dubrovnik', *Viator (Medieval and Renaissance Studies)*, 18 (1987), pp. 337–45, at pp. 339–44. The 1474 law was evidently influenced by the Venetian decree of 1464 (above, p. 92).
67. R. Jeremić and J. Tadić, *Prilozi za istoriju zdravstvene kulture starog Dubrovnika*, 2 vols. (Belgrade, 1938–9), i, p. 130 ('često se to spominje kao uvreda medju muškarcima', 'Turci').
68. J. Chiffoleau, *Les Justices du Pape: délinquance et criminalité dans la région d'Avignon au quatorzième siècle* (Paris, 1984), p. 192 (few cases); T. Burton, *Chronica monasterii de Melsa, a fundatione usque ad annum 1396*, ed. E. A. Bond, 3 vols. (Cambridge, 1866–8), ii, p. 321 (cook; both cook and boy were burnt at the stake but, as the chronicle recorded, the boy, protected by the Virgin Mary, emerged from the fire with body and clothes unscathed.)
69. D. Bouliau, 'Sorcellerie et sodomie en Languedoc (1485–1791): de la répression à la dépénalisation', 2 vols. ('mémoire de master', University of Toulouse, 2016), i, pp. 296 (statistics), 300 (ages), 302 (boys). I am extremely grateful to Damien Bouliau for sending me a copy of his work.
70. Ibid., i, pp. 252 (Muret), 253–5 (Rochette), 256–9 (Bacon), 303 (Italian); R. A. Mentzer, 'Heresy Proceedings in Languedoc, 1500–1560', *Transactions of the American Philosophical Society*, n.s., 74, no. 5 (1984), pp. 1–183, at pp. 140, 161 (deputy). The title 'Inquisitor' here referred to a local role dealing with heresy; there was no national Inquisition in France.
71. Zysberg, *Les Galériens*, pp. 161–2.
72. Puff, *Sodomy in Reformation Germany*, pp. 81, 118 (quotations).
73. J. Duvernoy, ed. and trans., *Le Registre d'inquisition de Jacques Fournier, évêque de Pamiers (1318–1325)*, 3 vols. (Paris, 1978), iii, pp. 1039–68, esp. pp. 1057, 1061; cf. M. Goodich, *The Unmentionable Vice: Sodomy in the Late Medieval Period* (Santa Barbara, CA, 1979), pp. 89–123; E. Le Roy Ladurie, *Montaillou: Cathars and Catholics in a French Village, 1294–1324*, trans. B. Bray (Harmondsworth, 1980), pp. 144–9.
74. Above, p. 88; and cf. the discussion of bestiality statistics on p. 230.
75. Fernandez, 'Repression of Sexual Behavior', pp. 476 (360,000), 483 (40%); Carrasco, *Inquisición y represión*, p. 14 ('muy estrecha vigilancia de la población rural'); J.-P. Dedieu, *L'Administration de la foi: l'Inquisition de Tolède (XVIe–XVIIIe siècle)* (Madrid, 1989), p. 261 ('l'Office exerce sur les villes une pression quatre à cinq fois supérieure à celle qu'il fait subir aux campagnes').
76. Alves Dias, 'Para uma abordagem do sexo proibido', p. 156.
77. Carol Lansing comments: 'Women at low social levels who were not domestics in wealthy households had more independence than the closely guarded wives and daughters of the elite, though to be outside of patriarchal control meant

that they were less protected by family and community and more at risk' ('Gender and Civic Authority: Sexual Control in a Medieval Italian Town', *Journal of Social History*, 31 (1997), pp. 33–59, at p. 37).

78. Higgs, 'Lisbon', p. 114 ('overwhelmingly'); Boswell, *Christianity, Social Tolerance*, pp. 34–5, 207–10; B.-U. Hergemöller, *Einführung in die Historiographie der Homosexualitäten* (Tübingen, 1999), p. 42.

79. In Florence only 36% were in the home: Rocke, *Forbidden Friendships*, p. 153. On the precarious nature of early modern urban privacy see also the comments in A. Farge, *Vivre dans la rue à Paris au XVIIIᵉ siècle* (Paris, 1979), pp. 20, 31.

80. Pizzolato, '"Lo diavolo mi ingannao"', p. 451 ('Nelle campagne la sodomia si inscrive nelle relazioni sociali che scaturiscono dall'economia agro-pastorale').

CHAPTER 9

1. See D. S. Bailey, *Homosexuality and the Western Christian Tradition* (London, 1955), pp. 2–4, and the comments on this in T. Horner, *Jonathan Loved David: Homosexuality in Biblical Times* (Philadelphia, 1978), pp. 48–50. The mainstream view of modern scholarship seems to be that the sin of the men of Sodom was a larger one, of inhospitality and violence, containing a sexual element, but not narrowly focused on the same-sex nature of the sexual desire: see M. Nissinen, *Homoeroticism in the Biblical World: A Historical Perspective* (Minneapolis, 1998), pp. 45–9.

2. Horner, *Jonathan Loved David*, pp. 71–85; H. Lutterbach, 'Gleichgeschlechtliches sexuelles Verhalten: ein Tabu zwischen Spätantike und Früher Neuzeit?', *Historische Zeitschrift*, 267:2 (1998), pp. 281–311, at pp. 284–6.

3. Horner, *Jonathan Loved David*, pp. 59–70.

4. E. Ahern, 'The Sin of Sodom in Late Antiquity', *JHS*, 27 (2018), pp. 209–33 (Orosius, Augustine); Boswell, *Christianity, Social Tolerance*, pp. 140–61 (Clement, Augustine, nature, rejection of Alexandrian rule); J. Chiffoleau, '*Contra naturam*: pour une approche casuistique et procédurale de la nature médiévale', *Micrologus*, 4 (1996), pp. 265–312, at pp. 268–70 (Augustine, nature).

5. Above, p. 47 (Basil); S. Morris, *'When Brothers Dwell in Unity': Byzantine Christianity and Homosexuality* (Jefferson, NC, 2016), pp. 6, 20 (Desert Fathers), 110 (Chrysostom).

6. Boswell, *Christianity, Social Tolerance*, p. 164.

7. P. J. Payer, *Sex and the Penitentials: The Development of a Sexual Code, 550–1150* (Toronto, 1984), pp. 5 (code), 40 ('sodomitae'), 136 (penances), 134–9 (against Boswell); H. Lutterbach, *Sexualität im Mittelalter: eine Kulturstudie anhand von Bussbüchern des 6. bis 12. Jahrhunderts* (Cologne, 1999), pp. 147–61, esp. 153 (penances). Elsewhere Lutterbach argues that the early Middle Ages saw a revival of the biblical notion of 'pollution' in relation to sodomy: 'Gleichgeschlechtliches sexuelles Verhalten', pp. 288–93.

8. P. A. Quinn, *Better than the Sons of Kings: Boys and Monks in the Early Middle Ages* (New York, 1989), pp. 115 (raising of age), 126 (quotation), 165 (clapper).

9. See Jordan, *Invention of Sodomy*, pp. 45–66.

10. A. Gauthier, 'La Sodomie dans le droit canonique médiévale', in B. Roy, ed., *L'Érotisme au Moyen Âge* (Paris, 1977), pp. 109–22, at p. 119.

11. Jordan, *Invention of Sodomy*, p. 46.

12. Chiffoleau, '*Contra naturam*', pp. 276–8 (1170; Chiffoleau writes that the link with heresy was made in the 11th century, but his first example is from the trial of a heretical monk in the early 12th); Boswell, *Christianity, Social Tolerance*, pp. 283–5 (Cathars); B. Spreitzer, *Die stumme Sünde: Homosexualität im Mittelalter* (Göppingen, 1988), pp. 48–57 (Cathars, also Waldensians). For the development of this link in the 13th century see B.-U. Hergemöller, *Krötenkuss und schwarzer Kater: Ketzerei, Götzendienst und Unzucht in der inquisitorischen Phantasie des 13. Jahrhunderts* (Warendorf, 1996).

13. Connor, 'Les Molles et les chausses', p. 132 (le Leu); Spreitzer, *Die stumme Sünde*, pp. 57–8 (Augsburg); Puff, *Sodomy in Reformation Germany*, p. 13 (*ketzern*). Angela Taeger notes that in French legal compilations of the 13th century sodomy was, although not identified with heresy, closely associated with it: *Intime Machtverhältnisse. Moralstrafrecht und administrative Kontrolle der Sexualität im ausgehenden Ancien Régime* (Munich, 1999), p. 24.

14. See F. Molina, 'La *herejización* de la sodomía en la sociedad moderna: consideraciones teológicas y *praxis* inquisitorial', *Hispania sacra*, 62 (2010), pp. 539–62, at pp. 556–62 (discussing the *factum hereticale* concept but, I believe, exaggerating its significance); P. Scaramella, 'Sodomia', in A. Prosperi, ed., *Dizionario storico dell'Inquisizione*, 5 vols. (Pisa, 2010), iii, pp. 1445–50, at p. 1448 (Spain, Portugal); Monter, *Frontiers of Heresy*, p. 280 (Navarre).

15. A. de Sousa, *Opusculum circa constitutionem Pontificis Pauli V, in confessarios ad actus inhonestos foeminas in sacramentali confessione allicientes* (Lisbon, 1623), p. 143, quoted in V. Lavenia, 'Indicibili *mores*. Crimini contro natura e tribunali della fede in età moderna', *Cristianesimo nella storia*, 30 (2009), pp. 513–41, at p. 526.

16. J. Benedicti, *La Somme des pechez, et le remede d'iceux* (Paris, 1595), p. 149.

17. Puff, *Sodomy in Reformation Germany*, p. 55. On the development of this argument see D. Elliott, *Fallen Bodies: Pollution, Sexuality and Demonology in the Middle Ages* (Philadelphia, 1990), pp. 150–3.

18. J. Matthijssen, *Rechtsboek van Den Briel beschreven in vijf tractaten*, ed. J. A. Fruin and M. S. Pols (The Hague, 1880), pp. 206–7 ('Het is also vuylen onaerdige sonde, dat so wanneer die duvel een daartoe gebrocht heeft, dat hy ommekeert ende en mach die vuylicheyt der sonden niet zien'), quoted in H. J. Kuster, *Over homoseksualiteit in middeleeuws West-Europa* (Utrecht, 1977), p. 32.

19. H. Kramer [and J. Sprenger, attrib.], *Malleus maleficarum*, trans. M. Summers (London, 1971), part 1, qu. 4, p. 88. Incubi were demons who took human (male) form to penetrate women; succubi or succubae took human (female) form to be penetrated by men.

20. Ibid., p. 288; Spreitzer, *Die stumme Sünde*, p. 64; W. Stephens, *Demon Lovers: Witchcraft, Sex, and the Crisis of Belief* (Chicago, 2002), p. 332. In Kramer's account the relic is a column from Solomon's Temple, held in 'the church of St Peter';

this may be a garbled reference to the chains from which St Peter was miraculously freed—a relic, displayed in the church of San Pietro in Vincoli, which was used to exorcise demons.

21. T. Herzig, 'The Demons' Reaction to Sodomy: Witchcraft and Homosexuality in Gianfrancesco Pico della Mirandola's "Strix"', *The Sixteenth Century Journal*, 34 (2003), pp. 53–72.

22. Ibid., p. 67.

23. M. Delrio, *Disquisitionum magicarum libri sex*, 3 vols. (Mainz, 1603), iii, p. 79 ('vos viri cum succubis, vos mulieres cum incubis fornicati estis, Sodomiam veram & nefandissimu[m] crimen miserè cum illis... exercuistis', 'Sodomiticos'); this was quoted from S. Michaelis, *Pneumalogie* (1587), reprinted in his *Histoire admirable de la possession et conversion d'une penitente... ensemble la Pneumalogie, ou discours des esprits* (Paris, 1613), sep. pag., here at pp. 150–1.

24. Carrasco, *Inquisición y represión*, p. 43(n.) (1610); Spreitzer, *Die stumme Sünde*, p. 67 ('cum impuro spiritu et bestiis', 'alzeit in hindtern sodomitisch gebraucht wovon er kalt empfünden hab'). I can see no evidence to support Gisela Bleibtreu-Ehrenberg's claim that sodomy was generally subsumed under witchcraft in this period (*Homosexualität: die Geschichte eines Vorurteils* (Frankfurt, 1981), pp. 276–7).

25. J. Michelsen, 'Von Kaufleuten, Waisenknaben und Frauen in Männerkleidern: Sodomie im Hamburg des 18. Jahrhunderts', *Zeitschrift für Sexualforschung*, 9 (1996), pp. 205–37, at p. 215.

26. Pizzolato, '"Lo diavolo mi ingannao"', p. 466 (1620: 'Lo diavolo mi ingannao, futtivi allo figlio di Stassi'); Perry, *Gender and Disorder*, p. 125 (1603); Molina, *Cuando amar era pecado*, pp. 131 ('un demonio lo atormentava y... le necesitava a actos torpes... lo qual no tenia por pecado mortal diziendo no tenia en aquello libertad'), 134–5 (debate). Jean-Jacques Bouchard was told by a physician in Rome in 1632 that many men had themselves buggered as a remedy for haemorrhoids: *Journal*, i, p. 149.

27. B.-U. Hergemöller, *Sodom and Gomorrah: On the Everyday Reality and Persecution of Homosexuals in the Middle Ages*, trans. J. Phillips (London, 2001), pp. 148–9 (Incarnation), 152 (birth of Jesus, life of Mary, Golden Legend); Benedicti, *La Somme des pechez*, p. 149; the present work, p. 192 (Bernardino).

28. Antoninus [Florentinus], *Summae sacrae theologiae, iuris pontificij, & Caesarei, secunda pars* (Venice, 1582), fo. 213v; Hergemöller, *Sodom and Gomorrah*, pp. 150–1; Mormando, *The Preacher's Demons*, p. 123 (tracing this to Peter Comestor, who got it from (Pseudo-)Methodius).

29. Hergemöller, 'Sodomiter', p. 385 (1333); Antoninus, *Summae sacrae theologiae*, fo. 214r ('fortè ista est causa, quare in multis ciuitatibus Italiae frequenter super veniunt pestes, quia magis abundat tale vitium, quam in aliquibus aliis').

30. Above, p. 95 (Naples); Solorzano Telechea, '*Fama publica*', p. 410 ('hambres e pestylençias e otros males e dannos'); Krekić, 'Abominandum crimen', p. 341 (1534); Rocke, *Forbidden Friendships*, pp. 232–3 (1542); Scaramella, 'Sodomia', pp. 1445–6 (1566); Boon, '*Dien godlosen hoop*', p. 242 (Dutch writers).

31. Chiffoleau, '*Contra naturam*', pp. 272–3 (*Inst.* 4.18.14: 'cum masculis nefandam libidinem exercere audent'). Strangely, this statement claimed to be summarizing a component of the 'lex Julia' on adultery, a law from the reign of Augustus which in fact said nothing about sodomy: see S. Troianos, 'Kirchliche und weltliche Rechtsquellen zur Homosexualität in Byzanz', *Jahrbuch der österreichischen Byzantinistik*, 39 (1989), pp. 29–48, at pp. 32–3.

32. Jordan, *Invention of Sodomy*, p. 98 (Paul); Puff, *Sodomy in Reformation Germany*, p. 54 (Perault).

33. Jordan, *Invention of Sodomy*, pp. 150–1. The word 'uncleanness' accurately translated the Greek *akatharsia*, which could mean either physical or moral filthiness. Aquinas's interpretation clearly misses the point of Paul's injunction, where the reason for 'naming' or mentioning the sins would have been their actual occurrence.

34. Puff, *Sodomy in Reformation Germany*, p. 54 (Jerome); Antoninus, *Summae sacrae theologiae*, fo. 213v ('Sodomia interpraetatur muta, quia facit hominem mutum, vt excusare se non possit sicut de quibusdam alijs malis').

35. Puff, *Sodomy in Reformation Germany*, pp. 66–7 (William); A. Krass, 'Sprechen von der stummen Sünde: das Dispositiv der Sodomie in der deutschen Literatur des 13. Jahrhunderts (Berthold von Regensburg/Der Stricker)', in L. M. Thoma and S. Limbeck, eds., '*Die Sünde, der sich der tiuvel schamet in der helle*': *Homosexualität in der Kultur des Mittelalters und der frühen Neuzeit* (Ostflidern, 2009), pp. 123–36, at pp. 125–6 (Berthold).

36. T. Linkinen, *Same-Sex Sexuality in Later Medieval English Culture* (Amsterdam, 2015), pp. 99–100 (Mirk).

37. Mormando, *Preacher's Demons*, pp. 110 (9 sermons and a treatise), 122 (worst sin); L. M. Thoma, '"Das seind die sünd der vnküscheit". Eine Fallstudie zum Umgang mit der Sodomie in der Predigt des ausgehenden Mittelalters—Die "Brösamlin" Johannes Geilers von Kayserberg', in L. M. Thoma and S. Limbeck, eds., '*Die Sünde, der sich der tiuvel schamet in der helle*': *Homosexualität in der Kultur des Mittelalters und der frühen Neuzeit* (Ostflidern, 2009), pp. 137–53, at pp. 140–1.

38. Benedicti, *La Somme des pechez*, pp. 147–8 ('Ce ne sont pas les liures, qui enseignent les pechez, c'est nostre nature helas! par trop vitiee'), 150.

39. Puff, *Sodomy in Reformation Germany*, p. 67.

40. P. Payer, *Sex and the New Medieval Literature of Confession, 1150–1300* (Toronto, 2009), pp. 137–8 (discretion).

41. Antoninus [Florentinus], *Summa confessionalis* (Lyon, 1546), p. 332 ('de vicijs carnalibus cum masculis & foeminis, vel per seipsos co[m]missis, vel adinuicem quae hodie abu[n]da[n]t', 'Interroga[n]di sunt cu[m] magna cautela, & à longe vt non addisca[n]t, qua[e] ignorant').

42. J. Gerson, *Oeuvres complètes*, ed. Mgr Glorieux, 10 vols. (Paris, 1960–73), viii, pp. 71–2 ('quemadmodum pueri solent', 'pollutio', 'si fricaverit virgam alterius socii sui similiter, aut si aliquis fricuerit suam; et consequenter descendendo ad species magis speciales peccati sodomitici').

43. G. ['H.'] Savonarola, *Confessionale pro instructione confessorum* (Venice, 1543), fo. 31r–v ('vt placeat alicui mulieri, vel adolescenti, quam vel quem desiderat ad p[e]c[catu]m tale inducere').

44. M. de Azpilcueta, *Manual de confesores, y penitentes* (Medina del Campo, 1554), p. 111 ('detenerse mucho en las pregu[n]tas desta materia es peligroso para el co[n]fesor, y para el penite[n]te: por e[n]de deuese despedir presto, pregunta[n]dole solamente lo necessario, sin particularizar, ni desmenuzar demasido').

45. Estienne, *Apologie pour Herodote*, i, p. 114 ('d'autant plus meschants sont les prestres, qui en la confession auriculaire, qu'ils appellent, par leurs interrogats esueillent les esprits, & les aduisent de plusieurs vilanies'). On solicitation in Spain see Haliczer, *Sexuality in the Confessional*.

46. Above, pp. 110–11 (Peter Damian); Jordan, *Invention of Sodomy*, p. 97 (Paul).

47. Thomas Aquinas, St, *Summa theologiae*, in *S. Thomae Aquinatis opera omnia*, ed. R. Busi, 7 vols. (Stuttgart, 1980), ii, pp. 184–926, at p. 713, IIa IIae, qu. 154, art. 11, resp. ('vitium contra naturam', 'rationi rectae', 'ordini naturali venerei actus', 'puta masculi ad masculum vel feminae ad feminam, ut apostolus dicit ad rom. i. quod dicitur sodomiticum vitium', 'si non servetur naturalis modus concumbendi, aut quantum ad instrumentum non debitum aut quantum ad alios monstruosos et bestiales concumbendi modos').

48. J. Cadden, *Meanings of Sex Difference in the Middle Ages: Medicine, Science, and Culture* (Cambridge, 1993), p. 219. The meanings of the last two descriptions are clarified in the commentary by Tommaso de Vio (Cardinal Cajetan), who numbers them as the 4th and 5th forms: *Commentaria*, in St Thomas Aquinas, *Summa theologica cum commentariis Thomae de Vio cardinalis Cajetani*, 10 vols. (Rome, 1773), vi, p. 487.

49. Payer, *Sex and the New Medieval Literature*, p. 135 (mediaeval guides); C. Reinle, 'Zur Rechtspraxis gegenüber Homosexuellen. Eine Fallstudie aus dem Regensburg des 15. Jahrhunderts', *Zeitschrift für Geschichtswissenschaft*, 44 (1996), pp. 307–26, at p. 319 (German guide); Boccaccio, *Esposizioni*, p. 682 ('secondo la ordinaria regola della natura e ancora delle leggi canoniche').

50. A. da Montalcino, *Lucerna dell'anima: somma de' casi di conscientia, necessaria a i confessori, & molto utile a i penitenti* (Venice, 1590), p. 62 ('fra persone dell'istesso sesso consumato comunque si uoglia').

51. Thomas Aquinas, *Summa theologiae*, p. 713, IIa IIae, qu. 154, art. 11, resp. ad 3 ('luxuriosus non intendit generationem humanam, sed delectationem veneream, quam potest aliquis experiri sine actibus ex quibus sequitur humana generatio. et hoc est quod quaeritur in vitio contra naturam').

52. de Vio, *Commentaria*, vi, p. 487 ('mollem movet delectatio sola expletio voluptatis veneriae; *Sodomitam* movet persona indebiti sexus').

53. P. Hurteau, 'Catholic Moral Discourse on Male Sodomy and Masturbation in the Seventeenth and Eighteenth Centuries', *JHS*, 4 (1993), pp. 1–26, at pp. 12–13.

54. de Vio, *Commentaria*, vi, p. 488 ('subordinatum morosae delectationi'). For a good discussion of 'lingering delectation' in early modern Catholic theology, see

F. V. García and A. Moreno Mengíbar, *Sexo y razón: una genealogía de la moral sexual en España (siglos XVI–XX)* (Madrid, 1997), pp. 77–84.

55. Agostino da Montalcino, *Lucerna dell'anima*, p. 35 ('pensando a maschi, è Sodomito pessimo'); Benedicti, *La Somme des pechez*, p. 141.

56. T. M. Sánchez, *Disputationum de sancto matrimonii sacramento libri tres*, 3 vols. (Antwerp, 1620), iii, p. 217.

57. H. Busenbaum ['Busembaum'], *Medulla theologiae moralis* (Padua, 1723), p. 178 ('mutua pollutio', 'Si fiat ex solo affectu ad veneream libidinem absque concubitu, esse tantum mollitiem: si vero fiat ex affectu ad personam illam indebiti sexus (praesertim si adsit aliqua conjunctio, & commixtio corporum) est quoad malitiam Sodomia'). Busenbaum's work was very widely read, running to 200 printings by 1776: see A. R. Jonsen and S. Toulmin, *The Abuse of Casuistry: A History of Moral Reasoning* (Berkeley, CA, 1988), pp. 155–6.

58. Sánchez, *Disputationum libri tres*, iii, pp. 312–15 ('beneuolentia, & amicitia honesta habita secundum patriae consuetudinem', 'à fortiori dicendum est, oscula & amplexus inter personas eiusdem sexus habita ex praedicta delectatione venerea, quae ex ipsis sentitur, esse peccata mortalia', 'inchoatio', 'ioco pudenda arripientibus', 'ob vehementem propensionem ad sodomiam').

59. M. Rocke, 'Sodomites in Fifteenth-Century Tuscany: The Views of Bernardino of Siena', *JH*, 16 (1989), pp. 7–32, at p. 12; Benedicti, *La Somme des pechez*, p. 137; Hurteau, 'Catholic Moral Discourse', p. 13 (n.).

CHAPTER 10

1. On the Visigothic edicts of 650 and 693, which decreed castration for consensual sodomy, see Bailey, *Homosexuality and Western Tradition*, pp. 92–4; Boswell, *Christianity, Social Tolerance*, pp. 174–6.

2. S. M. Oberhelman, 'Hierarchies of Gender, Ideology, and Power in Ancient and Medieval Greek and Arabic Dream Literature', in J. M. Wright and E. K. Rowson, eds., *Homoeroticism in Classical Arabic Literature* (New York, 1997), pp. 55–93, at p. 63 (quotation); Bailey, *Homosexuality and Western Tradition*, pp. 73–5 (texts), 78–9 (debate); Boswell, *Christianity, Social Tolerance*, pp. 172–4 (debate).

3. Troianos, 'Kirchliche und weltliche Rechtsquellen', p. 36.

4. C. J. von Hefele, *Conciliengeschichte, nach den Quellen bearbeitet*, 2nd edn., 9 vols. (Freiburg im Breisgau, 1873–90), i, pp. 234–5 (canon 15).

5. Payer, *Sex and the Penitentials*, p. 43; Payer, *Sex and the New Medieval Literature*, p. 133.

6. Gauthier, 'La Sodomie dans le droit canonique', pp. 116–17 (16th Council of Toledo, 693); F. Leroy-Forgeot, *Historie juridique de l'homosexualité en Europe* (Paris, 1997), p. 29.

7. van Eickels, 'Die Konstruktion des Anderen', p. 49.

8. Gauthier, 'La Sodomie dans le droit canonique', pp. 120–1.

9. Puff, *Sodomy in Reformation Germany*, p. 40; Scaramella, 'Sodomia', p. 1447.

10. C. Coquelines, ed., *Bullarium privilegiorum ac diplomatum romanorum pontificum amplissima collectio*, 6 tomes (Rome, 1739–62), tome 4, part 2, p. 285 ('crimen nefandum contra naturam', 'simili poena subiiciatur'); tome 4, part 3, p. 33 ('tam dirum nefas exercentes', 'potestati statim saeculari tradantur'). *Cum primum Apostolatus*'s stipulation that cases could be brought to trial even on the basis of secret denunciations was widely objected to, and was dropped from vernacular translations distributed to the public: see S. Manzi, 'Controllare la sessualità, controllare l'Inquisizione? Il caso di due bolle pontificie in lingua volgare (1566–1588)', in U. Grassi, V. Lagioia and G. P. Romagnani, eds., *Tribadi, sodomiti, invertite e invertiti, pederasti, femminelle, ermafrodite . . . Per una storia dell'omosessualità, della bisessualità e delle trasgressioni di genere in Italia* (Pisa, 2017), pp. 41–57, at pp. 46–51.

11. M. de Azpilcueta ['Navarrus'], *Enchiridion, sive manuale confessariorum et poenitentium* (Venice, 1600), fos. 332v–333r ('tam dirum nefas . . . exercentes', 'tantum . . . eos, q[ui] quasi ex vsu co[n]tinuato id exerce[n]t', 'eu[m] qui toties, vt vulgi opinione habeatur pro tali', 'actum sodomiticum', 'copulam sodomiticum').

12. Benedicti, *La Somme des pechez*, pp. 148–9.

13. J. Azor ['I. Azorius'], *Institutionum moralium*, 3 vols. (Lyon, 1616–25), part 3, bk 3, ch. 19, vol. iii, col. 163 ('haec pollutio licet sit contra naturam, non est tamen sodomiticum peccatum'); Coquelines, ed., *Bullarium privilegiorum*, tome 4, part 3, p. 33 ('illa incontinentia, quae contra naturam est'). On Azor's work, which enjoyed 'vast popularity', see Jonsen and Toulmin, *Abuse of Casuistry*, pp. 153–5.

14. Riera i Sans, *Sodomites catalans*, pp. 326–32 (witness statements, sentence); Carrasco, *Inquisición y represión*, p. 48 ('La *mollicies* y sodomía convienen en echar el semen con deleite que es la razón de la lujuria y es el mismo en cada una. Diferéncianse en el modo que la *mollicies* echa el semen *omnino extra vas*, la sodomía *intra vas spurcissimum et nefandum*. Y así la una no es subordinada a la otra, ni los atentados de la una se pueden decir atentados de la otra sino que son dos vías diferentes por donde se puede llegar al deleite carnal torpe y si el derecho las llama sodomías y a sus actos sodomíticos es *improprie et figurate* tomando el nombre de la *specie* sodomía por el género *peccatum contra naturam*, el cual no tiene nombre sino por circunloquio se declara y esto *brevitatis causa* por el tropo o figura que llaman los retóricos sinécdoque').

15. Garza Carvajal, *Butterflies will Burn*, p. 218(n.14) ('contra naturam', 'pecado en que caen los omes yaziendo vnos con otros contra natura, e costubre natural'); cf. Solorzano Telechea, '*Fama publica*', pp. 403–4; F. Soyer, *Ambiguous Gender in Early Modern Spain*, pp. 29–30. The phrasing seems influenced by the injunctions in Leviticus, which referred to 'lying with mankind' (see above, p. 108).

16. Pérez Cánovas, *Homosexualidad*, p. 12.

17. For a balanced assessment of that whole affair, noting some confessions of sodomy in France and Italy but dismissing the general charge against the order, see A. Gilmour-Bryson, 'Sodomy and the Knights Templar', *JHS*, 7 (1996), pp. 151–83.

18. M. Goodich ['Goodrich'], 'Sodomy in Medieval Secular Law', *JH*, 1 (1976), pp. 295–302 (confraternities); above, p. 111 (Augsburg).

19. L. Zdekauer, 'Il frammento degli ultimi due libri del più antico constituto senese (1262–1270)', *Bulletino senese di storia patria*, 3 (1896), pp. 79–92, at p. 86 (Siena); G. Fasoli and P. Sella, *Statuti di Bologna dell'anno 1288*, 2 vols. (Vatican City, 1937–9), i, p. 195 (Bologna); J. P. Grundman, *The Popolo at Perugia, 1139–1309* (Perugia, 1992), p. 438 (Perugia).

20. Lansing, 'Gender and Civic Authority', pp. 38–9 (noting also that death by burning was introduced in the 16th century: p. 54(n.51)).

21. Grassi, *L'Offizio sopra l'Onestà*, p. 40.

22. Rocke, *Forbidden Friendships*, pp. 21–2 (Florence); Goodich, 'Sodomy', p. 299 (Ascoli Piceno); Fasoli and Stella, *Statuti di Bologna*, i, p. 196 (Bolognese law); Bernardino of Siena, *Opera omnia*, 9 vols. (Quaracchi, 1950–65), viii, p. 298 (Condulmier). Venice also introduced rewards for informers in 1408: see B.-U. Hergemöller, '*Accusatio* und *denunciatio* im Rahmen der spätmittelalterlichen Homosexuellenverfolgung in Venedig und Florenz', in G. Jerouschek, I. Marssolek and H. Röckelein, eds., *Denunziation: historische, juristische und psychologische Aspekte* (Tübingen, 1997), pp. 64–79, at p. 66.

23. Above, pp. 92–3 (Italian cities); Rocke, *Forbidden Friendships*, pp. 231–4 (1527, 1542).

24. Ferguson, *Same-Sex Marriage*, p. 78.

25. Hergemöller, 'Sodomiter', p. 376; Thoma, '"Das seind die sünd der vnküscheit"', p. 143.

26. Ruggiero, *Boundaries of Eros*, p. 132 (1407, noting however that the man was freed by some of his friends); L. Frati, *La vita privata di Bologna dal secolo XIII al XVII* (Bologna, 1900), pp. 81 (burnt), 88–9 (cage).

27. Fasoli and Stella, *Statuti di Bologna*, i, p. 195 ('nisi etas patientem excuset').

28. A. Terry, 'The Craft of Torture: Bronze Sculptures and the Punishment of Sexual Offense', in A. Levy, ed., *Sex Acts in Early Modern Italy: Practice, Performance, Perversion, Punishment* (Abingdon, 2010), pp. 209–23, at pp. 217–18.

29. Rocke, *Forbidden Friendships*, pp. 21–2 (1325, 1365), 63 (1459), 72 (quotation).

30. Ruggiero, *Boundaries of Eros*, pp. 121–3 (distinction, legal principle); Martini, *Il 'vitio nefando'*, pp. 30–1 (distinction); Tortorici, *Sins against Nature*, pp. 67–8.

31. Krekić, 'Abominandum crimen', p. 339.

32. Grassi, *L'Offizio sopra l'Onestà*, p. 82 (1500, 1516); Labalme, 'Sodomy and Venetian Justice', p. 240(n.).

33. Grassi, *L'Offizio sopra l'Onestà*, pp. 41–2.

34. Mormando, *Preacher's Demons*, p. 156.

35. Baldassari, *Bande giovanili*, pp. 59 (sentences), 123 (1580).

36. Mazzi, *'Gente a cui si fa notte innanzi sera'*, p. 122, case of 1496 ('zoveneto', 'bruxatto per havere sottomità uno garzoneto in chiesia la note del venerdì santto').

37. Garza Carvajal, *Butterflies will Burn*, p. 219(n. 16) ('por el qual la nobleza se pierde, y el corazon se acobarda', 'el delito nefando contra naturam', 'perfecto', 'actos muy propinquos y cercanos a la conclusion del').

38. Solorzano Telechea, '*Fama publica*', p. 411 (1510); above, p. 75 (1579). Enrique Villalba Pérez notes that among the cases tried in Madrid in 1581–1621 were four men accused of 'suspected' sodomy (as opposed to sodomy *tout court*) and two accused of 'intended' sodomy: *¿Pecadoras o delincuentes?*, p. 251.

39. Garza Carvajal, *Butterflies will Burn*, p. 221(n. 25) ('de su naturaleza de muy dificultosa probanza', 'aunque el dicho delito no fuese probado con testigos, sino por otras formas establecidas y aprobadas en Derecho, de las quales pudiese resultar bastante probanza para poderese imponer en el la pena ordinaria'), giving the date as 1592.

40. Perry, '"Nefarious Sin"', p. 78; de León, *Grandeza y miseria*, pp. 473 ('mozuelo'), 475 ('de bien poca edad') (and cf. p. 520 for a case of 1596, where two boys, aged 8 and 9, who had been sodomized by a 22-year-old, were whipped 50 times and made to pass through the fire).

41. Solorzano Telechea, '*Fama publica*', pp. 405–6 (1505), 411 (1503).

42. Canosa, *Sessualità e Inquisizione*, pp. 53–4; Soyer, *Ambiguous Gender in Early Modern Spain*, p. 31.

43. Monter, *Frontiers of Heresy*, pp. 276–7; Canosa, *Sessualità e Inquisizione*, pp. 53–4. Many historians state that the Mallorca tribunal was also given jurisdiction, but this is an error. Sodomy arose in Mallorcan cases either as an aggravating point mentioned when a man was prosecuted on other charges, or in relation to heretical statements about it (i.e. that it was not a mortal sin), or when it had been solicited by priests: see Pérez, Muntaner and Colom, eds., *El Tribunal de la Inquisición en Mallorca*, e.g. pp. 21, 68, 113, 169, 269–72.

44. Scaramella, 'Sodomia', pp. 1445–6.

45. Monter, *Frontiers of Heresy*, pp. 278–82.

46. Above, pp. 96 (Sicily), 98 (death, galleys); Rosselló, *L'homosexualitat a Mallorca*, pp. 10–12.

47. Monter, *Frontiers of Heresy*, p. 279 (anonymity, defence lawyer). On the normal principles of anonymity and secrecy see Bethencourt, *Inquisition*, pp. 61, 369; T. F. Mayer, *The Roman Inquisition: A Papal Bureaucracy and its Laws in the Age of Galileo* (Philadelphia, 2013), pp. 160–1, 176–7.

48. Monter, *Frontiers of Heresy*, p. 285; Riera i Sans, *Sodomites catalans*, p. 530.

49. M. Escamilla-Colin, *Crimes et châtiments dans l'espace inquisitoriale: essai de typologie délictive et punitive sous le dernier Habsbourg et le premier Bourbon*, 2 vols. (Paris, 1992), ii, p. 287 (Barcelona rules); García Cárcel, *Herejía y sociedad*, p. 290 (one witness); V. Lavenia, 'Tra eresia e crimine contro natura: sessualità, islamofobia e inquisizioni nell'Europa moderna', in U. Grassi and G. Marcocci, eds., *Le trasgressioni della carne: il desiderio omosessuale nel mondo islamico e cristiano, secc. XII–XX* (Rome, 2015), pp. 103–30, at p. 121(n.60), citing F. de Castro Palao, *Operis moralis pars prima* (Lyon, 1656), p. 370 (one witness).

50. García Cárcel, *Herejía y sociedad*, p. 215 (30%); Riera i Sans, *Sodomites catalans*, pp. 191–293. On the use of torture see H. Kamen, *The Spanish Inquisition* (London, 1976), pp. 174–6.

51. Escamilla-Colin, *Crimes et châtiments*, ii, pp. 283–4. Note, however, that according to García Cárcel torture was used in 5% of cases in the secular courts: *Herejía y sociedad*, p. 215.

52. Drumond Braga, 'Pelo universo da sexualidade proibida', pp. 10–11 ('molícies e os tocamentos desonestos'). Since 'shameful touching' usually referred to mutual masturbation, the separate reference to *mollities* appears to have denoted solitary masturbation, as well as other forms of same-sex non-penetrative activity. A special law of 1606 confirmed this, prescribing whipping, galley service and even death for such an offence (Mott, '*Justitia et misericórdia*', p. 67). This was the only example of an early modern state criminalizing ordinary masturbation, though there is no evidence of people actually being prosecuted for it.

53. Drumond Braga, 'Pelo universo da sexualidade proibida', pp. 11–12 (1550s); Alves Dias, 'Para uma abordagem do sexo proibido', p. 152 (breves). 'Regular' here means those who belonged to religious orders.

54. Ibid., p. 152 (1553); Mea, *A Inquisição de Coimbra*, p. 321 (1568).

55. I. Rosa Pereira, *A Inquisição em Portugal, séculos XVI–XVII—período filipino* (Lisbon, 1993), pp. 65–7.

56. Mott, '*Justitia et misericórdia*', pp. 90–1 (incarceration), 99 (percentages); cf. also the comments above (p. 58) on Inquisition prison sentences.

57. Mea, *A Inquisição de Coimbra*, p. 323.

58. Above, pp. 99–100 (procedure); Mott, 'Misadventures', pp. 319 (minor), 320–1 (rebuttal, two acts).

59. Mott, '*Justitia et misericórdia*', p. 91 (10%); Vainfas, *Trópico dos pecados*, pp. 207 (*Regimento*, confessors), 259 (*conatos nefandos*).

60. Mott, '*Justitia et misericórdia*', pp. 73, 98 (15%).

61. On the principle of exemplary punishment and the ceremonializing of executions in the early modern period, see P. Spierenburg, *The Spectacle of Suffering. Executions and the Evolution of Repression: From a Preindustrial Metropolis to the European Experience* (Cambridge, 1984), esp. pp. 43–80.

62. See the rich account in Bethencourt, *Inquisition*, pp. 246–315.

63. Mott, '*Justitia et misericórdia*', p. 83.

64. Dedieu, *L'Administration de la foi*, pp. 270–1.

65. Berco, 'Social Control', p. 348.

66. Molina, *Cuando amar era pecado*, p. 71 ('sean traydos por las calles publicas y acostumbrados de esta ciudad . . . y en el sitio y parte de esta ciudad acostumbrado sean puestos dos palos en los quales sean arrimados y se les de garrote hasta que naturalmente mueran y después sus cuerpos sean quemados en llamas de fuego hasta que se conbiertan en polbo y zeniça para que perezca su memoria').

67. Rosa Pereira, *A Inquisição em Portugal*, p. 111 ('para que a pública demonstração de castigo nos culpados preserve a outros').

CHAPTER 11

1. R. M. Mérida, 'Sodomy and the Sick Body of Women', *Imago temporis: medium aevum*, 7 (2013), pp. 323–41, at pp. 325–6 ('la indicible, | pudent, horrible, | fort llebrosia | —la sodomía—, | pecat no poc, | digne de foc, | del mundanal | e infernal | a l'arma i cos'). Much less typical, however, as Mérida points out, was Roig's argument that sodomy had been introduced into the world by women.

2. García Cárcel, *Herejía y sociedad*, p. 289 (Valencian literature); J. I. Díez Fernández, *La poesía erótica de los Siglos de Oro* (Madrid, 2003), pp. 253–5 ('dominante, y casi totalmente exclusiva'); M. J. Delgado and A. Saint-Saëns, eds., *Lesbianism and Homosexuality in Early Modern Spain: Literature and Theater in Context* (New Orleans, 2000), *passim* (specialists).

3. Martín, 'Sodomitas, putos, doncellos', esp. pp. 110–15; K. Vaiopoulos, 'L'Italiano sodomita nella poesia satirica di Quevedo', in M. G. Profeti, ed., *Giudizi e pregiudizi. Percezione dell'altro e stereotipi tra Europa e Mediterranea: atti del seminario, Firenze, 10–14 giugno 2008*, i (Florence, 2010), pp. 183–209. On Quevedo's strong sense of disgust for human sexuality, which he harnessed to Counter-Reformation purposes, see A. Morel D'Arleux, 'Obscenidad y desengaño en la poesía de Quevedo', *Edad de Oro*, 9 (1990), pp. 181–94.

4. Anon., *Cancionero de obras de burlas provocantes a risa* (Madrid, n.d. [c.1900]), pp. 155–6 ('encendido en lujuría', 'adonde el triste s'está remendando el culo hasta hoy'); this is briefly discussed in Berco, *Jerarquías sexuales*, pp. 68–9.

5. A. Martínez de Toledo, Arcipreste de Talavera, *Corbacho*, ed. J. González Muela (Madrid, 1970), pp. 233–4 ('desean conpaña de omes por su vil acto, como ombres con los tales cometer', 'abominables obras e sodemíticos fechos', 'aborrecen las mugeres, escupen dellas, e algunos non comen cosa alguna [que] ellas aparejasen, nin vestirían ropa blanca que ellas xabonasen, nin dormirían en cama que ellas fiziesen. Sy les fablan de mugeres, ¡alça, Dios, tu yra!, que se dexan dezir e fazer de ficta onestad; e después andan tras los moçuelos, besándolos, falagándolos, dándoles joyuelas, dineros, cosyllas que a su hedad conviene').

6. Martín, 'Sodomitas, putos, doncellos', p. 113 ('Ningún coño jamás le vio arrecho').

7. D. Alighieri, *Commedia*, ed. E. Pasquini and A. Quaglio (Milan, 1987), p. 129 (*Inferno*, XI, ll. 46–8) ('Puossi far forza nella deïtade, | col cor negando e bestemmiando quella, | e spregiando natura e sua bontade'), 50 ('Sodoma e Caorsa').

8. G. Boccaccio, *Decameron*, ed. A. Quondam, M. Fiorilla and G. Alfano (Milan, 2013), I.1, p. 202 ('del contrario più che alcuno altro tristo uomo si dilettava'), I.2, p. 224 ('del Papa e de' cardinali e degli altri prelati e di tutti i cortigiani', 'tutti disonestissimamente peccare in lussuria, e non solo nella naturale ma ancora nella sogdomitica, senza freno alcuno di rimordimento o di vergogna').

9. Above, p. 94.

10. G. Sabadino degli Arienti, *Novelle porretane*, ed. P. Stoppelli (L'Aquila, 1975), nov. 12, pp. 63–71 (p. 70: 'quanto sei degno di eterna vituperazione!').

11. Cellini, *La vita*, pp. 65 ('di forma oltra'modo bello'), 67 ('il detto misser Giovanni si scopri seco d'amore sporco et non virtuoso: perché si vedeva ogni giorno mutare veste di velluto et di seta al ditto giovane, et si conosceva ch'el s'era dato in tutto alla scelleratezza...io lo havevo ripreso, dicendogli che s'era dato impreda a brutti vitii, i quali gli harien fatto rompere il collo').

12. Boccaccio, *Decameron*, I.1, p. 204 ('Delle femine era così vago come sono i cani de' bastoni'), V.10, pp. 931 ('più per ingannare altrui e diminuire la generale oppinion di lui avuta da tutti i perugini che per vaghezza che egli n'avesse'), 932 ('perché per moglie mi prendeva se le femine contro all'animo gli erano?'), 941 ('sè così vago di noi come il can delle mazze').

13. N. Cartlidge, 'Homosexuality and Marriage in a Fifteenth-Century Italian Humanist Comedy: *The Debate between Cavichiolus and his Wife*', *The Journal of Medieval Latin*, 15 (2005), pp. 25–66, at pp. 54 ('Rumpebat sompnos femina nulla meos. | Nil praeter pueros mea mentula noverat aureos, | Cum quibus aeternum uiuere uelle sedet', 'Et fiet cornix candida, pullus olor, | Quam queat ignotis mea se miscere latebris | Arrigat et cunnot mentula clara tuo...Sola meos poterunt conuertere Fata calores, | Obstabit uotis mors nisi sola meis'), 64–5 (translations).

14. Sabadino degli Arienti, *Novelle porretane*, nov. 13, pp. 72–6 (p. 73: 'voi perdeti tempo in ciò adimandarme, ché questo è vero e non ve ne maravigliati, perché non voglio dire me sia dispiaciuto le donne, ma me hano pur a mirarle astomacato', 'nefando vicio contra natura', 'sì...e non tanto peccato ho io per piacere, quanto per seguire il nostro motto fiorentino che al mio tempo si dicea: Quando vòi prendere trastullo, usa spesso col fanciullo').

15. B. Penman, ed. and trans., *Five Italian Renaissance Comedies* (Harmondsworth, 1978), pp. 118, 122, 189.

16. K. Borris, ed., *Same-Sex Desire in the English Renaissance: A Sourcebook of Texts, 1470–1650* (New York, 2004), p. 13.

17. See M. Sherberg, 'Il potere e il piacere: la sodomia del "Marescalco"', in S. Zatti, ed., *La rappresentazione dell'altro nei testi del Rinascimento* (Lucca, 1998), pp. 96–110, esp. pp. 97–8.

18. A. Luzio, *Pietro Aretino nei primi suoi anni a Venezia e la corte del Gonzaga* (Turin, 1888), pp. 23(n.) ('Isabella Sforza ha convertito | L'Aretin da ch'ei nacque sodomito'), 45, 102 (*bardassa*); P. Larivaille, *Pietro Aretino* (Rome, 1997), pp. 308–15 (catamites).

19. A. Beccadelli, *The Hermaphrodite*, ed. and trans. H. Parker (Cambridge, MA, 2010), pp. viii–ix (biographical details), pp. 26 ('Quintium, turpem et deformem puerum', 'mentula perpetuo tibi quam contracta iacebit, | tu sibi dumtaxat basia fige semel! | I procul hinc, Quinti, foedum putensque lupanar...Quis numeret quot hians absorpserit inguina podex?'), 27 (translation).

20. Ibid., pp. xiii–xvi (attacks, recantation), 42 ('Tuscus es, et populo iocunda est mentula Tusco'), 43 (translation), 56–8 ('res adeo impudicas, adeo ineptas, tam venuste, tam composite', 'ne arguatur vita impura libelli obscenitate', 'non licere idem nobis, qui Christiani sumus'), 57–9 (translation).

21. P. Massimi, *Les Cent Élégies: Hecatelegium, Florence, 1489*, ed. and trans. J. Desjardins (Grenoble, 1986), pp. 1–18 (biography).

22. Ibid., pp. 184 (Heaven, Hell), 198 (erection), 214 (orgasms), 226 (bridges).

23. Ibid., pp. 208 ('Ad Cynedum'), 210 ('ta[n]tillum', 'audes | Poscere porrecta sordidus aera manu', 'fellator'), 212 ('Hoc quoq[ue] nos fuimus. spes (ne co[n]temne) p[re]corum | Mille (mihi credas) inuidiosa fui'), 216 ('Et patres, matresq[ue] etia[m]: si munera defers: | Lenones fient, executientq[ue] thorum'), 346–50 (passive adult).

24. Ibid., pp. 8 (rarity, 1501 letter), 358–60 ('saepe salutat, | Et saepe arridet, dat digitisq[ue] notas. | Et modo subsequit[ur], modo me praecedit', 'Fama mea est teneris semp[er] munerare cinaedis'), 362 ('Saepe ego paedico (fateor) nec uera negabo, | Sed tame[n] electa no[n] nisi pascor aue. | Vuidus & pinguis, calidusq[ue] & candidus esse, | Et puer in culo debet habere focum').

25. J. Hankins, *Plato in the Italian Renaissance*, 2 vols. (Leiden, 1990), i, pp. 56, 138, 313 (bowdlerizations and omissions by Italian humanists); U. Pfisterer, *Lysippus und seine Freunde. Liebesgaben und Gedächtnis im Rom der Renaissance, oder: Das erste Jahrhundert der Medaille* (Berlin, 2008), pp. 273–4 (passages censored, gender changed); K. Hollewand, 'Sex and the Classics: The Approaches of Early Modern Humanists to Ancient Sexuality', in D. Levitin and I. Maclean, eds., *The Worlds of Knowledge and the Classical Tradition in the Early Modern Age: Comparative Approaches* (Leiden, 2021), pp. 48–69, at pp. 55–6 (quotation). Gender-switching was a tactic used by English translators of Theocritus, Anacreon, Martial and Horace in the 17th and early 18th centuries: see Hammond, *Figuring Sex between Men*, pp. 45, 53; M. H. Loughlin, *Same-Sex Desire in Early Modern England, 1550–1735* (Manchester, 1988), p. 146.

26. A. Grafton, *Defenders of the Text: The Traditions of Scholarship in an Age of Science, 1450–1800* (Cambridge, MA, 1991), p. 38. On the various strategies adopted by Renaissance commentators and poets to deal with this problematic text, see E. Fredericksen, 'Finding Another Alexis: Pastoral Tradition and the Reception of Vergil's Second Eclogue', *Classical Receptions Journal*, 7 (2015), pp. 422–41, esp. pp. 427–9.

27. J. Davidson, *The Greeks and Greek Love: A Radical Reappraisal of Homosexuality in Ancient Greece* (London, 2007), p. 171 (quotation).

28. A. Kruszynski, *Der Ganymed-Mythos in Emblematik und mythographischer Literatur des 16. Jahrhunderts* (Worms, 1985), pp. 24–5 (Landino), 31–2 (Ficino), 33–48 (emblems, 'Vera in Cognitione Dei Cultuque Voluptas'). On the iconography see also M. Marongiu, *Il mito di Ganimede prima e dopo Michelangelo* (Florence, 2002).

29. J. C. Nelson, *The Renaissance Theory of Love: The Context of Giordano Bruno's Eroici furori* (New York, 1958), pp. 69–70; G. Dall'Orto, ' "Socratic Love" as a Disguise for Same-Sex Love in the Italian Renaissance', in K. Gerard and G. Hekma, eds., *The Pursuit of Sodomy: Male Homosexuality in Renaissance and Enlightenment Europe* (New York, 1989), pp. 33–65, at pp. 36–7; Hankins, *Plato*,

i, p. 355 (Ficino); Hankins discusses also (pp. 259–61) the contemporaneous development of a very similar approach by Cardinal Bessarion.

30. Nelson, *Renaissance Theory of Love*, p. 71 ('nefaria scelerateza, la quale Platone nelle sue leggi, come spezie di omicidio, agramente bestemmia'); Nelson notes similar remarks in the treatises on love by Mario Equicola, Tullia d'Aragona and Giuseppe Betussi (pp. 71–2). On Ficino's strategies for desexualizing Plato's account of male–male love, see T. W. Reeser, *Setting Plato Straight: Translating Ancient Sexuality in the Renaissance* (Chicago, 2016), pp. 87–149.

31. Dall'Orto, '"Socratic Love"', p. 40; Hankins, *Plato*, i, pp. 213, 240; Pfisterer, *Lysippus und seine Freunde*, pp. 277–80.

32. B. Castiglione, *Il libro del cortegiano, con una scelta delle Opere minori*, ed. B. Maier (Turin, 1964), p. 401 ('ché pur strano loco e tempo era il letto e la notte per contemplar quella pura bellezza, la qual si dice che amava Socrate senza alcun desiderio disonesto; massimamente amando più la bellezza dell'animo che del corpo, ma nei fanciulli e no nei vecchi, ancor che siano più savi').

33. M. Accame, *Pomponio Leto: vita e insegnamento* (Tivoli, 2008), pp. 43–8; V. Zabughin, *Giulio Pomponio Leto, saggio critico*, 2 vols. (Rome, Grottaferrata, 1909–10), i, p. 32 ('manifesto sospetto di sodomia'); I. D. Rowland, *The Culture of the High Renaissance: Ancients and Moderns in Sixteenth-Century Rome* (Cambridge, 1998), pp. 11–16, 25 (quotation).

34. I. Carini, 'La "Difesa" di Pomponio Leto pubblicata ed illustrata', in *Nozze Cian-Sappa-Flandinet* (Bergamo, 1894), pp. 151–93, at pp. 186–7 ('ut praeceptoris officium est, ut filios tractabam; horum alimentis nutriebar, horum domo tege-bar, horum strato requiescebam', 'Hos merito laudavi binis litteris, tum munere naturae idest a forma, tum virtute idest litterarum studio, tum assiduitate', 'Is enim formosis adolescentibus speculum admovebat inquiens: ubi natura tale tibi donum dedit, age ne in moribus ac litteris turpis videaris. Et informibus dicere solebat: ubi natura pulchritudinem denegavit, fac animo pulcher sis').

35. Pfisterer, *Lysippus und seine Freunde*, pp. 280–4.

36. L. Barkan, *Transuming Passion: Ganymede and the Erotics of Humanism* (Stanford, CA, 1991), esp. pp. 53–9, 66, 70. For contrary views of Dante on Latini see A. Pézard, *Dante sous la pluie de feu* (Paris, 1950); R. Kay, *Dante's Swift and Strong: Essays on 'Inferno' XV* (Lawrence, KS, 1978). The most thorough study of Latini insists that Dante saw him as a usurer, not a sodomite: J. B. Holloway, *Twice-Told Tales: Brunetto Latino and Dante Alighieri* (New York, 1993), pp. 8, 24.

37. Barkan, *Transuming Passion*, pp. 67–8.

38. See A. Campana, 'The Origin of the Word "Humanist"', *Journal of the Warburg and Courtauld Institutes*, 9 (1946), pp. 60–73, esp. pp. 61–4.

39. Barkan, *Transuming Passion*, pp. 70–1.

40. See J. Hankins, 'The Myth of the Platonic Academy of Florence', *Renaissance Quarterly*, 44 (1991), pp. 429–75, and his 'Humanist Academies and the "Platonic Academy of Florence"', in M. Pade, ed., *On Renaissance Academies: Proceedings of the International Conference 'From the Roman Academy to the Danish Academy in*

Rome, Dall'Accademia Romana all'Accademia di Danimarca a Roma' (Rome, 2011), pp. 31–45.

41. A. Vignali, *La cazzaria*, ed. P. Stoppelli (Rome, 1984); on the *Intronati* see A. Vignali, *The Book of the Prick*, trans. I. F. Moulton (New York, 2003), pp. 13–17. The word 'sodo' could be a coded term meaning 'arse': see J. Toscan, *Le Carnaval du langage: lexique érotique des poètes de l'équivoque de Burchiello à Marino (XVe–XVIIe siècles)*, 4 vols. (Lille, 1981), i, p. 559. On Vignali's text see also D. O. Frantz, *Festum Voluptatis: A Study of Renaissance Erotica* (Columbus, OH, 1989), pp. 38–42; R. Buranello, 'The Hidden Ways and Means of Antonio Vignali's *La cazzaria*', *Quaderni d'italianistica*, 26 (2005), pp. 59–76; M. T. Ricci, 'Antonio Vignali e *La Cazzaria*', in E. Boillet and C. Lastraioli, eds., *Extravagances amoureuses: l'amour au-delà de la norme à la Renaissance* (Paris, 2010), pp. 181–90.

42. Vignali, *Book of the Prick*, p. 83 (translation).

43. Vignali, *La cazzaria*, pp. 154–5 (printing history, including a non-extant Neapolitan edition); Vignali, *Book of the Prick*, pp. 46–50 (publication history, including just 2 MSS), 88–90 (friars).

44. Rocco, *Alcibiade*, pp. 27–8, 32–3 (biography), 95 (date of composition).

45. Ibid., pp. 47 (Cupid), 51 (nature, beauty, vagina), 59 ('datici dalla natura e da Dio'), 81–2 ('l'abito di timore imbevutogli da chi per leggi o per altro li persuade che sia vergogna e peccato'). Paolo Fasoli connects the naturalistic argument here with Rocco's Paduan philosophical background: 'Body Language: Sex-Manual Literature from Pietro Aretino's *Sixteen Positions* to Antonio Rocco's *Invitation to Sodomy*', in A. Levy, ed., *Sex Acts in Early Modern Italy: Practice, Performance, Perversion, Punishment* (Abingdon, 2010), pp. 27–42, at pp. 31–2.

46. Rocco, *Alcibiade*, pp. 57 (nations), 58 (legislators), 60 (Israelites), 61 ('fu dunque castigata la violenza, non il piacere; la crudeltà, non l'amore; l'inumanità, non gl'amplessi').

47. Ibid., pp. 53 ('piú a loro che a' fanciulli inclinano', 'svanisce con la puerizia il bello e il grazioso de' putti; dura piú longo tempo nella donna'), 71 (despotic), 72 (infectious), 73 (marriage).

48. Ibid., pp. 95–6. The title pages identify the author using only the initials 'D.P.A.'—'di Padre Antonio' ('by Father Antonio').

49. Above, p. 81; C. Mutini, 'Berni, Francesco', *Dizionario biografico degli italiani*, 100 vols. (Rome, 1960–2020), ix, pp. 343–57, at p. 345 (1523).

50. Berni, *Poesie e prose*, p. 48 ('Entra a sua posta ove la vòle, et esce... | Ch'ella sguizza per forza e passa via | Quant'un piú con la man la stringe e serra').

51. Ibid., p. 54 ('O frutto sopra gli altri benedetto, | Buono inanzi, nel mezzo e dietro pasto; | Ma inanzi buone e di dietro perfetto!... | Le pesche eran già cibo da prelati; | Ma, perché ad ognun piace i buon bocconi, | Voglion oggi le pesche insino a i frati').

52. Frantz, *Festum Voluptatis*, pp. 33–4; L. Wolk-Simon, ' "Rapture to the Greedy Eyes": Profane Love in the Renaissance', in A. Bayer, ed., *Art and Love in Renaissance Italy* (New York, 2008), pp. 43–58, at p. 50; W. Fisher, 'Peaches and

Figs: Bisexual Eroticism in the Paintings and Burlesque Poetry of Bronzino', in A. Levy, ed., *Sex Acts in Early Modern Italy: Practice, Performance, Perversion, Punishment* (Abingdon, 2010), pp. 151–64, at p. 158 (fruits); cf. also L. Giannetti Ruggiero, 'The Forbidden Fruit or the Taste for Sodomy in Renaissance Italy', *Quaderni d'italianistica*, 27:1 (2006), pp. 31–52.

53. Parker, *Bronzino: Renaissance Painter as Poet* (Cambridge, 2000), pp. 17–18 (publication), 24–7 (paintbrush, frying-pan), 28 ('giunto in galea non bisogna conforto | altro, a tal male: un guarisce in un tratto | con un po' po' di dondol corto corto').

54. Fisher, 'Peaches and Figs', p. 158.

55. Toscan, *Le Carnaval du langage*, esp. i, pp. 21–57 (Berni), 72–95 (Burchiello), 99–107 (carnival songs). The genre of nonsense poetry to which Burchiello contributed was a different matter; his poems remain nonsensical even when the sexual images are decoded. See N. Malcolm, *The Origins of English Nonsense* (London, 1997), pp. 69–72.

56. Rocke, *Forbidden Friendships*, p. 33 (satires); G. Dall'Orto, *Tutta un'altra storia. L'omosessualità dall'antichità al secondo dopoguerra* (Milan, 2015), pp. 207–8 (satires); Boccaccio, *Decameron*, V.10, p. 932 ('Questo dolente abbandona me per volere con le sue disonestà andare in zoccoli per l'asciutto, e io m'ingegnerò di portare altrui in nave per lo piovoso'). On the complicated history of the phrase 'andare in zoccoli per l'asciutto', meaning to commit sodomy, see Toscan, *Le Carnaval du langage*, i, pp. 532–6.

57. Toscan, *Le Carnaval du langage*, i, pp. 229 (modern-style), 233 (strong, dextrous), 529–59 (wet/dry), 561–606 (water/earth), 710–11 (south/north), 727–32 (light/dark).

58. C. S. Singleton, ed., *Canti carnascialeschi del Rinascimento* (Bari, 1936), p. 472 ('E che diavolo sono eglino poi altro che Canti Carnascialeschi? composizione plebeia, e del volgo; e come voi diceste giá, quanto peggio stanno, tanto è meglio, e tanto piú piacciono'). This is the Grazzini, also known as Lasca, whose *novella* involving the punishment of a schoolmaster for 'betraying sodomy' was quoted above (p. 64).

59. R. Bruscagli, ed., *Trionfi e canti carnascialeschi toscani del Rinascimento*, 2 vols. (Rome, 1986), i, pp. xxxviii ('ossessione sodomitica del Carnevale fiorentino', 'l'invito alla sodomia omoerotica si riveli sporadico e sempre incluso o sottinteso all'interno di un'aspirazione sodomitica indifferenziata'), 127–9 (Fig, Hole), 196–8 (*calcio*).

60. C. Fuhrmann, 'Gossip, *Erotica*, and the Male Spy in Alessandro Striggio's *Il Cicalamento delle donne al bucato* (1567)', in T. C. Borgerding, ed., *Gender, Sexuality, and Early Music* (New York, 2002), pp. 167–97.

61. Toscan, *Le Carnaval du langage*, i, pp. 211–12.

62. F. Berni et al., *Tutte le opere del Bernia in terza rima* (n.p., 1540), pp. 136 ('piccino', 'chi fa questo mestier diuino | Sa ben trouar doue l'hanno nascosto | Cola dirieto un certo fornellino'), 137 ('un certo uescouaccio ... | ... perche uuol del pan taluolta in fretta | M'e stato detto, che l'ha sempre drieto | Et tienla il suo garzon nella brachetta'). This work was first published in 1538.

63. See the definitive account of this episode in Puff, *Sodomy in Reformation Germany*, pp. 158–62, 260(n. 131) ('le laudi della Sodomia'). The charge about this non-existent treatise has continued to be made in modern times: see e.g. Greenberg, *Construction of Homosexuality*, p. 323.

64. E. Doumergue, *Jean Calvin: les hommes et les choses de son temps*, 7 vols. (Lausanne, 1899–1927), i, pp. 428–9, 433–9 (Calvin); Cocks, *Visions of Sodom*, pp. 149–52 (Calvin, Beza).

65. For all these details see D. Romei, 'Saggi di poesia omoerotica volgare del Cinquecento', in E. Boillet and C. Lastraioli, eds., *Extravagances amoureuses: l'amour au-delà de la norme à la Renaissance* (Paris, 2010), pp. 235–62; S. Lo Re, 'Gli amori omosessuali del Varchi: storia e legenda', ibid., pp. 279–95 (p. 281: 'quello star sempre a parlar d'occhi, di fronte, di guance, di labra non mi sembra che habbi niente del sano, né che quel bacione habbia del casto, dicano i platonici quel che ne vogliono'); on Beccuti see also Dall'Orto, *Tutta un'altra storia*, pp. 289–91. A valuable collection of works by these poets is available online: D. Romei, ed., *Antologia di poesia erotica volgare del Cinquecento* (2008), <http://www.nuovorinascimento.org/n-rinasc/testi/pdf/omoerotici/antologia.pdf>; for the two Beccuti poems see pp. 267–75.

66. G. Masi, 'Marignolli, Curzio (Curzio da Marignolle)', *Dizionario biografico degli italiani*, 100 vols. (Rome, 1960–2020), lxx, pp. 359–63 (p. 359: 'improbus amator'); G. Masi, '"Gente scapigliatissima e bizzarra": la poesia libertina di Curzio Marignolli', in E. Boillet and C. Lastraioli, eds., *Extravagances amoureuses: l'amour au-delà de la norme à la Renaissance* (Paris, 2010), pp. 341–70; G. Masi, 'Testi libertini di Curzio Marignolli inediti o editi con censure', ibid., pp. 371–414 (p. 377: 'bellissimo mio vezzoso Adone').

67. Masi, 'Testi libertini', pp. 372–3 (sonnet), 400–3 ('candelotto', 'e quivi sfibbïato | gl'ebbi i calzoni, e senza alcun schiamazzo | gli spinse in culo un gran palmo di cazzo; | e in tanto sollazzo | stetti un gran pezzo, e a punto su l'aurora | volle meco compir due volte ancora').

68. C. Galderisi, ed., *Il piacevol ragionamento de l'Aretino: Dialogo di Giulia e di Maddalena* (Rome, 1987), pp. 31 (1577), 63–4 (boys), 94–6 (banker). This edn. is of the only surviving manuscript, which appears to be late-16th- or early-17th-century.

69. Anon., *Vita di Pietro Aretino del Berni*, ('Perugia, 1537' [19th-century reprinting]), pp. 36–7; the attribution of this work to Berni was false. It may have been influenced by Aretino's former protégé Niccolò Franco, who published scurrilous accusations against Aretino; in 1540 Franco published a book of obscene poems, some of them targeting Aretino as a passive sodomite: see I. F. Moulton, *Before Pornography: Erotic Writing in Early Modern England* (Oxford, 2000), pp. 139–41. Franco has also been suggested as the author of *Il piacevol ragionamento*: Pfisterer, *Lysippus und seine Freunde*, p. 343(n.).

70. See the summary account by Moulton in Vignali, *Book of the Prick*, pp. 47–9; for the text's rather minimal mentions of male–female sex see Rocke, *Forbidden Friendships*, p. 125.

71. The 1660 printing called the work *La puttana errante*, borrowing that title from a 16th-century bawdy poem about a prostitute by a friend and follower of Aretino. See D. Foxon, *Libertine Literature in England, 1660–1745* (New York, 1965), pp. 27–30 (*La puttana*), 51–63 (Cleland; esp. p. 61 on the sodomitical passage, but not noticing the debt to the earlier work). On early modern pornography see ibid., pp. 19–27; P. Findlen, 'Humanism, Politics and Pornography in Renaissance Italy', in L. Hunt, ed., *The Invention of Pornography: Obscenity and the Origins of Modernity, 1500–1800* (New York, 1993), pp. 49–108 (esp. pp. 95–102 on Aretino); J. DeJean, *The Reinvention of Obscenity: Sex, Lies, and Tabloids in Early Modern France* (Chicago, 2002), pp. 56–83. (Note that the definition of pornography offered here excludes Beccadelli and Vignali, both of whom are called pornographic by Findlen.)

72. See above, p. 61; for the text, see p. 184.

73. R. Mills, *Suspended Animation: Pain, Pleasure and Punishment in Medieval Culture* (London, 2005), pp. 85–9 (Giotto, Buffalmacco); R. Mills, 'Acts, Orientations and the Sodomites of San Gimignano', in A. Levy, ed., *Sex Acts in Early Modern Italy: Practice, Performance, Perversion, Punishment* (Abingdon, 2010), pp. 195–208, at pp. 195–6 (di Bartolo).

74. D. Romano, 'A Depiction of Male Same-Sex Seduction in Ambrogio Lorenzetti's "Effects of Bad Government" Fresco', *JHS*, 21 (2012), pp. 1–15 (p. 7: photograph).

75. J. Manca, 'Sacred vs. Profane: Images of Sexual Vice in Renaissance Art', *Studies in Iconography*, 13 (1989–90), pp. 145–90, at pp. 149–52. A similar significance has been claimed for two scantily clad men who stand with arms intertwined in the background of the mid-15th-century 'Tondo Cook' (*Adoration of the Magi*) by Fra Angelico and Filippo Lippi: J. Saslow, *Pictures and Passions: A History of Homosexuality in the Visual Arts* (New York, 1999), p. 85.

76. A. Sternweiler, *Die Lust der Götter: Homosexualität in der italienischen Kunst, von Donatello zu Caravaggio* (Berlin, 1993), pp. 161–6. Sternweiler also draws attention (pp. 168–9) to a scene from the life of St Benedict, at Monte Oliveto Maggiore, where the saint presents a model of a church to two monks who are asleep in the same bed. He claims that this scene has a sexual significance; but the monks are fully clothed and fast asleep. On Sodoma see also Wittkower and Wittkower, *Born under Saturn*, pp. 173–5; and for a recent study of this painting, emphasizing its dynastic, and therefore in sexual terms thoroughly male–female, implications, see J. James, 'Bedding Agostino Chigi: Sodoma's *Marriage of Alexander and Roxanne* in the Villa Farnesina', *The Sixteenth Century Journal*, 52 (2021), pp. 647–66.

77. Sotheby's, New York, 'Master Paintings & Sculpture Evening Sale', 25 Jan. 2017, lot 3: <https://www.sothebys.com/en/auctions/2017/master-paintings-n09601.html?p=3&locale=en>; Rocke, *Forbidden Friendships*, p. 166.

78. P. L. Rubin, *Seen from Behind: Perspectives on the Male Body and Renaissance Art* (New Haven, CT, 2018). Rubin's argument is also weakened by the scant attention it gives to the importance in Mannerist art of *repoussoir* framing figures,

people placed in the foreground, turning away from the viewer, whose function it is to direct attention to the central event which takes place in the middle ground.

79. L. Bersani and U. Dutoit, *Caravaggio's Secrets* (Cambridge, MA, 1998), p. 2 ('erotically provocative'); D. Posner, 'Caravaggio's Homo-erotic Early Works', *The Art Quarterly*, 34 (1971), pp. 301–24; C. E. Gilbert, *Caravaggio and His Two Cardinals* (University Park, PA, 1995), esp. pp. 191–214 (criticizing Posner). More generally, Gilbert's study shows that some of the most apparently homoerotic paintings have other, much more complex, iconographic back-stories and significances. The homoerotic interpretation is only marginally strengthened by a suggestion that the presence of two peaches in one painting is a Berniesque coded allusion to young male buttocks: A. von Lates, 'Caravaggio's Peaches and Academic Puns', *Word & Image*, 11 (1995), pp. 55–60.

80. See for example the series known as the 'lascivie' of Agostino Carracci: D. DeGrazia Bohlin, *Prints and Related Drawings by the Carracci Family: A Catalogue Raisonné* (Washington, DC, 1979), pp. 289–305; cf. also B. Furlotti, G. Rebecchini and L. Wolk-Simon, eds., *Giulio Romano: arte e desiderio* (Mantua, 2019).

81. A. Matteoli, *Lodovico Cardi-Cigoli, pittore e architetto: fonti biografiche, catalogo delle opere, documenti, bibliografia, indici analitici* (Pisa, 1980), p. 31.

82. R. E. Spear, *The 'Divine' Guido: Religion, Sex, Money and Art in the World of Guido Reni* (New Haven, CT, 1997), pp. 57 ('latent sado-masochism'), 67–76. It is not clear why invoking sado-masochism here is more relevant than in the case of any other vivid depiction, in Renaissance art, of the sufferings of a martyr.

83. G. Vasari, *Lives of the Painters, Sculptors and Architects*, trans. G. du C. De Vere, ed. D. Ekserdjian, 2 vols. (New York, 1996), i, p. 676.

84. A small number of such cases feature in the illustrations to F. Le Targat, *Saint Sébastien dans l'histoire de l'art depuis le XVᵉ siècle* (Paris, 1979).

85. One likely exception is a painting of St Sebastian by Carlo Saraceni, of c.1606, now in the Prague Castle Museum, where the young man, alone under some trees, leans back with closed eyes and an intense but distant expression which might denote pleasure rather than suffering, his hand on a solitary arrow which rises at a suggestive angle from his groin; with its apparent allusion to masturbation, this was presumably commissioned by an individual for private delectation, not for public display. See M. G. Aurigemma, ed., *Carlo Saraceni, 1579–1620: un veneziano tra Roma e l'Europa* (Rome, 2013), pp. 189–92 (entry by M. Fratarcangeli).

86. S. Ferino Pagden, 'Giulio Romano und das künstlerische Vermächtnis Raffaels', in S. Ferino Pagden and K. Oberhuber, eds., *Fürstenhöfe der Renaissance: Giulio Romano und die klassische Tradition* (Vienna, 1989), pp. 46–87, at p. 67, plate II/73.

87. See D. Ekserdjian, *Parmigianino* (New Haven, CT, 2006), pp. 109–17, here p. 111 (and cf. the ambiguously gendered drawing on p. 110).

88. Barkan, *Transuming Passion*, p. 89 ('an image…'); Gilbert, *Caravaggio*, pp. 229–31 (pp. 230–1: 'The eagle…holds him against the left side of its bird body…if

indeed it touched the boy from behind, the area would meet his right leg, about a third of the way down to the knee. It will not be argued that the artist was weak in anatomical drawing...'). Paul Joannides notes that in a painting of 1538 Battista Franco used Michelangelo's Ganymede 'as an image of the divine elevation of Cosimo de' Medici', and comments that 'he would hardly have done so had the image carried an exclusively homosexual meaning': *Michelangelo and His Influence: Drawings from Windsor Castle* (Washington, DC, 1996), p. 74.

89. C. Monbeig Goguel, ed., *Francesco Salviati (1510–1563) o la bella maniera* (Paris, 1998), pp. 202–3 (entry by A. Nova).

90. A. Canevari and G. Fusconi, 'Un disegno licenzioso di Pietro Testa: gli amori di Pan e Venere', in S. Albl and S. Ebert-Schifferer, eds., *La fortuna dei baccanali di Tiziano nell'arte e nella letteratura del seicento* (Rome, 2019), pp. 129–47.

CHAPTER 12

1. Above, p. 141.

2. Berco, *Jerarquías sexuales*, p. 70; Pizzolato, '"Lo diavolo mi ingannao"', p. 450 ('una diffusa tolleranza a livello del popolo minuto'); Baldassari, *Bande giovanili*, p. 121; Davidson, 'Sodomy in Early Modern Venice', p. 75.

3. Bruscagli, ed., *Trionfi e canti carnascialeschi*, i, p. xxxviii ('Sia ringraziato Iddio, che ora si potrà soddomitare!'); Rocke, *Forbidden Friendships*, pp. 228–9.

4. Antoninus, *Summae sacrae theologiae*, fo. 214r ('Est autem infectiuum caeterorum quia vnus deditus huic vitio est sufficiens inficere totam vnam ciuitatem').

5. F. Tomás y Valiente, 'El crimen y pecado contra natura', in F. Tomás y Valiente et al., *Sexo barroco y otras transgresiones premodernas* (Madrid, 1990), pp. 33–55, at p. 52.

6. Jordan, *Invention of Sodomy*, pp. 100–1; Hergemöller, 'Sodomiter', p. 388.

7. Haliczer, *Sexuality in the Confessional*, p. 168.

8. Quoted in Rocke, 'Sodomites', pp. 22–3.

9. See D. Herlihy and C. Klapisch-Zuber, *Les Toscans et leurs familles: une étude du 'catasto' florentin de 1427* (Paris, 1978), pp. 439–42; S. K. Cohn, *Women in the Streets: Essays on Sex and Power in Renaissance Italy* (Baltimore, 1996), p. 152.

10. R. C. Trexler, 'La Prostitution florentine au XVᵉ siècle: patronages et clientèles', *Annales. Histoire, sciences sociales*, 36 (1981), pp. 983–1015, at pp. 983–4.

11. Berco, *Jerarquías sexuales*, pp. 169–82. I leave aside here the claim by the Brazilian scholar Luiz Mott that the main reason why the Portuguese Inquisition prosecuted sodomy was that it was seen as representing a 'counterculture feared to be revolutionary': L. Mott, 'Sodomia não é heresia: dissidência moral e contracultura', in R. Vainfas, B. Feitler and L. Lage da Gama Lima, eds., *A Inquisição em xeque: temas, controvérsias, estudos de caso* (Rio de Janeiro, 2006), pp. 253–66, at p. 253 ('uma contracultura temida como... revolucionária'). Little evidence is given for that claim, and the general argument has been adequately refuted by Ronaldo Vainfas, 'Inquisição como fábrica de hereges: os sodomitas foram exceção?', ibid., pp. 267–80.

12. Above, p. 80.
13. Mott, 'Misadventures', p. 308.
14. Above, p. 88.
15. Alves Dias, 'Para uma abordagem do sexo proibido', p. 154 (censored, suppressed); Rosa Pereira, *A Inquisição em Portugal*, p. 180–1 ('pessoa de qualidade').
16. García Cárcel, *Herejía y sociedad*, p. 293.
17. See above, pp. 46, 67. Both those men, unusually, were prosecuted; but in neither case does the accusation of occasional passivity seem to have made any special contribution to that fact.
18. Toscan, *Le Carnaval du langage*, i, pp. 193–201 (trope); T. Scaramella, ' "La sodomia è boccone da principi". Voci libertine fuori dall'Accademia: il caso veneziano tra Sei e Settecento', in U. Grassi, V. Lagioia and G. P. Romagnani, eds., *Tribadi, sodomiti, invertite e invertiti, pederasti, femminelle, ermafrodite . . . Per una storia dell'omosessualità, della bisessualità e delle trasgressioni di genere in Italia* (Pisa, 2017), pp. 111–28, at p. 116 (friar).
19. Cellini, *Vita*, p. 461 ('Iddio 'l volessi che io sapessi fare una così nobile arte, perchè e' si legge ch' e' l'usò Giove con Ganimede in paradiso, e qui in terra e' la usano i maggiori imperatori ed i più gran re del mondo: io sono un basso ed umile uomiciattolo, il quale nè potrei nè saprei impacciarmi d'una così mirabil cosa'). Cellini puts this story in a chapter describing events of 1546–7, a decade before the actual conviction for sodomy which, understandably, he never mentions.
20. Richard Trexler discusses 'homosexual rape' in the ancient world as a form of 'punitive gendering', commenting that 'sexual punishments in antiquity and in traditional Europe often aimed at branding living males as dependent and thus not fully male: either as defenseless, passive males, or as women': *Sex and Conquest*, pp. 14, 19.
21. Pius II, *Commentaries*, ed. and trans. M. Meserve and M. Simonetta, i (Cambridge, MA, 2003), pp. 326–7 ('libidinis ita impatiens fuit, ut filiabus ac generis vim intulerit'; note also his comment, probably implying not so much a causal theory as a picture of lifelong depravity, that 'As a boy he often played the bride; later, he who had so often taken the woman's part used other men like whores' ('adolescens nupsit in feminam, et saepe muliebria passus saepe masculos effeminavit')).
22. Carrasco, *Inquisición y represión*, p. 131 ('El sodomita era una cri[a]tura de lujuria, un esclavo de los apetitos sensuales, pero de unos apetitos que naturaleza provocaba en la comunidad universal de los hombres').
23. The quotation from Pius II, above, does seem to imply sex with adult males, but this surely reflects Pius's desire to portray Malatesta as the most extreme and monstrous kind of sinner.
24. K. Borris, 'Sodomizing Science: Cocles, Patricio Tricasso, and the Constitutional Morphologies of Renaissance Male Same-Sex Lovers', in K. Borris and G. Rousseau, eds., *The Sciences of Homosexuality in Early Modern Europe* (London, 2008), pp. 137–64, at pp. 146–7. Thomas Laqueur has claimed that mediaeval

and early modern Europe adhered to a 'one-sex' anatomical theory, in which the female body was a variant of, not a binary alternative to, the male: *Making Sex: Body and Gender from the Greeks to Freud* (Cambridge, MA, 1990). This might be taken to support the view that some early modern men saw the bodies of pre-pubertal boys as essentially equivalent to female ones; but Laqueur's claim has been strongly contested (see A. Ragab, 'One, Two, or Many Sexes: Sex Differentiation in Medieval Islamicate Medical Thought', *JHS*, 24 (2015), pp. 428–54, esp. pp. 428, 447).

25. Voltaire, *Dictionnaire philosophique*, ed. G. Stenger (Paris, 2010), pp. 94–5 ('Souvent un jeune garçon par la fraîcheur de son teint, par l'éclat de ses couleurs, & par la douceur de ses yeux, ressemble pendant deux ou trois ans à une belle fille; si on l'aime, c'est parce que la nature se méprend; on rend hommage au sexe en s'attachant à ce qui en a les beautés, & quand l'âge a fait évanouir cette ressemblance, la méprise cesse'). The immediate context here is an explanation of why boys, brought up with other boys and developing sexual feelings in the absence of girls, may be sexually attracted to male friends; but the basic argument seems capable of further extension, even though Voltaire was a censorious critic of sodomy.

26. Above, p. 48; Ottonelli, *Della christiana moderatione*, p. 195 ('huomini casti... dal guardar liberamente la bellezza de' Giouanetti').

27. Basil of Caesarea, *De renunciatione saeculi*, 6, cited in Boswell, *Christianity, Social Tolerance*, p. 159.

28. Above, p. 162.

29. Rocco, *Alcibiade*, pp. 40–1. The only difference involves a comment which is not itself a description of beauty: he writes that the boy's nose made him think of his penis, and adds a number of other anatomical associations of that kind.

30. Above, p. 145; Sabadino degli Arienti, *Novelle porretane*, nov. 12, p. 63 ('una bellissima dongella').

31. Penman, ed. and trans., *Five Italian Renaissance Comedies*, pp. 193–278, esp. pp. 244–8. This play was a significant influence on Shakespeare's *Twelfth Night*.

32. Cellini, *Vita*, pp. 72–5 ('bello di persona, maraviglioso di color di carne', 'con ingiuriose parole quali si usano dire ai belli giovanetti').

33. M. Martelli, 'Un caso di "amphibolatio": la canzone a ballo "Ragionavasi di sodo"', in G. C. Garfagnini, ed., *Lorenzo de' Medici. Studi* (Florence, 1992), pp. 309–27, at p. 324 ('La sua moglie si dolea | Che faceva un certo giuoco, | Che veder non lo potea; | E dicea pur: "Muta loco". Il marito disse poco: | "Seguir vo' l'usanza mia: | Nol vo' far per altra via, | Se miglior ragion' non odo"').

34. Rocke, *Forbidden Friendships*, p. 215 (statistics); Trexler, 'La Prostitution florentine', p. 995 (further cases).

35. Anon. [Lorenzi], *Leggi e memorie*, pp. 65–7 (1470), 82 (1496, 'lenones puerorum et feminarum in vitio sodomie tam mares quam femine'), 86–7 (1500, 'in domo sua tenuerit scolam sodomitij hominum cum feminis').

36. Ruggiero, *Boundaries of Eros*, pp. 119–20 (1484 case); Anon. [Lorenzi], *Leggi e memorie*, p. 89 (1500 case).

37. Trexler, 'La Prostitution florentine', pp. 995, 998 (Florence, statistics, carnival); Crouzet-Pavan, *'Sopra le acque salse'*, ii, p. 841 (beards); cf. also G. Ruggiero, 'Marriage, Love, Sex, and Renaissance Civic Morality', in J. G. Turner, ed., *Sexuality and Gender in Early Modern Europe* (Cambridge, 1993), pp. 10–30, at p. 25. Among the sexual escapades recounted in Aretino's classic work, two involve women using male dress for assignations with male lovers, and in a third story a courtesan wears male clothing for the Carnival (P. Aretino, *The Ragionamenti*, trans. I. Liseux and P. Stafford (London, 1971), pp. 56, 124, 148).

38. Bernardino, *Le prediche volgari*, ed. Cannarozzi, ii, p. 141; Rosselló, *L'homosexualitat a Mallorca*, p. 13 ('per provocar los homes a pecat').

39. Dean, 'Sodomy in Renaissance Bologna', p. 440; Dutra, 'Sodomy and the Portuguese Nobility', pp. 172–3.

40. Aretino, *Ragionamenti*, p. 149.

41. Rocke, *Forbidden Friendships*, pp. 215–16.

42. Toscan, *Le Carnaval du langage*, i, pp. 245–68; cf. Ruggiero, *Boundaries of Eros*, pp. 118–19, for evidence that it was an accepted method of birth control in Venice.

43. J. Bale, *A Mysterye of Inyquyte Contayned within the Heretycall Genealogye of Ponce Pantolabus* ('Geneva' [Antwerp], 1545), sigs. D5v–D6r ('a dispensacyon for the whole howsholde of the cardinall of Saynt Lucie | to haue the fre occupyenge of buggerye boyes for the .iii. hotter monthes of the yeare'). The claim was popular among Huguenot writers (see G. Mathieu-Castellani, 'Éros masqué: figures mystiques de l'homosexualité', in P. Ford and P. White, eds., *Masculinities in Sixteenth-Century France* (Cambridge, 2006), pp. 181–97, at pp. 195–6), and was still being discussed in 18th-century Holland (see Boon, *'Dien godlosen hoop van menschen'*, p. 223).

44. Aretino, *Ragionamenti*, pp. 30–1, 43–4, 54, 74, 87, 126, 149.

45. Romeo, *Amori proibiti*, pp. 108–9 ('esponendo querela contra tutti i priapi per aver pervertito le regole', 'perpetui calori').

46. Carrasco, *Inquisición y represión*, pp. 37–8.

47. Perry, 'The "Nefarious Sin"', p. 79.

48. Drumond Braga, 'Foreigners, Sodomy', p. 155.

49. Ruggiero, *Boundaries of Eros*, p. 119.

50. Mazzi, *'Gente a cui si fa notte innanzi sera'*, p. 103 ('vilan sodomito, el quale usò con la moglie et fu impichato et poi brusatto').

51. See the discussion in Sánchez, *Disputationum de sancto matrimonii sacramento*, iii, pp. 217–21.

52. J. Merrick and B. T. Ragan, *Homosexuality in Early Modern France: A Documentary Collection* (New York, 2001), pp. 102–3. Azpilcueta seems to have acquired a reputation as a lax or exculpatory writer on sexual sins: a few years later, a man who told the Sicilian Inquisition that masturbation was not a sin said that he had read this in Azpilcueta's work (Canosa, *Sessualità e Inquisizione*, p. 22).

53. Monter, *Frontiers of Heresy*, pp. 174–5.

54. Canosa, *Sessualità e Inquisizione*, p. 19 ('cosa santa e giusta').

55. Monter, *Frontiers of Heresy*, p. 176; Riera i Sans, *Sodomites catalans*, pp. 282–3 (' "Adam, nuestro primer padre, ¿no se lo hizo a su muger por la parte trassera?"; y que si Dios no hubiera hecho el culo, no se alegrerían con él, y que Dios le avia criado para que se olgassen y se sirviessen dél'). The Sicilian Inquisition noted 6 statements of this claim about Adam: F. Renda, *L'Inquisizione in Sicilia* (Palermo, 1997), p. 386.

56. Monter, *Frontiers of Heresy*, p. 175(n.) (1618); Grassi, *L'Offizio sopra l'Onestà*, pp. 26–7 ('que no lo tenía por pecado porqué la naturaleza lo permitía (entendiendo por el pecado contra natura) replicando diversas vezes').

57. Rocke, *Forbidden Friendships*, pp. 128–9.

58. Aristotle, *The Complete Works*, ed. J. Barnes, 2 vols. (Princeton, NJ, 1984), 4.26, 879a36–7, ii, p. 1356; Cadden, *Meanings of Sex Difference*, pp. 214–16 (d'Abano); Borris, *Same-Sex Desire*, pp. 130–40 (d'Abano text).

59. B. Nathan, 'Medieval Arabic Medical Views on Male Homosexuality', *JH*, 26 (1996), pp. 37–9; J. Cadden, *Nothing Natural is Shameful: Sodomy and Science in Late Medieval Europe* (Philadelphia, 2013), pp. 3–4. For a late Renaissance treatment emphasizing habit (apparently for moral–religious reasons), see F. Wallis, 'Giulio Guastavini's Commentary on Pseudo-Aristotle's Account of Male Same-Sexual Coitus, *Problemata* 4.26', in K. Borris and G. Rousseau, eds., *The Sciences of Homosexuality in Early Modern Europe* (London, 2008), pp. 57–73.

60. Borris, 'Sodomizing Science', pp. 144–5; for other relevant texts by Cocles see Borris, *Same-Sex Desire*, pp. 184–91.

61. Borris, *Same-Sex Desire*, p. 34.

62. M. Bandello, *La prima parte de le novelle*, ed. D. Maestri (Alessandria, 1992), nov. 6, pp. 68 ('enormi vizii', 'sempre la carne del capretto gli piaceva molto più che altro cibo che gli potesse dare, di maniera che questo era il sommo suo diletto d'andar in zoccoli per l'asciutto'), 71 ('Oh, oh, padre reverendo, voi non mi sapreste interrogare. Il trastullarmi con i fanciulli a me è più naturale che non è il mangiar e il ber a l'uomo, e voi mi domandavate se io peccava contra natura'); above, pp. 48 (Rocco), 159 (Boccaccio).

63. Bandello, *La prima parte*, nov. 6, p. 71 ('sono io assicurato che tu sei più vago mille volte dei fanciulli che non è la capra del sale').

64. Rocco, *Alcibiade*, pp. 55 (animals), 59 ('Le inclinazioni sono contrapesi datici dalla natura e da Dio, chi segue quelli non s'allontana dai propri principii, non fa contro l'istitutore').

65. Above, p. 186 (Lombard); Grassi, *L'Offizio contra l'Onestà*, p. 26 (1559); G. Romeo, *Aspettando il boia: condannati a morte, confortatori, inquisitori nella Napoli della Controriforma* (Florence, 2003), p. 240 ('che era cosa naturale et che se havesse potuto havere una dispensa se l'haveria pigliato per moglie').

66. Above, p. 103 (de Verniolles); Molina, *Cuando amar era pecado*, p. 86 ('abia de ser en el puño o en el culo'); T. Scaramella, *Un doge infame: sodomia e nonconformismo sessuale a Venezia nel Settecento* (Venice, 2021), p. 119 ('erano cose naturali, [praticate] per diletto naturale').

67. Drumond Braga, 'Foreigners, Sodomy', p. 150 (1596); Davidson, 'Sodomy', p. 74 (1618); above, p. 185 (1597–8); Pérez, Muntaner and Colom, eds., *El Tribunal de la Inquisición en Mallorca*, pp. 169–70 (Mallorca).

68. Archivio di Stato, Venice, Savi all'eresia (Santo Ufficio) busta 8, fasc. 28, fos. 1r ('ch[e] no[n] ge [*sic*] fu mai Christo, et che q[ue]llo christo ch[e] cossi e ditto dale persone, era homo carnale, et che conosceua spesse uolte carnalme[n]te S. Gioa[n]ni et che lo teneua per Cinedo', 'ha detto che Vn bel Culo, era suo Altar', la sua messa, l'hostia, Calice, et la patena. Ite[m] ch[e] adora piu presto vn bel putto carnalmente conoscendolo, che Domenedio'), 3r ('matto', 'erano p[er]sone d[e]l Diauolo, et ch[e] faceuano q[ue]sto p[er] far star la gente in timor[e], et governar il mondo a loro modo, et me diceua spesso quel uerso de lucretio, Primus in orbe deos fecit timor'), 3v ('Tutt'il mondo, ch[e] era vna bestia, et ch[e] il vulgo credeua in queste cose ch[e] lui diceua, et ch[e] il papa, et q[ue]sti homini grandi credeuano come lui, cioe ch[e] no[n] ui è Dio, et ch[e] non ui era ne paradiso, ne altro, ma ch[e] morto il corpo, è morta l'anima, et ch[e] il Tutto se gouernaua a caso').

69. Ibid., fos. 5r–v (denied, forgot), 6r ('ch[e] Xr[ist]o era homo, come li altri, et che S. Gioa[n]n era sta [*sic*] suo Cinedo'), 6v ('in vn libro chiamato la Cazzaria').

70. L. Rostagno, *Mi faccio Turco: esperienze ed immagini dell'Islam nell'Italia moderna* (Rome, 1983), p. 74 (1571: 'va in culo alla scrofa'); Renda, *L'Inquisizione in Sicilia*, p. 389 (Sicily); W. Christian, *Local Religion in Sixteenth-Century Spain* (Princeton, NJ, 1981), p. 258(n. 41) (proclamation); S. T. Nalle, *God in La Mancha: Religious Reform and the People of Cuenca, 1500–1650* (Baltimore, 1992), p. 61 (wool-comber, María).

71. John 19: 26; 20: 2; 21: 7 (loved); 21: 20 ('which also leaned on his breast at supper'). Separate representations of Jesus and John in this position were also made: see Saslow, *Pictures and Passions*, pp. 68–9.

72. Davidson, *Greeks and Greek Love*, p. 177 (Ganymede); Kruszynski, *Der Ganymed-Mythos*, unpaginated, n. 159 (Ganymede); Romeo, *Aspettando il boia*, p. 241 (Naples: 'bogerone'); Scaramella, *Un doge infame*, pp. 167–8 (Venice, 1627); Mott, 'Misadventures', p. 309 (Brazil); F. da Rocha Peres, *Gregório de Mattos e a Inquisição* (Salvador, 1987), p. 18 (Mattos: 'Jesus Cristo nosso Redentor fora Nefando').

73. Bernardino, *Le prediche volgari*, ed. Cannarozzi, ii, p. 143 ('al suo tempo non era sodomiti'); V. Lavenia, *Un'eresia indicibile: Inquisizione e crimini contro natura in età moderna* (Bologna, 2015), p. 60 (Macerata).

74. Mott, 'Misadventures', p. 309 (Brazil); Tortorici, *Sins against Nature*, p. 186 (Yucatán); Pérez, Muntaner and Colom, eds., *El Tribunal de la Inquisición en Mallorca*, p. 86 ('Pedro tan cerca del culo le enclavas').

75. Scaramella, 'Sodomia', p. 1449 (Naples, 1567, 1578); F. Barbierato, 'Follie della natura tra Sei e Settecento', in U. Grassi, V. Lagioia and G. P. Romagnani, eds., *Tribadi, sodomiti, invertite e invertiti, pederasti, femminelle, ermafrodite... Per una storia dell'omosessualità, della bisessualità e delle trasgressioni di genere in Italia* (Pisa, 2017), pp. 61–7, at p. 62 (Venice, 1587).

76. Renda, *L'Inquisizione in Sicilia*, p. 390; Lavenia, *Un'eresia indicibile*, p. 61 (weaver).

77. García Fuentes, *La Inquisición en Granada*, p. 120 (Granada); Pérez, Muntaner and Colom, eds., *El Tribunal de la Inquisición en Mallorca*, pp. 21, 68.

78. See E. Behrend-Martinez, 'Making Sense of the History of Sex and Gender in Early Modern Spain', *History Compass*, 7:1 (1999), pp. 1306–16, esp. pp. 1307–8.

CHAPTER 13

1. N. J. Dawood, trans., *The Koran*, 3rd revd edn. (Harmondsworth, 1968), pp. 358–9.

2. Ibid., pp. 203, 247.

3. See Schmitt, '*Liwāṭ* im *Fiqh*', pp. 60–4; A. Schmitt, 'Different Approaches to Male–Male Sexuality/Eroticism from Morocco to Usbekistān', in A. Schmitt and J. Sofer, eds., *Sexuality and Eroticism among Males in Moslem Societies* (Binghamton, NY, 1992), pp. 1–24, at pp. 8, 13–18; El-Rouayheb, *Before Homosexuality*, pp. 124–5.

4. Note however that this verse 'was simply not considered by Islamic scholars to be the basis for legal opinions on the punishment of sodomy' (El-Rouayheb, *Before Homosexuality*, p. 122).

5. J. Wafer, 'Muhammad and Male Homosexuality', in S. O. Murray and W. Roscoe, eds., *Islamic Homosexualities: Culture, History and Literature* (New York, 1997), pp. 87–96, at p. 89.

6. El-Rouayheb, *Before Homosexuality*, pp. 120, 125.

7. J. A. Bellamy, 'Sex and Society in Islamic Popular Literature', in A. L. al-Sayyid-Marsot, ed., *Society and the Sexes in Medieval Islam* (Malibu, CA, 1979), pp. 23–42, at pp. 37–8.

8. J. Robson, trans., *Tracts on Listening to Music, being* Dhamm al-malāhī *by Ibn abī 'l-Dunyā and* Bawāriq al-ilmā' *by Majd al-Dīn al-Ṭūsī al-Ghazālī* (London, 1938), p. 38.

9. Bellamy, 'Sex and Society', p. 37; 'Daily Hadith Online', <https://www.abuaminaelias.com/dailyhadithonline/2019/07/03/lowering-gaze-beardless-youth>, citing *Dhamm al-malāhī*, p. 140; cf. also Bouhdiba, *La Sexualité*, pp. 46, 146.

10. Bellamy, 'Sex and Society', p. 38.

11. Dawood, trans., *The Koran*, pp. 108, 115. On the influence of these passages on the trope of the handsome cupbearer in Islamic literature see Andrews and Kalpaklı, *Age of Beloveds*, pp. 156–7.

12. El-Rouayheb, *Before Homosexuality*, pp. 129 (depopulation), 131–2 (debate); A. Arjona Castro, *La sexualidad en la España musulmana*, 2nd edn. (Cordova, n.d.), pp. 78–9 (depopulation).

13. El-Rouayheb, *Before Homosexuality*, p. 129.

14. Ibid., pp. 88 (*ḥadīth*), 139 ('Falling in love…'); cf. Berger, *Gesellschaft und Individuum*, p. 242.

15. S. D. Goitein, *A Mediterranean Society: The Jewish Communities of the Arab World as Portrayed in the Documents of the Cairo Geniza*, 6 vols. (Berkeley, CA, 1967), v, pp. 317–20.

16. El-Rouayheb, *Before Homosexuality*, pp. 95–6.

17. On this theme in the Sufi tradition see H. Ritter, *Das Meer der Seele: Mensch, Welt, und Gott in den Geschichten des Fariduddin 'Attar* (Leiden, 1955), pp. 434–87; A. Schimmel, 'Eros—Heavenly and not so Heavenly—in Sufi Literature and Life', in A. L. al-Sayyid-Marsot, ed., *Society and the Sexes in Medieval Islam* (Malibu, CA, 1979), pp. 119–41, at pp. 122–4, 131–3.

18. Ritter, *Das Meer der Seele*, pp. 449–58.

19. J. N. Bell, *Love Theory in Later Ḥanbalite Islam* (Albany, NY, 1979), pp. 19–31, 128–9.

20. Ibid., pp. 139–40 (noting that Ibn 'Arabī 'specifically condemned keeping company with youths'); cf. also El-Rouayheb, *Before Homosexuality*, p. 103.

21. Schimmel, 'Eros', pp. 131–2.

22. Ze'evi, *Producing Desire*, p. 88.

23. Andrews and Kalpaklı, *Age of Beloveds*, pp. 138–40.

24. See the important work by C. Tortel, *L'Ascète et le bouffon: qalandars, vrais et faux renonçants en Islam, ou l'Orient indianisé* (Paris, 2009); more generally, on the qalandars and other related groups, see A. T. Karamustafa, *God's Unruly Friends: Dervish Groups in the Islamic Later Middle Period, 1200–1550* (Salt Lake City, 1994).

25. M. Febvre, *L'État présent de la Turquie, où il est traité des vies, moeurs et coûtumes des Ottomans, et autres peuples de leur empire* (Paris, 1675), p. 84 ('sur tout, ils sont tres-enclins aux vices de la chair, & aux pechez contre nature. Car la Sodomie & autres abominations, que l'honnesteté ne permet pas de nommer, leur sont si ordinaires qu'ils leurs sont devenus comme en habitude, & ils les commettent sans aucun remords de conscience').

26. El-Rouayheb, *Before Homosexuality*, pp. 96–8, 100–4 (p. 104: 'eager to ...'); on the traditional idea of Adam as a beardless boy see Ritter, *Das Meer der Seele*, pp. 445–7.

27. See especially Schmitt, '*Liwāṭ* im *Fiqh*', pp. 69–90; also D. Ze'evi, 'Changes in Legal–Sexual Discourses: Sex Crimes in the Ottoman Empire', *Continuity and Change*, 16 (2001), pp. 219–42, at pp. 225–7; El-Rouayheb, *Before Homosexuality*, pp. 118–21; M. Mezziane, 'Sodomie et masculinité chez les juristes musulmans du IXe au XIe siècle', *Arabica*, 55 (2008), pp. 276–306, at pp. 282–90; E. Semerdjian, '*Off the Straight Path': Illicit Sex, Law, and Community in Ottoman Aleppo* (Syracuse, NY, 2008), pp. 7–8, 13–14; S. Omar, 'From Semantics to Normative Law: Perceptions of *Liwāṭ* (Sodomy) and *Siḥāq* (Tribadism) in Islamic Jurisprudence (8th–15th Century CE)', *Islamic Law and Society*, 19 (2012), pp. 222–56, at pp. 229–36; I. A. Rabb, *Doubt in Islamic Law: A History of Legal Maxims, Interpretation, and Islamic Criminal Law* (Cambridge, 2015), pp. 148(n.), 191–2. As Rabb notes (pp. 275–6), the most severe view of sodomy was to be found in the Shi'ite legal tradition, where it was argued that God's destruction of Sodom and Gomorrah showed that this was a worse offence than any other sexual crime.

28. El-Rouayheb, *Before Homosexuality*, p. 123; Schmitt, '*Liwāṭ* im *Fiqh*', pp. 104–5. Mohammed Mezziane argues that a major concern of Islamic jurists was the damage to social order that might be caused by publicizing sexual offences ('Sodomie et masculinité', pp. 296–7); but Sara Omar notes that while such a

concern may have been present, it did not determine actual judgments ('From Semantics to Normative Law', p. 225).

29. Ze'evi, 'Changes in Legal–Sexual Discourses', pp. 227–8; U. Heyd, *Studies in Old Ottoman Criminal Law*, ed. V. L. Ménage (Oxford, 1973), pp. 102–3 (p. 102: quotation).

30. Ş. Pamuk, *A Monetary History of the Ottoman Empire* (Cambridge, 2000), pp. 136–42 (debasement); C. Finkel, *The Administration of Warfare: The Ottoman Military Campaigns in Hungary, 1596–1606* (Vienna, 1988), p. 76 (Janissary); R. C. Jennings, *Christians and Muslims in Ottoman Cyprus and the Mediterranean World, 1571–1640* (New York, 1993), pp. 101–2 (judge).

31. Mott, 'Musulmani sodomiti', p. 157 ('perché ciò nella sua terra non era punito se non con l'arresto e la liberazione dietro pagamento'). I correct the dating given by Mott.

32. Ze'evi, 'Changes in Legal–Sexual Discourses', pp. 230–2.

33. F. Zarinebaf, *Crime and Punishment in Istanbul, 1700–1800* (Berkeley, CA, 2011), pp. 116–18; Semerdjian, *'Off the Straight Path'*, p. 98 (giving as the other reason 'the lack of consensus among jurists as to whether homosexuality constituted *zina*'; she does note, however (p. 54), that the great Ottoman jurist Ebu's Su'ud declared that sodomitical rape, causing physical damage to the boy victim, was *zinā* and merited the death penalty).

34. Tolan, *Saracens*, p. 238 (Martí); Spandounes, *Origin of the Ottoman Emperors*, pp. 130–1; G. Postel, *De la république des Turcs: et là où l'occasion s'offrera, des meurs et loy de tous Muhamedistes* (Paris, 1560), p. 127; Bodleian Library, Oxford, MS Rawl. D 618, fos. 106r–111v: 'Del Turco. Alcune Particolarita estratte dalla Relazione fatta da Francesco Bandola [*sic*] ritornato da Ragusa delli 1574. à P.P Gregorio 13:°', at fo. 108v ('libidinosi et nel piu peruerso modo se bene la legge loro comanda che siano puniti insieme col patiente dalla piu alta torre della città ma si richiedono circonstanze quasi impossibili alla proua'); M. Febvre, *Theatre de la Turquie* (Paris, 1682), p. 159.

35. Rowson, 'Categorization', p. 74 (quotation); V. Boškov, 'Zum Problem des Objekts der Liebe in der osmanischen Divan-Poesie', in W. Voigt, ed., *XVIII. deutscher Orientalistentag, vom 1. bis 5. Oktober 1972 in Lübeck: Vorträge* (*Zeitschrift der Deutschen Morgenländische Gesellschaft*, Supplement II) (Wiesbaden, 1974), pp. 124–30, at pp. 124–5; Berger, *Gesellschaft und Individuum*, p. 242.

36. J. W. Wright, 'Masculine Allusion and the Structure of Satire in Early 'Abbāsid Poetry', in J. W. Wright and E. K. Rowson, eds., *Homoeroticism in Classical Arabic Literature* (New York, 1997), pp. 1–23, at p. 21 (n. 44); Bellamy, 'Sex and Society', p. 40 (quotation).

37. Szombathy, *Mujūn*, p. 41; cf. also Bouhdiba, *La Sexualité*, p. 157. The term was not essentially literary; it referred to a way of behaving and expressing oneself.

38. Szombathy, *Mujūn*, pp. 134 (quotation), 138, 194 (real preference); E. Wagner, *Abū Nuwās: eine Studie zur arabischen Literatur der frühen Neuzeit* (Wiesbaden, 1965), p. 175 (real preference).

39. Szombathy, Mujūn, p. 138. Szombathy comments (p. 139, n. 69) that the sexual metaphors of sea and land here, which recur in other poets, seem to have been invented by Abū Nuwās, and suggests that they contrast travelling in the belly of a ship with riding on the back of an animal. The Florentine code (see above, p. 159) offers a different explanation. Whether the Arabic and Italian schemes of metaphor just formed independently, or were in some way related, seems impossible to tell.

40. Wright, 'Masculine Allusion', p. 12.

41. Ibid., p. 12.

42. Ibid., p. 9 (*islam*); Abū Nuwās, *Poèmes bachiques et libertins*, trans. O. Merzoug (Paris, 2002), p. 115 (afterlife).

43. Wagner, *Abū Nuwās*, pp. 180–6.

44. J. C. Bürgel, 'Abglanz Gottes oder Fallstrick Satans? Zum homoerotischen Element in der Dichtung des islamischen Mittelalters', in T. Stemmler, ed., *Homoerotische Lyrik: 6. Kolloquium der Forschungsstelle für europäische Lyrik des Mittelalters* (Mannheim, 1992), pp. 103–18, at p. 105 (al-Jāḥiẓ); Szombathy, Mujūn, pp. 138 (b. Hindū), 139(n. 70), 149 (al-Ṣaymarī); on such works see also F. Rosenthal, 'Male and Female: Described and Compared', in J. W. Wright and E. K. Rowson, eds., *Homoeroticism in Classical Arabic Literature* (New York, 1997), pp. 24–54, at pp. 24–9.

45. Oberhelman, 'Hierarchies of Gender', p. 68. Bouhdiba remarks on a lengthy section of the commentary on the poems of al-Tughrai by the eminent 14th-century Palestinian scholar al-Safadi, which contains 'a veritable anthology of salacious stories, riddles and verse compositions, in short, of everything written by earlier poets on...the size of the holes of women and boys': *La Sexualité*, p. 157 ('une véritable anthologie d'anecdotes salaces, de devinettes, de pièces en vers, bref de tout ce qui a été écrit par les poètes du temps jadis sur...la largeur des trous de femmes et de garçons').

46. Bürgel, 'Abglanz Gottes', p. 108. Again, the similarity to the popular Italian belief about the hottest months of the year (above, p. 183) is intriguing.

47. El-Rouayheb, *Before Homosexuality*, pp. 60–5. See also Boswell, *Christianity, Social Tolerance*, pp. 18–19(n.) on the attempts by modern editors and translators of the classic Persian poet Hafiz to falsify the gender of the beloved in his *ghazals*.

48. N. Roth, '"Deal Gently with the Young Man": Love of Boys in Medieval Hebrew Poetry of Spain', *Speculum*, 57 (1982), pp. 20–51, at pp. 31, 38, 45. Cf. Goitein, *A Mediterranean Society*, v, p. 320 (for similar Hebrew poems from the Cairo Geniza); Tov Assis, 'Sexual Behaviour', p. 50 (for a poem by Todros Ben Judah Halevi Abulafia on the advantages of male youths over women). On the Islamic writers of homoerotic poetry in Spain see Boswell, *Christianity, Social Tolerance*, pp. 194–8 (commenting on p. 197: 'Many of the authors...were teachers of the Qur'an, religious leaders, or judges'); for numerous examples see A. R. Nykl, *Hispano-Arabic Poetry and its Relations with the Old Provençal Troubadours* (Baltimore, 1946), *passim*.

49. Rosenthal, 'Male and Female', p. 35.

50. Andrews and Kalpaklı, *Age of Beloveds*, pp. 40–4 (Persian origins; mentioning 46 examples, one about women); Sariyannis, 'Prostitution', p. 48 (prostitutes); S. S. Kuru, 'Il genere del desiderio. L'amore per i bei ragazzi nella letteratura ottomana della prima età moderna', in U. Grassi and G. Marcocci, eds., *Le trasgressioni della carne: il desiderio omosessuale nel mondo islamico e cristiano, secc. XII–XX* (Rome, 2015), pp. 81–102, at pp. 91–3 (mentioning more than 60 examples).

51. See Kuru, 'Sixteenth Century Scholar', pp. 72–104, 183–214.

52. Andrews and Kalpaklı, *Age of Beloveds*, p. 72.

53. Ibid., p. 146.

54. Above, p. 75 (2 boys). On solitary masturbation, Selim Kuru comments that it was not regarded as a sin in the Ottoman Empire; 'fetwas (law collections) testify to this, and suggest that one must follow such acts with ablutions, as one would follow any approved sexual act' ('Sixteenth Century Scholar', p. 20).

55. El-Rouayheb, *Before Homosexuality*, p. 77.

56. Lithgow, *Totall Discourse*, p. 325; Thévenot, *L'Empire*, p. 165.

57. de Nicolay, *Dans l'empire*, p. 65.

58. S. Schweigger, *Ein newe Reyssbeschreibung auss Teutschland nach Constantinopel und Jerusalem*, ed. R. Neck (Graz, 1964), p. 97; R. Lubenau, *Beschreibung der Reisen*, ed. W. Sahm, 2 vols. (Königsberg, 1914–30), i, p. 208.

59. Laṭīfī ('Lâtifî'), *Éloge d'Istanbul*, ed. and trans. S. Yerasimos (Paris, 2001), p. 115.

CHAPTER 14

1. Above, pp. 92 (Venice, Rome), 97 (Valencia), 98 (Seville); Riera i Sans, *Sodomites catalans*, pp. 182–416 (Barcelona).

2. W. von Rosen, *Månens kulør: studier i dansk bøssehistorie, 1628–1912*, 2 vols. (Copenhagen, 1993), i, pp. 47–71; W. von Rosen, 'Almost Nothing: Male–Male Sex in Denmark, 1550–1800', in K. O'Donnell and M. O'Rourke, eds., *Queer Masculinities, 1550–1800* (Basingstoke, 2006), pp. 77–93, at pp. 79–81; Ø. Rian, 'Mellom straf og fortielse: homoseksualitet i Norge fra vikingtiden til 1930-årene', in M. C. Brantsæter et al., eds., *Norsk homoforskning* (Oslo, 2001), pp. 25–56, at pp. 33–5 (p. 35: 'legemlig omgængelse på sodomie maner').

3. F. Silverstolpe, 'Inledning', in F. Silverstolpe et al., *Sympatiens hemlighetsfulla makt: Stockholms homosexuella, 1860–1960* (Stockholm, 1999), pp. 15–26, at pp. 18–20 (p. 20: 'femb åtskillige gånger... såsom när een qwinna').

4. J. Meek, *Queer Voices in Post-War Scotland* (Basingstoke, 2015), p. 14.

5. C. Reinle, 'Zur Rechtspraxis gegenüber Homosexuellen. Eine Fallstudie aus dem Regensburg des 15. Jahrhunderts', *Zeitschrift für Geschichtswissenschaft*, 44 (1996), pp. 307–26.

6. R. van Dülmen, *Theater des Schreckens: Gerichtspraxis und Strafrituale in der frühen Neuzeit* (Munich, 1988), pp. 190–3; H. Puff, 'Homosexuality: Homosocialities in Renaissance Nuremberg', in B. Talvecchia, ed., *A Cultural History of Sexuality in the Renaissance* (London, 2011), pp. 51–72.

7. W. Behringer, 'Mörder, Diebe, Ehebrecher: Verbrechen und Strafen in Kurbayern vom 16. bis 18. Jahrhundert', in R. van Dülmen, ed., *Verbrechen, Strafen und soziale Kontrolle* (Frankfurt, 1990), pp. 85–132, 287–93, at p. 290(n. 85) (but note that Puff dates the first case to 1378, not 1363: *Sodomy in Reformation Germany*, p. 23); B.-U. Hergemöller, 'Leoncelli, Astor', in B.-U. Hergemöller and N. Clarus, eds., *Mann für Mann: biographisches Lexikon zur Geschichte von Freundesliebe und mannmännlicher Sexualität im deutschen Sprachraum*, 2 vols. (Berlin, 2010), i, pp. 741–2; R. Heydenreuter, *Kriminalität in München: Verbrechen und Strafen im alten München (1180–1800)* (Regensburg, 2014), pp. 98–9. One other Bavarian case was investigated in 1649–51, but the man concerned died before the investigation was complete: see the present work, pp. 266–7.

8. H. Schnabel-Schüle, *Überwachen und Strafen im Territorialstaat: Bedingungen und Auswirkungen des Systems strafrechtlicher Sanktionen im frühneuzeitlichen Württemberg* (Cologne, 1997), pp. 79(n.), 320–3, 326.

9. S. Hehenberger, *Unkeusch wider die Natur: Sodomieprozesse im frühneuzeitlichen Österreich* (Vienna, 2006), pp. 81, 157–8. All the other 'sodomy' cases presented in Hehenberger's book are of bestiality; see the present work, p. 229.

10. Puff, *Sodomy in Reformation Germany*, p. 90 (16th century); W. Schneider-Lastin and H. Puff, '"Vnd solt man alle die so das tuend verbrennen, es bliben nit funffzig mannen jn Basel": Homosexualität in der deutschen Schweiz im Spätmittelalter', in H. Puff, ed., *Lust, Angst und Provokation: Homosexualität in der Gesellschaft* (Göttingen, 1993), pp. 79–103, at p. 87 (1489).

11. D. Guggenbühl, *Mit Tieren und Teufeln: Sodomiten und Hexen unter Basler Jurisdiktion in Stadt und Land, 1399 bis 1799* (Basel, 2002), *passim*; Schneider-Lastin and H. Puff, '"Vnd solt man alle die so das tuend verbrennen"', p. 86, notes 8 cases between 1399 and 1449.

12. Puff, *Sodomy in Reformation Germany*, pp. 25, 90; T. Lau, '"Da erhob sich ein gross Geschrei über Sodom": Sodomitenverfolgung in Zürich in der zweiten Hälfte des 17. Jahrhunderts', *Invertito: Jahrbuch für die Geschichte der Homosexualitäten*, 11 (2009), pp. 8–21, at p. 10. After 1668 there was a sudden increase; this will be discussed later.

13. E. W. Monter, 'Sodomy and Heresy in Early Modern Switzerland', *JH* (1981), pp. 41–55, at pp. 44–5, 54–5.

14. D. J. Noordam, 'Homosexualiteit en sodomie in Leiden, 1533–1811', *Leids jaarboekje (Jaarboekje voor geschiedenis en oudheidkunde van Leiden en omstreken)*, 75 (1983), pp. 72–105, at pp. 76–8, 99.

15. van der Meer, *Sodoms zaad*, pp. 21, 459–60.

16. Vanhemelryck, *De criminaliteit*, pp. 56 (*ammanie*), 159–60 (statistics).

17. J. Roelens, 'Fornicating Foreigners: Sodomy, Migration, and Urban Society in the Southern Low Countries (1400–1700)', *Dutch Crossing: Journal of Low Countries Studies*, 41 (2017), pp. 229–46, at pp. 230, 240.

18. M. Naessens, 'Seksuele delicten in het laatmiddeleeuwse Gent: de grenzen van een kwantitatieve benadering van de bronnen', in A. Musin, X. Rousseaux and F. Vesentini, eds., *Violence, conciliation et répression: recherches sur l'histoire du crime,*

de l'Antiquité au XXIᵉ siècle (Louvain-la-Neuve, 2008), pp. 155–89, at p. 182 (executed); M. Boone, 'State Power and Illicit Sexuality: The Persecution of Sodomy in Late Medieval Bruges', *Journal of Medieval History*, 22 (1996), pp. 135–53, at p. 141 (fined).

19. J. Roelens, 'Middeleuwse brandstapels', in W. Dupont, E. Hofman and J. Roelens, *Verzwegen verlangen: een geschiedenis van homoseksualiteit in België* (Antwerp, 2017), pp. 23–55, at p. 37 (half the convictions); Boone, 'State Power', pp. 143 (women, *mollities*), 145 (1395–1515), 152 (1475); Naessens, 'Seksuele delicten', pp. 182–3 (73, women, *mollities* in Ghent), 185–6 (politics, Italy, 15%), 187 (acquittal rates); Roelens, 'Fornicating Foreigners', pp. 236–7 (6–8 men from Mediterranean region).

20. C. Gauvard, *'De grace especial': crime, état et société en France à la fin du Moyen Âge*, 2 vols. (Paris, 1991), ii, p. 597.

21. Y. G. Lepage, 'François Villon et l'homosexualité', *Le Moyen Âge*, 92 (1986), pp. 69–89, at pp. 73–4, citing Jacques du Clercq.

22. S. McDougall, 'Prosecution of Sex in Late Medieval Troyes', in A. Classen, ed., *Sexuality in the Middle Ages and Early Modern Times* (Berlin, 2008), pp. 691–714, at pp. 698–9.

23. Merrick and Ragan, *Homosexuality in Early Modern France*, pp. 32–3.

24. Coward, 'Attitudes to Homosexuality', p. 251 (n.13); the relevant documents are in Bibliothèque Sainte-Geneviève, Paris, MS 1775, Suppl. F33, with other papers relating to the priest, Antoine Ransson, which emphasize his piety, zeal and long career in the Church. The youth was described as 'debauched and taken away by the said Ransson' (fo. 13r: 'desbauché & enleué par Le dit Ransson'), but the same passage explains that this was to enable him to attend a meeting of the town council in Compiègne. The term 'desbauché' probably meant 'perverted from his monastic vocation'; otherwise the documentation yields no sexual, or even potentially sexual, reference at all.

25. G. Poirier, *L'Homosexualité dans l'imaginaire de la Renaissance* (Paris, 1996), pp. 46–8 (p. 48: 'une portion… infime des crimes liés à la famille ou à la sexualité des Français de cette époque').

26. T. Hamilton, 'Sodomy and Criminal Justice in the Parlement of Paris, ca. 1540–ca. 1700', *JHS*, 29 (2020), pp. 303–34, at pp. 307 (quotation), 314–15.

27. A. J. Finch, 'Sexual Morality and Canon Law: The Evidence of the Rochester Consistory Court', *Journal of Medieval History*, 20:3 (1994), pp. 261–75, at pp. 267–9.

28. Linkinen, *Same-Sex Sexuality*, citing A. Ryan, 'Vicars and Prostitutes: Sexual Immorality in and around the Close of York Minster, 1396–1489', MA thesis, Centre for Medieval Studies, University of York (1995).

29. L. R. Poos, 'Sex, Lies, and the Church Courts of Pre-Reformation England', *Journal of Interdisciplinary History*, 25 (1995), pp. 585–607.

30. R. M. Wunderli, *London Church Courts and Society on the Eve of the Reformation* (Cambridge, 1981), pp. 83–4. It is possible that some sodomy cases would have been heard by the bishop himself, rather than by this court; but that would not explain the almost complete absence of defamation cases relating to sodomy.

31. S. McSheffrey, *Marriage, Sex, and Civic Culture in Late Medieval London* (Philadelphia 2006), p. 148.

32. K. Jones, *Gender and Petty Crime in Late Medieval England: The Local Courts in Kent, 1460–1560* (Woodbridge, 2006), p. 129 (Kent); L. Patterson, 'Chaucer's Pardoner on the Couch: Psyche and Clio in Medieval Literary Studies', *Speculum*, 76 (2001), pp. 638–80, at p. 663 (reporting the findings of David Klausner on Heref., Worcs.).

33. See the relevant volumes of J. S. Cockburn (ed.), *Calendar of Assize Records* (London, 1975–).

34. P. Griffiths, 'The Structure of Prostitution in Elizabethan London', *Continuity and Change*, 8 (1993), pp. 39–63, at p. 43 (charter); A. L. Beier, *Masterless Men: The Vagrancy Problem in England, 1560–1640* (London, 1985), pp. 164–9 (vagrants, punishments); F. Dabhoiwala, 'Sex, Social Relations and the Law in Seventeenth- and Eighteenth-Century London', in M. J. Braddick and J. Walter, eds., *Negotiating Power in Early Modern Society: Order, Hierarchy, and Subordination in Britain and Ireland* (Cambridge, 2001), pp. 85–101, at p. 86 (1600–1). Ian Archer calculates that in sample years from the Elizabethan period the proportion of sexual offences averaged 46%; this fell steeply in the early 17th century, as street crimes rapidly grew. See his *The Pursuit of Stability: Social Relations in Elizabethan London* (Cambridge, 1991), p. 239, and the comments in P. Griffiths, *Lost Londons: Change, Crime, and Control in the Capital City, 1550–1650* (Cambridge, 2008), p. 202.

35. Bethlem Royal Hospital Archives and Museum, Beckenham, London, Bridewell Hospital records, Courtbook 1, fos. 128v (indictment), 130r (sentence, quotation). This is the only case I have found. Paul Griffiths refers to three others (*Youth and Authority: Formative Experiences in England, 1560–1640* (Oxford, 1996), p. 271), but I have not been able to locate these, either by using the references he gives or by searching more widely in Courtbooks 1–4—though my search has not been exhaustive.

36. A. Shepard, *Meanings of Manhood in Early Modern England* (Oxford, 2003), pp. 116–19.

37. L. Gowing, *Domestic Dangers: Women, Words, and Sex in Early Modern London* (Oxford, 1996), p. 65.

38. M. Ingram, *Carnal Knowledge: Regulating Sex in England, 1470–1600* (Cambridge, 2017), pp. 36–7.

39. P. Burke, *The Historical Anthropology of Early Modern Italy: Essays on Perception and Communication* (Cambridge, 1987), p. 105.

40. R. Trumbach, 'Renaissance Sodomy, 1500–1700', in M. Cook, ed., *A Gay History of Britain: Love and Sex between Men since the Middle Ages* (Oxford, 2007), pp. 45–75, at pp. 50–1 (calculation); R. Trumbach, 'The Transformation of Sodomy from the Renaissance to the Modern World and its General Sexual Consequences', *Signs: Journal of Women in Culture and Society*, 37 (2012), pp. 832–48, at p. 834 (quotation).

41. A. N. Shaw, 'The *Compendium compertorum* and the Making of the Suppression Act of 1536', Warwick University PhD thesis (2003), pp. 53–4 (women), 66 (confession), 92 (absent).

42. Ibid., pp. 93, 335, 341, 345–7 (masturbation), 349–50 (procedure), 446–51 (statistics used here, with nunneries excluded: 4 out of 365 (Norwich), 19 out of 1,432 (Northern)).

43. R. Trumbach, *Sex and the Gender Revolution: Heterosexuality and the Third Gender in Enlightenment London* (Chicago, 1998), pp. 3–4.

44. See Bleibtreu-Ehrenberg, *Homosexualität*, pp. 297–8 (Bamberg, Carolina); I. V. Hull, *Sexuality, State, and Civil Society in Germany, 1700–1815* (Ithaca, NY, 1996), pp. 61–4 (Carolina); Puff, *Sodomy in Reformation Germany*, pp. 29–30 (Bamberg, Carolina).

45. Boone, 'State Power', pp. 137–8.

46. Silverstolpe, 'Inledning', p. 16.

47. T. Pastorello, *Sodome à Paris, fin XVIIIᵉ–milieu XIXᵉ siècle: l'homosexualité masculine en construction* (Paris, 2011), p. 84 (Breton law).

48. Boone, 'State Power', p. 151 (Bruges); Roelens, 'Middeleuwse brandstapels', p. 39 (Antwerp); Guggenbühl, *Mit Tieren und Teufeln*, pp. 99–100 (Basel); Poirier, *L'Homosexualité*, p. 50 (de Coras).

49. Roelens, 'Middeleuwse brandstapels', pp. 46–7.

50. G. J. Durston, *Jacks, Knaves and Vagabonds: Crime, Law, and Order in Tudor England* (Hook, 2020), pp. 220–1.

51. Above, pp. 137, 140.

52. F. Helbing and M. Bauer, *Die Tortur: Geschichte der Folter im Kriminalverfahren aller Zeiten und Völker* (Berlin, 1926), pp. 164–77; J. H. Langbein, *Prosecuting Crime in the Renaissance: England, Germany, France* (Cambridge, MA, 1974), pp. 179–86 (Carolina), 241 (quotation).

53. W. Naphy, 'Sodomy in Early Modern Geneva: Various Definitions, Diverse Verdicts', in T. Betteridge, ed., *Sodomy in Early Modern Europe* (Manchester, 2002), pp. 94–111, at pp. 97–8.

54. P. O. Träskman, 'Om "menniskior som af sathan och sin onda begiärelse låter förföra sigh"', *Historisk Tidskrift för Finland*, 75 (1990), pp. 248–63, at p. 252.

55. Langbein, *Prosecuting Crime*, pp. 239–41 (less routine); Hamilton, 'Sodomy and Criminal Justice', p. 319 (40 of 131); on the use of torture in France, which declined from the 16th to the 17th century, see A. Soman, 'La Justice criminelle aux XVIᵉ–XVIIᵉ siècles: le Parlement de Paris et les sièges subalternes', in A. Soman, *Sorcellerie et justice criminelle: le Parlement de Paris (16ᵉ–18ᵉ siècles)* (Aldershot, 1992), item 7 (pp. 16–52), at pp. 38–49.

56. M. DiGangi, 'How Queer was the Renaissance?', in K. O'Donnell and M. O'Rourke, eds., *Love, Sex, Intimacy, and Friendship between Men, 1550–1800* (Basingstoke, 2003), pp. 128–47, at p. 132 (summarizing Smith, *Homosexual Desire*, pp. 50–3).

57. Borris, *Same-Sex Desire*, p. 87 (Buggery Act quotation); Griffiths, *Lost Londons*, p. 95 (Farrar).

58. Kenneth Borris writes that 'The norms for conducting criminal proceedings *in general* under English common law inadvertently made prosecution of the crime of sodomy very problematic by continental standards' (*Same-Sex Desire*, p. 81), but gives no further details to substantiate this claim.

59. van der Meer, *Sodoms zaad*, pp. 60–1 (suppression); Boon, *'Dien godlosen hoop van menschen'*, pp. 31 (many lost), 93 (kept separately).

60. J. Hashagen, 'Aus Kölner Prozessakten: Beiträge zur Geschichte der Sittenzustände in Köln im 15. und 16. Jahrhundert', *Archiv für Kulturgeschichte* 3 (1905), pp. 301–21, at pp. 309–10.

61. Puff, *Sodomy in Reformation Germany*, pp. 93 (code), 103 (quotation), 180 (judges).

62. J. Michelsen, 'Von Kaufleuten, Waisenknaben und Frauen in Männerkleidern: Sodomie im Hamburg des 18. Jahrhunderts', *Zeitschrift für Sexualforschung*, 9 (1996), pp. 205–37, at p. 216 (Hamburg); M. R. Boes, 'On Trial for Sodomy in Early Modern Germany', in T. Betteridge, ed., *Sodomy in Early Modern Europe* (Manchester, 2002), pp. 27–45, at pp. 40–1 (Frankfurt, 1598, 1645).

63. This is implicit in Bray's argument; cf. also Poirier, *L'Homosexualité*, p. 58; Hull, *Sexuality, State, and Civil Society*, p. 70 ('consensual homosexual acts or bestiality would usually have left no traces, such as pregnancy, to attract official attention').

64. Ingram, *Carnal Knowledge*, p. 37.

65. J. S. Cockburn, ed., *Calendar of Assize Records: Kent Indictments, Charles I* (London, 1995), p. 471.

66. Puff, *Sodomy in Reformation Germany*, *passim*.

67. T. Hamilton, 'A Sodomy Scandal on the Eve of the French Wars of Religion', *The Historical Journal*, 64 (2021), pp. 844–64, at p. 855 (France); Blastenbrei, *Kriminalität in Rom*, pp. 278, 280 (Rome).

68. J. Liliequist, 'Peasants against Nature: Crossing the Boundaries between Man and Animal in Seventeenth- and Eighteenth-Century Sweden', *JHS*, 1 (1991), pp. 393–423, at pp. 394–5.

69. P. G. Maxwell-Stuart, '"Wild, filthie, execrabil, detestabil, and unnatural sin": Bestiality in Early Modern Scotland', in T. Betteridge, ed., *Sodomy in Early Modern Europe* (Manchester, 2002), pp. 81–93, at p. 89.

70. J. S. Cockburn, ed., *Calendar of Assize Records*, individual volumes as follows: *Essex Indictments, Elizabeth I* (1978), *Essex Indictments, James I* (1982), *Hertfordshire Indictments, Elizabeth I* (1975), *Kent, Elizabeth I* (1979).

71. Hehenberger, *Unkeusch wider die Natur*, pp. 81–102 (male–female), 114–56 (bestiality), 157–8 (male–male); H. Haustein, 'Strafrecht und Sodomie vor zwei Jahrhunderten. Eine archivalische Studie auf Grund der Akten des Preussischen Geheimen Staatsarchivs in Berlin-Dahlem', *Zeitschrift für Sexualwissenschaft und Sexualpolitik*, 16 (1929–30), pp. 98–105.

72. Guggenbühl, *Mit Tieren und Teufeln*, pp. 51 (46 and 5), 98 (4).

73. Puff, *Sodomy in Reformation Germany*, p. 90.

74. Monter, 'Sodomy and Heresy', p. 47.

75. H. Hiegel, *Le Bailliage d'Allemagne de 1600 à 1632: l'administration, la justice, les finances et l'organisation militaire* (Saarguemines, 1961), pp. 183–4 ('sodomitischen Sünden'). The dates of these cases range from 1586 to 1627.

76. Gauvard, *'De grace especial'*, ii, p. 598.

77. See A. Soman, 'Pathologie historique: le témoignage des procès de bestialité aux XVIe et XVIIe siècles', in A. Soman, *Sorcellerie et justice criminelle: le Parlement de Paris (16e–18e siècles)* (Aldershot, 1992), item 8 (pp. 149–61), at p. 156.

78. Monter, 'Sodomy and Heresy', pp. 54–5.

79. Vanhemelryck, *De criminaliteit*, pp. 159, 162.

80. G. Dubois-Desaulle, *Étude sur la bestialité au point de vue historique, médical et juridique* (Paris, 1905), pp. 211–13.

81. A. Borges Coelho, 'Repressão ideológica e sexual na Inquisição de Évora entre 1533–1668. As primeiras gerações de vítimas cristãs-novas', in *Inquisição: comunicações apresentadas ao 1.º Congresso Luso-Brasileiro sobre Inquisição realizado em Lisboa, de 17 a 20 de Fevereiro de 1987*, 2 vols. (Lisbon, 1989–90), i, pp. 423–46, at pp. 428–32.

82. Perry, '"The "Nefarious Sin"'', p. 72.

83. Fernandez, 'Repression of Sexual Behavior', p. 480 (percentages); Liliequist, 'Peasants against Nature', p. 422 (Monter quotation).

84. Carrasco, *Inquisición y represión*, pp. 34 (85, 'con una agresividad increíble'), 49 (3).

85. Hamilton, 'Sodomy Scandal', p. 851 (France); Puff, *Sodomy in Reformation Germany*, pp. 24, 84, 86 (Germany); J. Roelens, 'Gossip, Defamation and Sodomy in the Early Modern Southern Netherlands', *Renaissance Studies*, 32:2 (2017), pp. 235–52, at p. 250 (southern Netherlands).

86. See J. C. Vitiello, *Public Justice and the Criminal Trial in Late Medieval Italy: Reggio Emilia in the Visconti Age* (Leiden, 2016), pp. 88–113 (p. 90: Bartolus); R. H. Helmholz, 'Crime, Compurgation and the Courts of the Medieval Church', *Law and History Review*, 1 (1983), pp. 1–26, at pp. 13–14 (compurgation); L. I. Stern, 'Public Fame in the Fifteenth Century', *The American Journal of Legal History*, 44:2 (2000), pp. 198–222.

87. Bray, *Homosexuality*, p. 76.

88. C. Reinle, 'Das mittelalterliche Sodomiedelikt im Spannungsfeld von rechtlicher Norm, theologischer Deutung und gesellschaftlicher Praxis', in L. M. Thoma and S. Limbeck, eds., *'Die Sünde, der sich der tiuvel schamet in der helle': Homosexualität in der Kultur des Mittelalters und der frühen Neuzeit* (Ostfildern, 2009) pp. 13–42, at p. 39.

89. Schnabel-Schüle, *Überwachen und Strafen*, pp. 320–3.

90. Silverstolpe, 'Inledning', p. 16 ('Tu skalt icke liggia när Drängiar såsom när enne qwinno'). Cf. the legal codes of the New England colonies: see the present work, p. 312.

91. Naphy, 'Sodomy in Early Modern Geneva', p. 108. One modern study seeks to differentiate Calvin from Luther on this issue, portraying the former as someone who, concerned with sodomy as a form of general sinfulness (threatening the community), downplayed its essentially 'unnatural' quality; yet at the same time it quotes him describing sodomites as worse than beasts, because they 'subverted the whole order of nature' (C. Elwood, 'A Singular Example of the Wrath of God: The Use of Sodom in Sixteenth-Century Exegesis', *The Harvard*

Theological Review, 98 (2005), pp. 67–93 (p. 78: quotation)). In practice there was no significant difference between Lutheran and Calvinist approaches.

92. See above, p. 161.

93. Bleibtreu-Ehrenburg, *Homosexualität*, p. 302.

94. G. Cardano ['H. Cardanus'], *Libelli quinque* (Nuremberg, 1547), fo. 64r ('minus in Italia').

CHAPTER 15

1. I. K. Ben-Amos, *Adolescence and Youth in Early Modern England* (New Haven, CT, 1994), pp. 62 (ages, London), 69 (households), 81 (small towns), 84 (London).

2. Beier, *Masterless Men*, p. 217.

3. Above, pp. 50, 68.

4. W. G. Walker, *A History of the Oundle Schools* (London, 1956), pp. 127–8; Cockburn, ed., *Calendar* (indexed under 'sodomy'); Bray, *Homosexuality*, pp. 38, 43, 72–3; G. R. Quaife, *Wanton Wenches and Wayward Wives: Peasants and Illicit Sex in Early Seventeenth Century England* (London, 1979), pp. 176–7; Wunderli, *London Church Courts*, p. 84; B. Smith, *Homosexual Desire in Shakespeare's England*, 2nd edn. (Chicago, 1994), 51–3, 84; Griffiths, *Youth and Authority*, p. 271; D. L. Boyd and R. M. Karras, 'The Interrogation of a Male Transvestite Prostitute in Fourteenth-Century London', *GLQ: A Journal of Lesbian and Gay Studies*, 1 (1995), pp. 459–65, at pp. 461–2; R. M. Karras, *From Boys to Men: Formations of Masculinity in Late Medieval Europe* (Philadelphia, 2002), pp. 81–2; P. Lake with M. Questier, *The Antichrist's Lewd Hat: Protestants, Papists and Players in Post-Reformation England* (New Haven, CT, 2002), p. 305 (with boys: the accused said he had acquired the habit in Italy); Shepard, *Meanings of Manhood*, pp. 116–18; McSheffrey, *Marriage, Sex, and Civic Culture*, p. 244(n. 67); R. Mills, 'Male–Male Love and Sex in the Middle Ages, 1000–1500', in M. Cook, ed., *A Gay History of Britain: Love and Sex between Men since the Middle Ages* (Oxford, 2007), pp. 1–43, at p. 35. I omit two 'galleymen' convicted of attempted or actual sodomy in Southampton in the 1490s, as they were Italian or Ragusan (C. Butler, ed., *The Book of Fines: The Annual Accounts of the Mayors of Southampton*, i: *1488–1540* (Southampton, n.d. [2008]), pp. 17, 38); I also omit one Frenchman (Bray, *Homosexuality*, pp. 73–4), whose precise geographical origins are unknown, and the French culprit whipped at Bridewell (probably a youth who had sex with another youth: above, p. 221). I include the case of the headmaster of Oundle School, who in 1625 was accused of 'wanton behaviour' towards boys and confessed to some improper 'touching'; the trial records do not survive, so we do not know whether he was actually charged with sodomy. And in the case of the two middle-aged men in Kent (above, p. 227) I treat this as only one adult having sex with an adult, though each was separately charged. Including the second of these men, or excluding the headmaster, would yield an absolute majority of adult–adult cases. On the other hand I exclude cases on board ships,

as these were untypical environments, strongly age-hierarchical with boys at the bottom of the hierarchy, liable to 'situational' sex in the prolonged absence of women, and capable of being much more closely policed. Known cases up to 1650 yield 7 men accused of sex with boys, and 1 accused of sex with another man; see C. Fury, ' "To Sett Downe All the Villanie": Accounts of the Sodomy Trial on the Fourth East India Company Voyage (1609)', *The Mariner's Mirror*, 102 (2016), pp. 74–80, at pp. 75, 77; see the present work, pp. 259–60, 311 (excluding the case where the perpetrator was an Indian Muslim).

5. Rocke, *Forbidden Friendships*, p. 243 (or 3% if the transitional age ends at 20).

6. Puff, *Sodomy in Reformation Germany*, *passim*. Note that whereas the English cases analysed above were confined to charges of sodomy, the range of sexual acts here is wider, being sometimes unspecified in the documentation, and sometimes described as mutual masturbation.

7. Guggenbühl, *Mit Tieren und Teufeln*, pp. 52–3, 99, 178. These include two cases from the 18th century.

8. Lau, ' "Da erhob sich ein gross Geschrei" ', pp. 14–15.

9. T. van der Meer, ' "Are Those People like Us": Early Modern Homosexuality in Holland', in K. O'Donnell and M. O'Rourke, eds., *Queer Masculinities, 1550–1800: Siting Same-Sex Desire in the Early Modern World* (Basingstoke, 2006), pp. 58–76, at p. 60.

10. Above, pp. 323–3.

11. Quaife, *Wanton Wenches*, pp. 175–7; on this case see also Bray, *Homosexuality*, pp. 132–3 (n. 60).

12. Hamilton, 'Sodomy and Criminal Justice', pp. 323–4.

13. J. Merrick, 'Chaussons in the Streets: Sodomy in Seventeenth-Century Paris', *JHS*, 15 (2006), pp. 167–203, at pp. 170–7.

14. Ibid., p. 177; 'L. Hernandez' [F. Fleuret and L. Perceau], ed., *Les Procès de sodomie aux XVIᵉ, XVIIᵉ et XVIIIᵉ siècles, publiés d'après les documents judiciaires conservés à la Bibliothèque Nationale* (Paris, 1920), pp. 71, 79. Note, however, that the source-document here, an 18th-century compilation, is unreliable: see Soman, 'Pathologie historique', pp. 149–52. For a description of the execution, which began with the men's tongues being torn out, see M. de Lescure, ed., *Journal et mémoires de Mathieu Marais, avocat au Parlement de Paris, sur la régence et le règne de Louis XV (1715–1737)*, 4 vols. (Paris, 1863–8), iii, p. 65.

15. Merrick and Ragan, *Homosexuality in Early Modern France*, pp. 33–7.

16. G. B. Primi Visconti, *Mémoires sur la cour de Louis XIV*, trans. J. Lemoine (Paris, 1908), p. 136 (' "Monsieur, en Espagne les moines, en France les grands, en Italie tout le monde" ', 'je répondis en plaisantant que cette pensée était loin de moi, que j'avais vingt-cinq ans et de la barbe. Il me répliqua que les Français de bon goût ne regardent ni aux années, ni aux poils; bref, je n'eus pas peu à faire pour m'échapper').

17. J. Merrick, 'Sodomitical Inclinations in Early Eighteenth-Century Paris', *Eighteenth-Century Studies*, 30 (1997), pp. 289–95, at p. 291. The document cited by Merrick gives his age as 30; another report described him as 25 or 26 in

1702, when he was regularly prostituting himself to young men in his lodgings: see the present work, p. 248.

18. N. Hammond, *Gossip, Sexuality and Scandal in France (1610–1715)* (Oxford, 2011), p. 98 ('le meilleur bougre du monde', 'car le grand plaisir de ce Duc étoit de se faire enculer, et se servoit pour cela de Valets et de paysans, faute de plus gentils ouvriers', 'se tenoient avec soin sur son chemin lorsqu'il y alloit à la chasse, parce qu'il les écartoit souvent dans les bois pour se faire f[outre] et leur donnoit à chacun un Pistole pour le prix de leur travail').

19. Schneider-Lastin and Puff, '"Vnd solt man alle die so das tuend verbrennen"', p. 84.

20. Reinle, 'Zur Rechtspraxis', p. 312.

21. B.-U. Hergemöller, 'Das Verhör des "Sodomiticus" Franz von Alsten (1536/37)— ein Kriminalfall aus dem nachtäuferischen Münster', *Westfälische Zeitschrift*, 140 (1990), pp. 31–47, at pp. 36, 40.

22. Naphy, 'Sodomy in Early Modern Geneva', pp. 101–2.

23. Roelens, 'Middeleuwse brandstapels', p. 27.

24. G. Tallement des Réaux, *Historiettes*, ed. A. Adam, 2 vols. (Paris, 1960), i, pp. 417–18 ('"Je pourrois me vanter d'avoir f… [*sic*] le plus grand Roy de la chrestienté." Il disoit que M. le Prince et luy avoient faict *volta per volta* à Venise'; attempt at mutual masturbation with a boy).

25. Ibid., i, pp. 417–18 ('Je ne voudrois pas asseurer qu'il fust bougaron tout à fait, mais il estoit grand masturbateur').

26. A. Niederhäuser, '"…nemlich das ÿedtwederer dem anndern sin mennlich glid jn die hand genomen…": gleichgeschlechtliche Sexualität zwischen Männern im Spätmittelalter', in U. Heider, S. Micheler and E. Tuider, eds., *Jenseits der Geschlechtergrenzen: Körper, Identitäten und Perspektiven von* Queer Studies (Hamburg, 2001), pp. 30–49, at pp. 30–1 ('ÿedtwederer dem anndern sin mennlich glid jn die hand genomen vnnd also ainanndern daran gemolchen habend, bis jnen die natur entgangen sig').

27. Above, p. 217 (Lucerne); Puff, *Sodomy in Reformation Germany*, pp. 23 (Bavaria), 97–8 (Steiner).

28. van der Meer, *Sodoms zaad*, p. 148 (mistakenly stating that this offence was not punished anywhere else in Europe).

29. Niederhäuser, '"…nemlich das ÿedtwederer"', p. 38 ('sinen swancz haruss ze ziehende und jn den lassen ze sehende', 'da er nocht da jn der brüche was'); for the date see Schneider-Lastin and Puff, '"Vnd solt man alle die so das tuend verbrennen"', p. 88.

30. Roelens, 'Gossip, Defamation', p. 251 (Bruges); Wunderli, *London Church Courts*, p. 84.

31. Puff, *Sodomy in Reformation Germany*, pp. 80 (1547), 82 (1537), 93 (1592). As is noted later (p. 393), this 'grabbing' practice was probably modelled on similar interactions between men and female prostitutes—in which, again, each party was feeling (or at least, in the prostitute's case, simulating) sexual desire for the other.

32. Rocke, *Forbidden Friendships*, pp. 154, 156.

33. Puff, *Sodomy in Reformation Germany*, pp. 23 (1381, 'mit ainander'), 40 (1409), 41 (1489), 78–9 (1530s); L. Roper, *The Holy Household: Women and Morals in Reformation Augsburg* (Oxford, 1989), pp. 255–6 (1530s, 9 men).

34. Naphy, 'Sodomy in Early Modern Geneva', p. 105.

35. D. Booy, ed., *The Notebooks of Nehemiah Wallington, 1618–1654* (Aldershot, 2007), p. 92.

36. 'B. C.', *Puritanisme the Mother, Sinne the Daughter* (n.p., 1633), sig. *2r.

37. Ibid., sigs. *4v–*5v. The traditional identification of 'B. C.' with the convert Benjamin Carier is untenable, as Carier died in 1614: see M. Questier, 'Crypto-Catholicism, Anti-Calvinism and Conversion at the Jacobean Court: The Enigma of Benjamin Carier', *Journal of Ecclesiastical History*, 47 (1996), pp. 45–64, at p. 57. The pamphlet is discussed in A. Stewart, 'A Society of Sodomites: Religion and Homosexuality in Renaissance England', in L. Gowing, M. Hunter and M. Rubin, eds., *Love, Friendship and Faith in Europe, 1300–1800* (Basingstoke, 2005), pp. 88–109, and G. Stanivuković, 'Between Men in Early Modern England', in K. O'Donnell and M. O'Rourke, eds., *Queer Masculinities, 1550–1800: Siting Same-Sex Desire in the Early Modern World* (Basingstoke, 2006), pp. 232–51; Stanivuković remains agnostic about whether the episode was real or fictitious. On Wallington and his religiously inflected but omnivorous interest in contemporary events, see P. Seaver, *Wallington's World: A Puritan Artisan in Seventeenth-Century London* (Stanford, CA, 1985) (p. 42 on this report).

38. London Metropolitan Archives, MJ/SB/R/005 (Middlesex Sessions of the Peace registers, 1629–33); The National Archives, Kew, ASSI 35/73/6 (12 July 1631); ASSI 35/75/6 (27 Feb. 1633); ASSI 35/76/12 (10 Mar. 1634). The same is true of the indictments for the Surrey Assize at Croydon of 24 July 1633: ASSI 35/75/7.

39. R. Norton, *Mother Clap's Molly House: The Gay Subculture in England, 1700–1830*, 2nd edn. (Stroud, 2006), p. 178.

40. See above, pp. 51–3.

41. Boyd and Karras, 'Interrogation', pp. 461–2 ('stallum', 'nominans ipsum Alianoram'); D. Crowther, 'Medieval Price and Wages', https://thehistory-ofengland.co.uk/resource/medieval-prices-and-wages/, 1st table. Rykener's case is also discussed in C. Dinshaw, *Getting Medieval: Sexualities and Communities, Pre- and Postmodern* (Durham, NC, 1999), pp. 100–12.

42. G. L. Stringer et al., eds., *The Variorum Edition of the Poetry of John Donne*, iii, *The Satyres*, (Bloomington, 2016), p. 6 (Satyre 1, l. 40); [T. Middleton,] *Micro-cynicon: Sixe Snarling Satyres* (London, 1599), sigs. C4r–C6r.

43. Bray, *Homosexuality*, p. 74.

44. Hergemöller, 'Das Verhör des "Sodomiticus"', p. 46, items 8, 14.

45. Naphy, 'Sodomy', p. 106.

46. A. Adam, *Théophile de Viau et la libre pensée française en 1620* (Paris, 1935), p. 87. On de Viau see the present work, pp. 295–6.

47. Above, p. 240 (1704); F. Ravaisson, *Archives de la Bastille: documents inédits*, xi: *Règne de Louis XIV (1702 à 1710)* (Paris, 1880), pp. 2–3 ('beau de visage', 'se prostitue à tous les jeunes gens qui le viennent trouver dans son lit', 'commerce abominable').

48. P. Cottin, ed., *Rapports inédits du lieutenant de police René d'Argenson (1697–1715)* (Paris, 1891), p. 127 ('après avoir passé sa jeunesse dans une sodomie honteuse, prostituoit des jeunes gens').

49. 'Hernandez', *Les Procès de sodomie*, pp. 72 ('un jeune garçon fort beau'), 73 ('l'on entendoit ledit garçon crier et pleurer'), 75–6 (14-year-old), 78 (sales). Again, it should be noted that the manuscript printed here may not be reliable on points of detail. On Charles du Bellay, prince d'Yvetot, whose interest in youths and young men was notorious, see M. Lever, *Les Bûchers de Sodome: histoire des 'infâmes'* (Paris, 1985), pp. 140–1.

50. D. Van der Cruysse, *Madame Palatine, princesse européenne* (Paris, 1988), p. 169 ('il était athée et sodomite; il en tenait école, et vendait des garçons comme des chevaux. Il allait au parterre de l'Opéra pour y conclure ses marchés').

51. Cottin, ed., *Rapports inédits*, pp. 72 ('séduits', 'après les avoir employés aux usages les plus criminels, pour son propre compte, il…les eût vendus au sieur de la Guillaumie, son ami, et à quelques autres scélérats qui font depuis longtems ce commerce infâme'), 73 (Irish).

52. Ravaisson, *Archives de la Bastille*, xi, pp. 3 ('un beau garçon', 'un lieu ou l'on voit tous les jours entrer des jeunes garçons avec des gens de qualité et même des moines'), 5 (24, 'débauché'), 6 ('Comme ils n'ont aucun bien, et qu'ils ne subsistent que de cette intrigue, ils livrent les jeunes gens qu'ils ont débauchés à des personnes qui les payent bien, et ils en partagent le prix', 'celui-là envoie de beaux laquais à des seigneurs de province, lorsqu'on lui en demande, et fait ici les conditions de leurs engagements').

53. T. Durfey, *The Royalist* (London, 1682), p. 5.

54. J. Marston, *The Poems*, ed. A. Davenport (Liverpool, 1961), p. 112. 'Cynedian' is derived from the Graeco-Latin *cinaedus*, meaning a catamite.

55. C. Walker ['T. Verax'], *Anarchia anglicana, Or, The History of Independency, being a Continuation of Relations and Observations Historical and Politique upon this Present Parliament* (n.p., 1649), pp. 251–2.

56. See Tacitus, *Annals*, 6.1; Suetonius, *Tiberius*, 43.1, *Caligula*, 16.1, *Vitellius*, 3.2; Talvacchia, *Taking Positions*, p. 58 (medals).

57. See the detailed account in J. Evelyn, *The Diary*, ed. E. S. de Beer, 6 vols. (Oxford, 1955), iii, pp. 96–7(n. 7), and the plan of 1675 (after the 'Mulberry Garden' had moved eastwards; its location in 1649 was in the 'Goring Great Garden' on the plan): <https://www.rct.uk/collection/918910/d-goring-house-estate-and-mulberry-garden-1675>.

58. J. Wilmot, Earl of Rochester, *Works*, ed. H. Love (Oxford, 1999), pp. 76–80, 'A Ramble in St. James's Park' (p. 77: quotation).

59. M. Bly, *Queer Virgins and Virgin Queans on the Early Modern Stage* (Oxford, 2000), pp. 18–19, 154(n. 91); cf. M. Drayton, *The Battaile of Agincourt…[and] The Moone-Calfe* (London, 1627), p. 228.

CHAPTER 16

1. Osman ağa of Timişoara ['Osmân Agha de Temechvar'], *Prisonnier des infidèles: un soldat ottoman dans l'Empire des Habsbourg*, trans. F. Hitzel (Paris, 1998), pp. 101–2 ('Si un dévergonde avait été à ma place, il n'aurait pas pu se retenir tant le désir eût été fort car le gars était attirant', 'm'interrogea sur les moeurs avilissantes des Turcs dont il avait entendu parler et il voulait que je lui apprenne... comment on procédait!', 'même si j'étais par moments très excité'.)

2. J. Liliequist, 'State Policy, Popular Discourse, and the Silence on Homosexual Acts in Early Modern Sweden', *JH*, 35:3–4 (1998), 15–52, at p. 20.

3. J. S. Cockburn, ed., *Calendar of Assize Records: Sussex Indictments, Elizabeth I* (London, 1975), p. 156 (1580); Bray, *Homosexuality*, pp. 43, 66, 69, 126–7 (1643).

4. S. Pepys, *Diary*, ed. R. Latham and W. Matthews, 11 vols. (London, 1970–83), viii, p. 596 (30 Dec. 1667); note, once again, the reference to the 'grabbing' of another man's genitals.

5. Lever, *Les Bûchers de Sodome*, pp. 177–9; cf. also M. Daniel, *Hommes du grand siècle: études sur l'homosexualité sous les règnes de Louis XIII et Louis XIV* (Paris, 1957), pp. 46–7.

6. Puff, *Sodomy in Reformation Germany*, pp. 79 (1530s), 130 (1506), 243 (n. 44) (1507).

7. T. Sterneck, 'Hříšní sodomité: Jaké tresty čekaly homosexuály v raném novověku', *100+1 zahraniční zajímavost* (16 Dec. 2018) (<https://www.stoplusjednicka.cz/hrisni-sodomite-jake-tresty-cekaly-homosexualy-v-ranem-novoveku>).

8. van der Meer, *Sodoms zaad*, pp. 22–3 (Wielant accusations), 217–18 (Arnhem, Wielant), 302–3 ('tot alle publyke beroepingen (daer ick te bevoor met eeren, naer aspireeren mochte) als Professoratus, Pastoratus, Rectoratus etc. nu voortaen voor mijn gansche leeven sal onwaerdig geestimeert werden').

9. Hamilton, 'Sodomy and Criminal Justice', pp. 324–5.

10. Ibid., pp. 327–8; cf. also Poirier, *L'Homosexualité*, p. 48.

11. Bray, *Homosexuality*, p. 52; see also A. Stewart, *Close Readers: Humanism and Sodomy in Early Modern England* (Princeton, NJ, 1997), pp. 92 (on the unclear nature of the 1594 case), 116–19 (on Udall).

12. Bray, *Homosexuality*, pp. 51–2; 'R. C.', *The Times' Whistle: Or, A New Daunce of Seven Satires, and Other Poems, Compiled by R. C., Gent.*, ed. J. M. Cowper (London, 1871), p. 79 ('In Academie...'). Cowper proposes that 'R. C.' was Richard Corbet (pp. xiv–xviii).

13. Bray, *Homosexuality*, pp. 34–5.

14. J. S. Cockburn, ed., *Calendar of Assize Records: Surrey Indictments, James I* (London, 1982), p. 102 (Willington, found not guilty). Willington was described as a gentleman, but the venue suggests that he was working as a teacher, and this is confirmed by another document of the same year, calling him 'schoolmaster and servant of an apothecary': M. Pelling with F. White, *Medical Conflicts in Early Modern London: Patronage, Physicians, and Irregular Practitioners, 1550–1640* (Oxford, 2003), p. 147. (Four years earlier, implicated in a Star Chamber case involving forgery and poisoning, he was described as a 'professor of phisicke': The National Archives, Kew, STAC 8/291/29, Walker v Dawson, 1609.)

15. Walker, *History of Oundle Schools*, p. 127 (Death); Hammond, *Figuring Sex*, p. 151 (Lincoln). I omit here one case described as involving a schoolmaster by Alan Stewart (*Close Readers*, p. 100(n. 46)); the record (of a presentment at an ecclesiastical court in 1471) merely said 'cum magistro Thoma Tunley' (see Wunderli, *London Church Courts*, p. 84), and 'magister' (master) could have a range of meanings.

16. H. E. Salter, ed., *Registrum annalium collegii Mertonensis, 1483–1521*, Oxford Historical Society, lxxvi (Oxford 1923), pp. 162–4 (p. 162: 'varios & diuersos juvenes ad peccatum contra naturam incitasti & prouocasti, et eis vel saltem eorum quibusdam in eodem peccato variis temporibus miserabiliter abusus es in maximam tue anime periculum & in collegii nostri immensum scandalum & infamiam non mediocrem'). Edmund had graduated BA; undergraduates typically entered the University at 17, so he may have been only a few years older than his (alleged) sexual partners. I assume that the 'sin against nature' here was sodomy, though it is possible that it was mutual masturbation.

17. Shepard, *Meanings of Manhood*, pp. 116–18. Shepard also notes (p. 122) the temporary suspension of two fellow-commoners of St John's for 'seducing young schollers'. But a search for examples of this verb during this period shows that the religious meaning heavily predominated; more generally, 'seducing' could mean leading astray or enticing to some wrong, e.g. disobedience, but it is hard to find any example of the modern sexual meaning.

18. J. McCann and H. Connolly, eds., *Memorials of Father Augustine Baker, and Other Documents Relating to the English Benedictines*, Publications of the Catholic Record Society, xxxiii (1933), pp. 20 ('much lesse…'), 34 (master, 'the greatest…'), 43 (Oxford); Stewart, *Close Readers*, pp. 90 (motive), 104(n.) (quotation).

19. Bray, *Homosexuality*, p. 52.

20. H. Nicolas, ed., *Proceedings and Ordinances of the Privy Council of England*, 7 vols. (London, 1834–7), vii, p. 153 (14 Mar. 1541).

21. Bray, *Homosexuality*, p. 52 ('indicative of…'). On Udall see W. L. Edgerton, *Nicholas Udall* (New York, 1965), pp. 37–45; Stewart, *Close Readers*, pp. 116–19. Edgerton's suggestion (pp. 39–40) that 'buggery' in the Privy Council minutes was a mistranscription of 'burglary' is not absurd, given the initial robbery charge and the fact that the Privy Council register was written up, apparently quite hastily, on the basis of rough notes. (The passage printed by Nicolas as 'he did com[m]itt buggery' is 'he [had *deleted, replaced above the line with* did] com[m]itt [a certain felony th *deleted*] buggery' in the manuscript register: The National Archives, London, PC 2/1, p. 153.) But the balance of probabilities seems to weigh against it.

22. Fury, ' "To Sett Downe All the Villanie" ', pp. 74–7.

23. The National Archives, Kew, HCA 1/5, no. 224 (1608: William Audley); HCA 1/7, nos. 120–2 (1630s: Robert Hewitt), 164, 171 (1638: Robert Stone), 170 (1638: Richard Seawell); HCA 1/9, nos. 37–8, 40–1 (1661: Richard Kingston); *Calendar of State Papers, Domestic, of the Reign of Charles I, 1639*, ed. W. Douglas Hamilton (London, 1873), p. 482 (reprieved).

24. B. R. Burg, *Sodomy and the Pirate Tradition: English Sea Rovers in the Seventeenth-Century Caribbean* (New York, 1984), pp. 148–9.

25. *The Laws, Ordinances, and Institutions of the Admiralty of Great Britain, Civil and Military*, 2 vols. (London, 1746), i, p. 470 (following similar standard provisions of the death penalty for theft, sleeping on the watch, etc.). Burg misdates this to 1627, bizarrely writing: 'the propensity of King James I for male lovers may have provided the example that convinced the Navy homosexual behavior was a problem. Significantly, they did not move to restrict or eliminate it until 1627, after James was cold in his grave' (*Sodomy*, p. 144). As the cases just mentioned show, the naval authorities had no difficulty in prosecuting sodomy long before the death penalty was specified in regulations.

26. The National Archives, Kew, HCA 1/7, no. 120 ('sceleratissime et felonice, ac contra naturae ordinem, crimen illud detestabile, et abhominabile Sodomiae anglice of Buggery, inter homines non nominandu[m],...felonice comisit et perpetravit'); HCA 1/9, no. 41 ('peccatum illud detestabile et abhominabile Sodomiae (Anglice of Buggery) inter Christianos non nominand[um]...felonice nequiter et diabolice et contra naturae ordinem...com[m]isit et perpetravit, In magnam Dei omnipotentis displicentiam ac totius generis humani dedecus contra pacem dicti domini Regis').

27. Hammond, *Figuring Sex*, pp. 150–1.

28. *Calendar of State Papers Colonial, America and West Indies*, x, *1677–80*, ed. W. N. Sainsbury and J. W. Fortescue (London, 1896), pp. 329–30, item 894.

29. Anon., *An Account of the Proceedings against Capt. Edward Rigby ... for Intending to Commit the Abominable Sin of Sodomy, on the Body of one William Minton* (London, 1698), pp. [1–2]. 'Alexander' was Alexander Danilovich Menshikov, a good-looking man of allegedly plebeian origins. He was taken up by Peter the Great (who was one year older) and accompanied Peter on his lengthy visit to The Netherlands and England in 1697–8. The Jesus–John suggestion is made by Cocks, *Visions of Sodom*, p. 83, but the source he gives for this (Anon., *The Sodomites Shame and Doom, Laid before Them with Great Grief and Compassion by a Minister of the Church of England* (London, 1702), p. 1) refers only to Rigby's 'unparallell'd Blasphemies'.

30. Norton, *Mother Clap*, pp. 61–8. On this episode see also A. G. Craig, 'The Movement for the Reformation of Manners, 1688–1715' (Edinburgh University PhD dissertation, 1980, revd and re-formatted, 2015: https://era.ed.ac.uk/bitstream/handle/1842/6840/Craig-PhD-1980-reformatted-2015.pdf), pp. 95–8. Norton writes that Rigby had been tried for sodomy, and acquitted, at a court martial 'early in 1698'; on that basis he suggests that vigilantes from the Society for the Reformation of Manners (on which see the present work, pp. 340–2) had targeted him, using Minton as bait. However, Rigby's court martial was announced on 24 Nov. 1698, and his acquittal took place by 3 Dec. (British Library, London, MS Add. 70035, fo. 321r–v: Navy Board correspondence of those dates). That was between his arrest on 7 Nov. and his criminal trial on 7 Dec.

31. P. Boomgaard, 'Male–Male Sex, Bestiality and Incest in the Early-Modern Indonesian Archipelago: Perceptions and Penalties', in R. A. G. Reyes and W. G. Clarence-Smith, eds., *Sexual Diversity in Asia, c.600–1950* (London, 2012), pp. 141–60, at pp. 150–2.

32. J. S. Wurffbain, *Reise nach den Molukken und Vorder-Indien, 1632–1646*, ed. R. P. Meyjes, 2 vols. (The Hague, 1931), ii, pp. 144–5; Boomgaard, 'Male–Male Sex', p. 152.

33. I leave aside a case of 1681, where both partners were executed at sea; one was a 15-year-old boy, and the other was a man who was not Dutch but Italian. See K. Van der Stighelen and J. Roelens, 'Made in Heaven, Burned in Hell: The Trial of the Sodomite Sculptor Hiëronymus Duquesnoy (1602–1654)', in H. Magnus and K. Van der Stighelen, eds., *Facts & Feelings: Retracing Emotions of Artists, 1600–1800* (Turnhout, 2015), pp. 101–38, at p. 120.

34. L. Dingli, *Colbert, marquis de Seignelay, le fils flamboyant* (Paris, 1997), p. 135.

35. Puff, *Sodomy in Reformation Germany*, p. 84.

36. Above, p. 55.

37. J. M. Hýzrle z Chodů, *Příběhy Jindřicha Hýzrla z Chodů*, ed. V. Petráčková and J. Vogeltanz (Prague, 1979), pp. 76–80 (p. 76: 'Načež pachole tuto odpověd dalo, že ped někderejm dnem málo jemu jest takové násilí učinil').

38. van der Meer, *Sodoms zaad*, pp. 23, 219–20.

39. Above, p. 217; Rian, 'Mellom straf og fortielse', pp. 34–5; von Rosen, *Månens kulør*, i, pp. 47 (Scots), 67–71 (captain). The majority of the Danish–Norwegian cases involved soldiers, and were investigated by the military authorities. That does not mean that the ordinary judiciary was reluctant to punish sodomy; it did prosecute and punish bestiality cases in this period (see von Rosen, i, pp. 48–9).

40. Liliequist, 'State Policy', pp. 19–20, 25–7.

41. Ibid., pp. 28–9. What makes it even stranger is that some of these sexual acts took place in the corporal's marital bed, with his wife present on his other side. It was an angry private conversation between her and the dragoon that finally persuaded the latter that he might have been mistaken.

42. D. Godard, *Le Goût de Monsieur: l'homosexualité masculine au XVIIᵉ siècle* (Béziers, 2002) p. 171; Bély, 'Homosexuelle Netzwerke', pp. 112–13; cf. also Daniel, *Hommes du grand siècle*, pp. 26–8, 42.

43. Schneider-Lastin and Puff, ' "Vnd solt man alle die so das tuend verbrennen" ', p. 85; Puff, *Sodomy in Reformation Germany*, pp. 45–7.

44. *Letters and Papers Foreign and Domestic of the Reign of Henry VIII*, xv, *1540*, ed. J. Gairdner and R. H. Brodie (London, 1896), pp. 216 (item 498), 458 (item 926); see also C. B. Herrup, *A House in Gross Disorder: Sex, Law, and the 2nd Earl of Castlehaven* (New York, 1999), p. 36. The ages of the servants were not given.

45. A. H. Nelson, *Monstrous Adversary: The Life of Edward de Vere, 17th Earl of Oxford* (Liverpool, 2003), pp. 155–7 (Italian boy), 209–10 (blasphemies), 213–17 (sodomy, bestiality). Nelson quotes a statement that Ralph Hopton had once had to defend himself against a sexual advance by Oxford, and takes this as another

example of adult–boy desire; but Hopton, who accompanied Oxford on his Italian journey, was of roughly the same age as him (see N. Green, 'Oxmyths Involving Oxford Personally', pp. 32–3, at <www.oxford-shakespeare.com/Oxmyths/OxmythsOxford.pdf>.

46. Herrup, *House in Gross Disorder*, pp. 44, 46, 61, 95; British Library, London, MS Hargrave 226, fos. 311r–313v, 'The Manner of the Trial of Marven Lord Audley Earle of Castlehauen', at fos. 311v–312r (quotation).

47. Herrup, *House in Gross Disorder*, *passim*, esp. p. 89; British Library, London, MS Hargrave 226, fo. 312v (quotation). The usual definition was established in the classic text by Sir Edward Coke; see his *The Third Part of the Institutes of the Laws of England*, 3rd edn. (London, 1660), p. 59: '*Emissio seminis* [ejaculation] maketh it not Buggery…there must be penetration'. Cf. C. Bingham, 'Seventeenth-Century Attitudes toward Deviant Sex', *Journal of Interdisciplinary History*, 3 (1971), 447–68, at p. 459.

48. H. Puff, 'Sodomie und Herrschaft—eine Problemskizze: das Verfahren Pappenheim contra Pappenheim (1649–1651)', in I. Bauer, C. Hämmerle and G. Hauch, eds., *Liebe und Widerstand: Ambivalenzen historischer Geschlechterbeziehungen* (Vienna, 2005), pp. 175–93 (pp. 182–3: 'Wie man es in Hispania vnnd Jtalia mache', 'Kurzwail und Narrethey' [literally: amusement and foolishness]).

49. Daniel, *Hommes du grand siècle*, p. 42.

50. Primi Visconti, *Mémoires*, p. 91 ('Voyons qui de nous blasphémera le mieux').

51. Van der Cruysse, *Madame Palatine*, p. 176 ('La débauche des jeunes seigneurs à Versailles a contribué à en éloigner encore quelques-uns…de ladite troupe, accusés de dessins infâmes de sodomie').

52. G.-J., comte de Cosnac, and A. Bertrand, eds., *Mémoires du marquis de Sourches sur le règne de Louis XIV*, 13 vols. (Paris, 1882–93), i, pp. 110–12 ('l'exil d'un grand nombre de personnes considérables accusées de débauches ultramontaines', 'fort mêlé dans ces débauches').

53. G. de Courtilz de Sandras, *Les Intrigues amoureuses de la cour de France* ('Cologne', n.d. [1684]), pp. 6 ('caballe'), 7 ('Confrairie', 'Ordre'), 8–13.

54. Ibid., pp. 13–16 (p. 14: 'aux rigueurs du Noviciat').

55. See J. Lombard, *Courtilz de Sandras et la crise du roman à la fin du grand siècle* (Paris, 1980), pp. 83, 86, 320–1; for the political dimension see also B. M. Woodbridge, *Gatien de Courtilz, sieur du Verger: étude sur un précurseur du roman réaliste en France* (Baltimore, 1925), pp. 18–26 (commenting on p. 26, about this and a similar text recounting sexual scandals, that 'These books were made to amuse the general public, and the author is not much concerned with telling the truth' ('Ces livres sont faits pour amuser le vulgaire, et l'auteur se soucie peu de dire la vérité')). The whole story is accepted by, for example, Lever, *Les Bûchers de Sodome*, pp. 158–62; Van der Cruysse, *Madame Palatine*, pp. 175–6; Godard, *Le Goût de Monsieur*, pp. 167–8; and C. Denton, *Decadence, Radicalism, and the Early Modern French Nobility: The Enlightened and Depraved* (Lanham, MD, 2017), pp. 70–1 (attributing it to the 'informed and contemporary observer at the court, the Comte de Bussy-Rabutin').

56. Van der Cruysse, *Madame Palatine*, p. 165 ('Séduisant, brutal et dénué de scrupules').

57. Ibid., p. 163; Lever, *Les Bûchers de Sodome*, p. 146.

58. V. L. Bullough, *Sexual Variance in Society and History* (New York, 1976), p. 478 ('who, angered...'); Coward, 'Attitudes to Homosexuality', p. 234 ('ever ready...').

59. O. Amiel, ed., *Lettres de Madame, duchesse d'Orléans, née princesse Palatine* (Paris, 1981), pp. 126 ('il n'y a pas de plus grand sodomite que lui dans toute la France'), 167 ('Quel prince, en effet, trouve-t-on qui aime uniquement son épouse et qui n'ait pas autre chose à côté, soit maîtresses, soit mignons'), 257 ('en vogue'); Van der Cruysse, *Madame Palatine*, p. 171 ('Ils le considèrent comme un simple divertissement. Ils s'en cachent tant qu'ils peuvent pour ne pas scandaliser le vulgaire [*den gemein Mann*], mais ils en parlent ouvertement entre gens de qualité [*unter Leütte von Qualitet*]').

60. See R. M. Karras, 'The Lechery that Dare not Speak its Name: Sodomy and the Vices in Medieval England', in R. Newhauser, ed., *In the Garden of Evil: The Vices and Culture in the Middle Ages* (Toronto, 2005), pp. 193–205, at pp. 193–4; Linkinen, *Same-Sex Sexuality*, pp. 112–21; K. Heyam, *The Reputation of Edward II, 1305–1697: A Literary Transformation of History* (Amsterdam, 2020), pp. 26–39, 241–76; D. B. R. Kouamenan, 'The Reproach of Sodomy in the Deposition of Edward II of England and its Repercussions in the Historiography of the Middle Ages to the Twentieth Century', in N. Domeier and C. Mühling, eds., *Homosexualität am Hof: Praktiken und Diskurse vom Mittelalter bis heute* (Frankfurt, 2020), pp. 151–77.

61. Rian, 'Mellom straf og fortielse', pp. 32–3.

62. Gilmour-Bryson, 'Sodomy and the Knights Templar', esp. p. 163; J. Coste, ed., *Boniface VIII en procès: articles d'accusation et dépositions des témoins (1303–1311)* (Rome, 1995), p. 915 (multiple index entries for sodomy with both boys and men). Other charges against Boniface included sacrilege, blasphemy, idolatry, necromancy and murder.

63. See P. Chevallier, *Henri III, roi shakespearien* (Paris, 1985), pp. 432–41; Poirier, *L'Homosexualité*, pp. 109–61 (pp. 132–3: changing connotations of *mignon*); J. Cady, 'The "Masculine Love" of the "Princes of Sodom" "Practising the Art of Ganymede" at Henri III's Court: The Homosexuality of Henri III and his *Mignons* in Pierre de l'Estoile's *Mémoires-Journaux*', in J. Murray and K. Eisenbichler, eds., *Desire and Discipline: Sex and Sexuality in the Premodern West* (Toronto, 1996), pp. 123–54 (sexual allegations); K. B. Crawford, 'Love, Sodomy, and Scandal: Controlling the Sexual Reputation of Henry III', *JHS*, 12 (2003), pp. 513–42 (p. 524: L'Estoile quotation; pp. 536–9: Joyeuse; *passim*: three factors).

64. King James VI [and I], *Basilikon doron, Devided into Three Bookes* (Edinburgh, 1599), pp. 37–8 ('so is there some horrible Crymes that yee are bounde in Conscience neuer to forgiue: such as Witch-craft, wilfull-murther, Incest... Sodomie, Poysoning, and false coyne').

65. M. B. Young, *James VI and I and the History of Homosexuality* (Basingstoke, 2000), pp. 39, 41; Trumbach, 'Renaissance Sodomy', p. 53 (two others).

66. See K. van Eickels, 'Tender Comrades: Gesten männlicher Freundschaft und die Sprache der Liebe im Mittelalter', *Invertito: Jahrbuch für die Geschichte der Homosexualitäten*, 6 (2004), pp. 9–48; A. Bray, 'Homosexuality and the Signs of Male Friendship in Elizabethan England', in J. Goldberg, ed., *Queering the Renaissance* (Durham, NC, 1994), pp. 40–61. Sir Keith Thomas notes a decline in the use of kissing between men as a casual salutation in 17th-century England, but also cites a mid-century text which recorded a range of circumstances for it ('In *Salutation, Valediction, Reconciliation* or *renewing of Love, Congratulation, Approbation, Adulation, Subjection, Confederation*, but more especially and natur-ally *in token of Love*' (Bulwer, J. ['J. B.'], *Pathomyotomia, Or: A Dissection of the Significative Muscles of the Affections of the Minde* (London, 1649), p. 220, referring to male–female as well as male–male kissing)): see K. Thomas, 'Afterword', in K. Harvey, ed., *The Kiss in History* (Manchester, 2005), pp. 187–203, at pp. 192–3.

67. R. Shephard, 'Sexual Rumours in English Politics: The Cases of Elizabeth I and James I', in J. Murray and K. Eisenbichler, eds., *Desire and Discipline: Sex and Sexuality in the Premodern West* (Toronto, 1996), pp. 101–22, at p. 110 (quoting Lord Thomas Howard); A. W. Beasley, 'The Disability of James VI and I', *The Seventeenth Century*, 10 (1995), pp. 152–62 (p. 157: 'fiddling').

68. For gossip portraying his attitude as unbecoming, see E. Bourcier, ed., *The Diary of Sir Simonds D'Ewes, 1622–1624: journal d'un étudiant londonien sous le règne de Jacques 1ᵉʳ* (Paris, 1974), pp. 57, 87.

69. Young, *James VI and I*, pp. 44–5. In a rare lapse of judgement, Rictor Norton suggests that the reference to Jesus and John may have been a conscious invo-cation of the sexual blasphemy about them: *The Myth of the Modern Homosexual: Queer History and the Search for Cultural Unity* (London, 1997), p. 221. It is inconceivable that James, a pious theologian, would have intended such an implication.

70. Shephard, 'Sexual Rumours', pp. 111–12; Anon., *Tom Tell Troath: Or, a Free Discourse Touching the Manners of the Tyme. Directed to His Majestie by Way of Humble Advertisement* (n.p., n.d. [1622]), pp. 25–6; Bourcier, ed., *Diary of Sir Simonds D'Ewes*, pp. 92–3. Young claims (*James VI and I*, pp. 52–3) that the accus-ation against James was also made in another pamphlet of the same year: Anon. [attrib. T. Scott], *The Belgicke Pismire Stinging the Slothfull Sleeper, and Awaking the Diligent to Fast, Watch, Pray* (n.p., 1622). This is incorrect; the only references there to sodomy and sodomites (pp. 40, 47–8) are part of a very general moral-rhetorical denunciation of English society, not a criticism of the King.

71. Hammond, *Figuring Sex*, pp. 141–3. This appears in a MS collection containing topical poems from 1612–23: see N. K. Farmer, ed., 'Poems from a Seventeenth-Century Manuscript with the Hand of Robert Herrick', *Texas Quarterly*, 16:4 (1973), Supplement, pp. 1–185, esp. pp. 7, 137–41. Hammond also cites another poem (*Figuring Sex*, pp. 144–6) about an imminent revolt by the gods against Jove and Ganymede; this may have been a political allegory, as Hammond

argues, but the application of most of its specific elements to Jacobean politics is far from clear.

72. Shephard, 'Sexual Rumours', pp. 112–13.
73. Young, *James VI and I*, p. 43, referring to M. Lee, *Great Britain's Solomon: King James VI and I in His Three Kingdoms* (Urbana, IL, 1990), p. 249.
74. D. M. Bergeron, *King James and Letters of Homoerotic Desire* (Iowa City, IA, 1999), pp. 87, 134.
75. S. Handley, *Sleep in Early Modern England* (New Haven, CT, 2016), pp. 176, 178.
76. van der Meer, *Sodoms zaad*, pp. 220 (older), 302–3 (tutor, officer); T. Hamilton, 'A Sodomy Scandal on the Eve of the French Wars of Religion', *The Historical Journal*, 64 (2021), pp. 844–64, at pp. 860–1 (monastery official).
77. Young, *King James VI and I*, pp. 36 ('King James...'), 44 ('George I...', 'never one...'), 135 ('he did...').

CHAPTER 17

1. Patterson, 'Chaucer's Pardoner on the Couch', p. 663; for a classic account of the puzzlement, see C. D. Benson, 'Chaucer's Pardoner and Modern Critics', *Mediaevalia*, 8 (1982), pp. 337–49.
2. D. G. Neal, *The Masculine Self in Late Medieval England* (Chicago, 2008), p. 139.
3. Spreitzer, *Die stumme Sünde*, p. 107 ('das beinahe vollständige Fehlen des Themas der Homosexualität in der mittelalterlichen deutschsprachigen Literatur') (and cf. also p. 77); Krass, 'Sprechen von der stummen Sünde', pp. 130–1 (Der Stricker). Robert Mills notes also a 12-line denunciation of sodomy by the 13th-century poet known as 'Der Tugentschrîber': *Seeing Sodomy in the Middle Ages* (Chicago, 2015), p. 149.
4. Karras, 'Lechery', pp. 193–8 (p. 193: quotation), 201 (fornication, adultery).
5. H. Martin, *Le Métier de prédicateur en France septentrionale à la fin du moyen âge (1350–1520)* (Paris, 1988), p. 381.
6. Puff, *Sodomy in Reformation Germany*, p. 69.
7. Ibid., p. 69 (Geiler); Kramer, *Malleus maleficarum*, p. 89; Rocke, 'Sodomites', p. 17 (Bernardino); Thomas of Cantimpré ['Cantipratanus'], *Bonum universale de apibus* (Douai, 1627), p. 381 ('irretitos'). The connection with Thomas was first made by Thoma, '"Das seind die sünd der vnküscheit"', p. 145; Thoma also notes (p. 144) that Geiler's comments about boys and masturbation were based on textual borrowings from Gerson.
8. Cited in Williams, *Dictionary of Sexual Language*, s.v. 'Sodom'.
9. A. Hill, *The Crie of England: A Sermon Preached at Paules Cross in September 1593* (London, 1595), p. 24 ('Sodometrie also...'). 'Sodometry' was a word for sodomy, derived apparently from the French word *sodomiterie* (Mills, *Seeing Sodomy*, p. 67), which was also Germanicized as *Sodomiterei*.
10. R. Milles, *Abrahams Sute for Sodom: A Sermon Preached at Paules Crosse, the 25 of August 1611* (London, 1612), sig. E5r (quotation).

11. J. Harris, *The Destruction of Sodome: A Sermon Preached at a Publicke Fast, before the Honourable Assembly of the Commons* (London, 1629), pp. 9 ('A sinne...'), 34 ('If I...').

12. On the sense of theological urgency, involving parallels between the people of England and the people of Israel (and with further examples from sermons), see Cocks, *Visions of Sodom*, pp. 62–6.

13. Coke, *Third Part of the Institutes*, p. 59.

14. Smith, *Homosexual Desire*, p. 166; Herrup, *House in Gross Disorder*, p. 30 (referring on p. 175(n. 15) to other works which also followed Ezekiel).

15. DiGangi, 'How Queer was the Renaissance?', pp. 137–8.

16. P. Stubbes, *The Anatomie of Abuses*, in J. P. Collier, ed., *Illustrations of Early English Literature*, 3 vols. (London, 1867–70), i, item 1, pp. 51 (hats; 'pearking' = perking, projecting), 145–6 (church-ales), 184 (football).

17. Ibid., pp. 94 ('consumed with...'), 100 ('Whylest these...'), 149 ('in drunkennesse...').

18. T. Beard and T. Taylor, *The Theatre of Gods Judgements, wherein is Represented the Admirable Justice of God against Notorious Sinners*, 4th edn. (London, 1648), pp. 253 (adultery), 280–2 (sodomy). The initial text produced by Beard was an augmented translation of Jean Chassanion, *Histoires memorables des grans et merveilleux jugemens et punitions de Dieu avenues au monde*, first published in Geneva in 1581; hence the detail from French history (p. 387 in the 2nd edn. (Geneva, 1586)). But what is significant is that neither in 1587 nor in any later edition were any examples added that related to English sodomites.

19. G. W. Bredbeck, *Sodomy and Interpretation: Marlowe to Milton* (Ithaca, NY, 1991), p. 34.

20. See Smith, *Homosexual Desire*, pp. 174–84, 216 ('Only in...').

21. H. Cockeram, *The English Dictionarie: Or, An Interpreter of Hard English Words* (London, 1623), s.v. 'catamite'.

22. 'J.' [G.] Florio, *A Worlde of Wordes, Or, Most and Exact Dictionarie, in Italian and English* (London, 1598), s.vv.

23. T. Nashe, *Nashe's Lenten Stuffe, Containing the Description and First Procreation and Increase of the Towne of Great Yarmouth in Norffolke* (London, 1599), sig. A3r ('Hugge it, ingle it, kisse it, and cull it now thou hast it'); Anon., *The First Part of the True and Honorable Historie, of the Life of Sir John Old-Castle, the Good Lord Cobham* (London, 1600), sig, C4r (Dorothy: 'Oh if I wist this old priest would not sticke to me, by Ioue I would ingle this old seruing-man'); 'I. H.', *This Worlds Folly: Or, A Warning-Peece Discharged upon the Wickedness thereof* (London, 1615), sig. B2r ('these are they, who by their wantonizing Stage-gestures, can ingle and seduce men to heaue vp their heartes and affections'); J. Donne ['J. D.'], *Poems* (London, 1633), p. 49 (Elegie IV: 'Thy little brethren, which like Faiery Sprights | Oft skipt into our chamber, those sweet nights, | And kist, and ingled on thy fathers knee').

24. Anon. ['Jack Dawe'], *Vox graculi: Or, Jack Dawe's Prognostication* (London, 1623), p. 9 ('When the first word that a Punke speakes at her Ingles comming into her

Chamber in a Morning, *I pray thee send for some Fagots'*); J. Earle, *Micro-Cosmographie: Or, A Peece of the World Discovered in Essayes and Characters* (London, 1628), sig. 8v (on a gentleman student: 'His companion is ordinarily some stale fellow, that ha's beene notorious for an Ingle to gold hatbands'); Anon., *Merrie Conceited Jests of George Peele Gentleman sometimes a Student in Oxford* (London, 1627), p. 20 ('There was a Gentleman, whom GOD had indued with good liuing...and hee was in a manner an Ingle to *George,* one that tooke great delight to haue the first hearing of any worke that *George* had done, himselfe being a writer'); G. Wither, *The Schollers Purgatory Discovered in the Stationers Common-wealth* (London, 1624), p. 98 (on the Stationers' Company: 'So much oppertunity (by meanes of their Trade and Customers) to possesse the generality on their behalfes; Such a Brood of Ingles (by reason of their many troublesome suites) in euery Court of Iustice, and about euery eminent person, ready to serue their turnes').

25. B. Jonson, *Every Man in His Humor*, sig. B3r ('I doubt, *Apollo* hath got thee to be his *Ingle*...For his Retayners, I am sure, I haue knowne some of them, that haue followed him, three, foure, fiue yeere together, scorning the world with their bare heeles, & at length bene glad for a shift'); Anon., *A Pill to Purge Melancholy: Or, Merry News from Newgate* (London, 1652), p. 9 ('giving his Ningle charge to keep her station').

26. B. Jonson, *A Pleasant Comedy, Called: The Case is Alterd* (London, 1609), sigs. A2v, A4r, F4v; T. Dekker, *Satiro-mastix: Or, The Untrussing of the Humorous Poet* (London, 1602) sigs. B4r, D1v, D2r.

27. B. Jonson, *The Fountaine of Selfe-Love: Or, Cynthia's Revels* (London, 1601), sig. A4r; T. Dekker, *Newes from Graves-End Sent to Nobody* (London, 1604), sig. A3r.

28. B. Jonson, *Poetaster: Or, The Arraignment* (London, 1602), sigs. B1r, F3r.

29. Griffiths, *Lost Londons*, p. 95.

30. Kathleen McLuskie comments: 'It may be, as the moralists asserted, that the boys were subject to homosexual exploitation by the adult players...If that was the case it is remarkable that no specific charge of homosexuality was ever brought against an actor or a boy player' ('The Act, the Role, and the Actor: Boy Actresses on the Elizabethan Stage', *New Theatre Quarterly*, 3 (2009), pp. 120–30, at p. 126).

31. Bly, *Queer Virgins*, pp. 70 (citing J. Webster, 'The Induction' to J. Marston, *The Malcontent. Augmented by Marston* (London, 1604), sig. A3v: adults); T. Middleton, *Father Hubburds Tales: Or, The Ant and the Nightingale* (London, 1604), sig. D1r: 'after dinner, he must venture...to the Bank-side, where he must sit out the breaking vp of a Comedie, or the first cut of a Tragedie; or rather (if his humour so serue him) to call in at the Black-fryers, where he should see a neast of Boyes, able to rauish a man'; T. Dekker, *The Guls Horne-Booke* (London, 1609), p. 29: 'By sitting on the stage, you may (with small cost) purchase the deere acquaintance of the boyes: haue a good stoole for sixpence: at any time know what particular part any of the infants present: get your match lighted, examine the play-suits lace, and perhaps win wagers vpon laying tis copper'), 70–1 (citing

J. Wright, *Historia histrionica: An Historical Account of the English Stage* (London, 1699), p. 4: Hammerton), 74 ('a theatrical...').

32. Stubbes, *Anatomie*, p. 139 (where 'fleering' = laughing impudently; 'bussing' = kissing vigorously; 'clipping' = hugging; 'culling' = hugging or fondling). For the standard—mistaken—interpretation see e.g. Smith, *Homosexual Desire*, p. 155; L. Levine, *Men in Women's Clothing: Anti-Theatricality and Effeminization, 1579–1642* (Cambridge, 1994), p. 22; Young, *James VI and I*, p. 71; Cocks, *Visions of Sodom*, p. 70.

33. S. Gosson, *The Schoole of Abuse: Conteining a Pleasaunt Invective against Poets, Pipers, Plaiers, Jesters, and such like Caterpillers of the Commonwelth* (London, 1579), p. 18 (where 'cheapen' = bargain for; 'quean' = impudent woman, prostitute); S. Gosson, *Playes Confuted in Five Actions, Proving that they are not to be Sufferd in a Christian Common Weale* (London, 1582), sig. G5r, summarizing Xenophon's description of the effects of a dramatic performance depicting the dalliance of Bacchus and Ariadne: 'the company presently was set on fire, they that were married posted home to theire wiues.' Note that while Gosson's first comment presupposes the presence of women in the theatre audience, the second does not; nor, apparently, does the passage from Stubbes.

34. J. Rainolds, *Th'Overthrow of Stage-Playes* (Middelburg, 1599), pp. 10–11, 17–18, 96 (quotation); on the exchanges with his opponents see J. W. Binns, 'Women or Transvestites on the Elizabethan Stage?: An Oxford Controversy', *The Sixteenth Century Journal*, 5:2 (1974), pp. 95–120.

35. Rainolds, *Th'Overthrow*, pp. 34–5.

36. W. Prynne, *Histrio-mastix: The Players Scourge, or Actor's Tragaedie* (London, 1633), pp. 208 (quotation), 209 (extenuation argument).

37. Ibid., pp. 211–12.

38. S. Orgel, *Impersonations: The Performance of Gender in Shakespeare's England* (Cambridge, 1996), p. 29.

39. M. Shapiro, 'Lady Mary Wroth Describes a Boy Actress', *Medieval and Renaissance Drama in England*, 4 (1989), pp. 187–94, at p. 187 (quoting her *The Countesse of Mountgomeries Urania* (London, 1621), sig. I2r); T. Heywood, *An Apology for Actors* (London, 1612), sig. C3v.

40. Orgel, *Impersonations*, p. 70. He adds (p. 71) that 'The love of men for boys is all but axiomatic in the period', a claim for which English evidence is notably lacking, and goes on to offer a version of Alan Bray's argument that male–male sexual relations were accepted as common and untroubling in England—a claim based only on the extreme paucity of evidence of any such sexual relations at all.

41. M. Shapiro, *Gender in Play on the Shakespearian Stage: Boy Heroines and Female Pages* (Ann Arbor, MI, 1994), pp. 2–7, 39 (quotation).

42. Ibid., pp. 85, 120–2, 170–1 (statement).

43. Trumbach, 'Renaissance Sodomy', pp. 56–8. He also writes (p. 45) that 'about one-third of the 300 plays for which texts exist for the period from 1601 to 1642 have some reference to sexual relations between men and boys', giving no reference for this extraordinary claim.

44. Martial, *Epigrammata*, IX.25 ('Hyllum…mollem…ministrum'); J. P. Sullivan and A. J. Boyle, eds., *Martial in English* (Harmondsworth, 1996), p. 12 (from T. Kendall, *Flowers of Epigrammes* (London, 1577)); Hammond, *Figuring Sex*, p. 45 ('Thomas Stanley's…'); C. J. Summers, 'Homosexuality and Renaissance Literature, Or the Anxieties of Anachronism', *South Central Review*, 9 (1992), pp. 2–23, at p. 8 ('most of…').

45. C. Marlowe, *The Complete Works*, ed. F. Bowers, 2nd edn., 2 vols. (Cambridge, 1981), ii, pp. 19 (I.1, l. 144), 29 (I.4, l. 180), 35 (I.4, l. 390).

46. Ibid., ii, pp. 449–50 (sest. 2, ll. 181–93).

47. Hammond, *Figuring Sex*, p. 48, citing L. Machin, 'Three Eglogs', in W. Barksted, *Mirrha the Mother of Adonis* (London, 1607), sigs. E5r–E6v. The phrase about melting into amorous dew may suggest ejaculation.

48. R. Barnfield, *The Affectionate Sheapheard, Containing the Complaint of Daphnis for the Love of Ganymede* (London, 1594), sig. C1r. For a good discussion of the nature of the eroticism in Barnfield's poetry see Smith, *Homosexual Desire*, pp. 99–113.

49. R. Barnfield, *Cynthia, with Certaine Sonnets, and the Legend of Cassandra* (London, 1595), sig. A3r.

50. M. Drayton, *Peirs Gaveston Earle of Cornwall, His Life, Death and Fortune* (London, 1594), sigs. C1v–C2r. See the discussion in Hammond, *Figuring Sex*, pp. 121–6. Hammond's explanation of the revision is that Drayton feared the original version might be read as a critique of King James; this seems unlikely, given that Robert Carr would not become James's favourite until 1607.

51. For the dating see Colin Burrow's summary in W. Shakespeare, *Complete Sonnets and Poems*, ed. C. Burrow (Oxford, 2002), pp. 103–6; for Barnfield echoes, Hammond, *Figuring Sex*, pp. 80–4, and Smith, *Homosexual Desire*, p. 250.

52. Shakespeare, *Complete Sonnets*, p. 421.

53. Stephen Orgel proposes that 'pricked thee out for women's pleasure' means 'selected you for the pleasure which women receive in the sexual act' (*Impersonations*, p. 57); this is a very strained interpretation, requiring us somehow to exclude the obvious link between 'pricked thee out' here and the reference in the previous line to Nature endowing the young man with a penis. In this case a critic who would normally be quick to accept a bawdy meaning (however tentative) prefers, for the sake of finding same-sex implications, to ignore one that is surely obvious.

54. Masi, 'Marignolli, Curzio', p. 360.

55. T. de Viau, *Oeuvres poétiques*, ed. G. Saba (Paris, 1990), p. 358: 'Philis, tout est…tu [*sic*], je meurs de la vérole; | Elle exerce sur moi sa dernière rigueur: | Mon v. baisse la tête et n'a point de vigueur […] Philis, le mal me vient de vous avoir…tue [*sic*]. | Mon Dieu, je me repens d'avoir si mal vécu: | Et si votre courroux à ce coup ne me tue, | Je fais voeu désormais de ne…tre [*sic*] qu'en cul.' There is a larger local poetic context, the vogue for so-called satires which saw the publication of many anthologies in Paris between 1600 and 1626, including many humorous, sexually explicit poems: see D. Foucault, *Histoire du*

libertinage (Paris, 2007), pp. 256–64. But none of the examples cited there has quite the same scathing intensity as Théophile's poem.

56. For examples from, respectively, 1707, 1726 and 1794 see Norton, *Mother Clap's Molly House*, p. 72; 'Hernandez', *Les Procès de Sodome*, p. 99; R. C. Bleys, *The Geography of Perversion: Male-to-Male Sexual Behaviour outside the West and the Ethnographic Imagination, 1750–1918* (London, 1996), p. 66.

57. See C. L. Gaudiani, *The Cabaret Poetry of Théophile de Viau: Texts and Traditions* (Tübingen, 1981).

58. See L. C. Seifert, 'Masculinity and Satires of "Sodomites" in France, 1660–1715', *JH*, 42 (2001), pp. 37–52 (p. 38: from late 16th century).

59. DeJean, *The Reinvention of Obscenity*, pp. 29–55 (sonnet, trial), 149 ('Faire des vers de sodomie ne rend pas un homme coupable du fait; poète et pédéraste sont deux qualités différentes').

60. See L. Godard de Donville, *Le Libertin des origines à 1665: un produit des apologètes* (Paris, 1989), pp. 112–327; I. Moreau, *'Guérir du sot': les stratégies d'écriture des libertins à l'âge classique* (Paris, 2007), pp. 50–73.

61. For the heterodox beliefs see Moreau, *'Guérir du sot'*, pp. 73–80.

62. See for example T. Gregory, *Genèse de la raison classique de Charron à Descartes*, tr. M. Raiola (Paris, 2000), pp. 94–5; J.-P. Cavaillé, *Postures libertines: la culture des esprits forts* (Toulouse, 2011), pp. 95–6.

63. Lever, *Les Bûchers de Sodome*, pp. 121–2 ('sans contraindre mes désirs | Je me donne entier aux plaisirs', 'Caliste m'ayant aujourd'hui | Surpris avec son jeune frère, | M'a reproché tout en colère, | Qu'elle avait un cul comme lui…'). The poem about Calista, which ends with the poet telling her that she has two cunts, is loosely adapted from Martial, *Epigrammata*, XI.43.

64. Hammond, *Gossip, Sexuality and Scandal*, pp. 56 ('Je suis bougre de vieille roche'), 58 ('Tous nos docteurs l'ont défendu, | Mais un auteur plus entendu | Dit qu'il est pour l'individu | Et le c[on] pour l'espèce'). The former example is from one of a number of openly irreligious poems by him: see A. Adam, *Les Libertins au XVIIᵉ siècle* (Paris, 1964), pp. 75–9 (here p. 76).

65. On the claimed or alleged connection with Hobbes, see N. Malcolm, 'Hobbes and Sexual Desire', *Hobbes Studies*, 28 (2015), pp. 77–102.

66. T. Shadwell, *The Complete Works*, ed. M. Summers, 5 vols. (London, 1927), pp. 29 ('He owns…'), 45 ('There's nothing…'), 85 ('I know…').

67. See Hammond, *Figuring Sex*, p. 231.

68. Pepys, *Diary*, iv, pp. 209–10, 1 July 1663.

69. Ibid., iv, p. 209; A. Wood, *The Life and Times of Anthony Wood, Antiquary, of Oxford, 1632–1695, Described by Himself*, ed. A. Clark, 5 vols. (Oxford, 1891–1900), ii, p. 335. Wood also writes that on being fined £500, 'Sidley therfore answered that he thought he was the first man that paid for shiting'.

70. Young, *James VI and I*, p. 146 (on T. Hitchcock, *English Sexualities, 1700–1800* (Basingstoke, 1997), p. 65).

71. J. Treglown, ed., *The Letters of John Wilmot, Earl of Rochester* (Oxford, 1980), pp. 160 ('un bougre lasse'), 230 ('this pretty…').

72. Hammond, *Figuring Sex*, p. 246.

73. Wilmot, *Works*, p. 38.

74. Ibid., p. 45.

75. Ibid., pp. 15 ('Stiffly Resolv'd...'), 117 (MS tradition), 118 (MS readings). The 'nor' construction requires an implied punctuation mark (semicolon or dash) after the intransitive verb 'invade'; the 'or' version takes 'Woman, or man/Boy' as the object of the transitive verb. Taking 'Woman' as the sole object, followed by 'nor Man', would remove the implication that males were also invaded, but the third line implies that they were.

76. See H. Love, 'But Did Rochester *Really* Write *Sodom?*', *The Papers of the Bibliographical Society of America*, 87 (1993), pp. 319–36 (not Rochester); N. D. Nace, 'The Author of *Sodom* among the Smithfield Muses', *The Review of English Studies*, 68 (2016), pp. 296–321 (Jordan, Fishbourne); Foxon, *Libertine Literature*, p. 11(n.) (1684 printing, non-extant); D. S. Thomas, 'Prosecutions of *Sodom: Or, The Quintessence of Debauchery*, and *Poems on Several Occasions by the E. of R.*, 1689–1690 and 1693', *The Library*, 24 (1969), pp. 51–5 (1689 printing, suppressed).

77. Wilmot, *Works*, pp. 302–33.

78. Ibid., p. 305 (quotation); Love, 'But Did Rochester?', pp. 326–9 (on the unconvincing attempts).

79. Hammond, *Figuring Sex*, p. 29 (translating 'sumus omnes expergefacti, et salutavimus alter alterum (sicut mos est apud bene educatos): sed erant ex nobis qui salutabant socios per viam de retro, quod non erat, meo judicio, valde honestum, quamvis nonnulli dicunt esse bonum pro lumbis; sed nihil male fit quod non male accipitur'), from Bishop Reeves, 'Bodley's Visit to Lecale, County of Down, A.D. 1602–3', *Ulster Journal of Archaeology*, 2 (1854), pp. 73–95, at p. 87.

80. T. Middleton, *Michaelmas Term*, ed. R. Levin (London, 1967), pp. 13 (I.i, ll. 123–4, 127–8), 75 (III.ii, ll. 15–16), 84 (III.iv, ll. 98), 94 (III.v, l. 45).

81. Sir Keith Thomas writes that kissing between men was going out of fashion in early-17th-century England, except on formal occasions; he cites the traveller Thomas Coryate expressing surprise at seeing men in Venice routinely kiss when parting ('Afterword', pp. 192–3). But it was still unremarkable to impart a kiss as a form of special emotional emphasis: in Middleton's play the draper, when given the news he has been waiting for by a servant boy, exclaims: 'The land's mine; that's sure enough, boy. | Let me advance thee, knave, and give thee a kiss' (p. 79 (III.iv, l. 3–4)).

82. DiGangi, 'How Queer was the Renaissance?', p. 136.

83. DiGangi, *The Homoerotics of Early Modern Drama* (Cambridge 1997), p. 9.

84. E. K. Sedgwick, *Between Men: English Literature and Male Homosocial Desire*, 2nd edn. (New York, 2016), pp. 1–2. Sedgwick's actual argument, which draws on psychoanalytic forms of thought as well as 'dialectical' reasoning about power relations, resists easy simplification. But its value to the historian may be slight, as the historical argument is (professedly) dependent on the 'readings of the literary texts' (pp. 15–16), and the methods of reading are dependent on pre-formed theories.

85. G. V. Stanivukovic, '"Knights in Armes": The Homoerotics of the English Renaissance Prose Romances', in C. C. Relihan and G. V. Stanivukovic, eds., *Prose Fiction and Early Modern Sexualities in England, 1570–1640* (New York, 2003), pp. 171–92.

86. W. Shakespeare, *The Complete Works*, ed. S. Wells and G. Taylor (Oxford, 1986), p. 1227 (IV.iv, ll. 12–16). On the strength of early-modern expressions of friendship, which could go far beyond modern norms, see K. Thomas, *The Ends of Life: Roads to Fulfilment in Early Modern England* (Oxford, 2009), pp. 199–205.

87. M. de Montaigne, *The Essays*, trans. M. A. Screech (London, 1991), I.28, pp. 210 ('abhorrent'), 211–12 ('In the...') 214 ('one soul...') (*Essais*, ed. J.-V. Leclerc, 2 vols. (Paris, 1931), pp. 201 ('abhorree'), 203 ('En l'amitié de quoy je parle, elles se meslent et confondent l'une en l'aultre d'un meslange si universel, qu'elles effacent et ne retrouvent plus la cousture qui les a joinctes. Si on me presse de dire pourquoy je l'aymoys, je sens que cela ne se peult exprimer qu'en respondant, "Parce que c'estoit luy; parce que c'estoit moy" '), 206 ('une ame en deux corps... ils ne se peuvent ny prester ny donner rien')).

88. Sir Thomas Browne, *Selected Writings*, ed. G. Keynes (London, 1968), p. 75 (*Religio medici*, II.5–6).

89. A. Sinfield, *Shakespeare, Authority, Sexuality: Unfinished Business in Cultural Materialism* (New York, 2006), p. 97.

90. A. Bray, *The Friend* (Chicago, 2003), pp. 6 ('To let...'), 67 ('The language...').

91. M. E. Novak, G. R. Guffey and A. Roper, eds., *The Works of John Dryden*, xiii, *All for Love; Oedipus; Troilus and Cressida* (Berkeley, CA, 1984), p. 58 (III.1, ll. 91–8).

92. G. E. Haggerty, *Men in Love: Masculinity and Sexuality in the Eighteenth Century* (New York, 1999), pp. 25–6. Space here does not permit a discussion of Haggerty's further claims about this play (pp. 27–9), which are no less questionable.

93. G. L. Stringer et al., eds., *The Variorum Edition of the Poetry of John Donne*, vii, part 1, *The Holy Sonnets* (Bloomington, IN, 2005), p. 105.

94. Loughlin, *Same-Sex Desire*, pp. 340–50 (p. 350: 'Holy Sonnet 14'), 360–3.

95. For striking examples of this in mediaeval sermons on the Song of Songs, see C. W. Bynum, *Jesus as Mother: Studies in the Spirituality of the High Middle Ages* (Berkeley, CA, 1982), pp. 117–19.

96. T. Webster, '"Kiss Me with Kisses of His Mouth": Gender Inversion and Canticles in Godly Spirituality', in T. Betteridge, ed., *Sodomy in Early Modern Europe* (Manchester, 2002), pp. 148–63, at pp. 152–3 (Rogers); J. G. Turner, *One Flesh: Paradisal Marriage and Sexual Relations in the Age of Milton* (Oxford, 1987), p. 79 (Rous).

97. W. Bradford, *Of Plymouth Plantation*, ed. S. E. Morison (New York, 1952), pp. 224–5 (Gott letter), 316 ('even sodomy...'), 320–1 (bestiality, 'had made...').

98. J. Goldberg, *Sodometries: Renaissance Texts, Modern Sexualities* (Stanford, CA, 1992), p. 237.

CHAPTER 18

1. 'W. S.', *The Proceedings of the English Colonie in Virginia since their First Beginning from England in the Yeare of Our Lord 1606, till this Present 1612* (Oxford, 1612), appended to J. Smith, *A Map of Virginia: With a Description of the Countrey, the Commodities, People, Government and Religion* (Oxford, 1612), p. 9, partly cited in J. N. Katz, *Gay/Lesbian Almanac: A New Documentary* (New York, 1983), p. 66.

2. Katz, *Gay/Lesbian Almanac*, pp. 66–7.

3. To support his case, Katz draws attention to a marginal note next to this passage which reads: 'The sailers abuses'; but this stands precisely next to the line containing the word 'pilfer'. Katz himself also records (ibid., p. 68) that the Virginia legal code of 1610—issued two years before this text was published—imposed the death penalty for 'the horrible, detestable sin of Sodomie'.

4. Katz, *Gay/Lesbian Almanac*, pp. 69–70 (noting also two subsequent complaints that the captain was wrongfully executed; we cannot infer that the complainants thought all executions for sodomy were wrong, as they may have spoken on the basis of particular knowledge of this case); Smith, *Homosexual Desire*, pp. 194–5 (meaning of 'boy'). James Saslow writes that the alleged victim was 'referred to as a "rascally boy" though he was twenty-nine years old, suggesting that the pederastic construct was applied even where chronologically tenuous' ('Homosexuality in the Renaissance: Behavior, Identity, and Artistic Expression', in M. B. Duberman, M. Vicinus and G. Chauncey, eds., *Hidden from History: Reclaiming the Gay and Lesbian Past*, pp. 90–105, at p. 94); this is both to ignore the common usage of the period, and to treat the age-differentiated model as dominant *a priori*.

5. V. D. Anderson, 'New England in the Seventeenth Century', in N. Canny and A. Low, eds., *The Origins of Empire: British Overseas Enterprise to the Close of the Seventeenth Century* (Oxford, 1998), pp. 193–217, at p. 211.

6. J. Winthrop, *The History of New England from 1630 to 1639*, ed J. Savage, 2 vols. (Boston, 1853), ii, p. 324 ('unclean practices', 'to some...'); R. Godbeer, '"The Cry of Sodom": Discourse, Intercourse, and Desire in Colonial New England', *The William and Mary Quarterly*, 52 (1995), pp. 259–86, at p. 272 ('corrupted a...'); B. C. Steiner, *History of the Plantation of Menunkatuck and of the Original Town of Guilford, Connecticut* (Baltimore, 1897), p. 47 (corrupting boys).

7. Godbeer, '"Cry of Sodom"', p. 272.

8. Anderson, 'New England', p. 203 ('intensely rigorous...').

9. Godbeer, '"Cry of Sodom"', pp. 266–8.

10. Ibid., p. 270 ('an contactus et fricatio usque ad effusionem seminis sit sodomia morte plectenda').

11. R. Godbeer, *Sexual Revolution in Early America* (Baltimore, 2002), p. 108.

12. See M. Warner, 'New English Sodom', in J. Goldberg, ed., *Queering the Renaissance* (Durham, NC, 1994), pp. 330–58, esp. pp. 330–1, 337.

13. Turner, *One Flesh*, p. 73; cf. K. Verduin, '"Our Cursed Natures": Sexuality and the Puritan Conscience', *New England Quarterly*, 56 (1983), pp. 220–37.

14. T. Shepard, 'The Autobiography of Thomas Shepard', *Publications of the Colonial Society of Massachusetts*, 27 (1927–30), pp. 343–400, at p. 393.
15. A. Bray, 'The Curious Case of Michael Wigglesworth', in M. Duberman, ed., *A Queer World: The Center for Lesbian and Gay Studies Reader* (New York, 1997), pp. 205–16, at p. 213 (n. 5); cf. the rather routine listing of student sins in Shepard's earlier description of Cambridge life ('Autobiography', p. 361): 'I . . . fell from god to loose & lewd company to lust & pride & gaming & bowling & drinking'.
16. Bray, 'Curious Case', pp. 205–6 (where 'fond' is a negative term meaning 'foolish', and 'affection' has the sense of 'feeling' or 'passion'). Bray also quotes a passage from the diary about troubling dreams and self-pollution (p. 207); Bray describes the dreams as sodomitical, but the text does not quite say that.
17. Godbeer, *Sexual Revolution*, p. 89.
18. J. J. McCusker, and R. R. Menard, *The Economy of British America, 1607–1789* (Chapel Hill, NC, 1985), p. 103 (statistics).
19. W. M. Billings, ed., *The Old Dominion in the Seventeenth Century: A Documentary History of Virginia, 1606–1689* (Chapel Hill, NC, 1975), pp. 69–81 (system), 102–3 (fornication, adultery).
20. Bradford, *Of Plymouth Plantation*, pp. 316–17.
21. R. Thompson, 'Attitudes towards Homosexuality in the Seventeenth-Century New England Colonies', *Journal of American Studies*, 23 (1989), pp. 27–40, at pp. 30–1; R. Thompson, *Sex in Middlesex: Popular Mores in a Massachusetts County, 1646–1699* (Amherst, MA, 1986), pp. 74–5, 82.
22. R. Godbeer, ' "Sodomitical Actings", "Inward Disposition", and "The Bonds of Brotherly Affection": Sexual and Emotional Intimacy between Men in Colonial and Revolutionary America', in K. O'Donnell and M. O'Rourke, eds., *Queer Masculinities, 1550–1800: Siting Same-Sex Desire in the Early Modern World* (Basingstoke, 2006), pp. 191–210, at p. 198.
23. See the listing in Godbeer, ' "Cry of Sodom" ', pp. 285–6. I omit here the case of the five 'beastly Sodomiticall boyes' who were on a ship which came to Massachusetts in 1629, and were sent back to England for punishment; their actual ages, status (were they part of the crew?) and the nature of their offence (mutual masturbation?) are unknown. See F. Higginson, 'A True Relation of the Last Voyage to New England', in *Proceedings of the Massachusetts Historical Society*, ser. 3, vol. 62 (1928–9), pp. 281–99, at p. 295; N. B. Shurtleff, ed., *Records of the Governor and Company of the Massachusetts Bay in New England*, 5 vols. (Boston, 1853–4), i, pp. 52, 54.
24. Godbeer, ' "Cry of Sodom" ', pp. 271–2 (1641); Godbeer, *Sexual Revolution*, p. 73 (1658).
25. N. B. Shurtleff and D. Pulsifer, eds., *Records of the Colony of New Plymouth in New England*, 12 vols. (Boston, 1855–61), i, p. 64.
26. R. F. Oaks, ' "Things Fearful to Name": Sodomy and Buggery in Seventeenth-Century New England', *Journal of Social History*, 12 (1978–9), pp. 268–81, at p. 270.

27. R. Godbeer and D. L. Winiarski, 'Documents from the Sodomy Trial of Nicholas Sension, May 1677', *Early American Studies*, 12 (2014), pp. 444–57, at pp. 445–6 (cases 20, 19 years previously), 449 (Pond, 'did often...'), 451 (Saxton).

28. Godbeer, '"Cry of Sodom"', pp. 260 (reprimands, trial result), 276 (quotations).

29. Katz, *Gay/Lesbian Almanac*, pp. 90 (Creoli: his victim was named Manuel Congo—probably also a slave, or the son of one, from Spanish territory), 103 (soldiers); D. L. Noorlander, *Heaven's Wrath: The Protestant Reformation and the Dutch West India Company in the Atlantic World* (Ithaca, NY, 2019), p. 152 (Creoli, merchant, second soldier). On the merchant see T. O'Reilly, 'The "Bad Fate" of Harmen Meyndertsz van den Bogaert', <https://www.nyhistory.org/blogs/the-bad-fate-of-harmen-meyndertsz-van-den-bogaert>, which reproduces a letter of 1647 euphemistically describing his offence: he 'had goings-on with his black boy [presumably a slave], and also with another one called Smist Jan; both ran away to the savages, but the boy has been captured' ('heeft met sijn swarte jongen te don [*sic*] gehadt en noch een ander genannt smist [*sic*] Jan beijde bij de wilde geloopen maer de jongen is gevangen'). For a fuller narrative account see R. Shorto, *The Island at the Center of the World: The Epic Story of Dutch Manhattan and the Forgotten Colony that Shaped America* (New York, 2005), pp. 187–9.

30. P. Corriveau, *La Répression des homosexuels au Québec et en France: du bûcher à la mairie* (Sillery, 2006), pp. 57–8 ('debaucher plusieurs hommes', 'par un espace de temps').

31. Ibid., pp. 59 (1690s, dispersion), 64 ('la forte autorégulation du milieu colonial, caractérisé par son mode de vie rural où l'unité familiale est au centre de la régulation sociale et où les actes répréhensibles sont moins portés à l'attention des officiels').

32. W. Benemann, *Male–Male Intimacy in Early America: Beyond Romantic Friendships* (New York, 2006), p. 1 (citing the commonplace book of Augustus John Foster).

33. Katz, *Gay/Lesbian Almanac*, pp. 128–30.

34. Ibid., p. 133.

35. Ibid., pp. 127–8 (1712); T. A. Foster, 'Antimasonic Satire, Sodomy, and Eighteenth-Century Masculinity in the "Boston Evening-Post"', *The William and Mary Quarterly*, 60 (2003), pp. 171–84, at p. 174(n.) (1714, 1740); T. A. Foster, *Sex and the Eighteenth Century Man: Massachusetts and the History of Sexuality in America* (Boston, 2006), pp. 158–9.

36. Godbeer, '"Cry of Sodom"', p. 279.

37. Ibid., p. 277.

38. C. A. Lyons, 'Mapping an Atlantic Sexual Culture: Homoeroticism in Eighteenth-Century Philadelphia', *The William and Mary Quarterly*, 60 (2003), pp. 119–54, at pp. 121 (cosmopolitan), 131–4 (*Select Trials*), 137 and n. (no evidence).

39. Molina, *Cuando amar era pecado*, pp. 55–7, 126 (Aragonese Inquisition, Lima); Tortorici, *Sins against Nature*, p. 13 (Mexico); Giraldo Botero, *Deseo y represión*,

pp. 14–15 (Cartagena; other cases are found in the records of the criminal courts).

40. For a detailed study of the staffing and functioning of the Inquisition, see J. E. Wadsworth, 'In the Name of the Inquisition: The Portuguese Inquisition and Delegated Authority in Colonial Pernambuco, Brazil', *The Americas: Quarterly Review of Inter-American Cultural History*, 61 (2004), pp. 19–54.

41. M. J. Horswell, *Decolonizing the Sodomite: Queer Tropes of Sexuality in Colonial Andean Culture* (Austin, TX, 2006), p. 77 ('podrían con pleno derecho los cristianos…destruirla por sus nefandos delitos y barbarie'); for similar statements by Sarmiento de Gamboa and Acosta see Trexler, *Sex and Conquest*, p. 181(n. 4).

42. Garza Carvajal, *Butterflies will Burn*, pp. 145–8 (Vitoria).

43. F. Guerra, *The Pre-Columbian Mind* (London, 1971), *passim* (early accounts), p. 242 (quotation).

44. Ibid., pp. 223–4.

45. For examples of such exiles, see Mott, 'Crypto-Sodomites', p. 173; Higgs, 'Tales of Two Carmelites', p. 153. Some other colonial powers adopted this measure: in the 18th century France sent some convicted sodomites to Martinique, Guadeloupe, Santo Domingo and Mississippi (Pastorello, *Sodome à Paris*, p. 100).

46. Above, p. 80 (González de Sosa); Molina, *Cuando amar era pecado*, pp. 92–3, 103 (Ponce de León).

47. Vainfas, *Trópico dos pecados*, p. 172; Vainfas, 'The Nefarious and the Colony', p. 353; see also Mott, 'Crypto-Sodomites', pp. 183–9.

48. Vainfas, 'The Nefarious and the Colony', pp. 355–6.

49. Above, p. 76.

50. Vainfas, 'The Nefarious and the Colony', p. 340 (quotation); Vainfas, *Trópico dos pecados*, pp. 161, 165.

51. See pp. 392–8.

52. Above, p. 66.

53. Molina, *Cuando amar era pecado*, p. 85 ('muchos frayleçitos ynoçentes', 'porque eran moçuelos y como yndios gente facil').

54. Ibid., pp. 92–3, 103.

55. Ibid., pp. 84–5. The Dominican was in his 60s.

56. Tortorici, *Sins against Nature*, pp. 194, 288(n. 83) ('gente rustica y desconocida en quienes huviesse menos peligro de que lo delatassen').

57. J. S. Trevisan, *Perverts in Paradise*, trans. M. Foreman (London, 1986), p. 55.

58. Tortorici, *Sins against Nature*, pp. 47–9, 54–63.

59. Arquivo Nacional da Torre do Tombo, PT/TT/TSO-IL proc. 6366, fo. 19r ('grande numero de vezes em djuersos lugares co[m] mujtos homens sendo sempre elle Reo o Pacjente'); Vainfas, *Trópico dos pecados*, p. 164.

60. Vainfas, *Trópico dos pecados*, p. 163.

61. Molina, *Cuando amar era pecado*, p. 72.

62. Vainfas, *Trópico dos pecados*, p. 159. Luiz Mott takes a contrary view, arguing that a fragile colonial ruling class, seeking to strengthen its social and moral authority, placed an increasing emphasis on patriarchy and machismo, thereby encouraging

'homophobic repression' ('Crypto-Sodomites', pp. 178–9). Yet there is no evidence of a moral campaign against sodomy by the authorities in this period.

63. See Guerra, *Pre-Columbian Mind, passim*; Bleys, *Geography of Perversion*, pp. 22–8.

64. P. Sigal, '(Homo)Sexual Desire and Masculine Power in Colonial Latin America: Notes toward an Integrated Analysis', in P. Sigal, ed., *Infamous Desire: Male Homosexuality in Colonial Latin America* (Chicago, 2003), pp. 1–24, at p. 1.

65. Trexler, *Sex and Conquest*, pp. 118–39 (pp. 121: quotation; 125: northern plains). For differing perspectives on Latin American *berdaches*, see R. C. Trexler, 'Gender Subordination and Political Hierarchy in Pre-Hispanic America', in P. Sigal, ed., *Infamous Desire: Male Homosexuality in Colonial Latin America* (Chicago, 2003), pp. 70–101, and M. J. Horswell, 'Toward an Andean Theory of Ritual Same-Sex Sexuality and Third-Gender Subjectivity', ibid., pp. 25–69.

66. V. Woodard, *The Delectable Negro: Human Consumption and Homoeroticism within US Slave Culture* (New York, 2014), p. 230 ('possessed since ...'); Vainfas, *Trópico dos pecados*, pp. 159 (early reports), 165–6 (Manicongo, Antônio); H. Furtado de Mendoça, *Primeira visitação do Santo Offício ás partes do Brasil: denunciações da Bahia (1591–1593)* (São Paulo, 1925), p. 407 ('os negros somitigos que no peccado nefando servem de molheres pacientes, aos quais pacientes chamão na lingoa de Angola e Congo jinbandaa que quer dizer sometigos pacientes', 'hum pano cingido assim como na sua terra em Congo trazem os sometigos pacientes').

67. C. Giraldo Botero, 'Esclavos sodomitas en Cartagena colonial. Hablando del pecado nefando', *Historia crítica: revista del Departamento de Historia de la Universidad de los Andes*, 20 (2000), pp. 171–8, at pp. 174–5.

68. Mott, 'Crypto-Sodomites', pp. 178–9; P. Beattie, 'Conflicting Penile Codes: Modern Masculinity and Sodomy in the Brazilian Military, 1860–1916', in D. Balderston and D. J. Guy, eds., *Sex and Sexuality in Latin America* (New York, 1997), pp. 65–85, esp. pp. 73, 79.

69. Trexler, *Sex and Conquest*, p. 126.

70. Garza Carvajal, *Butterflies will Burn*, pp. 131–4, 174–83.

71. S. Gruzinski, 'Las cenizas del deseo. Homosexuales novohispanos a mediados del siglo XVII', in S. Ortega, ed., *De la santidad a la perversión, o de porqué no se cumplía la ley de Dios en la sociedad novohispana* (Mexico City, 1985), pp. 255–81.

72. Gruzinski refers to 'a subculture which has its secret geography, its network of information and informers, its language and its codes of behaviour' (ibid., p. 278: 'una subcultura que tiene su geografia secreta, su red de información e informantes, su lenguaje y su códigos').

73. Lage da Gama Lima, 'Sodomia e pedofilia no século XVII'.

74. Boomgaard, 'Male–Male Sex, Bestiality and Incest', pp. 150, 152.

75. W. van Rossum, *Werkers van de wereld: globalisering, arbeid en interculturele ontmoetingen tussen Aziatische en Europse zeelieden in dienst van de VOC, 1600–1800* (Hilversum, 2014), pp. 323 (1747: 'twee malen de vinger in sijn fondament gestoken, waardoor hij genoodsak was geweest om te schreuwen door smert en peijn'), 329 (1748).

76. Ibid., pp. 331–3 (1735), 334 (1746), 335–9 (1779). Kerry Ward also notes a case from 1735–6 in which a Company slave was accused of attempted sodomy: *Networks of Empire: Forced Migration in the Dutch East India Company* (Cambridge, 2008), p. 106.

77. A. Chan, 'Chinese–Philippine Relations in the Late Sixteenth Century and to 1603', *Philippine Studies*, 26 (1978), pp. 51–82, at pp. 70–1.

78. Ward, *Networks of Empire*, pp. 32, 34.

79. Boomgaard, 'Male–Male Sex, Bestiality and Incest', pp. 142–5.

80. Boon, *'Dien godlosen hoop van menschen'*, p. 191.

81. T. M. Aerts, '"Het verfoeijelijke crimen van sodomie": sodomie op VOC-schepen in de 18e eeuw', *Leidschaft* (Apr. 1988), pp. 5–21, at pp. 12 (totals), 12–17 (Mediterranean examples); Boon, *'Dien godlosen hoop van menschen'*, p. 192 (1729, 1733; the term 'Indian' here could cover a range of southern and south-eastern Asian peoples). Jan Oosterhoff discusses several 18th-century cases heard at Cape Town, some of which may have involved colonists there rather than mariners. At least one (in 1753) related to seemingly consensual sex—mutual masturbation—between a Dutchman and a slave from southern India: 'Sodomy at Sea and at the Cape of Good Hope during the Eighteenth Century', in K. Gerard and G. Hekma, eds., *The Pursuit of Sodomy: Male Homosexuality in Renaissance and Enlightenment Europe* (New York, 1989), pp. 229–35, at p. 231.

82. C. R. Boxer, *Race Relations in the Portuguese Colonial Empire, 1415–1825* (Oxford, 1963), p. 59 (norm); C. Nocentelli, 'The Erotics of Mercantile Imperialism: Cross-Cultural Requitedness in the Early Modern Period', *Journal for Early Modern Cultural Studies*, 8 (2008), pp. 134–52, at pp. 139–40 (incentives).

83. A. S. Willis, 'Abusing Hugh Davis: Determining the Crime in a Seventeenth-Century American Morality Case', *JHS*, 28 (2019), pp. 117–47, at pp. 118 (statute), 133 (1640s, 1650s).

84. Ibid.

85. T. A. Foster, 'The Sexual Abuse of Black Men under American Slavery', *JHS*, 20 (2011), pp. 445–64, at pp. 453–4 (referring to the planter Thomas Thistlewood).

86. The National Archives, Kew, HCA 1/64, item 17, fos. [1r–2v].

87. Ibid., fo. [3r–v].

88. Ibid., fo. [4r].

CHAPTER 19

1. Trumbach, 'Transformation of Sodomy', p. 832 ('Europeans before...'); Trumbach, 'Renaissance Sodomy', p. 49 ('In the...It is...').

2. R. Trumbach, 'Sodomitical Subcultures, Sodomitical Roles, and the Gender Revolution of the Eighteenth Century: The Recent Historiography', in R. P. Maccubbin, ed., *'Tis Nature's Fault: Unauthorized Sexuality during the Enlightenment* (Cambridge, 1987), pp. 109–21, at p. 118 ('a profound...'); Trumbach, *Sex and the Gender Revolution*, p. 6 (1690s); R. Trumbach, 'Modern

Sodomy: The Origins of Homosexuality, 1700–1800', in M. Cook, ed., *A Gay History of Britain: Love and Sex between Men since the Middle Ages* (Oxford, 2007), pp. 77–105, at p. 77 ('a new...'); R. Trumbach, 'Gender and the Homosexual Role in Modern Western Culture: The 18th and 19th Centuries Compared', in D. Altman et al., *Which Homosexuality?* (Amsterdam, 1989), pp. 149–69, at p. 150 (1700, 'it is...').

3. Trumbach, 'Modern Sodomy', p. 77 ('England, France...'); Trumbach, 'Gender and the Homosexual Role', p. 150 ('fully established...'); Trumbach, 'Transformation of Sodomy', p. 833 (Central Europe, 'but it...').

4. Trumbach, 'Modern Sodomy', p. 78 ('entirely with...', 'Half of...'); Trumbach, 'Gender and the Homosexual Role', p. 163 ('the men...'); R. Trumbach, 'The Birth of the Queen: Sodomy and the Emergence of Gender Equality in Modern Culture, 1660–1750', in M. B. Duberman, M. Vicinus and G. Chauncey, eds., *Hidden from History: Reclaiming the Gay and Lesbian Past*, pp. 129–40, at p. 130 ('at the...').

5. Trumbach, 'Birth of the Queen', p. 130 ('either seduced...'); Trumbach, 'Gender and the Homosexual Role', p. 153 ('the presumption...', 'it seems...').

6. R. Trumbach, 'London's Sodomites: Homosexual Behavior and Western Culture in the 18th Century', *Journal of Social History*, 11:2 (1977), pp. 1–33, at p. 18 ('the majority...'); Trumbach, 'Birth of the Queen', p. 130 ('markedly effeminate...'); R. Trumbach, 'England', in W. Dynes, ed., *Encyclopedia of Homosexuality*, 2 vols. (New York, 1990), i, pp. 354–8, at p. 356 ('Adult males...'); R. Trumbach, 'The Heterosexual Male in Eighteenth-Century London and his Queer Interactions', in K. O'Donnell and M. O'Rourke, eds., *Love, Sex, Intimacy, and Friendship between Men, 1550–1800* (Basingstoke, 2003), pp. 99–127, at p. 105 ('an effeminate...').

7. Trumbach, 'Modern Sodomy', p. 88 ('were able...'); R. Trumbach, 'Are Modern Western Lesbian Women and Gay Men a Third Gender?', in M. Duberman, ed., *A Queer World: The Center for Lesbian and Gay Studies Reader* (New York, 1997), pp. 87–99, at p. 91 ('almost all...'); Trumbach, 'Gender and the Homosexual Role', pp. 153–4 (transvestite, *berdache*, 'the sodomite...').

8. Trumbach, 'Are Modern Western Lesbian Women?', p. 92 ('allowed sodomites...').

9. Trumbach, 'Birth of the Queen', pp. 137 (active role), 139 ('after 1700...'); Trumbach, 'Heterosexual Male', p. 105 ('perhaps mainly'); Trumbach, 'Modern Sodomy', p. 86 ('It is...').

10. Trumbach, 'Birth of the Queen', p. 140 (gender roles, equality); Trumbach, 'Heterosexual Male', p. 104 (equality); Trumbach, 'Modern Sodomy, p. 78 ('No one...').

11. As Trumbach himself has acknowledged, the first pioneer here was Mary McIntosh, who in an influential article challenged the claims of Foucault and others that modern homosexuality emerged only in the late 19th century; it was McIntosh who argued for a turning-point around 1700. See her 'The Homosexual Role', *Social Problems*, 16 (1968), pp. 182–92.

12. See for example van der Meer, *Sodoms zaad*, pp. 280–3, 319–20, 448; Bleys, *Geography of Perversion*, pp. 82–3. Cf. also its basic acceptance in one of the best recent studies of early modern sex in England: F. Dabhoiwala, *The Origins of Sex: A History of the First Sexual Revolution* (London, 2012), p. 128.

13. J. Cady, '"Masculine Love", Renaissance Writing, and the "New Invention" of Homosexuality', *JH*, 26 (1992), pp. 9–40. Similar objections have been raised, more tentatively, by Gary Ferguson: see *Same-Sex Marriage*, pp. 154–8.

14. Norton, *Mother Clap*, pp. 107 ('around 1700...'), 108 ('The "shift"...', 'all of...', surveillance), 109 ('fully grown...').

15. See T. C. Curtis and W. A. Speck, 'The Societies for the Reformation of Manners: A Case Study in the Theory and Practice of Moral Reform', *Literature and History*, 3 (1976), pp. 45–64, esp. pp. 46 ('to consult...'), 47 (16 in 1694); F. Dabhoiwala, 'Sex and Societies for Moral Reform, 1688–1800', *Journal of British Studies*, 46 (2007), pp. 290–319, esp. pp. 297–9 (Tower Hamlets, national and international expansion), 300, 303–4 (informers, agents); Norton, *Mother Clap*, p. 91 (costs, government); Craig, 'Movement', p. 65 (791). Craig's dissertation remains a fundamental study, though superseded on some points by Dabhoiwala's article.

16. Norton, *Mother Clap*, p. 105 (94,322); Dabhoiwala, 'Sex and Societies' (nearly 2,000).

17. Craig, 'Movement', pp. 95–6.

18. McFarlane, *The Sodomite*, pp. 147–50 (prurient); Norton, *Mother Clap*, p. 82 (n. 34) (accurate); Craig, 'Movement', pp. 96–9 (widely discussed, Castlehaven); Herrup, *House in Gross Disorder*, pp. 134–5 (Castlehaven).

19. Anon., *The Sodomites Shame and Doom*, p. 2.

20. Cited in Craig, 'Movement', p. 99.

21. See <https://www.oldbaileyonline.org>.

22. See Cocks, *Visions of Sodom*, pp. 107–11, 115, 119–22 (attempted sodomy, sodomitical assault); N. M. Goldsmith, *The Worst of Crimes: Homosexuality and the Law in Eighteenth-Century London* (London, 1998), p. 40 (discretion); on 'assault' see also Norton, *Mother Clap*, p. 170 (noting that in consensual cases each partner could be charged separately with committing an assault on the other).

23. Anon., *The Tryal and Conviction of Several Reputed Sodomites, before the Right Honourable the Lord Mayor, and Recorder of London, at Guild-Hall, the 20th Day of October, 1707* (London, 1707). Possibly this was the same William Huggins who, 23 years later, was found being sodomized in St Paul's Cathedral and convicted at the Old Bailey: <https://www.oldbaileyonline.org/browse.jsp?id=t17301204-22-off114&div=t17301204-22#highlight>.

24. Norton, *Mother Clap*, p. 71. He suggests the figure of 'nearly 100' for the whole year, but the evidence for that, beyond a phrase in a satirical poem, is not clear.

25. Ibid., pp. 118, 138–9.

26. 'Proceedings of the Old Bailey, 1674–1913' <https://www.oldbaileyonline.org>, 11 July 1726: <https://www.oldbaileyonline.org/browse.jsp?div=t17260711-77>.

27. See above, pp. 238, 242–3.

28. Above, pp. 250, 251, 260. There may well have been some quantitative change over that period, as London grew and Puritan moral standards weakened; but the point made here is about the nature of the behaviour itself.

29. Rictor Norton points out that several of the traditional low-life locations, where same-sex encounters were also sought, centred on what had been the 'sanctuaries' of mediaeval monastic houses: Southwark, Whitefriars, Holborn, the Savoy and Covent Garden (*Mother Clap*, p. 116). These had long been sites of female prostitution too.

30. K. Briggs, 'OE and ME *cunte* in Place Names', *Journal of the English Place Name Society*, 41 (2009), pp. 26–39; Trumbach, 'Sodomitical Assaults', p. 425 (quotation).

31. Norton, *Mother Clap*, p. 229 (c.50); Anon., ed., *Select Trials, for Murders, Robberies, Rapes, Sodomy, Coining, Frauds and Other Offences, at the Sessions-House in the Old-Bailey*, 2nd edn., 4 vols. (London, 1742), i, p. 161 (quotation)

32. Norton, *Mother Clap*, p. 230.

33. Netta Goldsmith, selecting only Old Bailey cases from the period 1730–50, notes that the greatest number of prosecutions for sodomy or attempted sodomy were brought by teenaged boys: *Worst of Crimes*, p. 68.

34. Anon., ed., *Select Trials*, i, pp. 158–60.

35. Ibid., i, p. 329. For further examples of attempted seductions of boys (where the boys' reactions covered the whole spectrum from complete incomprehension to understanding), see R. Trumbach, 'Sodomitical Assaults, Gender Role, and Sexual Development in Eighteenth-Century London', in K. Gerard and G. Hekma, eds., *The Pursuit of Sodomy: Male Homosexuality in Renaissance and Enlightenment Europe* (New York, 1989), pp. 407–29, at pp. 409–22.

36. Gilbert, 'Buggery and the British Navy', pp. 75 (boys), 79 (1703–10), 86–8 (wartime, indiscipline: Britain was at war from 1701 to 1714); N. A. M. Rodger, *The Wooden World: An Anatomy of the Georgian Navy* (London, 1986), pp. 80–1 (quotation).

37. Norton, *Mother Clap*, p. 69.

38. Anon., *A Full and True Account of the Discovery and Apprehending a Notorious Gang of Sodomites in St James's* (London, 1709).

39. E. Ward, *The Secret History of Clubs* (London, 1709), pp. 284–8.

40. Norton, *Mother Clap*, p. 87.

41. *Oxford English Dictionary*, 'molly', *n.1*, 2 (citing Ward's *London Terrae-filius*, no. 5.11); 1 Cor. 6: 9 (St Paul); Anon., *Dolly and Molly: Or, The Two Country Damosels Fortunes at London* (London, n.d. [1670–96]). In that ballad, Dolly remains virtuous and is eventually happily married; Molly is seduced by 'a kiss and a Guiny' from a young man, and ends up as a whore.

42. Norton, *Mother Clap*, pp. 87–9 (p. 88: quotation), 94–5, 101 (trials).

43. R. Norton, 'Homosexuality', in J. Peakman, ed., *A Cultural History of Sexuality in the Enlightenment* (London, 2011), pp. 57–83, at p. 65.

44. Nationaal Archief, The Hague, Hof van Holland, MS 5420.3, 'Informaties inzake een aantal personen te den Haag schuldig aan crimen nefandum, 1730',

examination of Dirk van Wanrooij, 31 May 1730, fo. [3v] ('persoonen hem onbekendt, die hy van agteren heeft gebruykt').

45. Norton, *Mother Clap*, pp. 92–3, 96 (quotation).

46. Trumbach, 'Heterosexual Male', p. 110.

47. Norton, *Mother Clap*, p. 159; the fullest discussion of Cooper's case is Goldsmith, *Worst of Crimes*, pp. 58–65.

48. T. Castle, 'The Culture of Travesty: Sexuality and Masquerade in Eighteenth-Century England', in G. S. Rousseau and R. Porter, eds., *Sexual Underworlds of the Enlightenment* (Manchester, 1987), pp. 156–80.

49. Norton, *Mother Clap*, pp. 149, 156–7.

50. Ibid., pp. 147–9.

51. Ibid., pp. 148 ('cement relations...'), 162 ('self-identification...', 'vigorous and...'). Cameron McFarlane suggests that the imitation of women was satirical and therefore misogynistic (*The Sodomite*, pp. 66–8); but this interpretation depends on passing comments by Ned Ward, whose knowledge of molly house life may have been superficial at best.

52. Norton, *Mother Clap*, pp. 154–6 (mock births, cheese); D. Rollison, 'Property, Ideology and Popular Culture in a Gloucestershire Village, 1660–1740', *Past & Present*, 93 (1981), pp. 70–97, at pp. 72–3.

53. Cf. Goldsmith, *Worst of Crimes*, p. 93; K. M. Phillips and B. Reay, *Sex before Sexuality: A Premodern History* (London, 2011), pp. 84–5.

54. S. Poole, '"Bringing Great Shame upon This City": Sodomy, the Courts and the Civic Idiom in Eighteenth-Century Bristol', *Urban History*, 34 (2007), pp. 114–26, at p. 118.

55. Dabhoiwala, 'Sex and Societies', pp. 311–14 (resistance); F. Azfar, 'Genealogy of an Execution: The Sodomite, the Bishop, and the Anomaly of 1726', *Journal of British Studies*, 51 (2012), pp. 568–93 (1726 pardon attempt; p. 574: 'outstandingly draconian').

56. Goldsmith, *Worst of Crimes*, p. 9 (1738); Dabhoiwala, 'Sex and Societies', p. 307 (system strengthened); Norton, *Mother Clap*, p. 334 (quotation).

57. Poole, '"Bringing Great Shame"', pp. 119, 122. Of the 58, 6 were convicted of the capital felony, and 16 of the misdemeanour; of the 22, 1 was convicted of the capital felony and 3 of the misdemeanour. Norton describes the SRM as 'particularly active' in Bristol: *Mother Clap*, p. 113.

58. For elements of the debate see Trumbach, 'Birth of the Queen', pp. 133–5; L. Senelick, 'Mollies or Men of Mode? Sodomy and the Eighteenth-Century London Stage', *JHS*, 1 (1990), pp. 33–67; Haggerty, *Men in Love*, pp. 44–80. The best discussion is S. O'Driscoll, 'The Molly and the Fop: Untangling Effeminacy in the Eighteenth Century', in C. Mounsey, *Developments in the Histories of Sexualities: In Search of the Normal, 1600–1800* (Lewisburg, PA, 2013), pp. 145–72.

59. See P. Carter, *Men and the Emergence of Polite Society, Britain 1660–1800* (Harlow, 2001), pp. 138–56.

60. On Hervey see Norton, *Mother Clap*, pp. 255–64.

CHAPTER 20

1. P. Piasenza, 'Juges, lieutenants de police et bourgeois à Paris aux XVIIᵉ et XVIIIᵉ siècles', *Annales. Histoire, sciences sociales*, 45:5 (1990), pp. 1189–1215, at pp. 1194–9; A. Taeger, 'Die Karrieren von Sodomiten in Paris während des 18. Jahrhunderts', in W. Schmale, ed., *MannBilder: ein Lese- und Quellenbuch zur historischen Männerforschung* (Berlin, 1998), pp. 113–29, at pp. 121–2; Taeger, *Intime Machtverhältnisse*, pp. 96–9, 103–5; Pastorello, *Sodome à Paris*, pp. 88–9.

2. M. Rey, 'Parisian Homosexuals Create a Lifestyle, 1700–1750: The Police Archives', *Eighteenth-Century Life*, 9 (1985), pp. 179–91, at pp. 179–80; M. Sibalis, 'Homosexuality in Early Modern France', in K. O'Donnell and M. O'Rourke, eds., *Queer Masculinities, 1550–1800: Siting Same-Sex Desire in the Early Modern World* (Basingstoke, 2006), pp. 211–31, at pp. 217–19; Pastorello, *Sodome à Paris*, pp. 61–2.

3. Bibliothèque de l'Arsenal, Paris, MSS 10255, fo. 21r (Dupuis); 10256, fo. 77r ('asseure que c'est la p.ʳᵉ fois cepend.ᵗ il sçait toutes les manoeuvres des Infames'); 10257, fo. 84r (Desprez: 'a fait plusieurs tours a tour de moy, ma donné un coup de coude, et m'a fait signe auec son mouchoir de le suiure'). Cf. also Rey, 'Parisian Homosexuals', p. 181; Sibalis, 'Homosexuality', pp. 219–20.

4. Bibliothèque de l'Arsenal, Paris, MS 10256, fos. 22r ('en luy souhaitant le bon soir et luy demandant sans autre complim.ᵗ s'il bandoit voulant luy mettre la main dans la Culotte'), 46r ('a qui il a dit quil bandoit et voulu luy mettre la main dans la Culotte pour voir s'il étoit de même').

5. Rey, 'Parisian Homosexuals', p. 181 (exceptional case).

6. Bibliothèque de l'Arsenal, Paris, MS 10255, fo. 145v ('que pour luy il aimoit le changement tantost d'une façon tantost d'un [*sic*] autre').

7. Rey gives statistical analyses of propositions in sample years ('Parisian Homosexuals', p. 183), but misses at least one passive-only request (Bibliothèque de l'Arsenal, Paris, MS 10254, *fiche* of 4 May 1723, Nicolas Debrie, who said 'people did it to him sometimes, but he didn't do it to others' ('que l'on luy metoit quelques fois, mais qu'il ne le metoit pas')), and interprets as 'kissing' what were more probably references to fellatio. For a range of examples see the reports printed in C. Courouve, *Les Gens de la manchette* (Paris, 1981).

8. M. Rey, 'Police et sodomie à Paris au XVIIIᵉ siècle: du péché au désordre', *Revue d'histoire moderne et contemporaine*, 29 (1982), pp. 113–24, at p. 122 ('de ce...').

9. Bibliothèque de l'Arsenal, Paris, MSS 10254, *fiche* of 28 Oct. 1723 ('tous les plaisirs de la Sod.', 'il n[']aimoit nullement les femmes, me disant...qu'il connoissoit plusieurs Jeunes Gens qui estoient de ce Goust la'); 10257, fo. 76v ('il n'auoit Jammais eu D'Inclination que celle la, qu'il n'auoit Jammais aimé les femmes, et que leur compagnie même luy étoit a charge').

10. Bibliothèque de l'Arsenal, Paris, MSS 10254, *fiche* of 26 Oct. 1723 ('ou le garçon quy les seruit sestoit trouué du meme gout, que luy...le mit au Page et le page au garçon touts les trois a la fois'); 10255, fo. 22r ('sept B...les plus rudes de Paris'). This was Louis, duc de Villars-Brancas (1663–1739).

11. Bibliothèque de l'Arsenal, Paris, MS 10255, fo. 21v (Richelieu); 10254, *fiche* of 14 July 1723 ('un prince allemant, qui étoit tres Genereux').

12. Bibliothèque de l'Arsenal, Paris, MSS 10254, *fiche* of 9 Sept. 1723 ('pourueu qu'il y ait de l'argent à gagnier'; 'qu'il lauoit mis Il y a quelques Jours a un homme de Condition qui luy auoit donné 7^{ll} 10^s mais que cest sorte de rencontres estoit rare'); 10256, fos. 22v (26 sous), 34v (26 sous), 67v (40 sous); 10257, fo. 44r (2 louis); J. J. McCusker, *Money and Exchange in Europe and America, 1600–1775: A Handbook* (Chapel Hill, NC, 1978), pp. 9, 11, 88, 96 (values); J. Burnett, *A History of the Cost of Living* (Harmondsworth, 1969), pp. 164–5 (1s.).

13. Bibliothèque de l'Arsenal, Paris, MS 10256, fos. 19r–v (marquis), 26r–27r (*chevalier*), 30r–v (marquis), 44r–45r (comte d'Autry: 'et qu'en s'en allant chez luy il luy mettroit, que demain il luy mettroit dans la bouche et après demain dans le Cul'; these details came from subsequent questioning of the boy, who was an impoverished student at the Collège des quatre nations), 67r–v (comte).

14. Ibid., fos. 26–27r ('et menacé le dit Sr Haimier de le faire chasser de sa charge disant au surplus qu'il vouloit f... dans le milieu des Thuilleries sans que personne osat l'en en empescher').

15. Pastorello, *Sodome à Paris*, pp. 48 (servants), 51 (clergy), 55 (artisans etc.); Rey, 'Parisian Homosexuals', p. 187.

16. Rey, 'Police et sodomie', p. 119; Pastorello, *Sodome à Paris*, p. 55.

17. The age of the *mouche* is very seldom stated. In one case, a man said that he had seen the *mouche* in the park ten years earlier, which suggests that he was now in his later 20s at least; in another the *mouche* recorded that, asked his age by the man who approached him, he said 25: Bibliothèque de l'Arsenal, Paris, MS 10255, fos. 55r (later 20s), 145r (25).

18. Above, pp. 238–9.

19. Taeger, 'Die Karrieren von Sodomiten', p. 115 (serious offence); Coward, 'Attitudes to Homosexuality', p. 235 ('policy of...', punishments); Sibalis, 'Homosexuality', p. 221 (punishments).

20. P. d'Estrées, *Les Infâmes sous l'ancien régime: documents historiques recueillis à la Bibliothèque Nationale et à l'Arsenal* (Paris, 1902), p. 20 (Bicêtre); Pastorello, *Sodome à Paris*, pp. 99–100 (Bicêtre); for a study based on 60 cases of imprisonment in the Bicêtre by *lettres de cachet*, see Merrick, 'Sodomitical Inclinations'.

21. Above, pp. 248–9.

22. 'Hernandez', ed., *Les Procès de sodomie*, pp. 88–188, esp. pp. 89 (16), 96 (false title), 99 (strong young man), 111–13 (14), 112 (Italians), 132 (10–11), 139 (sex with servant), 149–52 (7), 169 (urchins), 183 (opium), 186 (14), 187 (10–11), 188 (7, clergyman). See also d'Estrées, *Les Infâmes*, pp. 26–37.

23. Coward, 'Attitudes to Homosexuality', pp. 236–7; on the 1722 scandal, involving six young aristocrats engaging in mutual sodomy in the park at Versailles, see D. Godard, *L'Amour philosophique: l'homosexualité masculine au siècle des lumières* (Paris, 2005), pp. 130–1.

24. R. Hérault, *Jugement à mort en dernier ressort, rendu par Monsieur Herault, Lieutenant general de police de la ville, prevosté et vicomté de Paris* (Paris, 1726) (placard). There

is some evidence of a deterrent effect: in June 1737 a 38-year-old man told a *mouche* that 'after a man was burnt for sodomy in Paris, he didn't want to do anything more than masturbate, and have someone masturbate him; he said it had been the man called Deschauffours, and he had known him' (Bibliothèque de l'Arsenal, Paris, MS 10257, fo. 74v: 'depuis qu'il y auoit un homme de Brule a paris, pour la Sod^e ..., qu'il ne veut plus que Branler, et se faire branler le v ..., que cestoit le nommé Du Chaufour, qu'il le connoissoit').

25. E.-J.-F. Barbier, *Chronique de la Régence et du règne de Louis XV (1718–1763)*, 8 vols. (Paris, 1858), i, p. 425 ('n'étant pas possible de punir tous ceux qui étoient déclarés, parce que cela feroit trop de fracas', 'illustrer ce crime et le rendre plus commun, la plupart de ce peuple même ne sachant pas ce que c'est').

26. Taeger, 'Die Karrieren von Sodomiten', pp. 128–9; Taeger, *Intime Machtverhältnisse*, pp. 55–64 (p. 56: not divulged; p. 64: trial statistics); Merrick and Ragan, *Homosexuality in Early Modern France*, pp. 77–9.

27. Barbier, *Chronique de la Régence*, i, p. 425 ('car, en général, ce n'est pas là l'amusement du petit bourgeois').

28. Rey, 'Parisian Homosexuals', p. 186; Courouve, *Les Gens de la manchette*, no. 27 ('tous ont eu affaire les uns avec les autres soit dans ce cabaret soit après en être sortis'; the precise kind of sex was not specified).

29. Ferguson, *Same-Sex Marriage*, pp. 144 (translation; 'il y en a qui mettent des serviettes sur leurs testes, contrefont les femmes, faisant des minauderies et des reverences comm'elles... quand il s'y trouve quelque nouveau jeune homme on l'appelle la mariée et, dans ce cas, il devient l'object des complaisances d'un chacun'), 145–6 (translation; 'dans lesdites assemblées il s'y en est trouvé qui ont contrefait les manieres des femmes').

30. Rey, 'Parisian Homosexuals', p. 188.

31. Bibliothèque de l'Arsenal, Paris, MSS 10254, undated petition (1723) for release of a lackey called Chamousset, saying that he had been 'arrested for what people call *la Manchette*' ('pris pour ce que l'on apelle la Manchette'); 10256, fo. 88r, letter of complaint from François Bodin (May 1725) about the arrest of his lackey 'as a criminal of *La Manchette*' ('comme criminel de La Manchette'); cf. also C. Courouve, *Vocabulaire de l'homosexualité masculine* (Paris, 1985), pp. 156–8.

32. Ferguson, *Same-Sex Marriage*, pp. 146–53 (p. 147: 'parties de plaisir', 'parties de cabaret', 'chacun s'habilla differament et prirent des noms convenables à leurs habits de masque'; p. 148: 'Mme la Générale', 'Mr le Grand-Maître').

33. Rey, 'Parisian Homosexuals', p. 187.

34. Ibid., pp. 185–6.

35. van der Meer, *Sodoms zaad*, pp. 187 (1710), 223 (Rotterdam, Amsterdam), 224 ('geselschap'), 461 (blackmail; one was executed); D. J. Noordam, 'Sodomy in the Dutch Republic, 1600–1725', in K. Gerard and G. Hekma, eds., *The Pursuit of Sodomy: Male Homosexuality in Renaissance and Enlightenment Europe* (New York, 1989), pp. 207–28, at p. 214 (Amsterdam).

36. van der Meer, *Sodoms zaad*, pp. 248–9; Boon, *'Dien godlosen hoop'*, pp. 95, 110 (bumping). Exceptionally, one person tried in 1730 described a much more

organized form of sexual behaviour in the wood on the edge of The Hague: up to 20 men would gather on a summer evening 'around a great tree', and then 'make a selection' of their sexual partners, with one of the upper-class participants having the first choice: Nationaal Archief, The Hague, Hof van Holland, MS 5420.3, examination of Piet van Steyn, 10 June 1730, fo. [2r–v] ('omtrendt een grooten boom', 'te maaken een verkiesingh').

37. van der Meer, *Sodoms zaad*, pp. 223 (1715), 285 (1717).
38. Ibid., pp. 242–3 (Dutch cities), 285 (1717); Trumbach, 'Birth of the Queen', p. 136 (London); Norton, *Mother Clap*, pp. 72, 102, 116–17 (London).
39. Above, pp. 242–3.
40. Puff, *Sodomy in Reformation Germany*, pp. 23–4 (1400); Reinle, 'Zur Rechtspraxis gegenüber Homosexuellen', p. 312 (1471); Hergemöller, 'Das Verhör des Franz von Alsten', p. 46 (1536); Lau, '"Da erhob sich ein gross Geschrei"', p. 12 (Zurich).
41. Boon, *'Dien godlosen hoop'*, pp. 37–45.
42. van der Meer, *Sodoms zaad*, pp. 14–15; Boon, *'Dien godlosen hoop'*, pp. 62–3.
43. F. J. A. M. van der Helm, *Gesodomieter in Den Haag: over homofilie en de homovervolging in Den Haag anno 1730* (The Hague, 2011), pp. 79–80 (Wilsma, noting on p. 79 his probable baptism in Apr. 1707—hence he was 22 when arrested, not 23 as he said), 89–91 (Backer), 93–4 (Backer and Wilsma); Boon, *'Dien godlosen hoop'*, pp. 99 (Backer), 188 (three years older); Nationaal Archief, The Hague, Hof van Holland MS 5661, Register van de crimineele sententien, July 1729–Oct. 1731, fos. 47r–48v (sentence, 'vuÿl gewin').
44. Boon, *'Dien godlosen hoop'*, pp. 108–10; Hof van Holland, MS 5420.3, examination of Zacharias Wilsma, 26 June 1730, fo. [1r–v] (Gurck account of Hague).
45. van der Helm, *Gesodomieter*, pp. 94–8; Boon, *'Dien godloosen hoop'*, pp. 99–100. 'Seneschal' here is a rough translation of *drost*, a senior administrative officer.
46. Boon, *'Dien godlosen hoop'*, pp. 127–8, 370(n. 42).
47. Ibid., pp. 145–53 (decree), 255–8 (Groningen).
48. See G. M. Cohen Tervaart, *De grietman Rudolf de Mepsche: historisch-juridische beschouwingen over een reeks crimineele processen, gevoerd in 1731 in den rechtstoel Oosterdeel-Langewold* (The Hague, 1921), noting that, notwithstanding his arbitrary misuse of power, de Mepsche did make use of the services of at least four legal advisers: pp. 61–2, 132–3; Boon, *'Dien godlosen hoop'*, pp. 251 (21), 260–90 (p. 285: 24 Sept., detachment), 318 (died from torture).
49. Nationaal Archief, The Hague, Hof van Holland, MS 5420.3, examination of Hermanus Moljon, 26 May 1730, fo. [2v] ('dat de Kruysbaan onder dat volk werdt genoemdt'); a sentence issued on 5 Oct. 1731 said that the Voorhout was known as the 'grand salon', another nearby street as the 'little salon', and both together as the 'cruising route' (MS 5661, fo. 104v: 'groote Zaal', 'Kleÿn Sael', 'Kruÿsbaan').
50. van der Meer, *Sodoms zaad*, p. 224 ('het welke weeckelyx by beurten aan malcanders huizen bij een quaam en daar den anderen oneerlyck behandelden').

51. Boon, *'Dien godlosen hoop'*, pp. 45 (Utrecht), 130 (Amsterdam, list), 188–9 (Leeuwarden).

52. Above, pp. 241–2, 244; Puff, *Sodomy in Reformation Germany*, p. 29.

53. van der Meer, *Sodoms zaad*, pp. 232 (*lolhuizen*, prostitution etc.), 246–7 (Utrecht, Amsterdam), 254, 255(n. 259) (uncertain derivation). What is here called informal prostitution was managed, for example, by Jan Schut in The Hague, who allowed his house to be used for sex. He had no regular prostitutes there, and no tariff, but would ask any man who received payment there to give him half, or at least a quarter, of the amount: Nationaal Archief, The Hague, Hof van Holland, MS 5420.3, examination of Piet van Steyn, 1 June 1730, fo. [2r] (½); examination of Jan Schut, 2 June 1730, fo. [2r] (c.¼).

54. van der Meer, *Sodoms zaad*, p. 223 (*vlaggeman*); Boon, *'Dien godlosen hoop'*, p. 211 (*een glas ..., cousijn, neef, nicht*).

55. van der Meer, *Sodoms zaad*, pp. 254 (*op sijn ...*), 257 (nicknames). Van der Meer notes (pp. 254–5) one comment by prostitutes in the late 1740s, using a similar phrase to describe the speech of their pimp and his friend, and one description of effeminate speech from 1776.

56. Ibid., pp. 247 (hats, aprons), 256 (de Berger, Hague *lolhuis*); on de Berger's *modus operandi* see Boon, *'Dien godlosen hoop'*, pp. 93–5.

57. Nationaal Archief, The Hague, Hof van Holland, MS 5420.3, examination of Dirk van Wanrooij, 31 May 1730, fos. [2r–3v]; Boon, *'Dien godlosen hoop'*, pp. 95 (de Berger), 115 (Wanrooij) 161–2 (Irish news); van der Meer, *Sodoms zaad*, pp. 239 (Wanrooij), 249 (de Berger), 298 (Backer), 299(n. 106) (Backer); van der Helm, *Gesodomieter*, pp. 188–9 (Wanrooij); Goldsmith, *Worst of Crimes*, p. 56 (pillory case); G. S. Rousseau, 'The Pursuit of Homosexuality in the Eighteenth Century: "Utterly Confused Category" and/or Rich Repository?', in R. P. Maccubbin, ed., *'Tis Nature's Fault: Unauthorized Sexuality during the Enlightenment* (Cambridge, 1987) pp. 132–68, at p. 154 (2,000 articles).

58. I. Schöffer, 'Conclusie', in L. J. Boon, *'Dien godlosen hoop van menschen'. Verfolging van homoseksuelen in de Republiek in de jaren dertig van de achttiende eeuw*, ed. I. Schöffer et al. (Amsterdam, 1997) pp. 327–59, at p. 327 (totals arrested, executed), 332 (400); Boon, *'Dien godlosen hoop'*, p. 204 (Holland, *in absentia*).

59. van der Meer, *Sodoms zaad*, pp. 469–79 (cases, by date).

60. Lau, '"Da erhob sich ein gross Geschrei"', pp. 10 (100), 12 (baths, etc.), 14 (1630s, no molly houses), 18 (Winterthur).

61. J. Michelsen, '"Wider die Natur": gleichgeschlechtliche Sexualität im früh-neuzeitlichen Hamburg', in J. A. Steiger and S. Richter, eds., *Hamburg: eine Metropolregion zwischen Früher Neuzeit und Aufklärung* (Berlin, 2012), pp. 805–23, at pp. 809–10 ('keine speziell von Sodomitern frequentierten Lokale ... auch keine festen Treffpunkte wie Grünanlagen, öffentliche Toiletten oder bestimmte Kirchen'), 810 (1760).

62. [J. Friedel,] *Briefe über die Galanterien von Berlin, auf einer Reise gesammelt von einem österreichischen Offizier* (Gotha, 1782), pp. 146–87; J. D. Steakley, 'Sodomy in Enlightenment Prussia: From Execution to Suicide', in K. Gerard and

G. Hekma, eds., *The Pursuit of Sodomy: Male Homosexuality in Renaissance and Enlightenment Europe* (New York, 1989), pp. 163–75, at pp. 168–70 (treated as genuine); P. Derks, *Die Schande der heiligen Päderastie. Homosexualität und Öffentlichkeit in der deutschen Literatur, 1750–1850* (Berlin, 1990), pp. 92–3, 103–5 (fictitious); Michelsen, ' "Wider die Natur" ', p. 810(n. 12) (fictitious).

63. Silverstolpe, 'Inledning', p. 17.

64. Träskman, 'Om "menniskior" ', pp. 248–52 (1734 code), 255 ('Lagen byggde ju trots allt överlag på en rätt pragmatisk uppfattning om sexualiteten i samhället. De sexuella handlingar som belades med straff var sådana som kunde ge upphov till avkomma'). Omitting a direct reference to sodomy from the law-code did not mean decriminalizing it; two men were executed for it in 1734, and two more in 1735 (Liliequist, 'State Policy', p. 20).

65. W. Sjögren, ed., *Förarbetena till Sveriges Rikes lag, 1686–1736*, 8 vols. (Uppsala, 1901–9), ii, p. 160 ('At införa om de flere sodomistiske synder, synes ingalunda rådeligit, utan bättre at förtijga som okunnige, och finna de wäl sitt straff, om det händer så illa, at de begås'); Liliequist, 'State Policy', pp. 18 (1699, translation), 19 (1713), 19–20 (1719).

66. Liliequist, 'State Policy', p. 21 (Denmark); Rian, 'Mellom straf og fortielse', p. 36 (Jutland case, where the younger man was freed and the older one was sentenced to 2 years' hard labour).

67. van der Meer, *Sodoms zaad*, p. 158 ('met de uiterste omzigtigheit behandelt opdat doch niemand weten zou, dat het geschieden kon'); Norton, *Mother Clap*, p. 77 (Defoe).

68. Boon, *'Dien godlosen hoop'*, p. 130 (Amsterdam).

69. Above, p. 361.

70. Michelsen, ' "Wider die Natur" ', p. 816 ('eine Menge Menschen und insonderheit die Jugend aus der glückseeligen Unwissenheit, dass sie höchstens den Nahmen der Sodomie kennen, mögte zu einer schädlichen Wissenschaft gelangen').

71. Above, pp. 263–4.

72. Boon, *'Dien godlosen hoop'*, pp. 192 (Cape Town), 289 (Faan); van Rossum, *Werkers van de wereld*, p. 329 ('dat bij aldien hij geweten hadde desen misdaad soo verfoeijlijk, en onnatuurlijk was, hij zijn lighaam nooijt daar meede soude hebben laten besmette', 'daar van geheel onkundig'). Cf. the case of another 15-year-old on a VOC ship in 1681, who was sentenced to death despite the plea of an observer that 'he had not known what wrong he did': Van der Stighelen and Roelens, 'Made in Heaven', p. 120 ('niet...hadde geweten wat quaet dat hy dede').

73. 'Hernandez', *Les Procès de sodomie*, p. 109.

74. Nationaal Archief, The Hague, Hof van Holland, MS 5420.3, examination of Wanrooij, 10 June 1730, fo. [1r] ('aan syn ouders niet en heeft geklaaght, alsoo hy meynde dat daar geen quaadt in was').

75. Norton, *Mother Clap*, pp. 199 ('at the...'), 200 (extortioners), 204 (1763).

76. <https://www.oldbaileyonline.org/browse.jsp?div=t17260711-77>

77. Liliequist, 'State Policy', p. 25 (captain); S. S. LeJacq, 'Buggery's Travels: Royal Navy Sodomy on Ship and Shore in the Long Eighteenth Century', *Journal for Maritime Research*, 17:2 (2015), pp. 103–16, at p. 103 (carpenter).

78. van der Meer, *Sodoms zaad*, pp. 194–5 (1757–9, dreams), 315 (David), 316 ('hem van natuuren eygen was', 'overgeërft').

79. Ibid., pp. 193 (not a sin), 314 (Leviticus), 314–15 (Sodom); Boon, *'Dien godlosen hoop'*, p. 233 (Israel).

80. Amiel, ed., *Lettres de Madame*, p. 312 ('n'était un péché que tant que le monde n'était pas peuplé').

81. [A. Radicati,] *A Philosophical Dissertation upon Death, Composed for the Consolation of the Unhappy* [trans. J. Morgan] (London, 1732), pp. 29–31 (moral notions, Cretans), 39 (quotation); Goldsmith, *Worst of Crimes*, p. 18 (custody).

82. C. Lauriol, *La Beaumelle: un protestant cévenol entre Montesquieu et Voltaire* (Geneva, 1978), p. 176 ('mettez à part l'Ecriture Sainte et Gomorrhe, vous verrez qu'il n'y a pas plus de mal dans la sodomie que dans le péché d'Onan. Si cette action était contraire à la Nature, elle serait condamnée par toutes les nations auxquelles la voix de la Nature se fait entendre; or elle n'est condamnée que par les Chrétiens').

83. H. Gladfelder, 'In Search of Lost Texts: Thomas Cannon's *Ancient and Modern Pederasty Investigated and Exemplify'd*', *Eighteenth-Century Life*, 31 (2007), pp. 22–38, at pp. 26–8 (printing, exile arrest); H. Gladfelder, 'The Indictment of John Purser, containing Thomas Cannon's *Ancient and Modern Pederasty Investigated and Exemplify'd*', *Eighteenth-Century Life*, 31 (2007), pp. 39–61, at pp. 40 ('Demolition...Prejudice'), 51 (rhapsodic), 52–3 (male beauty; women's psychology), 54 ('Unnatural...Desire'; depopulation), 55–6 (rhapsodic).

84. B. T. Ragan, 'The Enlightenment Confronts Homosexuality', in J. Merrick and B. T. Ragan, *Homosexuality in Modern France* (Oxford, 1996), pp. 8–29, at pp. 15 (Mirabeau), 21 (Helvétius), 24 (Diderot); M. Delon, trans. N. Stéphane, 'The Priest, the Philosopher, and Homosexuality in Enlightenment France', in R. P. Maccubbin, ed., *'Tis Nature's Fault: Unauthorized Sexuality during the Enlightenment* (Cambridge, 1987), pp. 122–31, at p. 126 (Diderot).

85. Godard, *L'Amour philosophique*, pp. 171 (Voltaire), 192 (Condorcet); Ragan, 'Enlightenment Confronts Homosexuality', p. 22 (Condorcet); Norton, *Mother Clap*, pp. 218–20 (Bentham).

86. J. Israel, *Enlightenment Contested: Philosophy, Modernity, and the Emancipation of Man, 1670–1752* (Oxford, 2006), p. 586.

87. Godard, *L'Amour philosophique*, pp. 183–4 (Montesquieu); Taeger, 'Die Karrieren von Sodomiten', pp. 120–1 (mainstream); Michelsen, 'Wider die Natur', p. 819 (mainstream); Bleibtreu-Ehrenberg, *Homosexualiät*, pp. 325–6 (new line).

88. M. D. Sibalis, 'The Regulation of Male Homosexuality in Revolutionary and Napoleonic France, 1789–1815', in J. Merrick and B. T. Ragan, *Homosexuality in Modern France* (Oxford, 1996), pp. 80–101, at p. 82.

89. Michelsen, 'Die Verfolgung', p. 244; see also Traeger, *Intime Machtverhältnisse*, pp. 152–3. The thinking expressed here seems quite separable in principle from

the sympathy which Frederick himself may have felt for sodomites, in view of his own intensely affectionate relationships with men and his taste for young male beauty. On his sexual orientation see W. Burgdorf, 'Königliche Liebschaften. Friedrich der Grosse und seine Männer', in N. Domeier and C. Mühling, eds., *Homosexualität am Hof: Praktiken und Diskurse vom Mittelalter bis heute* (Frankfurt, 2020), pp. 133–48.

90. [L. de Clapiers, marquis de Vauvenargues,] *Introduction à la connoissance de l'esprit humain, suivie de réflexions et de maximes* (Paris, 1746), p. 319, maxim 70 ('Ce qui n'offense pas la société n'est pas du ressort de sa justice').

91. Higgs, 'Lisbon', p. 126; Mott, '*Justitia et misericórdia*', p. 99 (statistics).

CHAPTER 21

1. See N. Malcolm, *Kosovo: A Short History* (London, 1998), p. 52.

2. E. Levin, *Sex and Society in the World of the Orthodox Slavs, 900–1700* (Ithaca, NY, 1989), pp. 197–202 (p. 201: quotations; p. 202: shaving); D. Healey, 'Moscow', in D. Higgs, ed., *Queer Sites: Gay Urban Histories since 1600* (London, 1999), pp. 38–60, at p. 41 (shaving).

3. G. Turberville, *Tragicall Tales Translated by Turberville in his Time of Troubles* (London, 1587), fo. 184r.

4. A. Olearius, *The Travels of Olearius in Seventeenth-Century Russia*, ed. and trans. S. H. Baron (Stanford, CA, 1967), p. 142.

5. S. Collins, *The Present State of Russia, in a Letter to a Friend at London* (London, 1671), p. 105.

6. Liliequist, 'State Policy', p. 46; above, pp. 263–4.

7. Above, pp. 97, 100; at least 29 sodomy cases were considered by the Barcelona tribunal between 1717 and 1790 (Riera i Sans, *Sodomites catalans*, pp. 459–518).

8. M. Cattaneo, '"Vitio nefando" e Inquisizione romana', in M. Formica and A. Postigliola, eds., *Diversità e minoranze nel Settecento: atti del seminario di Santa Margherita Ligure, 2–4 giugno 2003* (Rome, 2006), pp. 55–77; Cattaneo comments (p. 75) that this evidence confirms the long continuation of the paederastic form of sodomy. Cf. above, p. 192.

9. Scaramella, *Un doge infame*, pp. 142–3 (milder), 146–56 (analysis).

10. G. Casanova, *Histoire de ma vie jusqu'à l'an 1797*, ed. G. Lahouati and M.-F. Luna (Paris, 2013), p. 250.

11. G. ['J.'] Gorani, *Mémoires secrets et critiques des cours, des gouvernemens, et des moeurs des principaux états d'Italie*, 3 vols. (Paris, 1793), ii, pp. 299–300 (p. 299: 'Ce penchant connu et avoué est presque général. On le nomme le *péché noble*, le *péché gentil*').

12. See R. Aldrich, *The Seduction of the Mediterranean: Writing, Art and Homosexual Fantasy* (London, 1993).

13. El-Rouayheb, *Before Homosexuality*, pp. 62–3 (14 poets), 82–3 (writers).

14. Rafeq, 'Public Morality', p. 187.

15. Bleys, *Geography of Perversion*, pp. 79–80 (travellers); C.-N.-S. ['C. S.'] Sonnini, *Voyage dans la haute et basse Égypte, fait par l'ordre de l'ancien gouvernement*, 3 vols. (Paris, 1799), i, p. 278 ('généralement répandue', 'le riche, comme le pauvre, en est infecté; au contraire de l'effet qu'elle produit dans des climats moins chauds, celui d'être exclusive, elle s'y allie avec l'inclination pour les femmes').

16. El-Rouayheb, *Before Homosexuality*, p. 156; G. De Martino, 'An Italian in Morocco', trans. A. Schmitt, in A. Schmitt and J. Sofer, eds., *Sexuality and Eroticism among Males in Moslem Societies* (Binghamton, NY, 1992), pp. 25–32 (p. 33: 'there are the boys between 9 and 17, who get fucked by their cousins, teachers, and neighbors—whether they like it or not (not necessarily by force, but by intimidation, by seduction, by making presents, or as a "natural right"). These boys are called *zamel*. By the age of 15 or 16 a *zamel* loses his admirers or he starts refusing advances: becomes a "man", i.e., he fucks boys and courts girls'). Only the lower threshold age differentiates this from the older Mediterranean pattern; it would seem that in Morocco, as elsewhere, modern nutrition reduced the age at which facial hair began to appear.

17. M. Foucault, *La Volonté du savoir* (Paris, 1976). For a thorough response to Foucault, pointing out that the category of homosexuality was developed primarily by homosexual activists and law reformers seeking to express existing facts, not by anti-homosexual forces developing new ways of exercising control, and that in any case the category did not determine thinking or behaviour for a long time after its late-19th-century formulation, see Norton, *Myth of the Modern Homosexual*, esp. pp. 9–11, 61–78.

18. Foucault, *La Volonté du savoir*, p. 59 ('La sodomie—celle des anciens droits civil ou canonique—était un type d'actes interdits; leur auteur n'en était que le sujet juridique. L'homosexuel du XIXe siècle est devenu un personnage: un passé, une histoire et une enfance, un caractère, une forme de vie... Rien de ce qu'il est au total n'échappe à sa sexualité. Partout en lui, elle est présente: sous-jacente à toutes ces conduites... Elle lui est consubstantielle, moins comme un péché d'habitude que comme une nature singulière... Le sodomite était un relaps, l'homosexual est maintenant une espèce').

19. D. M. Halperin, *How to Do the History of Homosexuality* (Chicago, 2002), pp. 28–32.

20. Anon., *Tryal and Conviction of Several Reputed Sodomites*.

21. van der Meer, *Sodoms zaad*, p. 327 ('dat volck'); Boon, *'Dien godlosen hoop'*, pp. 43 ('sulcken volk'), 116 ('van 't volck'), 133 ('van dat soort'); Nationaal Archief, The Hague, Hof van Holland, MS 5420.3, examination of Jacobus Backer, 24 May 1730 ('is hy dan mede van het volk?').

22. Above, p. 357.

23. Merrick and Regan, eds., *Homosexuality in Early Modern France*, p. 64 (38); Courouve, *Les Gens de la manchette*, no. 14 (50).

24. Noordam, 'Sodomy in the Dutch Republic', p. 220 (80s); Puff, 'Nature on Trial', pp. 242–3 (minister).

25. R. von Krafft-Ebing, *Lehrbuch der Psychiatrie, auf klinischer Grundlage für praktische Ärzte und Studirende*, 5th edn. (Stuttgart, 1893), p. 83 ('von der Art und Weise

geschlechtlichen Fühlens zum grossten Theil die geistige Individualität, speciell ihr ethisches, ästhetisches und sociales Fühlen und Streben bedingt wird'). Cf. the intriguingly similar remark in Nietzsche's *Jenseits von Gut und Böse* (written in 1885–6): 'The degree and nature of a person's sexuality reaches up into the highest summit of his spirit' (F. Nietzsche, *Werke*, ed. G. Stenzel, 2 vols. (Salzburg, 1952), ii, p. 736: 'Grad und Art der Geschlechtlichkeit eines Menschen reicht bis in den letzten Gipfel seines Geistes hinauf').

26. On Winckelmann see D. M. Sweet, 'The Personal, the Political, and the Aesthetic: Johann Joachim Winckelmann's German Enlightenment Life', in K. Gerard and G. Hekma, eds., *The Pursuit of Sodomy: Male Homosexuality in Renaissance and Enlightenment Europe* (New York, 1989), pp. 147–62; Derks, *Die Schande*, pp. 174–92; on Beckford see Norton, *Mother Clap*, pp. 379–89.

27. Above, pp. 187–8.

28. See Borris, ed., *Same-Sex Desire*, pp. 122–7, 165–75; and cf. the essays on medical and astrological issues in K. Borris and G. Rousseau, eds., *The Sciences of Homosexuality in Early Modern Europe* (London, 2008).

29. See above, pp. 30 (*ubnah*), 187 (Ibn Sina); Nathan, 'Medieval Arabic Medical Views'. See also, on the work of Ibn Sina's predecessor Abu Bakr al-Razi or ar-Razi ('Rhazes'), F. Rosenthal, 'Ar-Râzî on the Hidden Illness', *Bulletin of the History of Medicine*, 52 (1978), pp. 45–60.

30. Above, p. 73.

31. Above, pp. 73, 327.

32. Hergemöller, 'Sodomiter', p. 378 (Ronchaia); above, pp. 246, 326.

33. Ottonelli, *Della christiana moderatione*, p. 191 ('fingendosi Femmina, andaua per le Chiese con vesti, con gesti, e con portamenti femminili').

34. Gauthier, 'La Sodomie', p. 116; Lutterbach, *Sexualität im Mittelalter*, p. 154; Quinn, *Better than the Sons of Kings*, p. 162.

35. Jordan, *Invention of Sodomy*, p. 52 (Burchard); Vainfas, *Trópico dos pecados*, p. 260 ('habituado'); above, p. 127 (Azpilcueta).

36. Above, pp. 278–9.

37. Above, pp. 121–2; Rocke, *Forbidden Friendships*, pp. 173–4.

38. Rocke, 'Sodomites', pp. 12 ('Send your...'), 20 ('The sodomite...'). Similarly, Puff notes Antoninus of Florence saying that 'such men are said to be more consumed by passion for other men than others [are] for women': *Sodomy in Reformation Germany*, p. 207(n.6).

39. Above, pp. 146–7.

40. Molina, *Cuando amar era pecado*, p. 151 (Lima, noting also that only a small minority of the sodomites processed there were married); D. Clarke, ' "The Sovereign's Vice Begets the Subject's Error": The Duke of Buckingham, "Sodomy" and Narratives of Edward II, 1622–8', in T. Betteridge, ed., *Sodomy in Early Modern Europe* (Manchester, 2002), pp. 46–64, at p. 46 (Ashley).

41. Baldassari, *Bande giovanili*, p. 163 ('il termine "sodomizzatore" individuava chi era conosciuto per la sua particolare "inclinazione" verso i ragazzi').

42. Goldberg, *Sodometries*, p. 19.

43. Hergemöller, *Einführung*, p. 36 (Stocker); Bouliau, 'Sorcellerie et sodomie', i, p. 258 ('n'estre point mal faict d'estre bougre et sodomite'); above, pp. 147 (Aretino), 166 (Bazzi), 296 (de Blot).

44. Above, pp. 82–3.

45. Above, p. 241.

46. R. A. Padgug, 'Sexual Matters: On Conceptualizing Sexuality in History', *Radical History Review*, 20 (1979), pp. 3–23, at p. 14.

47. Trexler, 'La Prostitution florentine', p. 996 (hat-grabbing by female prostitutes).

48. Jeffrey Weeks writes that a 'sexual subculture' is formed specifically 'as a response to the emergence of hostile norms: in the case of homosexuality, of a sharpening social oppression' (*Coming Out: Homosexual Politics in Britain, from the Nineteenth Century to the Present* (London, 1977), pp. 35–6). This seems broadly true of periods before the late 20th century in Western societies, though perhaps too general a statement otherwise.

49. de León, *Grandeza y miseria*, pp. 437–8 ('por el tacto se conocen unos a otros, y por cierta señal que hace el uno al otro en el toque de la mano, sabe si es del trato o si no, y si se puede atrever a él o no, y…huelen y entienden los pensamientos, como si los leyesen y en el mismo hablar, andar y en otros meneos').

50. Above, p. 150.

51. Our knowledge of most of these cases derives, admittedly, from the fact that eventually they approached someone who did comprehend their purpose, and reported them to the authorities; this introduces an inevitable evidential bias. But the subsequent testimonies in court often showed that they had been making such approaches to strangers over many years.

52. Above, pp. 61 (1591), 77 (1655, 1578).

53. Higgs, 'Lisbon', p. 121.

54. It is true that Volpino's group did include boys, though seemingly not in its core membership, which consisted of priests and friars; and they may have had a more carefree attitude, feeling relatively protected by their clerical status. Also, the witness in the Lisbon case was aged 16; but he seems to have been a visitor, not a regular member.

55. Above, pp. 327–8.

56. Above, pp. 244–5.

57. Above, p. 365.

58. J. Boswell, 'Revolutions, Universals, and Sexual Categories', in M. B. Duberman, M. Vicinus and G. Chauncey, eds., *Hidden from History: Reclaiming the Gay and Lesbian Past* (New York, 1989), pp. 17–36, at pp. 34–5. Note that Boswell also abandoned here a distinction he had previously tried to make between gay people, who had a self-conscious sexual orientation, and homosexuals.

59. L. Stone, *The Family, Sex and Marriage in England, 1500–1800* (London, 1977), p. 483.

60. Borris, 'Introduction' (medical, scientific); Garza Carvajal, *Butterflies will Burn*, p. 70 (effeminate sodomite), Berco, *Jerarquías sexuales*, p. 45 (effeminate sodomite);

Phillips and Keay, *Sex before Sexuality*, pp. 68–9 (male-oriented); Dall'Orto, *Tutta un'altra storia*, pp. 252–3 (male-oriented).

61. Carrasco, *Inquisición y represión*, p. 9 ('cierto atavismo pagano', 'la gran cultura del viejo Mediterráneo'); Rocke, *Forbidden Friendships*, p. 88.

62. Halperin, *How to Do the History*, p. 115.

63. M. Kuefler, 'Sex with Eunuchs, Sex with Boys, and the Implications of Sexual Difference', in *Comportamenti e immaginario della sessualità nell'Alto Medievo* (Spoleto, 2006), pp. 139–72, at p. 153; M. den Hartog, '"Overvallen door onzedige ondeugd". Opvattingen over "homoseksualiteit" in Italië, 1450–1500', *Madoc: tijdschrift over de Middeleeuwen*, 31:1 (2017), pp. 2–9, at p. 4.

64. Davidson, *Greeks and Greek Love*, pp. 26 (shocking), 80–1 (words, ages).

65. C. A. Williams, *Roman Homosexuality*, 2nd edn. (Oxford, 2010), pp. 19 (20th year), 79 (quotation).

66. Davidson, *Greeks and Greek Love*, pp. 68–71, 83–6 (not under 18), 184 (death), 300–43 (Crete, Sparta); Williams, *Roman Homosexuality*, p. 19.

67. Above, p. 179 (Basil); Morris, *'When Brothers Dwell in Unity'*, pp. 20 (injunction), 110 (Chrysostom); C. T. Schroeder, *Monastic Bodies: Discipline and Salvation in Shenoute of Atripe* (Philadelphia, 2007), pp. 36–7 (Shenoute); Kuefler, 'Sex with Eunuchs', p. 149 (Salvian).

68. M. Rosenblum, ed. and trans., *Luxorius: A Latin Poet among the Vandals* (New York, 1961), pp. 116, 132, 140; H. Behlmer, 'Koptische Quellen zu (männlicher) "Homosexualität"', *Studien zur altägyptischen Kultur*, 28 (2000), pp. 27–53, at p. 50.

69. M. Lautermann, 'Ninth-Century Classicism and the Erotic Muse', in L. James, ed., *Desire and Denial in Byzantium* (Aldershot, 1999), pp. 161–70 (epigrams); Morris, *'When Brothers Dwell in Unity'*, pp. 18 ('as true…'), 30 (Athos). However, Angeliki Laiou notes that male–male sexual relations feature much less in Byzantine sources of the 11th–13th centuries than they had done in the 4th–5th: *Mariage, amour et parenté à Byzance aux XIᵉ–XIIIᵉ siècles* (Paris, 1992), p. 78.

70. Schmitt, 'Liwāṭ im Fiqh', pp. 49–50.

71. J. Hajnal, 'European Marriage Patterns in Perspective', in D. V. Glass and D. E. C. Eversley, eds., *Population in History: Essays in Historical Demography* (London, 1965), pp. 101–43.

72. R. M. Smith, 'The People of Tuscany and Their Families in the Fifteenth Century: Medieval or Mediterranean?', *Journal of Family History*, 6 (1981), pp. 107–28, at p. 111.

73. Rocke, *Forbidden Friendships*, pp. 28 (men 30–1), 97 (girls 17–18); A. Molho, *Marriage Alliance in Late Medieval Florence* (Cambridge, MA, 1994), pp. 137–9 (general view).

74. D. Martelli, *Polifonie: le donne a Venezia nell'età di Moderata Fonte (seconda metà del secolo XVI)* (Padua, 2011), pp. 239, 260(n. 9). Joanne Ferraro gives 30 as the typical minimum age for the men, but only 15 as typical for the woman: *Marriage Wars in Late Renaissance Venice* (Oxford, 2001), p. 62.

75. D. Rheubottom, *Age, Marriage, and Politics in Fifteenth-Century Ragusa* (Oxford, 2000), pp. 87, 107.

76. M. Chojnacka, *Working Women of Early Modern Venice* (Baltimore, 2001), p. 4 (own home); Martelli, *Polifonie*, p. 242 (dowries).

77. Hajnal, 'European Marriage Ages', p. 111 (village of Riana). In rural and small-town southern Italy the typical age of marriage for a woman was in the range 16–20 in the 16th and 17th centuries; the men's ages varied more, in accordance with the nature of their work, as professionals waited until they were established in their professions, but day-labourers did not need to do so. See G. Da Molin, 'Family Forms and Domestic Service in Southern Italy from the Seventeenth to the Nineteenth Centuries', *Journal of Family History*, 15 (1990), pp. 503–27, at p. 512.

78. E. A. Wrigley and R. Schofield, *The Population History of England, 1541–1871: A Reconstruction* (Cambridge, 1981), pp. 255, 422–4 (age difference); Ben-Amos, *Adolescence and Youth*, p. 227 (men in later 20s); A. Kussmaul, *Servants in Husbandry in Early Modern England* (Cambridge, 1981), p. 111 (median ages).

79. A. E. Imhof, 'Remarriage in Rural Populations and in Urban Middle and Upper Strata in Germany from the Sixteenth to the Twentieth Century', in J. Dupaquier et al., eds., *Marriage and Remarriage in Populations of the Past* (London, 1981), pp. 35–46.

80. McSheffrey, *Mariage, Sex, and Civic Culture*, p. 5 (general estimate).

81. M. Kowaleski, 'Singlewomen in Medieval and Early Modern Europe: The Demographic Perspective', in J. M. Bennett and A. M. Froide, eds., *Singlewomen in the European Past, 1250–1800* (Philadelphia, 1998), pp. 38–81, at pp. 42 (Prato), 46 (Coventry etc., poll tax).

82. D. Youngs, *The Life Cycle in Western Europe, c.1300–c.1500* (Manchester, 2006), p. 139 (London); Ben-Amos, *Adolescence and Youth*, pp. 201–2 (initiative).

83. P. J. P. Goldberg, *Women, Work and Life Cycle in a Medieval Economy: Women in York and Yorkshire c.1300–1520* (Oxford, 1992), pp. 226–7. Some of the 47 were second marriages, which could involve a greater age-gap.

84. S. Morpurgo, ed., *Il libro di buoni costumi di Paolo di Messer Pace da Certaldo: documento di vita trecentesca fiorentina* (Florence, 1921), p. 77 ('La femina è chosa molto vana e leggiere a muovere, e però quand'ella sta sanza il marito sta a grande pericolo. E però se ài femine in chasa, tielle appresso il più che tu puoi, e torna spesso in chasa, e provedi i fatti tuoi, e tielle in tremore e in paura tuttavia').

85. Quoted in M. Rocke, 'Gender and Sexual Culture in Renaissance Italy', in J. J. Martin, ed., *The Renaissance at Home and Abroad* (London, 2003), pp. 139–58, at p. 141.

86. F. Moryson, *An Itinerary written by Fynes Morison Gent. . . . Containing his Ten Yeeres Travell* (London, 1617), p. 70.

87. Haliczer, *Sexuality in the Confessional*, pp. 107 (quotations), 108 (case).

88. Above, p. 67.

89. See Da Molin, 'Family Forms and Domestic Service'. Domestic service seems to have been both a cause and a consequence of the later marriage age in the North; on the importance of this factor see J. L. Viret, 'Children Leaving Home in Europe in the Modern Age: Towards a Typology Taking into Account Western

European Forms of Authority', in D. Albera, L. Lorenzetti and J. Mathieu, eds., *Reframing the History of Family and Kinship: From the Alps to Europe* (Bern, 2016), pp. 187–202, esp. pp. 189–91.

90. J.-L. Flandrin, 'Repression and Change in the Sexual Life of Young People in Medieval and Early Modern Times', *Journal of Family History*, 2 (1977), pp. 196–210, at p. 199 (price, unmarried); J. Rossiaud, 'Prostitution, Youth, and Society in the Towns of Southeastern France in the Fifteenth Century', in R. Forster and O. Ranum, eds., *Deviants and the Abandoned in French Society*, tr. E. Forster and P. M. Ranum (Baltimore, 1978), pp. 1–46, at p. 23 (unmarried); Farr, *Authority and Sexuality*, p. 139 (1561); Perry, *Gender and Disorder*, p. 150 (1623).

91. Rocke, 'Gender and Sexual Culture', p. 147.

92. J. E. Tucker, 'Marriage and Family in Nablus, 1720–1856: Toward a History of Arab Marriage', *Journal of Family History* 13 (1988), pp. 165–79; A. Marcus, *The Middle East on the Eve of Modernity: Aleppo in the Eighteenth Century* (New York, 1989), p. 196; A. Duben and C. Behar, *Istanbul Households: Marriage, Family and Fertility, 1880–1940* (Cambridge, 1991), p. 126; M. N. Todorova, *Balkan Family Structure and the European Pattern: Demographic Developments in Ottoman Bulgaria* (Budapest, 2006), p. 39.

93. Peirce, 'Seniority, Sexuality, and Social Order', pp. 184–6; Andrews and Kalpaklı, *Age of Beloveds*, p. 178.

94. Ben-Naeh, 'Moshko the Jew', pp. 96–7.

95. El-Rouayheb, *Before Homosexuality*, p. 29.

96. S. A. Spectorsky, *Women in Classical Islamic Law: A Survey of the Sources* (Leiden, 2010), pp. 67–8 (father); L. Peirce, *A Spectrum of Unfreedom: Captives and Slaves in the Ottoman Empire* (Budapest, 2021), pp. 13–14 (Ebu's Su'ud).

97. Cited in Andrews and Kalpaklı, *Age of Beloveds*, p. 167.

98. Above, p. 173 (Italians); Dols, *Majnūn*, pp. 97–8.

99. Ben-Naeh, 'Moshko the Jew', p. 96.

100. Radicati, *Philosophical Dissertation*, pp. 67–8.

101. Above, p. 36.

AFTERWORD

1. While disagreeing with Bray's central claim, I should nevertheless like to pay tribute to the admirably thoughtful and scholarly nature of his pioneering work.

2. J. Ellis, 'Desire in Translation: Friendship in the Life and Work of Spenser', *English Studies in Canada*, 20 (1994), pp. 171–86, at p. 175, quoted in McFarlane, *Sodomite in Fiction*, p. 175.

3. B. R. Smith, 'Premodern Sexualities', *Publications of the Modern Languages Association of America*, 115 (2000), pp. 318–29, at p. 321.

4. Trexler, 'Gender Subordination', p. 72.

5. Padgug, 'Sexual Matters', p. 18.

6. Halperin, *How to Do the History*, p. 10 (referring to D. M. Halperin, *One Hundred Years of Homosexuality and Other Essays on Greek Love* (New York, 1990)).

7. Valerie Traub's important study *The Renaissance of Lesbianism in Early Modern England* (Cambridge, 2002) brings together a number of literary texts; but a significant proportion of these might best be described as expressions of male fantasy or male anxiety. For an interesting work of male fantasy which has remained unnoticed by scholars in this field since its publication nearly 30 years ago, see also François du Verdus's 'Iride innamorata de Fenice', in T. Hobbes, *The Correspondence*, ed. N. Malcolm, 2 vols. (Oxford, 1994), pp. 637–49, 654–66.

8. See Puff, *Sodomy in Reformation Germany*, pp. 31–5; above, p. 218.

9. Perry, ' "Nefarious Sin" ', p. 79 (Spain: Seville); Garza Carvajal, *Butterflies will Burn*, pp. 55–6 (Spain); García Cárcel, *Herejía y sociedad*, p. 290 (Valencian Inquisition); Tortorici, *Sins against Nature*, p. 243 (Latin America); L. Bellini, *A coisa obscura: mulher, sodomia e Inquisição no Brasil colonial* (São Paulo, 1989) (Brazil); R. Vainfas, 'Homoerotismo feminino e o Santo Ofício', in M. Del Priore, ed., *História das mulheres no Brasil* (São Paulo, 1997), pp. 115–40, esp. pp. 125–39 (Brazil).

List of Manuscripts

ARCHIVIO DI STATO, VENICE [ASV]

Capi del Consiglio dei Dieci, Dispacci (Lettere) di Ambasciatori ['CCD, DA'], busta 6 (Costantinopoli, 1581–99), item 99: letter of *bailo* Giovanni Moro, 10 Sept. 1588.
Savi all'eresia (Santo Ufficio) busta 8, fasc. 28: Francesco Calcagno trial, 1550.

ARCHIVIO SEGRETO VATICANO, VATICAN CITY

Misc., Arm. II, vol. 110, fos. 385r–399v: report on fleet, 1571–2.

ARQUIVO NACIONAL DA TORRE DO TOMBO, LISBON

PT/TT/TSO-IL proc. 141 (caderno 14º de nefandos), fos. 226r–237v: Mathias de Mattos confession, 1690.
PT/TT/TSO-IL proc. 2033: Gil trial, 1576.
PT/TT/TSO-IL proc. 4026: Francisco trial, 1557–9.
PT/TT/TSO-IL proc. 5106: António de Matos trial, 1703–6.
PT/TT/TSO-IL proc. 6366: Baltazar da Lomba trial, 1595.

BETHLEM ROYAL HOSPITAL ARCHIVES AND MUSEUM, BECKENHAM, LONDON

Bridewell Hospital records, Courtbooks 1–4.

BIBLIOTECA AMBROSIANA, MILAN

Q 116 sup., fos. 136r–146v: [G. Barelli,] 'Relatione delle cose di Constantinopoli'

BIBLIOTHÈQUE DE L'ARSENAL, PARIS

10254: Administration du Lieutenant Général de Police, sodomy reports, 1723.
10255: Administration du Lieutenant Général de Police, sodomy reports, 1724.
10256: Administration du Lieutenant Général de Police, sodomy reports, 1725–6.
10257: Administration du Lieutenant Général de Police, sodomy reports, 1727–35.

BIBLIOTHÈQUE SAINTE-GENEVIÈVE, PARIS

1775, Suppl. F33: Antoine Ransson documents.

BODLEIAN LIBRARY, OXFORD

Rawl. D 618, fos. 106r–111v: 'Del Turco. Alcune Particolarita estratte dalla Relazione fatta da Francesco Bandola [*sic*, for Gondola] ritornato da Ragusa delli 1574. à P.P Gregorio 13:°'.

BRITISH LIBRARY, LONDON

Add. 6877: Giovanni Francesco Graziani, report to Pope Paul V, 1610.
Add. 70035, fos. 321r–322v: Navy Board correspondence about Captain Rigby.
Hargrave 226, fos. 311r–313v: 'The Manner of the Trial of Marven Lord Audley Earle of Castlehauen'.

LONDON METROPOLITAN ARCHIVES

MJ/SB/R/005: Middlesex Sessions of the Peace registers, 1629–33.

NATIONAAL ARCHIEF, THE HAGUE

Hof van Holland, 5420.3: 'Informaties inzake een aantal personen te den Haag schuldig aan crimen nefandum, 1730'.
Hof van Holland, 5661: Register van de crimineele sententien, July 1729–Oct. 1731.

THE NATIONAL ARCHIVES, KEW

ASSI 35/73/6: Surrey Assize Indictments, Southwark, 12 July 1631.
ASSI 35/75/6: Surrey Assize Indictments, Southwark, 27 Feb. 1633.
ASSI 35/75/7: Surrey Assize Indictments, Croydon, 24 July 1634.
ASSI 35/76/12: Surrey Assize Indictments, Southwark, 10 Mar. 1634.
HCA 1/5: William Audley case.
HCA 1/7: Robert Hewitt case; Robert Stone case; Richard Seawell case.
HCA 1/9: Richard Kingston case.
HCA 1/64: Abdul Rahim case.
PC 2/1: Privy Council register, 1540–2.
STAC 8/291/29: Walker v Dawson, 1609.

STADSARCHIEF, AMSTERDAM

Arch. 5075, inv. no. 378A (Jacob en Nicolaes Jacobs), fo. 267r–v: statement by Samuel Cohen, Isaac Farcha and Alexander Falcon, 1 May 1615.

Bibliography

This bibliography is confined to listing works quoted or referred to in this book. Authors' names are listed by the first element of the name to bear a capital letter. The two most frequently cited journals are abbreviated as follows: *JH*: *Journal of Homosexuality*; *JHS*: *Journal of the History of Sexuality*.

Abū Nuwās, *Poèmes bachiques et libertins*, trans. O. Merzoug (Paris, 2002).

Accame, M., *Pomponio Leto: vita e insegnamento* (Tivoli, 2008).

Adam, A., *Théophile de Viau et la libre pensée française en 1620* (Paris, 1935).

Adam, A., *Les Libertins au XVIIᵉ siècle* (Paris, 1964).

Aerts, T. M.,'"Het verfoeijelijke crimen van sodomie": sodomie op VOC-schepen in de 18e eeuw', *Leidschaft* (Apr. 1988), pp. 5–21.

Agostino da Montalcino, *Lucerna dell'anima: somma de' casi di conscientia, necessaria a i confessori, & molto utile a i penitenti* (Venice, 1590).

Ahern, E., 'The Sin of Sodom in Late Antiquity', *JHS*, 27 (2018), pp. 209–33.

Albèri, E., ed., *Relazioni degli ambasciatori veneti al Senato durante il secolo decimosesto*, ser. 3, *Relazioni dagli Stati Ottomani*, 3 vols. (Florence, 1840–55).

Aldrich, R., *The Seduction of the Mediterranean: Writing, Art and Homosexual Fantasy* (London, 1993).

Alighieri, D., *Commedia*, ed. E. Pasquini and A. Quaglio (Milan, 1987).

Alonso Cortés, N., *La muerte del conde de Villamediana* (Valladolid, 1928).

Alves Dias, J. J., 'Para uma abordagem do sexo proibido em Portugal, no século XVI', in *Inquisição: comunicações apresentadas ao 1.º Congresso Luso-Brasileiro sobre Inquisição realizado em Lisboa, de 17 a 20 de Fevereiro de 1987*, 2 vols. (Lisbon, 1989–90), i, pp. 151–9.

Amiel, O., ed., *Lettres de Madame, duchesse d'Orléans, née princesse Palatine* (Paris, 1981).

Anderson, S. P., *An English Consul in Turkey: Paul Rycaut at Smyrna, 1667–1678* (Oxford, 1989).

Anderson, V. D., 'New England in the Seventeenth Century', in N. Canny and A. Low, eds., *The Origins of Empire: British Overseas Enterprise to the Close of the Seventeenth Century* (Oxford, 1998), pp. 193–217.

Andrews, W. G., and M. Kalpaklı, *The Age of Beloveds: Love and the Beloved in Early-Modern Ottoman and European Culture and Society* (Durham, NC, 2005).

Anon., *Ausszug eynes Briefes, wie eyner so in der Türckey wonhafft, seynem freünd in dise land geschriben* (Nuremberg, 1526).

Anon., *The First Part of the True and Honorable Historie, of the Life of Sir John Old-Castle, the Good Lord Cobham* (London, 1600).

Anon. [attrib. T. Scott], *The Belgicke Pismire Stinging the Slothfull Sleeper, and Awaking the Diligent to Fast, Watch, Pray* (n.p., 1622).

Anon., *Tom Tell Troath: Or, a Free Discourse Touching the Manners of the Tyme. Directed to His Majestie by Way of Humble Advertisement* (n.p., n.d. [1622]).

Anon. ['Jack Dawe'], *Vox graculi: Or, Jack Dawe's Prognostication* (London, 1623).

Anon., *Merrie Conceited Jests of George Peele Gentleman sometimes a Student in Oxford* (London, 1627).

Anon., *A Pill to Purge Melancholy: Or, Merry News from Newgate* (London, 1652).

Anon., *Capricciosi e piacevoli ragionamenti di M. Pietro Aretino* (Cosmopoli, 1660).

Anon., *Dolly and Molly: Or, The Two Country Damosels Fortunes at London* (London, n.d. [1670–96]).

Anon., *An Account of the Proceedings against Capt. Edward Rigby . . . for Intending to Commit the Abominable Sin of Sodomy, on the Body of one William Minton* (London, 1698).

Anon., *The Sodomites Shame and Doom, Laid before Them with Great Grief and Compassion by a Minister of the Church of England* (London, 1702).

Anon., *The Tryal and Conviction of Several Reputed Sodomites, before the Right Honourable the Lord Mayor, and Recorder of London, at Guild-Hall, the 20th Day of October, 1707* (London, 1707).

Anon., *A Full and True Account of the Discovery and Apprehending a Notorious Gang of Sodomites in St James's* (London, 1709).

Anon., ed., *Select Trials, for Murders, Robberies, Rapes, Sodomy, Coining, Frauds and Other Offences, at the Sessions-House in the Old-Bailey*, 2nd edn., 4 vols. (London, 1742).

Anon. [G. Lorenzi], *Leggi e memorie venete sulla prostituzione fino alla caduta della republica* (Venice, 1870–2).

Anon., *Vita di Pietro Aretino del Berni*, (n.p., n.d. ['Perugia, 1537']; 19th century).

Antoninus [Florentinus], *Summa confessionalis* (Lyon, 1546).

Antoninus [Florentinus], *Summae sacrae theologiae, iuris pontificij, & Caesarei, secunda pars* (Venice, 1582).

al-Aqhiṣārī, A., *Against Smoking: An Ottoman Manifesto*, trans. Y. Michot (Markfield, 2010).

d'Aranda, E., *Relation de la captivité et liberté du sieur Emanuel d'Aranda, jadis esclave à Alger*, 3rd edn. (Brussels, 1666).

Arberry, A. J., *The Koran Interpreted* (Oxford, 1998).

Archer, I., *The Pursuit of Stability: Social Relations in Elizabethan London* (Cambridge, 1991).

Aretino, P., *The Ragionamenti*, trans. I. Liseux and P. Stafford (London, 1971).

Aristotle, *The Complete Works*, ed. J. Barnes, 2 vols. (Princeton, NJ, 1984).

Arjona Castro, A., *La sexualidad en la España musulmana*, 2nd edn. (Cordova, n.d.).

Atlas, M., *Die Femminielli von Neapel: zur kulturellen Konstruktion von Transgender* (Frankfurt, 2010).

Aurigemma, M. G., ed., *Carlo Saraceni, 1579–1620: un veneziano tra Roma e l'Europa* (Rome, 2013).

Azfar, F., 'Genealogy of an Execution: The Sodomite, the Bishop, and the Anomaly of 1726', *Journal of British Studies*, 51 (2012), pp. 568–93.

Aznar Cardona, P., *Expulsion justificada de los moriscos españoles* (Huesca, 1612).

Azor, J. ['I. Azorius'], *Institutionum moralium*, 3 vols. (Lyon, 1616–25).

de Azpilcueta, M., *Manual de confesores, y penitentes* (Medina del Campo, 1554).

de Azpilcueta, M. ['Navarrus'], *Enchiridion, sive manuale confessariorum et poenitentium* (Venice, 1600).

'B. C.', *Puritanisme the Mother, Sinne the Daughter* (n.p., 1633).

Babayan, K., '"In Spirit we Ate Each Other's Sorrow": Female Companionship in Seventeenth-Century Safavi Iran', in K. Babayan and A. Najmabadi, eds., *Islamicate Sexualities: Translations across Temporal Geographies of Desire* (Cambridge, MA, 2008), pp. 238–74.

Badakçı, M., *Osmanlı'da seks: sarayda gece dersleri* (Istanbul, 1993).

Bailey, D. S., *Homosexuality and the Western Christian Tradition* (London, 1955).

Baldassari, M., *Bande giovanili e 'vizio nefando': violenza e sessualità nella Roma barocca* (Rome, 2005).

Bale, J., *A Mysterye of Inyquyte Contayned within the Heretycall Genealogye of Ponce Pantolabus* ('Geneva' [Antwerp], 1545).

Bandello, M., *La prima parte de le novelle*, ed. D. Maestri (Alessandria, 1992).

Barahona, R., *Sex Crimes, Honour, and the Law in Early Modern Spain: Vizcaya, 1528–1735* (Toronto, 2003).

Barbero, A., *Lepanto: la battaglia dei tre imperi* (Rome, 2010).

Barbier, E.-J.-F., *Chronique de la Régence et du règne de Louis XV (1718–1763)*, 8 vols. (Paris, 1858).

Barbierato, F., 'Follie della natura tra Sei e Settecento', in U. Grassi, V. Lagioia and G. P. Romagnani, eds., *Tribadi, sodomiti, invertite e invertiti, pederasti, femminelle, ermafrodite... Per una storia dell'omosessualità, della bisessualità e delle trasgressioni di genere in Italia* (Pisa, 2017), pp. 61–7.

Barnfield, R., *The Affectionate Sheapheard, Containing the Complaint of Daphnis for the Love of Ganymede* (London, 1594).

Barnfield, R., *Cynthia, with Certaine Sonnets, and the Legend of Cassandra* (London, 1595).

de Barrionuevo, J., *Avisos de Jerónimo de Barrionuevo (1654–1658)*, ed. A. Paz y Mélia, 2 vols. (Madrid, 1892).

Bassano, L., *Costumi et i modi particolari della vita de' Turchi*, ed. F. Babinger (Munich, 1963).

Baudier, M., *Histoire generale de la religion des Turcs* (Paris, 1625).

Baudier, M., *Histoire génralle du serrail et de la cour du Grand Seigneur empereur des Turcs* (Paris, 1652).

Bazan Díaz, I., *Delincuencia y criminalidad en el Pais Vasco en la transición de la Edad Media a la moderna* (Vitoria-Gasteiz, 1995).

Beard, T., and T. Taylor, *The Theatre of Gods Judgements, wherein is Represented the Admirable Justice of God against Notorious Sinners*, 4th edn. (London, 1648).

Beasley, A. W., 'The Disability of James VI and I', *The Seventeenth Century*, 10 (1995), pp. 152–62.

Beattie, P., 'Conflicting Penile Codes: Modern Masculinity and Sodomy in the Brazilian Military, 1860–1916', in D. Balderston and D. J. Guy, eds., *Sex and Sexuality in Latin America* (New York, 1997), pp. 65–85.

Beccadelli, A., *The Hermaphrodite*, ed. and trans. H. Parker (Cambridge, MA, 2010).

Behar, C., *Ali Ufkî ve mezmurlar* (Istanbul, 1990).

Behlmer, H., 'Koptische Quellen zu (männlicher) "Homosexualität"', *Studien zur altägyptischen Kultur*, 28 (2000), pp. 27–53.

Behrend-Martinez, E., 'Making Sense of the History of Sex and Gender in Early Modern Spain', *History Compass*, 7:1 (1999), pp. 1306–16.

Behringer, W., 'Mörder, Diebe, Ehebrecher: Verbrechen und Strafen in Kurbayern vom 16. bis 18. Jahrhundert', in R. van Dülmen, ed., *Verbrechen, Strafen und soziale Kontrolle* (Frankfurt, 1990), pp. 85–132, 287–93.

Beier, A. L., *Masterless Men: The Vagrancy Problem in England, 1560–1640* (London, 1985).

Bell, J. N., *Love Theory in Later Ḥanbalite Islam* (Albany, NY, 1979).

Bellamy, J. A., 'Sex and Society in Islamic Popular Literature', in A. L. al-Sayyid-Marsot, ed., *Society and the Sexes in Medieval Islam* (Malibu, CA, 1979), pp. 23–42.

Bellini, L., *A coisa obscura: mulher, sodomia e Inquisição no Brasil colonial* (São Paulo, 1989).

Bély, L., 'Homosexuelle Netzwerke am Hof Ludwigs XIV.', in N. Domeier and C. Mühling, eds., *Homosexualität am Hof: Praktiken und Diskurse vom Mittelalter bis heute* (Frankfurt, 2020), pp. 101–18.

Ben-Amos, I. K., *Adolescence and Youth in Early Modern England* (New Haven, CT, 1994).

Benedicti, J., *La Somme des pechez, et le remede d'iceux* (Paris, 1595).

Benemann, W., *Male–Male Intimacy in Early America: Beyond Romantic Friendships* (New York, 2006).

Ben-Naeh, Y., 'Moshko the Jew and his Gay Friends: Same-Sex Sexual Relations in Ottoman-Jewish Society', *Journal of Early Modern History*, 9 (2005), 79–105.

Bennassar, B., 'L'Esclavage des femmes en Europe à l'époque moderne', *Storia delle donne*, 5 (2009), pp. 131–46.

Bennassar, B., and L. Bennassar, *Les Chrétiens d'Allah: l'histoire extraordinaire des renégats, XVIᵉ–XVIIᵉ siècles* (Paris, 1989).

Benson, C. D., 'Chaucer's Pardoner and Modern Critics', *Mediaevalia*, 8 (1982), pp. 337–49.

Benvenuto da Imola, *Comentum super Dantis Aldigherij Comoediam*, ed. J. P. Lacaita, 5 vols. (Florence, 1887).

Berco, C., 'Social Control and its Limits: Sodomy, Local Sexual Economies, and Inquisitors during Spain's Golden Age', *The Sixteenth Century Journal*, 36 (2005), pp. 331–58.

Berco, C., *Jerarquías sexuales, estatus público: masculinidad, sodomía y sociedad en la España del Siglo de Oro*, trans. E. Cano Miguel (Valencia, 2009).

Berger, L., *Gesellschaft und Individuum in Damaskus, 1550–1791* (Würzburg, 2007).

Bergeron, D. M., *King James and Letters of Homoerotic Desire* (Iowa City, IA, 1999).

Bernardino of Siena, *Le prediche volgari*, ed. C. Cannarozzi, 2 vols. (Pistoia, 1934).

Bernardino of Siena, *Opera omnia*, 9 vols. (Quaracchi, 1950–65).

Berni, F., et al., *Tutte le opere del Berni in terza rima* (n.p., 1540).

Berni, F., *Poesie e prose*, ed. E. Chiòrboli (Geneva, 1934).

Bersani, L., and U. Dutoit, *Caravaggio's Secrets* (Cambridge, MA, 1998).

Berthier, A., and S. Yerasimos, 'Introduction', in A. Bobovius, *Topkapi: relation du sérail du Grand Seigneur*, ed. A. Berthier and S. Yerasimos (Arles, 1999), pp. 9–22.

Bertuzzi, M., *I femminielli: il labile tra il sacro e l'umano*, 2nd edn. (Florence, 2018).

Bethencourt, F., *The Inquisition: A Global History, 1478–1834*, trans. J. Birrell (Cambridge, 2009).

Bibliander, T., ed., *Machumetis Sarracenorum principis vita ac doctrina omnis, quae & Ismahelitarum lex, & Alcoranum dicitur*, 3 vols. (Basel, 1543).

Billings, W. M., ed., *The Old Dominion in the Seventeenth Century: A Documentary History of Virginia, 1606–1689* (Chapel Hill, NC, 1975).

Bingham, C., 'Seventeenth-Century Attitudes toward Deviant Sex', *Journal of Interdisciplinary History*, 3 (1971), pp. 447–68.

Binns, J. W., 'Women or Transvestites on the Elizabethan Stage? An Oxford Controversy', *The Sixteenth Century Journal*, 5:2 (1974), pp. 95–120.

Biow, D., *On the Importance of Being an Individual in Renaissance Italy: Men, Their Professions, and Their Beards* (Philadelphia, 2015).

Blastenbrei, P., *Kriminalität in Rom, 1560–1585* (Tübingen, 1995).

Bleibtreu-Ehrenberg, G., *Homosexualität: die Geschichte eines Vorurteils* (Frankfurt, 1981).

Bleys, R. C., *The Geography of Perversion: Male-to-Male Sexual Behaviour outside the West and the Ethnographic Imagination, 1750–1918* (London, 1996).

Bloch, I., *Die Prostitution*, 2 vols. (Berlin, 1912–25).

Blount, Sir Henry, *A Voyage into the Levant* (London, 1636).

Blumenthal, D., *Enemies and Familiars: Slavery and Mastery in Fifteenth-Century Valencia* (Ithaca, NY, 2009).

Bly, M., *Queer Virgins and Virgin Queans on the Early Modern Stage* (Oxford, 2000).

Boccaccio, G., *Esposizioni sopra la Comedia di Dante*, ed. G. Padoan (Milan, 1965).

Boccaccio, G., *Decameron*, ed. A. Quondam, M. Fiorilla and G. Alfano (Milan, 2013).

Boes, M. R., 'On Trial for Sodomy in Early Modern Germany', in T. Betteridge, ed., *Sodomy in Early Modern Europe* (Manchester, 2002), pp. 27–45.

Bombín Pérez, A., *La Inquisición en el País Vasco: el tribunal de Logroño, 1570–1610* (Bilbao, 1997).

Bono, S., *Schiavi musulmani nell'Italia moderna: galeotti, vu' cumprà, domestici* (Naples, 1999).

Boomgaard, P., 'Male–Male Sex, Bestiality and Incest in the Early-Modern Indonesian Archipelago: Perceptions and Penalties', in R. A. G. Reyes and W. G. Clarence-Smith, eds., *Sexual Diversity in Asia, c.600–1950* (London, 2012), pp. 141–60.

Boon, L. J., *'Dien godlosen hoop van menschen'. Vervolging van homoseksuelen in de Republiek in de jaren dertig van de achttiende eeuw*, ed. I. Schöffer et al. (Amsterdam, 1997).

Boone, M., 'State Power and Illicit Sexuality: The Persecution of Sodomy in Late Medieval Bruges', *Journal of Medieval History*, 22 (1996), pp. 135–53.

Booy, D., ed., *The Notebooks of Nehemiah Wallington, 1618–1654* (Aldershot, 2007).

Borges Coelho, A., 'Repressão ideológica e sexual na Inquisição de Évora entre 1533–1668. As primeiras gerações de vítimas cristãs-novas', in *Inquisição: comunicações apresentadas ao 1.° Congresso Luso-Brasileiro sobre Inquisição realizado em Lisboa, de 17 a 20 de Fevereiro de 1987*, 2 vols. (Lisbon, 1989–90), i, pp. 423–46.

Borris, K., ed., *Same-Sex Desire in the English Renaissance: A Sourcebook of Texts, 1470–1650* (New York, 2004).

Borris, K., 'Introduction: The Prehistory of Homosexuality in the Early Modern Sciences', in K. Borris and G. Rousseau, eds., *The Sciences of Homosexuality in Early Modern Europe* (London, 2008), pp. 1–40.

Borris, K., 'Sodomizing Science: Cocles, Patricio Tricasso, and the Constitutional Morphologies of Renaissance Male Same-Sex Lovers', in K. Borris and G. Rousseau, eds., *The Sciences of Homosexuality in Early Modern Europe* (London, 2008), pp. 137–64.

Borris, K., and G. Rousseau, eds., *The Sciences of Homosexuality in Early Modern Europe* (London, 2008).

Boškov, V., 'Zum Problem des Objekts der Liebe in der osmanischen Divan-Poesie', in W. Voigt ed., *XVIII. deutscher Orientalistentag, vom 1. bis 5. Oktober 1972 in Lübeck: Vorträge (Zeitschrift der Deutschen Morgenländische Gesellschaft*, Supplement II) (Wiesbaden, 1974), pp. 124–30.

Boswell, J., *Christianity, Social Tolerance, and Homosexuality: Gay People in Western Europe from the Beginning of the Christian Era to the Fourteenth Century* (Chicago, 1980).

Boswell, J., 'Revolutions, Universals, and Sexual Categories', in M. B. Duberman, M. Vicinus and G. Chauncey, eds., *Hidden from History: Reclaiming the Gay and Lesbian Past* (New York, 1989), pp. 17–36.

Bouchard, J.-J., *Journal*, ed. E. Kanceff, 2 vols. (Turin, 1976–7).

Bouhdiba, A., *La Sexualité en Islam* (Paris, 1975).

Bouliau, D., 'Sorcellerie et sodomie en Languedoc (1485–1791): de la répression à la dépénalisation', 2 vols. ('mémoire de master', University of Toulouse, 2016).

Bourcier, E., ed., *The Diary of Sir Simonds D'Ewes, 1622–1624: journal d'un étudiant londonien sous le règne de Jacques 1ᵉʳ* (Paris, 1974).

Boxer, C. R., *Race Relations in the Portuguese Colonial Empire, 1415–1825* (Oxford, 1963).

Boyar, E., and K. Fleet, *A Social History of Ottoman Istanbul* (Cambridge, 2010).

Boyd, D. L., and R. M. Karras, 'The Interrogation of a Male Transvestite Prostitute in Fourteenth-Century London', *GLQ: A Journal of Lesbian and Gay Studies*, 1 (1995), pp. 459–65.

Bradford, W., *Of Plymouth Plantation*, ed. S. E. Morison (New York, 1952).

Bray, A., 'Homosexuality and the Signs of Male Friendship in Elizabethan England', in J. Goldberg, ed., *Queering the Renaissance* (Durham, NC, 1994), pp. 40–61.

Bray, A., *Homosexuality in Renaissance England*, 2nd edn. (New York, 1995).

Bray, A., 'The Curious Case of Michael Wigglesworth', in M. Duberman, ed., *A Queer World: The Center for Lesbian and Gay Studies Reader* (New York, 1997), pp. 205–16.

Bray, A., *The Friend* (Chicago, 2003).

Bredbeck, G. W., *Sodomy and Interpretation: Marlowe to Milton* (Ithaca, NY, 1991).

Brennan, M. G., ed., *The Travel Diary of Robert Bargrave, Levant Merchant (1647–1656)* (London, 1999).

Breuning, H. J., *Orientalische Reyss* (Strasbourg, 1612).

Briggs, K., 'OE and ME *cunte* in Place Names', *Journal of the English Place Name Society*, 41 (2009), pp. 26–39.

Brookes, D. S., ed. and trans., *The Ottoman Gentleman of the Sixteenth Century: Mustafa Ali's Meva'idü'n-nefa'is fi kava'idi'l-mecalis*, 'Tables of Delicacies concerning the Rules of Social Gatherings' (Cambridge, MA, 2003).

Browne, Sir Thomas, *Selected Writings*, ed. G. Keynes (London, 1968).

Bruscagli, R., ed., *Trionfi e canti carnascialeschi toscani del Rinascimento*, 2 vols. (Rome, 1986).

Bullough, V. L., *Sexual Variance in Society and History* (New York, 1976).

Bulwer, J. ['J. B.'], *Pathomyotomia, Or: A Dissection of the Significative Muscles of the Affections of the Minde* (London, 1649).

de Bunes Ibarra, M. A., *La imagen de los musulmanes y del Norte de África en la España de los siglos XVI y XVII: los caracteres de una hostilidad* (Madrid, 1989).

Buranello, R., 'The Hidden Ways and Means of Antonio Vignali's *La cazzaria*', *Quaderni d'italianistica*, 26 (2005), pp. 59–76.

Burg, B. R., *Sodomy and the Pirate Tradition: English Sea Rovers in the Seventeenth-Century Caribbean* (New York, 1984).

Burgdorf, W., 'Königliche Liebschaften. Friedrich der Grosse und seine Männer', in N. Domeier and C. Mühling, eds., *Homosexualität am Hof: Praktiken und Diskurse vom Mittelalter bis heute* (Frankfurt, 2020), pp. 133–48.

Bürgel, J. C., 'Abglanz Gottes oder Fallstrick Satans? Zum homoerotischen Element in der Dichtung des islamischen Mittelalters', in T. Stemmler, ed., *Homoerotische Lyrik: 6. Kolloquium der Forschungsstelle für europäische Lyrik des Mittelalters* (Mannheim, 1992), pp. 103–18.

Burke, P., *The Historical Anthropology of Early Modern Italy: Essays on Perception and Communication* (Cambridge, 1987).

Burnett, J., *A History of the Cost of Living* (Harmondsworth, 1969).

Burton, T., *Chronica monasterii de Melsa, a fundatione usque ad annum 1396*, ed. E. A. Bond, 3 vols. (Cambridge, 1866–8).

Busenbaum ['Busembaum'], H., *Medulla theologiae moralis* (Padua, 1723).

Butler, C., ed., *The Book of Fines: The Annual Accounts of the Mayors of Southampton*, i: *1488–1540* (Southampton, n.d. [2008]).

Bynum, C. W., *Jesus as Mother: Studies in the Spirituality of the High Middle Ages* (Berkeley, CA, 1982).

Cadden, J., *Meanings of Sex Difference in the Middle Ages: Medicine, Science, and Culture* (Cambridge, 1993).

Cadden, J., *Nothing Natural is Shameful: Sodomy and Science in Late Medieval Europe* (Philadelphia, 2013).

Cady, J., '"Masculine Love", Renaissance Writing, and the "New Invention" of Homosexuality', *JH*, 26 (1992), pp. 9–40.

Cady, J., 'The "Masculine Love" of the "Princes of Sodom" "Practising the Art of Ganymede" at Henri III's Court: The Homosexuality of Henri III and his *Mignons* in Pierre de l'Estoile's *Mémoires-Journaux*', in J. Murray and K. Eisenbichler, eds., *Desire and Discipline: Sex and Sexuality in the Premodern West* (Toronto, 1996), pp. 123–54.

Calendar of State Papers Colonial, America and West Indies, x, *1677–80*, ed. W. N. Sainsbury and J. W. Fortescue (London, 1896).

Calendar of State Papers, Domestic, of the Reign of Charles I, 1639, ed. W. Douglas Hamilton (London, 1873).

Campana, A., 'The Origin of the Word "Humanist"', *Journal of the Warburg and Courtauld Institutes*, 9 (1946), pp. 60–73.

Canevari, A., and G. Fusconi, 'Un disegno licenzioso di Pietro Testa: gli amori di Pan e Venere', in S. Albl and S. Ebert-Schifferer, eds., *La fortuna dei baccanali di Tiziano nell'arte e nella letteratura del seicento* (Rome, 2019), pp. 129–47.

Canosa, R., *Storia di una grande paura: la sodomia a Firenze e a Venezia nel Quattrocento* (Milan, 1991).

Canosa, R., *Sessualità e Inquisizione in Italia tra Cinquecento e Seicento* (Rome, 1994).

Carboni, F., *L'umanità negata: schiavi mori, turchi, neri, ebrei e padroni cristiani nella Sardegna del '500* (Cagliari, 2008).

Cardano, G. ('H. Cardanus'), *Libelli quinque* (Nuremberg, 1547).

Carini, I., 'La "Difesa" di Pomponio Leto pubblicata ed illustrata', in *Nozze Cian-Sappa-Flandinet* (Bergamo, 1894), pp. 151–93.

Carlier de Pinon, J., *Voyage en orient*, ed. E. Blochet (Paris, 1920).

Carnoy, D., *Représentations de l'Islam dans la France du XVIIᵉ siècle* (Paris, 1998).

Carrasco, R., *Inquisición y represión sexual en Valencia: historia de los sodomitas (1565–1786)* (Barcelona, 1985).

Carter, P., *Men and the Emergence of Polite Society, Britain 1660–1800* (Harlow, 2001).

Cartlidge, N., 'Homosexuality and Marriage in a Fifteenth-Century Italian Humanist Comedy: *The Debate between Cavichiolus and his Wife*', *The Journal of Medieval Latin*, 15 (2005), pp. 25–66.

Casanova, G., *Histoire de ma vie jusqu'à l'an 1797*, ed. G. Lahouati and M.-F. Luna (Paris, 2013).

Castiglione, B., *Il libro del cortegiano, con una scelta delle Opere minori*, ed. B. Maier (Turin, 1964).

Castle, T., 'The Culture of Travesty: Sexuality and Masquerade in Eighteenth-Century England', in G. S. Rousseau and R. Porter, eds., *Sexual Underworlds of the Enlightenment* (Manchester, 1987), pp. 156–80.

de Castro Palao, F., *Operis moralis pars prima* (Lyon, 1656).

Cattaneo, M., '"Vitio nefando" e Inquisizione romana', in M. Formica and A. Postigliola, eds., *Diversità e minoranze nel Settecento: atti del seminario di Santa Margherita Ligure, 2–4 giugno 2003* (Rome, 2006), pp. 55–77.

Cavaillé, J.-P., *Postures libertines: la culture des esprits forts* (Toulouse, 2011).

Çelebi, Evliya: *see* Evliya Çelebi.

Cellini, B., *La vita di Benvenuto Cellini, scritta da lui medesimo, nuovamente riscontrata sul codice Laurenziano*, ed. G. Guasti (Florence, 1890).

Chan, A., 'Chinese–Philippine Relations in the Late Sixteenth Century and to 1603', *Philippine Studies*, 26 (1978), pp. 51–82.

Chassanion, J., *Histoires memorables des grans et merveilleux jugemens et punitions de Dieu avenues au monde*, 2nd edn. (Geneva, 1586).

Cherubini, P., 'Un fonte poco noto per la storia di Roma: i processi della curia del Campidoglio (sec. XV)', in L. Biancini et al., *Roma memoria e oblio* (Rome, 2001), pp. 157–82.

Chevallier, P., *Henri III, roi shakespearien* (Paris, 1985).

Chiffoleau, J., *Les Justices du Pape: délinquance et criminalité dans la région d'Avignon au quatorzième siècle* (Paris, 1984).

Chiffoleau, J., '*Contra naturam*: pour une approche casuistique et procédurale de la nature médiévale', *Micrologus*, 4 (1996), pp. 265–312.

Chojnacka, M., *Working Women of Early Modern Venice* (Baltimore, 2001).

Christian, W., *Local Religion in Sixteenth-Century Spain* (Princeton, NJ, 1981).

Cian, V., 'Una lettera di Carlo Sigonio contro i pedanti', *Giornale storico della letteratura italiana*, 15 (1890), pp. 459–61.

Cicuta, A. ['A. Adriano'], *Della disciplina militare del Capitano Alfonso Adriano* (Venice, 1566).

[de Clapiers, L., marquis de Vauvenargues,] *Introduction à la connoissance de l'esprit humain, suivie de réflexions et de maximes* (Paris, 1746).

Clarke, D., '"The Sovereign's Vice Begets the Subject's Error": The Duke of Buckingham, "Sodomy" and Narratives of Edward II, 1622–8', in T. Betteridge, ed., *Sodomy in Early Modern Europe* (Manchester, 2002), pp. 46–64.

Cockburn, J. S., ed., *Calendar of Assize Records* (London, 1975–).

Cockburn, J. S., ed., *Calendar of Assize Records: Hertfordshire Indictments, Elizabeth I* (London, 1975).

Cockburn, J. S., ed., *Calendar of Assize Records: Essex Indictments, Elizabeth I* (London, 1978).

Cockburn, J. S., ed., *Calendar of Assize Records: Kent Indictments, Elizabeth I* (London, 1979).

Cockburn, J. S., ed., *Calendar of Assize Records: Essex Indictments, James I* (London, 1982).

Cockburn, J. S., ed., *Calendar of Assize Records: Surrey Indictments, James I* (London, 1982).

Cockburn, J. S., ed., *Calendar of Assize Records: Kent Indictments, Charles I* (London, 1995).

Cockeram, H., *The English Dictionarie: Or, An Interpreter of Hard English Words* (London, 1623).

Cocks, H. G., *Visions of Sodom: Religion, Homoerotic Desire, and the End of the World in England, c.1550–1850* (Chicago, 2017).

Cohen, A., *The Guilds of Ottoman Jerusalem* (Leiden, 2001).

Cohen Tervaart, G. M., *De grietman Rudolf de Mepsche: historisch-juridische beschouwingen over een reeks crimineele processen, gevoerd in 1731 in den rechtstoel Oosterdeel-Langewold* (The Hague, 1921).

Cohn, S. K., *Women in the Streets: Essays on Sex and Power in Renaissance Italy* (Baltimore, 1996).

Cohn, S. K., review of M. Rocke, *Forbidden Friendships*, *Speculum*, 74 (1999), pp. 481–3.

Coke, Sir Edward, *The Third Part of the Institutes of the Laws of England*, 3rd edn. (London, 1660).

Colavizza, G., R. Cella and A. Bellavitis, 'Apprenticeship in Early Modern Venice' (2017): <https://www.researchgate.net/publication/318284139_Apprenticeship_in_Early_Modern_Venice>.

Collins, S., *The Present State of Russia, in a Letter to a Friend at London* (London, 1671).

Conner, R., 'Les Molles et les chausses: Mapping the Isle of Hermaphrodites in Premodern France', in A. Livia and K. Hall, eds., *Queerly Phrased: Language, Gender, and Sexuality* (New York, 1997), pp. 127–46.

Coquelines, C., ed., *Bullarium privilegiorum ac diplomatum romanorum pontificum amplissima collectio*, 6 tomes (Rome, 1739–62).

Corriveau, P., *La Répression des homosexuels au Québec et en France: du bûcher à la mairie* (Sillery, 2006).

Cosnac, G.-J., comte de, and A. Bertrand, eds., *Mémoires du marquis de Sourches sur le règne de Louis XIV*, 13 vols. (Paris, 1882–93).

Coste, J., ed., *Boniface VIII en procès: articles d'accusation et dépositions des témoins (1303–1311)* (Rome, 1995).

Cottin, P., ed., *Rapports inédits du lieutenant de police René d'Argenson (1697–1715)* (Paris, 1891).

Courouve, C., *Les Gens de la manchette* (Paris, 1981).

Courouve, C., *Vocabulaire de l'homosexualité masculine* (Paris, 1985).

de Courtilz de Sandras, G., *Les Intrigues amoureuses de la cour de France* (Cologne, n.d. [1684]).

Coward, D. A., 'Attitudes to Homosexuality in Eighteenth-Century France', *Journal of European Studies*, 10, no. 40 (1980), pp. 231–55.

Craig, A. G., 'The Movement for the Reformation of Manners, 1688–1715' (Edinburgh University PhD dissertation, 1980, revd and re-formatted, 2015: <https://era.ed.ac.uk/bitstream/handle/1842/6840/Craig-PhD-1980-reformatted-2015.pdf>).

Crawford, K. B., 'Love, Sodomy, and Scandal: Controlling the Sexual Reputation of Henry III', *JHS*, 12 (2003), pp. 513–42.

Crouzet-Pavan, E., *'Sopra le acque salse': espaces, pouvoirs et société à Venise à la fin du Moyen Âge*, 2 vols. (Rome, 1992).

Crowther, D., 'Medieval Price and Wages', <https://thehistoryofengland.co.uk/resource/medieval-prices-and-wages/>.

Cunha de Azevedo Mea, E., *A Inquisição de Coimbra no século XVI: a instituição, os homens e a sociedade* (Porto, 1997).

Curtis, T. C., and W. A. Speck, 'The Societies for the Reformation of Manners: A Case Study in the Theory and Practice of Moral Reform', *Literature and History*, 3 (1976), pp. 45–64.

Dabhoiwala, F., 'Sex, Social Relations and the Law in Seventeenth- and Eighteenth-Century London', in M. J. Braddick and J. Walter, eds., *Negotiating Power in Early Modern Society: Order, Hierarchy, and Subordination in Britain and Ireland* (Cambridge, 2001), pp. 85–101.

Dabhoiwala, F., 'Sex and Societies for Moral Reform, 1688–1800', *Journal of British Studies*, 46 (2007), pp. 290–319.

Dabhoiwala, F., *The Origins of Sex: A History of the First Sexual Revolution* (London, 2012).

'Daily Hadith Online': <https://www.abuaminaelias.com/dailyhadithonline/2019/07/03/lowering-gaze-beardless-youth/>.

Dall'Orto, G., '"Socratic Love" as a Disguise for Same-Sex Love in the Italian Renaissance', in K. Gerard and G. Hekma, eds., *The Pursuit of Sodomy: Male Homosexuality in Renaissance and Enlightenment Europe* (New York, 1989), pp. 33–65.

Dall'Orto, G., *Tutta un'altra storia. L'omosessualità dall'antichità al secondo dopoguerra* (Milan, 2015).

Da Molin, G., 'Family Forms and Domestic Service in Southern Italy from the Seventeenth to the Nineteenth Centuries', *Journal of Family History*, 15 (1990), pp. 503–27.

Daniel, M., *Hommes du grand siècle: études sur l'homosexualité sous les règnes de Louis XIII et Louis XIV* (Paris, 1957).

Dankoff, R., *An Ottoman Mentality: The World of Evliya Çelebi* (Leiden, 2006).

Davidson, J., *The Greeks and Greek Love: A Radical Reappraisal of Homosexuality in Ancient Greece* (London, 2007).

Davidson, N. S., 'Sodomy in Early Modern Venice', in T. Betteridge, ed., *Sodomy in Early Modern Europe* (Manchester, 2002), pp. 65–81.

Dawood, N. J., trans., *The Koran*, 3rd revd edn. (Harmondsworth, 1968).

Dean, T., 'Sodomy in Renaissance Bologna', *Renaissance Studies*, 31 (2016), pp. 426–43.

Dedieu, J.-P., *L'Administration de la foi: l'Inquisition de Tolède (XVIᵉ–XVIIIᵉ siècle)* (Madrid, 1989).

DeGrazia Bohlin, D., *Prints and Related Drawings by the Carracci Family: A Catalogue Raisonné* (Washington, DC, 1979).

DeJean, J., *The Reinvention of Obscenity: Sex, Lies, and Tabloids in Early Modern France* (Chicago, 2002).

Dekker, T., *Satiro-mastix: Or, The Untrussing of the Humorous Poet* (London, 1602).

Dekker, T., *Newes from Graves-End Sent to Nobody* (London, 1604).

Dekker, T., *The Guls Horne-Booke* (London, 1609).

Delgado, M. J., and A. Saint-Saëns, eds., *Lesbianism and Homosexuality in Early Modern Spain: Literature and Theater in Context* (New Orleans, 2000).

Della Porta, G. B., *Della fisionomia dell'uomo*, ed. M. Cicognani (Parma, 1988).

Delon, M., trans. N. Stéphane, 'The Priest, the Philosopher, and Homosexuality in Enlightment France', in R. P. Maccubbin, ed., *'Tis Nature's Fault: Unauthorized Sexuality during the Enlightenment* (Cambridge, 1987), pp. 122–31.

Delrio, M., *Disquisitionum magicarum libri sex*, 3 vols. (Mainz, 1603).

De Luca, G. B., *Il dottor volgare, libro decimoquinto* (Rome, 1673).

De Martino, G., 'An Italian in Morocco', trans. A. Schmitt, in A. Schmitt and J. Sofer, eds., *Sexuality and Eroticism among Males in Moslem Societies* (Binghamton, NY, 1992), pp. 25–32.

Denton, C., *Decadence, Radicalism, and the Early Modern French Nobility: The Enlightened and Depraved* (Lanham, MD, 2017).

Derks, P., *Die Schande der heiligen Päderastie. Homosexualität und Öffentlichkeit in der deutschen Literatur, 1750–1850* (Berlin, 1990).

Derosas, R., 'Moralità e giustizia a Venezia nel '500–'600: gli esecutori contra la bestemmia', in G. Cozzi, ed., *Stato, società e giustizia nella repubblica veneta (sec. XV–XVIII)* (Rome, 1980), pp. 431–528.

Díez Fernández, J. I., *La poesía erótica de los Siglos de Oro* (Madrid, 2003).

DiGangi, M., *The Homoerotics of Early Modern Drama* (Cambridge 1997).

DiGangi, M., 'How Queer was the Renaissance?', in K. O'Donnell and M. O'Rourke, eds., *Love, Sex, Intimacy, and Friendship between Men, 1550–1800* (Basingstoke, 2003), pp. 128–47.

Dingli, L. *Colbert, marquis de Seignelay: le fils flamboyant* (Paris, 1997).

Dinshaw, C., *Getting Medieval: Sexualities and Communities, Pre- and Postmodern* (Durham, NC, 1999).

van der Does, J. ['G. Dousa'], *De itinere suo constantinopolitano epistola* (Leiden, 1599).

Dols, M. W., *Majnūn: The Madman in Medieval Islamic Society*, ed. D. E. Immisch (Oxford, 1992).

Domínguez Ortiz, A., 'La esclavitud en Castilla durante la Edad Moderna', *Estudios de historia social de España*, 2 (1952), pp. 369–428.

Donne, J. ['J. D.'], *Poems* (London, 1633).

Doumergue, E., *Jean Calvin: les hommes et les choses de son temps*, 7 vols. (Lausanne, 1899–1927).

Drayton, M., *Peirs Gaveston Earle of Cornwall, His Life, Death and Fortune* (London, 1594).

Drayton, M., *The Battaile of Agincourt...* [and] *The Moone-Calfe* (London, 1627).

Drumond ['Drummond'] Braga, I. M. R., 'Foreigners, Sodomy, and the Portuguese Inquisition', in H. Johnson and F. A. Dutra, eds., *Pelo vaso traseiro: Sodomy and Sodomites in Luso-Brazilian History* (Tucson, AZ, 2006), pp. 145–64.

Drumond Braga, I. M., 'Pelo universo da sexualidade proibida: os Mouriscos portugueses e o pecado nefando de sodomia', *Revista lusófona de ciência das religiões*, 21 (2018), pp. 7–25.

Duben, A., and C. Behar, *Istanbul Households: Marriage, Family and Fertility, 1880–1940* (Cambridge, 1991).

Dubois-Desaulle, G., *Étude sur la bestialité au point de vue historique, médical et juridique* (Paris, 1905).

van Dülmen, R., *Theater des Schreckens: Gerichtspraxis und Strafrituale in der frühen Neuzeit* (Munich, 1988).

Dupuy, J., and P. Dupuy, eds., *Scaligeriana, sive excerpta ex ore Josephi Scaligeri* (Geneva, 1666).

Durfey, T., *The Royalist* (London, 1682).

Dursteler, E. R., *Venetians in Constantinople: Nation, Identity and Coexistence in the Early Modern Mediterranean* (Baltimore, 2006).

Durston, G. J., *Jacks, Knaves and Vagabonds: Crime, Law, and Order in Tudor England* (Hook, 2020).

Dutra, F. A., 'Sodomy and the Portuguese Nobility: The Case of Dom Filipe de Moura and His Circle', in H. Johnson and F. A. Dutra, eds., *Pelo vaso traseiro: Sodomy and Sodomites in Luso-Brazilian History* (Tucson, AZ, 2006), pp. 165–94.

Duvernoy, J., ed. and trans., *Le Registre d'inquisition de Jacques Fournier, évêque de Pamiers (1318–1325)*, 3 vols. (Paris, 1978).

Eamon, W., 'Science and Medicine in Early Modern Venice', in E. R. Dursteler, ed., *A Companion to Venetian History, 1400–1797* (Leiden, 2013), pp. 701–41.

Earle, J., *Micro-Cosmographie: Or, A Peece of the World Discovered in Essayes and Characters* (London, 1628).

Edgerton, W. L., *Nicholas Udall* (New York, 1965).

van Eickels, K., 'Tender Comrades: Gesten männlicher Freundschaft und die Sprache der Liebe im Mittelalter', *Invertito: Jahrbuch für die Geschichte der Homosexualitäten*, 6 (2004), pp. 9–48.

van Eickels, K., 'Die Konstruktion des Anderen: (Homo)sexuelles Verhalten als Element des Sarazenenbildes zur Zeit der Kreuzzüge und die Beschlüsse des Konzils von Nablus 1120', in L. M. Thoma and S. Limbeck, eds., *'Die Sünde, der sich der tiuvel schamet in der helle': Homosexualität in der Kultur des Mittelalters und der frühen Neuzeit* (Ostflidern, 2009), pp. 43–68.

Eisenberg, D., 'Juan Ruiz's Heterosexual "Good Love"', in J. Blackmore and G. S. Hutcheson, eds., *Queer Iberia: Sexualities, Cultures, and Crossings from the Middle Ages to the Renaissance* (Durham, NC, 1999), pp. 250–74.

Ekserdjian, D., *Parmigianino* (New Haven, CT, 2006).

Elliott, D., *Fallen Bodies: Pollution, Sexuality and Demonology in the Middle Ages* (Philadelphia, 1990).

Ellis, J., 'Desire in Translation: Friendship in the Life and Work of Spenser', *English Studies in Canada*, 20 (1994), pp. 171–86.

El-Rouayheb, K., *Before Homosexuality in the Arab-Islamic World, 1500–1800* (Chicago, 2005).

Elwood, C., 'A Singular Example of the Wrath of God: The Use of Sodom in Sixteenth-Century Exegesis', *The Harvard Theological Review*, 98 (2005), pp. 67–93.

Erdoğan, S. N., *Sexual Life in Ottoman Society* (Istanbul, 1996).

Escamilla-Colin, M., *Crimes et châtiments dans l'espace inquisitoriale: essai de typologie délictive et punitive sous le dernier Habsbourg et le premier Bourbon*, 2 vols. (Paris, 1992).

Estienne, H., *Apologie pour Herodote, ou traité de la conformité des merveilles anciennes avec les modernes*, 2 vols. (The Hague, 1735).

d'Estrées, P., *Les Infâmes sous l'ancien régime: documents historiques recueillis à la Bibliothèque Nationale et à l'Arsenal* (Paris, 1902).

Evelyn, J., *The Diary*, ed. E. S. de Beer, 6 vols. (Oxford, 1955).

Everard, M., *Ziel en zinnen: over liefde en lust tussen vrouwen in de tweede helft van de achttiende eeuw* (Groningen, 1994).

Evliya Çelebi, *An Ottoman Traveller: Selections from the Book of Travels of Evliya Çelebi*, ed. and trans. R. Dankoff and S. Kim (London, 2010).

Falkner, S. A., ' "Having It Off" with Fish, Camels, and Lads: Sodomitic Pleasures in German-Language *Turcica*', *JHS*, 13 (2004), pp. 401–27.

Farge, A. *Vivre dans la rue à Paris au XVIIIᵉ siècle* (Paris, 1979).

Farmer, N. K., ed., 'Poems from a Seventeenth-Century Manuscript with the Hand of Robert Herrick', *Texas Quarterly*, 16:4 (1973), Supplement, pp. 1–185.

Fasoli, G., and P. Sella, *Statuti di Bologna dell'anno 1288*, 2 vols. (Vatican City, 1937–9).

Fasoli, P., 'Body Language: Sex-Manual Literature from Pietro Aretino's *Sixteen Positions* to Antonio Rocco's *Invitation to Sodomy*', in A. Levy, ed., *Sex Acts in Early Modern Italy: Practice, Performance, Perversion, Punishment* (Abingdon, 2010), pp. 27–42.

Febvre, M., *L'État présent de la Turquie, où il est traité des vies, moeurs et coûtumes des Ottomans, et autres peuples de leur empire* (Paris, 1675).

Febvre, M., *Theatre de la Turquie* (Paris, 1682).

Ferguson, G., *Same-Sex Marriage in Renaissance Rome: Sexuality, Identity, and Community in Early Modern Europe* (Ithaca, NY, 2016).

Ferino Pagden, S., 'Giulio Romano und das künstlerische Vermächtnis Raffaels', in S. Ferino Pagden and K. Oberhuber, eds., *Fürstenhöfe der Renaissance: Giulio Romano und die klassische Tradition* (Vienna, 1989), pp. 46–87.

Fernandez, A., 'The Repression of Sexual Behavior by the Aragonese Inquisition between 1560 and 1700', *JHS*, 7 (1997), pp. 469–501.

Ferraro, J. M., *Marriage Wars in Late Renaissance Venice* (Oxford, 2001).

Finch, A. J., 'Sexual Morality and Canon Law: The Evidence of the Rochester Consistory Court', *Journal of Medieval History*, 20:3 (1994), pp. 261–75.

Findlen, P., 'Humanism, Politics and Pornography in Renaissance Italy', in L. Hunt, ed., *The Invention of Pornography: Obscenity and the Origins of Modernity, 1500–1800* (New York, 1993), pp. 49–108.

Finkel, C., *The Administration of Warfare: The Ottoman Military Campaigns in Hungary, 1596–1606* (Vienna, 1988).

Fisher, W., 'Peaches and Figs: Bisexual Eroticism in the Paintings and Burlesque Poetry of Bronzino', in A. Levy, ed., *Sex Acts in Early Modern Italy: Practice, Performance, Perversion, Punishment* (Abingdon, 2010), pp. 151–64.

Flandrin, J.-L., 'Repression and Change in the Sexual Life of Young People in Medieval and Early Modern Times', *Journal of Family History*, 2 (1977), pp. 196–210.

Florio, 'J.' [G.], *A Worlde of Wordes, Or, Most and Exact Dictionarie, in Italian and English* (London, 1598).

Foster, T. A., 'Antimasonic Satire, Sodomy, and Eighteenth-Century Masculinity in the "Boston Evening-Post" ', *The William and Mary Quarterly*, 60 (2003), pp. 171–84.

Foster, T. A., *Sex and the Eighteenth-Century Man: Massachusetts and the History of Sexuality in America* (Boston, 2006).

Foster, T. A., 'The Sexual Abuse of Black Men under American Slavery', *JHS*, 20 (2011), pp. 445–64.

Foucault, D., *Histoire du libertinage* (Paris, 2007).

Foucault, M., *La Volonté du savoir* (Paris, 1976).

Foxon, D., *Libertine Literature in England, 1660–1745* (New York, 1965).

Frajese, V., *Une Histoire homosexuelle: Paolo Sarpi et la recherche de l'individu à Venise au XVIIᵉ siècle*, trans. J. Castiglione (Paris, 2022).

Frantz, D. O., Festum Voluptatis: *A Study of Renaissance Erotica* (Columbus, OH, 1989).

Frati, L., *La vita privata di Bologna dal secolo XIII al XVII* (Bologna, 1900).

Fredericksen, E., 'Finding Another Alexis: Pastoral Tradition and the Reception of Vergil's Second Eclogue', *Classical Receptions Journal*, 7 (2015), pp. 422–41.

[Friedel, J.,] *Briefe über die Galanterien von Berlin, auf einer Reise gesammelt von einem österreichischen Offizier* (Gotha, 1782).

Fuhrmann, C., 'Gossip, *Erotica*, and the Male Spy in Alessandro Striggio's *Il Cicalamento delle donne al bucato* (1567)', in T. C. Borgerding, ed., *Gender, Sexuality, and Early Music* (New York, 2002), pp. 167–97.

Furlotti, B., G. Rebecchini and L. Wolk-Simon, eds., *Giulio Romano: arte e desiderio* (Mantua, 2019).

Furtado de Mendoça, H., *Primeira visitação do Santo Offício ás partes do Brasil: denunciações da Bahia (1591–1593)* (São Paulo, 1925).

Fury, C., ' "To Sett Downe All the Villanie": Accounts of the Sodomy Trial on the Fourth East India Company Voyage (1609)', *The Mariner's Mirror*, 102 (2016), pp. 74–80.

Galán, D., *Cautiverio y trabajos de Diego Galán, natural de Consuegra y vecino de Toledo, 1589 a 1600*, ed. M. Serrano y Sanz (Madrid, 1913).

Galderisi, C., ed., *Il piacevol ragionamento de l'Aretino: Dialogo di Giulia e di Maddalena* (Rome, 1987).

Gallucci, M. A., 'Cellini's Trial for Sodomy: Power and Patronage at the Court of Cosimo I', in K. Eisenbichler, ed., *The Cultural Politics of Duke Cosimo I de' Medici* (Aldershot, 2001), pp. 37–46.

García, F. V., and A. Moreno Mengíbar, *Sexo y razón: una genealogía de la moral sexual en España (siglos XVI–XX)* (Madrid, 1997).

García Cárcel, R., *Herejía y sociedad en el siglo XVI: la Inquisición en Valencia 1530–1609* (Barcelona, 1980).

García Fuentes, J. M., *La Inquisición en Granada en el Siglo XVI: fuentes para su estudio* (Granada, 1981).

Garza Carvajal, F., *Butterflies will Burn: Prosecuting Sodomites in Early Modern Spain and Mexico* (Austin, TX, 2003).

Gaudiani, C. L., *The Cabaret Poetry of Théophile de Viau: Texts and Traditions* (Tübingen, 1981).

Gauthier, A., 'La Sodomie dans le droit canonique médiévale', in B. Roy, ed., *L'Érotisme au Moyen Âge* (Paris, 1977), pp. 109–22.

Gauvard, C., *'De grace especial': crime, état et société en France à la fin du Moyen Âge*, 2 vols. (Paris, 1991).

Gerlach, S., *Stephan Gerlachs dess Aeltern Tage-Buch*, ed. S. Gerlach (Frankfurt, 1674).

Gerson, J., *Oeuvres complètes*, ed. Mgr Glorieux, 10 vols. (Paris, 1960–73).

Giannetti Ruggiero, L., 'The Forbidden Fruit or the Taste for Sodomy in Renaissance Italy', *Quaderni d'italianistica*, 27:1 (2006), pp. 31–52.

Gilbert, A. N., 'Buggery and the British Navy, 1700–1861', *Journal of Social History*, 10 (1976), pp. 72–98.

Gilmour-Bryson, A., 'Sodomy and the Knights Templar', *JHS*, 7 (1996), pp. 151–83.

Giraldo Botero, C., 'Esclavos sodomitas en Cartagena colonial. Hablando del pecado nefando', *Historia crítica: revista del Departamento de Historia de la Universidad de los Andes*, 20 (2000), pp. 171–8.

Giraldo Botero, C., *Deseo y represión. Homoeroticidad en la Nueva Granada (1559–1822)* (Bogotá, 2002).

Giuffredi, A., *Avvertimenti cristiani*, ed. L. Natoli (Palermo, 1896).

Gladfelder, H., 'The Indictment of John Purser, containing Thomas Cannon's *Ancient and Modern Pederasty Investigated and Exemplify'd*', *Eighteenth-Century Life*, 31 (2007), pp. 39–61.

Gladfelder, H., 'In Search of Lost Texts: Thomas Cannon's *Ancient and Modern Pederasty Investigated and Exemplify'd*', *Eighteenth-Century Life*, 31 (2007), pp. 22–38.

Glünz, M., 'Das männliche Liebespaar in der persischen und türkischen Diwanlyrik', in T. Stemmler, ed., *Homoerotische Lyrik: 6. Kolloquium der Forschungsstelle für europäische Lyrik des Mittelalters* (Mannheim, 1992), pp. 119–28.

Godard, D., *Le Goût de Monsieur: l'homosexualité masculine au XVIIᵉ siècle* (Béziers, 2002).

Godard, D., *L'Amour philosophique: l'homosexualité masculine au siècle des lumières* (Paris, 2005).

Godard de Donville, L., *Le Libertin des origines à 1665: un produit des apologètes* (Paris, 1989).

Godbeer, R., '"The Cry of Sodom": Discourse, Intercourse, and Desire in Colonial New England', *The William and Mary Quarterly*, 52 (1995), pp. 259–86.

Godbeer, R., *Sexual Revolution in Early America* (Baltimore, 2002).

Godbeer, R., '"Sodomitical Actings", "Inward Disposition", and "The Bonds of Brotherly Affection": Sexual and Emotional Intimacy between Men in Colonial and Revolutionary America', in K. O'Donnell and M. O'Rourke, eds., *Queer Masculinities, 1550–1800: Siting Same-Sex Desire in the Early Modern World* (Basingstoke, 2006), pp. 191–210.

Godbeer, R., and D. L. Winiarski, 'Documents from the Sodomy Trial of Nicholas Sension, May 1677', *Early American Studies*, 12 (2014), pp. 444–57.

Goitein, S. D., *A Mediterranean Society: The Jewish Communities of the Arab World as Portrayed in the Documents of the Cairo Geniza*, 6 vols. (Berkeley, CA, 1967).

Goldberg, J., *Sodometries: Renaissance Texts, Modern Sexualities* (Stanford, CA, 1992).

Goldberg, P. J. P., *Women, Work and Life Cycle in a Medieval Economy: Women in York and Yorkshire c.1300–1520* (Oxford, 1992).

Goldsmith, N. M., *The Worst of Crimes: Homosexuality and the Law in Eighteenth-Century London* (London, 1998).

Gonzalez-Raymond, A., *La Croix et le croissant: les inquisiteurs des îles face à l'Islam, 1550–1700* (Paris, 1992).

Goodich ['Goodrich'], M., 'Sodomy in Medieval Secular Law', *JH*, 1 (1976), pp. 295–302.

Goodich, M., *The Unmentionable Vice: Sodomy in the Late Medieval Period* (Santa Barbara, CA, 1979).

Gorani, G. ['J.'], *Mémoires secrets et critiques des cours, des gouvernemens, et des moeurs des principaux états d'Italie*, 3 vols. (Paris, 1793).

Gosson, S., *The Schoole of Abuse: Conteining a Pleasaunt Invective against Poets, Pipers, Plaiers, Jesters, and such like Caterpillers of the Commonwelth* (London, 1579).

Gosson, S., *Playes Confuted in Five Actions, Proving that they are not to be Sufferd in a Christian Common Weale* (London, 1582).

Gowing, L., *Domestic Dangers: Women, Words, and Sex in Early Modern London* (Oxford, 1996).

Gracián de la Madre de Dios, J. ['G.'], *Tractado de la redempcion de captivos* (Rome, 1597).

Graf, T. P., *The Sultan's Renegades: Christian-European Converts to Islam and the Making of the Ottoman Elite, 1575–1610* (Oxford, 2017).

Grafton, A., *Defenders of the Text: The Traditions of Scholarship in an Age of Science, 1450–1800* (Cambridge, MA, 1991).

Gramaye, J.-B.: *see* ben Mansour, A.

Grassi, U., *L'Offizio sopra l'Onestà: il controllo della sodomia nella Lucca del Cinquecento* (Milan, 2014).

Grassi, U., *Bathhouses and Riverbanks: Sodomy in a Renaissance Republic* (Toronto, 2021).

Grazzini, A., *Le cene*, ed. G. B. Squarotti and E. Mazzali (Milan, 1989).

Green, N., 'Oxmyths Involving Oxford Personally': <www.oxford-shakespeare. com/Oxmyths/OxmythsOxford.pdf>.

Greenberg, D. F., *The Construction of Homosexuality* (Chicago, 1988).

Gregory, T., *Genèse de la raison classique de Charron à Descartes*, trans. M. Raiola (Paris, 2000).

Griffiths, P., 'The Structure of Prostitution in Elizabethan London', *Continuity and Change*, 8 (1993), pp. 39–63.

Griffiths, P., *Youth and Authority: Formative Experiences in England, 1560–1640* (Oxford, 1996).

Griffiths, P., *Lost Londons: Change, Crime, and Control in the Capital City, 1550–1650* (Cambridge, 2008).

Grundman, J. P., *The Popolo at Perugia, 1139–1309* (Perugia, 1992).

Gruzinski, S., 'Las cenizas del deseo. Homosexuales novohispanos a mediados del siglo XVII', in S. Ortega, ed., *De la santidad a la perversión, o de porqué no se cumplía la ley de Dios en la sociedad novohispana* (Mexico City, 1985), pp. 255–81.

Guerra, F., *The Pre-Columbian Mind* (London, 1971).

Guggenbühl, D., *Mit Tieren und Teufeln: Sodomiten und Hexen unter Basler Jurisdiktion in Stadt und Land, 1399 bis 1799* (Basel, 2002).

Gundersheimer, W., 'Crime and Punishment in Ferrara, 1440–1500', in L. Martines, ed., *Violence and Civil Disorder in Italian Cities, 1200–1500* (Berkeley, CA, 1972), pp. 104–28.

de Haedo, D.: *see* de Sosa, A.

Haggerty, G. E., *Men in Love: Masculinity and Sexuality in the Eighteenth Century* (New York, 1999).

Hajnal, J., 'European Marriage Patterns in Perspective', in D. V. Glass and D. E. C. Eversley, eds., *Population in History: Essays in Historical Demography* (London, 1965), pp. 101–43.

Haliczer, S., *Sexuality in the Confessional: A Sacrament Profaned* (New York, 1996).

Halperin, D. M., *One Hundred Years of Homosexuality and Other Essays on Greek Love* (New York, 1990).

Halperin, D. M., *How to Do the History of Homosexuality* (Chicago, 2002).

Hamilton, T., 'Sodomy and Criminal Justice in the Parlement of Paris, ca. 1540–ca. 1700', *JHS*, 29 (2020), pp. 303–34.

Hamilton, T., 'A Sodomy Scandal on the Eve of the French Wars of Religion', *The Historical Journal*, 64 (2021), pp. 844–64.

Hammond, P., *Figuring Sex between Men from Shakespeare to Rochester* (Oxford, 2002).

Hammond, N., *Gossip, Sexuality and Scandal in France (1610–1715)* (Oxford, 2011).

Handley, S., *Sleep in Early Modern England* (New Haven, CT, 2016).

Hankins, J., *Plato in the Italian Renaissance*, 2 vols. (Leiden, 1990).

Hankins, J., 'The Myth of the Platonic Academy of Florence', *Renaissance Quarterly*, 44 (1991), pp. 429–75.

Hankins, J., 'Humanist Academies and the "Platonic Academy of Florence"', in M. Pade, ed., *On Renaissance Academies: Proceedings of the International Conference 'From the Roman Academy to the Danish Academy in Rome, Dall'Accademia Romana all'Accademia di Danimarca a Roma'* (Rome, 2011), pp. 31–45.

Harris, J., *The Destruction of Sodome: A Sermon Preached at a Publicke Fast, before the Honourable Assembly of the Commons* (London, 1629).

den Hartog, M., '"Overvallen door onzedige ondeugd". Opvattingen over "homoseksualiteit" in Italië, 1450–1500' *Madoc: tijdschrift over de Middeleeuwen*, 31:1 (2017), pp. 2–9.

Hashagen, J., 'Aus Kölner Prozessakten: Beiträge zur Geschichte der Sittenzustände in Köln im 15. und 16. Jahrhundert', *Archiv für Kulturgeschichte* 3 (1905), pp. 301–21.

Haustein, H., 'Strafrecht und Sodomie vor zwei Jahrhunderten. Eine archivalische Studie auf Grund der Akten des Preussischen Geheimen Staatsarchivs in Berlin-Dahlem', *Zeitschrift für Sexualwissenschaft und Sexualpolitik*, 16 (1929–30), pp. 98–105.

Healey, D., 'Moscow', in D. Higgs, ed., *Queer Sites: Gay Urban Histories since 1600* (London, 1999), pp. 38–60.

von Hefele, C. J., *Conciliengeschichte, nach den Quellen bearbeitet*, 2nd edn., 9 vols. (Freiburg im Breisgau, 1873–90).

Hehenberger, S., *Unkeusch wider die Natur: Sodomieprozesse im frühneuzeitlichen Österreich* (Vienna, 2006).

Helbing, F., and M. Bauer, *Die Tortur: Geschichte der Folter im Kriminalverfahren aller Zeiten und Völker* (Berlin, 1926).

van der Helm, F. J. A. M., *Gesodomieter in Den Haag: over homofilie en de homovervolging in Den Haag anno 1730* (The Hague, 2011).

Helmholz, R. H., 'Crime, Compurgation and the Courts of the Medieval Church', *Law and History Review*, 1 (1983), pp. 1–26.

Hérault, R., *Jugement à mort en dernier ressort, rendu par Monsieur Herault, Lieutenant general de police de la ville, prevosté et vicomté de Paris* (Paris, 1726).

Hergemöller, B.-U., 'Das Verhör des "Sodomiticus" Franz von Alsten (1536/37)— ein Kriminalfall aus dem nachtäuferischen Münster', *Westfälische Zeitschrift*, 140 (1990), pp. 31–47.

Hergemöller, B.-U., 'Sodomiter: Erscheinungsformen und Kausalfaktoren des spätmittelalterlichen Kampfes gegen Homosexuelle', in B.-U. Hergemöller, ed., *Randgruppen der spätmittelalterlichen Gesellschaft*, 2nd edn. (Warendorf, 1994), pp. 361–403.

Hergemöller, B.-U., *Krötenkuss und schwarzer Kater: Ketzerei, Götzendienst und Unzucht in der inquisitorischen Phantasie des 13. Jahrhunderts* (Warendorf, 1996).

Hergemöller, B.-U., '*Accusatio* und *denunciatio* im Rahmen der spätmittelalterlichen Homosexuellenverfolgung in Venedig und Florenz', in G. Jerouschek, I. Marssolek and H. Röckelein, eds., *Denunziation: historische, juristische und psychologische Aspekte* (Tübingen, 1997), pp. 64–79.

Hergemöller, B.-U., *Einführung in die Historiographie der Homosexualitäten* (Tübingen, 1999).

Hergemöller, B.-U., *Sodom and Gomorrah: On the Everyday Reality and Persecution of Homosexuals in the Middle Ages*, trans. J. Phillips (London, 2001).

Hergemöller, B.-U., 'Leoncelli, Astor', in B.-U. Hergemöller and N. Clarus, eds., *Mann für Mann: biographisches Lexikon zur Geschichte von Freundesliebe und mann-männlicher Sexualität im deutschen Sprachraum*, 2 vols. (Berlin, 2010), i, pp. 741–2.

Herlihy, D., and C. Klapisch-Zuber, *Les Toscans et leurs familles: une étude du 'catasto' florentin de 1427* (Paris, 1978).

'Hernandez, L.' [F. Fleuret and L. Perceau], ed., *Les Procès de sodomie aux XVIᵉ, XVIIᵉ et XVIIIᵉ siècles, publiés d'après les documents judiciaires conservés à la Bibliothèque Nationale* (Paris, 1920).

Herrero García, M., *Ideas de los Españoles del siglo XVII* (Madrid, 1966).

Herrup, C. B., *A House in Gross Disorder: Sex, Law, and the 2nd Earl of Castlehaven* (New York, 1999).

Herzig, T., 'The Demons' Reaction to Sodomy: Witchcraft and Homosexuality in Gianfrancesco Pico della Mirandola's "Strix"', *The Sixteenth Century Journal*, 34 (2003), pp. 53–72.

Hewlett, M., 'The French Connection: Syphilis and Sodomy in Late-Renaissance Lucca', in K. Siena, ed., *Sins of the Flesh: Responding to Sexual Disease in Early-Modern Europe* (Toronto, 2005), pp. 239–60.

Heyam, K., *The Reputation of Edward II, 1305–1697: A Literary Transformation of History* (Amsterdam, 2020).

Heyd, U., *Studies in Old Ottoman Criminal Law*, ed. V. L. Ménage (Oxford, 1973).

Heydenreuter, R., *Kriminalität in München: Verbrechen und Strafen im alten München (1180–1800)* (Regensburg, 2014).

Heywood, T., *An Apology for Actors* (London, 1612).

Hiegel, H., *Le Bailliage d'Allemagne de 1600 à 1632: l'administration, la justice, les finances et l'organisation militaire* (Saarguemines, 1961).

Higginson, F., 'A True Relation of the Last Voyage to New England', *Proceedings of the Massachusetts Historical Society*, ser. 3, vol. 62 (1928–9), pp. 281–99.

Higgs, D., 'Lisbon', in D. Higgs, ed., *Queer Sites: Gay Urban Histories since 1600* (London, 1999), pp. 112–37.

Higgs, D., 'Rio de Janeiro', in D. Higgs, ed., *Queer Sites: Gay Urban Histories since 1600* (London, 1999), pp. 138–63.

Higgs, D., 'Tales of Two Carmelites: Inquisitorial Narratives from Portugal and Brazil', in P. Sigal, ed., *Infamous Desire: Male Homosexuality in Colonial Latin America* (Chicago, 2003), pp. 152–67.

Higgs, D., 'The Historiography of Male–Male Love in Portugal, 1550–1800', in K. O'Donnell and M. O'Rourke, eds., *Queer Masculinities, 1550–1800: Siting Same-Sex Desire in the Early Modern World* (Basingstoke, 2006), pp. 37–57.

Hill, A., *The Crie of England: A Sermon Preached at Paules Cross in September 1593* (1595).

Hill, A., *A Full and Just Account of the Present State of the Ottoman Empire in All its Branches* (London, 1709).

Hitchcock, T., *English Sexualities, 1700–1800* (Basingstoke, 1997).

Hobbes, T., *The Correspondence*, ed. N. Malcolm, 2 vols. (Oxford, 1994).

Hollewand, K., 'Sex and the Classics: The Approaches of Early Modern Humanists to Ancient Sexuality', in D. Levitin and I. Maclean, eds., *The Worlds of Knowledge and the Classical Tradition in the Early Modern Age: Comparative Approaches* (Leiden, 2021), pp. 48–69.

Holloway, J. B., *Twice-Told Tales: Brunetto Latino and Dante Alighieri* (New York, 1993).

Horner, T., *Jonathan Loved David: Homosexuality in Biblical Times* (Philadelphia, 1978).

Horswell, M. J., 'Toward an Andean Theory of Ritual Same-Sex Sexuality and Third-Gender Subjectivity', in P. Sigal, ed., *Infamous Desire: Male Homosexuality in Colonial Latin America* (Chicago, 2003), pp. 25–69.

Horswell, M. J., *Decolonizing the Sodomite: Queer Tropes of Sexuality in Colonial Andean Culture* (Austin, TX, 2006).

Howell, J. ['J. H.'], *Paroimiographia: Proverbs; Or, Old Sayed Sawes & Adages in English (or the Saxon Toung), Italian, French and Spanish* (London, 1659).

Hull, I. V., *Sexuality, State, and Civil Society in Germany, 1700–1815* (Ithaca, NY, 1996).

Hurteau, P., 'Catholic Moral Discourse on Male Sodomy and Masturbation in the Seventeenth and Eighteenth Centuries', *JHS*, 4 (1993), pp. 1–26.

Hýzrle z Chodů, J. M., *Příběhy Jindřicha Hýzrla z Chodů*, ed. V. Petráčková and J. Vogeltanz (Prague, 1979).

'I. H.', *This Worlds Folly: Or, A Warning-Peece Discharged upon the Wickedness thereof* (London, 1615).

Imhof, A. E., 'Remarriage in Rural Populations and in Urban Middle and Upper Strata in Germany from the Sixteenth to the Twentieth Century', in J. Dupaquier et al., eds., *Marriage and Remarriage in Populations of the Past* (London, 1981), pp. 35–46.

Imola, Benvenuto da: *see* Benvenuto da Imola.

Ingram, M., *Carnal Knowledge: Regulating Sex in England, 1470–1600* (Cambridge, 2017).

Israel, J., *Enlightenment Contested: Philosophy, Modernity, and the Emancipation of Man, 1670–1752* (Oxford, 2006).

James, J., 'Bedding Agostino Chigi: Sodoma's *Marriage of Alexander and Roxanne* in the Villa Farnesina', *The Sixteenth Century Journal*, 52 (2021), pp. 647–66.

James VI [and I], King, *Basilikon doron, Devided into Three Bookes* (Edinburgh, 1599).

Jennings, R. C., *Christians and Muslims in Ottoman Cyprus and the Mediterranean World, 1571–1640* (New York, 1993).

Jeremić, R., and J. Tadić, *Prilozi za istoriju zdravstvene kulture starog Dubrovnika*, 2 vols. (Belgrade, 1938–9).

Joannides, P., *Michelangelo and His Influence: Drawings from Windsor Castle* (Washington, DC, 1996).

Johnson, H., and F. A. Dutra, eds., *Pelo vaso traseiro: Sodomy and Sodomites in Luso-Brazilian History* (Tucson, AZ, 2006).

Jones, K., *Gender and Petty Crime in Late Medieval England: The Local Courts in Kent, 1460–1560* (Woodbridge, 2006).

Jonsen, A. R., and S. Toulmin, *The Abuse of Casuistry: A History of Moral Reasoning* (Berkeley, CA, 1988).

Jonson, B., *Every Man in His Humor* (London, 1601).

Jonson, B., *The Fountaine of Selfe-Love: Or, Cynthia's Revels* (London, 1601).

Jonson, B., *Poetaster: Or, The Arraignment* (London, 1602).

Jonson, B., *A Pleasant Comedy, Called: The Case is Alterd* (London, 1609).

Jordan, M. D., *The Invention of Sodomy in Christian Theology* (Chicago, 1997).

Karamustafa, A. T., *God's Unruly Friends: Dervish Groups in the Islamic Later Middle Period, 1200–1550* (Salt Lake City, 1994).

Karras, R. M., *From Boys to Men: Formations of Masculinity in Late Medieval Europe* (Philadelphia, 2002).

Karras, R. M., 'The Lechery that Dare not Speak its Name: Sodomy and the Vices in Medieval England', in R. Newhauser, ed., *In the Garden of Evil: The Vices and Culture in the Middle Ages* (Toronto, 2005), pp. 193–205.

Karras, R. M., *Unmarriages: Women, Men, and Sexual Unions in the Middle Ages* (Philadelphia, 2012).

Katz, J. N., *Gay/Lesbian Almanac: A New Documentary* (New York, 1983).

Kay, R., *Dante's Swift and Strong: Essays on 'Inferno' XV* (Lawrence, KS, 1978).

Kendall, T., *Flowers of Epigrammes* (London, 1577).

Khoury, A.-T., *Polémique byzantine contre l'Islam (VIIIᵉ–XIIIᵉ s.)*, 2nd edn. (Leiden, 1972).

Koen, E. M., 'Notarial Records Relating to the Portuguese Jews in Amsterdam up to 1639', *Studia Rosenthaliana*, 8 (1974), pp. 138–45.

Koenigsberger, H. G., *The Government of Sicily under Philip II of Spain: A Study in the Practice of Empire* (London, 1951).

Kouamenan, D. B. R., 'The Reproach of Sodomy in the Deposition of Edward II of England and its Repercussions in the Historiography of the Middle Ages to the Twentieth Century', in N. Domeier and C. Mühling, eds., *Homosexualität am Hof: Praktiken und Diskurse vom Mittelalter bis heute* (Frankfurt, 2020), pp. 151–77.

Kowaleski, M., 'Singlewomen in Medieval and Early Modern Europe: The Demographic Perspective', in J. M. Bennett and A. M. Froide, eds., *Singlewomen in the European Past, 1250–1800* (Philadelphia, 1998), pp. 38–81.

von Krafft-Ebing, R., *Lehrbuch der Psychiatrie, auf klinischer Grundlage für praktische Ärzte und Studirende*, 5th edn. (Stuttgart, 1893).

Kramer, H., [and J. Sprenger, attrib.], *Malleus maleficarum*, trans. M. Summers (London, 1971).

Krass, A., 'Sprechen von der stummen Sünde: das Dispositiv der Sodomie in der deutschen Literatur des 13. Jahrhunderts (Berthold von Regensburg/Der Stricker)', in L. M. Thoma and S. Limbeck, eds., *'Die Sünde, der sich der tiuvel schamet in der helle': Homosexualität in der Kultur des Mittelalters und der frühen Neuzeit* (Ostfildern, 2009), pp. 123–36.

Krekić, B., 'Abominandum crimen: Punishment of Homosexuals in Renaissance Dubrovnik', *Viator (Medieval and Renaissance Studies)*, 18 (1987), pp. 337–45.

Kritzeck, J., *Peter the Venerable and Islam* (Princeton, NJ, 1964).

Kruszynski, A., *Der Ganymed-Mythos in Emblematik und mythographischer Literatur des 16. Jahrhunderts* (Worms, 1985).

Kuefler, M., 'Sex with Eunuchs, Sex with Boys, and the Implications of Sexual Difference', in *Comportamenti e immaginario della sessualità nell'Alto Medievo* (Spoleto, 2006), pp. 139–72.

Kuru, S. S., 'A Sixteenth Century Scholar: Deli Birader and his *Dāfi 'ü'l-ġumūm ve rāfi 'ü'l-humūm*', Harvard University PhD dissertation (2000).

Kuru, S. S., 'Il genere del desiderio. L'amore per i bei ragazzi nella letteratura ottomana della prima età moderna', in U. Grassi and G. Marcocci, eds., *Le trasgressioni della carne: il desiderio omosessuale nel mondo islamico e cristiano, secc. XII–XX* (Rome, 2015), pp. 81–102.

Kussmaul, A., *Servants in Husbandry in Early Modern England* (Cambridge, 1981).

Kuster, H. J., *Over homoseksualiteit in middeleeuws West-Europa* (Utrecht, 1977).

Labalme, P. H., 'Sodomy and Venetian Justice in the Renaissance', *The Legal History Review*, 52 (1984), pp. 217–54.

Lage da Gama Lima, L., 'Sodomia e pedofilia no século XVII: o proceso de João da Costa', in R. Vainfas, B. Feitler and L. Lage da Gama Lima, eds., *A Inquisição em xeque: temas, controvérsias, estudos de caso* (Rio de Janeiro, 2006), pp. 237–52.

Laiou, A. E., *Mariage, amour et parenté à Byzance aux XIᵉ–XIIIᵉ siècles* (Paris, 1992).

Lake, P., with M. Questier, *The Antichrist's Lewd Hat: Protestants, Papists and Players in Post-Reformation England* (New Haven, CT, 2002).

Lamansky, V., *Secrets d'état de Venise: documents, extraits, notices et études* (St Petersburg, 1884).

Langbein, J. H., *Prosecuting Crime in the Renaissance: England, Germany, France* (Cambridge, MA, 1974).

Lansing, C., 'Gender and Civic Authority: Sexual Control in a Medieval Italian Town', *Journal of Social History*, 31 (1997), pp. 33–59.

Laqueur, T., *Making Sex: Body and Gender from the Greeks to Freud* (Cambridge, MA, 1990).

Larivaille, P., *Pietro Aretino* (Rome, 1997).

von Lates, A., 'Caravaggio's Peaches and Academic Puns', *Word & Image*, 11 (1995), pp. 55–60.

Laṭīfī ('Lâtifî'), *Éloge d'Istanbul*, ed. and trans. S. Yerasimos (Paris, 2001).

Lau, T., '"Da erhob sich ein gross Geschrei über Sodom": Sodomitenverfolgung in Zürich in der zweiten Hälfte des 17. Jahrhunderts', *Invertito: Jahrbuch für die Geschichte der Homosexualitäten*, 11 (2009), pp. 8–21.

Laugier de Tassy, J. P., *Histoire du royaume d'Alger, avec l'état présent de son gouvernement* (Amsterdam, 1725).

Lauriol, C., *La Beaumelle: un protestant cévenol entre Montesquieu et Voltaire* (Geneva, 1978).

Lautermann, M., 'Ninth-Century Classicism and the Erotic Muse', in L. James, ed., *Desire and Denial in Byzantium* (Aldershot, 1999), pp. 161–70.

Lavenia, V., 'Indicibili *mores*. Crimini contro natura e tribunali della fede in età moderna', *Cristianesimo nella storia*, 30 (2009), pp. 513–41.

Lavenia, V., 'Tra eresia e crimine contro natura: sessualità, islamofobia e inquisizioni nell'Europa moderna', in U. Grassi and G. Marcocci, eds., *Le trasgressioni della carne: il desiderio omosessuale nel mondo islamico e cristiano, secc. XII–XX* (Rome, 2015), pp. 103–30.

Lavenia, V., *Un'eresia indicibile: Inquisizione e crimini contro natura in età moderna* (Bologna, 2015).

The Laws, Ordinances, and Institutions of the Admiralty of Great Britain, Civil and Military, 2 vols. (London, 1746).

Lee, M., *Great Britain's Solomon: King James VI and I in His Three Kingdoms* (Urbana, IL, 1990).

LeJacq, S. S., 'Buggery's Travels: Royal Navy Sodomy on Ship and Shore in the Long Eighteenth Century', *Journal for Maritime Research*, 17:2 (2015), pp. 103–16.

de León, P., *Grandeza y miseria en Andalucia: testimonio de una encrucijada historia (1578–1616)*, ed. P. Herrera Puga (Granada, 1981).

Lepage, Y. G., 'François Villon et l'homosexualité', *Le Moyen Âge*, 92 (1986), pp. 69–89.

Leroy-Forgeot, F., *Histoire juridique de l'homosexualité en Europe* (Paris, 1997).

Le Roy Ladurie, E., *Montaillou: Cathars and Catholics in a French Village, 1294–1324*, trans. B. Bray (Harmondsworth, 1980).

de Lescure, M., ed., *Journal et mémoires de Mathieu Marais, avocat au Parlement de Paris, sur la régence et le règne de Louis XV (1715–1737)*, 4 vols. (Paris, 1863–8).

Le Targat, F., *Saint Sébastien dans l'histoire de l'art depuis le XVᵉ siècle* (Paris, 1979).

Letters and Papers Foreign and Domestic of the Reign of Henry VIII, xv, 1540, ed. J. Gairdner and R. H. Brodie (London, 1896).

Lever, M., *Les Bûchers de Sodome: histoire des 'infâmes'* (Paris, 1985).

Levin, E., *Sex and Society in the World of the Orthodox Slavs, 900–1700* (Ithaca, NY, 1989).

Levine, L., *Men in Women's Clothing: Anti-Theatricality and Effeminization, 1579–1642* (Cambridge, 1994).

Liliequist, J., 'Peasants against Nature: Crossing the Boundaries between Man and Animal in Seventeenth- and Eighteenth-Century Sweden', *JHS*, 1 (1991), pp. 393–423.

Liliequist, J., 'State Policy, Popular Discourse, and the Silence on Homosexual Acts in Early Modern Sweden', *JH*, 35:3–4 (1998), pp. 15–52.

Limbeck, S., '*Sacrista—Hypocrita—Sodomita*. Komödiantische Konstruktion sexueller Identität in Mercurino Ranzos *De falso hypocrita*', in A. Bihrer, S. Limbeck and P. G. Schmidt, eds., *Exil, Fremdheit und Ausgrenzung in Mittelalter und früher Neuzeit* (Würzburg, 2000), pp. 91–112.

Limbeck, S., '"Ein seltzam wunder vnd monstrum, welches beide mannlichen vnd weiblichen geschlecht an sich hett": Tetralogie, Sodomie und Allegorese in der Medienkultur der frühen Neuzeit', in L. M. Thoma and Sven Limbeck, eds., *'Die Sünde, der sich der tiuvel schamet in der helle': Homosexualität in der Kultur des Mittelalters und der frühen Neuzeit* (Ostfildern, 2009), pp. 199–247.

Linkinen, T., *Same-Sex Sexuality in Later Medieval English Culture* (Amsterdam, 2015).

Lithgow, W., *The Totall Discourse of the Rare Adventures and Painefull Peregrinations of Long Nineteen Yeares Travayles from Scotland to the Most Famous Kingdomes in Europe, Asia and Affrica* (Glasgow, 1906).

Lombard, J., *Courtilz de Sandras et la crise du roman à la fin du grand siècle* (Paris, 1980).

Lo Re, S., 'Gli amori omosessuali del Varchi: storia e legenda', in E. Boillet and C. Lastraioli, eds., *Extravagances amoureuses: l'amour au-delà de la norme à la Renaissance* (Paris, 2010), pp. 279–95.

Loughlin, M. H., *Same-Sex Desire in Early Modern England, 1550–1735* (Manchester, 1988).

Love, H., 'But Did Rochester *Really* Write *Sodom*?', *The Papers of the Bibliographical Society of America*, 87 (1993), pp. 319–36.

Lubenau, R., *Beschreibung der Reisen*, ed. W. Sahm, 2 vols. (Königsberg, 1914–30).

Lucchetta, F., 'La scuola dei "giovani di lingua" veneti nei secoli XVI e XVII', *Quaderni di studi arabi*, 7 (1989), pp. 19–40.

Lutterbach, H., 'Gleichgeschlechtliches sexuelles Verhalten: ein Tabu zwischen Spätantike und Früher Neuzeit?', *Historische Zeitschrift*, 267: 2 (1998), pp. 281–311.

Lutterbach, H., *Sexualität im Mittelalter: eine Kulturstudie anhand von Bussbüchern des 6. bis 12. Jahrhunderts* (Cologne, 1999).

Luzio, A., *Pietro Aretino nei primi suoi anni a Venezia e la corte del Gonzaga* (Turin, 1888).

Lyons, C. A., 'Mapping an Atlantic Sexual Culture: Homoeroticism in Eighteenth-Century Philadelphia', *The William and Mary Quarterly*, 60 (2003), pp. 119–54.

Macaraig, N., *Çemberlitaş hamamı in Istanbul: The Biographical Memoir of a Turkish Bath* (Edinburgh, 2019).

McCann, J., and H. Connolly, eds., *Memorials of Father Augustine Baker, and Other Documents Relating to the English Benedictines*, Publications of the Catholic Record Society, xxxiii (1933).

McCusker, J. J., *Money and Exchange in Europe and America, 1600–1775: A Handbook* (Chapel Hill, NC, 1978).

McCusker, J. J., and R. R. Menard, *The Economy of British America, 1607–1789* (Chapel Hill, NC, 1985).

McDougall, S., 'Prosecution of Sex in Late Medieval Troyes', in A. Classen, ed., *Sexuality in the Middle Ages and Early Modern Times* (Berlin, 2008), pp. 691–714.

McFarlane, C., *The Sodomite in Fiction and Satire, 1660–1750* (New York, 1997).

McIntosh, M., 'The Homosexual Role', *Social Problems*, 16 (1968), pp. 182–92.

McKee, S., 'The Implications of Slave Women's Sexual Service in Late Medieval Italy', in M. E. Kabadayi and T. Reichardt, eds., *Unfreie Arbeit: ökonomische und kulturgeschichtliche Perspektiven* (Hildesheim, 2007), pp. 101–14.

McKee, S., 'The Familiarity of Slaves in Medieval and Early Modern Households', in S. Hanss and J. Schiel, eds., *Mediterranean Slavery Revisited (500–1800). Neue Perspektiven auf mediterrane Sklaverei (500–1800)* (Zurich, 2014), pp. 501–14.

McLuskie, K., 'The Act, the Role, and the Actor: Boy Actresses on the Elizabethan Stage', *New Theatre Quarterly*, 3 (2009), pp. 120–30.

McSheffrey, S., *Marriage, Sex, and Civic Culture in Late Medieval London* (Philadelphia 2006).

Malcolm, N., *The Origins of English Nonsense* (London, 1997).

Malcolm, N., *Kosovo: A Short History* (London, 1998).

Malcolm, N., 'Hobbes and Sexual Desire', *Hobbes Studies*, 28 (2015), pp. 77–102.

Malcolm, N., *Useful Enemies: Islam and the Ottoman Empire in Western Political Thought, 1450–1750* (Oxford, 2019).

Malcolm, N., 'Forbidden Love in Istanbul: Male–Male Sexual Relations in the Early-Modern Mediterranean World', *Past & Present*, 257:1 (2022), pp. 52–88.

Manca, J., 'Sacred vs. Profane: Images of Sexual Vice in Renaissance Art', *Studies in Iconography*, 13 (1989–90), pp. 145–90.

ben Mansour, A. [Abd el Hadi], ed., *Alger, XVIᵉ–XVIIᵉ siècle: journal de Jean-Baptiste Gramaye, 'évêque d'Afrique'* (Paris, 1998).

Mantecón Movellán, T. E., 'Los mocitos de Galindo: sexualidad *contra natura*, culturas proscritas y control social en la edad moderna', in idem, ed., *Bajtín y la historia de la cultura popular: cuarenta años de debate* (Santander, 2008), pp. 209–39.

Manzi, S., 'Controllare la sessualità, controllare l'Inquisizione? Il caso di due bolle pontificie in lingua volgare (1566–1588)', in U. Grassi, V. Lagioia and G. P. Romagnani, eds., *Tribadi, sodomiti, invertite e invertiti, pederasti, femminelle, ermafrodite . . . Per una storia dell'omosessualità, della bisessualità e delle trasgressioni di genere in Italia* (Pisa, 2017), pp. 41–57.

Marcocci, G., 'Matrimoni omosessuali nella Roma del tardo cinquecento: su un passo del "Journal" di Montaigne', *Quaderni storici*, n.s., no. 133, year 45 (2010), pp. 107–37.

Marcus, A., *The Middle East on the Eve of Modernity: Aleppo in the Eighteenth Century* (New York, 1989).

Marlowe, C., *The Complete Works*, ed. F. Bowers, 2nd edn., 2 vols. (Cambridge, 1981).

Marongiu, M., *Il mito di Ganimede prima e dopo Michelangelo* (Florence, 2002).

Marrone, G., *La schiavitù nella società siciliana dell'età moderna* (Caltanissetta, 1972).

Marston, J., *The Malcontent. Augmented by Marston* (London, 1604).

Marston, J., *The Poems*, ed. A. Davenport (Liverpool, 1961).

Martelli, D., *Polifonie: le donne a Venezia nell'età di Moderata Fonte (seconda metà del secolo XVI)* (Padua, 2011).

Martelli, M., 'Un caso di "amphibolatio": la canzone a ballo "Ragionavasi di sodo"', in G. C. Garfagnini, ed., *Lorenzo de' Medici. Studi* (Florence, 1992), pp. 309–27.

Martín, A. L., 'Sodomitas, putos, doncellos y maricotes en algunos textos de Quevedo', *La Perinola*, 12 (2008), pp. 107–22.

Martin, H., *Le Métier de prédicateur en France septentrionale à la fin du moyen âge (1350–1520)* (Paris, 1988).

Martínez de Toledo, A., Arcipreste de Talavera, *Corbacho*, ed. J. González Muela (Madrid, 1970).

Martini, G., *Il 'vitio nefando' nella Venezia del Seicento: aspetti sociali e repressione di giustizia* (Rome, 1988).

Mas, A., *Les Turcs dans la littérature espagnole du siècle d'or*, 2 vols. (Paris, 1967).

Masi, G., 'Marignolli, Curzio (Curzio da Marignolle)', *Dizionario biografico degli italiani*, 100 vols. (Rome, 1960–2020), lxx, pp. 359–63.

Masi, G., '"Gente scapigliatissima e bizzarra": la poesia libertina di Curzio Marignolli', in E. Boillet and C. Lastraioli, eds., *Extravagances amoureuses: l'amour au-delà de la norme à la Renaissance* (Paris, 2010), pp. 341–70.

Masi, G., 'Testi libertini di Curzio Marignolli inediti o editi con censure', in E. Boillet and C. Lastraioli, eds., *Extravagances amoureuses: l'amour au-delà de la norme à la Renaissance* (Paris, 2010), pp. 371–414.

Massimi, P., *Les Cent Élégies: Hecatelegium, Florence, 1489*, ed. and trans. J. Desjardins (Grenoble, 1986).

Masson, M., 'Barda, bardache et bredindin: la base "BRD" dans les langues romanes', *La Linguistique*, 51 (2015), pp. 41–88.

Matar, N., *Turks, Moors, and Englishmen in the Age of Discovery* (New York, 1999).

Mathieu-Castellani, G., 'Éros masqué: figures mystiques de l'homosexualité', in P. Ford and P. White, eds., *Masculinities in Sixteenth-Century France* (Cambridge, 2006), pp. 181–97.

Matteoli, A., *Lodovico Cardi-Cigoli, pittore e architetto: fonti biografiche, catalogo delle opere, documenti, bibliografia, indici analitici* (Pisa, 1980).

Matthijssen, J., *Rechtsboek van Den Briel beschreven in vijf tractaten*, ed. J. A. Fruin and M. S. Pols (The Hague, 1880).

Maxwell-Stuart, P. G., '"Wild, filthie, execrabil, detestabil, and unnatural sin": Bestiality in Early Modern Scotland', in T. Betteridge, ed., *Sodomy in Early Modern Europe* (Manchester, 2002), pp. 81–93.

Mayer, T. F., *The Roman Inquisition: A Papal Bureaucracy and its Laws in the Age of Galileo* (Philadelphia, 2013).

Mazzi, S. M., *'Gente a cui si fa notte innanzi sera': esecuzioni capitali e potere nella Ferrara estense* (Rome, 2003).

Mea, E. C. de A.: *see* Cunha de Azevedo Mea.

Meek, J., *Queer Voices in Post-War Scotland* (Basingstoke, 2015).

van der Meer, T., *Sodoms zaad in Nederland: het ontstaan van homoseksualiteit in de vroegmoderne tijd* (Nijmegen, 1995).

van der Meer, T., ' "Are Those People like Us": Early Modern Homosexuality in Holland', in K. O'Donnell and M. O'Rourke, eds., *Queer Masculinities, 1550–1800: Siting Same-Sex Desire in the Early Modern World* (Basingstoke, 2006), pp. 58–76.

Mendoza Garrido, J. M., *Delincuencia y represión en la Castilla bajomedieval (los territorios castellano-manchegos)* (Granada, 1999).

Mentzer, R. A., 'Heresy Proceedings in Languedoc, 1500–1560', *Transactions of the American Philosophical Society*, n.s., 74, no. 5 (1984), pp. 1–183.

Mérida, R. M., 'Sodomy and the Sick Body of Women', *Imago temporis: medium aevum*, 7 (2013), pp. 323–41.

Merrick, J., 'Sodomitical Inclinations in Early Eighteenth-Century Paris', *Eighteenth-Century Studies*, 30 (1997), pp. 289–95.

Merrick, J., and B. T. Ragan, *Homosexuality in Early Modern France: A Documentary Collection* (New York, 2001).

Merrick, J., 'Chaussons in the Streets: Sodomy in Seventeenth-Century Paris', *JHS*, 15 (2006), pp. 167–203.

Mezziane, M., 'Sodomie et masculinité chez les juristes musulmans du IXe au XIe siècle', *Arabica*, 55 (2008), pp. 276–306.

Michaelis, S., *Histoire admirable de la possession et conversion d'une penitente... ensemble la Pneumalogie, ou discours des esprits* (Paris, 1613).

Michelsen, J., 'Von Kaufleuten, Waisenknaben und Frauen in Männerkleidern: Sodomie im Hamburg des 18. Jahrhunderts', *Zeitschrift für Sexualforschung*, 9 (1996), pp. 205–37.

Michelsen, J., ' "Wider die Natur": gleichgeschlechtliche Sexualität im frühneuzeitlichen Hamburg', in J. A. Steiger and S. Richter, eds., *Hamburg: eine Metropolregion zwischen Früher Neuzeit und Aufklärung* (Berlin, 2012), pp. 805–23.

Michelsen, J., 'Die Verfolgung des Delikts Sodomie im 18. Jahrhundert in Brandenburg-Preussen', in N. Finzsch and M. Velke, eds., *Queer/Gender/Historiographie: aktuelle Tendenzen und Projekte* (Berlin, 2016), pp. 217–52.

[Middleton, T.,] *Micro-cynicon: Sixe Snarling Satyres* (London, 1599).

Middleton, T., *Father Hubburds Tales: Or, The Ant and the Nightingale* (London, 1604).

Middleton, T., *Michaelmas Term*, ed. R. Levin (London, 1967).

Milles, R., *Abrahams Sute for Sodom: A Sermon Preached at Paules Crosse, the 25 of August 1611* (London, 1612).

Mills, R., *Suspended Animation: Pain, Pleasure and Punishment in Medieval Culture* (London, 2005).

Mills, R., 'Male–Male Love and Sex in the Middle Ages, 1000–1500', in M. Cook, ed., *A Gay History of Britain: Love and Sex between Men since the Middle Ages* (Oxford, 2007), pp. 1–43.

Mills, R., 'Acts, Orientations and the Sodomites of San Gimignano', in A. Levy, ed., *Sex Acts in Early Modern Italy: Practice, Performance, Perversion, Punishment* (Abingdon, 2010), pp. 195–208.

Mills, R., *Seeing Sodomy in the Middle Ages* (Chicago, 2015).

Molho, A., *Marriage Alliance in Late Medieval Florence* (Cambridge, MA, 1994).

Molina, F., 'La *herejización* de la sodomía en la sociedad moderna: consideraciones teológicas y *praxis* inquisitorial', *Hispania sacra*, 62 (2010), pp. 539–62.

Molina, F., 'La sodomía a bordo. Sexualidad y poder en la Carrera de Indias (siglos XVI–XVII)', *Revista de estudios marítimos y sociales*, 3:3 (2010), pp. 9–19.

Molina, F., *Cuando amar era pecado: sexualidad, poder e identidad entre los sodomitas coloniales (Virreinato del Perú, siglos XVI–XVII)* (La Paz, 2017).

Moller, H., 'The Accelerated Development of Youth: Beard Growth as a Biological Marker', *Comparative Studies in Society and History*, 29 (1987), pp. 748–62.

Monbeig Goguel, C., ed., *Francesco Salviati (1510–1563) o la bella maniera* (Paris, 1998).

de Montaigne, M., *Essais*, ed. J.-V. Leclerc, 2 vols. (Paris, 1931).

de Montaigne, M., *The Essays*, trans. M. A. Screech (London, 1991).

da Montalcino, A.: *see* Agostino da Montalcino.

Monter, E. W., 'Sodomy and Heresy in Early Modern Switzerland', *JH* (1981), pp. 41–55.

Monter, W., *Frontiers of Heresy: The Spanish Inquisition from the Basque Lands to Sicily* (Cambridge, 1990).

Moreau, I., *'Guérir du sot': les stratégies d'écriture des libertins à l'âge classique* (Paris, 2007).

Morel D'Arleux, A., 'Obscenidad y desengaño en la poesía de Quevedo', *Edad de Oro*, 9 (1990), pp. 181–94.

Mormando, F., *The Preacher's Demons: Bernardino of Siena and the Social Underworld of Early Renaissance Italy* (Chicago, 1999).

Morpurgo, S., ed., *Il libro di buoni costumi di Paolo di Messer Pace da Certaldo: documento di vita trecentesca fiorentina* (Florence, 1921).

Morris, S., *'When Brothers Dwell in Unity': Byzantine Christianity and Homosexuality* (Jefferson, NC, 2016).

Moryson, F., *An Itinerary written by Fynes Morison Gent. . . . Containing his Ten Yeeres Travell* (London, 1617).

Mott, L., *O sexo proibido: virgens, gays e escravos nas garras da Inquisição* (Campinas, 1988).

Mott, L., 'Meu menino lindo: cartas de amor de um Frade sodomita, Lisboa, 1690', *Luso-Brazilian Review*, 38:2 (2001), pp. 97–115.

Mott, L., 'Crypto-Sodomites in Colonial Brazil', trans. S. Popat, in P. Sigal, ed., *Infamous Desire: Male Homosexuality in Colonial Latin America* (Chicago, 2003), pp. 168–96.

Mott, L., 'Le Pouvoir inquisitorial et la répression de l'abominable péché de sodomie dans le monde luso-brésilien', in G. Audisio, ed., *Inquisition et pouvoir* (Aix-en-Provence, 2004), pp. 203–18.

Mott, L., '*Justitia et misericórdia*: The Portuguese Inquisition and the Repression of the Nefarious Sin of Sodomy', in H. Johnson and F. A. Dutra, eds., *Pelo vaso traseiro: Sodomy and Sodomites in Luso-Brazilian History* (Tucson, AZ, 2006), pp. 63–104.

Mott, L., 'The Misadventures of a Portuguese Man in Seventeenth-Century Brazil', in H. Johnson and F. A. Dutra, eds., *Pelo vaso traseiro: Sodomy and Sodomites in Luso-Brazilian History* (Tucson, AZ, 2006), pp. 293–335.

Mott, L., 'My Pretty Boy: Love Letters from a Sodomite Friar, Lisbon (1690)', in H. Johnson and F. A. Dutra, eds., *Pelo vaso traseiro: Sodomy and Sodomites in Luso-Brazilian History* (Tucson, AZ, 2006), pp. 231–61.

Mott, L., 'Sodomia não é heresia: dissidência moral e contracultura', in R. Vainfas, B. Feitler and L. Lage da Gama Lima, eds., *A Inquisição em xeque: temas, controvérsias, estudos de caso* (Rio de Janeiro, 2006), pp. 253–66.

Mott, L., 'Musulmani sodomiti in Portogallo e bardassi cristiani in Africa del Nord nei secoli dell'età moderna', in U. Grassi and G. Marcocci, eds., *Le trasgressioni della carne: il desiderio omosessuale nel mondo islamico e cristiano, secc. XII–XX* (Rome, 2015), pp. 155–86.

Mott, L., and A. Assunção, 'Love's Labors Lost: Five Letters from a Seventeenth-Century Portuguese Sodomite', in K. Gerard and G. Hekma, eds., *The Pursuit of Sodomy: Male Homosexuality in Renaissance and Enlightenment Europe* (Binghamton, NY, 1989), pp. 91–101.

Moulton, I. F., *Before Pornography: Erotic Writing in Early Modern England* (Oxford, 2000).

Mutini, C., 'Berni, Francesco', *Dizionario biografico degli italiani*, 100 vols. (Rome, 1960–2020), ix, pp. 343–57.

Nace, N. D., 'The Author of *Sodom* among the Smithfield Muses', *The Review of English Studies*, 68 (2016), pp. 296–321.

Naessens, M., 'Seksuele delicten in het laatmiddeleeuwse Gent: de grenzen van een kwantitatieve benadering van de bronnen', in A. Musin, X. Rousseaux and F. Vesentini, eds., *Violence, conciliation et répression: recherches sur l'histoire du crime, de l'Antiquité au XXIᵉ siècle* (Louvain-la-Neuve, 2008), pp. 155–89.

Nalle, S. T., *God in La Mancha: Religious Reform and the People of Cuenca, 1500–1650* (Baltimore, 1992).

Naphy, W., 'Sodomy in Early Modern Geneva: Various Definitions, Diverse Verdicts', in T. Betteridge, ed., *Sodomy in Early Modern Europe* (Manchester, 2002), pp. 94–111.

Nashe, T., *Nashe's Lenten Stuffe, Containing the Description and First Procreation and Increase of the Towne of Great Yarmouth in Norffolke* (London, 1599).

Nathan, B., 'Medieval Arabic Medical Views on Male Homosexuality', *JH*, 26 (1996), pp. 37–9.

Neal, D. G., *The Masculine Self in Late Medieval England* (Chicago, 2008).

Nelson, A. H., *Monstrous Adversary: The Life of Edward de Vere, 17th Earl of Oxford* (Liverpool, 2003).

Nelson, J. C., *The Renaissance Theory of Love: The Context of Giordano Bruno's Eroici furori* (New York, 1958).

Niccoli, O., *Il seme della violenza: putti, fanciulli e mammoli nell'Italia tra Cinque e Seicento* (Rome, 1995).

Nicolas, H., ed., *Proceedings and Ordinances of the Privy Council of England*, 7 vols. (London, 1834–7).

de Nicolay, N., *Dans l'empire de Soliman le Magnifique*, ed. M.-C. Gomez-Géraud and S. Yérasimos (Paris, 1989).

Niederhäuser, A., '"...nemlich das ÿedtwederer dem anndern sin mennlich glid jn die hand genomen...": gleichgeschlechtliche Sexualität zwischen Männern im Spätmittelalter', in U. Heider, S. Micheler and E. Tuider, eds., *Jenseits der Geschlechtergrenzen: Körper, Identitäten und Perspektiven von* Queer Studies (Hamburg, 2001), pp. 30–49.

Nietzsche, F., *Werke*, ed. G. Stenzel, 2 vols. (Salzburg, 1952).

Nissinen, M., *Homoeroticism in the Biblical World: A Historical Perspective* (Minneapolis, 1998).

Nocentelli, C., 'The Erotics of Mercantile Imperialism: Cross-Cultural Requitedness in the Early Modern Period', *Journal for Early Modern Cultural Studies*, 8 (2008), pp. 134–52.

Noordam, D. J., 'Homosexualiteit en sodomie in Leiden, 1533–1811', *Leids jaarboekje (Jaarboekje voor geschiedenis en oudheidkunde van Leiden en omstreken)*, 75 (1983), pp. 72–105.

Noordam, D. J., 'Sodomy in the Dutch Republic, 1600–1725', in K. Gerard and G. Hekma, eds., *The Pursuit of Sodomy: Male Homosexuality in Renaissance and Enlightenment Europe* (New York, 1989), pp. 207–28.

Noorlander, D. L., *Heaven's Wrath: The Protestant Reformation and the Dutch West India Company in the Atlantic World* (Ithaca, NY, 2019).

Norton, R., *The Myth of the Modern Homosexual: Queer History and the Search for Cultural Unity* (London, 1997).

Norton, R., *Mother Clap's Molly House: The Gay Subculture in England, 1700–1830*, 2nd edn. (Stroud, 2006).

Norton, R., 'Homosexuality', in J. Peakman, ed., *A Cultural History of Sexuality in the Enlightenment* (London, 2011), pp. 57–83.

Novak, M. E., G. R. Guffey and A. Roper, eds., *The Works of John Dryden*, xiii, *All for Love; Oedipus; Troilus and Cressida* (Berkeley, CA, 1984).

Nykl, A. R., *Hispano-Arabic Poetry and its Relations with the Old Provençal Troubadours* (Baltimore, 1946).

Oaks, R. F., '"Things Fearful to Name": Sodomy and Buggery in Seventeenth-Century New England', *Journal of Social History*, 12 (1978–9), pp. 268–81.

Oberhelman, S. M., 'Hierarchies of Gender, Ideology, and Power in Ancient and Medieval Greek and Arabic Dream Literature', in J. W. Wright and E. K. Rowson, eds., *Homoeroticism in Classical Arabic Literature* (New York, 1997), pp. 55–93.

O'Driscoll, S., 'The Molly and the Fop: Untangling Effeminacy in the Eighteenth Century', in C. Mounsey, *Developments in the Histories of Sexualities: In Search of the Normal, 1600–1800* (Lewisburg, PA, 2013), pp. 145–72.

Old Bailey, Proceedings of the: *see* 'Proceedings of the Old Bailey'.

Olearius, A., *The Travels of Olearius in Seventeenth-Century Russia*, ed. and trans. S. H. Baron (Stanford, CA, 1967).

Omar, S., 'From Semantics to Normative Law: Perceptions of *Liwāṭ* (Sodomy) and *Siḥāq* (Tribadism) in Islamic Jurisprudence (8th–15th Century CE)', *Islamic Law and Society*, 19 (2012), pp. 222–56.

Oosterhoff, J., 'Sodomy at Sea and at the Cape of Good Hope during the Eighteenth Century', in K. Gerard and G. Hekma, eds., *The Pursuit of Sodomy: Male Homosexuality in Renaissance and Enlightenment Europe* (New York, 1989), pp. 229–35.

O'Reilly, T., 'The "Bad Fate" of Harmen Meyndertsz van den Bogaert', <https://www.nyhistory.org/blogs/the-bad-fate-of-harmen-meyndertsz-van-den-bogaert>.

Orgel, S., *Impersonations: The Performance of Gender in Shakespeare's England* (Cambridge, 1996).

Osman ağa of Timişoara ['Osmân Agha de Temechvar'], *Prisonnier des infidèles: un soldat ottoman dans l'Empire des Habsbourg*, trans. F. Hitzel (Paris, 1998).

Ottonelli, G. D., *Della christiana moderatione del theatro libro primo, detto la qualità delle Comedie*, 2nd edn. (Florence, 1655).

Oxford English Dictionary: <https://www.oed.com>.

Padgug, R. A., 'Sexual Matters: On Conceptualizing Sexuality in History', *Radical History Review*, 20 (1979), pp. 3–23.

Pamuk, Ş., *A Monetary History of the Ottoman Empire* (Cambridge, 2000).

Parker, D., *Bronzino: Renaissance Painter as Poet* (Cambridge, 2000).

Pastorello, T., *Sodome à Paris, fin XVIIIᵉ–milieu XIXᵉ siècle: l'homosexualité masculine en construction* (Paris, 2011).

Patterson, L., 'Chaucer's Pardoner on the Couch: Psyche and Clio in Medieval Literary Studies', *Speculum*, 76 (2001), pp. 638–80.

Payer, P. J., *Sex and the Penitentials: The Development of a Sexual Code, 550–1150* (Toronto, 1984).

Payer, P. J., *Sex and the New Medieval Literature of Confession, 1150–1300* (Toronto, 2009).

Pedani, M. P., *In nome del Gran Signore: inviati ottomani a Venezia dalla caduta di Costantinopoli alla guerra di Candia* (Venice, 1994).

Pedani-Fabris, M. P., ed., *Relazioni di ambasciatori veneti al Senato*, xiv: *Costantinopoli: relazioni inedite (1512–1789)* (Padua, 1996).

Peirce, L., 'Seniority, Sexuality, and Social Order: The Vocabulary of Gender in Early Modern Ottoman Society', in M. C. Zilfi, ed., *Women in the Ottoman Empire: Middle Eastern Women in the Early Modern Era* (Leiden, 1997), pp. 169–96.

Peirce, L., *A Spectrum of Unfreedom: Captives and Slaves in the Ottoman Empire* (Budapest, 2021).

Pelling, M., with F. White, *Medical Conflicts in Early Modern London: Patronage, Physicians, and Irregular Practitioners, 1550–1640* (Oxford, 2003).

Penman, B., ed. and trans., *Five Italian Renaissance Comedies* (Harmondsworth, 1978).

Penrose, M. A., *Masculinity and Queer Desire in Spanish Enlightenment Literature* (Farnham, 2014).

Pepys, S., *Diary*, ed. R. Latham and W. Matthews, 11 vols. (London, 1970–83).

Pérez, L., L. Muntaner and M. Colom, eds., *El Tribunal de la Inquisición en Mallorca: relación de causas de fe, 1578–1806*, i (Palma de Mallorca, 1986).

Pérez Cánovas, N., *Homosexualidad: homosexuales y uniones homosexuales en el Derecho español* (Granada, 1996).

Perry, M. E., 'The "Nefarious Sin" in Early Modern Seville', *JH*, 16 (1989), pp. 67–89.

Perry, M. E., *Gender and Disorder in Early Modern Seville* (Princeton, NJ, 1990).

Pézard, A., *Dante sous la pluie de feu* (Paris, 1950).

Pfisterer, U., *Lysippus und seine Freunde. Liebesgaben und Gedächtnis im Rom der Renaissance, oder: Das erste Jahrhundert der Medaille* (Berlin, 2008).

Phillips, K. M., and B. Reay, *Sex before Sexuality: A Premodern History* (London, 2011).

Piasenza, P., 'Juges, lieutenants de police et bourgeois à Paris aux XVIIe et XVIIIe siècles', *Annales. Histoire, sciences sociales*, 45:5 (1990), pp. 1189–1215.

Pius II, *Commentaries*, ed. and trans. M. Meserve and M. Simonetta, i (Cambridge, MA, 2003).

Pizzolato, N., '"Lo diavolo mi ingannao": la sodomia nelle campagne siciliane (1572–1664)', *Quaderni storici*, 122 (year 41, no. 2) (2006), pp. 449–80.

Poirier, G., *L'Homosexualité dans l'imaginaire de la Renaissance* (Paris, 1996).

Poole, S., '"Bringing Great Shame upon This City": Sodomy, the Courts and the Civic Idiom in Eighteenth-Century Bristol', *Urban History*, 34 (2007), pp. 114–26.

Poos, L. R., 'Sex, Lies, and the Church Courts of Pre-Reformation England', *Journal of Interdisciplinary History*, 25 (1995), pp. 585–607.

Posner, D., 'Caravaggio's Homo-erotic Early Works', *The Art Quarterly*, 34 (1971), pp. 301–24.

Postel, G., *De la république des Turcs: et là où l'occasion s'offrera, des meurs et loy de tous Muhamedistes* (Paris, 1560).

Potter, D., *Der minnen loep*, ed. P. Leendertz, 4 vols. (Leiden, 1845–7).

Primi Visconti, G. B., *Mémoires sur la cour de Louis XIV*, trans. J. Lemoine (Paris, 1908).

'Proceedings of the Old Bailey, 1674–1913': <https://www.oldbaileyonline.org>.

Prynne, W., *Histrio-mastix: The Players Scourge, or Actor's Tragaedie* (London, 1633).

Puff, H., *Sodomy in Reformation Germany and Switzerland, 1400–1600* (Chicago, 2003).

Puff, H., 'Nature on Trial: Acts "Against Nature" in the Law Courts of Early Modern Germany and Switzerland', in L. Daston and F. Vidal, eds., *The Moral Authority of Nature* (Chicago, 2004), pp. 232–53.

Puff, H., 'Sodomie und Herrschaft—eine Problemskizze: das Verfahren Pappenheim contra Pappenheim (1649–1651)', in I. Bauer, C. Hämmerle and G. Hauch, eds., *Liebe und Widerstand: Ambivalenzen historischer Geschlechterbeziehungen* (Vienna, 2005), pp. 175–93.

Puff, H., 'Homosexuality: Homosocialities in Renaissance Nuremberg', in B. Talvecchia, ed., *A Cultural History of Sexuality in the Renaissance* (London, 2011), pp. 51–72.

Quaife, G. R., *Wanton Wenches and Wayward Wives: Peasants and Illicit Sex in Early Seventeenth Century England* (London, 1979).

Questier, M., 'Crypto-Catholicism, Anti-Calvinism and Conversion at the Jacobean Court: The Enigma of Benjamin Carier', *Journal of Ecclesiastical History*, 47 (1996), pp. 45–64.

Quinn, P. A., *Better than the Sons of Kings: Boys and Monks in the Early Middle Ages* (New York, 1989).

Quintana Toret, F. J., 'De los delitos y las penas. La criminalidad en Málaga y su tierra durante los siglos de oro', *Estudis: revista de historia moderna*, 15 (1989), pp. 245–70.

'R. C.', *The Times' Whistle: Or, A New Daunce of Seven Satires, and Other Poems, Compiled by R. C., Gent.*, ed. J. M. Cowper (London, 1871).

Rabb, I. A., *Doubt in Islamic Law: A History of Legal Maxims, Interpretation, and Islamic Criminal Law* (Cambridge, 2015).

[Radicati, A.,] *A Philosophical Dissertation upon Death, Composed for the Consolation of the Unhappy* [trans. J. Morgan] (London, 1732).

Rafeq, A.-K., 'Public Morality in the [*sic*] 18th Century Damascus', *Revue du monde musulman et de la Méditerranée* 55–6 (1990), pp. 180–96.

Ragab, A., 'One, Two, or Many Sexes: Sex Differentiation in Medieval Islamicate Medical Thought', *JHS*, 24 (2015), pp. 428–54.

Ragan, B. T., 'The Enlightenment Confronts Homosexuality', in J. Merrick and B. T. Ragan, *Homosexuality in Modern France* (Oxford, 1996), pp. 8–29.

Rainolds, J., *Th'Overthrow of Stage-Playes* (Middelburg, 1599).

Ravaisson, F., *Archives de la Bastille: documents inédits*, xi: *Règne de Louis XIV (1702 à 1710)* (Paris, 1880).

Rebhorn, W. A., *The Emperor of Men's Minds: Literature and the Renaissance Discourse of Rhetoric* (Ithaca, NY, 1995).

Reeser, T. W., *Setting Plato Straight: Translating Ancient Sexuality in the Renaissance* (Chicago, 2016).

Reeves, Bishop, 'Bodley's Visit to Lecale, County of Down, A.D. 1602–3', *Ulster Journal of Archaeology*, 2 (1854), pp. 73–95.

Reinle, C., 'Zur Rechtspraxis gegenüber Homosexuellen. Eine Fallstudie aus dem Regensburg des 15. Jahrhunderts,' *Zeitschrift für Geschichtswissenschaft* 44 (1996), pp. 307–26.

Reinle, C., 'Das mittelalterliche Sodomiedelikt im Spannungsfeld von rechtlicher Norm, theologischer Deutung und gesellschaftlicher Praxis', in L. M. Thoma and S. Limbeck, eds., *'Die Sünde, der sich der tiuvel schamet in der helle': Homosexualität in der Kultur des Mittelalters und der frühen Neuzeit* (Ostflidern, 2009) pp. 13–42.

Renda, F., *L'Inquisizione in Sicilia* (Palermo, 1997).

Rey, M., 'Police et sodomie à Paris au XVIIIe siècle: du péché au désordre', *Revue d'histoire moderne et contemporaine*, 29 (1982), pp. 113–24.

Rey, M., 'Parisian Homosexuals Create a Lifestyle, 1700–1750: The Police Archives', *Eighteenth-Century Life*, 9 (1985), pp. 179–91.

Rheubottom, D., *Age, Marriage, and Politics in Fifteenth-Century Ragusa* (Oxford, 2000).

Rian, Ø., 'Mellom straf og fortielse: homoseksualitet i Norge fra vikingtiden til 1930-årene', in M. C. Brantsæter et al., eds., *Norsk homoforskning* (Oslo, 2001), pp. 25–56.

Ricci, G., *I Turchi alle porte* (Bologna, 2008).

Ricci, M. T., 'Antonio Vignali e *La Cazzaria*', in E. Boillet and C. Lastraioli, eds., *Extravagances amoureuses: l'amour au-delà de la norme à la Renaissance* (Paris, 2010), pp. 181–90.

Riera i Sans, J., *Sodomites catalans: història i vida (segles XIII–XVIII)* (Barcelona, 2014).

Ritter, H., *Das Meer der Seele: Mensch, Welt, und Gott in den Geschichten des Fariduddin 'Attar* (Leiden, 1955).

Rivero Rodríguez, M., *La batalla de Lepanto: cruzada, guerra santa e identidad confesional* (Madrid, 2008).

Robson, J., trans., *Tracts on Listening to Music, being* Dhamm al-malāhī *by Ibn abī 'l-Dunyā and* Bawāriq al-ilmā' *by Majd al-Dīn al-Ṭūsī al-Ghazālī* (London, 1938).

Roby, A., *La Prostitution au Moyen Âge: le commerce charnel en Midi toulousain du XIIIe au XVIe siècle* (Villemur-sur-Tarn, 2021).

Rocco, A., *L'Alcibiade fanciullo a scola*, ed. L. Coci (Rome, 1988).

da Rocha Peres, F., *Gregório de Mattos e a Inquisição* (Salvador, 1987).

Rochester, Lord: *see* Wilmot, J., Earl of Rochester.

Rocke, M., 'Sodomites in Fifteenth-Century Tuscany: The Views of Bernardino of Siena', *JH*, 16 (1989), pp. 7–32.

Rocke, M., *Forbidden Friendships: Homosexuality and Male Culture in Renaissance Florence* (New York, 1996).

Rocke, M., 'Gender and Sexual Culture in Renaissance Italy', in J. J. Martin, ed., *The Renaissance at Home and Abroad* (London, 2003), pp. 139–58.

Rodger, N. A. M., *The Wooden World: An Anatomy of the Georgian Navy* (London, 1986).

Roelens, J., 'Fornicating Foreigners: Sodomy, Migration, and Urban Society in the Southern Low Countries (1400–1700)', *Dutch Crossing: Jounral of Low Countries Studies*, 41 (2017), pp. 229–46.

Roelens, J., 'Gossip, Defamation and Sodomy in the Early Modern Southern Netherlands', *Renaissance Studies*, 32:2 (2017), pp. 235–52.

Roelens, J., 'Middeleuwse brandstapels', in W. Dupont, E. Hofman and J. Roelens, *Verzwegen verlangen: een geschiedenis van homoseksualiteit in België* (Antwerp, 2017), pp. 23–55.

Rollison, D., 'Property, Ideology and Popular Culture in a Gloucestershire Village, 1660–1740', *Past & Present*, 93 (1981), pp. 70–97.

Romano, D., 'A Depiction of Male Same-Sex Seduction in Ambrogio Lorenzetti's "Effects of Bad Government" Fresco', *JHS*, 21, pp. 1–15.

Romei, D., 'Saggi di poesia omoerotica volgare del Cinquecento', in E. Boillet and C. Lastraioli, eds., *Extravagances amoureuses: l'amour au-delà de la norme à la Renaissance* (Paris, 2010), pp. 235–62.

Romeo, G., *Aspettando il boia: condannati a morte, confortatori, inquisitori nella Napoli della Controriforma* (Florence, 2003).

Romeo, G., *Amori proibiti: i concubini tra Chiesa e Inquisizione, Napoli 1563–1656* (Bari, 2008).

Roper, L., *The Holy Household: Women and Morals in Reformation Augsburg* (Oxford, 1989).

Rosa Pereira, I., *A Inquisição em Portugal, séculos XVI–XVII—período filipino* (Lisbon, 1993).

von Rosen, W., *Månens kulør: studier i dansk bøssehistorie, 1628–1912*, 2 vols. (Copenhagen, 1993).

von Rosen, W., 'Almost Nothing: Male–Male Sex in Denmark, 1550–1800', in K. O'Donnell and M. O'Rourke, eds., *Queer Masculinities, 1550–1800* (Basingstoke, 2006), pp. 77–93.

Rosenblum, M., ed. and trans., *Luxorius: A Latin Poet among the Vandals* (New York, 1961).

Rosenthal, F., 'Ar-Râzî on the Hidden Illness', *Bulletin of the History of Medicine*, 52 (1978), pp. 45–60.

Rosenthal, F., 'Male and Female: Described and Compared', in J. W. Wright and E. K. Rowson, eds., *Homoeroticism in Classical Arabic Literature* (New York, 1997), pp. 24–54.

Rosselló, R., *L'homosexualitat a Mallorca a l'edat mitjana* (Felanitx, 1977).

Rosselló, R., ed., *Procés contra Ponç Hug Comte d'Empúries per pecat de sodomia* (Palma, 2003).

Rossiaud, J., 'Prostitution, Youth, and Society in the Towns of Southeastern France in the Fifteenth Century', in R. Forster and O. Ranum, eds., *Deviants and the Abandoned in French Society*, trans. E. Forster and P. M. Ranum (Baltimore, 1978), pp. 1–46.

van Rossum, W., *Werkers van de wereld: globalisering, arbeid en interculturele ontmoetingen tussen Aziatische en Europse zeelieden in dienst van de VOC, 1600–1800* (Hilversum, 2014).

Rostagno, L., *Mi faccio Turco: esperienze ed immagini dell'Islam nell'Italia moderna* (Rome, 1983).

Roth, N., '"Deal Gently with the Young Man": Love of Boys in Medieval Hebrew Poetry of Spain', *Speculum*, 57 (1982), pp. 20–51.

Rousseau, G. S., 'The Pursuit of Homosexuality in the Eighteenth Century: "Utterly Confused Category" and/or Rich Repository?', in R. P. Maccubbin, ed., *'Tis Nature's Fault: Unauthorized Sexuality during the Enlightenment* (Cambridge, 1987), pp. 132–68.

Rowland, I. D., *The Culture of the High Renaissance: Ancients and Moderns in Sixteenth-Century Rome* (Cambridge, 1998).

Rowson, E. K., 'The Categorization of Gender and Sexual Irregularity in Medieval Arabic Vice Lists', in J. Epstein and K. Straub, eds., *Body Guards: The Cultural Politics of Gender Ambiguity* (New York, 1991), pp. 50–79.

Rowson, E. K., 'Omoerotismo ed élite mamelucca tra Egitto e Siria nel tardo medievo', in U. Grassi and G. Marcocci, eds., *Le trasgressioni della carne: il desiderio omosessuale nel mondo islamico e cristiano, secc. XII–XX* (Rome, 2015), pp. 23–51.

Rubin, P. L., *Seen from Behind: Perspectives on the Male Body and Renaissance Art* (New Haven, CT, 2018).

Ruggiero, G., *The Boundaries of Eros: Sex Crime and Sexuality in Renaissance Venice* (New York, 1985).

Ruggiero, G., 'Marriage, Love, Sex, and Renaissance Civic Morality', in J. G. Turner, ed., *Sexuality and Gender in Early Modern Europe* (Cambridge, 1993), pp. 10–30.

Rycaut, P., *The Present State of the Ottoman Empire* (London, 1668).

Sabadino degli Arienti, G., *Novelle porretane*, ed. P. Stoppelli (L'Aquila, 1975).

Said, E., *Orientalism*, 2nd edn. (London, 1995).

Salter, H. E., ed., *Registrum annalium collegii Mertonensis, 1483–1521*, Oxford Historical Society, lxxvi (Oxford 1923).

Sánchez, T. M., *Disputationum de sancto matrimonii sacramento libri tres*, 3 vols. (Antwerp, 1620).

a Sancto Felice, J., *Triumphus misericordiae, id est sacrum ordinis SSS. Trinitatis institutum redemptio captivorum* (Vienna, 1704).

Sandys, G., *A Relation of a Journey Begun An: Dom: 1610* (London, 1621).

Sariyannis, M., 'Prostitution in Ottoman Istanbul, Late Sixteenth—Early Eighteenth Century', *Turcica*, 40 (2008), pp. 37–64.

Sarrión Mora, A., *Sexualidad y confesión: la solicitación ante el Tribunal del Santo Oficio (siglos XVI–XIX)* (Madrid, 1994).

Saslow, J. M., 'Homosexuality in the Renaissance: Behavior, Identity, and Artistic Expression', in M. B. Duberman, M. Vicinus and G. Chauncey, eds., *Hidden from History: Reclaiming the Gay and Lesbian Past* (New York, 1989), pp. 90–105.

Saslow, J., *Pictures and Passions: A History of Homosexuality in the Visual Arts* (New York, 1999).

Saunders, A. C. de C. M., *A Social History of Black Slaves and Freedmen in Portugal, 1441–1555* (Cambridge, 1982).

Savonarola, G. ['H.'], *Confessionale pro instructione confessorum* (Venice, 1543).

Savonarola, G., *Scelta di prediche e scritti di Fra Girolamo Savonarola*, ed. P. Villari and E. Casanova (Florence, 1898).

Scarabello, G., 'Devianza sessuale ed interventi di giustizia a Venezia nella prima metà del XVI secolo', in S. Bettini et al., *Tiziano e Venezia: convegno internazionale di studi, Venezia, 1976* (Vicenza, 1980), pp. 75–84.

Scaramella, P., *Le lettere della Congregazione del Sant'Ufficio ai Tribunali di Fede di Napoli, 1563–1625* (Trieste, 2002).

Scaramella, P., 'Sodomia', in A. Prosperi, ed., *Dizionario storico dell'Inquisizione*, 5 vols. (Pisa, 2010), iii, pp. 1445–50.

Scaramella, T., '"La sodomia è boccone da principi". Voci libertine fuori dall'Accademia: il caso veneziano tra Sei e Settecento', in U. Grassi, V. Lagioia and G. P. Romagnani, eds., *Tribadi, sodomiti, invertite e invertiti, pederasti, femminelle, ermafrodite… Per una storia dell'omosessualità, della bisessualità e delle trasgressioni di genere in Italia* (Pisa, 2017), pp. 111–28.

Scaramella, T., *Un doge infame: sodomia e nonconformismo sessuale a Venezia nel Settecento* (Venice, 2021).

Schick, İ. C., 'Three Genders, Two Sexualities: The Evidence of Ottoman Erotic Terminology', in A. Kreil, L. Torbero and S. Tolino, eds., *Sex and Desire in Muslim Cultures: Beyond Norms and Transgression from the Abbasids to the Present Day* (London, 2021), pp. 87–110.

Schimmel, A., 'Eros—Heavenly and not so Heavenly—in Sufi Literature and Life', in A. L. al-Sayyid-Marsot, ed., *Society and the Sexes in Medieval Islam* (Malibu, CA, 1979), pp. 119–41.

Schleiner, W., 'Linguistic "Xenohomophobia" in Sixteenth-Century France: The Case of Henri Estienne', *The Sixteenth Century Journal*, 34 (2003), pp. 747–60.

Schmitt, A., 'Appendix', in A. Schmitt and J. Sofer, eds., *Sexuality and Eroticism among Males in Moslem Societies* (Binghamton, NY, 1992), pp. 164–7.

Schmitt, A., 'Different Approaches to Male–Male Sexuality/Eroticism from Morocco to Usbekistān', in A. Schmitt and J. Sofer, eds., *Sexuality and Eroticism among Males in Moslem Societies* (Binghamton, NY, 1992), pp. 1–24.

Schmitt, A., '*Liwāṭ* im *Fiqh*: Männliche Homosexualität?', *Journal of Arabic and Islamic Studies*, 4 (2001–2), pp. 49–110.

Schnabel-Schüle, H., *Überwachen und Strafen im Territorialstaat: Bedingungen und Auswirkungen des Systems strafrechtlicher Sanktionen im frühneuzeitlichen Württemberg* (Cologne, 1997).

Schneider-Lastin, W., and H. Puff, '"Vnd solt man alle die so das tuend verbrennen, es bliben nit funffzig mannen jn Basel": Homosexualität in der deutschen Schweiz im Spätmittelalter', in H. Puff, ed., *Lust, Angst und Provokation: Homosexualität in der Gesellschaft* (Göttingen, 1993), pp. 79–103.

Schöffer, I., 'Conclusie', in L. J. Boon, *'Dien godlosen hoop van menschen'. Vervolging van homoseksuelen in de Republiek in de jaren dertig van de achttiende eeuw*, ed. I. Schöffer et al. (Amsterdam, 1997), pp. 327–59.

Schroeder, C. T., *Monastic Bodies: Discipline and Salvation in Shenoute of Atripe* (Philadelphia, 2007).

Schweigger, S., *Ein newe Reyssbeschreibung auss Teutschland nach Constantinopel und Jerusalem*, ed. R. Neck (Graz, 1964).

Seaver, P., *Wallington's World: A Puritan Artisan in Seventeenth-Century London* (Stanford, CA, 1985).

Sedgwick, E. K., *Between Men: English Literature and Male Homosocial Desire*, 2nd edn. (New York, 2016).

Seidel, F., *Denckwürdige Gesandtschafft an die Ottomanische Pforte* (Görlitz, 1711).

Seifert, L. C., 'Masculinity and Satires of "Sodomites" in France, 1660–1715', *JH*, 42 (2001), pp. 37–52.

Seijas, C., and J. Melchor Toledo, *Demencia nefanda: estudios sobre la homosexualidad en Guatemala del siglo XVII al XXI* (n.p., n.d.).

Semerdjian, E., *'Off the Straight Path': Illicit Sex, Law, and Community in Ottoman Aleppo* (Syracuse, NY, 2008).

Senelick, L., 'Mollies or Men of Mode? Sodomy and the Eighteenth-Century London Stage', *JHS*, 1 (1990), pp. 33–67.

Šerović, P. S., 'Paštrovići, njihovo plemensko uredjenje i pomorska tradicija', *Godišnjak pomorskog muzeja u Kotoru*, 5 (1956), pp. 25–37.

Shadwell, T., *The Complete Works*, ed. M. Summers, 5 vols. (London, 1927).

Shapiro, M., *Gender in Play on the Shakespearian Stage: Boy Heroines and Female Pages* (Ann Arbor, MI, 1994).

Shaw, A. N., 'The *Compendium compertorum* and the Making of the Suppression Act of 1536', Warwick University PhD thesis (2003).

Shepard, A., *Meanings of Manhood in Early Modern England* (Oxford, 2003).

Shepard, T., 'The Autobiography of Thomas Shepard', *Publications of the Colonial Society of Massachusetts*, 27 (1927–30), pp. 343–400.

Shephard, R., 'Sexual Rumours in English Politics: The Cases of Elizabeth I and James I', in J. Murray and K. Eisenbichler, eds., *Desire and Discipline: Sex and Sexuality in the Premodern West* (Toronto, 1996), pp. 101–22.

Sherberg, M., 'Il potere e il piacere: la sodomia del "Marescalco"', in S. Zatti, ed., *La rappresentazione dell'altro nei testi del Rinascimento* (Lucca, 1998), pp. 96–110.

Sherley, T., 'Discours of the Turkes', ed. E. Denison Ross, *Camden Miscellany* 16 (Camden ser. 3, vol. 52), item 2 (London, 1936).

Shorto, R., *The Island at the Center of the World: The Epic Story of Dutch Manhattan and the Forgotten Colony that Shaped America* (New York, 2005).

Shurtleff, N. B., ed., *Records of the Governor and Company of the Massachusetts Bay in New England*, 5 vols. (Boston, 1853–4).

Shurtleff, N. B., and D. Pulsifer, eds., *Records of the Colony of New Plymouth in New England*, 12 vols. (Boston, 1855–61).

Sibalis, M. D., 'The Regulation of Male Homosexuality in Revolutionary and Napoleonic France, 1789–1815', in J. Merrick and B. T. Ragan, *Homosexuality in Modern France* (Oxford, 1996), pp. 80–101.

Sibalis, M., 'Homosexuality in Early Modern France', in K. O'Donnell and M. O'Rourke, eds., *Queer Masculinities, 1550–1800: Siting Same-Sex Desire in the Early Modern World* (Basingstoke, 2006), pp. 211–31.

Sieber-Lehmann, C., *Spätmittelalterlicher Nationalismus: die Burgunderkriege am Oberrhein und in der Eidgenossenschaft* (Göttingen, 1995).

Sigal, P., '(Homo)Sexual Desire and Masculine Power in Colonial Latin America: Notes toward an Integrated Analysis', in P. Sigal, ed., *Infamous Desire: Male Homosexuality in Colonial Latin America* (Chicago, 2003), pp. 1–24.

Silverstolpe, F., 'Inledning', in F. Silverstolpe et al., *Sympatiens hemlighetsfulla makt: Stockholms homosexuella, 1860–1960* (Stockholm, 1999), pp. 15–26.

Simon, B., 'Les Dépêches de Marin Cavalli Bayle à Constantinople, 1558–1560', École Pratique des Hautes Études, Paris, doctoral thesis, 2 vols. (1985).

Sinfield, A., *Shakespeare, Authority, Sexuality: Unfinished Business in Cultural Materialism* (New York, 2006).

Singleton, C. S., ed., *Canti carnascialeschi del Rinascimento* (Bari, 1936).

Sjögren, W., ed., *Förarbetena till Sveriges Rikes lag, 1686–1736*, 8 vols. (Uppsala, 1901–9).

Smith, B., *Homosexual Desire in Shakespeare's England*, 2nd edn. (Chicago, 1994).

Smith, B. R., 'Premodern Sexualities', *Publications of the Modern Languages Association of America*, 115 (2000), pp. 318–29.

Smith, R. M., 'The People of Tuscany and Their Families in the Fifteenth Century: Medieval or Mediterranean?', *Journal of Family History*, 6 (1981), pp. 107–28.

Solorzano Telechea, J. A., '*Fama publica*, Infamy and Defamation: Judicial Violence and Social Control of Crimes against Sexual Morals in Medieval Castile', *Journal of Medieval History*, 33 (2007), pp. 398–413.

Soman, A., 'La Justice criminelle aux XVIᵉ–XVIIᵉ siècles: le Parlement de Paris et les sièges subalternes', in A. Soman, *Sorcellerie et justice criminelle: le Parlement de Paris (16ᵉ–18ᵉ siècles)* (Aldershot, 1992), item 7.

Soman, A., 'Pathologie historique: le témoignage des procès de bestialité aux XVIᵉ et XVIIᵉ siècles', in A. Soman, *Sorcellerie et justice criminelle: le Parlement de Paris (16ᵉ–18ᵉ siècles)* (Aldershot, 1992), item 8.

Sonnini, C.-N.-S. ['C. S.'], *Voyage dans la haute et basse Égypte, fait par l'ordre de l'ancien gouvernement*, 3 vols. (Paris, 1799).

de Sosa, A. ['D. de Haedo'], *Topographia e historia general de Argel, repartida en cinco tratados* (Valladolid, 1612).

Sotheby's, New York, 'Master Paintings & Sculpture Evening Sale', 25 January 2017: <https://www.sothebys.com/en/auctions/2017/master-paintings-n09601.html?p=3&locale=en>.

de Sousa, A., *Opusculum circa constitutionem Pontificis Pauli V, in confessarios ad actus inhonestos foeminas in sacramentali confessione allicientes* (Lisbon, 1623).

Soyer, F., *Ambiguous Gender in Early Modern Spain and Portugal: Inquisitors, Doctors and the Transgression of Gender Norms* (Leiden, 2012).

Spandounes, T., *On the Origin of the Ottoman Emperors*, ed. and trans. D. M. Nicol (Cambridge, 1997).

Spear, R. E., *The 'Divine' Guido: Religion, Sex, Money and Art in the World of Guido Reni* (New Haven, CT, 1997).

Spectorsky, S. A., *Women in Classical Islamic Law: A Survey of the Sources* (Leiden, 2010).

Spierenburg, P., *The Spectacle of Suffering. Executions and the Evolution of Repression: From a Preindustrial Metropolis to the European Experience* (Cambridge, 1984).

Sprachman, P., '*Le beau garçon sans merci*: The Homoerotic Tale in Arabic and Persian', in J. W. Wright and E. K. Rowson, eds., *Homoeroticism in Classical Arabic Literature* (New York, 1997), pp. 192–209.

Spreitzer, B., *Die stumme Sünde: Homosexualität im Mittelalter* (Göppingen, 1988).

Stadtwald, K., *Roman Popes and German Patriots: Antipapalism in the Politics of the German Humanist Movement from Gregor Heimburg to Martin Luther* (Geneva, 1996).

Stanivukovic, G. V., '"Knights in Armes": The Homoerotics of the English Renaissance Prose Romances', in C. C. Relihan and G. V. Stanivukovic, eds., *Prose Fiction and Early Modern Sexualities in England, 1570–1640* (New York, 2003), pp. 171–92.

Stanivuković, G., 'Between Men in Early Modern England', in K. O'Donnell and M. O'Rourke, eds., *Queer Masculinities, 1550–1800: Siting Same-Sex Desire in the Early Modern World* (Basingstoke, 2006), pp. 232–51.

Steakley, J. D., 'Sodomy in Enlightenment Prussia: From Execution to Suicide', in K. Gerard and G. Hekma, eds., *The Pursuit of Sodomy: Male Homosexuality in Renaissance and Enlightenment Europe* (New York, 1989), pp. 163–75.

Steiner, B. C., *History of the Plantation of Menunkatuck and of the Original Town of Guilford, Connecticut* (Baltimore, 1897).

Steinhausen, G., ed., *Briefwechsel Balthasar Paumgarnters des jüngeren mit seiner Gattin Magdalena, geb. Behaim (1592–1598)* (Tübingen, 1895).

Stern, L. I., 'Public Fame in the Fifteenth Century', *The American Journal of Legal History*, 44:2 (2000), pp. 198–222.

Sterneck, T., 'Hříšní sodomité: Jaké tresty čekaly homosexuály v raném novověku', *100+1 zahraniční zajímavost* (16 Dec. 2018) (<https://www.stoplusjednicka.cz/hrisni-sodomite-jake-tresty-cekaly-homosexualy-v-ranem-novoveku>).

Sternweiler, A., *Die Lust der Götter: Homosexualität in der italienischen Kunst, von Donatello zu Caravaggio* (Berlin, 1993).

Stewart, A., *Close Readers: Humanism and Sodomy in Early Modern England* (Princeton, NJ, 1997).

Stewart, A., 'A Society of Sodomites: Religion and Homosexuality in Renaissance England', in L. Gowing, M. Hunter and M. Rubin, eds., *Love, Friendship and Faith in Europe, 1300–1800* (Basingstoke, 2005), pp. 88–109.

Stone, L., *The Family, Sex and Marriage in England, 1500–1800* (London, 1977).

Stringer, G. L., et al., eds., *The Variorum Edition of the Poetry of John Donne*, vii, part 1, *The Holy Sonnets* (Bloomington, IN, 2005).

Stringer, G. L., et al., eds., *The Variorum Edition of the Poetry of John Donne*, iii, *The Satyres* (Bloomington, IN, 2016).

Stubbes, P., *The Anatomie of Abuses*, in J. P. Collier, ed., *Illustrations of Early English Literature*, 3 vols. (London, 1867–70), i, item 1.

Sullivan, J. P., and A. J. Boyle, eds., *Martial in English* (Harmondsworth, 1996).

Summers, C. J., 'Homosexuality and Renaissance Literature, Or the Anxieties of Anachronism', *South Central Review*, 9 (1992), pp. 2–23.

Sweet, D. M., 'The Personal, the Political, and the Aesthetic: Johann Joachim Winckelmann's German Enlightenment Life', in K. Gerard and G. Hekma, eds., *The Pursuit of Sodomy: Male Homosexuality in Renaissance and Enlightenment Europe* (New York, 1989), pp. 147–62.

Szombathy, Z., *Mujūn: Libertinism in Mediaeval Muslim Society and Literature* (n.p., 2013).

Taeger, A., 'Die Karrieren von Sodomiten in Paris während des 18. Jahrhunderts', in W. Schmale, ed., *MannBilder: ein Lese- und Quellenbuch zur historischen Männerforschung* (Berlin, 1998), pp. 113–29.

Taeger, A., *Intime Machtverhältnisse. Moralstrafrecht und administrative Kontrolle der Sexualität im ausgehenden Ancien Régime* (Munich, 1999).

Tallement des Réaux, G., *Historiettes*, ed. A. Adam, 2 vols. (Paris, 1960).

Talvacchia, B., *Taking Positions: On the Erotic in Renaissance Culture* (Princeton, NJ, 1999).

Teply, K., 'Vom Loskauf osmanischer Gefangener aus dem Grossen Türkenkrieg, 1683–1699', Südost-Forschungen, 32 (1973), pp. 33–72.

Terry, A., 'The Craft of Torture: Bronze Sculptures and the Punishment of Sexual Offense', in A. Levy, ed., Sex Acts in Early Modern Italy: Practice, Performance, Perversion, Punishment (Abingdon, 2010), pp. 209–23.

Thévenot, J., L'Empire du Grand Turc vu par un sujet de Louis XIV, ed. F. Billacois (Paris, 1965).

Thoma, L. M., ' "Das seind die sünd der vnküscheit". Eine Fallstudie zum Umgang mit der Sodomie in der Predigt des ausgehenden Mittelalters—Die "Brösamlin" Johannes Geilers von Kayserberg', in L. M. Thoma and S. Limbeck, eds., 'Die Sünde, der sich der tiuvel schamet in der helle': Homosexualität in der Kultur des Mittelalters und der frühen Neuzeit (Ostfildern, 2009), pp. 137–53.

Thomas, K., 'Afterword', in K. Harvey, ed., The Kiss in History (Manchester, 2005), pp. 187–203.

Thomas, K., The Ends of Life: Roads to Fulfilment in Early Modern England (Oxford, 2009).

Thomas Aquinas, St, Summa theologiae, in S. Thomae Aquinatis opera omnia, ed. R. Busi, 7 vols. (Stuttgart, 1980), ii, pp. 184–926.

Thomas of Cantimpré ['Cantipratanus'], Bonum universale de apibus (Douai, 1627).

Thompson, R., Sex in Middlesex: Popular Mores in a Massachusetts County, 1646–1699 (Amherst, MA, 1986).

Thompson, R., 'Attitudes towards Homosexuality in the Seventeenth-Century New England Colonies', Journal of American Studies, 23 (1989), pp. 27–40.

Tietze, A., ed. and trans., Muṣṭafā ʿĀlī's Description of Cairo of 1599 (Vienna, 1975).

Todorova, M. N., Balkan Family Structure and the European Pattern: Demographic Developments in Ottoman Bulgaria (Budapest, 2006).

Tolan, J. V., Saracens: Islam in the Medieval European Imagination (New York, 2002).

Tomás y Valiente, F., 'El crimen y pecado contra natura', in F. Tomás y Valiente et al., Sexo barroco y otras transgresiones premodernas (Madrid, 1990), pp. 33–55.

Tortel, C., L'Ascète et le bouffon: qalandars, vrais et faux renonçants en Islam, ou l'Orient indianisé (Paris, 2009).

Tortorici, Z., Sins against Nature: Sex and Archives in Colonial New Spain (Durham, NC, 2018).

Toscan, J., Le Carnaval du langage: lexique érotique des poètes de l'équivoque de Burchiello à Marino (XVᵉ–XVIIᵉ siècles), 4 vols. (Lille, 1981).

Tov Assis, Y., 'Sexual Behaviour in Mediaeval Hispano-Jewish Society', in A. Rapoport-Albert and S. J. Zipperstein, eds., Jewish History: Essays in Honour of Chimen Abramsky (London, 1988), pp. 25–59.

Träskman, P. O., 'Om "menniskior som af sathan och sin onda begiärelse låter förföra sigh" ', Historisk Tidskrift för Finland, 75 (1990), pp. 248–63.

Traub, V., The Renaissance of Lesbianism in Early Modern England (Cambridge, 2002).

Treglown, J., ed., The Letters of John Wilmot, Earl of Rochester (Oxford, 1980).

Trevisan, J. S., Perverts in Paradise, trans. M. Foreman (London, 1986).

Trexler, R. C., 'La Prostitution florentine au XVe siècle: patronages et clientèles', *Annales. Histoire, sciences sociales*, 36 (1981), pp. 983–1015.

Trexler, R. C., *Sex and Conquest: Gendered Violence, Political Order, and the European Conquest of the Americas* (Ithaca, NY, 1995).

Trexler, R. C., 'Gender Subordination and Political Hierarchy in Pre-Hispanic America', in P. Sigal, ed., *Infamous Desire: Male Homosexuality in Colonial Latin America* (Chicago, 2003), pp. 70–101.

Troianos, S., 'Kirchliche und weltliche Rechtsquellen zur Homosexualität in Byzanz', *Jahrbuch der österreichischen Byzantinistik*, 39 (1989), pp. 29–48.

Trumbach, R., 'London's Sodomites: Homosexual Behavior and Western Culture in the 18th Century', *Journal of Social History*, 11:2 (1977), pp. 1–33.

Trumbach, R., 'Sodomitical Subcultures, Sodomitical Roles, and the Gender Revolution of the Eighteenth Century: The Recent Historiography', in R. P. Maccubbin, ed., *'Tis Nature's Fault: Unauthorized Sexuality during the Enlightenment* (Cambridge, 1987), pp. 109–21.

Trumbach, R., 'The Birth of the Queen: Sodomy and the Emergence of Gender Equality in Modern Culture, 1660–1750', in M. B. Duberman, M. Vicinus and G. Chauncey, eds., *Hidden from History: Reclaiming the Gay and Lesbian Past* (New York, 1989), pp. 129–40.

Trumbach, R., 'Gender and the Homosexual Role in Modern Western Culture: The 18th and 19th Centuries Compared', in D. Altman et al., *Which Homosexuality?* (Amsterdam, 1989), pp. 149–69.

Trumbach, R., 'Sodomitical Assaults, Gender Role, and Sexual Development in Eighteenth-Century London', in K. Gerard and G. Hekma, eds., *The Pursuit of Sodomy: Male Homosexuality in Renaissance and Enlightenment Europe* (New York, 1989), pp. 407–29.

Trumbach, R., 'England', in W. Dynes, ed., *Encyclopedia of Homosexuality*, 2 vols. (New York, 1990), i, pp. 354–8.

Trumbach, R., 'Are Modern Western Lesbian Women and Gay Men a Third Gender?', in M. Duberman, ed., *A Queer World: The Center for Lesbian and Gay Studies Reader* (New York, 1997), pp. 87–99.

Trumbach, R., *Sex and the Gender Revolution: Heterosexuality and the Third Gender in Enlightenment London* (Chicago, 1998).

Trumbach, R., 'The Heterosexual Male in Eighteenth-Century London and his Queer Interactions', in K. O'Donnell and M. O'Rourke, eds., *Love, Sex, Intimacy, and Friendship between Men, 1550–1800* (Basingstoke, 2003), pp. 99–127.

Trumbach, R., 'Modern Sodomy: The Origins of Homosexuality, 1700–1800', in M. Cook, ed., *A Gay History of Britain: Love and Sex between Men since the Middle Ages* (Oxford, 2007), pp. 77–105.

Trumbach, R., 'Renaissance Sodomy, 1500–1700', in M. Cook, ed., *A Gay History of Britain: Love and Sex between Men since the Middle Ages* (Oxford, 2007), pp. 45–75.

Trumbach, R., 'The Transformation of Sodomy from the Renaissance to the Modern World and its General Sexual Consequences', *Signs: Journal of Women in Culture and Society*, 37 (2012), pp. 832–48.

Tucker, J. E., 'Marriage and Family in Nablus, 1720–1856: Toward a History of Arab Marriage', *Journal of Family History* 13 (1988), pp. 165–79.

Turberville, G., *Tragicall Tales Translated by Turberville in his Time of Troubles* (London, 1587).

Turbet-Delof, G., *L'Afrique barbaresque dans la littérature française aux XVIe et XVIIe siècles* (Geneva, 1973).

Turner, J. G., *One Flesh: Paradisal Marriage and Sexual Relations in the Age of Milton* (Oxford, 1987).

de Turre, A. M., *Orbis seraphicus*, tome 2, part 2, ed. A. Chiappini (Quaracchi, 1945).

Vainfas, R., *Trópico dos pecados: moral, sexualidade e Inquisição no Brasil* (Rio de Janeiro, 1989).

Vainfas, R., 'Homoerotismo feminino e o Santo Ofício', in M. Del Priore, ed., *História das mulheres no Brasil* (São Paulo, 1997), pp. 115–40.

Vainfas, R., 'Inquisição como fábrica de hereges: os sodomitas foram exceção?', in R. Vainfas, B. Feitler and L. Lage da Gama Lima, eds., *A Inquisição em xeque: temas, controvérsias, estudos de caso* (Rio de Janeiro, 2006), pp. 267–80.

Vainfas, R., 'The Nefarious and the Colony', in H. Johnson and F. A. Dutra, eds., *Pelo vaso traseiro: Sodomy and Sodomites in Luso-Brazilian History* (Tucson, AZ, 2006), pp. 337–67.

Vaiopoulos, K., 'L'Italiano sodomita nella poesia satirica di Quevedo', in M. G. Profeti, ed., *Giudizi e pregiudizi. Percezione dell'altro e stereotipi tra Europa e Mediterranea: atti del seminario, Firenze, 10–14 giugno 2008*, i (Florence, 2010), pp. 183–209.

Van der Cruysse, D., *Madame Palatine, princesse européenne* (Paris, 1988).

Van der Stighelen, K., and J. Roelens, 'Made in Heaven, Burned in Hell: The Trial of the Sodomite Sculptor Hiëronymus Duquesnoy (1602–1654)', in H. Magnus and K. Van der Stighelen, eds., *Facts & Feelings: Retracing Emotions of Artists, 1600–1800* (Turnhout, 2015), pp. 101–38.

Vanhemelryck, F., *De criminaliteit in de ammanie van Brussel van de Late Middeleeuwen, tot het einde van het Ancien Regime (1404–1789)* (Brussels, 1981).

Vasari, G., *Lives of the Painters, Sculptors and Architects*, trans. G. du C. De Vere, ed. D. Ekserdjian, 2 vols. (New York, 1996).

Veinstein, G., *Les Esclaves du Sultan chez les Ottomans: des mamelouks aux janissaires (XIVe–XVIIe siècles)* (Paris, 2020).

Verduin, K., '"Our Cursed Natures": Sexuality and the Puritan Conscience', *New England Quarterly*, 56 (1983), pp. 220–37.

de Viau, T., *Oeuvres poétiques*, ed. G. Saba (Paris, 1990).

Vieira, A., 'Contributions to the Study of Daily Life and Sexuality on the Island of São Miguel in the Seventeenth Century: The Case of the Count of Vila Franca', in H. Johnson and F. A. Dutra, eds., *Pelo vaso traseiro: Sodomy and Sodomites in Luso-Brazilian History* (Tucson, AZ, 2006), pp. 105–44.

Vignali, A., *La cazzaria*, ed. P. Stoppelli (Rome, 1984).

Vignali, A., *The Book of the Prick*, trans. I. F. Moulton (New York, 2003).

Villalba Pérez, E., *¿Pecadoras o delincuentes?: delito y género en la Corte (1580–1630)* (Madrid, 2004).

de Villamont, J., *Les Voyages du Seigneur de Villamont*, 2nd edn. (Paris, 1596).

de Vio, T., *Commentaria*, in St Thomas Aquinas, *Summa theologica cum commentariis Thomae de Vio cardinalis Cajetani*, 10 vols. (Rome, 1773).

Viret, J. L., 'Children Leaving Home in Europe in the Modern Age: Towards a Typology Taking into Account Western European Forms of Authority', in D. Albera, L. Lorenzetti and J. Mathieu, eds., *Reframing the History of Family and Kinship: From the Alps to Europe* (Bern, 2016), pp. 187–202.

Vitiello, J. C., *Public Justice and the Criminal Trial in Late Medieval Italy: Reggio Emilia in the Visconti Age* (Leiden, 2016).

Vratislav, V., *Prihody Wáclawa Wratislawa swobodného pána z Mitrovic*, ed. F. M. Pelzel (Prague, 1777).

'W. S.', *The Proceedings of the English Colonie in Virginia since their First Beginning from England in the Yeare of Our Lord 1606, till this Present 1612* (Oxford, 1612), appended to J. Smith, *A Map of Virginia: With a Description of the Countrey, the Commodities, People, Government and Religion* (Oxford, 1612).

Wadsworth, J. E., 'In the Name of the Inquisition: The Portuguese Inquisition and Delegated Authority in Colonial Pernambuco, Brazil', *The Americas: Quarterly Review of Inter-American Cultural History*, 61 (2004), pp. 19–54.

Wafer, J., 'Muhammad and Male Homosexuality', in S. O. Murray and W. Roscoe, eds., *Islamic Homosexualities: Culture, History and Literature* (New York, 1997), pp. 87–96.

Wagner, E., *Abū Nuwās: eine Studie zur arabischen Literatur der frühen Neuzeit* (Wiesbaden, 1965).

Wallis, F., 'Giulio Guastavini's Commentary on Pseudo-Aristotle's Account of Male Same-Sexual Coitus, *Problemata* 4.26', in K. Borris and G. Rousseau, eds., *The Sciences of Homosexuality in Early Modern Europe* (London, 2008), pp. 57–73.

Walker, C. ['T. Verax'], *Anarchia anglicana, Or, The History of Independency, being a Continuation of Relations and Observations Historical and Politique upon this Present Parliament* (n.p., 1649).

Walker, W. G., *A History of the Oundle Schools* (London, 1956).

Ward, E., *The Secret History of Clubs* (London, 1709).

Ward, K., *Networks of Empire: Forced Migration in the Dutch East India Company* (Cambridge, 2008).

Warner, M., 'New English Sodom', in J. Goldberg, ed., *Queering the Renaissance* (Durham, NC, 1994), pp. 330–58.

Wassilowsky, G., 'Homosexualität am frühneuzeitlichen Hof des Papstes', in N. Domeier and C. Mühling, eds., *Homosexualität am Hof: Praktiken und Diskurse vom Mittelalter bis heute* (Frankfurt, 2020), pp. 79–99.

Webster, T., ' "Kiss Me with Kisses of His Mouth": Gender Inversion and Canticles in Godly Spirituality', in T. Betteridge, ed., *Sodomy in Early Modern Europe* (Manchester, 2002), pp. 148–63.

Weeks, J., *Coming Out: Homosexual Politics in Britain, from the Nineteenth Century to the Present* (London, 1977).

Wettinger, G., *Slavery in the Islands of Malta and Gozo, ca. 1000–1812* (San Gwann, 2002).

Wiesner-Hanks, M., *Christianity and Sexuality in the Early Modern World: Regulating Desire, Reforming Practice*, 2nd edn. (London, 2010).

Williams, C. A., *Roman Homosexuality*, 2nd edn. (Oxford, 2010).

Williams, G., *A Dictionary of Sexual Language and Imagery in Shakespearean and Stuart Literature*, 3 vols. (London, 2001).

Willis, A. S., 'Abusing Hugh Davis: Determining the Crime in a Seventeenth-Century American Morality Case', *JHS*, 28 (2019), pp. 117–47.

Wilmot, J., Earl of Rochester, *Works*, ed. H. Love (Oxford, 1999).

Winthrop, J., *The History of New England from 1630 to 1639*, ed J. Savage, 2 vols. (Boston, 1853).

Wither, G., *The Schollers Purgatory Discovered in the Stationers Common-wealth* (London, 1624).

Wittkower, M., and R. Wittkower, *Born Under Saturn* (New York, 1963).

Wolk-Simon, L., ' "Rapture to the Greedy Eyes": Profane Love in the Renaissance', in A. Bayer, ed., *Art and Love in Renaissance Italy* (New York, 2008), pp. 43–58.

Wood, A., *The Life and Times of Anthony Wood, Antiquary, of Oxford, 1632–1695, Described by Himself*, ed. A. Clark, 5 vols. (Oxford, 1891–1900).

Woodard, V., *The Delectable Negro: Human Consumption and Homoeroticism within US Slave Culture* (New York, 2014).

Wright, J., *Historia histrionica: An Historical Account of the English Stage* (London, 1699).

Wright, J. W., 'Masculine Allusion and the Structure of Satire in Early 'Abbāsid Poetry', in J. W. Wright and E. K. Rowson, eds., *Homoeroticism in Classical Arabic Literature* (New York, 1997), pp. 1–23.

Wrigley, E. A., and R. Schofield, *The Population History of England, 1541–1871: A Reconstruction* (Cambridge, 1981).

Wroth, Lady Mary, *The Countesse of Mountgomeries Urania* (London, 1621).

Wunderli, R. M., *London Church Courts and Society on the Eve of the Reformation* (Cambridge, 1981).

Wurffbain, J. S., *Reise nach den Molukken und Vorder-Indien, 1632–1646*, ed. R. P. Meyjes, 2 vols. (The Hague, 1931).

Young, M. B., *James VI and I and the History of Homosexuality* (Basingstoke, 2000).

Youngs, D., *The Life Cycle in Western Europe, c.1300–c.1500* (Manchester, 2006).

Zabughin, V., *Giulio Pomponio Leto, saggio critico*, 2 vols. (Rome, Grottaferrata, 1909–10).

Zarinebaf, F., *Crime and Punishment in Istanbul, 1700–1800* (Berkeley, CA, 2011).

Zdekauer, L., 'Il frammento degli ultimi due libri del più antico constituto senese (1262–1270)', *Bulletino senese di storia patria*, 3 (1896), pp. 79–92.

Ze'evi, D., 'Changes in Legal-Sexual Discourses: Sex Crimes in the Ottoman Empire', *Continuity and Change*, 16 (2001), pp. 219–42.

Ze'evi, D., *Producing Desire: Changing Sexual Discourse in the Ottoman Middle East, 1500–1900* (Berkeley, CA, 2006).

Zilfi, M., 'The Kadizadelis: Discordant Revivalism in Seventeenth-Century Istanbul', *Journal of Near Eastern Studies*, 45 (1986), pp. 251–69.

Zorach, R. E., 'The Matter of Italy: Sodomy and the Scandal of Style in Sixteenth-Century France', *Journal of Medieval and Early Modern Studies*, 28 (1998), pp. 581–609.

Zuccarello, U., 'La sodomia al tribunale bolognese del Torrone tra XVI e XVII secolo', *Società e storia*, no. 87 (2000), pp. 37–51.

Zysberg, A., *Les Galériens: vies et destins de 60,000 forçats sur les galères de France, 1680–1748* (Paris, 1987).

Index

d'Abano, Pietro 187
abbate Volpino 61, 165, 184
Abdul Rahim 333–5
Abū Nuwās 205–7
academies, Italian 152–3, 155, 156, 180
'Accademia Nobilissima e
    Onoratissima' 61, 165, 184
actors: *see* theatre/actors
Adam and Eve, alleged sodomy of 185
Africans
    in Iberian America 66–7, 325, 326
    in N. America 317, 318, 331–3
    in S. Europe 52, 65, 326
Aleppo 15, 203
Alexandrian rule 109
Al-Ghazali 197
Algiers 9, 11, 13, 14, 15, 19
Ali Piccinin 19
Alves Dias, João José 105
Americans, native: *see* indigenous
    Americans
Amsterdam 218, 226, 369, 370, 371, 373
Ancona 66, 383
Andalusia 33, 208
Andrews, Walter 211, 411
Angola 326
Antoninus of Florence 115, 117,
    118, 172
apprentices
    in N. Europe 236
    in Ottoman world 37–8
    in S. Europe 68
Aragon 45, 231; *see also* Inquisition,
    Aragonese
d'Aranda, Emanuel 11, 19, 99
Archpriest of Talavera 143–4
Aretino, Pietro 147–8, 183–4, 391
d'Argenson, Marc-René 355, 360, 363
Ariosto, Ludovico 154

aristocrats: *see* noblemen
Aristotle 178, 185
Arlington 254
Armengol, Melchor 128–9
Ashley, Sir Anthony 390–1
Aslborn, Rittermeister 262
Augsburg 111, 130, 244
Augustine, St 109
Austria 217, 229
autos-da-fé 140–1, 193
Avicenna: *see* Ibn Sina
Avignon 102, 114
Azor, Juan 128
Azores 45
de Azpilcueta, Martín 119, 127, 185

Backer, Jacob Cornelis 367, 371
Backer, Jacobus 367, 369
Bacon, Anthony 102, 391
Baghdad 205
bagno/bagni 55, 56–7
Bahia 66, 322, 324
bailo 1–2, 5–6, 10
Baker, Augustine 257
Baldassari, Marina 78, 92, 171, 391
Bandello, Matteo 188–9
barbers/barbershops 2, 36, 54, 74
Barcelona 57, 88–9, 97–8
bardache/bardascia/bardaxo 13, 240, 284
Bargrave, Robert 16
Barkan, Leonard 153–4
Barnfield, Richard 293
Basel 55, 217–18, 224, 229, 237,
    243, 391
Basil, St 109, 179, 404
Basque Country 98–9
Bassano, Luigi 17
Batavia (Jakarta) 261, 329
Bath, NC 318

baths, public
  in N. Europe 372
  in S. Europe 53–4
  see also *hamams*
Baudier, Michel 17–18
Bavaria 217, 241, 266
Bazzi, Giovanni Antonio 166–7, 391
'B. C.' 245
Beard, Thomas 282–3
beards/beardlessness 28–9, 31, 46–7, 206,
  208, 240, 381, 403–4
beau garçon sans merci 33, 199
Beccadelli, Antonio 148–9
Beccuti, Francesco 162–3
Beckford, William 385
bed-sharing 71, 153, 238, 242, 255, 273,
  274–5, 302–3
beggar-boys 50, 236
Benedicti, Jean 112, 115, 117–18, 122,
  124, 128
Benin 326
Ben-Naeh, Yaron 411, 412
Bentham, Jeremy 378
Benvenuto da Imola 54
Berco, Cristian 45, 47, 57, 85, 88–9, 174
berdaches (among indigenous
  Americans) 325–6
de Berger, Gabriel 370–1
Bergeron, David 275
Berlin 372
Bernardino of Siena 52, 90, 115, 117,
  123–4, 130, 133, 148, 173, 192,
  278, 390
Berni, Francesco 81, 158–9, 160
bestiality 120–1, 124, 228–31, 307, 317,
  319, 379, 381
Beza, Theodore 161
biblical passages: *see* Deuteronomy;
  Epistle to the Romans; Ezekiel;
  Genesis; Leviticus
Birader, Deli: *see* Deli Birader
blackmail 344–5, 365, 375
blasphemy 191, 192–3, 265
  about Jesus and St John 190–1, 192
blazon of beauty, poetic 179–80, 207
de Blot l'Eglise, Claude de Chouvigny,
  baron 196
Blount, Sir Henry 16–17
Boccaccio, Giovanni 64, 120, 144–5,
  146, 159

Bodley, Josias 302
Boindin, Nicolas 376
Bologna 43–4, 50, 54, 91, 93, 130–1, 182
Boniface VIII, Pope 271
Boomgaard, Peter 330
Boone, Marc 219
Boswell, John 105, 110, 398
Botelho, Diogo 322
Bouchard, Jean-Jacques 59–60, 95
Bouliau, Damien 102
'boy', meaning servant 300, 311
boys, attraction to
  extended from attraction to females
    178–81
  in Islamic law 29, 30, 35
  viewed as natural in Ottoman world
    29–30, 39–40, 198
  viewed as natural in S. Europe
    47–8, 179
Bradford, William 307–9, 314
Brandenburg-Prussia 229
Bray, Alan 214–15, 228, 247, 249–50,
  256–8, 271, 281, 283, 302, 305,
  313, 391
Brazil 80, 192, 320, 322–3, 325–7
  Inquisition in 320
  sexual use of slaves in 66–7
  sodomites exiled to 321
  statistics for 325
Breda 366–7
Brest 262
Bridewell Hospital 221, 226
Bristol 352, 352
Brocardo, Antonio 162
Bronzino, Agnolo 159
Browne, Sir Thomas 304–5
Bruges 218–19, 224, 241, 243
Brussels 218
  ammanie of 230
Buggery Act (1533) 220, 226
Buono, Giuseppe: *see* abbate Volpino
Burchard of Worms 389
Burford 246
Bursa 35, 36, 40
Byzantium/Byzantine empire 125–6, 405

Cadden, Joan 120, 187–8, 388
Cady, Joseph 339
Cairo 33, 37
Calcagno, Fra Francesco 190–1

Calvin, Jean 161, 234
Cambrai, court of archbishop of 239
Cambridge 221–2, 257, 313
Canada: see New France colony
Canal, Pierre 244, 247
Cannon, Thomas 376–7
Cape Town 330, 374
Caporali, Cesare 162
captives: see slaves/captives
Caravaggio, Michelangelo Merisi da
    167–8
Cardano, Girolamo 234
carnival songs, Florentine 159–60
'Carolina': see 'Constitutio criminalis
    Carolina'
Carpzov, Benedikt 234
Carr, Robert, Earl of
    Somerset 273–4, 275
Carrasco, Rafael 44–5, 49, 59, 74, 75, 82,
    89, 98, 104, 184, 231, 337, 403
Carriveau, Patrice 317–18
Cartagena (Colombia) 326
della Casa, Giovanni 160–1
Casanova, Giacomo 383
Castiglione, Baldassare 152
Castile 98
Castlehaven, Earl of: see Touchet, Mervin
Cathars 111
Catullus 148, 150, 283, 291
Çelebi, Evliya: see Evliya Çelebi
Cellini, Benvenuto 81–2, 145, 176, 180–1
Charles V, Emperor 136
Chaucer, Geoffrey 277–8
Chausson, Jacques 239, 248
Cheney, Thomas 258
Ciudad Real 98
Clap, 'Mother' 348, 352
Cleland, John 164–5
Clement of Alexandria, St 109
clergy 242, 244, 254–5, 359, 383
    punishment of 62–3, 127–9, 131,
        139, 233
    see also friars/friaries; monks/
        monasteries
Cocles: see della Rocca, Bartolomeo
coded language 369–70
    in poems, songs 158–61
coffee-houses 34–5
Coke, Sir Edward 281
Collins, Samuel 381–2

Cologne 226–7
Condé, Henri de Bourbon, prince de
    241
Condorcet, Jean Antoine Nicolas de
    Caritat, marquis de 378
confession 62, 118–19; see also
    penitentials; solicitation
Congo 326
'Constitutio criminalis Carolina' 224
constructionism 398–9, 402
Contrarietas elfolica 21
Cooper, John ('Princess Seraphina')
    348, 349–50
Coras, Jean 224
da Costa, João 45, 51
Councils of the Church
    Ancyra 126, 131
    Nablus 126
    Third Lateran 126
    Trent 122
de Courtilz de Sandras, Gatien 269, 363
courts, royal 270–5
Cresti, Domenico (Passignano) 167
criminal law: see law, criminal
'cruising' 343, 356–9, 365, 368–9, 395;
    see also signalling methods
Cuenca, law code of 129
'culture wars', Protestant–Catholic 86,
    161, 183, 234
Cuzco 189

Dadon, Nicolas 255
Damascus 16, 37, 383–4
Dante Alighieri 144, 153–4
Davidson, Nicholas 171
Davis, Hugh 332
Dean, Trevor 91, 93
'Debate between Cavichiolus and his
    Wife' 146
defamation
    in N. America 318
    in N. Europe 220–1, 221–3, 243, 257
    in S. Europe 102, 222
Defoe, Daniel 373
Dekker, Thomas 284, 285
delectatio morosa 122
Delgado, Luiz 80, 175
Deli Birader 33, 35, 36, 208
Della Porta, Giovanni Battista 73, 388
Delrio, Martin 114

De Luca, Cardinal Giovanni Battista
47–8, 179
Denmark 217, 373
denunciations, in S. Europe 52, 79
depopulation, argument concerning
173, 197
dervishes: see Sufis/Sufism
Deschauffours, Étienne-Benjamin 360–1,
362, 374
desire, undifferentiated 177–8
Deuteronomy 287
Devil/demons
in comic tale 143
offended by sodomy 112–13
'Dialogue between Giulia and
Maddalena' 164
Dionysius Carthusianus 287
'displacement' syndrome 87
van der Does (Dousa), Joris 9, 15, 30
Dominico of Vicenza 4
Donne, John 247, 251, 283, 306–7
Dowdeney, George 238, 344
Drayton, Michael 251, 293
Dryden, John 305–6
Dubrovnik 101–2, 116, 406
Durfey, Thomas 249
Dutch East Indies 261, 329–30

East India Company (Dutch):
see Vereenigde Oostindische
Compagnie
East India Company (English)
259, 333
Ebu's Su'ud 411
Edirne 9, 40
Edward II, King of England 271
effeminacy 73, 337–8, 347, 348, 349–52,
362–4, 370, 388–9; see also
transvestites/transvestism
Egypt 33–4, 37, 384
Elisabeth-Charlotte, Princess of the
Palatinate 270, 376
Ellis, Jim 416
El-Rouayheb, Khaled 28, 29, 39, 198,
200, 207, 211, 383, 384, 411
England 220–3, 223, 225–6, 227–8,
229, 236–7, 244–7, 249–52, 256–9,
260–1, 265–6, 273–6,
279–94, 297–307
ecclesiastical courts 220–1

marriage ages in 406
see also law, criminal, in England
Enlightenment 378
Epistle to the Romans, prohibition in
109, 120, 121, 257
Erasmus, Desiderius 151
de Espina, Alonso 22
essentialism 398–9, 402
Estienne, Henri 23, 119
Eugene IV, Pope 130–1, 148–9
Evliya Çelebi 32, 33–4, 36
Ezekiel, on sins of Sodom 108, 279,
280, 281

Faan 368, 374
fama/fame 231–2
fanchonos 73
Fathers of the Church 109
favourites, royal 270–6
Febvre, Michel 15, 200
fellatio 74, 267, 357, 359, 367
female–female sex 120, 121, 218, 312,
417–19
Ferdinand of Aragon, King 134–5
Ferguson, Gary 77, 363
Ferrara 93, 184
Fez 26, 49
Ficino, Marsilio 151–2
Fishbourne, Christopher 300–1
Fletcher, John 290
Florence 49, 52, 54–5, 65, 68, 70,
74, 75, 79
anti-sodomy measures 52, 53,
64, 90, 173
marriage ages in 70, 406
Office of the Night 42, 51, 90, 181
punishment regime 90, 131, 132–3
reputation for sodomy 86
statistics for 42, 43, 51, 90
fops 353
Foster, Thomas 333
Foucault, Michel 120, 123, 176, 384–6,
398, 402
France/Frenchmen 57, 59, 88, 219–20,
225, 267–70, 272, 295–7
northern 219–20, 224, 228, 230,
238, 355–64
southern 56–7, 102–4, 230
see also law, criminal, in France
Frankfurt 217, 227

Frederick II, King of Prussia 379
de Freitas Lessa, André 322
friars/friaries 60–2, 73, 75, 82, 115, 145,
    156, 176, 192, 241, 243, 323–4, 382
Fribourg, canton of 229

Gager, William 287–8
Galán, Diego 20
Galata 1, 7, 10, 213
Gallatin, Albert 318
galleys: see mariners
Ganymede, myth of 151
gaols: see prisons
Garasse, François 295–6
Garza Carvajal, Federico 58
gazel: see ghazal/gazel
'gazing': see nazar
Geiler von Keisersberg, Johannes
    117, 278–9
Genesis, story of Sodom 108
Geneva 218, 225, 230, 241, 244
Gerlach, Stephan 16
German lands 224, 225, 237–8, 244,
    369, 406
Gerson, Jean 118–19
ghazal/gazel 207–8
Ghent 218–19
Gianesino: see Salvego, Gianesino
gifts 3, 50–1, 149
Giotto 166
Giraldo Botero, Carolina 326
Giulio Romano 169
Gladfelder, Hal 377
Goa 45, 51, 175, 328
Godbeer, Richard 315, 316
Goffman, Erving 58
Goldberg, Jonathan 307–9, 391
Gomorrah, biblical city: see Sodom,
    biblical city
Gondola, Francesco 204
González de Sosa, Dr Gaspar 80, 174
Gorani, Giuseppe 383
Gosson, Stephen 287
Gott, Charles 308
Gowing, Laura 222
grabbing
    of genitals 242–3, 263, 344, 356,
        365–6, 371
    of hats 49, 393
    see also signalling methods

Gracián de la Madre de Dios, Jerónimo 13
Gramaye, Jean-Baptiste 14
Granada 193
Grassi, Umberto 91
Grazzini, Antonfrancesco 64, 160
Greece, ancient 403–4
Gregorio, barber 1–7, 50, 79–80, 213
Groningen 368
Gruzinski, Serge 328
Guatemala City 71
Gurck, Frederick 367

habit/habituation 187, 389–90
hadīths 196, 198, 199, 201
Haggerty, George 306
Hague, The 218, 226, 365, 366–7, 368,
    369, 370, 386
Hajnal, John 406
Haliczer, Stephen 62, 408–9
Halperin, David 403, 416–17
hamams 35–6, 206, 209
Hamburg 114, 227, 372, 373–4
Hamilton, Tom 220, 255
Hamm 241, 366
Handley, Sasha 275–6
Harris, John 280
den Hartog, Marlisa 403
Hehenberger, Susanne 229
Henri III, King of France 272–3
heresy
    factum hereticale 111
    linked with sodomy 111–12, 129–30,
        134, 172
Hergemöller, Bernd-Ulrich 105
Hewlett, Mary 91
Heywood, Thomas 290
hierarchy, social: see social
    hierarchy/order
Higgs, David 379
Hill, Aaron 9
Hill, Adam 279–80
Hitchcock, Tim 299
Hobbes, Thomas 197
von Hoen, Captain Johan 263
Holy Roman Empire: see German lands
Home Counties 221, 229, 254
homoeroticism
    concept of 303
    in English literature 283, 303–4
    in Islamic literature 205–8, 211–12

homosexuality/homosexual
  forerunners of 401–2
  modern concept of 384–6, 402
  and subculture 393
Hondius, Jacobus 373
Horace 283
Huamanga 322, 324
Hug, Ponç, Count of Empúries 67, 175
humanists/humanism 150–4, 254
Hungerford, Walter, Lord 265
Hurteau, Pierre 122

Ibn Abī al-Dunyā 196
Ibn ʿArabī, Muḥyī al-Dīn 198, 199
Ibn Ezra, Moses 208
Ibn Gabirol, Solomon 208
Ibn Sina 187
identity, sodomitical 384–92, 397–8
'Indians' (in Americas): see indigenous
  Americans
indigenous Americans 320–1, 322, 323–8
ingles 284–5
Ingram, Martin 222
Inquisition, Aragonese 136–7
  jurisdiction of 45, 136
  punishments by 57
  statistics for 97, 230–1
  torture, use of 137
  tribunal in Barcelona 11, 13–14, 63, 97,
    136, 137, 217
  tribunal in Cartagena (Colombia) 320
  tribunal in Lima 320, 323, 390
  tribunal in Mallorca 75
  tribunal in Mexico 320
  tribunal in Valencia 22, 63, 74, 97, 104,
    136, 184, 217, 231
  tribunal in Zaragoza 97, 136, 137,
    189, 231
  see also Inquisition, Sardinian;
    Inquisition, Sicilian
Inquisition, Castilian
  tribunal in Cuenca 192–3
  tribunal in Toledo 104–5, 191
Inquisition, Portuguese 22, 45–6, 69–70,
    73–4, 99–101, 138–40, 379
  and colonies 100, 175, 320
  rules of 99–100, 139, 175
  statistics for 100, 379
  tribunal in Coimbra 46, 100, 138, 184
  tribunal in Évora 80, 83, 230

tribunal in Lisbon 46, 63–4, 73, 85–6,
  100, 105, 396
Inquisition, Roman 136
  tribunal in Naples 189
Inquisition, Sardinian 1, 14
Inquisition, Sicilian 96–7, 191, 193
Inquisition, Venetian 189, 190
inns: see taverns/inns
interfemoral sex 69, 83, 111
irreligion, popular 191–3
Islam
  associated with sodomy by
    W. Europeans 10–11, 13, 20–2
  conversion to 5, 10–13
  expansion of, and hellenistic
    culture 405
Istanbul 1–2, 7, 15–16, 35, 40
Italy/Italians 42–4, 50–6, 61–2, 64–5,
    70–2, 75–7, 81–2, 89–96, 130–4,
    144–69, 181–4, 190–1, 382–3
  in Aragonese trials 88
  reputation for sodomy 85–7, 113
  sodomy widespread in 89, 93–6

Jamaica 260, 333
James VI, King of Scotland, and James I
  of England 273–6
Jerome, St 117
Jews
  associated with sodomy by mediaeval
    English 23
  homoerotic poetry by Andalusian
    208
  molested by Ottomans in Hague 8–9
  Ottoman 31, 33, 37–8, 411, 412
  warning Dutch about Ottoman
    sodomy 15–16
Jireček, Konstantin 380
John, St: see blasphemy, about Jesus
  and St John
John Chrysostom, St 109, 404
Jonson, Ben 283–5
Jordan, Thomas 300–1
de Joyeuse, Anne 272
Justinian, Emperor 116, 125–6

Kalpaklı, Mehmet 211, 411
Karras, Ruth Mazo 278
Katz, Jonathan Ned 311
Kent 221

kimbanda 326
kissing 273, 302–3, 307
Klink, Andreas 375–6
Knights Templar 130, 271
Koran 195–7, 201
  prejudicial interpretation of, by
    Christians 20–2
von Krafft-Ebing, Richard 387
Kramer, Heinrich 113, 279
Kuefler, Mathew 403

Languedoc 102
Laṭīfī 213
Latini, Brunetto 153–4
law, Byzantine 125–6
law, criminal
  in England 221, 225–6, 266
  in France 224, 360, 378
  in Holy Roman Empire 224
  in Italy 91–3
  in Netherlands 224
  in Portugal 75
  in Sweden/Finland 224, 372–3
law, Islamic
  on boys as temptation 29, 30, 35
  on interfemoral sex 70
  on punishment of sodomy 196, 201–2
  witnesses required by 202
  on women 411
Leeuwaarden 366, 369
legends, theological 115
Leiden 218, 254
de León, Pedro 54, 98, 135, 394
Lepanto campaign 56
lesbianism/lesbians: *see* female–female sex
lèse-majesté 134, 137–8
Leto, Pomponio 152–3
Levin, Eva 380
Leviticus, prohibitions in 108–9, 233, 376
libertines/libertinism 296–9
Lima 60, 62, 115, 321
Lincoln, court of bishop of 227
Lincoln's Inn Fields 343
lingering delectation: see *delectatio morosa*
Lisbon 60, 72, 75, 83, 190, 396
Lithgow, William 26, 49, 96, 101, 211
lolhuizen 369–70
London 221, 222, 244–5, 246, 250–1,
    279–80, 281, 298, 340–5, 347–52
  Commissary court, of bishop of 221

Lorenzetti, Ambrogio 166
Lorraine 229
de Lorraine-Armagnac, Philippe 270
Lot
  in Hebrew Bible 107–8
  'people of', in Islamic tradition 37
Louis XIV, King of France 268–9
Lubenau, Reinhold 213
Lucca 51, 53–4, 68, 91–2
  anti-sodomy measures in 70, 91
  Office for Virtue 91
  punishment regime 91, 133–4
  statistics for 43
Lucerne 89, 217, 229, 244
Luther, Martin 86, 118
Lutterbach, Hubertus 110
Luxorius 404–5
Lyons, Clare 319

ma'būn: see *ubnah/ma'būn*
Macerata 192, 382
Machin, Lewis 292–3
Machuco 52
Madrid 76, 77, 98
Magnus IV, King of Sweden (Magnus VII
    of Norway) 271
Malaga 98
Mallorca 75, 190, 193
Malleus maleficarum: *see* Kramer,
    Heinrich
Malta 65, 101, 406
Marcocci, Giuseppe 77
Marignolli, Curzio 163, 295
mariners
  in Dutch colonies 261, 329–31
  on East India Co. ship 333–5
  in Iberian America 321
  in N. America 311
  in N. Europe 259–62, 341–2,
    346, 375
  in Otttoman world 14
  in S. Europe 55–8
Marlowe, Christopher 292–3, 294
marriage
  ages of 70, 406–12
  companionate 407–8
  'inveterate' sodomites shunning
    70, 187
  as metaphor for sex 348, 349
  mock-ceremony 77, 348, 349

ben Mar-Saul,Yiṣḥaq 208
Marseille 56–7
Marston, John 249, 251, 256, 283
Martí, Ramon 204
Martial 283, 291
Maryland 311, 314
masquerades 350, 363–4
Massimi, Pacifico 149–50
masturbation, theological views of
    mutual 111, 118, 122–3
    solitary 111, 118, 120, 121–2
masturbation in N. America
    mutual 312, 315
masturbation in N. Europe 222
    mutual 217, 219, 229, 241–2, 244, 357,
        365, 366, 369, 375
    solitary 226, 387
masturbation in Orthodox Slav world
    mutual 380
masturbation in S. Europe
    mutual 75
    solitary 75
Matar, Nabil 25–7
de Mattos, Gregório 192
de Mattos, Matthias 60, 83–4
de' Medici, Lorenzo 181
van der Meer, Theo 370
de Mepsche, Rudolf 368
Mexico 323, 324
Mexico City 327–8, 396
Micanzio, Fulgenzio 61
Michelangelo 162, 169
Michelsen, Jakob 372
Middelburg 242
Middlesex, MA 315
Middleton, Thomas 247, 302–3
mignons 270, 272, 273
Milan 93
military campaigns, boys taken on 16–17,
    36–7, 56
Milles, Robert 280
Miloslavsky, Ilya Danilovich 381–2
Mirabeau, Honoré Gabriel Riqueti,
    comte de 377–8
'mixed jurisdiction' 126–7, 137, 138, 219
mock-ceremonies 77, 268–9, 347, 348,
    351, 363
Molina, Fernanda 97
mollies/molly houses 347–52
mollities 74, 100, 118, 122–3, 138, 139, 219

monks/monasteries 60, 83–4, 89, 99,
    222–3, 244
    anti-sodomy measures in 110
Monreale 96
de Montaigne, Michel 304, 306
Monter, William 88, 97, 185, 231
Montesquieu, Charles-Louis de
    Secondat, baron de 378
Montreal 317
Moorfields 343, 375
Moriscos 22
Morris, Stephen 404–5
Mörth, Ladislaus 10
Moryson, Fynes 408
Moscow 381
Mott, Luiz 100, 327
mouches 355–9
de Moura, Dom Felipe 46, 72, 175, 182
mujūn 205–6, 209
mukhannath 31, 34
Mulberry Garden 250–1
Muret, Marc-Antoine 102
Mustafa Ali of Gallipoli 32, 34, 36, 37, 38,
    39–40, 411
Muzio, Girolamo 162

'al-Nābulusī, 'Abd al-Ghanī 200–1
Naessens, Mariann 219
Naples 61, 88–9, 95, 191, 192, 193
native Americans: see indigenous
    Americans
nature
    sins against 109, 119–22, 129,
        188, 378
    sodomy said to accord with 186, 189,
        190, 375–6, 377
naẓar 198–9, 210
nefandus: see sodomy, not to be spoken of
Neoplatonism 151–2, 210
the Netherlands 224, 238, 262
    northern 226, 364–71
    southern 218
    statistics for 218–19, 371
New England 307–9, 311–17, 318–19
New France colony 317–18
New Haven, CT 311–12
New London, CT 318–19
New Netherland colony 317
nicknames, female 348, 350
de Nicolay, Nicolas 10, 17, 212–13

noblemen 67, 175, 255, 264–70, 358–9, 361, 362
Nordheim 232
Norton, Rictor 216, 246, 340, 342, 350–1, 352, 375
Norway 217
Nuremberg 217

Oaks, Robert 315
Old Bailey 342, 344
Olearius, Adam 381
Olinda 72
Ordenações Afonsinas 137
Ordenações Filipinas 138
Ordenações Manuelinas 137–8
order, social: see social hierarchy/order
Orgel, Stephen 289
orientation, same-sex 144, 146–8, 357, 384–92, 400–2; see also identity, sodomitical
d'Orléans, Philippe de Bourbon, duc 248, 269–70
Orthodox Slav world 280–2
Orvieto 130
Osman ağa of Timişoara 253
Ottoman Empire
  associated with sodomy by W. Europeans 17–18, 19–20, 23
  marriage ages in 410–11
  sodomy in 28–40, 199–200, 202–4, 207–9, 211–13, 383–4
Ottonelli, Giovanni Domenico 47, 179
Oundle 257
Oxford 246, 257–8

Padgug, Robert 416
Padua 96
  University of 156
pages: see servants/pages
Palatine, Princess: see Elisabeth-Charlotte, Princess of the Palatinate
Palermo 46
Palmieri, Matteo 408
Pamiers 103
Panuzzi, Salvi di Niccolò 72, 75
Paolo da Certaldo 408
Papon, Jean 220
von Pappenheim, Caspar Gottfried 267
Paradise, in Islamic doctrine 197
parents, complicity of 33, 51, 149

Paris 220, 239, 248–9, 255, 295, 355–64
  Parlement de 220, 225, 230, 238, 255, 356
Parmigianino 169
Passignano: see Cresti, Domenico
Pastorello, Thierry 359
Paulmier, Jacques 239, 248
Pavia 94–5
Payer, Pierre 110
Peirce, Leslie 411
Pelagius of Cordoba, St 15
penitentials 110, 381–2, 389
Pennsylvania 319
Pepys, Samuel 254, 298
Perault, Guillaume 112, 115, 116
Pernambuco 71, 324
Perry, Mary Elizabeth 135
Persia 22, 35–6
Peru 322
  statistics for 325
Perugia 130, 133–4
Peter Damian 110–11
Peter the Great, Tsar 261
Philadelphia 319
Philip II, King of Spain 57, 96, 135
Philip III, King of Spain (Philip II of Portugal) 138–9, 141
Pico della Mirandola, Gianfrancesco 113–14
Pisa 51
Pius V, Pope 116, 127
Pizarro, Pedro 73
Pizzolato, Nicola 106, 171
Plato 150–2, 377
Plymouth Colony 312, 315
polemics, Protestant 86; see also 'culture wars', Protestant–Catholic
Ponce de León, Juan 322, 323
pornography 164–5
Portugal 45–6, 60, 73, 83–4, 99–101, 137–40, 379; see also Inquisition, Portuguese; law, criminal, in Portugal
Posner, Donald 167–8
Postel, Guillaume 204
Potosí 76
Potter, Dirk 86–7
Primi Visconti, Giovanni Battista 239–40, 267
prisons 58–9, 253

Priuli, Girolamo 48, 90
prostitution, female 105, 163, 164, 246,
        344, 351, 393–4, 409
    as anti-sodomy measure 173, 409
    involving male–female sodomy
        181–2, 183
prostitution, male
    in Muslim world 22, 33
    in N. Europe 240, 246–52, 358, 365,
        367, 369
    in S. Europe 42, 51–2, 92, 393
Provence 102
Prynne, William 288
publicity, judicial 140–1, 373
Puebla 328
Puff, Helmut 87, 103, 227, 237, 254,
        278, 369
Puller von Hohenburg, Richard 264–5
punishments, divine: see sodomy, divine
        punishments for
punishments in Dutch colonies
    beating/whipping 261, 329, 330
    death 261, 330, 331
punishments in Iberian America
    death 321, 325, 328
    galleys 325
punishments in N. America
    beating/whipping 315, 332
    branding 315
    death 311–12
    exile 315
    loss of property rights 315
punishments in N. Europe
    beating/whipping 218, 221, 224, 261,
        371, 373
    death 217–20, 221, 223–4, 227, 254,
        255, 259, 260, 261, 262, 265, 342, 348,
        361–2, 368, 369, 371
    deportation 360
    exile 224, 371, 373
    fines 218, 224, 261, 342
    hard labour 373
    imprisonment 258, 259, 261, 342, 360
    loss of office 258
    of minors/passive partners 224, 261
    public shaming/pillory 227, 261,
        342, 375
punishments in Ottoman world
    beating/whipping 202–3
    death 196

fines 202–3
    in Islamic law 196, 201–2
    of minors/passive partners 202–3
    in Sultanic law 202–3
punishments in S. Europe
    banishment 91, 92, 93, 130
    beating/whipping 91, 93
    castration 129, 130
    confiscation 130, 134, 138
    death 57, 59, 70, 92, 93, 100, 101, 129,
        130, 131, 134, 137, 141, 321
    deportation 321
    exclusion from public office 130
    fines 70, 90, 91, 93, 130
    galley service 57, 92, 100, 131, 135, 138–9
    house-burning 130–1
    imprisonment 70, 90, 91, 93, 139
    infamy 138
    of minors/passive partners 91, 131–4,
        135, 139
    mutilation 92
    public shaming/pillory 70, 90,
        130, 140–1
    see also clergy, punishment of

Qur'ān: see Koran
Qusṭā ibn Lūqā al-Ba'labakkī 412

Radicati, Alberto, Count of Passerano
        376, 412
Rafeq, Abdul-Karim 383–4
Ragusa: see Dubrovnik
Rainolds, John 287–8
Ranzo, Mercurino 94–5, 145
Rayner, John 312
Regensburg 217, 240–1, 366
Reinle, Christine 232
'renegades' 10 11–13, 15, 212–13; see also
        Islam, conversion to
Rey, Michel 359, 364
Riccoldo da Monte Croce 21–2
Riera i Sans, Jaume 97
Rigby, Captain Edward 260–1, 341–2
Rio de Janeiro 80
Robert of Ketton 20–1
della Rocca, Bartolomeo ('Cocles') 188
Rocco, Antonio 44, 48, 50, 70–1,
        156–7, 189
Rochester 220
    Bishop of 254

Rochester, Earl of: *see* Wilmot, John, Earl
of Rochester
Rocke, Michael 42, 46–7, 49, 52, 65, 70,
71, 74, 79, 91, 106, 132–3, 149, 167,
183, 243, 386, 409
Roelens, Jonas 224
Rogers, Samuel 307
Roig, Jaume 142
Rome 51, 53, 68, 76, 78, 134, 222, 228,
383, 391
statistics for 44, 92
Rome, ancient 403–4
Ronchaia, Rolandinus/Rolandina 389
Rotterdam 365
Rous, Francis 307
Royal Navy 259–60, 346
Rubin, Patricia 167
Ruggiero, Guido 54, 69, 75, 76, 184
Russia 380–2
Rycaut, Paul 17, 32
Rykener, John/Eleanor 246

Sabadino degli Arienti, Giovanni 145,
146–7
Said, Edward 24–5
sailors: *see* mariners
St Gallen 241
St James's Park 250–1, 260, 343,
371, 395
de Saint-Pavin, Denis Sanguin 196
Salerno 59
Salvador, Brazil 322
Salvego, Giannesino 1–7, 50, 79–80, 213
Salvego, Matteca 1
Salvian of Marseille 404
Salviati, Francesco 169
Sánchez, Tomás 122, 123, 185
Sandys, George 17, 35, 54
Sani 209
San Sebastián 98–9
Santa Fe de Antioquia 80
Sarpi, Paolo 61–2
Sava, St 380
Savannah, GA 318
Savonarola, Girolamo 90, 118
Sa'yi 209
'Sayings of the Desert Fathers' 404
Scaliger, Joseph 85, 240
Scaramella, Tommaso 382
Schmitt, Arno 405

schoolmasters
in N. Europe 254–9
in S. Europe 63–5, 135
Schouten, Joost 261
Schweigger, Salomon 213
Scotland 217, 229
Sebastian, St 168
secrecy, judicial 141, 226–7, 361–2, 373–4
Sedgwick, Eve Kosofsky 303
Sedley, Sir Charles 298–9
Sension, Nicholas 315–16
de Sepúlveda, Juan Ginés 320–1
'Seraphina, Princess': *see* Cooper, John
servants/pages
in N. Europe 240, 248–9, 255, 262, 265,
266, 267, 359, 361, 366, 367, 369, 370
in Ottoman world 37–8
in S. Europe 66, 67, 409
Setúbal 22
Seville 52, 59, 75, 89, 98, 135, 141, 230, 394
Shadwell, Thomas 297
Shakespeare, William 294, 304
Shapiro, Michael 289–90, 291
shariah: *see* law, Islamic
Shenoute of Atripe 404
Shepard, Alexandra 221–2
Shepard, Thomas 313
Shephard, Robert 274–5
Sherley, Thomas 16, 26
Shirley, James 290
Sicily 66, 96–7, 104
marriage ages in 406
statistics for 96–7
see also Inquisition, Sicilian
Siena 51, 130
Siete Partidas 129
signalling methods
in N. Europe 343–4, 356, 365,
370, 394–5
in S. Europe 150, 394
Silves 83
Sinfield, Alan 304–5
sins against nature: *see* nature, sins against
slaves/captives
in Dutch colonies 329, 331
in Iberian America 66–7, 323, 325, 326
in N. America 318, 332–3
in N. Europe 253
in Ottoman world 11–15, 38–9
in S. Europe 52, 65–6

Slavs: *see* Orthodox Slav world
Slovakia 262
Smith, Bruce 416
Soares, António 46, 59, 60
social hierarchy/order 174–7, 215, 228,
    259, 271, 378; *see also:* noblemen
Societies for the Reformation of
    Manners 340–5
Socrates 152–3
Sodom, biblical city, sins of 107–8,
    157, 376
  in Christian doctrine 108, 144, 279–82
  in Islamic doctrine 195
'Sodoma' (artist): *see* Bazzi,
    Giovanni Antonio
Sodom and Gomorrah (play) 300–1
'Sodomites' Walk': *see* Moorfields
sodomy
  as abstract noun 110
  astrological theories about 388
  classification/definition of 111, 119–21,
    226, 266, 312
  contrasted with homosexuality 384–6
  defences of 156–7, 188–90, 375–8
  divine punishments for 115–16, 125,
    134, 172, 282–3
  male–female 92, 119–21, 155, 160,
    181–6, 217, 229, 382
  not to be spoken of 116–18, 227
  pan-Mediterranean 41
  'perfect' 99–100, 128, 134, 139, 226
  physiological theories about 187–8,
    388
  psychological view of 121–2, 187
  transformation of, c.1700, alleged
    336–40, 385, 399–400
  as unnatural: *see* nature, sins against
  as urban phenomenon 105–6
sodomy/sodomites in Dutch colonies
  adult–adult 261, 330
  passive adult 261
sodomy/sodomites in Iberian America
  feminine-behaving 326, 327–8
  groups 322, 327–8, 396
  loving/infatuated 80
  passive adults 322, 324, 326
sodomy/sodomites in N. America
  adult–adult 311, 315, 317, 319
  adult–boy 312, 315–16, 317, 318
  interfemoral 315

sodomy/sodomites in N. Europe
  adult–adult 227–8, 237–40, 345, 357–8,
    359, 363
  adult–boy 235–9, 345–6, 358–9, 360–1
  attitudes to 218–19, 228, 231–2, 262,
    263–4, 361–2, 364
  fellatio 267, 357, 359, 367
  feminine-behaving 362–3
  groups 243–5, 397
  ignorance of 263–4, 373–4
  interfemoral 357
  loving/infatuated 364
  passive adults 240, 349, 357, 358, 361, 387
  reciprocal 240–1
  woman-hating 357, 390–1
sodomy/sodomites in Orthodox
    Slav world
  adult–adult 381
  adult–boy 380–2
  interfemoral 380
sodomy/sodomites in Ottoman world
  age-differentiated 28–31
  attitudes to 12, 14, 196–8, 201–12,
    383–4
  diplomatic incidents involving 8–10
  loving/infatuated 32, 33, 37, 39, 198,
    199, 211–12
  passive adults 30, 206
sodomy/sodomites in S. Europe
  age-differentiated 42–7, 383
  attitudes to 6, 170–2, 186–90, 193–4,
    383
  experimental 70–1
  fellatio 74
  feminine-behaving 73, 388–9
  groups 76–7, 395–6
  'inveterate' 70, 186, 389
  loving/infatuated 78–84, 187, 391–2
  passive adults 45–6, 47–8, 52, 71–3,
    187–8
  'perfect' 69
  reciprocal 71
  same-age 70–1
  woman-hating 144, 146–8, 187, 390
Sofia 32, 36
soldiers
  in Iberian America 321
  in N. America 317
  in N. Europe 217, 262–4, 343, 357, 358,
    367, 373, 375

in Orthodox Slav world 382
in Ottoman world 36–7
in S. Europe 54–5, 56
solicitation 62, 75
Somerset 232, 238
Song of Songs 307
de Sonnini, Charles-Nicolas-Sigisbert 384
de Sosa, Antonio 10–11, 13, 14, 35, 54
Spain 44–5, 57–8, 59, 63, 73, 97–9, 129,
    134–7, 142–4; *see also*: Inquisition,
    Aragonese; Inquisition, Castilian
Spandounes, Theodore 17, 204
spintria 250
Spoleto 93
Spreitzer, Brigitte 113, 278
SRM: *see* Societies for the Reformation
    of Manners
Steiner, Werner 242
Stephens, Walter 113
Stewart, Alan 258
Stocker, Johannes 391
Stockholm 372
Stone, Lawrence 399
Strasbourg 117, 240
Stuart, Esmé, Lord d'Aubigny 273
Stubbes, Philip 282, 286–7, 288
subculture, sodomitical 322, 337–8, 340,
    369–70, 392–8
Sucre 66, 76, 80
Sufis/Sufism
    cult of boys' beauty 30, 198–201
    hostile views of 30, 199–200
Surinam 330
Sweden 217, 224, 225, 229, 233, 253,
    263–4, 372–3; *see also* law, criminal,
    in Sweden/Finland
Switzerland 89–90, 217–18, 237, 244
syphilis 51, 117
Szombathy, Zoltan 205

Talavera, Archpriest of: *see* Archpriest
    of Talavera
Tallard, Camille d'Hostun de La Baume,
    comte de 248, 268
Tallement des Réaux, Gédéon 241
Tangier 12
de Tassy, Laugier 12
taverns/inns
    in N. Europe 246, 247–8, 249, 347–8,
    357, 362–3, 369–70

in Ottoman world 34, 206
    in S. Europe 52–3
teachers: *see* schoolmasters
Testa, Pietro 169
theatre/actors 47, 285–91, 383
Thévenot, Jean 17, 211
Thomas Aquinas, St 116–17, 119–23
Thomas of Cantimpré 279
de Tilladet, Gabriel de Cassagnet,
    chevalier 268, 269
Toledo 62
tolerance
    social 39, 170–2, 193–4, 232–3, 325, 326
    theological, alleged 110
Tortorici, Zeb 79, 324
Tortosa 71
    law code of 129
torture 129, 225, 265, 368
Toscan, Jean 159, 183
Touchet, Mervin, Lord Audley, Earl of
    Castlehaven 266
Toulon 56
Toulouse 102, 103, 342
transvestites/transvestism 73, 145, 181,
    182, 246, 287–8, 290, 326, 337–8,
    349–50, 363–4, 367, 389
Trexler, Richard 326, 327, 416
Troyes, diocese of 219
Trumbach, Randolph 223, 290–1,
    336–40, 349, 366
Tunis 53
Turberville, George 381
Tuscany 90, 92, 104

ubnah/ma'būn 30, 31, 32
Udall, Nicholas 256, 258
Uluç Ali 14, 56
unspeakable sin: *see* sodomy, not to be
    spoken of
Utrecht 218, 226, 364–5, 371

Vainfas, Ronaldo 67, 69–70, 322,
    325, 326
Valencia 45, 48, 59, 66, 67, 172; *see also*
    Inquisition, Aragonese, tribunal
    in Valencia
Valladolid 98
Varchi, Benedetto 162
Vaughan, John, Lord (later 3rd Earl of
    Carbery) 297–8

Vauvenargues, Luc de Clapiers,
    marquis de 379
de la Vega, Juan 327–8
Vendôme, Louis Joseph de Bourbon,
    duc de 240
Venice 44, 61, 69, 72, 75, 76, 91, 190, 192,
    382–3, 389
    anti-sodomy measures 44, 48, 54,
    64–5, 92
    Florentines in 91
    marriage ages in 406
    punishment regime 93, 133
    'Turks' in 8
    statistics for 92, 382–3
venues for sodomy in N. Europe
    baths 372
    churches 366
    latrines 365–6, 372
    public places, urban 355–6, 361, 365
venues for sodomy in Ottoman world
    hamams 35–6
    public places, urban 26
    riverbanks 356
venues for sodomy in S. Europe
    churches 49
    public places, urban 49
    riverbanks 49
    see also taverns/inns
de Vere, Edward, Earl of Oxford 265–6
Vereenigde Oostindische Compagnie
    ('VOC') 261, 329–31, 374
Vergerio, Pietro Paolo 161
Vergil
    Dante's 144
    second Eclogue 150–1, 162, 293
Vermandois, Louis de Bourbon, comte
    de 268
de Verniolles, Arnaud 103–4, 189
de Viau, Théophile 247–8, 295–6
Vignali, Antonio 155–6
Vila Franca, Count of 45
Villiers, George, Duke of Buckingham
    273–6
de Vio, Tommaso 121–2, 390

Virginia 310–11, 314, 332
Visigoths 125, 129
Visitations of monasteries (1535–6) 222–3
de Vitoria, Francisco 321
VOC: see Vereenigde Oostindische
    Compagnie
Volpino, abbate: see abbate Volpino
Voltaire 178, 378
Vratislav, Václav 15

Walker, Clement 250–1
Wallington, Nehemiah 244–5
van Wanrooij, Dirk 370–1, 374
Ward, Ned 347–8
Wettinger, Godfrey 101
Wielant, Litius 254–5
Wielant, Philippe 224
Wigglesworth, Michael 313
Willis, Alan Scot 332
Wilmot, John, Earl of Rochester 251,
    298–300
Wilsma, Zacharias 366–8, 386
Winckelmann, Johann Joachim 385
Windsor, CT 315–16
Winterthur 372
witchcraft 112–14
women
    buggery of: see sodomy, male–female
    unavailability of 405–13
    see also female–female sex; prostitution,
    female
Wroth, Lady Mary 289
Württemberg, Duchy of 217

York 220
Young, Michael 273, 275, 276, 299
Yucatán Peninsula 74

Zaragoza 97
Ze'evi, Dror 203
Žehušice 254
zinā 201–2
Zurich 103, 217, 229, 237, 242, 243, 265,
    366, 371–2, 387